KOREA

ALSO BY JOSEPH C. GOULDEN

KOREA

The Untold Story
of the War

JOSEPH C. GOULDEN

Times
BOOKS

Maps by Arlo Greer
and Dewain Greer

Published by TIMES BOOKS, a division of
Quadrangle/The New York Times Book Co., Inc.
Three Park Avenue, New York, N.Y. 10016

Published simultaneously in Canada by
Fitzhenry & Whiteside, Ltd., Toronto

Library of Congress Cataloging in Publication Data

Goulden, Joseph C.
  Korea, the untold story of the war.

  Includes index.
  1. Korean War, 1950–1953. I. Title.
DS918.G69 1982   951.9'042   81–21262
ISBN 0–8129–0985–2   AACR2

Manufactured in the United States of America

For Leslie Cantrell Smith,

my wife and best friend—

thanks, dearest.

A WORD ABOUT ORIGINS

On Memorial Day, 1977, I had struggled hard, and not too happily, for a year on a book on America in the 1950's, an intended sequel to my *The Best Years,* which was about the country between V-J Day, August 1945, and the start of the Korean War, June 1950. Much of the problem was boredom, for the differences between immediate postwar America and the early 1950's were not all that distinct. So on Memorial Day I griped about the problem with an old journalistic acquaintance, Robert Sherrill.

"Hell," Sherrill counseled, "forget about the overall history. Do the Korean War." Sherrill, who reads everything published in the English language, noted that a complete book had not been done on this war. Some memoirs of generals and politicians existed, to be sure, as well as analyses and revisionist histories of varying quality and credibility. But the big picture? "No such book has been written," Sherrill said.

Sherrill's suggestion came at a propitious time. When I began rummaging around for Korean War material I found that an astounding volume—and quality—was either in the public domain for the first time under normal governmental declassification timetables, or could be brought there, via the Freedom of Information Act. For that reason, much of this book is based upon previously unpublished material, the "Pentagon Papers of the Korean War," in a sense. Through FOIA, I was able to read hundreds of previously top-secret cables between Washington and its field commanders in the Far East—first, General Douglas MacArthur, then his successors, Matthew Ridgway and Mark Clark. I read, in State Department messages, the U.S. government's true opinion of President Syngman Rhee of South Korea, officially a "gallant ally," privately, a "zealous, irrational and illogical fanatic" (as presidential envoy Walter Robertson called him in July 1953). I watched policy develop in briefing papers prepared at the staff levels of the National Security Council and the Joint Chiefs of Staff, and monitored the course of the war through periodic estimates by a relatively small and new Washington bureaucracy called the Central Intelligence Agency. A trip to a Federal archives dump in Suitland, Maryland, brought forth dusty packing crates containing the Daily Intelligence Summaries prepared by the Far East Command before and during the war, an outsider's rare glimpse at the raw intelligence data upon which important national decisions are made. A sketch map of my travels to military, presidential, and other libraries and archives, and for interviews, looks like the itinerary of a national political campaign, or the helter-skelter roamings of an on-the-loose bank robber with a fast car and a poor road map.

Inevitably, in any book involving research, dumb luck often played a crucial role. Through mutual acquaintances I enjoyed many lengthy interviews with Hans Tofte, a charming Danish-American spy master who ran CIA's covert operations in Korea the first part of the war. Tofte lived only a few short walking-blocks from my Georgetown home, and he supplemented his incredible memory with copies of old operational reports and even photographs. Why, I asked, haven't you used this material previously? "No one ever asked me for it," Tofte replied.

Other interesting material came in even more ricochet fashion. When Dean Acheson set out to write his memoir, *Present at the Creation,* he assembled old State Department colleagues at Princeton for free-wheeling discussions, transcribed in many thousands of pages, to buttress his own memory of his tenure as Secretary of State. One participant, Paul Nitze, made fleeting reference to the effect that Major General Charles Willoughby, MacArthur's intelligence chief, once admitted tailoring his estimates to fit the known desires of his superior. I sent Nitze a note asking if he recalled where he heard Willoughby make such a statement. Nitze replied with a two-page, single-spaced letter, answering my question, providing further Willoughby material, and closing with a by-the-way suggestion that I talk with Charles Burton Marshall, who had been his colleague on the State Department's Policy Planning Staff during the war.

My interview with Marshall several days later, in the suite of think-tank offices he shared with Nitze in suburban Virginia, dealt mainly with the Truman administration's attempts to initiate peace talks during the spring of 1951. After several fruitful hours I began gathering my notebooks and pencils, only to have Marshall interrupt me: "By the way, what do you know about Thomas Jefferson Davis, who was MacArthur's aide when he was chief of staff?"

Nothing, I confessed, the name was totally unfamiliar.

Marshall motioned me back to the seat and told me a story. Shortly after the Second World War he and Davis were both attached to a refugee aid office in Washington, and they lunched together frequently. Davis, then a brigadier general, had had a friendly but objective relationship with MacArthur for a decade; it ended with bitterness when MacArthur cashiered him from his staff for being so unfaithful as to wager that President Roosevelt, a man the general considered an enemy, would win re-election in 1940. Davis entertained Marshall with long anecdotes on MacArthur's . . . well, *nuttiness,* especially his dealings with women. Marshall considered the stories nothing more than amusing luncheon gossip until August 1950, when MacArthur's conduct caused uneasiness among Washington officials. So he persuaded Davis to write a memorandum for the Joint Chiefs of Staff recounting what he had observed while living in close proximity to MacArthur as his personal aide.

The implication of the Davis material—which appears in the Prologue—was that MacArthur was much too unstable a man to be trusted with a delicate military-political command. The JCS did not act on the Davis memo in 1950, nor did they use it against MacArthur the next spring during the stormy hearings following his dismissal. Now, in a chain that began when Dean Acheson asked Paul Nitze to help him write a book, Davis's observations of MacArthur's bizarre personal conduct are made public for the first time.

A more formal citation of sources and acknowledgments can be found in the Notes and Sources. But I would like to pay especial thanks to Leslie Cantrell Smith, my wife, who joined a four-year voyage in midcourse, and who served admirably in the flagship and elsewhere for the duration.

JOSEPH C. GOULDEN

Rileyville, Round Hill, and Arlington, Virginia
Washington, D.C.
June 1981

CONTENTS

ILLUSTRATIONS

Sixteen pages of photographs follow page 390.

"A Sour Little War"

"A sour little war," W. Averell Harriman, that ageless old crocodile of American politics, said of it. President Harry S. Truman stubbornly insisted it was nothing more than a "police action" and stuck to the infuriating euphemism even as American casualties passed the 50,000 mark. The Republicans called it "the foreign policy blunder of the century" and used it as a bludgeon to end sixteen years of Democratic control of the White House. "Frankly, a great military disaster," commented General Omar Bradley, Chairman of the Joint Chiefs of Staff, "the wrong war, in the wrong place, at the wrong time, with the wrong enemy."

The Korean War—let us call it what it was—was all these things. It was also the turning point for America's post-World War II military and diplomatic strategy. Korea marked the first time the United States went to arms to attempt to halt Communist military expansion. Korea was the first step on a long road of such ventures; indeed, two months after the start of fighting there, the United States was to send its first military aid to the French, who were fighting an insurgency in Indochina that ultimately was to become the Vietnam War. In the next decades, for better or for worse, America was to commit increasing amounts of its national resources—and prestige—to Southeast Asia, to Europe, to Africa, to Latin America. The Korean War marked the start of the construction of a military juggernaut the support of which consumed half the annual federal budget, even in "peacetime" years, and found American men and women at posts in the farthest reaches of the world.

But as is often true of unpleasant national experiences, the Korean War is one of those events which most Americans, once it ended, were eager to permit to slip through the crevices of memory. For one reason, Korea was the first time America fought a war to an unvictorious conclusion. America left Korea in stalemate, held to a draw by a huge but backward Asian nation, Communist China, which used masses of men and shrewd manipulation of international politics to overcome vastly more powerful U.S. technology. For the first time America fought a war without using the full range of weapons available. The atomic weapons which staggered the Japanese into surrender in 1945 were denied to the military. Nor could field commanders "take the war to the enemy" in his homeland (i.e., China). Korea shattered the American illusion that atomic weaponry had outmoded the foot soldier. Politically world opinion would not support use of such hellish weapons. Tactically atomic bombs were worthless against infantry units scattered over scores of miles of rugged mountains. Practically America's "nuclear umbrella" at the time the Korean War began consisted of only four atomic bombs— trump cards Washington strategists felt, perhaps wisely, should be reserved for any war with the Soviet Union.

To the American public, the Korean War was an unwelcome interruption of postwar prosperity. The five years 1945–50, from V-J Day to the start of the Korean War, indeed were among the most pleasant in American history, a few economic and political bumps notwithstanding. With the Depression over, Americans cherished buying cars and going to ball games; they wished no further worries about weighty affairs of state. So America did not reflexively spring to defend the colors, especially after the Korean War degenerated, in 1952 and 1953, into dreary and seemingly senseless battles for the same hills. To read that hundreds of American soldiers died at such geographical locales as Heartbreak Ridge and No-Name Ridge does not excite public support for a war. During a beery discussion soon after my graduation from high school in 1952, in a strongly militaristic Texas community, a classmate summed up the attitude of those of us who were now eligible for the draft. "Boys," he said, "there's two things we gotta avoid: Korea and gonorrhea."

Korea: The Untold Story of the War is an attempt to explore how the United States got into the conflict and how military and civilian leaders conducted themselves thereafter. It is not an inspiring story, for America suffered from uninspiring leadership during most of the war years. Foremost among the bunglers (a strong word, but the record supports it) were President Truman and his secretary of state, Dean Acheson. Both men were endowed with strong wills that under stress often turned to sheer pigheadedness, and both suffered for it (as did the nation). In the space of four days in June 1950, after the North Korean Army swept into South Korea, Truman and Acheson put the United States into a war that the American military was unprepared to fight and in fact had been told it would *not* have to fight. In those heady days of summer Truman and Acheson "drew the line" against Communist aggression. They considered the "real enemy" the Soviet Union (although they never said so publicly, so as to give Moscow a face-saving chance to call off the war), and they felt they had out-bluffed America's strongest adversary. By October 1950 the intervention seemed successful. The North Koreans were repulsed by an army flying the United Nations flag (albeit predominantly American), and Truman and Acheson applauded themselves for their shrewdness.

Then things changed, and in a hurry. In November and December 1950 the Chinese, a foe far more formidable than the North Koreans, intervened. For desperate weeks the UN Command was in danger of being thrown off the Korean peninsula; entire divisions were trapped in the mountains in thirty below zero weather. Only through superhuman effort—guided by an unsung hero of the war, Lieutenant General Matthew Ridgway—did the military stabilize itself and halt the Chinese. Now Acheson and Truman hurriedly scaled down their "display of American will" and put limits on the war that made victory impossible. Belatedly they realized that the United States was two years away from the capability of challenging the Soviet Union directly. So Korea was recast as a local war that must be confined to the Korean peninsula.

The rashness of the Truman-Acheson venture, the facile rationalization of the cause which they sold to the American people are aptly illustrated by an episode during their attempt to end the war by armistice in late 1952. The stated reason for the U.S. intervention was to preserve the integrity and independence of the Republic of Korea (or ROK), the formal name of the South Korean government. But the terms did not satisfy the ROK president, Syngman Rhee, an octogenarian and hypereccentric nationalist who made his first pleas for Korean independence to President Theodore Roosevelt in 1905. Rhee did not intend to abandon a half century fight under terms he felt left him vulnerable to further Communist aggression, and he felt Truman and Acheson were willing to sacrifice him to extricate the United States from a war that had gone astray. So he refused the armistice terms.

Whereupon the National Security Council (NSC), the governing council of America's national security apparatus, considered an alternative. If Rhee would not go along with the armistice plan, the Central Intelligence Agency would inspire a coup to topple him from office, to be replaced by a hopefully more amenable military government. If Rhee continued to resist, he would be "eliminated."

One of the more sobering moments of the Vietnam War involved a young American infantry officer who told a television interviewer, "We had to destroy the village to save it." This man spoke of a single hamlet; Truman and Acheson were willing to destroy an entire government to "save it." To America's credit, the suggestion that the obstinate Rhee be killed, although generative of much bureaucratic paper, was never approved by the NSC or President Truman. It was simply left in abeyance.

The Truman-Acheson decision to enter the Korean War was an act of honor. The North Korean regime, a satellite of an avowed enemy of the United States, committed a brutal act of aggression when it invaded the Republic of Korea. The North Koreans (and their Soviet mentors) had had the opportunity for free elections under UN supervision with the aim of creating a united and independent Korea. The North Koreans chose bullets rather than the ballot box, in deliberate defiance of the United Nations.

Yet national leaders must be judged on performance as well as motivation. Truman and Acheson set out to establish the point that international order could not be flouted with impunity. Their assumption from the outset was that the Soviet Union was responsible for the war, that the Soviets used a surrogate to test American will. Soviet complicity is a matter that can be established only by circumstantial evidence, which is abundant. The Soviets armed the North Koreans to the teeth, with tanks and attack planes and self-propelled guns—military hardware built for offense, not defense. More than 3,000 Soviet advisers worked closely with the North Korean People's Army. The Soviets supported the North Koreans politically, in the UN and elsewhere, for the duration of the war. Nonetheless, Truman and Acheson went to great lengths to avoid a direct accusation that the Soviets were the true culprits in the war, a failure that in essence proved the Soviets' point—that is, that the USSR could use satellites to nip at America's flanks without fear of provoking direct retaliation. Such was the basic flaw of the Truman-Acheson policy in Korea.

So who were these men who led us into the Korean War? The first focus must fall upon Truman and Acheson, a most unlikely political couple who functioned in total harmony—Truman with the dress, diction, and demeanor of the small-town Rotarian, coupled with the foppish, mustachioed Acheson, whose manner and clipped accent made him a central-casting double for an English lord. Truman's strength was an intuitive intelligence, the determination to achieve, on his own, with no formal schooling, what was perhaps the broadest grasp of history of any American President save Woodrow Wilson (an academician). Truman's problem was that few people took him seriously. Then, in 1948, Truman defeated Republican Thomas E. Dewey in the most astounding upset ever in American politics. No longer was Truman the weak-eyed, failed midwestern haberdasher who owed his political career to a corrupt Missouri machine. The "accidental President" now ruled in his own right and with the special confidence of a man who finally, in his sixties, was freed of the burden of having to convince other people of his worth. Self-doubt did not trouble Harry Truman after 1948; he trusted his own instincts, and he made major decisions—such as the Korean intervention—swiftly, almost compulsively. Act now, let us consider the consequences later.

Truman's confidence was that of a man who had overcome years of implied inferiority. By contrast, Dean Acheson's confidence seemed to come by birthright. A graduate of Groton and Yale, a protégé of Justice Louis Brandeis, Acheson had an intellect almost stunning in its intensity. Fifty-seven years old in 1950, he had served as a partner in Covington & Burling, perhaps Washington's premier law firm; as undersecretary of the treasury for Roosevelt; and in high State Department posts from 1941 to 1947. Acheson's strength was an ability to correlate intricate issues, such as the relationship between foreign and monetary policy. One Truman administration official said of him, "The Dean [his nickname] could have served as secretary of state and the treasury simultaneously."

Truman brought Acheson back into government as secretary of state in January 1949. Truman's knowledge of domestic politics notwithstanding, he had the sense to realize he needed expert guidance in foreign affairs. The time was ripe for a man of European perspective. The Marshall Plan, begun in 1947, was sending massive economic aid to Western Europe; the North Atlantic Treaty Organization, founded in 1949, was mustering opposition to the sort of Soviet expansionism that had subverted Czechoslovakia. Acheson knew Europe. He was also a man totally devoted to Truman. He frequently told State Department colleagues, "I have a constituency of one person. He is President Truman."

But Acheson had flaws. His abundant self-confidence often converted his intellect into arrogance, for he was blessed with neither humility nor the ability to know when to remain silent. Rather than placate foes— people whose support could help him—he preferred the acid bon mot. In a closed congressional hearing he once so infuriated Senator Kenneth Wherry that the Nebraska Republican lunged across a table in a rage, fists swinging; Acheson replied with his own roundhouse swing before peace was restored. As a result, Acheson had few friends in Washington, even in the White House—save, of course, for Harry Truman.

Acheson also had political problems in 1950. Republican opponents charged him with a good deal of the responsibility for "losing China" to the Communist regime that had ousted Generalissimo Chiang Kai-shek's Nationalist government the previous year. Acheson's sin, they charged, was the the issuance of a massive White Paper about U.S.-China relations that wrote off Chiang as corrupt and beyond salvation; this document, the Republicans said, was the final shove that toppled the generalissimo. Then, in early 1950, Acheson said (kindly, but politically unwisely) that he would not "turn his back" on Alger Hiss, a longtime friend and State Department official convicted for perjury during an investigation of charges he was a Soviet espionage agent. Thus, in June 1950, both Truman and Acheson were under a drumfire of Republican criticism for being "soft on communism" and for letting Asia's largest nation fall into the hands of Communists.

One supposed checkrein on executive impulsiveness in times of military crisis is the Joint Chiefs of Staff (JCS), the uniformed heads of the services, charged with being the President's chief advisers on military matters. The JCS bear much responsibility for what went wrong in the Korean War, beginning from the first days. In 1949 the JCS, after extensive study of how America's limited military strength could be deployed around the world, had written off South Korea as of "little strategic value" to the United States. Occupation troops there should be withdrawn, and the United States should not come to its defense if the North Koreans invaded. Acheson's State Department, the National Security Council, and Truman all concurred.

Then came June 1950. The JCS sat silently as Acheson persuaded Truman to reverse established national policy and intervene in the war. Not once did they caution the President he was giving the military a mission it was not equipped to perform.

Later, and even more dismally, the JCS lost control of America's field commander in the war—General Douglas A. MacArthur. They permitted him to evade the spirit, if not the letter, of his orders. They gave him a dangerously free hand in the handling of his army, even when his deployment risked the lives of scores of thousands of soldiers. They treated him not as a subordinate but as a petulant child who must be humored and coaxed into following directions. The Chairman of the Joint Chiefs of Staff, the man who permitted these intolerable events, was General Omar Bradley, who during the Second World War had commanded in Europe a ground force of 1.3 million men, largest ever to serve under a single American general. But Bradley was no match for MacArthur. "He treated us," Bradley once lamented, "like we were a bunch of kids."

MacArthur, of course, was not an ordinary field general. Seventy years old in 1950, the senior officer in the United States Army, MacArthur ranks as the most exasperatingly complex man ever produced by the American military, a blend of Caesar and Caligula, skittering along the thin line between brilliance and eccentricity. Flamboyantly theatrical ("He could have been another John Barrymore," remarked General J.

Lawton Collins, the army chief of staff), MacArthur inspired both adulation and contempt in persons around him. His mammoth ego permitted no intimation he could be wrong, on any subject at any time. His messianic oratory charmed doubters into following any scheme he proposed. The holder of thirteen medals for bravery (including the Medal of Honor), he seemed at times deliberately to taunt death—or, conversely, to have such a sense of immortality that he felt he could expose himself to enemy fire with impunity. (Despite such displays, marines who fought in his Pacific command derided him as "Dugout Doug," an absentee commander who was around for the photographers but not for the actual fighting. The epithet was unfair.) But to the U.S. Army, Douglas MacArthur was *sui generis*, the star-struck officer who had earned every honor, held every high post, from ranking cadet in his West Point class to the office of chief of staff. From 1945 to 1951, after his Pacific triumph, MacArthur served as the viceroy who rebuilt shattered Japan into a democracy. So devoted was MacArthur to his duty in Japan (or so he said) that he did not return to America after the war for the traditional hero's welcome. He had not been home in thirteen years, but no matter: He would stay at his post. Thus the American public knew him only as a figure of almost mythical proportion, whose very stature was amplified by his remoteness.*

Yet beneath MacArthur's proud, unflinching façade were murky pools of self-doubt and personal cruelty. MacArthur's hair shirt was a doting mother, Pinky MacArthur, and the available evidence suggests strongly she was daft. She felt that her husband, a Civil War general and hero, had been denied proper honors (although his awards included the Medal of Honor), and she badgered the army on his behalf for years, until the poor fellow died. Then she shifted to "Dougie," helping him win appointment to West Point, then following him there (she lived on campus at the Thayer Hotel, within eyeshot of his dormitory room). She harried and goaded him to "greater successes" throughout his career, writing superior officers letters urging promotions, following him from dreary post to post. MacArthur made one attempt to break away in the 1920's, marrying a svelte café society divorcée (Mrs. MacArthur refused to attend the wedding), who almost persuaded him to leave the military for banking. When gossip columnists wrote of his wife's continued gay social life—with other men—while he was overseas, MacArthur hurried to the divorce courts.

*A more likely explanation for MacArthur's long absence from the United States stems from the circumstances of his departure. Upon retirement from the post of chief of staff he intended to become "field marshal" of the Philippine Army, feeling that at age fifty-seven he had some useful military years left. To his rage, President Roosevelt relieved him of the chief's position under what MacArthur felt were hurried conditions. He vowed to aides, "I'll never return to the United States as long as Roosevelt is President." One MacArthur associate felt the antipathy carried over to Truman, FDR's choice as Vice President.

This was in 1929, and the episode cut MacArthur; only the laws of taste and libel prevented the much-decorated general from being publicly revealed as a husband who had been cuckolded and abandoned. How could an officer command an army if he could not control his own household? Another wound to his pride came in 1932, when MacArthur donned full battle regalia to command troops and tanks to march on impoverished veterans seeking bonuses in Washington and drive them from their pitiful campgrounds. MacArthur thought the task distasteful, but he followed orders and was ridiculed in the press as a bully beating up on the very enlisted men he had commanded in France.

So MacArthur retreated. As chief of staff he commanded an elegant house at Fort Myer, in the green Virginia countryside just across the Potomac from Washington. But MacArthur now desired privacy, not the goldfish-bowl existence of an army post, for he had some specific pleasures in mind.

With a trusted aide, Lieutenant Thomas Jefferson Davis, MacArthur rented an apartment on Kalorama Road NW in Washington, a hideaway known to only a few intimates. There MacArthur entertained a succession of prostitutes—two, three, even four at a time—but as a gloatingly superior male rather than as a sexual partner. Davis was to recall in memoirs of his days with MacArthur:

> His idea of a hot time was just to bring them in for the evening. He'd never screw them; he would just sit there in an arm chair and let the girls admire what a great man he was.
>
> He also had a sadistic streak. We'd go to Baltimore to a whore house, and MacArthur would pick one special girl and be nice to her—take her to dinner, quote poetry, buy her flowers, generally get her built up until she was enamored with him. The first time she said a pressuring word, as if she wanted something permanent from him, he would denounce her as a "little whore," and walk away. He'd laugh at her later, on the ride back to Washington.

Another MacArthur quirk was more serious stuff. Many nights he would summon Davis to the living room and sit with a loaded revolver in his hand and discourse on the hidden tribulations of being America's preeminent soldier. To fellow officers and the public he was the golden boy of the American military. But did he truly deserve the accolades? In the predawn hours MacArthur would claim despondently he was miscast as a hero, that only at the insistence of his mother had he become a "glorious Apollo, Roland and George Washington all in one." He felt himself overvalued, as man and as general, and he feared that at some climactic point in life he would face a testing point he could not achieve—and fail. But death at a time and means of his own choice —and here he would sometimes point the pistol at his temple—would spare him the ignominy of failure and give him peace of mind.

Davis's role was to persuade MacArthur to put down the pistol, that he was such a valuable soldier the country could not spare him. MacArthur would continue that he would "be comfortable" dying in the company of such a good friend, but that he agreed. He replayed the scene constantly during the 1930's.

Only once did Davis not recite his lines properly. The two officers were on a train bound through the South for Washington. MacArthur banged on the door of Davis's compartment. Once again he had the pistol in hand. "We are nearing the area where my father won his Medal of Honor," MacArthur told Davis. "I've done everything I can in the army and life, my term as chief of staff is ending. As we pass over the Tennessee River bridge, I intend to jump from the train. This is where my life ends, Davis."

"General," Davis replied, "would you hurry up and get it over with so I can get back to sleep?"

MacArthur slammed the door of the compartment. The next morning he apologized for "being so emotional." A short time later mother Pinky MacArthur died. Davis never heard another suicide threat.

But the peculiar episodes witnessed by Lieutenant Davis are relevant to the Korean War period because of some of the MacArthur personality quirks he displayed at critical turns of that conflict. Reading the scores of cables he sent to the Joint Chiefs of Staff during the war—most of them previously unpublished—one senses a man who had lost touch with reality; who wanted full credit for every victory on the battlefield but no fault for the failures; who cast every message in terms: "Give me what I want or *you* accept the consequences" (that is, American casualties). Archives of the Joint Chiefs of Staff point to an even more damning explanation for MacArthur's behavior: In November and December 1950, when a sudden invasion by the Chinese almost threw his army out of Korea, MacArthur had lost not his reason but his nerve. The golden boy of the military was on the brink of the public failure he had always feared. He was scared.

MacArthur reacted with desperate attempts at self-redemption. He demanded that the Joint Chiefs permit a sharp escalation of the war, including blockading and bombarding the Chinese mainland. He wished to put a "band of radioactive waste" along the southern banks of the Yalu River, the border between North Korea and Chinese Manchuria. And in his private conversations MacArthur talked of even meatier stuff: nuclear attacks on China. If these raids provoked war with Russia, so be it. MacArthur wanted no part of an Asian land war; his one confrontation with the massed armies of China had taught him the necessary lesson. But if the Soviets indeed had stirred up the Korean War (the consensus of the U.S. intelligence and diplomatic communities), the Soviets should pay the price. Unfortunately for MacArthur, as we shall see, he confided these views to Spanish and Portuguese diplomats in Tokyo, who in due course reported them to their governments. The National Security Agency (NSA), which routinely intercepted and decoded such diplomatic cables, in short order reported the messages to Truman. MacArthur was already in trouble with the President for public statements criticizing administration policy in Asia. Given direct evidence of even more gross perfidy, Truman fired MacArthur within the week (although security and diplomatic courtesy meant he could not mention the NSA intercepts). The "firing of MacArthur," the political *cause célèbre* of the era, was a torturing and confusing episode for the American public, one which shattered national unity to the extent that peace would not come for two more years.

But MacArthur left his command unrepentant, convinced that he had done nothing beyond the pale of the professional soldier. Indeed he confided to his successor, General Matthew Ridgway, that mental illness might have prompted President Truman to fire him. Speaking to Ridgway the day after his relief, MacArthur claimed to have been told by an "eminent medical man" that Truman suffered from a condition called "malignant hypertension." This affliction, MacArthur continued, "was characterized by bewilderment and confusion of mind." MacArthur blamed it for such Truman flares of temper as the profane letter he sent to a Washington *Post* music critic who panned a concert by his daughter, Margaret. (Ridgway, after listening to MacArthur, decided that it was not the President who suffered mental confusion.)

War by nature is a duplicitous undertaking, and Korea certainly contained its share of dark secrets, many of which came to light during the four years of research that produced this book. The story of the war is a mélange of warts and beauty spots:

—The newborn Central Intelligence Agency (CIA), given its first opportunity for field operations in time of war, devised devilish ways of tormenting the Chinese. One operation involved the hijacking, on the high seas, of a hospital ship bound for China at a time when an epidemic was felling thousands of Chinese soldiers. The ship flew the flag of Norway, a nation friendly to the United States, then and now. Unbeknownst to the Norwegians, the "Chinese bandits" who seized the ship just north of Formosa were hired and commanded by a CIA operative.

—At one frustrated juncture when the United States considered abandoning the war, the JCS approved a contingency plan for relocating the ROK government and military—600,000 people, including dependents—to a "new Korea" to be created on islands in the American Samoa group. The climate was suitable for farming, the islands were largely uninhabited, the Koreans could "probably" adjust to the new surroundings, the JCS said. Nonetheless, the plan was not discussed with any Korean officials "for fear of provoking adverse public reaction."

—Although President Truman frequently made public pledges not to use atomic weapons in Korea, in December 1950 nonassembled bombs were quietly transported to a U.S. aircraft carrier stationed off the peninsula. U.S. planes also made simulated nuclear bombing raids over Pyongyang, the North Korean capital, as part of contingency planning for atomic warfare.

—Truman was even more bellicose in the privacy of his diary, where his angry scrawls often read like, say, the nut mail received by newspapers. In January 1952 Truman was enraged at North Korean and Chinese intransigence in the armistice talks. He wrote:

> Dealing with Communist governments is like an honest man trying to deal with a numbers racket king or the head of a dope ring. It seems to me that the proper approach now would be an ultimatum with a ten-day expiration limit, informing Moscow that we intend to blockade the China coast from the Korean border to Indochina, and that we intend to destroy every military base in Manchuria, including submarine bases, by means now in our control, and if there is further interference, we shall eliminate any ports or cities necessary to accomplish our peaceful purposes.

Truman recognized the possible consequences:

> This means all out war. It means that Moscow, St. Petersburg [Leningrad by 1952], Mukden, Vladivostok, Pekin [sic], Shanghai, Port Arthur, Dairen, Odessa, Stalingrad and every manufacturing plant in China and the Soviet Union will be eliminated. This is the final chance for the Soviet government to decide whether it desires to survive or not.

Truman revisited the idea five months later, during another fit of pique. This time he would ask Soviet leaders a series of rhetorical questions: "Now do you want an end to hostilities in Korea or do you want China and Siberia destroyed? You may have one or the other which ever you want. . . . You either accept our fair and just proposal or you will be completely destroyed." Truman never took any actions to implement these private thoughts; however, they do give a clear insight into his ideas on deployment of nuclear weapons.

But under the Eisenhower administration, the use of nuclear weapons came close to reality. On May 20, 1953, the National Security Council discussed actions that should be taken if the Communists did not accept reasonable peace terms. The council decided upon air and naval operations "directly against China and Manchuria," including "extensive strategical and tactical use of atomic bombs." This major escalation would commence with a naval blockade of Chinese ports and gradually extend to the nuclear bombings, which would be undertaken so as to "obtain maximum surprise and maximum impact." Warned obliquely of the U. S. intentions, the Chinese quickly decided to end the war. An armistice was signed within a month.

The "sour little war"—to use Averell Harriman's phrase again—almost became America's nuclear war. The fighting ended by armistice in July 1953, with Korea still a divided nation. Now, almost three decades later, representatives of both Koreas—American officers accompanying the ROKs—once a month or so hold a *pro forma* meeting in a neutral zone. The ostensible reason is to seek a common ground for peace. In actuality, nothing is said except an occasional exchange of insults. Kim Il Sung continues as the North Korean dictator, and from time to time he issues harsh statements about his intention to seize South Korea by force, just as he attempted to do in 1950. South Korea has endured a succession of swinging-door dictators, one after the other, presidents and strong men who imprison dissidents and scoff at any mention of reconciliation with the North. Some 40,000 American troops remain on duty there as a trip-wire defense against any North Korean invasion. And from time to time the new generation of soldiers asks, "What am I doing in this obscure little part of the world?"—exactly what many Americans asked when it all began, in June 1950.

KOREA

CHAPTER ONE

"Shrimp Crushed in Battle of Whales"

Secretary of State Dean Acheson, a man capable of eloquent exasperation, rose from his chair with anger at one particularly frustrating juncture of the Korean War, slapped the desk smartly with his hand, and exclaimed, "If the best minds in the world had set out to find us the worst possible location in the world to fight this damnable war, politically and militarily, the unanimous choice would have been Korea!" Indeed, the United Nations' putative ally, the Republic of Korea, was a difficult partner, but with reason. Korea was—and is—one of those nations with the misfortune to lie at a crossroads of world power politics, repeatedly stomped over, brutalized, and occupied by stronger neighbors. In Korea's instance, the perpetual antagonists were China, Japan, and Russia. When the Japanese launched their periodic imperialistic adventures on the Asian mainland, Korea was the most convenient invasion route. Defensively Japan considered the Korean peninsula a dagger thrust in its direction from China. So each of these antagonists for centuries used Korea for its own selfish ends; none could be trusted to "protect" it without a *quid pro quo* such as trading monopolies or governmental subservience. As an ancient Korean proverb accurately laments, "A shrimp is crushed in the battle of the whales."[1]

Korea's abiding interest was simply to be left alone to nurture and enjoy its centuries-old culture and civilization. During one rare respite from foreign occupation in the seventeenth century, a Korean king even barred the mining of gold and silver, hoping to reduce the incentive for outsiders to enter his country. The attempt at a "hermit kingdom" failed. At another juncture, in 1882, in an attempt to blunt Japanese ascendancy, the Chinese even persuaded a frail Korean government to negotiate a somewhat vague treaty of "friendship" with the U.S. Although the U.S. had no economic or other interests in Korea at the time, American diplomats agreed to the treaty as affording a possible future toehold in the country. The operative clause read: "If other powers deal unjustly or oppressively with either government, the other will exert their good offices, on being informed of the case, to bring about an amicable agreement, thus showing their friendly feelings."

Such broad language, of course, means as much—or as little—as the stronger party cares to make of it. After signing the treaty, the U.S. promptly forgot it. The reason was practical and pragmatic: The U.S. had neither the ambition nor the power to exert any influence in the Far East. Thus it remained silent in 1896, when Russia and Japan signed a formal compact dividing their spheres of influence in Korea at the 38th parallel, which cuts across the peninsula roughly at the midriff. The Russians took the northern sector, the Japanese the southern, and each dominated the politics and the economy of its respective area. The Japanese, by virtue of their occupation of the capital of Seoul, controlled the puppet royal family, which ruled in name only, its main function the suppression of domestic dissent. Korea was a divided vassal state, with no control over its present nor any voice in its future.

Yet as occupying armies have learned throughout history, nationalistic pride is not a quality easily demolished by bayonets or jackboots. Koreans had a keen sense of their own past and delighted in summoning up memories of long-ago times when the nation boasted a culture uncontaminated by outside influences. And nowhere were these sentiments stronger than among members of an eccentric social class known as the *yangban.*

The *yangban,* who dressed in academic gowns and grew flowing beards, devoted their entire lives to a most special scholarship: memorizing the genealogy of one's own and other Korean families. One devoted *yangban,* Yi Kyung-sun, could sit for hours with crossed legs on a woven mat, eyes closed to slits, and recite in a singsong voice no less than twenty-four volumes of genealogical tables, including the glorious interlude seventeen generations earlier, when one of his paternal relatives briefly had been in the line of succession for the Korean throne.

But Yi's son—Syngman Rhee,* born on March 26, 1876—early in his young manhood recognized the absurdity in the *yangban* system. What possible value could there be in ancestor worship when the present family lived on a few handfuls of rice daily in a shack above Seoul? By

---

*The formal name given at birth was Yi Seung-man; as a child he was known as Yongi, the Korean term for "dragon." He became Syngman Rhee in his youth because Western missionary benefactors had trouble translating his Korean name into English. Rather than rename the man in midtext, I use the name Rhee hereafter.

what right did the *yangban* demand material support from other families simply because their lineage had brushed against royalty twenty,
even thirty centuries hence? As Rhee was to tell biographer Robert T.
Oliver, "this same disease of ancestor-worship" even extended to impoverished rice farmers.

So Rhee made what must have been a tremendously difficult decision
for a young Asian man. In his late teens he entered a middle school in
Seoul run by Methodist missionaries and gradually moved away from
the complementary faiths of Buddhism and Confucianism followed by
his parents. He cut off the traditional hair topknot worn by Korean
males. He read such American magazines as *McClure's* and *The Out-
look,* and as he learned about Western democracy, he found the medievalism of Korea's social and political system intolerable. In the space
of a few months he made the quantum jump from traditional Oriental-
ism to quasi Westerner.

Rhee's next move was into anti-imperialist politics. He edited a student newspaper at the missionary school; he led demonstrations demanding the ouster of the Japanese and the restoration of a greatly
reformed monarchy, speaking so fervently at one rally that Seoul newspapers called him "a radical and a fire-eater." The puppet king responded with a crackdown on the dissidents. Rhee was imprisoned,
friends smuggled in guns to the jail, there was an exchange of shots, a
guard suffered a leg wound, and Rhee and a companion escaped, only
to be swiftly recaptured.

Next commenced an ordeal brutal even by the demanding standards
of Oriental cruelty, with Rhee powerless in the hands of torturers of a
monarch barely advanced beyond medievalism. According to the account Rhee gave biographer Oliver, his arms were bound tightly behind his back with silken ropes that cut into his flesh. "Two sticks were
placed between his legs, which were then bound tightly together at the
knees and ankles, after which two policemen twisted the sticks. Trian-
gular pieces of bamboo were tied between his fingers, which then were
drawn so tightly together that the flesh sheared off from the bones."
Rhee was spread-eagled on the floor and lashed with bamboo rods until
his flesh oozed blood. At night his feet were placed in stocks, and his
hands into cuffs. Memory and hope faded. This solitary and bound
confinement lasted seven months, his wardens releasing him from the
bonds only five minutes daily. Then he was brought to trial with a
companion also involved in the break. Only the fact that Rhee's pistol
had not been fired saved his life. The companion was sentenced to
beheading; Rhee, to life imprisonment and 100 blows from a bamboo
rod. (A guard spared Rhee the flogging because of his weak condition.)

These tortures are related at length because they help explain the
dogged determination with which Rhee fought for Korean independence during his later years, including those of the Korean War. Torture

is an experience that can be comprehended only by those who have endured it. Rhee's ordeal left him with a permanent mind set. He would broach no compromise with anyone who wanted settlement of any Korean problem on any terms short of assured independence.

In all, Rhee spent six more years in jail, albeit under livable conditions. His American missionary friends visited frequently, bringing books and reinforcing his belief that adherence to Christian ideals was essential to political freedom. In manifestos and political tracts Rhee lamented the selfishness of his own people, who would not help one another because they did not comprehend that "what they do for others is most truly working for themselves." Political freedom, he felt, came only through a change of heart of the general populace, not from "laws and regulations."

Rhee's total acceptance of Christianity was significant for several reasons, some not relevant at the moment. With his new faith Rhee conceived of himself as an instrument through which God's will would be worked. He was helpless to guide his own destiny, yet God's guidance would always be at hand. When he quibbled with American officials half a century later, they often fumed at him for being "messianic," a man so convinced of his own certitude that he would listen to no outside voices. Essentially their estimate was correct, with one major caveat: Rhee's sense of mission stemmed not from himself personally but from what he felt to be a God-granted mission.

Whether one accepts that another human can in fact be a messenger of God is irrelevant; Rhee felt he was just that, and for the rest of his life he conducted himself accordingly.

Although Rhee had no reason to sense it at the time, his conversion later would be of immense political value. American public opinion toward Asia during the first half of this century was inordinately influenced by missionaries who had served in China, Korea, Japan, Indochina, and elsewhere. In the words of Ross Y. Koen, in his landmark study *The China Lobby:*

> Through schools and hospitals, missionaries from American churches introduced the education, science, and medicine of the Occident to China. The education carried on by the Protestant churches of the United States to acquaint their members, who were supporting the work, with the activities of the missionaries gave millions of Americans information about China.[2]

Public support of the Chinese Chiang Kai-shek—also a converted Christian—was easily transferable to Syngman Rhee in the late 1940's and early 1950's, when destinies of the two men seemed interwoven. In supporting Rhee, America stood behind not an "Asian potentate" but a "Christian statesman."

For Rhee's immediate purposes, the prime value of his Westerniza-tion was that it led to his release from prison in 1904. The circumstances were fraught with the ironies and inconsistencies of Korean politics. That year Japan and Russia appeared drifting toward war, and Korea once again feared it was to be the "shrimp crushed in the battle of whales." So one faction in the Korean puppet government decided to ask the U.S. to invoke the "friendship treaty" it had signed two decades earlier. The person deemed most qualified in all Korea was Syngman Rhee, a political prisoner to be sure, but one who spoke English, under-stood the American system, and was a Christian.

So Rhee was taken from his cell, given three months' rest to recuper-ate, and sent off to the U.S. as a "special emissary" but one with limited support. One government faction, the dominant one, was content to accept the economic benefits stemming from Japanese control of Korea. A smaller one—the impetus for Rhee's mission—wanted a more independent role for Korea. What neither faction knew was that the issue of U.S. intervention in the Japanese-Russian conflict was already resolved. President Theodore Roosevelt admired Japanese "strength and energy" and accepted the judgment of advisers that the Koreans were "unfit" for self-government. Roosevelt's chief goal in the Orient was maintaining U.S. control of the Philippines, recently wrested from the Spanish, which TR felt the U.S. had a "manifest destiny" to bring into the modern world. So Roosevelt made a trade with Japan: In return for his support of Japan's claim of a "special interest" in Korea and Manchuria, Japan would not try to take the Philippines. In terms of imperial pragmatism, the deal was a good one for the U.S., which did not have the military power to hold the Philippines should the Japanese attempt to seize them. In his memoirs Roosevelt offered another ratio-nale:

> To be sure, by treaty it was solemnly covenanted that Korea should remain independent. But Korea itself was helpless to enforce the treaty, and it was out of the question to suppose that any other nation, with no interests of its own at stake, would do for the Koreans what they were utterly unable to do for themselves.[3]

All this was unknown to the twenty-nine-year-old Rhee, who was to have a baptism in the realities of big-power diplomacy. Given only enough money to travel to Kobe, Japan, he had to pause there—and in Honolulu and San Francisco—to raise funds to continue his "mission." The pro-Japanese Korean minister in Washington refused to arrange any official introductions, so Rhee had to rely upon his Methodist contacts to gain an audience with the elderly Secretary of State John Hay, who gave a careful vow: "I will do everything I can to fulfill our treaty obligations, whether personally or me representing the

United States government, whenever the opportunity presents itself."

By this time Japan and Russia had blooded each other in a brief but furious sea war; recognizing the futility of further combat, both sides accepted Roosevelt's offer to oversee peace talks at his summer home at Oyster Bay, Long Island. Through Secretary Hay, Rhee managed to visit Roosevelt at Oyster Bay in the summer of 1905 to plead for American support of Korean independence. Roosevelt gave Rhee polite and totally misleading double-talk. As Rhee recounted years later, Roosevelt stated he "would be glad to do anything I can in behalf of your country," but any requests must come through official diplomatic channels. Roosevelt neglected to tell Rhee two things. Secretary of War William Howard Taft at that very moment was en route to Tokyo to formalize the agreement giving the U.S. free rein over the Philippines in return for Japanese control of Manchuria and Korea. And Roosevelt knew full well that the pro-Japanese Korean embassy in Washington would do nothing to disrupt the deal. (The formal Russian-Japanese treaty, signed at Portsmouth, New Hampshire, a few months later under Roosevelt's aegis, gave Japan *de facto* control of Korea.)

Roosevelt's vague statement sent Rhee racing to Washington in high excitement. But the Korean minister curtly refused to see him and ordered the doorman to "throw him out" if he returned. Thus Rhee's mission ended in dismal failure, victim of both U.S. duplicity and his own government's willingness to accept Japanese domination for economic reasons.

Years later Rhee was to say that those frantic weeks left a permanent scar on his belief in American credibility; regardless of the language of formal treaties or its diplomats, the U.S. could be trusted to protect only what it conceived to be its best interests. Nor would his church "friends" work to change American policy. "Accept reality," they told him time and again.

The Japanese, for their part, formally converted Korea into a "protectorate," renamed it Chosen, and said it would be governed like any other Japanese province. The United States and other nations withdrew their diplomatic missions from Seoul. Korea no longer existed as a nation.

The anguished Rhee could not return to his homeland, for he knew his political activities against the Japanese made him a marked man. The Methodist Mission Board, which had funded the church schools he attended in Korea, offered to maintain him as a student in the U.S. So for the next five years Rhee became an academic nomad. He studied theology at George Washington University in Washington, D.C., earning pocket money by giving slide shows and lectures on missionary work and Korean independence (one missionary admirer praised him as "an outstanding example of what the Gospel of Christ can do for the Korean people"). After graduation from GWU in 1907, he moved on to

Harvard, again with Methodist money, where he earned a master's degree in history and political science. Next, he received support for two years at Princeton, where he lived in the theological seminary and took doctoral courses in political science. He later called this period "the most tranquil" of his life, chiefly because of his friendship with the Princeton president, Woodrow Wilson, his wife, and three daughters. Austere in a black alpaca suit, Rhee would stand poker-faced at the piano in the Wilsons' parlor while other Princetonians sang, declining to join in despite the teasing of the Wilson girls. Wilson took a strong liking to the withdrawn Rhee, ten to fifteen years the senior of class-mates, and frequently introduced him as the "future redeemer of Korean independence."

The idyl ended in 1910. The International Young Men's Christian Association offered him a job with the Seoul YMCA as teacher and evangelist. Rhee's church friends subtly told him the time had come for a return on their investment: They had paid for his education as a missionary; they now expected him to perform.

Rhee lasted only seventeen months in Korea. The Japanese minded him constantly because of his record of political activism. Watching his countrymen live under conquerors made Rhee sick at heart. He could not function. He quit the YMCA to become principal of a small school. When the Japanese began arresting Christian leaders in 1912, Rhee slipped out of Korea, beginning a thirty-three-year exile that lasted until the end of the Second World War.

He settled in Hawaii, which had a considerable Korean community, and immersed himself in exile politics (supporting himself as headmaster of a Methodist school). The core issue among the scattered thousands of Korean exiles—in Hawaii, on the West Coast of the U.S., in China and Japan—was whether they should attempt to expel the Japanese by force or through Western diplomatic efforts. Despite his earlier disappointments with the Theodore Roosevelt administration, Rhee still believed the public language of Western diplomats. Thus he rejoiced when his old Princeton friend Woodrow Wilson—now President of the United States—announced that the Paris Peace Conference ending the First World War would concern itself with "the right of self-determination of peoples." Excited Korean nationalists met in Seoul and organized a "provisional government" and elected the absent Rhee as president. With this credential, Rhee asked the State Department for a passport so he could attend the peace talks in Paris. To his distress, President Wilson ordered that Rhee be kept away; he needed Japanese cooperation for peace in the Orient, and Rhee's presence would be "disturbing." (Another Asian, Ho Chi Minh of Indochina, managed to reach the conference site, but no one of substance would listen to him. The world learned more of him during the Vietnam War.)

Desperate, Rhee tried to organize mass meetings to mobilize American public opinion behind his cause. The Methodists who a decade earlier had enjoyed his slide shows of Korean missionary life now shunned Rhee; he spoke only to the pitiful handful of Koreans living in the United States. Rhee slipped into Shanghai to meet with "Cabinet" members of his provisional government; he found more jealous infighting than planning. And leadership was rapidly slipping away from Rhee. For two decades he had preached a gradualist approach toward independence, and he had gotten nowhere. Twice his "American friends" had had the opportunity to aid Korea; twice the U.S. had become but another whale that helped crush the Korean shrimp. For understandable reasons Rhee now began earning a reputation for being disputatious and hardheaded. He feuded constantly with other exiled politicians and even his Methodist friends. When Rhee finally returned to Hawaii in early 1922 at age forty-seven, to preach and to teach school, he was a man whose reputation was more of the past than of the present, much less the future.

Enter the Korean Communists

Given the collapse of Rhee's "gradualist" resistance to Japanese occupation, many Koreans looked elsewhere for a more dynamic opposition.[4] Two sources of support in the early 1920's were the fledgling Chinese Communist movement, in the early years of its opposition to the Nationalist regime, and the Soviet Union, eager to encourage any force that might discomfort the Japanese. The Korean Communists suffered many of the same internecine pains as did Rhee's "peaceful reform" group. Japanese repression forced them to operate in exile, in Shanghai, Japan, the Soviet Union, and Manchuria, and their ranks were constantly thinned by political cannibalism.

But the Communists had several advantages over Rhee. Many stayed in Korea, to oppose the Japanese to their faces. They promised not only to evict the Japanese from Korea but to create a "better"—i.e., communistic—society. Koon Woo Nam, an anti-Communist Korean historian, concedes that the Communists were favorably received by farmers and factory workers and managed to stir demonstrations and rent strikes even in the face of harsh police measures. Further, the exiled Korean Communists fought the Japanese military as guerrillas across the Manchurian frontier and as part of the Chinese Communist People's Liberation Army.

One guerrilla—the man who was to be North Korean premier during the Korean War—was born Kim Song-joo, in the northwestern province of Pyongan-namdo, in 1912, or so it is stated by modern North Korean propaganda media. No other sources exist[5]; in analyzing Kim and other North Korean leaders, the American intelligence community has long had to rely upon material with the inherent credibility of, say, 1930's Hollywood fan magazines. To the propagandists' credit, they do give Kim a background fitting a Communist titan. His father, impoverished but bold, taught youngsters history and culture by day and trained them to fight the Japanese by night. Arrested and tortured, then driven into exile in Manchuria, Kim's father used his rudimentary medical knowledge to open a clinic for the poor. Prison broke his body; he died at thirty-two.

Son Kim was said to learn to hate the Japanese early and to have his eyes "swell with tears" when his mother admonished him to "grow up fast to avenge your father." One part of the legacy has father handing son two pistols on his deathbed. Use them, he urged. I shall, the son replied.

Kim's first claimed political activities were said to come in 1928, when at age sixteen he supposedly led violent demonstrations in the Manchurian commercial city of Kirin against expansion of the main Korean railroad into Manchuria. He was jailed briefly, then retired to the countryside to "exhort farmers, students, and small merchants to organize to oppose the Japanese."

Kim's organizing apparently bore fruit, for when the Japanese invaded Manchuria in 1931–32, he commanded one of the many guerrilla bands which rose in opposition. The Chinese Communists, who exercised overall control of the partisan groups, called them the Northeast Anti-Japanese United Army, a title more formidable in sound than in reality, and gave them arms and political leadership. And the man who had been born Kim Song-joo twenty years earlier now assumed the name Kim Il Sung, after a fabled guerrilla leader who had fought the Japanese around the turn of the century.

The change of name had considerable psychological significance. It endowed Kim with the mystique of a national hero, so much so that when he appeared in his home country after the Second World War, many persons were surprised to see so young a man; they actually thought the Kim Il Sung they gathered to greet would be the original. Later, North Korean official histories even credited Kim as becoming, at age twenty-one, the leader who "solidified the unity of comrades" fighting in northern Manchuria in 1934 and 1935 (a claim which Korean historian Koon Woo Nam found dubious, for there appeared to be no overall leadership in the region during this period).

The validity of this claim aside,[6] the Communists did build a strong guerrilla force in Manchuria, using arms seized from the Japanese and occasionally assaulting garrisons with forces of more than 1,000 men.

Kim's specific actions—and whereabouts—are impossible to document, and the official North Korean biography credits him with an implausible series of heroic exploits. Regardless of Kim's direct role, official Japanese Army figures attest to the guerrillas' effectiveness. From the mid-1930's through the end of the war Communist guerrillas in Manchuria killed more than 60,000 Japanese soldiers, equivalent to six divisions.

The evidence suggests that Kim's guerrilla success convinced the Soviets he could be useful in the postwar period. The Soviets during the war operated on several different tracks concerning Korea. On the one hand, they supported the Korean independence movement as a means of harassing the Japanese. Simultaneously they displayed cautious self-interest. The Soviets wanted control of Manchuria once the Japanese were displaced, but they feared that Koreans living there might help deliver the country back to China or even lay claim to parts of it themselves. (People living along the Korean-Manchurian frontier paid little heed to the formal border, and there was much back-and-forth mixing of populations.) So for "security reasons"[7] the Soviets in the late 1930's summarily moved some 150,000 Korean men, women, and children from the maritime provinces adjacent to Manchuria far into the Soviet interior. The young men were drafted into military units for the ostensible purpose of fighting the Japanese should the USSR and Japan ever go to war.

The date of this massive population shift coincides with the claim, in Kim's state biography, of a forced "long march" by his guerrilla forces into North Manchuria to escape tightening Japanese military pressures. And this is the time at which Kim presumably came under direct Soviet control, as an officer in the Red Army. Whatever the circumstances, when Kim surfaced in North Korea in late 1945, as the Soviet-chosen leader of the Communist regime there, he wore the uniform of a major in the Red Army. Western experts who have studied the scant details available on Kim's career feel it unlikely that the Soviets would have imposed such responsibility in Kim had he not been under their tutelage for a considerable period.

Whatever the facts of Kim Il Sung's background, and his wartime career, he clearly was a man the Soviet Union could trust—and control.

Rhee's Exile Years

During Kim's guerrilla years the indomitable Syngman Rhee continued plodding around Western chanceries, hoping the Americans would recognize him as the legitimate Korean leader. He divided his time between his school in Hawaii and visits to Washington, where his provisional government maintained a Korean Commission to the United States. Despite almost universal rebuffs, Rhee still felt that "our efforts must more or less for the time being be concentrated on the United States." One sympathizes with the old man's zeal; one must question his sense of realism, for the U.S. demonstrated no interest whatsoever in aiding a subjugated nation that most citizens would have had difficulty locating on a map. The Los Angeles *Times*, perhaps piqued at Rhee's insistence on being interviewed each time he came to town, headlined a story, RHEE HERE IN KOREA'S LOST CAUSE. The first sentence read: "Leader of the lost cause of the Orient, Dr. Syngman Rhee, . . . is in Los Angeles meeting with Chinese merchants and leaders in an effort to enlist their aid in his campaign for Korean freedom." At one point he even turned to the Soviet Union, arguing to the ambassador in Paris that a united front was needed on the Asian mainland against the rising menace of Japan. Rhee managed to obtain a visa and make his way to Moscow, only to be told it was all a mistake; he must leave Russia at once.

The trip did produce one significant benefit for Rhee: Before entraining for Moscow, he chanced to sit at dinner one evening beside Francesca Donner, the eldest of three daughters of a wealthy Vienna manufacturer. Donner, a strict disciplinarian, taught his girls "the rudiments of business management and masculine self-reliance"[8] and emphasized self-responsibility. Francesca, a strong-faced woman with rolls of blond curls, knew something of international affairs as well, and she had read Rhee's articles about Korean independence. The appeal was mutual and immediate. Two years later, in 1934, they were married in New York. Thereafter she served Rhee as wife, secretary, housekeeper, comrade, "warmest supporter, adviser and caretaker."

By the late 1930's Rhee indeed appeared to lead a "lost cause." Members of his own provisional government turned to violent assaults and guerrilla warfare against the Japanese; some even moved under the banner of the Korean People's Liberation Army, which Rhee denounced as "Communist and unChristian." Others made common cause with the Chinese Communists. In the words of friendly biographer Robert T. Oliver:

> His policy of seeking to revive his lost nation through appeals to the self-interest and good sense of the West was seemingly bankrupt. His leadership never made any deep impression on the American officials to whom he tried to appeal, and as decade piled upon decade with his program barren of results, his own following began to disintegrate.

Even Rhee's friends began to call him a stubborn and obstinate old man, one who would cling to a discredited strategy in hopes of salvaging some ill-defined personal advantage.

At the start of the Second World War Rhee moved back to Washington, to a small house above the National Zoo, where he "listened to the roaring of the lions . . . and felt a kinship with their frustrations." Soon after Pearl Harbor he visited the State Department and asked Stanley Hornbeck, the head of the Office of Far Eastern Affairs, that his provisional government be recognized as the legitimate Korean regime. Surely the old argument about "affronting Japan" no longer had any validity. Hornbeck huffed and waffled[9]; in the end he gave Rhee no more attention than would have been afforded any citizen who wandered in from the street. Later Assistant Secretary of State Adolf Berle told Rhee, in a convolutedly formal letter, that the U.S. for the time being did not intend to recognize exile groups claiming to be the "legitimate" governments of nations caught up in the war; in sum, let us first win the war, then decide the politics.

Rhee even lost the support of the majority of the "provisional Korean government," which in 1942 voted him out as president, choosing in his stead Kim Koo, who was in refuge in Nationalist China. A moderate, Koo wanted to form a "representative assembly of all revolutionary organizations," including even the Communist Korean National Revolutionary Party. In late 1942 Hornbeck curtly informed Rhee that the State Department considered him wholly unknown inside Korea and that the provisional government was no more than a "self-constituted club with limited membership among a group of expatriates." Rhee clearly was not a favorite of the U.S. government.

The Korean Communists, meanwhile, were belly-deep in snow in Manchuria, fighting the Japanese.

Independence "in Due Course"

The State Department was not being coy with Rhee when it told him he had no standing to speak for any "government." Korea was but one of many orphaned nations the futures of which would be resolved with peace, and in 1942 it ranked high on no one's list of priorities. President Franklin Roosevelt shared his cousin Theodore's low esteem of the nationalist Koreans. At the Teheran Conference of 1943, he told Soviet Premier Joseph Stalin the Koreans "are not yet capable of exercising and maintaining independent government and . . . they should be placed under a forty-year tutelage."[10] At a conference later that year Roosevelt, Prime Minister Winston Churchill of Great Britain, and Generalissimo Chiang Kai-shek of China issued a final communiqué which reflected FDR's pessimism: "Mindful of the enslavement of the Korean people, the aforementioned Great Powers [the United States,

Great Britain, and China] are determined that Korea shall, *in due course,* be free and independent [emphasis added]."

To Rhee and other Korean nationalists, the "in due course" phrase was a direct insult; again the shrimp was being caught in the battle of the whales. What right, Rhee stormed to the State Department, did the Allied powers have to withhold independence from Korea?

Roosevelt's lack of enthusiasm for Korean independence did not alter his intention to deny the USSR the dominant postwar role in Korea. According to secret State Department documents, FDR wished to try a wide range of diplomatic strategies to pursue this goal. He told Secretary of State Cordell Hull, for instance, that Korea "might be placed under an international trusteeship, with China, the United States, and one or two other countries participating."[11] Other State Department planning documents went even further, calling for postwar U.S. domination of Korea, which meant a U.S. role in the military liberation of the country. A State Department planning paper stated in March 1944: "The assumption by the U.S. of a major part in civil affairs and in international supervision of an interim government would be greatly facilitated by the participation of the U.S. in such military operations as take place in and around Korea." The paper foresaw a military occupation of Korea potentially of "considerable duration" and probably shared with the Soviets, who could be expected to hold "considerable portions" of the country. Another document, written two months later, in May 1944, warned that if the Soviets occupied Korea alone, "the U.S. might consider such a development as a threat to the future security of the Pacific." This and other papers advocated that any occupation be through a shared central administration, not zonal governments.

Ultimately Korea was fitted into a broad strategic mosaic for the Pacific war, as part of attractive bait intended to lure the Soviet Union into the war with Japan. Here some background is in order. Given the desperate struggle with the Germans on the eastern front, the Soviets remained technically at peace with Japan even after the attack on Pearl Harbor and declarations of war on Tokyo by its major allies, the U.S. and Great Britain. Neither Japan nor the USSR seemed eager to go to war, the former tied down with fighting elsewhere in Asia, the latter not wishing to open a second battlefront. Nonetheless, from the outset of the war General Douglas MacArthur, commander of American ground forces in the Far East, urged Washington superiors to find a way to persuade Russia to enter the Pacific war. On December 10, 1941, only three days after Pearl Harbor, MacArthur sent a pleading cable to General George C. Marshall, the army chief of staff, from his headquarters in the Philippines:

The mass of enemy air and naval strength committed in the theater to the Philippines and eastward established his weakness in Japan proper and definite information available here shows that entry of Russia is enemy's greatest fear. Most favorable opportunity now exists and immediate attack on Japan from north would not only inflict heavy punishment but would at once relieve pressure from objectives of Jap drive to southward. . . .

Golden opportunity exists for a master stroke while the enemy is engaged in over-extended initial air efforts.

The request was unrealistic, what with the German Wehrmacht on the outskirts of Moscow, and Marshall ignored it. But the issue was raised again in late 1944, in advance of a Big Three strategy conference to be held early the next year at Yalta, in the Russian Crimea. State Department planning papers accepted the necessity of Soviet entry into the war, albeit under cautious terms.[12] The War Department by this time was far along with plans for an assault on the Japanese mainland, with a feared frightful cost of life (some estimates ran as high as 1 million American dead). At Teheran, two years earlier, Stalin had promised vaguely to enter the Pacific war at the "proper time." Now the JCS urged that Roosevelt hold him to the pledge. War Department intelligence officers asserted that Japanese strength was such that Russian intervention was "imperative." The Joint Chiefs' estimate was that the Pacific war would last eighteen months beyond the collapse of Germany and that Allied casualties would be reduced by 200,000 men if the Soviets entered the war before the invasion of Japan.

To the Roosevelt inner circle, such a saving of life warranted the political risks inherent in giving the Soviets an opportunity for expansion into Japanese-held areas. To the State Department officials planning the Yalta Conference, Korea was to be a bargaining pawn. According to Yalta planning papers,[13] State was willing to share postwar occupation of Korea with Great Britain and China (and the USSR, provided the latter entered the Pacific war). But the papers stressed that the United States should "play a leading role in the occupation and military government." It had no long-range interest in Korea; what it wished was a buffer against any Russian thrust against Japan.

Once again the Korean "shrimp" was caught between the whales.

A Deal at Yalta

When Franklin D. Roosevelt sailed to Yalta in February 1945, he was a sick man, his brain already damaged by a stroke suffered the previous summer, his final, fatal seizure only weeks away. During the ten-day cruise across the Atlantic and through the Mediterranean he stayed in his cabin; a "severe cold" was the official explanation. But British Prime

Minister Winston Churchill instinctively knew otherwise when he exchanged a wave with his old comrade at the harbor in Malta, a stopping-over point. Churchill felt the President looked "frail and ill."[14]

Roosevelt's physical condition at Yalta, and the agreements he made there, were to plague American foreign policy for three decades, with Republican critics accusing a befuddled Democratic President of "selling out" Eastern Europe and much of Asia to the wily Soviet Premier Stalin. The Soviet dictator certainly wore a variety of faces at the talks: He could be as charming in public as he could be ruthless in private, and he made repeated protestations of everlasting friendship. Through one freshet of vodka toasts he proposed that "our alliance . . . should not lose its character of intimacy. . . . May it be strong and stable."

Both Stalin and the Allies came to Yalta with self-interest paramount. Stalin wanted "buffer zones" in both Asia and Europe, satellite nations answerable to Moscow. The details on Europe are too complex to pursue here; essentially the "rights" accorded the USSR in Europe were what the Red Army already held, or would occupy by the war's end, a *fait accompli* which no one had any reasonable expectation of reversing.

Stalin and Roosevelt decided on the Asian buffer in a private talk. Earlier Stalin had told Averell Harriman, the American ambassador in Moscow, his desiderata for entering the Pacific war: the "return" of the southern half of Sakhalin and the Kurile Islands, territories he claimed Japan had seized from Russia in the 1904 war.[15] (Actually Japan had taken only southern Sakhalin then; it had obtained the Kuriles in a freely negotiated 1875 treaty.) Stalin told FDR he felt the Soviet Union should be "preeminent" in Manchuria; hence he wanted internationalization of the port of Dairen, use of Port Arthur as a Soviet naval base, and shared control of Chinese railroads in the country. In return, Russia would enter the war against Japan "two or three months after Germany has surrendered."

Roosevelt balked; he said he could make no promises on the ports or railroads without consulting Chiang Kai-shek, the Chinese president. But the remainder of the deal he accepted (to the dismay of adviser Charles Bohlen, who disliked the President's making a deal on Manchuria "behind the backs of our Chinese allies." Chiang's Nationalist government was under strong siege by the Chinese Communists; conceding Soviet domination of Manchuria could do nothing but harm Chiang's cause).

Bohlen, however, was a minority voice. The American military—especially General Douglas MacArthur, commander of U.S. forces in the Pacific theater—strongly endorsed bringing the Russians into the war. A few days after the Yalta talks ended, the War Department sent Colonel Paul L. Freeman, Jr., to MacArthur's headquarters to brief him on the decisions. MacArthur was well into his invasion planning but apprehensive about the "potency of the Japanese army" and the possibility of troops' being shifted from Manchuria and China to defend the home islands. In a dispatch to the War Department on February 13, 1945, Freeman quoted MacArthur: "He emphatically stated that we must not invade Japan proper unless the Russian army is previously committed to action in Manchuria." MacArthur realized the postwar political cost. Freeman's memorandum continued:

> He [MacArthur] understands Russia's aims: that they would want all of Manchuria, Korea, and possibly part of North China. This seizure of territory was inevitable; but the United States must insist that Russia pay her way by invading Manchuria at the earliest possible date after the defeat of Germany.

MacArthur spoke in the same vein several days later to another War Department representative, Brigadier General George A. Lincoln. Lincoln cabled superiors on February 25, 1945:

> General MacArthur pointed out that politically they [the Russians] want a warm water port, which would be Port Arthur. He considered that it would be impracticable to deny them such a port because of their great military power. Therefore, it was only right they should share the cost in blood of defeating Japan.

In June 1945, when the War Department agonized over whether to issue final orders for the Japan invasion, MacArthur again pleaded for Soviet support. He sent General George C. Marshall a cable which the chief of staff read at a White House meeting. MacArthur called his invasion plan "the most economical one in effort and lives that is possible." Again he pleaded for Russian help: "The hazard and loss will be greatly reduced if an attack is launched from Siberia sufficiently ahead of our target date to commit the enemy to major combat."*

Korea Is Divided

The fireballs of two atomic bombs rendered moot any plans for invasion of the Japanese homeland in August 1945. The first of these nuclear

---

*These statements notwithstanding, MacArthur audaciously stated in his autobiography, published in 1964: "From my viewpoint, any intervention by Russia during 1945 was not required. The substance of Japan had already been gutted, the best of its army and navy had been defeated, and the Japanese homeland was now at the mercy of air raids and invasion." MacArthur did concede he wanted Russian participation in late 1941 to draw the Japanese away from the South Pacific, but "by 1945 such intervention had become superfluous." In his book MacArthur does not mention the cables quoted above.

attacks came on August 6; two days later the Soviets finally entered the Pacific war, far too late to be of any practical military value, but a *de jure* fulfillment of their Yalta pledge. On August 10 the Japanese sued for peace, and several divisions of Russian troops began a rapid drive through Manchuria, bound for Korea.

Where would they stop? No one knew. Despite all the talks on Soviet entry into the war, no demarcation line in Korea had been decided. U.S. military advisers at the Potsdam Conference in East Germany less than a month earlier had suggested (to General Marshall) that the division be along the 38th parallel, which divides the country roughly in half. But this apparently was not discussed with the Soviets, for the Potsdam record is devoid of any mention of a demarcation line.

With peace, the issue took on sudden urgency. The U.S. ground troops nearest to Korea were on Okinawa, 600 miles distant. Late in the night of August 10–11[16] the State-War-Navy Coordinating Committee, created early in the war to do just what its name implied, held an emergency session in the Pentagon, with the Korean surrender high on the agenda. State Department representatives, for political reasons, wished to receive the Japanese surrender as far to the north as possible. But Dean Rusk, then a young colonel on Marshall's staff,* noted that the military was "faced with the scarcity of U.S. forces immediately available and time and space factors which would make it difficult to reach very far north before Soviet troops could enter the area." John J. McCloy, the assistant secretary of war, told Rusk and another colonel, C. H. Bonesteel III, to go into an anteroom and see if they could decide on a line compromising State's political desires with military reality. Rusk commented later: "The military view was that if our proposals for receiving the surrender greatly over-reached our probable military capabilities, there would be little likelihood of Soviet acceptance—and speed was the essence of the problem."

After talking, Rusk and Bonesteel recommended the 38th parallel "even though it was further north than could be realistically reached by U.S. forces in the event of Soviet disagreement." They chose this line because "we felt it important to include the capital of Korea in the area of responsibility of American troops."

To Rusk's surprise, the Russians accepted the 38th parallel without hesitation. Formal orders went out from MacArthur on September 2, the day the Japanese signed the surrender on the USS *Missouri* in Tokyo: Japanese soldiers north of the 38th parallel would surrender to the Russians; those to the south, to the Americans.

The 190-mile demarcation line, although neat on Dean Rusk's map,

*Although he intended to remain in the military as a career officer, Rusk followed Marshall to the State Department when the latter became secretary of state in 1947. During the Korean War he was assistant secretary for Far Eastern affairs; later, from 1961 to 1969, he was secretary of state during the Kennedy-Johnson administrations.

made no economic sense. The southern zone covered 37,000 square miles and contained some 21 million people, about two-thirds of them in farm families. Although the South contained twelve of Korea's twenty largest cities—including Seoul, the capital, with 2 million people —it was primarily agricultural and historically supplied rice for the entire country. The northern zone, although larger with 48,000 square miles, had only about 9 million population. But because of its highly developed hydroelectric plants, the North had most of Korea's industrial plants—chemical, steel, cement, and fertilizers, products that complemented the South's agrarian economy. Neither zone had the capacity for economic self-sufficiency.

Its flaws notwithstanding, the Rusk line served the desired political purpose. By the time surrender orders went to the field scattered Soviet units had crossed the parallel, moving down the highway toward Seoul. But they quickly withdrew when told the demarcation line. Such was to be veritably the last instance of Soviet-American cooperation in Korea.

The first American troops, units of the 7th Infantry Division, landed at the port of Inchon on September 8—an operation code-named Black List Forty—and the next day entered Seoul amid wild outpourings of Korean emotion. The Koreans had waited half a century for independence and dignity; they thought they had both in their grasp.

They had neither. The man chosen by MacArthur to head the occupation, Major General John R. Hodge, was a brave battle commander (he had led the invasion of Okinawa), but he was a tactless man unsuited for any diplomacy beyond the barracks level. His first blunder came the first day of occupation. The Japanese commander, after surrendering, asked for authority to keep Japanese police armed to protect his troops and the 600,000 Japanese civilians in Korea from reprisals. Already Korean street mobs were throwing rocks and garbage at the hated foreigners who had occupied their country.

No problem, replied Hodge. He said that he considered Koreans "breeds of the same cat as the Japanese"[17] and that he intended to treat them as conquered enemies. Besides, so many Koreans had fought with the Japanese Army that he wanted time to sort out just who was who. Hodge's statement, reported by the American press, stunned his superiors in Washington. General George Marshall ordered him to disband the Japanese police and to avoid further insulting comments about the Koreans. But the damage was done. Hodge was to remain in Korea as the titular American vice-consul another four years. His opinion of the Korean people—and vice versa—did not change perceptibly during that time.

In Hodge's defense, the lack of any guidance from Washington forced him to work in a vacuum his first months in Korea. He had no training as a military governor; his command lacked persons who could speak

Korean; the swift postwar demobilization stripped his division of the most experienced officers and men. Besides, the departure of the Japanese left Korea in economic chaos.

The long-exiled Syngman Rhee, meanwhile, spent the first postpeace weeks fretting in Washington. In June he had asked recognition as head of the Korean government by virtue of his old title of High Commissioner from Korea, bestowed on him by other exiles in the 1920's. But middle-level diplomats wrote him off as a carping old man (Rhee was sixty-nine years old) who had been away from his native land for three decades and whose claimed credentials were so dated as to be dubious. By order of President Truman (in June 1945) the State Department refused to recognize Rhee's "provisional government" (or any other group); to do so would "compromise the right of the Korean people to choose the ultimate form and personnel of the government which they may wish to establish."

But in October 1945 Rhee suddenly received support from an unexpected and powerful force. General MacArthur wanted a national leader in Korea whom he could trust. So he made inquiries of other Asians, particularly Chiang Kai-shek of China: Of all the men claiming Korean leadership, who would be the best choice?

Chiang at the time had never met Rhee, but he knew of him through several channels he considered reliable. One was an exile named Kim Koo, "president" of the Rhee provisional government, who had spent the war years in Chiang's capital of Chungking. Chiang, like Rhee, was a converted Christian, and Protestant missionaries in China spoke highly of the Korean. Many Korean exiles had prospered in business in China; they, too, strongly recommended Rhee. Rhee's strong anticommunism was also a selling point with Chiang, whose government was besieged by domestic Communists.

So at MacArthur's direction both Rhee and Kim Koo were returned to Seoul in mid-October 1945. Concurrently the State Department gave MacArthur a broad policy directive on Korea "to foster conditions which will bring about the establishment of a free and independent nation" in stages: civil administration by the U.S. and the USSR; a period of trusteeship under the U.S., the USSR, Britain, and China; and, finally, "to . . . eventual independence" and UN membership.

Despite Kim Koo's presence, MacArthur clearly intended Rhee to be the dominant figure. At MacArthur's orders, Hodge welcomed Rhee to Seoul in a histrionic ceremony, with Rhee stepping from behind a curtain after a laudatory introduction. Hodge urged that "all Koreans accept Rhee as their leader."

But official American policy—as Truman had stated in June—was that the U.S. should favor no individual or group. To Hodge this policy was dangerous. "The Koreans want their independence more than any one thing, and they want it now," he told the Joint Chiefs in December 1945.

At one point George Atcheson, a diplomat assigned to MacArthur's headquarters as a political adviser, suggested a coalition of Rhee, Kim Koo, and a resistance leader, Kim Kiu-sik. Rhee, however, would have no part of a coalition. He wanted supremacy, and he formed a party, the Society for the Rapid Realization of Independence, and held rallies around the country. He solicited support from a broad range of philosophies but rejected outright any alliance with the Communists.

To General Hodge, Korean politics was a morass he would just as soon not enter. By late December the bickering had him so frustrated that he suggested to the War Department that both the Soviets and the Americans vacate Korea simultaneously and leave the country to an "inevitable internal upheaval for its self-purification."

The Russians, however, were in no mood for cooperation. In the months after the war ended they swiftly constructed a satellite state in the Soviet image, headed by the returned guerrilla chieftain Kim Il Sung. Thousands of expatriate Koreans returned from Manchuria and the USSR, most of them completely communized during their years of exile. Dissidents were imprisoned or driven to the South. Kim's control was so taut by mid-1946 that the Russians had only about 10,000 occupation troops in North Korea. (Hodge, by contrast, had about 43,000 American soldiers.)

More important, the Soviets managed to push the United States into an untenable corner at a Moscow conference in December 1945 of the Big Four foreign ministers. The ministers agreed on a joint U.S.-USSR commission to consult with Korean leaders and devise a provisional government covering all the country. After a trusteeship of "up to five years," Korea would be united and independent, with a government of its own choosing.

The trusteeship proposal touched off wild rioting in South Korea, and Hodge had to send troops into the streets to quell mobs. The Soviets shrewdly made false propaganda statements that trusteeship was a U.S. idea (Stalin had accepted it at Yalta) and that the Americans actually wanted a ten-year period. The Soviets also claimed (again, falsely) they were ready for immediate Korean independence. The Russian success in this diplomatic gambit embittered Hodge, who told MacArthur in February 1946 that "the Korean people are feeling that the U.S. has again 'sold them down the river.'"

In formal bargaining sessions in January and February 1946 the United States asked for integration of the northern and southern zones; the Soviets, however, wanted no disruption of their tight satellite state. The Soviet intention was crystal-clear to MacArthur, Hodge, and American diplomats. Once the situation in South Korea became chaotic enough, and the United States unpopular enough, a friendly Communist regime could be installed.

The U.S. dilemma was multidimensional. Any government created in the political turmoil then raging in South Korea would be no match for the disciplined North Korean state, already well along toward building an army. MacArthur's original choice as leader, Syngman Rhee, was untrustworthy. In December 1945, for instance, the army's Counter Intelligence Corps (CIC), a security group, regularly tapped Rhee's phone and intercepted his mail as the old man prepared for a trip to the U.S. Rhee wrote to such dignitaries as Eleanor Roosevelt, FDR's widow; Paul Henri Spaak, president of the UN General Assembly; Trygve Lie, UN secretary-general; and Francis Cardinal Spellman of the Catholic Archdiocese of New York. William Langdon, political officer with the occupation, summarized Rhee's goals in a December 1945 telegram to the State Department. Rhee intended to "fight and wreck" U.S. attempts at a trusteeship, with the aim of arousing U.S. and UN opinion to end the American occupation. (Rhee managed audiences with the people he had courted by mail; none offered to help him.) To Hodge, Rhee's deliberate attempt to sabotage U.S. policy meant the occupation must cast its lot with another man. Kim Koo, the onetime Rhee ally who had spent the war years in Nationalist China, seemed a more pliable alternative. Political adviser Langdon, in a secret cable to the State Department in December 1945, offered a pragmatic reason for firm American guidance of any new Korean government:

> The old native regime internally was feudal and corrupt but the record shows that it was the best disposed towards foreign interests of the three Far Eastern nations, protecting foreign lives and property and enterprises and respecting treaties and franchises. I am sure that we count on at least as much from a native government evolved as above. . . .[18]

Kim Koo, however, could muster no popular support. For brief weeks he headed a "council" which the occupation hoped would evolve into a government. The idea failed. By early 1946 the occupation was at its wit's ends about creating any sort of interim government. The omnipresent Rhee, although of uncertain following, had the political resources to incite street mobs and to discourage other leaders. One outside observer, Mark Gayn of the Chicago *Sun,* thought him a "sinister and dangerous man, an anachronism who had strayed into this age to use the clichés and machinery of democracy for unscrupulous and undemocratic ends."[19] To Gayn, Rhee was an inexplicable figure: a thin man with spare white hair, pale lips, and almost no eyebrows; thin slits of eyelids concealed his eyes most of the time, so that he seemed asleep. Rhee spoke what one Korean described to Gayn as a "Hawaiian brand of pidgin Korean." But one of Hodge's political advisers assured Gayn that Rhee was no fascist. "He is two centuries before fascism—a pure Bourbon."

But Rhee had drawn the line: The shrimp was not to be crushed between the whales again.

The United States Disengages

The cable traffic between the State Department, the War Department, and the occupation the next two years—1946–48—is more easily measured in lineal feet than by page count. It is dreary and repetitive reading: words written by diplomats and military officers in search of a solution that one finally concludes did not exist. The occupation dealt with political hatreds and feuds dating back for decades; at one time South Korea had no less than 113 "political parties," few willing to coalesce with another. Periodic talks with the Soviets about putting the entire country under trusteeship were fruitless. Intelligence reports drifting down from North Korea led Hodge to believe that invasion threats were "more than mere rumor." To occupation political officers, the Soviets had settled down for a war of attrition, confident that America would finally write off Korea and leave. Hodge recognized in mid-1946 that although "Korea has been low on the agenda of national foreign policy . . . I feel that the situation here is reaching the point where Washington must become aware that it may soon reach the point of explosion."

Washington's decision, ultimately, was a forced one: It would shed itself of responsibility for South Korea because it had no alternative. The chief reason was the drastic cut in the American military in the immediate postwar years. Here Truman had definitely listened to the voice of the people, who cried, "Bring the boys home!" and shipped scores of hundreds of baby shoes to congressmen to emphasize they wanted their husbands and fathers home immediately. On V-J Day, in August 1945, the U.S. had slightly more than 12 million men and women under arms. In January 1946 Truman told the Pentagon he wanted a standing military of 2 million (the generals wanted about a million more). But Congress, even more sensitive to public opinion than the President, went further. In the spring of 1946 the appropriations committees of both houses set a limit (for all services) of 1,070,000 men by July 1, 1947. Thousands of ships, tanks, and planes went into mothballs, and the military became a constabulary, concerned mainly with occupation duties and training.

The State and Defense departments spent the first months of 1947 reviewing how these limited resources should be deployed. The first priority definitely was Europe. Since the end of the war the Soviets had consolidated their hold on Eastern Europe and showed signs of moving against weakened France and Italy. As a counter the U.S. could muster only two divisions—20,000 soldiers, give or take 1,000—against some sixty-five Soviet and satellite divisions.

The key decision was made on the basis of a memorandum sent to Defense Secretary James Forrestal on September 25, 1947, under the signature of General Dwight D. Eisenhower, then the Chairman of the Joint Chiefs of Staff, on behalf of the other chiefs. The memo concluded that given America's limited resources, the United States "has little strategic interest"[20] in keeping bases and troops in Korea. The National Security Council and Truman concurred. Forrestal cited these reasons:

> In the event of hostilities in the Far East, our present forces in Korea would be a military liability and could not be maintained there without substantial reinforcement prior to the initiation of hostilities. Moreover, any offensive operation the United States might wish to conduct on the Asiatic continent most probably would by-pass the Korean peninsula.

Forrestal conceded that enemy air and naval bases in Korea could interfere with American operations in the area. But such bases "would be subject to neutralization by air action," which he called "more feasible and less costly than large scale ground operations." The 45,000 American troops in Korea "could well be used elsewhere," and their withdrawal "would not impair the military position of the Far East Command." Under a phased withdrawal the 40,000-odd occupation troops would be out of there by June 1950. The import of this action was that the U.S. was shedding itself of responsibility for South Korea.

But the United States did not intend to leave the ROKs entirely on their own. A month later, in October 1947, the U.S. asked the United Nations to appoint a commission to conduct elections in all Korea before March 31, 1948. The resultant government would control the entire country, and U.S. and Soviet troops would withdraw. The Soviets argued that the UN had no jurisdiction in Korea because it was not a member state. Although the General Assembly approved the U.S. proposal, the Soviets said they would not take part in any elections.

The United States did not rise to the Soviet bait. Although a CIA estimate in February 1948 thought it "improbable that any South Korean government can maintain its independence after U.S. withdrawal,"[21] the State Department told the UN to proceed with elections in the South to choose members of a national assembly that would form a government. The Communists worked first for a boycott; nonetheless, more than four out of five eligible Koreans registered to vote. The boycott having failed, the Communists resorted to terror on election day, on May 10, killing more than 100 people in and around polling places. Nonetheless, the turnout exceeded 90 percent of the registered voters, and the UN Commission later called the election "a valid expression of the free will of the electorate."

The clear winner: Syngman Rhee, who won more than 90 percent of the vote for an assembly seat from Seoul. The Assembly convened on May 31, elected Rhee as chairman, and proceeded to write a constitution. The constitution was promulgated on July 17, 1948, and three days later Rhee was elected president of the Republic of Korea. After more than fifty years of struggle the old man finally had an independent country.

The question now became, with U.S. military support absent, how long could the Republic of Korea survive in the face of constant military buildups in North Korea? General Douglas MacArthur, while in Seoul for Rhee's inaugural in October 1948, gave a perhaps unwitting boost to the country's spirit, telling the new president, "Personally, I will do anything I can to help the Korean people and to protect them. I will protect them as I would protect the United States or California against aggression."

In actuality, of course, MacArthur could do no such thing, for the army was already beginning the swift withdrawal of its 40,000-man garrison. The intention was to leave a military mission of 61 officers and men. But these plans were abruptly interrupted in the fall of 1948 by two events in North Korea. First, the Soviets announced establishment of a government there under Premier Kim Il Sung. Secondly, they said they intended to have all Red Army troops out of the North by the end of the year and suggested that American troops leave the South at the same time. The sudden Russian eagerness for the withdrawal of foreign troops aroused suspicions of American officers in Seoul, who feared an invasion by Kim Il Sung's army. So the Joint Chiefs of Staff, in December 1948, decided to leave a regimental combat team of about 7,500 Americans in the country for the time being. But the JCS made plain the American military would not remain in South Korea indefinitely, only long enough to nurse the fledgling nation through its first months of independence.*

Rhee Takes Charge

America's new role in South Korea was emphasized in August 1948 by the formal end of the occupation and the arrival of John J. Muccio as

*General MacArthur disagreed with the JCS. In a December 4 cable he complained that a "small army force in Korea . . . will be subject to possible destruction in event of a major attack on this vulnerable salient. The force . . . must be considered a liability rather than an asset."

ambassador. Muccio, forty-eight years old that summer, had been in the Foreign Service since 1921, spending most of his time in Latin America and the Far East. He was a ruggedly handsome bachelor, who, colleagues said, had exquisite tastes in both women and whiskey. ("A chronic womanizer," one person said of him. "You'd go to a reception with him and realize, from the looks that passed back and forth between him and the women, that he'd probably bedded a sizable number of the females present.") Muccio got along well with the military[22]; he could drink and talk with field-grade officers, and he exuded a *machismo* that set him apart from the urbane diplomats that career soldiers tended to dismiss as "striped-pants cookie pushers."

Muccio had his baptism of fire with the mercurial Rhee almost immediately upon arrival in the country. Major General John Coulter, now the ranking U.S. military officer in Korea,* was trying to negotiate the pact under which the United States would supply defense aid to the ROKs. In brief, Rhee wanted money and equipment, but without any U.S. controls over their use. He was quite willing to have Americans assigned to his army as "advisers," but he did not want the word to be mentioned in the aid agreement. To do so would make him appear dependent upon the Americans. The United States yielded and struck the word "adviser" from the pact. On another issue, however, Muccio stood firm. The U.S. wanted to retain control of ROK troops, especially along the 38th parallel, during the time of American withdrawal to guard against a sudden North Korean strike. Rhee protested, but futilely.

Although painful, these sessions gave Muccio an appreciation of Rhee. His differences with the ROK president were to be frequent and often frustrating in the future, but at least he understood the man:

> Rhee had fought in what really amounted to a guerrilla operation so long that when he finally ended up as the duly elected president of Korea he was so old . . . that he could not change from his . . . revolutionary instincts to being a duly recognized head of state. When he was in a logical frame of mind, he had an excellent historical perspective. . . . But when he got emotional, then he reverted to his long-standing instincts of self-survival of himself as an individual. . . .

As his relationship with Rhee deepened, Muccio came to support the ROK desire for a continued U.S. military presence. In this dispute, which occupied the first months of 1949, the State Department and the Defense Department reversed what could have been their expected roles—the diplomats arguing for troops in Korea, the generals for prompt withdrawal.[23] The State Department, through W. Walton But-

---

*General Hodge asked to be relieved after independence, saying his relations with Rhee were so poor he was no longer effective.

terworth of the Far Eastern Office, argued that the Communist victory in China in 1949 put Korea in a new light: The Chinese would now be able to support a North Korean attempt to seize the ROK. He spoke of a "growing conviction . . . that the Soviet Union is now determined to bring about at the earliest possible moment the destruction of the new [ROK] government. . . ."

The military case, stated by William H. Draper, Jr., the army under-secretary, was that South Korea continued to be of "little strategic interest" to the United States. Leaving troops there invited trouble. Further, the army had made no budgetary provision for retaining troops in Korea past 1949.*

After months of study the National Security Council (and Truman) sided with the military. The NSC paper—NSC 8/2, approved by Tru-man on March 23, 1949—stressed the necessity of U.S. aid to help the ROKs build their own army. The risk of a North Korean invasion "will obtain equally at any time in the foreseeable future." The council cited the fear that U.S. forces "might be either destroyed or obligated to abandon Korea in the event of a major hostile attack, with serious damage to U.S. prestige in either case." It set a withdrawal deadline of June 30, 1949. The ROKs would be left with six months of supplies, and American advisers would help them build a military force of at least 65,000 men.

The significance of this NSC conclusion is that it marked the second time in three years that the administration had decided against any further U.S. military role in South Korea. Months of detailed staff study went into each decision. Nonetheless, as we shall see, American policy was to change 180 degrees in the space of twenty-four hours in June 1950.

Muccio was in Washington for the final days of the debate over troop withdrawal, and he returned to Seoul with the mission of making the decision palatable to Rhee. At his urging nothing was said publicly until "I had a chance to work on Rhee." Muccio decided to mousetrap the ROK president:

> When I got back to Korea, the first thing I did was start pointing out to Rhee the wonderful progress (and they were making good progress) the new Korean constabulary was making.
> Soon Rhee got up several times and publicly said that his boys were

---

*The JCS knew the probable consequences of withdrawal. One of their staff groups, the Joint Strategic Survey Committee, had reported in January 1948: "Present informa-tion indicates that the withdrawal of U.S. forces will probably result in Communist domination; and it is extremely doubtful that it would be possible to build up the con-stabulary in time and with facilities available . . . to prevent Soviet encroachment. There-fore eventual domination of Korea by the USSR will have to be accepted as a probability." The committee said an augmented constabulary "might be a deterrent to covert acts by North Korean forces."

doing mighty well and could take care of the situation. Once he publicly committed himself that way, then I started working on him. "Well, it's about time we could get our forces out of the way." He didn't like that a damned bit but could not back out.[24]

What Rhee could do, however, was to use the withdrawal as a basis for demanding far more arms than Washington would—or could—supply. He wanted a "full air command" of two fighter and one bomber squadrons, with thirty P-51 fighters, twelve B-25 bombers, two destroyer escorts, two submarines, five minesweepers, and various support vessels. He wanted an army of 100,000 men with a reserve of 50,000 more, all armed with modern U.S. weapons. All these requests the United States refused. Then, as the June 30 deadline for withdrawal approached, Rhee suddenly took a new tack, one intended publicly to embarrass the United States.

In an angry public statement Rhee accused the Americans of abandoning his country. Were it not for the Americans, he continued, there would be no Communists in the North since they had been "invited in by the division of our country . . . by Russian-American agreement." The usually unflappable Dean Acheson told Muccio to warn Rhee that such outbursts endangered the prospects of future American aid. Rhee "should be disabused of impression we willing to pay any price his concurrence . . ." Acheson cabled.

Rhee calmed. He invited Muccio to meet on May 17 with his Cabinet; there the ROK government learned for the first time that the last American troops would be leaving in the "next few weeks." Rhee pleaded for a Pacific Pact patterned after the North Atlantic Treaty Organization. He begged for assurances he would be protected in the event of an invasion.

Muccio could promise nothing. The last American troops sailed as scheduled on June 30. The only soldiers remaining in South Korea were a corporal's guard of advisers.

Refining America's Strategy

The testing of the first Soviet nuclear warhead in August 1949, followed a few months later by the fall of China to Mao Tse-tung's Chinese forces, set into motion plans that, while not dealing with Korea in other than passing terms, were to be of signal importance when war began there.

The first was a policy paper—NSC 48/2, approved by the National Security Council and President Truman on December 30, 1949—which sought to apply the doctrine of "containment" of Soviet expansionism

to the Far East. The basic U.S. objectives, defined in NSC 48/2, were
to strengthen non-Communist Asia and to reduce Soviet power in the
Far East. The means were to be nonmilitary, chiefly the promotion of
economic and political development and regional associations of
friendly nations. The Republic of Korea was listed as one of the nations
to receive military and economic aid. The United States would "develop and strengthen the security of the area from Communist external
aggression or internal subversion." Therefore, the U.S. should "improve" its position with respect to "Japan, the Ryukyus, and the Philippines." By omission, South Korea was left outside the chain of states to
be protected.

Another important decision was that the United States would not
commit itself to the military defense of the ousted Nationalist regime
of Generalissimo Chiang Kai-shek, which had taken refuge on Formosa.
In a public statement on January 5, 1950, Truman said the United States
"has no predatory designs" on any Chinese territories, an indirect way
of saying he would not try to turn back the Chinese Revolution by force.
The Nationalist government had ample means to defend itself; the U.S.
would provide economic help, but no military assistance.*

The United States was not reticent in proclaiming the new boundaries of what it intended to defend directly in Asia. Speaking to the
National Press Club on January 12, Secretary Acheson stressed the importance of defending Japan, which would not be abandoned under any
circumstances. The "defensive perimeter," he said, "runs along the
Aleutians to Japan and then goes to the Ryukyus. We hold important
defense positions in the Ryukyu Islands, and these we will continue to
hold. . . . The defensive perimeter runs from the Ryukyus to the Philippine Islands." Acheson was vague about U.S. commitment to defending
"other areas in the Pacific." But he did declare: "It must be clear that
no person can guarantee these areas against military attack. . . . Should
such an attack occur . . . the initial reliance must be on the people
attacked to resist it and then upon the commitments of the entire
civilized world under the charter of the United Nations."

When the Korean War erupted six months later, Republican critics
roundly denounced Acheson for "inviting" the Communists to move
south. General Matthew B. Ridgway, then a JCS staff officer, later field

---

*Truman was silent about which China his administration would recognize diplomati-
cally. NSC 48/2, however, recommended continued recognition of the Nationalists "until
the situation is further clarified" and silence on recognition of the Communist government "until it clearly is in the United States interest to do so." The USSR apparently took
Truman's public silence as a signal that the time was opportune to press for the Communist Chinese to replace the Nationalists as one of the permanent members of the United
Nations Security Council. On January 13, 1950, the Soviet delegate, Yakov A. Malik,
walked out of the council, saying the Soviets would not participate in or recognize the
validity of any proceedings until the Nationalists were ousted. The move proved a diplomatic blunder, for six months later the Soviets were still absent and thus powerless to
resist the UN decision to go to war in Korea.

commander in Korea, thought this a "gross and misleading simplification." But he also said that the timing of the statement was open to criticism and that "this clear indication that we had no intention of defending Korea did nothing to give the enemy even momentary pause."[25]

In his memoirs General Douglas MacArthur felt that Acheson was "badly advised about the Far East" for excluding Formosa and South Korea from the defense perimeter.[26] MacArthur apparently had a poor memory. Some ten months earlier, in an interview with the British journalist G. Ward Price, MacArthur had offered an almost identical perimeter. "Our line of defense," he said, "runs through the chain of islands fringing the coast of Asia."[27] He identified the islands as the Philippines, the Ryukyus, Japan, and the Aleutians. As did Acheson, he omitted Formosa. There was only one difference in their statements: MacArthur listed the islands from south to north; Acheson listed them north to south.

The omission of Korea drew no public comment at the time of Acheson's speech; indeed, Korea received little attention anywhere. Later in January, in fact, the House of Representatives, protesting the administration's decision to withhold military aid for Formosa, rejected a proposal for $60 million in assistance for Korea. Direct pleas from Truman and Acheson finally persuaded the House to reverse the vote. Ironically the Republicans who led the fight against Korean aid were foremost among the critics who a few months later berated Truman for "abandoning" the Koreans.

NSC 48/2 was confined to the Far East. Another National Security Council study—NSC 68, finished in April 1950—was a reaction to the Soviets' test of a nuclear warhead in August 1949, years ahead of U.S. expectations. Analysts in the State and Defense departments (Paul Nitze of the former was the dominant figure) studied an array of alternatives: withdrawal of all American troops back to the mainland; a preventive war; or a rapid expansion of American assistance to allied nations. The last was chosen as a means of permitting the United States to deal with the Soviets from a position of strength. The assumption was that no other deterrent would convince the Soviets the U.S. was serious about global defense. The anticipated costs were awesome. The Truman administration's budget for fiscal 1950 was slightly more than $13 billion. NSC 68 urged an increase to $50 billion annually, about 20 percent of the gross national product. It foresaw a "danger period" of four years before the U.S. and allied nations could come to full strength. And it accepted unhesitatingly the vision of a Soviet Russia bent on world domination, through a combination of direct aggression and gradual subversion.

Although the exact language of the 151-page document remained top secret until 1975, the general thrust was made known in speeches by

Acheson and other administration officials. They saw, as the main concern, the necessity to prepare public opinion for such massive defense expenditures. Acheson wished to gain public acceptance of the principle of NSC 68 before getting down to specific details; otherwise, as he put it, "the mice in the Budget Bureau will nibble to death the will to decide."[28] The theme of Acheson's frequent public speeches during the spring of 1950 was an outright rejection of isolation. He said in a talk in Dallas on June 13, "We should not pull down the blinds and sit in the parlor with a loaded shotgun, waiting." Appeasement of Soviet ambitions he saw as an "alternative form of isolation."

Revisionist historians in the 1970's viewed NSC 68 as a blueprint for American aggression, the seminal document which transformed the United States into a warfare state. "This may be true," Acheson commented wryly in his memoirs. "Fortunately, perhaps, these authors were not called upon to analyze a situation in which the United States had not taken the action which it did take."[29]

As it developed, NSC 68 was still in the formative stages when the war began. And Acheson gave the Korean War substantial credit for changing NSC 68 from plan into reality, stating: "It is doubtful whether anything like what happened in the next few years could have been done had not the Russians been stupid enough to have instigated the attack against South Korea and opened the 'hate America' campaign."[30]

So in essence the Truman administration was walking a two-track strategy in its planning. It would keep off the Asian mainland, on the one hand; on the other, it would prepare itself to strike at any signs of Soviet expansionism, with the response to be limited only by strategic realities. NSC 68 was not a trigger mechanism intended to take the United States into war automatically; nonetheless, it represented the mind-set of an administration that was determined to bow its back if challenged.

Building a ROK Army

When the U.S. military left Korea,[31] it turned over to the ROK Army what looks at first blush like a considerable arsenal: equipment with a 1949 replacement cost of $110 million, sufficient to outfit a ground force of 50,000 men. There were 100,000 rifles, 50 million rounds of small-arms ammunition, 2,000 rocket launchers, more than 40,000 vehicles, and a number of light artillery pieces and mortars. But to the ROKs' chagrin, the Americans left no tanks, no airplanes, no heavy naval craft. By American design, the ROK Army was to have only a limited defensive ability. As MacArthur stated in a directive on March 7, 1949, the ROK Army should be capable of offering "token resistance" to invasion but should "be so organized as to indicate clearly its peaceful purpose and to provide no plausible basis for allegations of being a threat to North Korea."

The Korean Military Advisory Group (KMAG, "kay-mag" to everyone in the country) had 472 officers and men, commanded by Brigadier General William L. Roberts, a tank officer during the Second World War, serving a final tour before retirement. Neither Roberts nor many of the men under him were happy about being in Korea. Few of the Americans spoke Korean; they found the Koreans indifferent students; politics dominated the Korean officer corps; facilities for their families were primitive; and, finally, the Korean air was constantly permeated by the stench of the night soil farmers used as fertilizers. "In sum," one former KMAG stated, "the whole place stank—and I don't mean just the ROK Army."

KMAG advisers were pessimistic about the progress of the ROK Army. Lieutenant Colonel Thomas D. McDonald wrote in a report in December 1949 that it "could have been the American Army in 1775." Another KMAG evaluation stated that "except for its intense national pride, there was little to recommend the ROKA as a military force." There had been no platoon or company training; marksmanship was haphazard; officers did not know how to lead their men.

These reports were passed to Washington (General Roberts even wrote a 2,300-word personal letter to Lieutenant General Charles Bolte of the JCS staff in March 1949 to warn him of the sorry plight of the ROK military). But the military had decided to abandon Korea, and Bolte was not about to go against policy, even after Roberts's warning. In congressional testimony in June 1949, Bolte stated, "We feel that the [South Korean] forces in Korea now are better equipped than the North Korean forces. . . . The point has been reached in the development of South Korean forces and in the supplying of material aid . . . that it has reached a point [*sic*] where the tactical [American] units can and should be withdrawn."

But a year later, on June 6, 1950—three weeks before the war began —Ambassador Muccio gave a more realistic assessment of the ROKs. Testifying before the Senate Armed Services Committee, Muccio warned that the "undeniable material superiority of the North Korean forces would provide North Korea with the margin of victory in the event of a full-scale invasion of [South Korea], particularly in the matter of heavy infantry support weapons, tanks, and combat aircraft which the USSR has supplied and continues to supply."

At about the same time Muccio was testifying, General Roberts gave a farewell interview to Frank Gibney, the *Time* correspondent in the

Far East. Roberts was retiring after leaving Korea; he obviously wished his last army mission to be depicted as a success. Gibney's article stated:

> Most observers now rate the 100,000-man South Korean army as the best of its size in Asia. Its fast-moving columns have mopped up all but a few of the Communist guerrilla bands. And *no one* [emphasis added] now believes that the Russian-trained North Korean army could pull off a quick, successful invasion of the South without heavy reinforcements. . . .

On June 15, 1950, KMAG warned the Defense Department that supplies were available for ROK combat units only on a "bare subsistence basis." It stated that 15 percent of the army's weapons and 35 percent of its vehicles were busted. With the equipment on hand, the ROK Army could defend itself no longer than fifteen days. "Korea," KMAG stated, "is threatened with the same disaster that befell China."

The American public, however, did not read Defense Department cables. Its source of information was *Time,* which in turn reported what it was told by American generals and diplomats. Thus the makings of a very rude awakening ere June ended.

Rhee Is Restless

President Rhee made no secret of his intention eventually to seize control of the North (nor, for that matter, was Premier Kim Il Sung silent about his designs on the South). Ambassador Muccio remembered a reception at Blue House, the ROK presidential mansion, late in 1949. A ROK defense official "came in joyfully exalting that his 'boys' had just taken over Haeju, which is just beyond the 38th parallel opposite Kaesong. . . . [H]e didn't go on to say that practically every one of them was killed on the spot. But that's the sort of thing that was going on from both sides."[32]

Both the Koreas subjected the other to constant guerrilla probes and spy missions. Here the North had the clear advantage, for two reasons. The tight population controls in North Korea made movements of strangers difficult, if not impossible; hence ROK agents operated at considerable peril. Secondly, once he gained the presidency, Syngman Rhee became increasingly autocratic, suppressing any group or individual that questioned his policies and devoting far more attention to the "Communist menace" to the north than he did to problems in the South.

The composition of the prewar North Korean guerrilla forces reflected the depth of discontent with the Rhee government.[33] Intelligence officers at MacArthur's Far East Command* in Tokyo estimated, for instance, that trainees at the Kangdong Political School, chief guerrilla training facility in the North, were "composed almost entirely of South Koreans who defected to North Korea." A handful crossed to the North for "personal reasons," were caught, and pressed into service. But about 60 percent of the entire guerrilla force consisted of people still living in the South, G-2 said. Some did little more than recruit other agents and find supplies. Others actively fought in skirmishes alongside northern guerrillas, often armed with nothing more than bamboo poles and makeshift clubs. Only about 1 percent were involuntary guerrillas, young men seized and forced to join the Communists "by fear of death and reprisal against their families."

G-2 felt the northern guerrillas squandered their support by indiscriminately looting and pillaging villages in the South. But these raids did lure regular ROK troops into short and pitched engagements, usually to the guerrillas' advantage. Further, villagers in many border areas helped the guerrillas slip into the South because they were "sympathetic and . . . desire their trade." The South Korean Navy was of little use in stopping the intruders because its patrol ships "are apt to allow the [guerrillas'] boats to enter South Korean waters in return for money."

These activities aside, Kim Il Sung spent 1949 and the first months of 1950 bolstering the strength of his army. In contrast with the low-key KMAG support of the ROK Army, the Soviets dominated the North Korean Army, with an estimated 3,000 officers and men assigned to the country (versus fewer than 500 Americans). As many as 15 Soviet officers were attached to each North Korean People's Army (NKPA) division. The Soviets gave the NKPA heavy tanks, heavy artillery, self-propelled guns, and some 180 aircraft, 110 of which were combat fighter planes or bombers. The end of the Chinese Civil War gave the NKPA another boost—the return to North Korea of some 29,500 combat-hardened soldiers of Korean origin. By the spring of 1950, according to U.S. intelligence reports, the NKPA numbered some 135,000 soldiers; the South Koreans, 64,697.

But the North Koreans' matériel advantage was even greater, especially in Soviet-built heavy and medium tanks. One KMAG officer asked General Roberts why he did not insist that the ROK Army be given tanks to counter those of the North. Roberts patiently explained that the South Korean terrain was unfit for tank warfare. The roads were too few and narrow; the rice paddies and mountains were impassable. Any army that brought tanks into South Korea, he stated, would have them blown away within hours.

*Although MacArthur did not have command responsibility for South Korea, his office kept in close coordination with KMAG, and his G-2 (intelligence) section closely monitored Korean activities.

A Communist Deception Operation

Diplomats and officers in the American community in South Korea noted a quickening of tensions in the spring of 1950. The country had enjoyed its first bumper rice crop since the end of the Second World War, and the freshets of money touched off an intense inflation. Worried about the impact on its economic aid program, Ambassador Muccio pressured Rhee into imposing price controls. As it happened, this unpopular move coincided with the May National Assembly elections, and an anti-Rhee majority was elected. But mindful of Rhee's strong grass-roots support, the new majority made no effort to oust the president. Nonetheless, the elections put Rhee on notice that he should pay more mind to public opinion.

According to circumstantial evidence, Kim Il Sung decided in the spring of 1950 to take advantage of both Rhee's weakened political condition and the departure of the American military to strike for unification. His media spoke of a "Fatherland Front" that would bring a peaceful merger, with only Rhee and a handful of "pro-American and pro-Japanese traitors" liquidated. South Koreans by this juncture had heard so many threats and promises that none seemed to take Kim seriously. Nor did the U.S. embassy or the ROK Army, both of which by June 1950 were lapsing into early-summer lassitude.

Then, on June 10, a surprise:[34] The North Koreans announced that three representatives of the Fatherland Front would come to the frontier to meet with any South Korean leaders who wished to discuss unification. Radio Pyongyang held out promises of free elections, unity, and land reform. Ambassador Muccio, although dismissing the initiative as propaganda, nonetheless said its "superficial reasonableness may be attractive" to South Koreans yearning for elimination of the artificial 38th parallel division.[35] He proposed—and the State Department agreed—that John P. Gaillard of the UN Commission on Korea be sent to the border to pick up the North Korean documents and in turn hand over copies of UN General Assembly resolutions on unification. Gaillard had to talk his way past ROK soldiers engaged in a fire fight with Communists across the frontier, but he walked into North Korea and found the Fatherland Front delegates waiting for him at a table set up in the rail station. They gave Gaillard a longish statement proposing unification but refused to accept the UN documents. Somewhat baffled, Gaillard returned to Seoul, where the "statement" proved to be nothing more than a transcript of old Radio Pyongyang broadcasts.

To the surprise of the U.S. embassy, Radio Pyongyang early the next morning (June 11) announced that since the "pro-Japanese imperialist Rhee regime" had not permitted any of its officials to come to North Korea, as invited, the three Fatherland representatives would cross into South Korea at ten o'clock that morning.

They did just that, only to be arrested immediately by a waiting ROK Army patrol. The ROKs were furious. According to Harold J. Noble of the U.S. embassy, ROK Defense Minister Shin Sung Mo stormed that he intended to have the men court-martialed and then shot, immediately: "The area was under military control, they . . . violated basic laws, they [are] Communist agents; the simplest thing [is] to arrange a firing squad." Shooting the men would only make them martyrs, Noble argued; interrogate them first and see what information they could offer.

Under questioning, the men proved to be low-level bureaucrats who acted solely as messengers and who knew little of the documents they had brought south. Interrogators from the ROK Army and the United States Army Counterintelligence Corps (CIC) decided the Kim Il Sung regime had sent the men south as "expendables" in the expectation they would be killed.

So several days later the North Koreans were given a jeep tour of Seoul, and they saw something entirely different from the poverty-stricken, fear-infested city regularly described on Radio Pyongyang. Voluntarily they recorded radio broadcasts describing the relative comforts of life in South Korea. They also told interrogators that the Fatherland Front was a propaganda gimmick intended to unsettle the South. And one of the men, a former sergeant in the North Korean People's Army (NKPA), volunteered that he knew of "no significant military moves" that portended any invasion soon of the South.

Here was where Harold Noble felt that the ROK Army—and his own embassy—were deceived. "[T]hey had nearly everyone believing what we wanted to believe: that having seen the free south, they had chosen freedom instead of communism. When that was believed, their testimony on military subjects also was believed. They did their job of confusing the ROK Army, government, and foreign observers, like us, magnificently."*

An Intelligence Lapse

Two intelligence organizations shared responsibility for forecasting what might happen in Asia in the spring and early summer of 1950: the G-2 section of General MacArthur's Far East Command (FEC), headquartered in Tokyo, and the Central Intelligence Agency, half a globe

*The UN Commission on Korea agreed.[36] Its observation team wired the secretary-general a few hours after fighting erupted: "The radio propaganda offensive calling for early unification by peaceful means seems to have been intended solely for its screening effect."

away, in Washington. For different reasons, each was ill-equipped to perform its task.

The CIA had been in existence only three short years, a creation of the National Security Act of 1947, a bastard offspring of the Office of Strategic Services (OSS) of the Second World War, with few friends in official Washington, and highly resented by the military intelligence services.[37] The CIA was staffed, in the main, by two types of person: academics who had enjoyed cloak-and-dagger work with the OSS and misfits and incompetents dumped there by other agencies. Dr. Ray Cline (of the former category), who joined the CIA in 1949, was as an analyst responsible for "mainly drafting a monthly report of four or five printed pages with a fancy cover page and the resounding title of 'Estimate of the World Situation.'" Korea was one of the countries covered from time to time, and Cline admits that the CIA worked at a distance. "Mostly I simply wrote down analytical comments based on my reading of the newspapers and periodical literature, adding items from the research analysts wherever possible."

To Cline, the Far East was a particularly ticklish area. "We had very little intelligence to go on, little concrete stuff. CIA never recovered in the Far East from the antagonism of MacArthur to the OSS. He never let OSS into his theater, and he had the same attitude towards CIA. He kept CIA out of Japan and Korea; CIA was not part of his headquarters apparat."

The CIA's low status in Washington was reflected by its first three directors. Sidney Souers was a reserve navy admiral whose civilian occupation was executive of the Piggly Wiggly grocery chain in Truman's native Missouri. He had influence with Truman, but no intelligence background. Souers was followed by General Hoyt Vandenberg of the air force, named chiefly because he was a nephew of the powerful Senator Arthur Vandenberg. But even Hoyt Vandenberg sensed the CIA was a dead-end job; within a year he left to become air force chief of staff. In June 1950 the director was Admiral Roscoe Hillenkoetter, who one agency insider said was a "third-rate naval guy who happened to get the job because it was the navy's turn." (Truman thought so little of Hillenkoetter—and the CIA—that the director was not invited to the meetings the first days after the North Korean invasion. The CIA apparently was thought to have little to add to the discussion.)

The CIA's estimates on the possibility of war in Korea were long on analysis, short on actual forecasts, concerned more with broad global concerns than the specifics of any given situation. In its defense, the agency lacked any significant presence in Asia; the Tokyo "station" consisted of three men working from a hotel room, denied even an office by MacArthur's Far East Command. Korea understandably received scant coverage:

—From March 1 through the outbreak of war there was no mention of Korea in the CIA's daily summaries.

—During the same period, the CIA weekly summary mentioned Korea six times. Three reports concerned the May National Assembly elections. A March 31 report dealt with the unstable political and economic situation and blamed President Rhee for his insistence on building up the armed forces to resist invasion. On June 2 the CIA commented on rumors that Chiang Kai-shek would take refuge in South Korea should he be driven from Formosa. "Korea is too close to the USSR and Communist China to be regarded as anything more than a most temporary and uncomfortable refuge," the CIA commented. On June 16 a brief paragraph referred to the North Korean campaign for a "peaceful" unification.

—The CIA's monthly "Review of the World Situation" forecast on May 17 that should Rhee's power be reduced in elections that month, it "would considerably lessen the chances for Communist exploitation in Southern Korea." Korea was not mentioned in the June review.

—The CIA's last prewar word on Korea was contained in an intelligence community report, "Current Capabilities of the Northern Korean Regime," dated June 19 but based on information only through May 15. This report cited a North Korean "capability for attaining limited objectives in short term military operations against Southern Korea, including the capture of Seoul." The report mentioned tanks on the border but said nothing about the evacuation of villages. And although the report bore the CIA's imprimatur, the military paragraph was prepared by military G-2 and was included "over CIA objections."

In sum, the CIA was not capable of warning the Truman administration that South Korea was on the brink of war chiefly because it lacked an intelligence-gathering capability.

By contrast, the Far East Command's intelligence section, or G-2, covered Asia much like a vast, undiscriminating vacuum cleaner, scooping up so much minutia, unconfirmed reports, and wild guesses that officers seldom had the time to do the cold analytic work that produces usable intelligence.[38] Much of the fault lay in a lack of competent leadership. FEC's chief intelligence officer in 1950 was Major General Charles Willoughby, a member of the MacArthur palace guard since 1941. Fifty-eight years old in 1950, the German-born Willoughby was a man of deliberately vague origins. He occasionally claimed to be the son of a German baron, a refugee from undefined political persecution. (A writer for *Reporter* magazine discovered in 1951 that Willoughby, in fact, was the bastard son of a ropemaker.[39]) Willoughby came to the U.S. in 1910, at age eighteen, joined the U.S. Army as "Adolph Charles Weidenbach," as a private, and eventually won a commission and changed his name. Willoughby was a master at writing the baroque communiqués favored by MacArthur, and colleagues noted he seemed to spend as much time ghostwriting as he did in intelligence work. And indeed, Willoughby had little interest in intelligence in 1949 and 1950; MacArthur had commissioned him to oversee the writing and production of a massive four-volume history of the Pacific campaign. As one former intelligence officer noted, "Willoughby was the ideal man to be MacArthur's G-2. He knew exactly what MacArthur wanted to hear, and he told him exactly that, and no more."

Willoughby and MacArthur had one strong common view on intelligence: They distrusted unconventional methods of information gathering, especially by such freebooter organizations as the Office of Strategic Services and its successor, the CIA. MacArthur was straightforward about the OSS during the Second World War. He did not want its agents in his theater, and those detected there were harassed. Both Willoughby and MacArthur preferred to gather intelligence through attachés, through interrogation of prisoners, through captured documents; they put little faith in the "deep-cover" agent who used high position or access to gain confidential material.

Willoughby's chief intelligence "product" in Tokyo was a "Daily Intelligence Summary" of some forty pages, covering the entire Far East. Reading through sheafs of these summaries, three decades after their publication, is akin to listening to the babble of old women in a marketplace: a potpourri of rumor, speculation, isolated items that are impossible to evaluate. A good deal of Willoughby's "intelligence" came from disgruntled Nationalist Chinese officers who had daily predictions about the imminent collapse of Mao Tse-tung's Communist regime. Lacking agents in place, in North Korea, Willoughby's G-2 relied upon dribbles of second- and thirdhand information from low-level defectors, refugees, and the few Western diplomats stationed in Pyongyang. Nonetheless, a careful reading of Willoughby's daily summaries does reveal a pattern of events that pointed strongly toward a North Korean attack.

The most striking evidence—all this is admittedly hindsight; the patterns nonetheless were clear—was a rapid buildup of North Korean tank units close to the frontier. An informant in late May gave an extraordinarily detailed report on the formation of a new North Korean People's Army (NKPA) tank brigade, with an estimated 180 medium and light tanks, 10,000 officers and men, and such support equipment as antitank guns, field guns, and motorcycles. But Willoughby's staff, in a "comment" in the May 25 "Daily Intelligence Summary," refused to accept this information as valid. The "personnel and armor totals are excessive," the report said; the NKPA would not form so large a tank unit. "Aside from the difficulties which would be involved in the employment of, say, a tank division, it is felt that creation of such a unit in North Korea would not be economically or militarily practicable,"

G-2 stated. Less than a month later NKPA tanks formed the cutting edge of the forces that smashed through ROK defenses.

In early 1950 G-2 detected—and dismissed—another sign of impending war: the displacement of all families living within two miles of the 38th parallel. One seemingly obvious reason was to provide a secure assembly area for an invasion force. But Willoughby's G-2 thought otherwise. Some farm families might have left voluntarily "to avoid the danger of land mines laid along the border" by the NKPA. Any forced evacuations were due to the "need for troop billets, the impracticality of farming [in] areas where border incidents occur, and the fear of armed conflict between North and South."

There were other items as well: the closing of rail lines linking Sariwon, a transportation center outside Pyongyang, and the 38th parallel to all but military traffic; the opening of a large factory that made North Korea self-sufficient in the manufacture of small-arms ammunition; the recruitment of women for communications and nursing positions; a hurried conscription into the military both of teenaged boys and of men with prior experience in the Japanese Army. G-2 called these moves "war-type regimentation" and added, "Such steps are reminiscent of similar pre-World War II activities in Germany."

But on the prospect of an invasion, Willoughby sounded consistent themes. Yes, G-2 heard constant reports of invasion threats; yes, the NKPA had the capability of striking; yes, there were repeated signs of a buildup. None of these factors, however, was considered strong enough to lead G-2 to issue any specific warning of an invasion.

The lack of concern was prevalent in the Truman administration. On Tuesday, June 20, Dean Rusk, the assistant secretary of state for Far Eastern affairs, testified before the House Foreign Affairs Committee concerning a Korean aid bill. He was questioned at length about the strength of the ROK Army and the possibility of the North Koreans' resorting to force to seize the South. Rusk stated: "We see no present intention that the people across the border have any intention of fighting a major war for that purpose." Even if the North Koreans attacked, Rusk continued, the ROKs "could meet credibly the kind of force which the North Koreans have established."

Unbeknownst to Rusk, the NKPA had issued orders to field commands two days earlier, on June 18: Prepare to invade South Korea.

CHAPTER TWO

The Communists Strike South

June marks the start of the monsoon season in North Asia, and showers fell across most of Korea during the predawn darkness the morning of Sunday, June 25. The South Korean Army, after months of false alerts, had relaxed for a weekend of vacation. The frontier defense force—four infantry divisions and a regiment—on paper consisted of just shy of 38,000 men.[1] In actuality, only about one-third that number occupied defensive bunkers on the frontier; the remainder were either in reserve ten to thirty miles below the 38th parallel or on leave. ROK Army headquarters on June 24 had authorized commanders to give fifteen-day leaves to enlisted men from farming communities to work in the rice paddies. Another event drew away most ROK officers: a festive celebration opening of a new officers' club at army headquarters in Seoul.

The North Korean People's Army (NKPA), meanwhile, had amassed an invasion force of some 90,000 men, supported by 150 T-34 tanks, a low-silhouette medium tank that had been the standard for the Soviet Army at the end of the Second World War. Heavily armored, the T-34 carried an 85 mm cannon and two 7.62 mm machine guns. The T-34 was formidable; it had stopped the German drive on Moscow, and the Soviets had continued it as a basic supply item thereafter.

Brigadier General William L. Roberts, who retired as head of the American military advisory group in Korea two days before the war began, had said tank warfare was impossible in the country. The roads were too narrow; the rice paddies were too soft. Roberts, wrongly, assumed the North Koreans had drawn a similar conclusion. They had not.

Because the North Korean attack erupted across the neck of the Korean peninsula in tightly coordinated assaults, no single soldier or unit can accurately claim to have heard the "first shot fired in anger." But for Jin Hak Kim, a young lieutenant serving in the ROK 1st Division, stationed around the western city of Kaesong, on one of the key invasion routes, "the war began with a sudden eruption of artillery fire, a barrage laid onto our lines all along our sector of the frontier. One minute there was rain and silence; the next, a hellish din and explosions all around us. I was sleeping in a dugout, built into the side of a hill and with sandbags on the top. The impact of the first rounds knocked me off my cot, and sand and dirt poured into the dugout. I managed to pull on my clothes and run outside. One of my sergeants was near the door, groaning and holding his shoulder. I reached down to move him out of my way. His arm fell off; it had been severed near the shoulder. He groaned again, and was dead."[2]

The only American adviser on the 38th parallel that morning was Captain Joseph R. Darrigo, attached to the ROK 12th Regiment, stationed just northeast of Kaesong.[3] Artillery fire awoke Darrigo around five o'clock, and soon shell fragments and small-arms fire hit his house. He dressed and drove his jeep into Kaesong to see what was happening.

In the center of Kaesong he abruptly braked. At the railroad station, several hundred yards away, North Korean soldiers were unloading from a train of some fifteen cars, with no attempt at concealment, almost 1,000 men in all. Under cover of darkness the North Koreans had relaid previously destroyed lengths of rail on their side of the parallel and now were bringing troops in behind the ROK soldiers to the north. Darrigo jerked his jeep back into gear and sped to the south. There was now no doubt in his mind that a war had begun.

But word of what was happening along the 38th parallel—only two score or so miles north of Seoul—filtered slowly to the capital city. Sunday in Seoul began with dreary rain, the sun invisible behind low-hanging clouds at first light, a dawn typical of Korean summers.

A few minutes before seven o'clock someone in the American military advisory group telephoned Lieutenant Colonel Robert Edwards, military attaché to Ambassador John Muccio. He told about reports of fighting along the border. But given the rash of false-alarm invasions the previous months, he did not know whether the North Koreans had started a war or were doing more probing. In any event he felt the embassy should be notified.

Edwards shook himself awake, puffed on a cigarette, then decided to call Muccio's deputy, Everett Drumright, rather than unnecessarily disturb the ambassador. The next hour Drumright made his own phone calls, to Korean military headquarters and the American military advisory group. Shortly before eight o'clock he reported to Muccio.

"Brace yourself for a shock," Drumright opened the conversation, "the communists are hitting all along the front!"[4]

Another American was stirring that morning.[5] Jack James, the United Press correspondent in Seoul for the past eleven months, had partied late the night before. But conscientious journalist that he was, he intended to go into the embassy press room that morning and write a "mailer"—a background piece to be sent by post, rather than the more expensive cable—for his wire service. James had composed a lead paragraph in his head: "Despite a quickened propaganda campaign by North Koreans, and their continual threats that zero hour would be on such and such a date, the best opinion did not believe there would be any invasion at least before the fall."

James intended to write his story, retrieve a misplaced umbrella, and spend the rest of the day at a picnic. His Korean assistant monitored routine happenings on weekends.

As was true of most Americans in Seoul, James had heard so many reports that "invasion is imminent"—a dozen in his stint there—that he put little credence in them. In fact, earlier that very day he had heard a rumor of an invasion but checked with a G-2 friend and received a negative reply.

James drove the United Press jeep to the embassy a few minutes past eight o'clock and dashed through the rain for the door. He encountered an intelligence officer who came out in a great haste, looking for his car and driver. James recounted later:

> He thought I was on the story. "What do you hear from the border?" he asked me.
>
> "Not very much yet. What do you hear?" I said.
>
> "Hell, they're supposed to have crossed everywhere except in the Eighth Division area," he told me.
>
> "That's more than I've heard," I said, and went into the press room to start phoning.

James spent a frantic ninety minutes telephoning sources (most of whom still were in bed and unaware of any incidents) and monitoring reports reaching the embassy. He even aroused an embassy public information officer and asked him to check what the North Korean radio might have said that morning about an outbreak of war. (The answer: nothing.) "First reports were spotty and difficult to pin down," James recollected later. "Most of them were police reports, which usually are extremely exaggerated. Rather than start a war where there was not one, I held it [any story] for an hour and a half."

A former naval aviator and a man with long experience in Asia, James enjoyed the trust of the military officers and diplomats in the embassy. Harold Noble, the embassy first secretary, considered him an "honest and conscientious reporter," not given to sensationalism. Hence James sat in the embassy inner sanctum and listened to the discussion about what was happening. Finally, one KMAG officer said to another, "I think we'd better let Washington know about this."

"If it's good enough for you to file, it's good enough for me," James said. He hurriedly drafted an "urgent" press cable, which meant it would go at the most expensive rate and that it would also receive priority handling by United Press. James handled the reported attack cautiously, and his message stressed that the information was "fragmentary." But the fact that "I sent the message at urgent rates . . . was an indication that I felt it was extremely important." James wrote:

URGENT PRESS UNIPRESS NEWYORK

25095 JAMES* FRAGMENTARY REPORTS EXTHIRTY EIGHTH PARALLEL INDICATED NORTH KOREANS LAUNCHED SUNDAY MORNING ATTACKS GENERALLY ALONG ENTIRE BORDER PARA REPORTS AT ZERO NINETHIRTY LOCAL TIME INDICATED KAESONG FORTY MILES NORTHWEST SEOUL AND HEADQUARTERS OF KOREAN ARMYS FIRST DIVISION FELL NINE AYEM STOP ENEMY FORCES REPORTED THREE TO FOUR KILOMETERS SOUTH OF BORDER ON ONGJIN PENINSULA STOP TANKS SUPPOSED BROUGHT INTO USE CHUNCHON FIFTY MILES NORTHEAST SEOUL STOP LANDING EXSEA ALSO REPORTED FROM TWENTY SMALL BOATS BELOW KANGNUNG ON EASTERN COAST WHERE REPORTEDLY OFFCUT HIGHWAY ENDITEM NOTE SHOULD STRESS THIS STILL FRAGMENTARY AND PICTURE VAGUE STET JAMES

James's cable was received almost instantaneously at the UP office in San Francisco, where it was relayed to New York. There a rewrite man on the foreign desk translated his taut cable language into a news story and dispatched it around the world.

Within an hour James's story returned over UP wires to Seoul, where Korean-language newspapers rushed out afternoon extra editions telling of the invasion.

Ambassador Muccio's cable announcing the invasion left Seoul about ten minutes after the news dispatch. Diplomatic cables moved more slowly than United Press. Muccio's message had to be encrypted, then sent to Tokyo for relay to Washington. Hence the United States government received its first information of the invasion not from its embassy but from a news service ticker.

Muccio's cable, once dispatched, carried the priority symbol NIACT, the State Department's code designation for "night action," for emergency use only. A NIACT designation required the Washington code room to give the message immediate precedence over other cable traffic and to report it immediately to the responsible officer—in this

---

*Under the United Press system, each day's cables were numbered with the day of the month and the hour, broken into ten-minute intervals. The 25095 indicates James wrote his cable at about 9:50 A.M. on June 25.

instance, Dean Rusk, the assistant secretary of state for Far Eastern affairs.

A Presidential Holiday

President Harry S. Truman's mind was far removed from foreign affairs the weekend the war began.[6] Republicans in Congress had bedeviled him for almost eighteen months, and Truman's famed temper was near the breaking point. Now he planned to escape steamy Washington for a respite at his Missouri home. The schedule was free; Truman intended to relax and to forget his office for a few fleeting days.

But ever the politician, he permitted himself to be drawn into a side event en route: the dedication of Friendship Airport near Baltimore. Before emplaning, Truman wrote a snappy note to Stanley Woodward, former chief of protocol in the State Department, recently named ambassador to Canada. "I am leaving for Baltimore shortly to dedicate an airport—why I don't know," he wrote. "I guess because the Governor of Maryland, the two Senators from that great state, all the Congressmen and the Mayor of Baltimore highpressured [sic] me into doing it."[7] He good-naturedly demanded that Woodward visit him in his vacation retreat at Key West, Florida, the coming winter. "Don't get the idea that just because you are now Mr. Ambassador that the guy in the White House still can't harass you." While in Missouri, Truman said, he intended to "oversee some fence building—not political, order a new roof on the farmhouse and tell some politicians to go to hell. A grand visit —I hope?"

Maryland officials met the presidential party at Washington National Airport for the short flight to Friendship. There was much joshing with Baltimore Mayor Thomas D'Alesandro, who admitted to being a "little scared" about making his first airplane flight.[8] The dedication took less than an hour, and Truman talked earnestly about the need for federal, state, and local cooperation in developing air and other transportation projects. He could not pass up the chance for an off-the-cuff jab at his Republican foes: "If we had listened to the old mossbacks . . . we would never have given up the stagecoach. Some of these old stagecoach mossbacks are still with us—still in Congress, if you please. But thank God they are not in the majority. . . ." Ironically Truman thereafter ended successive sentences with the words "peaceful future, peaceful purposes and peaceful world." The world would be at peace for scant hours more.

Peace ended at about three o'clock that hot Saturday afternoon, while the President's plane was cruising high over the Mississippi Valley, on the final leg of the trip to Kansas City.[9]

A Saturday Night Surprise

As a columnist for the New York *Herald Tribune* Joseph Alsop carried useful credentials: a distant relationship with the Roosevelt family, the right Ivy League education, a social presence (no one ever had to brief Joe Alsop on the sequence of fork usage), and, most important, a reportorial energy and intelligence that put him on an intellectual par with the people he interviewed.[10] Joseph Alsop shared the *Herald Tribune* column with his brother Stewart, an equally competent reporter and analyst, but a man not so concerned with the social whirl of Georgetown.

Joe Alsop, to the contrary, prided himself on being able to command the presence, at his dinner table, of the people whom Washington reporters saw only through jousting with secretaries and aides. The guest list this night was not untypical. Joe Alsop, "rotund but profound," in the words of a National Press Club wit, had just returned from a reportorial visit to Europe. He gave himself a party to celebrate his own homecoming. The guest list was impressive: Justice Felix Frankfurter, Secretary of the Army Frank Pace, Undersecretary of the Air Force John McCone, and Dean Rusk, the assistant secretary of state for Far Eastern affairs.

As Alsop was to describe the scene, "the night was marvelously beautiful. The talk on the terrace under the stars was growing lively."

But a servant interrupted. He announced a phone call for "Mr. Rush." Dean Rusk looked over the assemblage, decided he was the party sought, and went indoors to the telephone.

A few minutes later he returned to the terrace "as white as a sheet" (Alsop's description) and beckoned to Pace and McCone to come inside the house. After a few minutes they returned and said, vaguely, that "there had been a rather serious border incident in Korea." With proper excuses they left for the State Department.

The party, according to Alsop, "settled down to argue whether *this was it.*"

Other parts of the national security bureaucracy began to stir about the same time. John D. Hickerson, the assistant secretary of state for United Nations affairs, was at his house in the Cleveland Park section of Washington when the telephone rang about ten o'clock.[11] "In those days night calls weren't unusual. . . . I had by that time fallen into a habit that was somewhat descriptive of the hectic life we led. If the telephone rang after nine o'clock, as I started to the telephone I involuntarily picked up my car keys, just in case."

This time the caller was the watch officer in the Far Eastern Bureau, who said, "There's a development and I think that you would want to come in right away. I can't discuss it on the telephone."

As Hickerson drove through Rock Creek Park to the State Department building, "I passed in review in my mind what it might be." Because of the caller, he knew the problem was in the Far East. "The thing I thought the likeliest was that the Chinese Communists had attempted an invasion of Taiwan."

The Pentagon received news of the invasion with calm, almost with lassitude.[12] The JCS duty officer, Lieutenant Colonel Chester V. Clifton, first heard of the attack at 11:30 P.M. via press inquiries. Checking with the JCS message center, Clifton confirmed that the rumored invasion had been verified and that Rear Admiral Arthur C. Davis, director of the Joint Staff, had already been notified. Clifton next talked with his immediate superior, Colonel W. B. Matthews, who first thought it unnecessary to notify General Bradley, the JCS Chairman, but eventually agreed to do so. (By the time they finally got to Bradley he had already received the news from reporters, whom he could not enlighten.)

So all the Pentagon—in the person of Clifton—did those early hours was to prepare a brief news announcement that the U.S. government knew of the invasion and that no American troops were involved.

The other action of substance came about ten minutes after midnight. Brigadier General Thomas S. Timberman, the deputy chief of staff for operations, established what he called a "command post" in the army G-3 office. In actuality, all this "post" did was to ensure that whatever sparse information arrived from the State Department was relayed back across the Pacific to General MacArthur's headquarters.

Defense Secretary Louis Johnson had spent the preceding days on a fact-finding trip to the Far East, chiefly concerned with Formosan defense questions.[13] A phone call brought him from bed. He listened; then he telephoned the army secretary, Frank Pace, and in effect gave him responsibility for any decisions that must be made that night on behalf of the civilian defense establishment. Johnson was exhausted. Besides, as he said later, Defense could do very little that night because "we really had very little to go on." General Bradley was the only JCS member even to know of the invasion for hours.

The man who had to make the ultimate decision on U.S. reaction was President Truman, by Saturday evening a few hours deep into his long-planned rest at Independence. A telephone call interrupted the family's after-dinner small talk.[14] The caller was Secretary of State Acheson. "Mr. President," he said, "I have very serious news. The North Koreans have invaded South Korea."

Truman's first reaction was to rush back to Washington. But Acheson told him to wait. Information was scanty, and the North Koreans had made frequent raids against the South, often in battalion force. Conceivably the action reported by Muccio was only a routine border clash (although Acheson doubted it). More important, a hurried flight across the continent in the dead of night not only would be dangerous but could also panic the world.

Acheson did have concrete suggestions. He wanted to ask a special meeting of the United Nations Security Council to declare that an act of aggression had been committed against the Republic of Korea. Truman agreed and asked that Acheson report promptly the next morning —or sooner if he received more information.

The call ended the festive family evening. Margaret Truman reported, "My father made it clear, from the moment he heard the news, that he feared this was the opening round in World War Three."

After Truman approved putting Korea before the Security Council, John Hickerson began trying to call members of the U.S. delegation.[15] He knew that Senator Warren R. Austin, the permanent representative, was weekending in Vermont and could not be reached by telephone. So he called the home of Ernest Gross, the deputy. No luck. The only person there was a young daughter, and Hickerson was not quite sure that she understood his message that the call was urgent and that her father should get back to him immediately. "I don't know the age of the girl, and we just *couldn't wait,*" Hickerson said.

So around midnight Hickerson decided to jump bureaucratic channels and telephone Trygve Lie, the UN secretary-general, directly at his home. "I told him what had happened [the invasion] and his first words (in a strong Norwegian accent) were, 'My God, Jack, that's against the charter of the United Nations.'

"I couldn't think of anything more original to say than, 'You're telling me, Trygve, of course it is!' "

Long after midnight Hickerson finally contacted Ernest Gross. They briefly discussed strategy. Hickerson's staff was well into writing a draft resolution, which would be flown to New York a few hours later by State Department lawyer David Wainhouse. The United States had a strategic advantage. Months earlier the Soviet representative on the Security Council, Yakov Malik, had walked out in protest against continued seating of the Nationalist Chinese. The Soviets wanted the "China" seat on the council to go to the new Communist government. Were Malik to return, his veto could keep the council from taking any action.

They decided Malik would not likely appear. He would have to receive instructions from Moscow, a lengthy process. Also, Hickerson felt that since Malik knew the UN Security Council could not take any military action without unanimous vote, "he probably assumed that he'd have time to come in."

At this time no one knew what the President might ultimately ask the UN to do about the invasion. One reason is that no one knew exactly what was happening in Korea. By early Sunday morning nothing beyond the first telegram had been received from Muccio or the Seoul embassy, despite repeated efforts "to obtain a clearer picture of what was actually happening in Korea," in Dean Rusk's words.[16] Acheson and Rusk talked about public relations. They decided it was of "utmost importance" that the decision to put the case before the UN Security Council appear in the Sunday morning newspapers simultaneously with the news of the North Korean invasion. Thus Acheson made the final decision to go to the council "shortly in advance of the press deadline . . . on the strength of the single telegram from Muccio."

At 2:30 A.M. Hickerson telephoned Ambassador Gross and dictated a resolution for the Security Council.[17] At about the same time circular telegrams went to the other member states of the council (Nationalist China, Cuba, Ecuador, Egypt, France, India, Norway, and the USSR) informing them of the American decision to call a special session. They were urged to seek instructions from their governments so that prompt action could be taken. The formal request read:

> The American Ambassador to the Republic of Korea has informed the Department of State that North Korean forces invaded the territory of the Republic of Korea at several points in the early morning hours of June 25 (Korean time).
> Pyongyang Radio under the control of the North Korean regime, it is reported, has broadcast a declaration of war against the Republic of Korea effective 9 P.M. EDT June 24.
> An attack of the forces of the North Korean regime under the circumstances referred to above constitutes a breach of the peace and an act of aggression.
> Upon the request of my government, I ask you call an immediate meeting of the Security Council of the United Nations.

Washington clearly was headed toward a crisis, possibly even a war. But for the moment all the diplomats and the generals could do was await further word from the battlefront. The urgency did not ruffle Harry Truman. Before midnight he said good night to his family and was sound asleep seconds after his head touched the pillow.

The ROKs Are Routed

By late morning Sunday, Seoul time, the American military mission realized the ROK Army faced a critical situation.[18] Reports from the front gave a broad picture of North Korean invasion strategy—a multicolumn attack by tank-supported infantry down the two main highway corridors leading toward Seoul.

The main thrust came along the Charwan-Uijongbu-Seoul axis, a route through a broad valley that invaders had used for centuries. Two divisions and a regiment, some 28,000 men in all, composed this force. The Russian-made T-34 tanks rode at the head of the invasion column, supported by artillery, mortars, and heavy machine guns, also of Soviet origin. A substrength ROK division of no more than 6,000 men was their only opponent.

Another North Korean column struck down a highway through the coastal lowlands on the west side of the country, the main communications corridor between Pyongyang and Seoul. Again, the North Korean numerical advantage was about the same—two divisions and a regiment, with tank support, against one depleted ROK division. These were the two main strikes directed against Seoul. With South Korea's logistical grid—highways, railroads, communications—all centered in Seoul, loss of this city would endanger the country's survival.

Of less immediate concern were three other North Korean strikes: against a single ROK regiment on the Ongjin Peninsula, which was completely cut off from South Korea by the Yellow Sea; the central city of Chunchon; and down the coast highway along the Sea of Japan (the latter supported by two minor amphibious landings).

The overriding tragedy the first day of the war was the collapse of the ROK Army, which Brigadier General William L. Roberts, the advisory group commander, had pronounced "the best of its size in Asia." Blame must rest on both the Americans and the South Koreans. Because of Roberts's refusal to conceive of any tanks being used in Korea, the ROKs had only a handful of antitank equipment. The first hectic hours of the war some units tried to use American-made 105 mm howitzers, a weapon not designed for antitank warfare. As one American artilleryman explained, "Few people realize the expertness required of gunners firing over open sights [i.e., at point-blank range] against oncoming tanks and with a gun which is not designed for antitank work. The shot is not so easy as it sounds; only veteran gunners will remain calm enough to make the shot count, and even they have to have a bit of luck." The ROKs had only ninety-one of these howitzers; most were lost the first days of the war. The Americans had withheld heavy equipment from the ROKs for fear they would use it to invade the North; consequently, the ROKs could now not defend themselves.

To the American advisers, the chief surprise was the total collapse of morale and fighting spirit among the ROKs. There were laudable exceptions, instances of incredible man-versus-machine bravery. Defenders near Munsan, frustrated by their inability to halt the T-34 tanks, strapped satchel charges of explosives to their backs and hurled themselves under the tanks, to certain death. Others approached the tanks with satchels or pole charges, darting through machine-gun fire. Still others leaped on top of passing tanks and tried desperately to open the hatches with hooks to drop grenades inside. The volunteers managed to disable some of the tanks—but an estimated ninety of them died doing so. Soon there were no more volunteers.

The more typical sight was that depicted by Sydney Smith of the London *Daily Express*, one of the first war correspondents to arrive, describing a column of retreating ROKs: "On some trucks I saw senior Korean unit commanders sitting among their troops, wearing white gloves, and carrying an official sword in one hand, and in the other a tree bough held over their heads like an umbrella."[19] Incongruities abounded: South Koreans riding away on the front of cavalry horses, animals bolting and stamping at the frightful sounds of battle; ROK soldiers forcing civilians to yield their clothing at gunpoint so they could shed their uniforms and meld into the refugee stream, while officers stood by and did nothing.

Around noon came signs of another North Korean advantage. The cloud cover over Seoul broke, and two dirty silver-colored YAK fighters, propeller-driven Soviet craft from the Second World War, soared over the city and Kimpo Airport repeatedly but without firing. Four hours later the Yaks returned. Two of them concentrated deadly accurate fire on Kimpo, hitting the control tower, a gasoline dump, and an American C-54 transport. Others hit a smaller airport near Seoul, damaging or destroying seven of ten trainer aircraft. Then they ranged north over the roadways, firing at random at panicked ROK troops. The ROKs could not fight back; the United States had refused to supply them fighter craft, again for fear they would be used against North Korea in an invasion.

But American military advisers on the front did radio occasional encouraging reports. Several ROK battalions around Uijongbu were organizing an attempted counterattack. The few ROK units that occupied fortified positions had managed to slow the North Korean advance. Reserves were rushing to the front, and road and bridges along the invasion route were being destroyed per previous planning. The great uncertainty was whether the ROK Army could hold long enough to regroup or—an alternative strongly desired by the American advisers —to give the United States a chance to send military forces to their rescue.

An Unperturbed MacArthur

One person not shaken by these intimations of imminent disaster was General Douglas MacArthur, who twelve hours after the invasion ex- uded an aura of nonconcern.[20] At six o'clock on Sunday evening he met in his Tokyo office with John Foster Dulles, a prominent Republican spokesman on foreign affairs, recently recruited by Secretary Acheson (in a show of bipartisanship) to help negotiate the Japanese peace treaty. Dulles a few days earlier had taken a side trip to Korea and posed for photographers with ROK troops along the 38th parallel. (The Korean soldiers seemed bemused by Dulles's formal homburg.) Dulles had also addressed the South Korean Parliament and implied unspecified help in time of trouble:

> The United Nations considers you as, spiritually, one of them. . . . The American people welcome you as an equal partner in the great company of those who make up this free world. . . . Therefore, I say to you: you are not alone. You will never be alone, so long as you continue to play worthily your part in the great design of human freedom.

These generalities meant as much—or as little—as one cared to make of them, but John Allison, a career State Department officer traveling as Dulles's escort, felt that Dulles had "rather tried to make up for what he thought Dean Acheson had omitted in his January speech" to the National Press Club.

Now Dulles and Allison wished to discuss their Korean trip with the general, whom they found seemingly indifferent to the war that had erupted only a few hours away. Allison thought MacArthur "magnificent as he strode up and down his huge office, his khaki shirt open at the neck, and his famous corncob pipe gripped between his teeth." Reports from the front thus far had been fragmentary, and MacArthur did not appear worried. "This is probably only a reconnaissance in force," he told his visitors. "If Washington only will not hobble me, I can handle it with one arm tied behind my back." President Rhee had already asked for some fighter planes. MacArthur said he was certain the Koreans could not handle them properly, but he intended to send a few along anyway for morale purposes. (A visiting journalist chatted with MacArthur later that evening and found him primarily concerned with "those asses back in Washington." MacArthur told the journalist, William R. Matthews, "I hope the American people have the guts to rise to meet this situation.")

Dulles and Allison returned to their hotel and drafted a cable for Dean Acheson:

> It is possible that the South Koreans may themselves contain and repulse the attack and, if so, this is the best way. If, however, it appears that they cannot do so, then we believe that United States force should be used. . . . To sit by while Korea is overrun by unprovoked armed attack would start a disastrous chain of events leading most probably to world war.

(When Dulles's cable arrived in Washington before daybreak on Sunday, U.S. time, Dean Acheson paid it careful attention. Acheson knew Dulles as a primary foreign policy spokesman for the opposition party. Not a blind partisan, he deserved attention. Via this cable, written from his Tokyo hotel room, Dulles became the first person to recommend, on paper, that the U.S. intervene with military force in Korea.)

President Rhee Panics

Late Sunday afternoon Communist YAK fighter planes strafed the area around President Syngman Rhee's home, the Blue House (so called because of its blue tile exterior). The closeness of the attack panicked the old man. He was alarmed that Seoul might fall, and he decided he must flee to avoid capture. Harold Noble of the American embassy (who was not in Seoul that weekend) talked with other American and ROK officials later and concluded that Cabinet officers and assorted hangers-on in the Rhee house "were terrified and infected him with their fear."[21] But Rhee's primary stated concern was not his personal safety: He felt that if the invaders captured him, it would end his lifetime dream of an independent Korea.

Rhee debated through the early evening whether he should flee or stay. Around nine o'clock Shin Sung Mo, the acting defense minister, brought Muccio into the debate. Muccio relates:

> When I arrived, President Rhee said that the Cabinet had just had a meeting and decided that it would be disastrous for the Korean cause to have him fall into the hands of the Communists and their defense capabilities were such that they had better move on out of Seoul.
>
> I was jarred to hear this. I very carefully reminded Rhee what I had been pointing [out] to him in the course of the day, that his military was doing a super job in facing up to this onslaught; no single unit had given in. [Muccio exaggerated, but for a reason: He wanted Rhee to stay.] Some of them had been overwhelmed, it was true, and scattered. I agreed with him that the last thing in the world *I* wanted to do was to fall into the hands of the Communists. We faced a delicate question of timing—of staying on as long as we could to bolster our forces and at the same time not [being] caught by the enemy."[22]

Muccio told Rhee that if he fled, and the fact became known, "there wouldn't be a single South Korean soldier facing north." The entire ROK Army would quit fighting. Rhee continued to insist he would leave, whereupon the ambassador replied, "Well, Mr. President, you make up your own mind, but I'm staying here."

Muccio's firmness shored up Rhee. He agreed to remain in Seoul—through the night at least.

Ambassador Muccio returned to his embassy to decide what should be done about wives and children of American personnel. Should they be sent from the country, their departure might signal the South Koreans that the United States had given up. The community was already under alert. At 1:00 P.M. the embassy radio station, WVTP, had advised Americans to remain either at home or at their duty posts "as the situation may dictate," saying there was "no reason for alarm."

A top-secret evacuation plan existed, as was customary for all American missions abroad. The worst-possible-situation scenario called for evacuation via aircraft from the Kimpo Airfield. Dispatch of an emergency code word via radio supposedly would bring planes winging in from Japan. But Muccio wondered about the efficacy of this plan, for it depended upon the safeguarding of a bridge separating Seoul from the airport. Other scenarios called for dependents to leave by ship from the ports of Inchon or Pusan or by plane from another airdrome at Suwon.

Muccio designated Jack Seifert, the embassy naval attaché, to see what ships were available at the ports, for he feared that the strafing YAK jets could disrupt any attempted air evacuation. But for the moment he would make no decision on evacuation.

With darkness came a lull in battle action to the north. Night was bringing Seoul a brief respite from war. Washington officials, conversely, now faced the dawn of Sunday—and some hard decisions.

Acheson Takes Command

Decisions began to be made at a meeting convened at eleven-thirty Sunday morning at the State Department.[23] The Pentagon's secondary role is suggested by the relative ranks of the participants. For State, there were Acheson, James Webb, the undersecretary, and Rusk, an assistant secretary—the one, two, and three men in the department. For the Pentagon, there were only General J. Lawton Collins, the army chief of staff, and Brigadier General Thomas S. Timberman, the deputy chief for operations—competent officers, to be sure, but men with far less relative rank in the Defense Department than the diplomats they faced.

Even JCS papers concede that it was the State representatives who "suggested a program of action to provide a measure of U.S. support for the hard-pressed South Korean forces." Although other JCS members were consulted by phone during the meeting, the State Department put forth the "suggestions [that] were ultimately approved," even though most of them involved action by MacArthur. They were as follows:

—American air and naval forces should establish a protective cordon around Seoul, Kimpo Airport, and Inchon Harbor to ensure safe evacuation of U.S. dependents.

—MacArthur's command should be authorized to send to Korea any equipment recommended by the U.S. mission there, regardless of current programs.

—U.S. military advisers should remain with ROK forces so long as they were combat-effective.

—MacArthur's area of responsibility should include operational control of all U.S. military activities in Korea.

—If the UN Security Council voted for collective action in Korea, MacArthur was "authorized and directed" to use his forces, plus the Seventh Fleet, "to stabilize the combat situation, including if feasible the restoration of original boundaries at the 38th Parallel."

None of these "suggestions," it should be stressed, had presidential approval. Just what authority Acheson had in taking the lead at this meeting is mentioned in neither his memoirs nor those of Truman. Both memoirs depict the major decisions as having been made much later that day, in an evening meeting at Blair House between Truman and his top advisers. By the time the Blair House meeting got under way, however, the "suggestions" from the morning conference were already being relayed to MacArthur in Tokyo via a Teletype conference, or telecon, that began at 7:30 P.M., Washington time. (In a telecon, conferees thousands of miles distant sit in conference rooms and "converse" via a Teletype printer, with messages projected on a screen so they can be read by all participants.)

The directive did hedge.[24] It noted that President Truman had not approved the recommendations, which were transmitted for "planning purposes." But MacArthur was advised that State agreed he should send a "survey group" to South Korea to determine what military forces might be needed to hold an escape route from Seoul south to the port of Inchon.

The message continued:

> Washington: JCS and State now meeting with the President. This telecon is to let you know current thinking here, and that the situation is regarded of great consequence.
>
> Tokyo: Come over and join the fight. We are delighted with your lines of action and this aid should turn the trick. Thank you.

The exuberant closing sentence was vintage Douglas MacArthur.

Planning a Response

When the Joint Chiefs of Staff finally held a round-table talk about Korea on Sunday morning, Dean Acheson had emerged as the manager of the Washington end of the crisis, via his request for a diplomatic solution through the UN. The chiefs' meeting was casual, and they showed no interest in American military intervention. Months before, they had worked out a contingency plan for the eventuality of an invasion. The plan was no snap-judgment decision made under pressure of a crisis. Staff officers had reviewed U.S. policy toward Korea, as enunciated by the National Security Council and the President, and they were aware Korea had been deemed "of little strategic interest" to the U.S. The contingency plan (which had been approved by Truman) was as follows: In the event of an invasion the U.S. would withdraw all its personnel, military, diplomatic, and civilian, as quickly as possible, using American air cover if necessary. By no means would America be drawn into war in Korea.

The chiefs behaved that crisis Sunday—and, indeed, for several days afterward—as if they expected the contingency plan to be followed. Nothing had been said to them that indicated anyone in Washington felt that the carefully devised policy of nonintervention should be changed.

Nor, for that matter, did General Bradley see any reason for great alarm. Earlier that morning, before meeting his colleagues, Bradley wrote a memorandum sketching his survey tour of the Far East.[25] While in Korea he had talked with General Roberts, the just-reassigned commander of the Korean Military Advisory Group (KMAG). Roberts apparently chose to express none of the doubts about the efficacy of the ROK Army he had revealed to General Bolte in his pessimistic letter of March 8 (see page 33 above). To do so would have been a tacit admission he had not succeeded in his mission (perhaps an impossible one on its face) of building a viable ROK Army. So he gave his commander what he thought he wanted to hear: an everything-is-going-well report that was so inaccurate as to be mendacious.

With the expertise of the casual visitor prone to believe what he is told, Bradley left Asia optimistic about South Korea's ability to survive and skeptical about North Korea's military strength. In the memo for his colleagues, he wrote, "I am of the opinion that South Korea will not fall in the present attack unless the Russians actively participate in the operation." But if Korea should fall, the United States should reinforce Formosa to offset adverse affects elsewhere in Asia.

Assured they would not be needed for the remainder of the afternoon of crisis, General Bradley and Secretary Johnson flew off to Norfolk, Virginia, for a previously scheduled conference with assorted civilian dignitaries.

At about the time the informal JCS meeting ended, the Pentagon message center received a gush of cables from Seoul, the bulk of which "did not sound excessively alarming," in the words of General Lawton Collins. A summary from MacArthur's headquarters reaching the JCS intelligence section (G-2) at 10:35 A.M. was most encouraging—although also inaccurate. The report estimated the balance of forces as three North Korean divisions against four for the ROKs, with a fifth ROK division moving toward the lines. Actually the North Koreans threw more than seven divisions against four much-depleted ROK divisions. Losses of territory thus far had been expected under contingency defense plans and were not regarded as "vital." Although North Korea's attack was "serious in strength and strategic intent" and had achieved tactical surprise, the ultimate goals remained obscure—in MacArthur's headquarters, at any event. MacArthur reported he was expediting the shipment of munitions to Korea and suggested that the Seventh Fleet, then gathered mainly around the Philippines, be moved toward Korea as a precaution.

But the optimistic cable provided no respite, for even before it arrived, direct contact with Tokyo revealed that the reality of the Korean situation had suddenly become vivid to MacArthur and staff. The medium was a telecon with General Willoughby, MacArthur's intelligence officer.

Willoughby sounded alarmed. Two North Korean divisions were attacking along roads leading to an important road junction at Uijongbu, with forty tanks reported within five kilometers (slightly more than three miles) of the city. "General situation points to tank breakthrough via Uijongbu," he warned. But Willoughby summoned optimism: The ROKs were withdrawing in orderly fashion, civilian morale was good, and the government was "reported to be standing firm and maintaining internal order."

Truman's Holiday Interrupted

No one in Washington bothered to disturb President Truman's holiday, for the first reports he received in Independence were optimistic. Eben Ayers, a White House deputy press secretary, drove out to the Truman home in midmorning and had a leisurely chat with the President in his library. "The President was not one to show great concern about anything," Ayers said. "He wasn't going to get excited and carried away about anything. . . . [A] man who gets to the point where he is President . . . isn't going to get up and run around in little circles and get overly excited. He's going to keep his head."[26]

After his talk with Truman, Ayers went out to meet reporters clustered around the gate. He said the President was "concerned, but not alarmed."

President Truman's original vacation plans had called for him to go to brother Vivian's farm for a family dinner Sunday evening, but instinct brought him back to his own house in Independence before noon. "I thought Acheson might call, which he did."[27] At 12:35 P.M. Acheson suggested that the President return to Washington "as quickly as possible."

A scramble ensued. Truman gathered his official party for the sprint to the Kansas City airport; at 1:57 P.M. the *Independence* was airborne. The press, well into a leisurely nonnews weekend, was so scattered that its chartered American Airlines flight did not follow until after five o'clock. Several Truman aides were aboard the press plane as embarrassed passengers; they, too, had been caught napping by the sudden departure.

Alone with his thoughts during the flight to Washington, Truman had no doubt that the Russians inspired the invasion. "I was sure of it . . . and it had to be met forcefully," he said. "The conclusion I had come to was that force was the only language the Russian dictatorship could understand. We had to meet them on that basis and defeat them. . . ."

Truman whiled away the hours-long flight back to Washington that Sunday afternoon with thoughts about what he considered past analogous crisis situations: the Japanese invasion of Manchuria in 1931; Mussolini's entrance into Ethiopia and Emperor Haile Selassie's unheeded protest to the League of Nations; Hitler's march into the Saar Valley, "which could have been stopped by the French and British if they had acted in unison." Truman felt that "if the Russian totalitarian state was intending to follow in the path of the dictatorships of Hitler and Mussolini, they should be met head on in Korea as they had been met in the evacuation of Iran after the war and the ultimatum to Tito on Trieste after that. . . ."*

In mid-flight Truman radioed a message asking Acheson and the ranking military and diplomatic advisers to meet later that evening at Blair House for a strategy conference. The First Family was residing at Blair House, a handsome building a block west of the White House, normally quarters for visiting dignitaries, during White House renovation.

---

*After the Second World War ended, the Soviets showed no signs of honoring a promise of vacating the northern provinces of Iran. Truman forced a showdown in the UN, and the Soviets left. A similar tough stance caused Marshal Josip Broz Tito of Yugoslavia to abandon designs on Trieste.

Truman then beckoned Treasury Secretary John Snyder to join him in his private quarters. "I don't know how serious this is," the President said. "They seem to think that it is rather serious in Washington." He mused aloud. "I'm so puzzled about this," he told Snyder. "I really don't know just how much the Russians are in this. We know that the Chinese had been training them and that they have been amply supplied—the Russians have supplied tanks and airplanes and pilot training, but I still know that there's an awful lot of manpower there of the Chinese that might be available in case this develops seriously." Truman felt the invasion would be "the testing point for our United Nations agreement of protection against invasion of a member country."*

The President next turned to Snyder's own area of responsibility. "Suppose it is serious, what do you think the Treasury will have to do promptly?" They talked about stopping the congressional effort then under way to reduce excise taxes (a war would demand tax dollars); they agreed to withdraw the next year's budget, work on which had been completed only a few days earlier. Snyder suggested "that we should immediately start studies as to what kinds of increases we may need in present taxes and in new taxes, if this is a grave matter."

Truman agreed, then talked for a few moments about using "extreme care to try to avoid excessive deficits" if war should come. He looked at Snyder. "You and I both have seen two world wars started on less causes."

The *fact* of a North Korean invasion now established beyond any doubt, the Washington diplomatic and intelligence communities turned to the *why*. Truman's snap judgment that the Kremlin had ordered the new war was widely shared in Washington. The scores of pages of analysis churned out on Sunday all started from the assumption the Soviets, in fact, were responsible.

Signs of Soviet mischief as well as omens of moves elsewhere were clearly visible. George Kennan, the State Department's foremost Soviet specialist (he had served as ambassador in Moscow), received word that Truman wished to be briefed on prospects for "further Russian action in other areas . . . whether this was the beginning of a series of Russian moves."[28] Kennan summoned other Kremlinologists to review intelligence reports and recent cable traffic. Disturbing omens were visible.[29] The Soviets had been moving "significant shipments of weapons, equipment and supplies" into Albania, Rumania, and Bulgaria the past six months by sea and rail. But analysts could not agree why: whether the material was intended as replacements for worn-out weapons, for use

---

*Truman misspoke; the Republic of Korea was not a UN member. However, it had been created through elections held under UN auspices.

in summer maneuvers, for support of guerrilla operations, or for stock-piling for future combat use by indigenous or Soviet forces. The Soviets had also announced extensive maneuvers by its Black Sea Fleet in close proximity to the Turkish coast later in the summer. As one intelligence report said, the maneuvers were "proclaimed with menacing details of a proposed simulated attack upon Turkey accompanied by amphibious landing exercises." To amplify the scope of the threatened "invasion," the Soviets planned to use 2,500 planes and enough landing craft for a two-division assault. Iran, beset with political unrest and economic in-stability, also offered the Soviets a chance for a "cheap victory" should they choose to move there.

But were the Soviets in fact responsible for the invasion, as reflexively assumed by Truman, Acheson, and virtually everyone else in official Washington that Sunday? Evidence of Soviet complicity is sketchy—but nonetheless conclusive. Former Soviet Premier Nikita Khrushchev related the scenario in his "memoirs" published in the West in 1970, a document of uncertain origin, but deemed authentic by such Soviet specialists as Edward Crankshaw. By Khrushchev's account, Kim Il Sung visited Stalin toward the end of 1949 and told him the "North Koreans wanted to prod South Korea with the point of a bayonet." An attack would touch off an internal explosion in South Korea and swiftly topple Syngman Rhee from power. "Naturally Stalin couldn't oppose this idea," commented Khrushchev. "It appealed to his convictions as a Communist all the more because the struggle would be an internal matter which the Koreas would be settling among themselves."

But Stalin reacted cautiously. He told Kim to return to North Korea, to think over his idea, and to return with a concrete plan. Back in Moscow a few months later, Kim was "absolutely sure of success." Stalin still had doubts. He worried that the Americans "would jump in," in Khrushchev's words. Kim, however, argued that he could crush South Korea so swiftly that U.S. intervention could be avoided. Mao Tse-tung, the Communist Chinese leader, also talked with Kim, at Stalin's sugges-tion. He, too, supported the invasion and felt the U.S. would not inter-vene in what he considered a "Korean internal matter."

The final decision came at a high-spirited dinner at Stalin's dacha outside Moscow. Kim spoke passionately of what he could do with a united Korea—of the complementary industry of the North and agricul-ture of the South. Commented Khrushchev: "We wished every success to Kim Il Sung and toasted the whole North Korean leadership, looking forward to the day when their struggle would be won."

However, Stalin took one final step which indicated his continued misgivings about the scheme and his apparent wariness of being drawn into a direct confrontation with the United States. The Soviets had had as many as 150 advisers attached to a single North Korean level, serving as low as battalion level, some 7,000 in all in the country. As Kim Il Sung prepared for his march, Stalin ordered most of these advisers back to the USSR. The "incomprehensible" decision surprised Khrushchev, who asked Stalin about it.

Stalin snapped back, "It's too dangerous to keep our advisers there. They might be taken prisoner. We don't want there to be evidence for accusing us of taking part in this business. It's Kim Il Sung's affair."

In Khrushchev's view, the withdrawal of Soviet advisers doomed the North Korean invasion from the outside. The North Korean People's Army made swift advances during the first weeks of the war, then bogged down at UN defensive positions around the southern port of Pusan in mid-August. "If we hadn't refused him [Kim] aid in qualified personnel to assess the distribution of forces and to direct operations," Khrushchev said, "there's no doubt that North Korea would have been victorious." In his memoirs Khrushchev did stress one point: "The war wasn't Stalin's idea, but Kim Il Sung's. Kim was the initiator. Stalin, of course, didn't try to dissuade him."*[30]

Dean Acheson kept busy the first part of Sunday afternoon with meetings in his office, further refining the arguments he would offer the President that evening.[31] Finally, around 3:30 P.M., he shooed everyone away, saying he wished to be alone while he dictated. Acheson's memoirs give a somewhat misleading account of this solitary time: that he spent it marshaling the recommendations he would press upon the President. In fact, of course, his first series of recommendations—the "suggestions" sent to Tokyo that morning—were already on the table. What Acheson *did* do during the afternoon was to prepare arguments for even stronger military moves. He unhesitatingly blamed the USSR for the attack and considered it "an open, undisguised challenge" to the United States; to back away would be "highly destructive" to American power and prestige. He felt that the "shadow cast by power . . . is of great deterrent importance."

In the privacy of his office, scrawling notes on a lawyer's yellow pad, Acheson decided that America must cast such a shadow of power—he hoped in company with the UN, but alone if necessary. He knew that any troop contributions by allies would be "unimportant militarily." Neither his own memoirs nor notes of State Department meetings that day show any concern that the U.S. might not be able to find enough men to fight in South Korea should it chose to do so. This capability was to come into sharp question at crucial periods the next months. But Acheson chose to ignore it in his rush to put America into the Korean War.

---

*Interestingly Khrushchev did not repeat the frequent Communist propaganda claim that the North Koreans went to war only in reaction to an attempted invasion by the South Koreans—a view still argued by some revisionist historians.

* * *

The State Department's Office of Intelligence Research completed a rushed but gloomy prognosis in late afternoon. The South Koreans, because of their military inferiority and limited supplies, could offer only limited resistance.[32] Their defensive lines surely would break in a few days, with the resultant loss of Seoul and the collapse of organized resistance. "At the point when military defeat appears imminent, the will to resist among the South Korean people is also likely to collapse. U.S. withdrawal would signify the end of organized resistance in South Korea." The State intelligence people saw "no possibility" that the North Koreans acted without prior instruction from Moscow. "The move . . . must therefore be considered a Soviet move" and was part of "the increasing militancy that has marked Soviet policy during the past eight months." But it was unique in that "it clearly carries with it . . . the risk of a general war."

But did the Soviets realize the grave risk posed by the invasion? Acheson moved to put Moscow on notice that the United States government did not consider the Soviet Union aloof from the conflict. A cable went off to Ambassador Alan G. Kirk: He should interview Andrei Vishinsky, the Soviet foreign minister, immediately and formally notify him of the invasion. Vishinsky should be told, in effect, that the Soviets should call off their puppet. "In view of the universally known fact of USSR controlling influence over North Korean regime US Govt. asks assurance USSR disavows responsibility for this unprovoked and unwarranted attack and that it will use its influence with North Korean authorities to withdraw their invading forces immediately." If Vishinsky would not receive Kirk, "deliver message to any official you can reach."[33]

The message left Washington at 4:00 P.M. At 6:48 P.M. Walworth Barbour, counselor of the embassy, replied that no ranking Foreign Ministry officer could be found, that key people were "reported out of town."

With Muccio alternately reporting on evacuation plans and his attempts to bolster Rhee's spirits, Acheson stressed in a cable to Seoul for the need for the "Korean army [to] pull things together for brief period required for US decision and action or help."[34] He promised a decision within a matter of hours on authorizing MacArthur to supply the ROKs with ammunition and arms. He asked that the Koreans do a "superhuman job until other factors began to operate." Acheson was readying for adventure.

A UN Resolution

At Lake Success, New York, meanwhile, work proceeded apace on putting the war before the UN Security Council.[35] The U.S. delegation, working through Charles P. Noyes, found firm resistance to the State Department's draft resolution accusing North Korea of an "unprovoked aggression" and demanding that it halt the fighting.

The main opposition came from the British, French, Egyptians, Norwegians, and Indians. On the basis of the meager information available at midday Sunday, could the UN determine which side actually started the war? There were arguments that "this was a fight between Koreans" and should be treated as a civil war. The Egyptian delegate, Mahmoud Fawzi Bey, suggested dropping the word "unprovoked" in view of the long-standing hostilities between the two Koreas. The French delegate, Jean Chauvel, wanted to change the resolution to order both sides, not just the North Koreans, to cease firing. Noyes "argued vigorously" against this change. Conversely, the Turkish and Australian delegates wanted a "strong-line" resolution.

Secretary-General Trygve Lie, the Norwegian statesman, went to work on the wavering delegations.[36] To him the North Korea move was "clear-cut aggression—apparently well-calculated, meticulously planned, and with all the elements of surprise which reminded me of the Nazi invasion of Norway." Lie felt personally offended because the Soviets had given him a warm reception during a visit to Moscow only a month earlier and spoken glowingly of their desire for peace. The Soviets "had been building up a peaceful atmosphere well suited to the surprise attack," Lie felt.

The final version of the resolution, one satisfactory to the State Department, was approved by a 9–0 vote around six o'clock Sunday, an hour or so before Truman arrived in Washington from Independence. It noted "with great concern the armed attack on the Republic of Korea" by forces from North Korea and called for "the immediate cessation of hostilities" and the withdrawal of North Korean forces to the 38th parallel.

The Soviet delegate, to no one's surprise, did not return to the Security Council for the vote, thus forfeiting a chance to kill the resolution with a veto. The resolution committed the UN to use of nothing stronger than its moral support (and the Australian delegate, K. C. O. Shann, thought it "obvious" that the Communists would pay it no heed). But the resolution had the legal effect of putting blame for the outbreak of war on the North Koreans, which satisfied Acheson for the moment. Coaxing a firmer mandate from the UN was a chore that could be performed in due course.

Decisions at Blair House

President Truman arrived back in Washington around seven o'clock Sunday evening, and Acheson, Defense Secretary Louis Johnson, and Undersecretary of State James Webb managed a cursory briefing during the short limousine ride to Blair House. Truman nodded satisfaction at the UN Security Council vote. Once at Blair House he excused himself briefly to telephone his wife and report that he had arrived safely (Mrs. Truman was nervous about air travel, and Truman invariably gave her a reassuring call). Then he went downstairs to the living room, where awaited thirteen of the nation's top military and diplomatic leaders. There were eight from the Defense Department: Johnson, the secretaries of the army (Frank Pace), navy (Francis Matthews), and air force (Thomas Finletter); the chiefs of staff of the army (J. Lawton Collins), navy (Forrest Sherman), and air force (Hoyt Vandenberg), and the chairman (Omar Bradley). From State there were Acheson, Webb, Rusk, Hickerson, and Philip Jessup (the latter as recording secretary). But there were surprising absences. Rear Admiral R. H. Hillenkoetter, the director of central intelligence, was not invited. Nor was the State Department's foremost Soviet expert, George F. Kennan.* The omissions are remarkable in view of the paucity of information available in Washington that evening on exactly what had happened in Korea and the role of the Soviet Union in the invasion.

Peculiarly, the conference began on a tangential issue. Johnson and Bradley had returned the previous day from a trip to the Far East, during which MacArthur had pressed upon them a lengthy memorandum on Formosa, which Bradley (at Johnson's order) proceeded to read. What the assemblage heard was an impassioned plea for Truman to reverse his policy announced in January that the United States did not intend to defend Formosa. MacArthur likened the island to "an unsinkable aircraft carrier and submarine tender" the loss of which to an unfriendly power "would be a disaster of utmost importance to the United States." MacArthur expressed willingness—even eagerness—to visit Formosa to make a survey of "the need and extent of the military assistance" required to protect the island against attack. Everyone had heard the arguments before *ad nauseam,* so there were no interruptions or comment, and Acheson wondered to himself why Johnson even bothered raising the issue at this particular meeting.

Soon after Bradley finished, Alonzo Fields, butler and maître d'hôtel who had served presidents since the Hoover administration, inter-

---

*In his memoirs Kennan said that Acheson wanted him to attend but that his name was inexplicably stricken from the list. Kennan defined the situation as decision making by "social invitation."[37]

rupted to announce dinner. The Trumans had not been expected back for another day, and Fields was quietly proud of the dinner which his staff put together on a few hours' notice.

Dinner conversation was general: the chances of direct intervention by either the Russians or the Chinese; the possibility that Korea might be a feint to shield wider war elsewhere; hopes that U.S. arms might help the South Koreans save themselves.

Then the dishes were cleared away, and the large oval mahogany table became a formal conference table. The President opened the discussion by saying he had an "open mind" and wanted to hear everything anyone had to say about the situation. For the moment he did not intend to make any crucial decisions. (Earlier Undersecretary James Webb had cautioned Truman, *sotto voce*, "Let's not do it too fast." "Don't worry, I won't," the President replied.) Then he asked Acheson for a detailed picture of the situation.

Acheson swiftly reviewed what had happened since receipt of the first bulletin on the invasion, a "darkening report of great confusion." Then he listed three recommendations stemming from his day of talks with State and Defense officials:

—Authorizing MacArthur to send the South Koreans arms and other equipment beyond the supplies authorized by the military assistance program.

—Using the air force to provide cover to help evacuate American women and children and to attack any North Korean planes or tanks attempting to interfere with the operation.

—Directing the Seventh Fleet to proceed north from the Philippines to prevent any Chinese Communist attack on Formosa and also to dissuade the Nationalist Chinese from any moves against the mainland. MacArthur should not be permitted to make his fact-finding mission to Formosa "until further steps had been decided upon." Acheson was emphatic that the United States "should not tie up with the Generalissimo." He thought that the future of Formosa might be determined by the UN. ("Or by the Japanese peace treaty," Truman interposed.) Finally, Acheson recommended stepped-up aid to French Indochina, the government of which was fighting Communist and anti-French nationalist insurgents.

Bradley, the JCS Chairman, speaking next, said, "We must draw the line somewhere," and Korea was as good a place as any to do so. He did not think Russia ready for war. He agreed with the actions suggested by Acheson. Jets flying over South Korea would have a great "morale effect . . . even if they were unable to spot the North Korean tanks." But Bradley questioned the value of sending matériel (such as F-51 fighter planes) which the Koreans were not trained to use. Any supplies sent should be "under the guise of aid to the United Nations." Finally, Bradley "questioned the advisability of putting in ground units particularly if large numbers were involved."

Admiral Sherman agreed with Bradley that the Soviets did not want war now, "but if they do they will have it." He also felt Chiang Kai-shek should be held in check. He wanted to start moving the Seventh Fleet up from the Philippines so it would be available if needed.

General Vandenberg was not as certain as his colleagues that the Russians would not fight. The air force could take out tanks if only the North Korean Air Force were involved. However, Russian jets, if they came into action, would be operating from bases much closer to the battlefield than U.S. bases in Japan.

President Truman asked whether the United States could knock out the Soviet air bases in the Far East.

"This might take some time," General Vandenberg said, but "it could be done if we used A-bombs."*

According to Acheson, Sherman and Vandenberg argued that "this was a matter which could be handled by the navy and the air . . . that the South Koreans could be pulled together and when you gave the North Koreans a terrible pasting from the air, you sent the Navy in to give them heavy gun support from the shores, that this would probably end the thing." Collins, the army chief, was not so certain. As Acheson put it, "he thought this might be a lot more trouble than his air and navy colleagues thought."

Truman next turned to the civilian secretaries. Pace expressed doubt about committing ground troops. Matthews stressed the need for prompt action and said the administration would get popular approval. Finletter thought "we should take calculated risks hoping that our action will keep the peace"; nonetheless, he would make "only the necessary decisions" that night.

Johnson advocated keeping a tight rein on MacArthur; his instructions "should be detailed so as not to give him too much discretion." No presidential authority should be delegated to MacArthur. Johnson, too, opposed putting ground troops into Korea.

Summarizing, Truman confirmed a series of orders. MacArthur was to send the suggested supplies and also a survey group to the Koreans. Fleet elements were to be sent to Japan. The air force "should prepare plans to wipe out all Soviet air bases in the Far East." Truman stressed this "was not an order for action but an order to make the plans." Finally, State and Defense should make a "careful calculation . . . of the next probable place in which Soviet action might take place."

---

*Vandenberg, as true of many air force officers, realized the limitations of conventional U.S. aircraft, especially against the long-range targets in the Far East. According to the Blair House record, his statement drew no response, either pro or con. Truman did flash his nuclear hole card in late November but quickly took it off the table. See Chapter Sixteen below.

Truman stressed that all these actions were taken under authority of the UN resolution passed earlier that day. He was "not yet ready" to name MacArthur as Commander in Chief in Korea. He ordered that nothing be said to the press, even on a background basis. Nor should Acheson and Johnson say anything about Korea the next morning during scheduled congressional appropriations testimony. So the conferees slipped out of Blair House at 11:00 P.M. by a side entrance to avoid reporters clustered on Pennsylvania Avenue.

The military contingent went directly to the Pentagon for another telecon with MacArthur, during which the general was given confirmation that the President had approved the four "suggestions" transmitted earlier that day.[38] MacArthur was warned that "further high level decisions may be expected as military and political situations develop" —in other words, the administration remained uncertain how far the United States would become involved. Did MacArthur require any further instructions? "No," he replied. He gave a reassuring battle report. Both Muccio and the KMAG command reported "increased steadiness" of ROK troops around Seoul and that an attempted North Korean landing at Kangnung, on the east coast, had been repulsed.

General Matthew Ridgway, the army deputy chief of staff, had had passing encounters with MacArthur when he served under him as athletic director at West Point.[39] He did not entirely trust the general, for he knew his proclivity to press orders to the limit and to take advantage of loopholes, real and imagined. Ridgway was a silent observer at the telecon; in the transcript his name appears far down on the "among those present" list. But on the basis of MacArthur's record elsewhere, Ridgway felt the directive should have been more precise.

Breaking protocol, he approached General Bradley after the conference and asked if the instructions to MacArthur "were deliberately intended to exclude the use of ground forces in Korea."

"Yes," Bradley replied.

Ridgway said nothing further, but he felt uneasy that the JCS, at this early stage of the war, were giving MacArthur orders so loosely written that he could easily put them to uses not intended by the President.

Back at Blair House, meanwhile, President Truman had asked Acheson and John Hickerson of the State Department to discuss some non-Korea business.[40] That out of the way, Truman said, "Now, let's all have a drink. It's been a hard day."

Bourbon was poured, and Truman relaxed. "I have hoped and prayed," he said, "that I would never have to make a decision like the one I have just made today. But I saw nothing else that was possible for me to do except that."

He swirled the bourbon around his glass. "Now, with this drink," he continued, "that's out of my mind." He turned to Hickerson.

"Jack," the President said, "in the final analysis, I *did this* for the

United Nations." He continued. "I believed in the League of Nations. It failed. Lots of people thought that it failed because we weren't in it to back it up. Okay, now we started the United Nations. It was our idea, and in this first big test we just couldn't let them down.

"If a collective system under the UN can work, it must be made to work, and *now* is the time to call their bluff."

An American Evacuation

All day Monday reports from the battlefront north of Seoul told of continued ROK withdrawals and North Korean advances.[41] American military advisers doubted that the ROKs could hold their lines at the Han River, the only natural barrier between the 38th parallel and Seoul. Jack Seifert, the naval officer designated by Ambassador John Muccio to handle evacuation of American civilians and dependents, found Norwegian and Chinese freighters at the port of Inchon, just to the west of Seoul, whose captains agreed to take out the refugees. At about two o'clock Monday morning Muccio decided the time had come. The embassy radio station, WVTP, broadcast a directive: Trucks, buses, and cars would start arriving at previously designated pickup points within the hour. Each evacuee could bring only what he or she could carry; mothers were advised to bring blankets for children.

The caravan of vehicles assembled at Ascom City, an American-created logistical center equidistant between Seoul and Inchon. Chaos prevailed. According to one embassy source, several of the women drank to bolster their courage and "were somewhat of a problem." One couple broke down in hysteria and had to be put in restraint. By dawn about 700 people were in Ascom City.

Seifert's plan was for the women to be divided between a Norwegian fertilizer ship, the *Reinholte,* and a Chinese freighter, both moored in open waters several miles past the mudbanks caused by the twenty-eight-foot tides at Inchon. Ships' boats ferried the women through narrow channels to the vessels. The women panicked when the boats pulled alongside the Chinese vessel and they saw Oriental faces staring down at them; according to Noble, "They had had so much terror back in Seoul, and they now recalled half-forgotten tales of Chinese bandit vessels." So the entire frightened flock was crammed into the *Reinholte* —some 700 people in a vessel with accommodations for exactly 6 persons other than crew. The fetid stench of chemical fertilizers permeated every cranny of the ship. Noble's account is restrained, yet one gets hints of a vessel gripped by hysteria, with women bickering and quarreling and exchanging bitter comments about favoritism. Why should Mrs. X be permitted to have dozens of pieces of luggage when everyone else lugged paper bags and knapsacks?

But both the military and the diplomatic corps are imbued with strong strains of leadership and common sense, and eventually everyone was quieted down enough for the *Reinholte* to begin its voyage to Japan—an uncomfortable voyage, to be sure, one marked by the frightened cries of children and the nasty retching sounds of seasick men and women.

From his vantage point in Tokyo on Monday morning, General MacArthur strongly disagreed with Ambassador Muccio's decision to evacuate the civilians.[42] John Foster Dulles, the roaming diplomat, and escort John Allison visited MacArthur to be brought up-to-date on war news. The general seemed confident the ROKs could regroup and throw back the invaders. He thought Muccio had acted "prematurely," but he nonetheless would comply with orders from Washington to provide an air cover for the evacuation. MacArthur saw "no reason to panic." He did not think the attack was an "all-out effort supported by the Soviet Union."

MacArthur remained sanguine that evening, when Dulles went to his private residence for a dinner. Allison supped with old friends. George Foster, the National Broadcasting Company correspondent in Tokyo, had just come from MacArthur's headquarters and told the gathering there was "nothing of significance to report." Later, however, an Australian diplomat joined the company. He told of talking to his embassy in Seoul—it was evacuating all personnel, and the ROK Army was in full flight.

Alarmed, Allison telephoned Muccio, who said that the ROK Army indeed was in retreat and that the front was "disintegrating." Allison could hear the thud of artillery shells in the background as Muccio spoke. Allison made more phone calls and finally located Dulles in his guest quarters at the embassy. Since Dulles had just returned from MacArthur's residence, surely he would have up-to-date information.

"I suppose you've heard the bad news from Korea," Allison commenced.

"What are you talking about?" Dulles replied. He had heard nothing.

"But didn't you just have dinner with the General?"

"Yes, but after dinner we saw a movie, and we weren't interrupted all evening. I stopped in on the way back to have a nightcap with Colonel [Sidney] Huff [MacArthur's pilot] and he had heard nothing."

That MacArthur's staff had not interrupted the general's evening at the movies upon receipt of such news astounded Allison. But after hanging up, he reflected on what he had heard elsewhere: Postdinner movies were a long-standing part of MacArthur's life, and he did not like to be disturbed for anything while one was in progress.

Late on Monday night—General MacArthur had finished viewing his movie and retired—President Syngman Rhee decided his army could hold Seoul no longer.[43] His transportation minister was ordered to find special trains for the Cabinet, the top executive officers, and members of the National Assembly. The decision to withdraw touched off angry debate in the Assembly, where Rhee did not command a majority. Rhee and his circle were accused of abandoning the Korean people to save themselves. But more moderate voices argued that by retreating, Rhee could continue the battle; were he to be captured, the republic would be dead. After an hour of debate the Assembly voted: The majority would stay in Seoul "with the people."

Rhee, however, was adamant about leaving Seoul. Late on Monday night his staff assembled two special trains to carry him, his chief advisers, and their families south away from the battle. Despite their talk of the previous day, Rhee did not bother—or dare—to inform Muccio of his flight. "I didn't know until after they had left that they had actually gone," Muccio recounted. But he was able to use this fact to psychological advantage in coming months. "His failure to do so [inform Muccio of the flight] was one thing that I had over Rhee that stood me in good stead the next few months, that he had left Seoul before I did."

Washington's Worries Deepen

Modern warfare relies upon communications. Without a swift exchange of information, the players in different spheres must act in ignorance of the existent situation elsewhere. Monday, June 26, was the day when the Korean War fell victim of a tenuous, unreliable net of field telephones, rapidly collapsing commercial telegraph systems in South Korea, slow encrypting machines, and the delays inherent in trying to pass messages halfway around the world.

For instance, several hours after President Rhee fled Seoul, President Truman summoned the Korean ambassador, John M. Chang, to the White House for a pep talk.[44] Chang wanted to talk about his country's need for tanks, artillery, and aircraft. To Truman the more important point was that the ROKs must "fight effectively" so that any American aid could be used effectively. The war had lasted only forty-eight hours; "other men and other countries had defended their liberties under much more discouraging situations," Truman told Chang. Chang insisted the ROKs were fighting bravely but did not have adequate equipment. Truman repeated that help was on the way (actually another Blair House meeting was necessary first) and that the Koreans "must develop the steadfast leadership which would carry through this crisis."

Chang left the White House with such a long face that veteran correspondent Richard Strout of the *Christian Science Monitor* concluded the United States intended to let the South Koreans fight alone.[45]

Such was not the case. In highly misleading phone talks with Republican congressional leaders that Monday, Acheson pleaded that Truman be given diplomatic breathing room.[46] He said that the situation was "well in hand" (an assertion belied by Muccio's cables) and that the President did not wish to "appear to be urging a course of action on the UN" (which would suggest Sunday's Security Council action stemmed from diplomatic immaculate conception). In his talk with Senator Alexander Wiley (Republican of Wisconsin) of the Foreign Relations Committee, Acheson even managed to assign MacArthur responsibility for the decisions made thus far. (MacArthur had been born on an army post in Wisconsin; for terms of political registration, he considered it his home state.) Acheson told Wiley that "MacArthur was in charge of sending them [the Koreans] assistance and it was MacArthur's judgment that the President was relying on." Wiley wondered whether Truman intended to send in ground troops. No, Acheson replied, but "all of that is now before the President."

Muccio's cables became increasingly gloomy as Monday wore on.[47] The embassy was in "current danger" of being cut off, and Rhee and top officials had fled south. One army commander inquired about Rhee's moving to Japan as a "government in exile."

Alarmed, Acheson interrupted Truman's dinner at 7:29 P.M. and said the Korean situation was so bad that another meeting was advisable.[48] "Have them here at nine P.M.," Truman replied. So the same group as the night before (less Undersecretary Webb) returned to the mahogany table in Blair House.

Vandenberg opened the meeting by reporting that U.S. Air Force planes had shot down their first Russian-built YAK fighter.

"I hope it's not the last," the President said, and there were some chuckles around the table. Then the group turned to serious business. Acheson presented a series of recommendations drafted earlier in the day at staff conferences. A strong strain of caution ran through the proposals—and also through the comments of the officials who heard them.

First, Acheson asked that an "all-out order" be given the navy and air force to waive all restrictions in Korea and "offer the fullest possible support to the South Korean forces, attacking tanks, guns, columns . . . of the North Koreans" to give the ROKs the chance to regroup.

Truman approved, only to hear nervous questions. Secretary Pace and General Vandenberg wanted assurances that this meant "action only south of the 38th Parallel." Correct, responded the President; no action should be taken north of the parallel. He paused, then added, "Not yet."

Acheson next moved to the Nationalist Chinese. He wanted a two-way blockade by the Seventh Fleet, one that prevented either side from attempting an invasion of the other.

Truman agreed, then mused about some radical approaches to the Formosan problem. He wanted consideration given to the idea of "taking Formosa back as part of Japan," as it had been before World War II, and putting it under MacArthur's control. Truman then revealed a political bombshell. A month or so earlier, he said, he had received a secret letter from Generalissimo Chiang Kai-shek in which he offered to "step out of the situation if that would help"—i.e., resign, and let another less controversial figure assume command of the Nationalists. Although his offer was mistily defined, Truman saw Chiang's gesture as a means of bringing the Nationalists into the Korean War. "We might want to proceed along these lines in order to get Chinese forces helping us," Truman said. He felt Chiang would accept MacArthur as a successor.

The advantages of such a succession were staggeringly favorable to General MacArthur. Were Chiang to hand him the cloak of leadership of Nationalist China, he would become *de facto* viceroy of not one but *two* major Asian nations. Chiang's offer also gave MacArthur a major bargaining chip in his later attempts to bring the Nationalists into the war. If the liberal third worldists of Britain, India, and elsewhere opposed Nationalist entry because of Chiang's omniconservative presence, why would not MacArthur be a suitable substitute?

Acheson was skeptical. He considered Chiang "unpredictable" and "thought it possible that he might resist and 'throw the ball game.' " He did not think it "desirable that we should get mixed up in the question of the Chinese administration" of Formosa.

Acheson's brief but strong argument convinced Truman. The United States would not give the Chinese "a nickel" for any purpose whatever, for "all the money we had given them is now invested in United States real estate." "Or in banks in the Philippine Islands," interjected Secretary Johnson.

Turning back to Korea, General Collins depicted the military situation as "bad," and it was "impossible to say how much our air can do." The Korean chief of staff, General Chae Byong Duk, "has no fight left in him." Both Acheson and Johnson stressed that it "was important for us to do something even if the efforts were not successful." Johnson quickly canvassed the service chiefs: Did they object to any of the actions proposed? No.

The President next asked whether the National Guard should be mobilized; if so, he must ask Congress for funds. General Bradley said that if the United States put ground troops into Korea, it could not carry out commitments elsewhere, especially NATO, "without mobilization." He suggested waiting several days before making any decision. Truman agreed. "I don't want to go to war," the President said.

Acheson made two other recommendations, both of which appeared innocuous at the time. One was for an increase in the level of U.S. forces in the Philippines, the government of which had been fighting a combined nationalist-Communist insurgency for several years. The other was for a "strong military mission" and about $20 million in direct military aid to the French for their war in Indochina. The French had been asking for such help for three years as they fought to retain control of their prewar colonies of Laos, Cambodia, and Vietnam. Truman had resisted, saying the United States had no business protecting outdated colonial relics the people of which wished independence. Now he had second thoughts: Could the war in Indochina be but another version of the Communist expansionism the United States had decided to oppose in Korea? Truman approved Acheson's proposed aid. Thus did the United States take the unwitting first step toward involvement in the Vietnam War.

Once again Dean Acheson had been the dominant figure—winning approval for each idea he proposed, dissuading Truman from any dalliance with Chiang Kai-shek. At his recommendation, American air and navy forces were to combat the North Koreans, and the American Navy was to ensure that the two Chinese regimes stayed at arm's length. Each of these proposals was primarily military; each time the military service chiefs concurred without offering serious discussion or independent alternatives. America again moved closer to general war and under the impetus of a diplomat, not its generals.

MacArthur's Confidence Sags

Battlefield reports reaching Tokyo on Tuesday morning, and news of the flight of the Rhee government, staggered General MacArthur. When he arrived at the airport to bid farewell to John Foster Dulles, John Allison saw him as a "vastly different [person] from the jaunty, confident General" of Sunday night who had boasted he could handle the North Koreans "with one arm tied behind my back." All of Korea was lost, MacArthur said. "The only thing we can do is get our people safely out of the country." Allison commented, "I have never seen such a dejected, completely despondent man as General MacArthur was that . . . morning. . . ."[49]

But yet another bizarre episode was to come. A minor mechanical problem delayed departure of the plane. As the party waited and listened to MacArthur's glum comments, a courier told the general that a message from Washington had just arrived in his office stating that the secretary of the army wished to have a telecon in less than an hour. Important decisions were about to be made in Washington, and the Pentagon needed input from its field commander.

MacArthur brushed the messenger aside. "Tell them I'm engaged in seeing Ambassador Dulles off," he said. "If I don't get back in time, have the chief of staff talk to the secretary."

Allison and William J. Sebald, embassy political officer, looked at one another in astonishment. They exchanged nods, quietly slipped away from the party, and found the airline manager, who said it would be long after one o'clock before the plane could be repaired. So they hit upon a subterfuge: They had the public address system announce departure of the flight and ask that the Dulles party please board first. MacArthur escorted Dulles to the plane, bade him a gracious farewell, and sped back to Tokyo.

As soon as he was out of sight, Dulles marched back down the ramp and sat around the VIP lounge for another hour.

MacArthur, however, had built what he thought was a useful backfire. John Foster Dulles, although formally in service of a Democratic administration, was the Republican Party's equivalent of a shadow-government secretary of state. MacArthur treated him with a deference not given to other visitors from Washington, and with a reason: His political future, if any, lay with the Republicans.

MacArthur's fawning behavior at the airport did not fool Dulles for a moment. Back in Washington two days later, he gave President Truman a most uncomplimentary report on MacArthur's conduct. He told Truman of the confusion in Tokyo the day the war began, of MacArthur's ignorance about its progress, and of his (Dulles's) inability to persuade any staff officers that the general should be told of the seriousness of the situation. Dulles told Truman he would have MacArthur "hauled back to the United States immediately."[50]

If the strong disavowal of MacArthur by such a prominent Republican surprised the President, he did not say so. He noted that the general "is involved politically in this country and that he could not recall [him] without causing a tremendous reaction." MacArthur, Truman said, "has been built up to heroic stature." Dulles agreed. But he also made plain that—although he was of MacArthur's party*—he would support publicly any relief of the general. In terms of Republican foreign policy, Dulles's attitude was understandable. He was a stalwart of the GOP's

---

*MacArthur had been an absentee candidate for the GOP presidential nomination in 1948 but did not survive the first primary, winning less than 5 percent of the vote in Wisconsin. He later claimed, unconvincingly, the candidacy was not of his own making.

internationalist wing that believed in a strong American involvement abroad, especially in Europe. This wing did not share MacArthur's view that the future of America depended on closer ties to Asia. In this particular phase of foreign policy there was a strong commonality of views of Dulles and Acheson.

Dulles's suggestion that MacArthur be replaced also punches considerable holes in a favored revisionist theory: that Dulles had plotted with MacArthur and President Rhee to lure the North Koreans into war as a means of stirring the United States into an all-out attack on Communist China. Under this supposed plot, ROK losses the first days of the war were intended to intensify the crisis and to leave Truman no choice but to strike at China. If indeed such a plot existed, Dulles behaved most peculiarly in attempting to remove one of his co-ringleaders from power the first week of the war.

The Air War Begins

The "urgent" message for which MacArthur had been summoned back to his office proved to be the decisions made earlier in Washington directing the use of air and naval forces in support of the beleaguered ROKs. General Earle Partridge, the air commander, sat alongside MacArthur as the teletypewriter briskly ticked out orders. When the machine fell silent, MacArthur turned and issued what Partridge recalled as a "volley of oral orders."[51] He wanted the Far East Air Force (FEAF) to pound the North Koreans with "every resource at its disposal" during the next thirty-six hours, and he wanted the barrage to start immediately, so that the enemy would feel the sting of American air might that very evening. MacArthur was convinced that vigorous air action would "drive the North Koreans back into their own territory in disorder." He approved Partridge's request to shift in a bombardment group from Guam to bolster forces already in Japan, but he also sounded a word of caution: FEAF must remain in position to defend Japan against possible Soviet strikes as well.

As Partridge saluted and left the conference room, he felt that MacArthur looked "almost jubilant" at the return to action.

FEAF scurried. Commanders dispatched visual and photoreconnaissance missions to scan Korea for targets. Ground crews loaded B-26 bombers for strikes against tanks, artillery, supply dumps, bridges, and moving traffic between the 38th parallel and the front lines. Lumbering B-29's were assigned to prowl South Korea in search of targets of opportunity. By nightfall the air force was ready for action.

Unfortunately the first night's missions were a flop, for reasons beyond air force control. First, six of the ten B-26's available were diverted to flying cover for the fertilizer ship *Reinholte,* still plodding through the Sea of Japan toward refuge. The other B-26's set out from Ashiya at dusk in quest of a North Korean tank column said to be somewhere north of Seoul. But foul weather and darkness kept them from finding the target; they returned to base without having dropped a single bomb. Then low clouds settled over Ashiya, closing the field for hours. Five planes finally got aloft. One turned back because of mechanical troubles; the other four made it to Korea but found that thick clouds enshrouded the battle area. They turned back, bomb racks full.

What MacArthur felt about these act-of-God failures is not a matter of record. But the attitude relayed through his chief of staff, General Edward Almond, was cold fury. (In the tactful words of the air force's official historian, Almond found the lack of results "extremely annoying.") He called the hapless Partridge repeatedly during the night, saying the salvation of the ROKs depended upon some show of force by FEAF. Almond spoke bluntly; he "wanted bombs put on the ground in the narrow corridor between the 38th Parallel and Seoul, employing any means and without any accuracy." In other words, FEAF must bomb blindly through the clouds, if necessary, and hope the high explosives hit North Koreans, not friendly forces. Partridge in turn put pressure on his subordinates, urging a "full-out effort."

The next morning, June 28, the weather over the Japanese islands was the "foulest imaginable," in the words of Lieutenant Bryce Poe II, who flew off alone in the murk in an RF-80A reconnaissance plane to search out the vanguard of the North Korean columns. Fortunately the weather broke when he reached Korea, and he managed to complete the air force's first battle reconnaissance ever in a jet-powered craft. He relayed the news to Ashiya: If the pilots could get through the muck over Japan, they could find targets in Korea.

Thus FEAF finally went into action. A strike force of twelve B-26's flew to busy railyards at Munsan, near the 38th parallel, and inflicted heavy bomb damage on lines of trains. Then they roared southward at low level, strafing and rocketing targets of opportunity on the rail line and an adjacent highway. Enemy ground fire was heavy; virtually every plane received hits. One limped into Suwon Air Base near Seoul with a dead engine; another managed to creep back to Ashiya but was so badly damaged it was junked. Yet another lost its bearings trying to land at fog-cloaked Ashiya and crashed; every man aboard died.

The F-80 fighter planes had even rougher going. The 310 miles from Itazuke were at the very limit of their range, especially when they had to operate beneath a 200-foot ceiling. But once they reached the area north of Seoul, they found roads laden with North Korean tanks, trucks, and artillery, which they strafed and rocketed at will. When their day's work was done, flame and smoke arose from a 50-mile stretch of high-way.

The B-29, the so-called Superfortress of the Air, had been built as a strategic bomber. But at MacArthur's insistence, FEAF deployed them as crude tactical support planes. In late afternoon four of the Superforts flew along roadways and parallel rail lines north of Seoul, with crews dropping bombs on "anything that looked to be worth a bomb"—a truck, a tank, even a cluster of people who may or may not have been North Korean soldiers. A "strange employment of the strategic bomb-ers," the air force lamented, "but General MacArthur had called for a maximum show of force."

Muccio Heads South

In Seoul, meanwhile, Ambassador Muccio vacillated through Tuesday on what to do about his own safety.[52] Leaving Seoul meant his com-munications with Washington would be uncertain for the next critical hours. Also, should the United States (symbolically) be driven from a friendly capital by Communist invaders? Muccio was no coward; by the same token, he was a prudent man. His nation had sent him to Korea to perform a task; now he must decide how best to do it.

He consulted with Vyvyan Holt, the British minister, and Georges Perruche, the French chargé. Both intended to stay, "regardless." The Nationalist Chinese ambassador, Shao Yu-lin, had no choice: If the Com-munists caught him, they would have him blindfolded before a wall within the hour.

Muccio mentally worked through several scenarios. The United States was not formally at war with North Korea. Could he not remain in Seoul under a flag of neutrality, as the British and French intended? He thought of bringing the entire American mission, military and civil-ian, together at the embassy and claiming diplomatic immunity if and when the North Koreans captured Seoul. The Korean Military Advisory Group (KMAG) lacked any official guidance on what it should be in event of war. But officers did see three alternatives: take up arms and actively help the South Koreans repel the invaders; advise the ROK Army in its combat operations; or simply leave Korea and abandon the republic to its fate. Although Rhee had fled, he left behind an acting prime minister, along with the defense minister and key members of the army staff. Muccio's accreditation was to the ROK government, not to Rhee. So long as a remnant of authority remained in Seoul, he should stay with it.

Muccio chose the latter option. At about six in the morning on Tuesday he told Washington via cable that he "will stick it out here . . . with limited volunteer force until bitter end." He proposed sending his deputy, Everett Drumwright, and the few remaining Foreign Service officers south "to follow President." Military officers in KMAG would be evacuated by truck, "timing depending upon developments, to preclude potential accusation abandonment."

Acheson quickly demurred. He thought it "inadvisable" that Muccio and staff should become hostages. They should leave Seoul to join Rhee "before safe departure becomes impossible."

Muccio could not argue with a direct order. Clear out, he told subordinates, we're heading south. With the sound of gunfire thundering from the northern skies, the few remaining Americans stripped filing cabinets of classified documents, carried them into the embassy courtyard, and piled them in a heap. Army officers urged haste; the ROK Army said the Communists would be in the capital at any moment. Someone sloshed gasoline on the papers and tossed in a match; whatever "secrets" America had about Korea billowed into the night.

Upstairs, Robert Heavy, the embassy security officer, used thorium bombs (which burn with intense and swift heat) to destroy the embassy's two coding machines. Then he took a sledgehammer and methodically smashed the telephone exchange equipment; no sense in leaving a communications network in place for the North Koreans.

One blow of his hammer unwittingly cut off Ambassador Muccio in mid-sentence. Muccio cussed the suddenly silent receiver in his hand, then closed his office door and left. He had two goals. One was to find the fleeing South Korean government. Another was to be at Suwon Airport by 6:00 P.M. to meet the fact-finding group from General MacArthur's headquarters.

Soon after Muccio left, someone pulled down the massive iron shutters that shielded the doors and windows of the first two floors of the embassy building. In all the confusion no one had found time to raise the American flag that morning, so the colors need not be struck.

Nor did anyone take time to remove the Great Seal of the United States, positioned over the center of the main doorway. (The North Koreans apparently did not realize the symbolic importance of the seal. When U.S. forces reoccupied Seoul weeks later, it remained in place.)

To South Koreans, the sight of the shuttered embassy was a significant signal. Panicked civilians raced to the railway station and clambered atop any train heading south. People who could not find room on a train put their belongings on their backs and trudged south. Members of the National Assembly who had voted only hours earlier to remain in Seoul, regardless of the Communist advance, had second thoughts. By dusk a majority had fled south across the Han. (The handful of ROK assemblymen who chose to stay in Seoul were rounded up and shot by the North Korean invaders within days.)

* * *

With dependents safely at sea aboard the noxious but functionable *Reinholte,* and the bulk of the embassy staff at Kimpo Airfield awaiting flights to Tokyo, Muccio returned to his residence for the first time since the distant Sunday morning when he received the alert of a possible invasion.

"I opened up the food and liquor cabinets and told the servants to help themselves and not to be found there," Muccio said. He gave his chauffeur the official embassy limousine—Muccio knew a jeep would best suit his needs in the days ahead—and told him to "put his family in it and whatever supplies he needed and drive south." But Muccio did not ignore his personal needs. He grabbed a handful of cigars from a desktop humidor, told his military aide to get a case of scotch whiskey from embassy stores, and packed a bag with socks, underwear, and a few shirts.

Muccio stopped on the steps and listened for sounds of the MIG fighters that had strafed Seoul periodically the past day; twice he had dived beneath a desk to escape bullets. He heard nothing. He got into a jeep with the military aide and set out in quest of the South Korean government.

A few hours after Muccio's hasty departure, North Korean airplanes swept over the city, dropping leaflets demanding surrender. North Korean radio broadcasts made the same demand. The ROK 7th and 2nd divisions made last-ditch counterattacks north of the city; they failed, and the ROKs broke into disorderly retreat.

Disaster at the Han River

Contingency defense plans called for the ROKs to dynamite bridges and roads north of Seoul and to post roadblocks. But so great was the panic, according to Major Richard I. Crawford, a KMAG officer serving as chief engineer adviser to the ROK Army, that "prepared demolitions were not blown, roadblocks were erected but not manned, and obstacles were not covered by fire." A major handicap was a lack of antitank mines (although one valiant band of ROKs tied explosives to poles under oncoming North Korean tanks, destroying four of them on a bridge).

Four American correspondents—Frank Gibney of *Time,* Keyes Beech of the Chicago *Daily News,* Burton Crane of *The New York Times,* and Marguerite Higgins of the New York *Herald Tribune*—flew into Seoul on a courier plane just after sundown.[53] Crane noted an

American officer, "tight-lipped and haggard," burning stacks of documents on the rubble-strewn concrete at Kimpo Airport. When they reached KMAG headquarters, they found Lieutenant Colonel W. H. Sterling Wright—who had not been to sleep since leaving Tokyo in a rush on Sunday morning—serving as acting commander. He called the situation "fluid but hopeful" and departed for his quarters to try to snatch a few hours' rest. But the ranking Korean officer there—General Kim Paik Il, who had served in the Japanese Army as a captain— sounded more pessimistic. "Not very good . . . not very good," he repeated time and again. The correspondents also went off for a brief rest.

On surged the North Koreans, four or more tank-supported divisions against remnants of two ROK divisions, 40,000 men against 10,000. Sometime around midnight the ROKs finally broke; the orders came for the defenders to flee south across the Han River.

A day or so earlier Korean engineers had packed vast quantities of explosives around the concrete abutments of the bridge complex across the Han—a three-lane highway span and three separate railroad trestles. The order was to blow the bridges only after the army had managed to escape.

The plan fell apart. At midnight Major George R. Sedberry, Jr., attached to the ROK Army, telephoned KMAG headquarters with the alarming news that the South Koreans intended to destroy the Han River bridges at any moment, despite the fact that some 10,000 men (and their equipment) had yet to cross it.

The order touched off a fierce row in the ROK High Command, with the chief of staff, Major General Chae Byong Duk, loudly resisting. (A mammoth man who weighed not much less than 300 pounds, Chae accepted with good humor his nickname of Fats. According to Harold Noble of the U.S. embassy, he was "so fat he didn't walk, he waddled. His face was crinkled into folds with rolls that almost hid his eyes." Despite his unmilitary physique, however, Chae was a fighter; he knew that holding the bridges several hours longer would enable his army to preserve men and equipment that would be sorely needed the next few days. But a higher official in the ROK Ministry of Defense wanted the bridges blown immediately; his first priority was stopping the North Koreans from getting the tanks across the Han, even if the order meant sacrificing thousands of ROK soldiers. When Chae continued to protest, he was summarily ushered to a jeep and driven across the river. His deputy, General Kim Paik Il, agreed to blow the bridges.

The Americans added their voice to the protest. Colonel Wright, aroused from his sleep, hurriedly dispatched Lieutenant Colonel Walter Greenwood, Jr., the KMAG deputy chief of staff, to the ROKs to remind them of an earlier promise that the bridges would not be blown

until enemy tanks reached the street on which the ROK Army headquarters were located.

During this debate someone awoke the sleeping American correspondents as well. "It's bad," a KMAG major said. "Tanks have broken
into the city, and we don't know how much longer the lines will hold.
I have to stay here until the colonel [Wright] comes, but you had better
turn left at the headquarters road and get across the bridge as soon as
you can. Then make for Suwon."

The writers ran down the stairs. *Time*'s Frank Gibney noted a bright
new poster on the KMAG bulletin board: "Don't forget—Tuesday, June
27, bingo."

The three male correspondents (Gibney, Beech, and Crane) got into
one jeep; Miss Higgins elected to ride with KMAG officers. The streets
were so congested with pedestrians and vehicles that no one made
much progress. For a routed army, the ROKs seemed in good spirits.
Many soldiers sang as they marched. Military police at the intersections
kept cars and other vehicles in line. But the unfortunate civilians who
had to walk were not nearly so orderly. They stumbled along by the
thousands, women with bundles on their heads, men with wooden
frames containing household goods on their backs.

Eventually the correspondents' jeep reached the midpoint of the
bridge, only to stall between a six-by-six truck of soldiers in front and
other jeeps in the rear. The thunder of guns behind them grew louder,
and they wondered how much longer the delaying units in Seoul could
hold. They tried to check what was blocking traffic, but so many civilians were pressed together on the bridge they found it impossible to
walk. Gibney recounted what happened next: "We returned to the jeep
and sat waiting. Without warning the sky was lighted by a huge sheet
of sickly orange flame. There was a tremendous explosion immediately
in front of us. Our jeep was picked up and hurled fifteen feet by the
blast."

The explosion shattered Gibney's glasses, and he felt blood pouring
from his head. "I can't see," cried Crane, also bloodied about the face.
The ROK soldiers in the truck ahead all looked dead. Scores, hundreds
of bodies of the dead and the gravely wounded lay scattered over the
bridge. Other screaming refugees raced pell-mell for the north shore.
The middle section of the highway bridge, crammed with three solid
lanes of vehicular and pedestrian traffic, dropped into the river. The
railway bridges were also demolished.

Reconstructing the disaster later, KMAG officers estimated that from
500 to 800 soldiers and civilians were killed by the blast or drowned
when they fell into the river. For the ROK Army, the premature blowing of the bridges was a catastrophe of the gravest order. The main part
of the army, now isolated north of the river and dependent on haphazard ferries to get across it, lost nearly all its transport and supplies and

the bulk of its heavy weapons. Had the blowing been delayed another six to eight hours, most of this matériel—as well as two ROK divisions —could have been transported safely to new defensive lines. Eyewitnesses put the time of the explosion at 2:15 A.M. Enemy troops did not reach the center of Seoul until around noon, and the banks of the Han several hours later. The surviving troops straggled across the Han in small boats and rafts the next few days, arriving on the south bank in disordered units.

After an investigation (one hampered by wartime confusion and the lack of any written directives) the ROKs court-martialed and summarily executed their army's chief engineer for the "manner" in which he prepared the bridges for demolition. The U.S. Army's official history, based upon interviews with many KMAG officers, does not attempt to fix blame, although the order's "utter disregard for the tactical situation" suggested it came from a civilian (the deputy defense minister), not from within the army. Regardless, the history states, "The disintegration of the ROK army now set in with alarming speed."

A recapitulation by KMAG in early July showed the extent of the ROK disaster. The day the war began the ROK Army had some 98,000 men under arms. A week later, army headquarters could account for only 22,000 men south of the Han River. Several days later more stragglers assembled beyond the river, and the 6th and 8th divisions, fighting in the sector west of Seoul, came in with specific strength estimates that brought the ROK fighting force to 54,000 men. Nonetheless, the ROK Army losses the first week of the fighting were 44,000 men—killed, captured, or missing, almost half its total force. The 6th and 8th divisions, out of the main corridor of the North Korean attack, managed to pull back with most of their weapons, equipment, and transport intact. But save for these units, the ROK Army came out of the first days of the war battered physically and psychologically. Clearly survival of the Republic of Korea now depended upon American intervention.

CHAPTER THREE

"A Police Action"

That President Truman had decided to commit U.S. air and naval forces to defense of Korea was withheld from the American public for twelve hours, for reasons of political and diplomatic expediency.[1] The decision had been made after eleven o'clock Monday night, hardly the hour to arrange an in-depth congressional briefing. Truman knew he needed political support for entering the war; he did not wish to squander it by having key congressional allies learn of developments through the Tuesday morning Washington *Post.* Secretary Acheson also objected to having news of the Formosa blockade reach Generalissimo Chiang Kai-shek through the media. So a public announcement was held off until the President could brief the congressional leadership on Tuesday morning.

General MacArthur, in cables from Tokyo, vigorously protested the delay. The ROKs were on the ropes; they must be told at once American aid was en route lest they collapse. MacArthur argued his case in a postmidnight telecon with Undersecretary of State James Webb and Army Secretary Frank Pace. Within hours, he said, the war could be over unless he could give the ROKs an incentive to hold firm. Webb hit upon what his State Department colleague George Kennan called a "rather ingenious and desperate device." MacArthur was given permission to broadcast Truman's decision over South Korean radio stations, but only in the Korean language and without notifying Western correspondents in Tokyo. Meanwhile, a courier was sent posthaste to Formosa to brief Chiang.

Thus the Korean people—at least those in hearing range of the few radio stations still operating—learned of the U.S. intervention while the American people slumbered in blissful ignorance.

Congressional leaders had surprisingly few questions for Truman at the White House briefing Tuesday morning.[2] He had Acheson review events of the past few days. Truman "hoped there would be no Soviet involvement in the attack, but their possible next moves were being studied." In any event, the United States "could not let this matter go by default." Finally, Truman stressed he was acting under a UN mandate that member nations furnished "such assistance to the Republic of Korea as may be necessary to repel the armed attack and to restore international peace and security in the area."*

Even Truman's Republican critics left the briefing with high praise for the President. "I think it is a damned good action," declared Senator Styles Bridges of New Hampshire. When word spread to Capitol Hill, one observer likened the air of excitement to the day after Pearl Harbor. Joseph C. Harsch of the *Christian Science Monitor* summed up the mood of the day:

> I have lived and worked in and out of this city for twenty years. Never before in that time have I felt such a sense of relief and unity pass through this city.
>
> The most curious thing about the affair was the [Monday] gloom from a belief that the Administration would miss the boat and do something idle or specious. The decision to act already had been taken, yet almost everyone was assuming there would be no action. When it came there was a sense first of astonishment and then of relief.
>
> Mr. Truman obviously did much more than he was expected to do, and almost exactly what most individuals seemed to wish he would do. I have never seen such a large part of Washington so nearly satisfied with a decision of the government.

The next day, Wednesday, however, Senator Robert A. Taft, the Republican spokesman in the Senate, served notice that the Truman administration—and Acheson in particular—must answer ultimately for a war brought on by "bungling and inconsistent foreign policy." He hit Truman for failing to get a mandate from Congress before entering the war. Congressional participants in the Tuesday White House briefing were not consulted; they were simply told of a *fait accompli*. Taft concluded with words that would be often quoted in the 1960's by liberal senators protesting American involvement in another undeclared war, Vietnam:

> I merely do not wish to have this action go by with the approval of the Senate, if it is what it seems to me, namely, a complete usurpation by the President of authority to use the armed forces of this country.

*Actually, the UN Security Council was still some hours away from considering this new U.S. resolution. See below.

> If the incident is permitted to go by without protest, at least from this body, we would have finally terminated for all time the right of Congress to declare war, which is granted by Congress alone by the Constitution of the United States.

Taft took care to stress he did not oppose the decisions themselves; had the issues been put before the Senate for a vote, he would have approved them. But he made no effort to force the issue by offering a resolution disapproving Truman's procedures. Taft knew the President commanded a strong Senate majority and that the administration, by winning a pretext vote, could later point to it as affirmation of Truman's actions. A wily strategist with presidential ambitions, Taft chose simply to state his case for the record and let events take care of themselves.

Nor did Taft enjoy the support of many of his more prominent Republican colleagues—particularly William F. Knowland of California, a man also infected with presidential aspirations. Asked if he agreed with Taft, Knowland replied he saw no reason for a formal declaration of war by Congress. His only criticism was that the President had limited military activities below the 38th parallel. Knowland would not mind if Truman let the air force cross the border, as a policeman might chase a burglar away from the scene of a crime.

"The action this government is taking," Knowland said in a floor speech, "is a police action against a violator of the law of nations and the charter of the United Nations."

Late in the week Truman met reporters for the first time since the North Korean invasion. He was asked several times to characterize the U.S. response.

> Q. Mr. President, everybody is asking in this country, are we or are we not at war?
> A. We are not at war. . . . The members of the United Nations are going to the relief of the Korean republic to suppress a bandit raid on the Republic of Korea.
> Q. Mr. President, would it be correct under your explanation to call this a police action under the United Nations?
> A. Yes, that is exactly what it amounts to.

Thus did one of America's most unpopular wars acquire the sobriquet "police action," a euphemism not of Truman's coinage, but one to which he clung tenaciously during coming months of criticism, with characteristic (and unwarranted) stubbornness. To the more than 100,000 Americans who were to become casualties in Korea, the events there were far more than a "police action." Truman's pettiness in refusing to call it by its proper name—the Korean War—cost him dearly in terms of public and moral support the next eighteen months.

Back to the UN

One bit of business to which Truman had referred in his Tuesday public statement about U.S. intervention was the UN role. Contrary to what Truman stated, the Security Council had not yet called upon members to "furnish such assistance" as might be needed to repel the North Korean aggression. And at one point at midday on Tuesday, an unwitting blunder by UN Secretary-General Trygve Lie almost gave the Soviets the opportunity to return to the Security Council (which they had boycotted for six months) and cast a veto.[3]

The event developed in this fashion. Early on Tuesday (June 27) morning U.S. diplomats at the UN sounded out Security Council members and found general support for the resolution. The Indian representative, however, asked time to obtain formal instructions from his government; hence the Security Council meeting was put off until the afternoon. With Truman's congressional briefing and public statement already scheduled for late morning, administration officials decided to gamble that the Security Council would vote as expected. Hence Truman's advance claim of UN support.

Some days earlier a Soviet UN diplomat, Constantin E. Zinchenko, had arranged a private luncheon at the Stockholm Restaurant on Long Island, one of the periodic social occasions which permitted the Russians to maintain political contacts with other Security Council members during the boycott. Secretary-General Lie sat between the U.S. representative, Ernest Gross, and the USSR representative, Yakov Malik. Most of the talk was about Korea, with Malik insisting the North Koreans were fighting in response to "border attacks" by ROK forces. Lie and Gross both pointed out the "major nature" of the North Korean attacks. Malik then complained of the American bombings. Gross and Lie retorted they were prompted by the invasion and were carried out under UN authority.

As the party lingered over coffee and dessert, Lie remarked to Malik that he and the other diplomats were about to set off to the Security Council meeting. "Won't you join us?" Lie asked. "The interests of your country would seem to me to call for your presence."

Gross flinched and whitened. Were Malik to attend, he would surely veto the resolution and jettison the carefully drafted U.S. plan. He thought of kicking Lie under the table to signal him to get off the subject.

But Malik shook his head and said, "No, I will not go there."

Gross managed to suppress a sigh of relief, and he left the restaurant with Lie. "Think," he told Lie with considerable feeling, "what would have happened if he had accepted your invitation." Lie realized his mistake. He attempted to minimize it by saying the issue could have been taken to the General Assembly, where a majority vote would have prevailed. Gross made it plain he would prefer that the secretary-general not attempt any further *ad hoc* diplomacy.

The Security Council convened at about three o'clock that afternoon, Tuesday, debated for several hours, then recessed for several more hours while India and Egypt awaited government instructions. The resolution finally passed just before midnight—the vote validating what Truman had claimed had been in hand a full twelve hours earlier.

The U.S. now possessed a broad mandate for future actions in Korea: to "furnish such assistance . . . as may be necessary to repel the armed attack and to restore international peace and security in the area."

Chaos in Seoul

In South Korea, meanwhile, the U.S. air strikes delayed but did not stop the North Korean advance. ROK units continued to fall back on a broad front. After leaving Seoul, Ambassador Muccio drove south in his jeep in quest of the fleeing Syngman Rhee and remnants of his government.[4] He found the ROK president in a house in Taejon, some ninety miles south of Seoul on the west coast. Rhee was unhappy. He complained again about his "abandonment" by the United States; he swore again he would seize a pistol and fight the Communists personally. He made plain he did not put much faith in U.S. promises. If America wanted to save his republic, where was its army?

Muccio did not argue. All he wanted from Rhee was a promise that the ROK government would remain in existence while tacitly turning the war over to the Americans. The United States desperately needed to preserve the Rhee government as a vehicle through which to wage the war. If the government vanished, so did any U.S. pretense at legality. To diplomat Harold Noble, who was with Muccio, Muccio's greatest challenge that afternoon was "the battle of saving the Republic of Korea from the fears of its leaders."

Muccio told Rhee that so far as he was concerned, the Cabinet and the National Assembly could vanish for the time being. The war would be left to military professionals, U.S. and Korean, with minimal interference by Rhee, the Cabinet, or other civilians. An advance party of American officers would be arriving momentarily from Tokyo to survey how U.S. military equipment could best be used by the ROKs.

"I won't try to minimize the difficulties before you," Muccio stated. "But I and the government I represent are convinced that the Korean people have the determination and the will to see this through. If I didn't have this confidence, I wouldn't be here, and U.S. forces wouldn't be in Korea."

Rhee agreed, albeit reluctantly. He would give the Americans the time—and authority—Muccio requested. But Muccio knew the mercurial Rhee could change his attitude in an instant. Rhee had been, and would continue to be, a shaky ally.

Remarkably the Korean Military Advisory Group party had managed to escape Seoul with only three men suffering minor wounds, despite the chaos of the night. With the Han River bridges down, prematurely destroyed by the ROKs, Colonel William Wright and his party competed with panicked ROKs in the scramble for the few seats available on boats ferrying refugees. After unsuccessful attempts at polite persuasion, the Americans watched the South Korean techniques and adopted them. An officer attracted a boatman's attention by firing a rifle shot close to him.[5] He then gestured with his weapon: Either give us rides, or the next bullet will go through you. The Korean immediately made his boat available.

Eventually the KMAG party made its way to Suwon Airfield, some twenty miles south of Seoul. There it met with an advance survey group from Japan led by Brigadier General John H. Church. Church's group was to survey logistical needs of the ROK Army. Although small, with thirteen officers and two enlisted men, the unit carried a most impressive title: "General Headquarters, Advance Command and Liaison Group in Korea," or ADCOM.

Church spent a confused day on Wednesday trying to find who in the ROK Army could speak with authority or knowledge. ROK officers of all ranks were jittery; Church used much time giving them pep talks and assuring them that equipment was on the way. Late on Wednesday Church received an enigmatic message from Tokyo. A "high-ranking officer" would arrive the next morning for an inspection tour. Was the Suwon Airfield operational?

Church replied that it was. He also made a private and accurate guess as to the visitor's identity.

MacArthur Stretches an Order

Douglas MacArthur was restless.[6] The welter of messages coming into the Dai Ichi Building lacked the immediacy, the roar and thunder of battle that a commander can obtain only by personal observation at the front lines. Aside from a ceremonial visit to President Rhee's inaugural months earlier, MacArthur had no firsthand knowledge of the land where the war was erupting. He had read the prewar efficiency reports on the ROK Army, but he had never seen it in action. Could it be saved? Could retreating soldiers be remolded into fighting men?

At noon on Wednesday MacArthur called in his personal pilot, Lieutenant Colonel Anthony F. Story, and told him he would fly to Korea the next day for a personal inspection of the battlefield. Story was dubious. The weather forecast was for storms, heavy rain, heavy winds, and a low ceiling. But MacArthur would not be dissuaded; he intended a personal inspection tour. That evening he invited four correspondents* to his office, told them of his plans, and offered to take them along. MacArthur made the flight sound like something of a suicide mission.

"It will be an unarmed plane," he warned the reporters, "and we are not sure of getting fighter cover, not sure of where we will land. If you are not at the airport, I will know you have other commitments."

One of the reporters quickly assured the general that he and his colleagues would be there. According to Whitney, MacArthur smiled and replied, "I have no doubt of your courage. I just wanted to give your judgment a chance to work."

MacArthur's admonition about the dangers of the trip was calculated hokum. Warning the reporters that they risked death by flying with him enhanced their self-image of courage. And no competitive reporter dared decline an invitation to witness the commander's battlefield visit. His lack of assurance of fighter cover was nonsensical; given more than half a day's notice of the mission, the air force assuredly would free sufficient planes to provide cover for the ranking American officer in Asia. (As it happened, four air force fighter planes picked up the *Bataan* soon after takeoff and escorted it to Korea.)

Nonetheless, MacArthur left Japan under melodramatic circumstances. Rain swished over Haneda Airport, and the cautious pilot, Story, suggested they wait a day. MacArthur heard this message as he was shaving. "No," he said, "we go." At the airport, noted David Douglas Duncan of *Life* magazine, "MacArthur seemed buoyant. His eyes possessed that same luminous brilliance which I had sometimes seen in the faces of fever patients."[7] When the craft reached cruising level, MacArthur pulled out the famed corncob pipe which had been, along with his rumpled aviator's cap, his trademark during the Pacific campaign. Someone jested, "Haven't seen you smoke that pipe, General, for years!" MacArthur smiled. "I don't dare smoke it back in Tokyo. They'd think I was nothing but a farmer." (Actually the journalist William R. Matthews had heard the same comment in MacArthur's office four days earlier, as the general puffed the same pipe.)

MacArthur soon separated himself from the press people. He had

---

*Russel Brines of Associated Press; Ernest Holberecht, United Press; Howard Handleman, International News Service; and Roy R. MacCartney, Australian Associated Press and Reuters.

serious business to discuss with Lieutenant General George Stratemeyer, the Far East Air Force (FEAF) commander. Stratemeyer made a strong argument for lessened restrictions on the air force. To gain control of the air, Stratemeyer said, he needed clearance to attack airfields in North Korea. His planes were so busy providing air cover for ROK forces they could not seek out and attack Communist combat targets.

MacArthur pondered the problem. His instructions permitted him to destroy only North Korean targets south of the 38th parallel. He turned to General Willoughby and asked, "How can I bomb north of the 38th Parallel without Washington hanging me?"[8] Willoughby could not answer, so MacArthur talked through the problem aloud. In a few moments he shifted the question onto an abstract plane. The Joint Chiefs' directive, he decided, was *permissive,* rather than restrictive.

The JCS, although they had not *authorized* MacArthur to bomb beyond the 38th parallel, had not *forbidden* him to do so either. A field commander should be permitted his normal discretionary powers in a battle situation. If North Korea remained a sanctuary, the Communists could continue to mobilize and supply forces south of the 38th parallel. So long as this happened, MacArthur could not give the ROKs the "effective military assistance" ordered by Washington. The more MacArthur talked—to himself and to sympathetic listeners—the firmer he felt the ground of traditional military practice beneath him. At 8:00 A.M. he dictated a message: "Partridge* from Stratemeyer. Take out North Korean airfields immediately. No publicity. MacArthur approves."[9]

General Courtney Whitney, perhaps the most sycophantic admirer in MacArthur's palace guard, enthusiastically applauded the general's ingenuity in circumventing orders. "Here was no timid delay while authorization was obtained from Washington; here was the capacity for command decision and the readiness to assume responsibility which had always been MacArthur's forte." Whitney asserted that he saw a "glint of appreciation" in another officer's eye when he heard the decision, "and he spoke for all of us on the plane as he commented: 'MacArthur at his best—a commander who fights to win!' "

The episode also shows MacArthur at his worst, as a commander willing to perform intellectual gymnastics to evade doing as he was told. Ironically, the question of bombing beyond the 38th parallel had been discussed by the National Security Council only a few hours before MacArthur began his trip.[10] Air Force Secretary Thomas Finletter wanted the restriction lifted to give the ROK Army "the full value of our air support."

Truman was uncertain.[11] He asked General Vandenberg, the air

*Partridge was deputy FEAF commander.

chief of staff, to "survey the point." The United States "may have to" bomb North Korean air bases and fuel dumps, but Truman "didn't want to decide that now."

Vandenberg recognized the sensitivity of the issue. Since the North Korean air bases were thirty to forty miles north of the parallel, "our planes were not likely to cross the frontier even by mistake."

Dean Acheson, heretofore the hawk, hoped "we would not cross the 38th Parallel."

Truman said flatly, "We are not to do it."

As if to emphasize the President's statement, Defense Secretary Johnson reminded Vandenberg "that those were his orders."

As it happened, the sweep of events of Korea within twenty-four hours prompted Truman to reverse himself on the 38th parallel issue and permit bombing of North Korea—something MacArthur had already decided to do on his own anyway. That Truman reversed himself, however, was irrelevant. For the first time in the war—but by no means the last—MacArthur had exceeded his orders. Such arrogance was ultimately to ruin his effectiveness as a field commander.

A Battlefield Tour

As the *Bataan* approached Korea, the radio reported heavy strafing of the destination airfield, Suwon, twenty miles south of Seoul. As the *Bataan* approached its glide pattern, a Communist YAK propeller-driven fighter plane tried to dive through the four-plane U.S. escort, flying in a tight pattern overhead.

"Mayday!" someone shouted in the cabin, and everyone dived for the aisle—everyone, that is, save MacArthur, who strode to a window and watched one of the Mustangs contest the YAK. "We've got him cold," MacArthur exulted. The YAK was driven off before it could fire a shot; pilot Story made an abrupt evasive turn, and the danger passed.

But the Communist fighters had hit two U.S. transport planes at Suwon only moments earlier, and the *Bataan* taxied through clouds of oily smoke, passing within twenty feet of a blazing C-54, bouncing roughly down a runway pockmarked with bomb and shell holes.

The senior American military officer present, Brigadier General John Church, initially had not invited any ROK officers to meet MacArthur. In the view of Harold Noble, the embassy first secretary, Church seemed to know nothing about the ROK Army, nor did he wish to learn anything. Old Asia hand Noble, born to Presbyterian missionary parents in China and a longtime writer and intelligence officer in the Far East, tartly wrote him off as a "confused man who did not do justice to himself."[12] Noble dismissed him as a serious figure after a conversation during their flight to Korea several days earlier. Church, who had never even seen Korea, told Noble he would "rather have one hundred New York policemen than the whole Korean army." Disturbed by Church's snub of the Koreans, Noble intervened with Muccio, and the ROK chief of staff, General Chae Byong Duk, appeared at the airport with Muccio, a thoroughly shaken President Syngman Rhee, and other lesser American and ROK officials to greet MacArthur.

Shabbily elegant in faded khakis, crinkled leather jacket, and dilapidated cap with encrustations of gold braid, field glasses dangling around his neck, sunglasses shielding his eyes despite the general gloom of the day, MacArthur stepped down onto the Suwon tarmac with studied nonchalance. He spotted Rhee, walked over to the tottering Oriental, and put both his hands on his shoulders in an affectionate sign of greeting. Muccio led the party to a ramshackle schoolhouse on the air base perimeter that the Church advisory group had taken for a command post. MacArthur stirred with restlessness; he had come to Korea for something more substantial than the formal briefing Church offered, a recitation consisting of what MacArthur could have learned from the cable traffic.

President Rhee offered the best summary of the situation. "We are in a hell of a fix," he said.[13] Church, in his briefing, said the ROK Army was down to about 25,000 men, meaning about three-quarters of the 100,000-man army was unaccounted for. MacArthur asked General Chae what he intended to do about the situation. Chae replied he was going to round up 2 million South Korean youths, train them, and repel the invasion. The American officers listened to Chae in incredulous silence; although they were too polite to say so, they thought Chae's scheme impossible, a pathetically impractical gesture. Even the friendly Harold Noble had to admit that his "huge bulk and fat, sleepy face did not impress a stranger as the proper casing for a warrior." MacArthur appraised him without comment. (Later he told Rhee the ROKs needed a new chief of staff. Chae was dismissed within forty-eight hours.) The immediate tactical problem, Church continued, was to find a means of slowing the dreaded Soviet-built tanks, the clanking treads and steel shielding of which terrorized ROK foot soldiers. Otherwise, they would drive straight down the peninsula. Although KMAG had felt earlier that Korea's rice-paddy terrain made use of tanks unfeasible, the NKPA had managed to control the roads, and thus their tanks roamed at will.

No sooner had Church lowered his briefing stick than MacArthur was on his feet. Slapping his knees with impatience, he said, "Let's go to the front for a look." The cautious Church wanted him to remain in Suwon. The front, some twenty miles north, was so fluid the ROKs could be swept away at any moment. MacArthur was already closer to the front than prudent. MacArthur shook off the objections. "The only way to judge a fight is to see it yourself—to see the troops in action. Let's go."

Someone had found an old black Dodge sedan to transport the general. Aides and the press perched in a flotilla of jeeps, and the little convoy moved through what Whitney called "the dreadful backwash of a defeated and dispersed army," MacArthur sitting with his cob pipe clinched tightly in his teeth. The party reached the Han River at the height of the ROK's rearguard action to permit combatants and civilians to flee south. The Han River is to Seoul as the Potomac is to Washington. In comparative terms, MacArthur stood on the Virginia palisades just north of Chain Bridge and watched a defeated army retreating southward.

He saw an awful picture. Seoul was in flames; a city built six centuries ago now billowed columns of smoke and darting tongues of flame. MacArthur looked at the scene in contemplative silence, hearing the leaden thumps! of North Korean mortars. Then he took his pipe from his mouth and made a jabbing gesture toward a hill even closer to the Han. He spoke to Major General Edward M. Almond, his chief of staff. "What do you say we push up there, Ned?"

To suggest was to command, so the convoy pushed forward to the limits of the vehicles' ability; then everyone got out and walked.

General Whitney described the scene:

> The sky was resonant with shrieking missiles of death, and everywhere were the stench and utter desolation of a stricken battlefield. Clogging all the roads in a writhing dust-shrouded mass of humanity were the refugees. . . . This scene was enough to convince him [MacArthur] that the defensive potential of South Korea had already been exhausted. There was nothing to stop the Communists from pushing their tank columns straight down the few good roads from Seoul to Pusan at the end of the peninsula. All Korea would then be theirs.*

MacArthur stood on the hill for perhaps an hour, pondering both the immediate scene and his future strategy. Then he lowered his field glasses and gestured toward remnants of a railroad bridge across the Han, possible passage for North Korean tanks and trucks. "Take it out," he snapped, and returned to his Dodge for the ride back to Suwon.

General Matthew B. Ridgway, then the army vice chief of staff, later to succeed MacArthur in the Asian command, found these hair-raising descriptions "amusing,"[14] when compared with the contemporary report of General Edward Almond. In *Reminiscences* MacArthur talked

---

*Whitney's memoirs were published in 1956. Two years earlier his colleague Willoughby had used identical phraseology to describe the scene. MacArthur's memoirs, published in 1964, recycled the phraseology once more. The "coincidence" is not isolated. Many sections of the three supposedly independent memoirs are identical word after word.

about "the dreadful backwash of a defeated and dispersed army. The South Korean forces were in complete and disorganized flight." From his vantage point on the hill overlooking the Han River MacArthur saw "panting columns of disorganized troops . . . clogging all the roads in a writhing dust-shrouded mass of humanity." Almond, watching the same columns from the same hill, told the Joint Chiefs in a report submitted the same week that the ROKs were "all smiling, all with rifles, all with bandeliers of ammunition, all saluting." Mortar fire fell, as MacArthur said, but so sporadically and distant that everyone ignored it. In his own war memoirs Ridgway also wondered about the source of the dust plaguing the troops in MacArthur's vision in view of the sporadic rain falling around Seoul the past twelve hours. Ridgway found in MacArthur's "ghostwritten reports [a] tendency to paint the dark side blacker and the bright side shinier than in life. . . ."

As MacArthur's miniconvoy rolled south back toward Suwon, it was overtaken by a jeep of shouting reporters: Communist YAKs were approaching. The vehicles pulled into a protective copse of trees, and everyone except MacArthur scurried for cover. The general chose to sit in the old Dodge for half an hour while the YAKs buzzed overhead. No shots were fired, but MacArthur's coolness under potential fire impressed some observers, including the reporters, who included the incident in their stories. Such behavior can be interpreted other than as bravery: a high commander wantonly risking his life in a grandstanding gesture, or a subconscious reversion to the suicidal patterns he had repeatedly demonstrated to his decades-ago aide Tommy Davis (see the Introduction).

Back at the schoolhouse MacArthur and Rhee talked for about an hour in private. MacArthur did not sound any false note of optimism. The ROK Army was in trouble. MacArthur did not feel it could hold on its own, but he intended to bring all aid possible to its defense. They talked amid a heavy clatter of machine-gun fire from YAKs strafing near the airport and from aerial battles far overhead. Under the restrictions still governing his actions, MacArthur could not commit the United States to all-out support of South Korea. But, as he later wrote, during this mission he conceived the basic strategy for turning around the war: to throw piecemeal replacements into the breach, as a morale-boosting stopgap for the sagging South Koreans; to stabilize the battle in a defensive perimeter far to the south that would permit an American toehold on the peninsula; to augment U.S. strength until it balanced or offset that of the North Koreans; and, finally, to make an audacious strike far behind the North Korean lines via an amphibious assault of the sort he had used so successfully in the Pacific during the previous war. (By MacArthur's later account, he chose the landing site while on the hill: the port of Inchon, some twenty miles west of Seoul. See Chapter Seven, "A Winning Gamble at Inchon.")

Flying back to Tokyo that evening, MacArthur told Marguerite Higgins of the New York *Herald Tribune* his conviction that if America wanted to save Korea, ground troops would be needed. "Give me two American divisions and I can hold Korea," he said. "The moment I reach Tokyo, I shall send President Truman my recommendation for the immediate dispatch of American divisions to Korea. But I have no idea whether he will accept my recommendations."[15]

MacArthur arrived in Japan a few minutes past eight o'clock on Thursday evening, which would have been six o'clock in the morning, Washington time. Contrary to what he told Higgins, however, he did not immediately send his recommendation for troops to the Joint Chiefs. Once again MacArthur was to resort to duplicity to ensure he obtained what he wanted.[16] As it turned out, the Joint Chiefs and the President had already arrived at the same decision—to commit American ground troops in force—but by a tedious and most hesitant route.

The U.S. Commitment Deepens

After a review of overnight developments on the front, the Joint Chiefs of Staff on Wednesday, June 27, slowly faced the realization that air and naval forces alone would not save the ROKs. Air force fighters and bombers could pound North Korean tank columns by day, but they could not stop an infantry advance of some 100,000 men opposed by a quarter that number. At a morning meeting the JCS directed the Joint Strategic Survey Committee (JSSC) to answer within forty-eight hours the question, in the event that the current course of action now being undertaken in Korea is unsuccessful, what course of action, from a military point of view, should be taken? The committee should consider U.S. air operations north of the border as well as other actions *"in lieu of committing ground troops* [emphasis added]."[17] Rear Admiral Arthur C. Davis, the JCS director, emphasized the latter point in a handwritten note forwarding the assignment to the Joint Strategic Survey Committee. The JCS, he scribbled, "do *not* want to commit troops."

But within twenty-four hours the chiefs realized they really had no choice. The first sketchy reports from General Church's survey team in South Korea told of the ROK Army's being cut down to some 25,000 men (from 100,000) and of the continued North Korean tank advances. Ambassador Muccio, in a flash report, said that MacArthur appeared ready to make "momentous recommendations" about the course of the war. The Soviets had not responded to a U.S. query made two days earlier on whether they intended to try to restrain the North Koreans, as mandated in the UN Security Council resolution. (In a reply several days later the Soviets disclaimed any responsibility for the war and charged that the North Koreans had crossed the frontier in response to a South Korean invasion—a statement belied by the UN Commission in Korea, which was on the scene at the time.) Although the Central Intelligence Agency could detect no abnormal movements of Soviet or satellite troops in Europe,[18] the uneasy fear persisted in Washington that the Korean invasion was either a probe of U.S. willingness to resist expansion by the Communist bloc or a prelude to all-out war.

Whatever the Soviet intention, the Communist thrust into Korea caused a hurried rethinking of U.S. strategic planning. Prior to June 1950 the U.S. war plan—code named Offtackle[19]—was based upon what a Pentagon staff paper summarized as "a strategic defensive in the Far East and a strategic offensive in Western Europe." The latter area would be held, if possible, as a base for offensive operations against the Soviet Union. "It has been emphasized repeatedly," the planning paper stated, "that Western Europe is the area of the greatest strategic importance to the overall security of the U.S." The priority was to hold a defensive line "preferably no further west than the Rhine" and to deploy forces to Northwest Africa to keep open the western Mediterranean. Offtackle also provided for defense of the Western Hemisphere, "the delivery of an initial atomic offensive," and protection of essential communications lines. The Far East got short shrift; the primary tasks there were defending Japan, Okinawa, and the Philippines and denying Formosa to the Soviets or Chinese Communists. The Asian portion did not contemplate any offensive against either China or the western reaches of the Soviet Union.

In June 1950 the total strength of the U.S. Army was about 591,000 men, including ten combat divisions. About 360,000 of these troops were in the continental United States, the Zone of the Interior, or ZI in military parlance. The remaining 231,000 were in occupation duty overseas. The largest number, 108,500, more or less, were in the Far East. In Europe about 80,000 U.S. soldiers were in Germany; 9,500, in Austria; and 4,800, in Trieste. A few more than 7,000 were scattered over the Pacific, and about 7,500 in Alaska. Another 12,200 were in the Caribbean. And the remainder, several thousand, were in U.S. missions, as attachés, sentries, and support personnel.*

In view of this limited infantry strength, how much help could the U.S. give to Korea? Four of the United States' ten divisions were on garrison duty in Japan—the 7th, 24th, and 25th Infantry divisions and the 1st Cavalry Division (also infantry, despite its historic name). The 5th Regimental Combat Team was in Hawaii; another regiment, the 29th,

*These figures are derived from the "Weekly Estimate of Army Command Strength," June 26, 1950. Because of daily fluctuations, pinpointing the to-the-man strength of the U.S. Army on any given date is bureaucratically impossible. The key fact to remember is that North Korea, a much smaller nation, fielded an army of around 125,000 men.

on Okinawa. All units were understrength: Three of the divisions in Japan had 12,000 to 13,000 men; the fourth, 15,000. Their equipment—tanks, mortars, recoilless rifles, trucks—was mostly of World War II vintage and in poor condition. The four divisions had been sent to Japan chiefly to ensure against any resurgence of Japanese militarism. To call them combat units was to stretch the term.

Nonetheless, these troops were all the United States had under arms, and the Pentagon planning paper cited earlier saw direct strategic consequences if they were put into the Korean War. If Japan and Western Europe were stripped of troops to meet the challenge in Korea, the depletions "would seriously affect our war readiness." The U.S. position in Western Europe was already tenuous, given the enormous numerical superiority of Soviet ground troops in the East (400,000 men versus fewer than 100,000 Americans). Plan Offtackle, the basic European defense scheme, was based upon an "assumed possible early loss of Western Europe." Troops sent to Korea "would simply be subtracted from the very limited forces available to rescue our allies in Europe in the event of a hot war."

Thus an infinite variety of factors were fed into the decision faced by President Truman and the men around him. The military was of a certain size because of financial strictures imposed by the Congress, which responded to political strictures imposed by the public. These military limitations in turn determined diplomatic limitations. The people in charge of the United States government—the President foremost among them—had decided Europe had priority. Korea had been dismissed as a backwater of no strategic value. Since Sunday the United States had taken tentative steps toward direct military involvement in Korea. Now should the final steps be taken? Should the United States reverse established policy and go into Korea on the ground?

Ground Troops Approved

The turning point for the Joint Chiefs came on Thursday morning, June 28, with a cautious escalation recommendation from a staff committee.[20] For two days the Joint Strategic Survey Committee (JSSC) had tried to balance long-range strategic objectives with the immediacy of the war at hand. Hedged though it was, its recommendation was bolder than anything yet approved by the JCS. MacArthur should be authorized to "provide the fullest possible support" to the ROK Army with air and naval power. The U.S. would be in a "strong political position" if it could repel the North Koreans without taking the war across the 38th parallel. But MacArthur should be permitted to send planes against

North Korean bases if, in his judgment, "serious risk of loss of Southern Korea might be obviated thereby." Even so, he should ask JCS permission. (As noted, no one knew in Washington that MacArthur had already ordered air strikes north of the 38th parallel on his own initiative.)

The recommendation touched off brisk discussion among the Joint Chiefs and Secretary Louis Johnson. The consensus—reached with "considerable reluctance" in the words of a JCS document—was that the planning committee did not go far enough, that the time had come to put ground troops into the war. At Johnson's suggestion the meeting was moved to the White House, where Secretary Acheson and other diplomats joined the discussion.[21] Johnson took the lead. He argued that ground troops should be used, if only to establish a secure base for air operations. Planes flying from distant bases in Japan could spend extremely limited time over target areas and could not communicate with the ROK group troops they sought to support. Johnson also complained about restricting air and naval attacks to south of the 38th parallel, leaving untouched supplies and reinforcements moving down from the North. Providing a protected base would not only bolster the South Koreans but also ensure the safe evacuation of the remaining Americans, if need be. "We must have at least an American foothold in South Korea," Johnson concluded.

Truman worried that the Soviets might interpret these strong actions as indicative of a U.S. intent to attack the USSR.[22] Although he was ready to do what was necessary to push the North Koreans back across the parallel, he did not want the United States to become so involved in Korea that it "could not take care of such other situations as might develop." Truman did not want the "slightest implication" that "we were planning to go to war against the Soviet Union." Johnson and the Joint Chiefs told him they intended no such implication.

Army Secretary Pace also wanted to be very careful about operations north of the 38th parallel. Truman should let planes operate in the North but only to "destroy military supplies." Acheson seemed less cautious. He did not want the air force to be "restricted in its tasks by a rigid application of the 38th parallel as a restraining line," but operations should not spill over into Manchuria.

Acheson briefed the meeting on State Department estimates of Soviet action. A U.S. note two days earlier had reminded the Soviets of the Security Council resolution and urged that they use their influence with the North Koreans to halt the invasion. Responding, the Soviets blamed the invasion on the South Koreans but said they intended to adhere to the "principle of the impermissibility of interference by foreign powers in the internal affairs of Korea."[23] As interpreted by the State Department, the quoted sentence meant the Russians would stay out of Korea.

"This means," Truman commented, "that the Soviets are going to let the Chinese and the North Koreans do the fighting for them." Acheson said that although State and the CIA had seen no hint of any Chinese intervention, they "might" enter the war.

The final decisions were to permit air and naval forces to hit military targets in North Korea and to hurry American ground forces to Korea to secure the port, airfield, and communications facilities around the port of Pusan, which, Acheson noted, were "considerably south of the combat zone." MacArthur was to be told that should the Soviets intervene, he was to protect his troops and notify Washington, which would provide further instructions. If the U.S. were to go to war with the USSR, the decision would be made in Washington, not Tokyo. The directive sent to MacArthur did not specify the number of ground troops he could send to Korea. That decision would rely upon the recommendation MacArthur sent to Washington after his inspection tour.

By the time the White House meeting ended it was late afternoon in Washington and midmorning Tokyo time. Although MacArthur had been back in Tokyo for more than twelve hours, he had yet to say a word to his superiors in Washington about the debacle he saw in Korea and what he wanted.

Curious, the Joint Chiefs dispatched the results of the afternoon meeting and sat and waited to hear from their field commander.

MacArthur Demands Help

MacArthur's report, a cablegram of some 2,000 words, finally arrived at the Pentagon between midnight and one o'clock the morning of Friday, June 30.[24] MacArthur recounted the collapse of the ROK Army, which he called "entirely incapable of counter-action." The only hope of holding the present line (then just south of Seoul) "is through the introduction of U.S. ground combat forces into the Korean battle area." Without ground forces, U.S. air and naval might would not be effective. He proposed moving a regimental combat team, some 2,200 men, to Korea immediately. Next, he wished to "provide for a possible build-up to a two-division strength from the troops in Japan for an early counter-offensive."

MacArthur concluded with what General Lawton Collins called a "do-it-my-way-or-else" paragraph that was to become an infuriating (to the JCS) feature of many of his subsequent cables: "Unless provision is made for the full utilization of the Army-Navy-Air team in this shattered area, our mission will be needlessly costly in life, money and prestige. At worst it might even be doomed to failure."

A Pentagon duty officer roused General Collins from his bed, and the army chief of staff hurried to his office. He quickly read through MacArthur's message. He was "so concerned by the critical situation it depicted and the urgency of MacArthur's request" that he decided to communicate with the general directly.[25] Collins ordered that a teleconference be arranged for 3:00 A.M. Washington time (5:00 P.M. Tokyo time).

Collins gathered his staff in a conference room several floors below ground level of the Pentagon, the war room, which linked the military command with commanders in the field, a place of maps and exotic (for 1950) communications equipment. Collins sat at a long, low desk, flanked by his deputy, General Alfred Gruenther, and several generals from the army's general staff division. Although the decisions were military, the State Department was represented by Dean Rusk and Niles W. Bond, the Korean desk officer. Half a world away, in the Dai Ichi Building in Tokyo, General Almond gathered with five of his senior staff officers in a similar but smaller room.

The telecon got under way at 3:40 A.M., forty minutes late.[26] The lights dimmed. Collins had written his first query in longhand. He handed it to a communications sergeant, who typed the words rapidly on a keyboard not unlike that of an office typewriter. They were immediately projected onto a screen facing the Pentagon group and simultaneously appeared on an identical screen in Tokyo. No one had to be reminded of the gravity of the situation—that the decision made in the dead of night would determine whether American soldiers would fight, and die, in Korea. Collins said the "air was fraught with tension. . . . We instinctively spoke with hushed voices . . . and we pictured in our minds the gathering in Tokyo where answers were being framed that would vitally affect our participation in this strange new war." Washington sent the first message:

DA-1 [Department of the Army, No. 1]
Authorization proposed in your C56942* will require Presidential decision which will take several hours for consideration. Meanwhile, you are authorized in accordance [with a JCS directive transmitted earlier that evening] to move one Regimental Combat Team to Pusan base area. This will be amplified in our telecon set for [8 A.M. the same morning].

MacArthur responded impatiently; he had made a specific request, and he wanted a decision. That he had caught the Pentagon in the middle of the night was not his concern.

FECOM—1 [Far East Command, No. 1]
Your authorization, while establishing basic principle that U.S. ground combat troops may be used in Korea, does not give sufficient latitude for

*MacArthur's report of a few hours earlier.

efficient operation in present situation. It does not satisfy the basic requirements contained in my message. . . . Time is of the essence and a clear cut
decision without delay is imperative.

Collins suggested that MacArthur stood a better chance of receiving
what he asked if he did not try to rush the President. He tried to explain
the drift of official thinking in Washington and the caution with which
Truman was approaching major decisions.

DA-2
I was present at White House conference late afternoon June 29th when
decision was made by President to authorize action covered by JCS 84681.
Tenor of decision clearly indicated to me that the President would wish
carefully to consider with his top advisors before authorizing introduction
of American combat forces into battle area.

Collins asked if permission to move the regimental combat team
would do for the moment. By the time this movement was completed,
he felt, the President would have made a "definite decision" on the
request for two divisions. "Does this meet your requirement for the
present?" Collins asked.

The interrogatory ending of the message made plain Collins expected a reply. None came. The teleprinter stood still for long, embarrassing minutes. MacArthur was speaking through the eloquence of
scornful silence, and he clearly had Washington on the defensive. He
had asked for troops he said he needed to avert imminent military
disaster; should he be refused, the blood and blame would mar the
hands of the Pentagon, not CINCFE (Commander in Chief, Far East).
"We took this [silence] to mean that General MacArthur stood by his
emphatic plea for a decision 'without delay,'" Collins said.[27] There was
a brief discussion with staff and State Department men, and Collins
yielded. He would "proceed immediately" through Army Secretary
Pace to ask presidential approval for moving the regimental combat
team directly into the combat area. He promised a reply "as soon as
possible, perhaps within half hour."

Still no response from MacArthur. Collins left the conference room
and telephoned Pace, who had been alerted that the telecon was in
progress. Pace agreed to relay the request to the President.[28]

Truman, too, knew that the crisis that night was likely to require his
decision. So he had awakened early, shaved, and was sitting in his Blair
House bedroom when the phone rang at 4:57 A.M. Dawn had not yet
reached the city.

Pace read the cable from MacArthur, Truman interrupting with occasional grunts and uh-huhs. What did the JCS think? The full body had
not been consulted; because of the press of time, Collins decided to
bypass his colleagues. But he and other officers in the army hierarchy

felt the request should be granted. Truman did not hesitate. He ordered the regimental combat team committed to action and said he would decide upon the additional two divisions within the next several hours.

In the meanwhile, the Pentagon group used the telecon to ask MacArthur a host of routine questions. Air strikes on North Korean airfields had been made with "undetermined results," and naval operations in Korea waters so far were "not of positive nature" because of a paucity of targets. No barriers remained to keep the North Koreans from sweeping across the Han. MacArthur would not estimate how long it would take him to get the regimental combat team to the front. Airlifting troops would not be feasible because Suwon Airfield was not secure.

The pastime chatter lasted for the better part of an hour, until Pace relayed Truman's decision to General Collins. Another message:

> DA-10
> Your recommendation to move one regimental combat team to combat area is approved. You will be advised later on the further build-up.

> FECOM—8 Reur DA-10
> Acknowledged. Is there anything further new?

> DA-11
> Everyone here delighted your prompt action in personally securing firsthand view of situation. Congratulations and best wishes. We have full confidence in you and your command.
> Nothing further here. End DA-11.

Immediately after the conference ended, General Collins telephoned other JCS members to report what had happened. Admiral Forrest Sherman of the navy concurred—he had no real choice; the orders had already been dispatched—but nonetheless he felt qualms about the sudden acceleration.[29] Months later he recollected his reaction:

> The decision [to send troops] had been taken on the recommendation of General MacArthur, who was on the spot. I had some apprehensions about it, and in the following days I felt that the decision was a sound one. It was unavoidable, but I was fully aware of the hazards involved in fighting Asiatics on the Asiatic mainland, which is something that, as a naval officer, I have grown up to believe should be avoided if possible.

Another aspect of the decision worried General Collins. By delaying his report for hours, MacArthur forced his superiors in Washington to make a crucial decision in the dead of night. MacArthur's strategy smacks of the policeman who rouses someone from sleep and starts an interrogation. The subject is apt to give the intruder what he wants for the privilege of returning to bed. The JCS message limiting American troops to defense of the Pusan Perimeter signaled to MacArthur—as skilled a bureaucrat and politician as he was military strategist—that dramatic action was needed to obtain the troops he wanted. And what could be more dramatic than rousing the President of the United States from his bed at four in the morning?

MacArthur's ploy succeeded, but at high cost. Had his request been submitted in the light of day, the President and the JCS likely would have concurred, given the evolution of their thinking the past two days. MacArthur's gamesmanship, however, was so transparent to Collins and other superiors that it did dire damage to his credibility.

President Truman, however, was ready to give MacArthur even more than the two divisions. Shortly after seven o'clock he telephoned Defense Secretary Johnson and Army Secretary Pace. He told them to "consider giving MacArthur the two divisions he asked for and also to consider the advisability of accepting the two divisions offered by the Chinese Nationalist government."[30] As justification for using Chiang Kai-shek's troops, Truman noted that his government was still recognized as a permanent member of the UN Security Council. "Since Britain, Australia, Canada and the Netherlands have come in with ships and planes, we probably should use the Chinese ground forces," Truman reasoned.

He did see a possible backlash. "What that will do to Mao Tse-tung we do not know. We must be careful not to cause a general Asiatic war." Truman remained convinced that Korea was a diversion and that the main Soviet thrust would come either in the Black Sea area or toward the Persian Gulf—i.e., the Balkans or Iran. "Both are prizes Moscow has wanted since Ivan the Terrible, who is now their hero along with Stalin and Lenin."

When his war council assembled at the White House at 9:30 A.M., Truman asked for advice on MacArthur's request for two divisions.[31] He wondered "if it would not be worthwhile" to accept Chiang's offer of 33,000 Chinese troops since they could be ready for sailing within five days. "Time was all-important," the President felt.

Acheson did not want any Chinese involvement. To take Chiang's offer, he argued, would risk bringing Chinese Communists into either Korea or Formosa. Further, if Chiang sent troops to Korea, he would weaken his ability to defend Formosa. The Communists might take advantage of an opportunity to invade Formosa, thereby confronting the United States with the decision of whether to intervene there as well as in Korea.

The Joint Chiefs definitely wanted no involvement with Chiang. His troops were no better equipped than the South Koreans, who had proved unable to cope with North Korean armor; further, using them would occupy transport facilities that could more profitably bring American troops and supplies to Korea.

The arguments convinced Truman. He would reject Chiang's offer, but "politely."

The other agenda item, the dispatch of two divisions of American troops to Korea, took little discussion. Unlike the Chinese matter, no dissent was heard. Truman announced he would give MacArthur full authority to use the ground troops under his command, with no limit on the number of divisions to be sent to Korea. He also approved a suggestion by Admiral Sherman that the navy be permitted to blockade the coast of North Korea.

Arriving at these momentous decisions took less than half an hour. The United States was a significant step closer to total war.

Dissent from the Republicans

Truman was also a significant step closer to losing his unquestioning congressional support.[32] Later on Friday morning he called congressional leaders to the Cabinet Room for a somewhat misleading briefing on his recent decisions. He stressed the decision to bomb targets north of the 38th parallel.

But Senator Kenneth Wherry, the Nebraska Republican, was not satisfied. He rose from his chair and paced around the room as if he were addressing questions from the Senate floor. He wanted to know whether Congress would be advised before ground troops entered Korea. Truman replied that some ground troops were already there; if a "real emergency" arose, he would advise the Congress. Wherry unhappily mused that he "thought the Congress ought to be consulted" before the President made such moves. Defending himself, Truman said he had acted during a weekend crisis when "there was not time for lots of talk. I just had to act as commander-in-chief and I did. I told MacArthur to go to the relief of the Koreans and to carry out the instructions of the United Nations Security Council." Vice President Alben Barkley had a minor quibble. He wanted a presidential statement that Truman was in charge of the forces and issuing orders to them.

"This is all very delicate," Truman replied. "I don't want it stated any place that I am telling MacArthur what to do. He is not an American general now, he is acting for the United Nations. It would spoil everything if we said he was just doing what we tell him to do." Truman acknowledged the subterfuge: "Of *course* MacArthur was obeying [my] orders but we want to be careful not to let ourselves be put in [that] light to the rest of the world." No congressman questioned Truman's glaring inconsistency: American troops were in Korea without congressional approval to carry out a mandate of the UN Security Council. But concurrently the President admitted to the fiction of UN command.

As the meeting ended, Truman read a press statement being released at that very moment. The concluding sentence read: "General MacArthur has been authorized to use certain supporting ground units." The restrained wording failed utterly to spell out the authority actually granted MacArthur—specifically, to "utilize army forces available to you." These forces numbered four divisions, roughly 40 percent of the strength of the U.S. Army. Had this fact been revealed to the congressmen, Truman certainly would have heard protests from persons other than Senator Wherry.

Another Republican senator, Alexander Smith of New Jersey, asked whether it might be a good idea to have Congress approve what the administration was doing. Acheson deftly turned the question aside. The matter, he said, would "be taken under advisement."

Muted though they were, the congressional questions did cause the Truman inner circle to discuss whether Congress should be asked for a formal declaration of war. The politically astute Averell Harriman would have taken advantage of the ground swell of public opinion supporting the administration. He felt that "President Truman would have gotten such overwhelming support that it would have silenced some of those who later were critical."[33]

Truman, however, felt congressional action unnecessary. He had exercised his proper constitutional authority, and he wished to protect the powers of the President "against all comers including the Congress," as Harriman said. Harriman quoted the President as saying to him, "We cannot do that because if I do it will tie the hands of a successor president."

The State Department sided with Truman. Lucius D. Battle, a key aide to Dean Acheson, remarked, "The President had done what he did; why open up the question of whether he should have done it? It had been accepted; everyone had overwhelmingly supported it; therefore, there was no problem. . . ." Battle and Acheson feared that if Congress were given the opening to debate a joint resolution, "it might challenge what the President had done without a joint resolution."

According to Truman adviser George M. Elsey, the President and his key advisers were "too busy thinking of military action and United Nations action" to give any serious thought to Congress in the first hectic days of the war.[34] "The President's motivation was to stop the aggression, not to prepare for future political skirmishes." Further, the President had "no strong Congressional leadership to push one through." The matter was brought to mind "mostly by Republican sniping" beginning the first days of July. Even then, Acheson opposed going to Congress. He likened the situation to that faced by a lawyer cross-examining a hostile witness: whether to ask "the one more question which destroys you." Acheson elaborated:

> We had complete acceptance of the President's policy by everybody on both sides of both houses of Congress. We had to do this [intervene in Korea]; we were going ahead with it; everything was in good shape.
>
> Now the question is: should we bring a joint resolution . . . approving this? The hazards . . . seemed to me far greater than any possible good. . . . If a resolution was introduced, both armed services committees would have had great hearings, at which everybody would ask all sorts of ponderous questions; by the time you got through with this you might have completely muddied up the situation which seemed to be very clear at the time.
>
> So I recommended that we just drop the idea, since there was no great pressure about it, to go ahead on our own.[35]

Acheson cited another reason as well: No one in the military establishment could estimate how long the war might last or how many troops ultimately might be required. "Now the thing to do was to get on and do it as quickly and effectively as you could, and if you stopped to analyze what you were doing, you immobilized yourself. . . . All you did was to weaken and confuse your will and not get on anywhere with this."

Nonetheless, Acheson's disdain for the prospect of having to listen to "ponderous questions" from congressional committees and his unwillingness to pause to "analyze what you were doing" displayed a contempt toward Congress that ultimately cost the administration dearly.

To recapitulate the decisions from Sunday, June 25, through Friday, June 30, the full commitment of American prestige and arms to the defense of the Republic of Korea came in four separate phases:

—Air and naval protection for the evacuation of American civilians;
—Air and naval action against North Korean forces south of the 38th parallel, in support of the ROK Army;
—Extension of air and naval action north of the 38th parallel, in part from South Korean bases;
—Introduction of American ground troops into the combat zone.

According to a JCS analysis,[36] the second step was the most significant. It reversed a policy decision of several years earlier—to wit, that the United States had no strategic reason to involve itself with the defense of South Korea. What Truman and Acheson, his chief counsel during the early crisis days, did not realize was that once the United

States stepped over the threshold of war and fired upon the enemy, it was irrevocably committed to continue. The failure of Step Two to dissuade the North Koreans led inexorably to the following steps, ones that kept American forces tied down in Korea for three years, with an unsatisfactory armistice finally ending a deadly military stalemate.

Truman and Acheson had made a political decision. North Korea had openly defied the United States and the United Nations; should the defiance go unchallenged, they feared grave consequences for the future peace of the world.

As the JCS analysts concede, although Truman's military advisers were not prime movers in the decision to respond to the invasion, neither did they dissent from it. A year later, when Congress belatedly bestirred itself into a serious inquiry into the reasons America was bogged down in an undeclared war, Louis Johnson stated:

> Neither I nor any member of the military establishment recommended we go into Korea. The recommendation came from the Secretary of State, but I want to repeat that it was not opposed by the Defense Department, all the members of which had severally pointed out the trouble, the trials, tribulations and the difficulties.[37]

Once the political decision was made, however, the JCS moved promptly to implement it militarily. Their initial hope of repelling the invasion with air and naval strikes was soon dashed. The field commander, MacArthur, avowed ground troops were necessary. MacArthur wanted foot soldiers, and in quantity, and the JCS would provide them for him.

The cold war between the United States and the Soviet bloc had now become a hot war, with no assurance it would remain limited in scope.

CHAPTER FOUR

"An Arrogant Display of Strength"

Lieutenant Colonel Charles Bradford Smith was exhausted, and his wife had to shake him several times to rouse him from sleep.[1] It was early Friday evening, June 30. Smith had gone sleepless the previous night because of an alert of the unit he commanded—1st Battalion, 21st Infantry Regiment, 24th Infantry Division, based at Camp Wood, on the Japanese island of Kyushu. His wife said Colonel Richard W. Stephens, the regimental commander, was on the phone.

Stephens was brief: "The lid has blown off—get on your clothes and report to the CP [command post]." Smith glanced at his watch: nine o'clock.

As the thirty-four-year-old officer dressed, he had a vivid recollection of another surprise summons. On December 7, 1941, Brad Smith, then a young lieutenant only two years out of West Point, had commanded D Company of the 35th Infantry at Schofield Barracks in Hawaii. When the Japanese hit Pearl Harbor, he received a hurried order to take up a defense position on Barbers Point to repel possible Japanese invaders. Smith spent the remainder of the war as a combat infantry officer in the 25th Infantry Division in the South Pacific. His then-commander, General J. Lawton Collins, noted him as a "bright young officer who showed great promise."

At the regimental command post Colonel Stephens gave Smith sobering orders. He was to lead the first American combat troops into Korea. B and C companies of his battalion were to proceed to Itazuke Air Base, some seventy-five miles distant, and fly to Korea immediately. The division commander, General William F. Dean, would meet them at Itazuke with further instructions.

Smith coolly analyzed the status of his troops. He had gaps in several rifle platoons. No matter, Stephens told him, borrow replacements from the 3rd Battalion.

By three o'clock in the morning Smith and his officers and noncoms had roused 440 men from their barracks, with rifles and field equipment, and put them onto trucks for the ride to Itazuke. The trucks rumbled down the dark Japanese highways in a driving rainstorm, a deluge of monsoon proportion.

Smith did not know what would be expected of him when he reached Korea, but the unit he headed was pitifully meager and ill-armed. It consisted of two understrength rifle companies and half of the headquarters company, mainly support personnel such as cooks, clerks, and staff people; a 75 mm recoilless rifle platoon with four guns (only two of which were airlifted to Korea, as it turned out) and four 4.2-inch mortars. B and C companies had six other recoilless rifles (bazookas, in lay terms) and four 60 mm mortars. Each man carried 120 rounds of .30 caliber ammunition for his M-1 rifle and two days of C rations.

Probably one-third of the officers had combat experience in Europe or the Pacific; perhaps one-half the noncoms were Second World War veterans, but not all in combat—understandably, more clerks than riflemen thought reenlistment attractive. In total, about 75 of the 440 men on the jostling trucks had faced an enemy on the battlefield. And the vast majority were young, twenty years old or less.

America's peacetime army was off to the war—an inexperienced and unenthusiastic band of youngsters, grandiosely titled Task Force Smith, charged with blunting the driving advance of the entire North Korea Army.

What Brad Smith did not know for a fact—but surely suspected—was that he was being sent on the equivalent of a suicide mission. General Douglas MacArthur, the man who ordered it, really had no other choice if the ROKs were to be steadied. His intention was to move in troops swiftly by air to form a locus of resistance around which the ROKs could rally. He hoped, by an "arrogant display of strength, to fool the enemy into a belief that I had greater resources at my disposal than I did."[2] What Smith was supposed to do was halt the North Korean advance long enough to enable MacArthur to move the rest of the 24th Division, under General Dean, into Korea. The 1st Cavalry and 25th Infantry divisions would follow (although formal approval for use of the additional division was not to come for several more days).

Collectively these units would constitute a new command known as Eighth United States Army, Korea, or EUSAK (pronounced "you-sack" by the military). The Eighth Army had been the principal army command in Japan since the war ended. Now it would have primary responsibility for waging war in Korea. Lieutenant General Walton Harris Walker, who had led the Eighth Army since 1948, would go to Korea as commanding general. Walker carried a deserved reputation as one of the best fighting generals the army had. A chunky man who often fretted as his barrel chest sank irretrievably toward his waist, Walker had the lined face, if not the lithe figure, of a plainsman from his native Texas. He spoke with a Texas twang, and he was a tank commander of such ferocity in the Second World War that General George S. Patton frequently called him "my toughest son of a bitch." During peacetime Walker enjoyed lifting a glass: to comrades from the Old Army he was known as Johnnie Walker, after his favored scotch. (Walker left his whiskey bottle in Japan; Captain Eugene M. "Mike" Lynch, who served as his personal pilot during Walker's months in Korea and was with him daily, said, "I never saw the general take a drink, even at times when both of us damned well needed one."[3])

Walker was not a warm man, even with his troops. He considered newspaper correspondents an unnecessary appendage of war and did not mind telling them so; hence he suffered a poor press his entire time in Korea. But as a fighter who was willing to draw a line and stand on it Walker had no equal. During one critical period in September, when the North Koreans threatened to push through a U.S. division, Walker called down the division commander: "If the enemy gets into Taegu you will find me resisting him in the streets and I'll have some of my trusted people with me and you had better be prepared to do the same. Now get back to your division and *fight it!*"[4] Walker told another laggard general that he did not want to see him back from the front again unless it was in a coffin. In addition to his .45 automatic, he carried a repeating shotgun as he roared around the battle area in a jeep. "I don't mind being shot at," he told a subordinate, "but these bastards are not going to ambush me."

In sum, MacArthur was sending a fighter to Korea, a man very capable of an "arrogant display of strength."

But to the men of Task Force Smith, MacArthur's strategic design meant immediate physical discomfort and command confusion. The seventy-five-mile ride from Camp Wood to Itazuke consumed five rain-soaked hours; when the men finally climbed from their trucks, not a dry stitch of clothing existed. General William Dean greeted Smith with uneasy news. He did not even know the exact location of ROK Army headquarters, for conflicting reports from the battle zone placed it "somewhere between Seoul and Suwon." Dean also had his own problems. He was to assemble an entire division, the 24th, and truck it to six nearby Japanese ports. But no ships were there to transport the troops to Korea. In frustration Dean gave Smith orders that were a model of command brevity:

> When you get to Pusan, head for Taejon. We want to stop the North Koreans as far from Pusan as possible. Block the main road as far north as possible. Contact General Church in Korea as head of the advance party. If you can't locate him, go to Taejon and beyond if you can. Sorry I can't give you any more information. That's all I've got. Good luck to you, and God bless you and your men.

Only six C-54 transport planes were available, and Smith had the first of them loaded and airborne within forty minutes of his arrival. But this flight, and the second, which left minutes later, found the fog so dense over the small Pusan runway that they were unable to land and had to return to Japan. Later the weather began to break, and at eleven in the morning the first American combat troops stepped onto Korean soil.

Church's advance party had assembled a miscellaneous assortment of about 100 Korean trucks and other vehicles to transport Task Force Smith the seventeen miles from the landing strip to the Pusan rail station, where they would board a train for Taejon.

Korean civilians either did not know or did not care to recognize the gravity of the situation to the north. Thousands of them stood along the streets in holiday spirit, waving happily to the American soldiers and displaying flags, banners, and posters. At the railway station there was even an Oriental version of an oompah band: Task Force Smith might be embarking on an impossible mission, but its young, confused, and nervous soldiers went toward battle with the music and accolades of a grateful populace ringing in their ears.

Rhee in a Rage

But even as Task Force Smith moved north to confront the invaders, political confusion threatened to bring the war to an abrupt and inglorious end before MacArthur's "arrogant display of strength" could appear on the battlefield.

Politically the problem again was a disturbed President Syngman Rhee. On Saturday morning he angrily upbraided Harold Noble of the American embassy, the diplomat assigned to remain with the president in his exile quarters in Taejon.[5] Rhee stormed that he had listened to Ambassador Muccio, and to the "great god MacArthur," and to the promises of President Truman. All had betrayed him. What was being done to halt the Communist advance? Nothing. Rhee spoke nonstop for an hour. The Communists would soon be in the streets of Taejon, and he did not intend to run again. If he died in Taejon, so be it. Further retreat would only compound his humiliation.

To Noble's dismay, Mrs. Rhee—usually a calming influence during such outbursts—this time agreed with her husband. She preferred that she and Rhee be remembered for having faced the enemy without fear, and died, rather than as cowards. Their memories would inspire future Koreans to fight to reestablish an independent republic. Noble argued "against such acceptance of defeat, against such a fatalistic invitation to death." Rhee had no right to follow his individual preference; he owed a duty to his people to survive.

The arrival of two ROK Cabinet officers saved the day for Noble. They supported his arguments, and Noble managed a few private words with Mrs. Rhee. Better, he said, for her husband to continue as a leader than to die like a trapped animal. Rhee finally agreed. He would continue his retreat to the south and keep out of range of the advancing North Koreans.

Smith Readies to Fight

At about the same time on Sunday morning that Rhee and Noble left Taejon, the weary troops of Task Force Smith were clambering off a train in the same city, heavy barracks bags in hand. By this time they had reached the condition where a soldier does not give a damn about what he might be asked to do half a day hence. So long as the ground beneath their prone bodies was immobile, they would occupy it, and worry about the future when it appeared.

Brad Smith, meanwhile, had his initial meeting with General Church, who a couple of days earlier had suggested he would trade the entire ROK Army for 100 New York City policemen. Church apparently still felt that the presence of a few Caucasian soldiers should reverse the combat disasters of the past few days. Flicking his pointer at a map, toward the hamlet of Osan, eighty miles to the north, Church told Smith, "We have a little action [sic] up here. All we need is some men up there who won't run when they see tanks. We're going to move you up to support the ROKs and give them moral support."

Smith sensed that something more complicated might be involved. He politely heard out Church, then borrowed several jeeps so that he and staff officers could inspect the terrain where they might be fighting.

Smith drove up the main highway on the west coast of Korea, north from Taejon toward Suwon and Seoul, the most threatening advance route of the North Koreans. The North Koreans' major impediment seemed to be supplies; their tank and infantry columns would advance from four to eight miles daily, then pause while fuel and ammunition were brought in from the rear.

What Brad Smith wanted was an ambush point. He found it on the road just south of the Suwon Airfield, about three miles north of the tiny town of Osan. Viewed from the south, the road ran through a low saddle, then dropped down and canted toward Suwon. An irregular line of hills crossed the road at right angles, providing perfect infantry positions and observation posts for both the highway and the railroad almost the entire eight miles to Suwon.

Brad Smith had his position. Rough sketches went onto position maps; here Task Force Smith would make its stand, with the hope of slowing, if not stopping, the North Korean advance.

The other men of Task Force Smith, meanwhile, moved slowly north by train, awaiting orders from Colonel Smith on where they would deploy to try to stop the North Koreans. They moved through scenes of wild confusion, with civilian and military refugees walking south along the railroad embankment. And at midday they witnessed one of the many accidental tragedies that marked the first hectic weeks of the war.

A northbound train of nine ammunition cars had paused at the small town of Pyongtaek, some forty miles below Suwon. The engineer needed instructions; he did not know how far the North Koreans had advanced, and he did not want his precious cargo to fall into Communist hands. His stalled train was spotted by four fighter planes piloted by Royal Australian Air Force pilots on their first missions since joining the war under UN auspices. Uncertain of their location and uncontrolled by any guidance from the ground, the Australians thought they had found a splendid North Korean target. Six times their tight formation roared over the station, firing rockets and machine guns into the train. The entire train vanished in a sudden burst of flame and fury, as did the station and most of Pyongtaek, including uncountable hundreds of civilians. Displaced rounds of ammunition continued exploding through the night. The train carrying Task Force Smith crept through Pyongtaek on a secondary track, the Americans staring at the carnage in mute contemplation of their own imminent initiation into battle.

Accidents occurred elsewhere that day mostly because of the lack of communications between troops on the ground and American and other planes overhead. U.S. planes strafed an ROK tank column near Suwon. ROK troops angrily fired rifles into the air and caused a damaged plane to land. Their "prisoner" proved to be a very embarrassed U.S. pilot. One American military adviser at Suwon asserted that "friendly" planes attacked the base no less than five times on July 3. Writing a friend a few days later, this officer said, "The fly boys really had a field day! They hit friendly dumps, the Suwon air strip, trains, motor columns, and KA [Korean Army] Hq." In another attack U.S.

pilots strafed and burned thirty South Korean trucks and killed some 200 soldiers on the Suwon–Osan highway.

General Church angrily asked General Stratemeyer to curb his overly enthusiastic pilots. He demanded that air strikes be confined to the Han River area northward.* Stratemeyer agreed.

The Buildup Quickens

As Task Force Smith moved north, Major General William Dean, commander of the 24th Infantry Division, set up headquarters in Taejon to prepare for the arrival of his troops. Dean, a few weeks shy of his fifty-first birthday, was an anomaly among army generals, an officer who had risen to star rank after receiving his commission through the Reserve Officers Training Corps program.[6] A strapping six-footer who weighed more than 200 pounds, Dean had commanded infantry troops in Europe during the Second World War and had a reputation for discipline. He had run the American military government in South Korea in 1947 and 1948, then took command of the 24th Division, in Japan. His knowledge of Korea was limited—he spoke only a few words of the language, and he had little contact with anyone outside the government—and he did not especially like the place (the first night he returned there in July 1950, he said tartly, he slept in a Pusan warehouse "that had more bedbugs in it than any structure I've seen, before or since").

His first look at the ROK military during wartime was not very reassuring. Less than two weeks into the war, it already had its third chief of staff. The ROK headquarters "was torn by internal strife, with everyone shouting 'Communist' at one another, and everyone apparently quite willing for me to make all decisions, especially theirs." Each time Dean tried to encourage a ROK stand, commanders responded with a "fog of excuses for the backward march"—they were short of ammunition; they could not stop the North Korean tanks; they had been outflanked. Far too many ROK soldiers were "apparently making no effort to stand and fight." Dean would not even guess what was happening in the mountains in the east, although the Korean command repeatedly claimed its army was "fighting hard there" and produced an occasional captured armored vehicle. Dean was not fooled. He had been in combat, and he knew the indices. He found it disconcerting that despite all the ROK talk about fighting, the South Koreans "did not seem to be able

*The official U.S. Air Force history of its participation in the Korean War is silent about these mishaps. The army, albeit angry at the time, correctly faulted haphazard air-ground communications for the errant bombs.

to produce any prisoners of war for interrogation." In even the most savage of fighting, prisoners are captured. Dean could only conclude the ROKs were not telling the truth.

Luckily for his disposition, late on July 4 Dean greeted his first sizable contingent of American troops, 1,981 men of the 34th Regiment. He ordered them to move up behind Task Force Smith and take up positions blocking one road at Ansong and also the main highway at Pyongtaek. Dean sought to make an ally of geography. At Pyongtaek, an arm of the Asan Bay stretched almost to the highway, affording a barrier to any enemy attempt to slip westward around the city and then south. To the east of Ansong, mountains coming down to the edge of the city provided a similar shield. If the enemy broke through these two key cities, he could range freely over the network of roads to the south. Task Force Smith was in position where it hoped it could blunt the attack.

Dean carefully explained the strategy to the 34th Regiment's commanding officer, Colonel Jay B. Lovless. He warned that if the North Koreans did get around these blocking positions, delaying actions would be infinitely more difficult. The regiment's immediate mission was to slow the advance, to give MacArthur time to rush further reinforcements to Korea. Dean recognized the difficulties: The 1st Battalion of the 34th Regiment, which would be on line, had no tanks, no artillery, no antitank weapons; it was in a poor state of training. The North Korean force sweeping toward it was infinitely stronger. But the battalion commander, Lieutenant Colonel Harold B. Ayres, had fought bravely and skillfully in the Italian campaign of the Second World War, and Dean was confident he could do the job.

Ayres did not quibble. He called in his noncoms and said, "OK, get 'em on the trucks and get 'em rollin'."

The Americans' First Fight

On Tuesday—Task Force Smith's fourth day of travel—the weary troopers climbed off their train in Osan and boarded an assortment of wheezing commandeered Korean trucks. One welcome addition was a contingent from their division's 52nd Field Artillery Battalion—six 105 mm howitzers, seventy-three vehicles, and 108 artillerymen, all of whom had been rushed to Korea by small naval craft, then brought north by truck and train. Now, Colonel Smith thought, we are getting the kind of muscle we need. Brigadier General George B. Barth accompanied the artillery unit; despite Barth's superior rank, however, Colonel Smith continued as overall commander.

Colonel Smith had his men in the trucks and ready to move north at nightfall. But the Koreans driving the trucks balked. "You are stupid," one of them told Smith through an interpreter. "The war is that way. We should be going the *other* way," gesturing to the south. When Smith persisted, the drivers abandoned their trucks and bolted away into the darkness. "All right," bellowed a sergeant, "we need some volunteers who can drive." So the task force proceeded with GIs at the wheel.

The ROKs gave more problems as the advance continued. At several bridges Smith found ROK engineers busily emplacing explosive charges. They told him they "intended to stop the Communists' tanks by cutting the road from beneath them." Smith and Barth argued that cutting the bridges would also strand their task force; leave the demolitions in place, they said, and they would ensure their destructions if the Americans had to withdraw.

Barth was not a man to tolerate long argument. When one group of ROKs insisted the bridges must be blown immediately, he snatched up the cases of dynamite and hurled them into the river. No one argued with him.

At three in the morning on Wednesday, July 5, Task Force Smith finally arrived at its destination—five days almost to the exact hour from departure from Camp Wood in Japan. Despite their grinding exhaustion, the men immediately began emplacing their guns. They worked somberly. By this time the rawest recruit knew the attacking force that would be coming down the road from the north the next few days would be led by tanks. The combat veterans had advice: Shoot for the treads, try to stop them; otherwise, go for a lucky round through the aiming slit. The unspoken conclusion was that the men of Task Force Smith had drawn the ultimate of shitty missions; their unit had been plucked from occupation duty because of their commanding officer's reputation for tactical expertise, and frankly many wished they were back in Japan.

Nonetheless, the troopers fell to their work. Explaining the positions on the gun emplacements dug that evening is best done by reference to the human hand. Drop the right hand onto a flat surface, thumb and first two fingers extended. The Suwon–Osan highway runs from upper right downward through the web. The right thumb is one hill; the knuckles of the index finger and the adjoining finger are another hill. The artillery was stationed along the left side of the wrist—one gun 400 yards back, four others perhaps a mile.

Company B straddled the road. To its right, Company C went into an L formation—one-third its men facing the axis of the enemy advance, the others dropping off at a ninety-degree angle (along the course of the middle finger) to parallel a rail track leading south. The hilly terrain left a single corridor open from north to south, and that was where Brad Smith assembled his roadblock.

Smith ran short of men before all positions were occupied. He asked for volunteers from the headquarters to complement the artillery unit. Enough men stepped forward to form four .50 caliber and four 2.36-inch bazooka teams, which joined the infantry in the forward positions.

The artillerymen counted their rounds carefully. When drawing supplies at Sasebo, Japan, the battalion ammunition officer discovered that only eighteen rounds of high-explosive antitank (HEAT) shells were available. Six of these he issued to A Battery, to be used sparingly against Russian-built T-34 tanks. The 1,200-odd other rounds were conventional high explosives (HE) of questionable value against the Soviet-made armor.

At first light on Wednesday there were 540 American soldiers on the roadblock, Smith's original contingent augmented by the artillery troops. Heavy rain pounded down on the men as they crouched in their muddy slit trenches and behind trees, ate cold C ration breakfasts, and awaited the North Korea advance.

Smith saw the tanks first, a grayish blob on the road from Suwon, miles distant, but nonetheless discernible. This was around seven o'clock. Within half an hour forward observers relayed more detailed information: A column of eight tanks was slowly closing on the positions.

For thirty more nervous minutes Smith watched the column slowly move into range of his 105 mm howitzers. At about eight o'clock the forward observer radioed a fire order to the artillery: range 4,000 yards, about 2,000 yards in front of the forward U.S. infantry positions. As the first American artillery fire of the war hurtled at the tanks, General Barth instinctively glanced at his watch. It was 8:16 A.M.

The first few rounds went astray; but the forward observer quickly adjusted the range, and shell bursts sent up plumes of smoke and mud amid the oncoming tanks. To the horror of the watching infantrymen, the exploding artillery shells did not deter the enemy. The tanks continued clattering along the roadway. Smith decided the enemy commander thought he had run into another minor ROK delaying action.

Because of the limited ammunition, Smith had ordered the 75 mm bazookas to hold fire until the tanks closed to 700 yards. The first shots smashed into the lead tanks but did no apparent damage. Their 85 mm cannon and 7.62 mm machine guns spitting fire, the tanks rumbled on up the incline toward the top of the draw.

Second Lieutenant Ollie D. Connor had stationed himself in a ditch on the east side of the roadway with a bazooka. He let the lead two tanks pass him by, then squatted and fired twenty-two rockets at fifteen yards' range against the rear of the tanks, where their armor was weakest. Meanwhile, the single howitzer battery with the HEAT ammunition took the two tanks under fire; damaged, they pulled to the side of the road to clear the way for those following.

One of the damaged tanks burst into flames, and two of the crewmen emerged from the turret with their hands in the air. A third man followed with a burp gun in his hands, spraying fire toward a nearby U.S. machine-gun position as he leaped from the tank. The fire hit and killed one of the gunners—the first American ground soldier killed in action, one whose name was lost to history in the chaos of battle. American fire quickly killed the three North Koreans. (Reconstructing the incident later, Smith deduced that the HEAT rounds, not Connor's bazooka fire, had damaged the tanks. The bazooka ammunition, he said, had deteriorated with age.)

Within minutes the last of the HEAT rounds was exhausted; the conventional high-explosive shells ricocheted harmlessly off tanks. The North Koreans moved with supreme confidence; they fired haphazard volleys at the infantry positions as the column of tanks moved through the pass but did not stop to clear out their emplacements. In frustration, the GIs fired occasional M-1 rounds at the tanks, but the import of the battle was clear. The North Koreans went through the American lines with the ease of motorists out for a Sunday drive.

The first line of tanks vanished down the road toward the artillery positions, their tracks cutting the field telephone wires connecting the howitzer crews with the infantry. The radio sets were wet, worn-out, and malfunctioning; soon the only communication was via a single jeep radio. Tanks continued to come, now in groups of four, unimpeded by any American fire. By nine o'clock thirty-three of them had passed through the infantry position. Their fire killed or wounded twenty Americans.

Earlier that day, before the battle began, someone in the artillery asked an obvious question: What happened to the gun emplacements if the tanks broke through the infantry lines? Sergeant Edwin Eversole of the artillery was among those who thought the question academic. "Everyone thought the enemy would turn around and go back when they found out who was fighting"—that is, Americans rather than the ROKs. And one of the infantrymen assured the artillery, "Don't worry, they will never get back to you."

But the tanks did, and with an ease that infuriated Smith and other officers. Further, they did not seem particularly interested in destroying the American batteries. Time and again a tank would lurch over the crest of the draw, hatches closed, and rush down the road past the artillery. Their occasional fire was almost contemptuous, as if they did not even care about the location of the American guns; some even aimed at the wrong side of the highway. One tank did pause briefly when its crew spotted the howitzer position and moved off the road as if to overrun it. Instead, after a moment it swerved back onto the roadway and continued toward Osan.

The 105 mm howitzers, meanwhile, fired at point-blank range, thundering shell after shell at a distance of 150 to 300 yards. The shells jarred the tanks but bounced off harmlessly.

Only once did the defenders have any success. Lieutenant Colonel Miller O. Perry, of the artillery contingent, and Sergeant Ed Eversole led bazooka teams toward the highway with the hope of getting a closer shot at the tanks. A tank caught the men in a rice paddy separating the howitzer and the highway. Eversole dropped to his knees and hastily fired a round at a tank so close it looked "as big as a battleship." The tank's turret swung toward the sergeant, and a round from its 85 mm cannon knocked down a roadside telephone pole. Eversole flung himself into a water-filled drainage ditch. The pole fell harmlessly over him. At about the same time a 105 mm shell clipped the tracks of the tank and stopped it. Other tanks in the column passed on through the draw.

Once the action had quieted, Colonel Perry, through an interpreter, called upon the crew of the disabled tank to surrender. They did not respond. Perry ordered the 105 mm howitzer to destroy the tanks. After three jolting rounds of cannon fire hit the tank, two North Koreans jumped out and fled; an American squad tracked them down and shot them.

In the melee a round of small-arms fire wounded Perry in the leg. But he refused evacuation, insisting on preparing his beleaguered artillery for the appearance of yet even more enemy tanks. A seemingly endless string of tanks came up the road—sometimes in miniconvoys of three, sometimes singly.

The sight demoralized some of the howitzer crews, who began to "take off," in the words of Eversole. Perry and other officers and noncoms moved to crew the abandoned guns, dragging up rounds of ammunition from a dump some yards away and loading and firing the pieces. Again, however, the artillery was mostly ineffectual. But this time the tanks carried an occasional cluster of infantrymen. The close-range artillery fire blew off or killed most of them; the tanks continued toward Osan, but now dead bodies festooned their sides.

By 10:15 A.M. the last of the tanks had passed, some forty in all. Smith took inventory. Artillery and bazooka fire, or a combination of both, had destroyed or immobilized four tanks and damaged three others that remained serviceable. In addition to twenty dead or wounded, Task Force Smith lost a 105 mm howitzer and most of the contingent's vehicles.

Later Colonel Perry was to lament the absence of antitank mines, nonexistent in Korea at the time. A handful of well-placed mines, he felt, could have stopped the entire column. But for the moment the Far East Command had to continue to fight the war on the cheap, relying on the bravery of its troops and stopgap measures in the gamble for time.

* * *

As the North Korean tanks swept through Task Force Smith unimpeded, the 34th Regiment was trying to set up positions at the hamlet of Pyongtaek, some ten miles south of Osan on the main highway-rail corridor on the west coast. When Colonel Harold Ayres heard of the breakthrough, he sent out bazooka teams. A few infantrymen led by Lieutenant Charles E. Payne moved north and encountered a tank on a railroad track about five miles south of Osan.

Sergeant Ray Turnbull, an army photographer, went with the patrol, hoping to get an action photo of the destruction of an enemy tank by a bazooka team.[7] He followed Private Kenneth Shadrick, a nineteen-year-old high school dropout from Skin Fork, West Virginia. The team operated from a graveyard outside a tiny village. Turnbull said later:

> I was getting some good pictures but two enemy tanks had stopped a little further off and Shadrick and his partner went to another position to try to knock them out. I went along.
>
> They fired a couple of times. Then Shadrick agreed to count one-two-three and then fire so I could get a picture of the flame shooting from the rear end of the bazooka after the count of three. Shadrick said, "Three!" then raised up to see where the projectile had gone—whether he had scored a hit or not. A bullet caught him right in the chest. Another went through his right arm.
>
> Shadrick moaned, "Oh, my arm." I could see the bone above his elbow was shattered. He fell to the ground. A lieutenant rushed to him but I said, "It's too late—he got it right in the chest, too." I took a picture of the lieutenant trying to feel his pulse but there wasn't any. He died in less than 30 seconds.

"What a place to die!" exclaimed a medic.*

Task Force Smith Withdraws

Task Force Smith enjoyed a brief lull after the North Korean tanks vanished to the south, but Brad Smith knew enemy infantry was certain to be on the road shortly. His men spent the respite deepening their foxholes, trying to patch the broken communications lines, and checking their weapons and ammunition. The heavy rainfall continued. "Helluva place to fight a war," muttered a private, and no one argued with him.

*Because reporters were present when Shadrick was killed, he had posthumous fame as the first American ground soldier to die in the war, an error committed to history in several subsequent books on the war. According to war diaries of the units fighting on July 5, however, Task Force Smith infantrymen died some time between eight and eleven o'clock in the morning, Shadrick not until around four o'clock in the afternoon. Twenty Americans were killed that day.

The calm did not last long. Sweeping the horizon with his field glasses, Smith picked up the first signs of further enemy movement near Suwon at around eleven o'clock. As the minutes dragged on, Smith realized with mounting apprehension that an awesome force was bearing down on his little band: a column of trucks and foot soldiers stretching a full six miles or more, spearheaded by three tanks. (According to interrogations of captured prisoners later, what he saw was two full regiments, the 16th and 18th, of the North Korean 4th Division, about 4,000 men. One of these reports, on the questioning of a Senior Colonel Lee Hak Ku, revealed the North Koreans did not know—or anticipate —at the time that the United States would enter the war, and that it did so came as a "surprise" to the Pyongyang government.)

So Smith was caught in a vise: To the south of his task force was the tank column he had barely been able to delay, much less destroy. Now he would try to stop a force which outnumbered him perhaps ten to one.

A soldier of lesser fighting heart well could have sounded the retreat at this point. Smith, however, recognized his mission: to slow the North Korean advance as long as possible and to demonstrate to the enemy that he now faced a foe more formidable than the shattered ROK Army. With a gambler's steady nerves Smith watched the North Korean column draw closer and closer. Finally, when the convoy of enemy trucks was no more than 1,000 yards away, Smith "threw the book at them," in his words.

At the fire order mortars chugged shell after shell into the line of trucks, and .50 caliber machine-gun bullets raked the column. Trucks exploded into flames. North Korean soldiers leaped or were blown onto the roadway. The first furious seconds of fire killed uncountable scores of enemy troops.

But the North Koreans regrouped speedily. The three tanks turned on the American positions and rolled to within 200 to 300 yards of the gun emplacements; their cannon and machine-gun fire raked the ridge line. Shouted commands brought some 1,000 North Koreans out of the trucks and ditches, and they began moving up the ridge along the east side of the road. The other North Korean troops sat in trucks beyond the burning vehicles and waited; they apparently felt the defenders would eventually break and run, as had the ROKs earlier in the war.

The advancing Communist troops gradually worked their way around both sides of the American lines, forcing the defenders to compress their perimeter on the east side of the road. Enemy mortar fire intensified. The North Koreans inexorably were working away to the south so that Smith's task force would be completely cut off.

Novice soldiers though they were, the defenders fought valiantly. Private First Class Vern Mulligan had the tripod of his machine gun shot away by enemy fire. He propped the barrel across an empty ammunition box and continued firing. More fire demolished this makeshift prop, and six North Korean soldiers ran toward him. Mulligan draped the machine gun across his left forearm and fired. He killed all six.

A first lieutenant, Raymond "Bodie" Adams, had pitched for the regimental baseball team back in Japan. Now he threw the most important pitch of his career. He tossed a grenade the seemingly impossible distance of forty yards, square into a North Korean machine-gun position, destroying the gun and killing the crew.

Smith after two hours realized his situation was beyond salvation. To retain his position meant certain death for his men. He said later, "In an obviously hopeless situation, with many casualties, no communications, no transportation, ammo gone, and the enemy tanks now well behind me, I was faced with the decision, what the hell to do?

"To stand and die, or to try to get the remains of my task force out of there? I could last, at best, only another hour, and then lose everything I had. I chose to try to get out, in hopes that we would live to fight another day."

So Smith led a small group that, after abandoning all mechanized weapons, managed to blast clear a pathway to escape the Communist encirclement. One of Smith's lieutenants, himself badly wounded, dragged himself to the rear past six men lying on the ground, none able to walk. "Lieutenant, what is going to happen to us?" one of the men cried out.

The lieutenant passed him a hand grenade. "This is the best I can do for you," he said.

"That's the worst part of a deal like that," Smith said later, "to leave wounded and dying men yelling for you to help them, and there was no way to help them."

Abandoning the wounded on the battlefield also violated American military doctrine. If a soldier knows he will not be left on the ground when hurt, he understandably fights better. Smith's wounded, unfortunately, were not to be the last to be abandoned to the enemy.

The Advance Rolls On

Stragglers from Task Force Smith began drifting into the 34th Regiment area late on the night of July 5 and with initial gloomy reports: Some men said that the entire contingent had been wiped out and that an armada of enemy tanks followed closely behind. Then Smith himself came through with about eighty-six survivors, including four men so badly wounded they had to be left with the regiment.

Now the regiment commander, Colonel Lovless, faced another problem as well: a total loss of communications among the various units at Pyongtaek, Ansong, and elsewhere. Fleeing South Korean soldiers and civilians repeatedly cut out sections of telephone wire along the roadways to fashion packs to carry their possessions. Because of the long distances, the radio network would not work. So the commanders were forced to use messengers to inform one another of what was happening, and reporting fell far behind actual events.

Another problem was confusion over just who was commanding what. General George Barth, last seen putting artillery units into position in support of Task Force Smith, now had joined up with the 34th Regiment. In the absence of a higher commander he began giving orders to Colonel Ayres of the 1st Battalion. He did what he thought best in a crisis situation. He ordered the highway bridge north of the town to be destroyed. He told Ayres to hold as long as he could but to withdraw immediately if he felt his battalion was in danger of being cut off. Ayres was "not to end up like Brad Smith." Apparently neither Ayres nor Barth warned Colonel Lovless of what was happening to the north. Lovless had received no instructions from Dean on Barth's role; nonetheless, colonels in the field do not argue with generals, so Lovless set about drafting a withdrawal plan. One company would remain as a rear guard and withdraw on successive positions when the 1st Battalion left Pyongtaek.

Meanwhile, the men of the 1st Battalion crouched in water-filled slit trenches at the riverbank two miles north of Pyongtaek and felt generally miserable. Cold C rations at daybreak did little to relieve their gloom. Then through the mist and rain could be heard the sound of motors.

Ayres and the other men peered through the fog and saw the outline of tanks on the far side of the blown bridge; beyond them were marching troops and trucks. The lead tank stopped at the edge of the bridge, and the crew got out to look at the damage. The other tanks halted behind it, thirteen of them in all. The North Korean infantry did not pause. It marched directly to the stream, and individual soldiers began to wade through the water.

American mortars rained a brief barrage on the bridge area, destroying a single truck. The tanks swiftly returned fire and soon silenced the U.S. guns. North Koreans swarmed across the river; within minutes they were so close to the American lines that infantrymen could see them loading their rifles.

Ayres had seen enough. He ordered his battalion to withdraw to Chonan, along roads jammed with retreating Korean civilians and soldiers. The retreat was disorganized; by afternoon discarded equipment and clothing were littering the highway between Pyongtaek and Chonan.

An outmanned, outgunned Task Force Smith had failed to slow the

North Koreans significantly. So had a similarly overpowered 34th Regiment—but with a major difference. Smith's men fought until driven out of their positions. The 34th Regiment had relatively insignificant contact with the enemy; once the North Koreans appeared, it simply packed up and left.

And no one was more astonished—and angered—at the withdrawal than General Dean.[8] By the time he heard of it the 34th Regiment was already fifteen miles distant from the river defense line he had chosen along the sea. "Units that had been at Ansong were now a full twenty miles from where I had left them—without even waiting until the enemy hit them," Dean said.

Dean got into his jeep and rushed to Chonan to learn what had gone wrong and why the 34th had not held on the river. When he arrived, he found that the entire regiment was now south of Chonan. "I should have said, 'Turn around and get going now,' but rather than add to the confusion and risk night ambushes, I told them, 'All right, hold tight here until I give you further orders.'"

The official army history discreetly describes as "uncomfortable" the ensuing confrontation between Generals Dean and Barth and the other officers. Dean asked point-blank who had authorized the withdrawal from Pyongtaek. An awkward silence ensued. Ayres finally said he would accept responsibility.

Dean ordered the 34th to turn around the next morning, to advance until it met the enemy, and then to fight a delaying action. But the advantage of geography had slipped from his grasp, with results he called "tragic." The Communists swept down the west coast on the road network, opposed only by a curious paramilitary force known as the Northwest Youth Group—500 to 1,000 non-Communist North Koreans armed by the ROK government but not a part of the Regular Army. Some American and Korean officers had faith in the group; Dean did not. And in ensuing days North Koreans harried the Americans and ROKs constantly from the west flank.

Dean did something else the next morning. The 34th Regiment received a new commanding officer, Colonel Robert R. Martin, with whom Dean had served in Europe in the 44th Division, where he commanded a regiment in combat. Martin came to Korea in a hurry from a staff assignment in Tokyo; he arrived wearing low-cut shoes, an overseas cap, with no helmet, weapon, or field equipment. Within a few hours he was at the front. Lovless was formally relieved of command that afternoon.*

*To Lovless's credit, he had commanded the regiment less than two months and had "inherited a chaotic situation" with an unsatisfactory state of training and some officers "wholly unfitted for troop command," according to an army summary.[9] He did not have time to turn the regiment around before it went into battle. Nonetheless, the debacle cost Lovless his career.

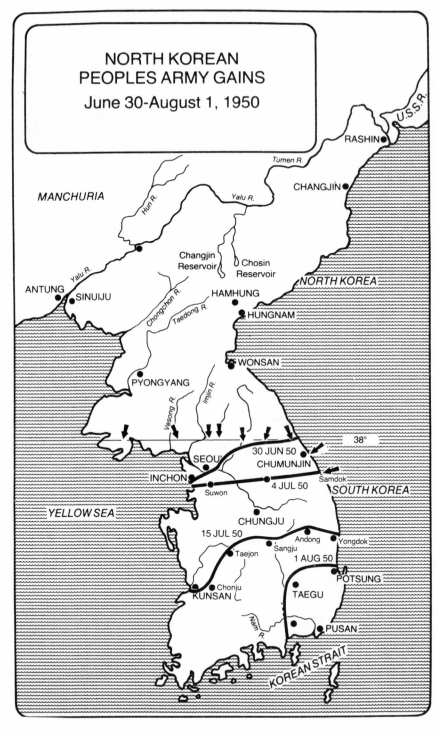

NORTH KOREAN
PEOPLES ARMY GAINS
June 30-August 1, 1950

"More Men!"—MacArthur

The speed of the North Korean advance unnerved MacArthur. On June 29 he had boasted to Marguerite Higgins of the New York *Herald Tribune,* "Give me two divisions and I can hold Korea." The JCS the next day authorized him to use two divisions of the four then in Japan. But even as advance elements of these divisions moved toward Korea, he pleaded for more help. On July 2 he wired the JCS: "Request if practicable immediate dispatch of one Marine RCT [regimental combat team] with comparable Marine air unit for tactical support. Earliest arrival here imperative due to pressure of impending operations."[10] He also endorsed a request by General Stratemeyer, the air commander, for some 700 aircraft to bring air force units to war strength.

On July 3 the JCS approved the dispatch of the marine regiment.[11] The chiefs also gave MacArthur about half the aircraft he requested for Stratemeyer, "all . . . that could be made available at that time."

Two days later—the day Task Force Smith went into combat—MacArthur again implored the JCS for more men.[12] This time he asked for the 2nd Infantry Division, the 2nd Engineer Special Brigade, and a regiment of the 82nd Airborne Division, for use in operations he planned between July 20 and August 10.

This time the JCS paused. The units he requested constituted a good portion of the army's General Reserve. Of the six divisions stationed outside Japan, one was on occupation duty in Germany, the remaining five were in the United States. The chiefs told MacArthur that while they gave "sympathetic consideration" to his request, it troubled them.[13] No increase in military manpower had been authorized, and the United States must continue to maintain a strong military posture in areas other than Korea. Nor did shipping exist to send him the requested troops by July 20. The JCS asked that MacArthur pause and try to arrive at an estimate of the total forces, from all branches of the service, that would be required to drive the invaders from South Korea.

In the eastern two-thirds of the country, defending along more rugged invasion routes, the ROK Army faced many of the same problems as the stopgap American effort along the west coast.[14] After the American 24th Division entered combat on July 5, the ROKs took responsibility for defending everything east of the main Seoul–Taegu highway and railroad.

The central section of Korea is mountainous, with two main north-south flows of highway and rail traffic, both commencing at Wonju, about forty-five miles southeast of Seoul. The central corridor runs almost due south, from Wonju to Kumchon. The other, slightly to the east, runs at a southeast slant to Yongchon. Seizure of either of these corridors would put the invader within striking range of Taegu.

The individual battles followed much the same pattern encountered by the 24th Division to the west: initial onslaughts by tanks, swift enveloping movements by infantry, and vastly superior manpower and firepower. Nonetheless, later prisoner of war interrogation reports gave a complimentary index of the increasing effectiveness of the ROK units (the 2nd, Capital, 3rd, 6th, and 8th divisions and the 17th Regiment). According to the POW reports, the North Korean Supreme Command relieved (and then probably shot) three divisional commanders for failure to push the advance as swiftly as planned.

When the ROKs had time to stand and fight and bring their scant artillery into play, they devastated the invaders. For instance, the ROK Capital Division fought a fierce three-day running battle with the North Korean 2nd Division south of Chunchon. ROK artillery set up an ambush at the edge of Chongu, calmly waited until the enemy walked into range, then methodically blasted away for more than an hour, killing 800 North Koreans.

MacArthur rushed 800 M-6 antitank mines to the front, but neither the ROKs nor their American military advisers had ever seen this particular model. Major Richard I. Crawford, of the advisory group, read the instructions printed on each case and set about to teach the ROKs how to use the strange weapons. Because of the press of combat—tanks clanked and rattled toward the training areas—Crawford dared not spend more than half an hour or so on the instruction. The time was not enough. The ROKs would place the mines and then either forget to put in the detonators or to arm them so they would fire under the weight of a tank. One of Crawford's men caught the ROKs throwing entire cases of the mines off the back of a truck, with no attempt at concealment.

The American method having proved unsatisfactory, the ROKs turned to what Crawford speciously called "a better idea," which worked as follows:

> Without our knowledge, they prepared charges designed to strap around the waist of a soldier and formed some "body contact squads." Members of these squads were to move into the side of a tank, pull a fuze lighter on a two-second fuze, perhaps disable the tank, and certainly join their honored ancestors.
>
> I never found out how many tanks were actually disabled by this method, but I do know that in the first four or five days we ran awfully short of "body contact" people. The ROK chief of engineers told me he was experiencing some difficulty in getting additional volunteers.*[15]

---

*Peer pressure perhaps contributed to the volunteers, for the ROK government offered a 100,000-won—about $300—bonus to any unit that destroyed a tank. One adviser

Another American adviser, Major David F. Campbell, taught booby-trap skills to the ROK 6th Engineer Combat Battalion.[16] The ROKs especially liked one device. Infiltrating teams would sneak behind North Korean lines and remove a wheel from one of the carts the enemy used to transport supplies. Then they would put the explosive under the cart and carefully lower the axle to the ground, trip wire attached. "When a group lifted the cart to replace the wheel the booby trap went off. This diabolical device was referred to by the ROKs as 'the shaver'—for the effect it had on one's head."

By the middle of the month, these diversions notwithstanding, the North Koreans, through bloody and protracted fighting, began to make their way through two key passes in the mountains—at Mungyong, in the central corridor, and at Tanyang, to the east. Along the east coast, beyond the Taebaek Mountains, North Korean units moved unopposed through some of the roughest country in Korea. One regiment marched 175 miles in an eight-day period before encountering opposing ROKs, who were withdrawing from the Tanyang area.

But the main force of the North Korean division in the coastal area moved so slowly, so cautiously, that it squandered a splendid opportunity to move south all the way to Pohangdong and flank the entire ROK and American line across the peninsula. The delays came from the commander's decision to send reconnaissance patrols into the rugged mountain defiles to ensure he would not be ambushed. The U.S. Army's war history called this delay "one of the enemy's major tactical mistakes" of the war. Because of it, the ROKs managed to rush into position a 3rd Division regiment commanded by Colonel Kim Chong Won—an unusually big and strong man, fierce enough a fighter to carry the nickname Tiger Kim. He blocked the enemy advance north of Pohangdong. General MacArthur, meanwhile, sent a fighter group to an air base near Pohangdong, and General Dean dispatched an infantry battalion there. The navy joined in with salvos from ships offshore when it could find targets.

Nonetheless, some of the ROK units broke on July 11 and withdrew, command post and all, into Yongdok. The ROK division commander solved the problem in direct fashion: He ordered his military police to shoot any ROK soldiers found in the town. The stragglers swiftly returned to the front.

But neither the ROKs nor the American troops could hold. All across Korea, from the Yellow Sea to the Sea of Japan, the defensive line was crumbling. By mid-July the question was: Could it hold until enough help arrived?

"thought it not unlikely" that the ROKs would draw straws to see who would sacrifice himself to earn money for the entire outfit.

A Red Regime in Seoul

Once Rhee's government had been routed from Seoul, the Communists moved to impose their own regime on South Korea, relying on friendly southerners when possible.[17] The North Koreans behaved confidently; they felt the southern masses preferred them to the "gangster government" of Rhee, and they rallied many converts. Won Sei Hun, a member of the National Assembly from Seoul, agreed to preside over the trials of "anti-Communist suspects" and former ROK officials. General Song Ho Song, relieved of command of the ROK 2nd Division early in the fighting, spoke over the North Korean state radio on July 4 to announce the formation of a "People's Volunteer Corps" to fight with the NKPA. According to a CIA analysis, Song's speech foreshadowed the North's future psychological and propaganda approach both to the Korean people and to the world at large: "As [ROK] forces are eliminated and administration officials are captured, every effort will be made by the Northern regime to establish a 'provisional' government for all Korea." As the ROK Army and government shrank, Communist charges that Rhee's republic was a "puppet regime" and that the United States was trying to superimpose its will on a united Korean people "will carry more weight." Meanwhile, the CIA also received reports of executions of prominent anti-Communists in Seoul.

Several days later the Communist invaders did what the CIA forecast. They established a Seoul People's Committee which, with the exception of the chairman, was made up of South Koreans, many of them public officials and assemblymen Rhee had imprisoned as Communists.

The Communists next began "recruiting" men for military service and a compulsory labor draft, primarily for emergency transport work to replace facilities damaged by U.S. air strikes. The People's Committee started a census to find families of ROK military, police, and government personnel.

But coercion was not always necessary. The CIA felt that the ROK government's "past failure . . . to win the support of its restless student class" could lie behind reports that more than half of Seoul's students "are actively aiding the Communist invaders, with many voluntarily enlisting in the Northern army. Apparently attracted by the glamor of a winning army, the morale of these recruits may suffer rapidly if the going gets rough." The agency noted similar disaffection in other segments of the Seoul population: The working class "generally supports the Northern Koreans, while merchants are neutral and the intelligentsia continue to be pro-Southern." One CIA informant, identified as a former Seoul policeman, reported that North Korean troops and policemen "are rather inconspicuous" in the city. Although most stores were closed, "the streets . . . are crowded, especially with youths engaging in Communist demonstrations."

The import of the CIA reports was clear: Sizable numbers of Seoul residents were happy to see Rhee and his government gone.

In propaganda broadcasts directed to the South, the North Korean radio warned that the United States could not be trusted. Northern broadcasts and publications stated that the U.S. had helped Chiang Kai-shek in China but withdrawn when Communist strength became apparent. They claimed the United States would withdraw from Korea once the northern forces pushed farther south.

But whatever chances the North Koreans had for massing broad popular support were soon squandered. Because of the NKPA's logistical problems, the army literally lived off the land. Soldiers went through Seoul house to house, confiscating all rice. "Since then," the CIA noted, "the people in Seoul have been subsisting without rice." Food prices skyrocketed; by late July, according to refugee reports reaching the CIA, Seoul rice prices were seven times that in Pusan, eleven times that in Taegu.

With the North Koreans clearly in the ascendancy during July, Pyongyang Radio drummed at the theme that ROK supporters were on the losing side. One broadcast, of a document supposedly signed by forty-eight former members of the National Assembly still in occupied Seoul, called on assemblymen in Taejon to withdraw their support of Rhee and come over to the side of the "people." For the world audience, the North Koreans brought in correspondents from Communist newspapers of France, England, and China who railed against American bombing of the North. These "newsmen" wrote that because the Americans bombed "from above the clouds," they clearly engaged in "terror bombing designed to kill the peaceful inhabitants." But by mid-August the CIA reported, "The 'victory is inevitable' theme is losing appeal, although the bombing and land distribution themes are still effective." The North Koreans also tried black propaganda: "spreading false rumors of UN victories in order to depress morale when the reports are proved false."

Although the North Korean regime made no attempt to distribute food, it executed black marketeers and hoarders in an attempt to alleviate shortages. Working through block committees, the new regime systematically conscripted reluctant laborers to repair the Han River bridges—an unpopular task because of the continuing American bombings. A CIA report in early August said leftists who initially endorsed the Communist regime "are being demoralized" by the bombings and "are removing their identification armbands and modifying their behavior" because of doubts about a final North Korean victory.

But for the besieged defenders still retreating toward the tip of the Korean peninsula, the specter of a North Korean victory remained real.

CHAPTER FIVE

"Act Now, Think Later"

Once the initial flush of euphoria about intervention had mellowed, the national security establishment began a series of sobering second thoughts about the obligation the United States had undertaken. One of the gloomier estimates came from the Central Intelligence Agency on July 10, 1950.[1] Still far inferior to the State Department and Defense Department intelligence units because of its youth and lack of size, the CIA had played a minimal role in the climactic meetings leading to intervention. Now that the United States was in the war, the agency had an opportunity to act as analytical critic, and what it said was not welcome reading at either the State or Defense departments. Given the fact of U.S. intervention, the CIA said, "voluntary or forced withdrawal . . . would be a calamity." U.S. commitments abroad no longer would be trusted, for allies would not believe America intended to back promises with military force. Friendly nations such as Iran and Indochina "might lose political control . . . or feel compelled to seek an accommodation with the USSR." The United States faced a firecracker string of Soviet-inspired incidents, for "the USSR will proceed with limited aggressions similar to the Korean incident if it does not estimate the risk of global war to be substantial. . . . Voluntary U.S. withdrawal from Korea probably would encourage rather than discourage Soviet initiation of limited wars in other areas."

To the CIA, withdrawal could trigger a drastic response from the Soviets. "It would be politically and psychologically more advantageous for the U.S. to mobilize in support of U.S. and UN intervention in Korea rather than to mobilize after a withdrawal," the estimate said. If the United States should withdraw and then begin partial mobilization, "Soviet leaders would be more likely to anticipate war aimed directly at the USSR than if the mobilization were begun in support of the UN intervention in Korea. It is possible that the USSR, if it should anticipate global war, would try to seize the initiative by attacking the U.S."

Ray Cline, then a China analyst for the CIA (he retired in 1969 as deputy director), was one of the many CIA line officers who supported Truman's decision to intervene as "a bold stroke" and a necessary one. But Cline had reservations about the administration's procedures. "Given the lack of serious analysis that went into the decision," he said, "it was a matter of 'act now, think later.' "[2]

For the moment, the CIA's main job was to look for signs that the Soviets would respond to the U.S. intervention by attacking. One sign that a nation is preparing for war is destruction of foreign embassy files and the evacuation of key personnel and women and children dependents.[3] (A classic case of intelligence hindsight was the FBI's belated observation early in the morning of December 7, 1941, of smoke billowing from the courtyard of the Japanese embassy in Washington. Vast quantities of papers apparently were being burned. The observing agent made a note; by the time he filed a report Japanese planes had destroyed much of the American fleet in Pearl Harbor.) As the Korean crisis deepened, both the CIA and the FBI kept close watch on Soviet diplomatic communities around the world. The agents collected a welter of scattered items:

—At 10:30 P.M. on July 4 agents noted "a large amount of smoke and an odor of burning paper" at the Soviet legation in Havana. Previously "a box containing six 35-mm Leica-type cameras was taken into the legation, indicating a possible micro-filming of documents prior to burning."

—On July 2 Soviet personnel in Tokyo assigned to the consular and cultural relations sections "were observed packing their personal effects."

—On July 7 the FBI reported that Soviet women at the embassy's camp at Woodland Beach, Maryland, across the Chesapeake Bay from Washington, had been summoned to a meeting at the embassy the evening of July 8. "Further, informant states that hammering sounds, possibly indicating packing or crating, have been heard at the home of Boris K. Sokolov, first secretary of the Soviet Embassy, attached to the Far Eastern Commission," at his home in Northwest Washington.

—CIA agents reported that in the past six weeks Soviet ambassadors had returned to the USSR from posts in Washington, France, Japan, Turkey, India, Syria-Lebanon, Siam, Poland, and Czechoslovakia.

Neither the CIA nor its director, Rear Admiral R. H. Hillenkoetter, made any attempt to analyze these disparate happenings. They were simply compiled and sent to the White House. President Truman grumped when he read the report, "I thought CIA was an intelligence agency, not a bulletin board." He telephoned General George C. Marshall, army chief of staff during the Second World War, secretary of state afterward, now living in retirement on his farm near Leesburg, Virginia. Truman said, in effect, I need a new man to run CIA. Do you have any ideas? Marshall said he "would think about it." As it turned out, Marshall did not have the chance to make a recommendation until mid-September. In the interim, Truman was to pay little attention to the CIA.

Not Enough Troops

For the moment Truman and his advisers had more pressing problems than intelligence. On July 9 MacArthur admitted in a cable to Washington that four divisions would not be enough to stop the North Koreans.[4] He asked for dispatch of an additional four divisions "without delay, and by every means of transportation available." The cable surprised the JCS, for only two days previously MacArthur had suggested four divisions would be sufficient; now he was doubling his demand. The JCS could not escape the basic strategical arithmetic: If MacArthur were given everything he wanted, the entire U.S. Army would be fighting in Korea, with not a single soldier left to defend Western Europe or the American continent. The rush to judgment of late June was appearing a more dubious decision all the while, and at least one of the chiefs, General Collins of the army, wished he had spoken more strongly against intervention.

But the JCS would have to live with the decision. MacArthur depicted his plight in terms so grave that the chiefs felt they had no choice but to send him any men who could be found and as rapidly as they could be airlifted to Korea.

The first act was to strip the General Reserve (the last-resort force retained in the U.S. for military emergency, the chief unit being the elite 101st Airborne Division) of the skilled officers and noncommissioned officers who normally would be training new recruits, reservists, and draftees.[5] These men are what the military calls cadre, soldiers who can impart their experience to newcomers and prepare them for combat. In the space of a single month, from June 25 to July 25, the General Reserve strength dropped from 140,000 men to 90,000. Even this figure is misleading. Of the 90,000 men left in the Strategic Reserve, 15,000 were required for the basic maintenance and clerical work that kept the army functioning. So the men who went to MacArthur meant a drain of about half the combat and support troops in the General Reserve.

The only alternative to domestic defenselessness was resumption of the draft. By coincidence, the Selective Service Act had expired on June 14, less than two weeks before hostilities began. When war erupted, Congress quickly rushed through a one-year extension of the act, thereby providing a statutory basis for conscription.

Congress at the same time gave Truman something he did not want: the authority to call to active duty both individuals and units of the National Guard. Truman's reluctance to use the guard was partly political. In the words of military analyst Colonel Roy K. Flint, "Federalizing the National Guard was a politically sensitive act. Guard units belonged to the states and their governors; they were primarily intended for internal security and for general mobilization, not partial mobilization."

Congress, however, favored federalizing the National Guard over increasing the size of the standing army, for fear of being stuck with a large military force when peace came. But the North Korean gains made these arguments academic; on July 20 Defense Secretary Louis Johnson ordered mobilization of four National Guard divisions and two regimental combat teams.*

The swiftest manpower gains, however, came from the draft. Although draft boards had not called anyone to active duty for some eighteen months, they had continued to register young men when they reached their eighteenth birthday. Now came the manpower calls from the Defense Department: 50,000 men for the September levy; the same number in October; 70,000 in November. The Marine Corps called up some 47,000 officers and men; the navy, 39,000. To free men for combat, the Defense Department hired 230,000 civilians for jobs that had been performed by uniformed servicemen.

Although the mass of the American public supported the Korean intervention—some two-thirds, according to a Gallup Poll in August— the average youth did not spring to the colors.[6] As Major General Lewis B. Hershey, the selective service director, succinctly put it, "Everyone wants out; no one wants in." Some of the loudest complaints came from guardsmen and reservists—many husbands and fathers among them— who had fought in the Second World War. Why, they asked, should they fight instead of younger men?

One answer was that they had enjoyed the pay and other benefits of reserve and guard service and the prospect of comfortable retirement

---

*The 28th Division of Pennsylvania, the 43rd of Rhode Island, the 45th of Oklahoma, and the 40th of California; the regimental combat teams came from Tennessee and South Dakota. The guard units added some 95,000 men to the army the first year of the war.

once they completed their terms. Many considered reserve "duty" a weekend lark. One unsympathetic congressman stated, "They drew the government's money for years to play at being soldiers. What the hell do they think Uncle Sam was financing—some kind of glorified boy scout camp for adults?"

Younger men did their own squirming to avoid the draft. Some enlisted in reserve and guard units, gambling that they would not be among those mobilized. Others made sudden midsummer decisions to enroll in college, knowing that most draft boards would not interrupt their studies.

Truman, however, realized that the military needed more than a few handfuls of conscripts and nationalized reservists; given the uncertainties of what the United States might have to face in coming months, the nation had to go on a war footing. On July 19 he sent a staggering message to the Congress. He wanted an emergency $10 billion defense appropriation (the entire fiscal 1951 budget, approved on July 1, had been for only $4 billion more). He wanted removal of the statutory limit of 2,005,882 on military manpower. He wanted authority to increase military and economic aid to troubled allies, to impose a broad range of economic and procurement programs, to raise taxes to finance defense spending, to give the government tacit control over strategic industries.

Truman's message caught Congress on the high tide of public support of the war, and even Republicans stood and cheered as the congressional clerks read the message. *Time* noted: "Republicans were tripping over Democrats in their eagerness to give President Truman what he thought he needed to win in Korea and prepare for the next Korea, whenever or wherever it might turn out to be."[7] Within days Truman received even more than he requested: $11 billion. The Pentagon was authorized to raise a force of 3.2 million men and women. Freshman Senator Lyndon Johnson of Texas summarized the national mood in a bellowing floor speech. Korea, he cried, would go down in history "as a slaughterhouse for democracy or as a graveyard for aggression." A colleague, Owen Brewster of Maine, would permit MacArthur to use the atomic bomb at his discretion. In the end, Truman received economic powers—to impose rationing and credit restrictions, to direct allocations of strategic materials, to control prices and wages, among others—equal to those wielded by President Roosevelt during the Second World War.

America in the space of a month had begun to correct the military neglect of five years. The machinery that won the Second World War might be rusty. But by late summer it had stirred into motion. MacArthur had bought the time required; now an army was on its way to him.

A Visit to MacArthur

Now that they had decided to put the great bulk of the U.S. Army under MacArthur's command, Truman and the Joint Chiefs of Staff decided in mid-July they needed more information before trying to satisfy an apparently insatiable appetite for men and equipment.[8] So Generals Collins and Vandenberg, accompanied by staff officers, flew to Japan and met with MacArthur, General Walton Walker, and various subordinates.

MacArthur impressed Collins as "cool and poised." As usual, MacArthur paced the floor when speaking. "He always gave me the impression of addressing not just his immediate listeners but a larger audience unseen," Collins noted.

By now—they met on July 13—MacArthur no longer considered the North Korean Army disorganized and ill-trained Oriental rabble. To the contrary, the North Korea soldier was a "tough opponent, well-led," who combined the infiltration expertise of the Japanese with the Russian tank tactics of the Second World War. The North Koreans could maneuver, march, and attack at night with cohesion, which even MacArthur admitted he "has never been able to do." The North Koreans handled their tanks with an effectiveness approximating the "standard in the Soviet army."

MacArthur had an excuse for the failure of Far East Command intelligence in its forecasts of both North Korean intentions and South Korean combat capabilities. The North Koreans deceived him by splitting their force into two components. The first consisted of local border patrols similar to those of South Korea. To the rear, "with the utmost secrecy," the North Koreans organized an offensive field force.

What he had done thus far, MacArthur continued, was a "desperate rear guard action . . . throwing everything in Japan into the fight." He knew the troops committed were "tailored for occupation duty, and not combat," but he put them into combat nonetheless with "maximum rapidity." So, too, with the air force, even directing heavy bombers to support the infantry "in violation of the norm."

MacArthur next turned to his long-range strategy. He wanted troops, and in a hurry. The degree of failure or delay in achieving success "will be in direct proportion to the degree of rapidity with which the U.S. sends reinforcements." The maximum commitment of troops from Japan "will have been made in August—if the U.S. picks up from there, there will be no question of the results."

He then added another of the on-the-other-hand alternatives that so infuriated members of the JCS in coming months. If he did not receive "full . . . support . . . the results will vary in direct proportion to the support received." If MacArthur were giving advice, it would be:

> In this matter, time is of the essence. The rapidity with which you can move will measure the strength of your stroke. Admittedly, we are playing a poor hand here, but long experience has shown . . . that it is how you play your poor hands rather than your good ones which counts in the long run.

MacArthur would "grab every ship on the Pacific, would pour the support into the Far East." He would not "start modestly," but rather "would make the complete effort at the beginning." As MacArthur said: "Business as usual—to hell with that concept."

In his monologue he also expressed an intention to make a quantum jump beyond his directive from Truman and the United Nations—that is, to repel the North Korean invaders and to restore peace to South Korea. According to notes of the conference: "He hopes to destroy North Korea, to block off the hope of relief from Manchuria or China —that the enemy will try to reinforce he is sure, but he is equally sure that it can be prevented with medium bomber effort.* He is convinced that the Soviets will not go to war at this time although he expects that the maximum underground effort will be made."

MacArthur recognized U.S. obligations elsewhere in the world. But he cited his "belief that success here will slow the Commy down on other fronts." He used the analogy of a metropolis of four districts, of which Number One was the most important and Number Four the least. "Should a fire in Number Four not be stamped out because you are saving your fire equipment for Number One, you may find the fire out of control by the time your equipment is sent to Number One." (The Washington visitors needed no annotation for the analogy: The Far East was Number Four; the European theater, Number One.)

His monologue completed, MacArthur answered questions. General Vandenberg, the air force chief of staff, wondered about the probability of Chinese Communists' getting into the war. "Do you visualize cutting them off at the North Korean border or a further U.S. advance into Manchuria?"

"I would cut them off in North Korea," MacArthur replied. "In Korea I would visualize a cul-de-sac. The only passages leading from Manchuria and Vladivostok have many tunnels and bridges. I see here a unique use for the atomic bomb to strike a blow, which would require a six months' repair job.

"Sweeten up my B-29 force—we'll give them back—perhaps by a rotational feature, and we can isolate the Korean peninsula."

General Collins asked when MacArthur could move to the counter-offensive and how many troops would have to be left in Korea when he concluded operations.

---

*MacArthur's statement about a possible North Korean "hope of relief from Manchuria or China" indicates his awareness that the Soviets and Chinese Communists could enter the war—a possibility he rejected at a crucial juncture in the fall.

MacArthur said a categorical answer was impossible, although he felt he could "stabilize" once three divisions had arrived. He repeated his intention to annihilate the North Korean Army. Once the front stabilized, he said, it is

then my purpose to infiltrate to the North—to follow any North Korean withdrawal. We will need reinforcements to undertake an amphibious operation.

I intend to destroy and not to drive back the North Korean forces. I may need to occupy all of North Korea. In the aftermath of operations, the problem is to compose and unite Korea (of course, this is purely speculative at this time).

Once again MacArthur's statement went far beyond the authorization given him by Truman and the UN Security Council. Nonetheless, neither General Collins nor General Vandenberg challenged him. Upon return to Washington they told Truman they agreed with MacArthur that the Pusan bridgehead could be held but urged "prompt reinforcements."

In the meanwhile, however, the U.S. Army endured some of the worst defeats of its long history.

Death of a U.S. Battalion

Of the many disasters that befell the U.S. Army in July 1950, perhaps the cruelest of all blows fell upon the 3rd Battalion of the 29th Infantry Regiment, the destruction of which was stomach-turning evidence of the disaster inherent in sending untrained, ill-armed soldiers into combat.[9] The "regiment," on garrison duty in Okinawa, more properly should have been called a battalion, for it had only about one-half its authorized strength of 1,200 men. In any event, the unit was alerted in mid-July for movement to Japan, with the promise of six weeks' training before being sent to Korea.

The regiment certainly needed some preparation. Its men had spent minimal time in field training; some knew the army's basic M-1 rifle by hearsay only. As garrison troops they performed clerical and routine security chores, and no one of authority in the Far East Command gave any thought—much less priority—to the needs of a few hundred troops on an occupied island.

MacArthur's sudden demand for troops—*any* troops—brought the 29th Regiment priority attention. Midday on July 20 a transport ship arrived on Okinawa, carrying 400 untrained recruits for assignment to the regiment. These men were permitted to carry only toilet articles from the ship. They were marched, in uneven ranks, to supply depots and arbitrarily assigned to the regiment's only two battalions, the 1st and the 3rd. Supply officers issued them weapons and field equipment, and within a few hours they were back aboard the transport ships and bound for Korea—not training areas in Japan, as had been promised.

Officers entered sharp protests. Major Tony J. Raibl, executive officer of the 3rd Battalion, told Eighth Army superiors many of the men had completed only eight weeks of basic training; few of them had the skills that would enable them to go into combat. All he could wheedle from Colonel Allan D. MacLean, the EUSAK assistant G-3, was the promise of three days' intensive training around Pusan before battle.

The promise was no sooner given than broken. The troops arrived at Pusan on July 24 and were immediately ordered to proceed to Chinju, the heart of the combat zone. Apparently reflecting pressures being put on him by General Walton Walker—who in turn was hearing hurry-up demands from MacArthur—MacLean was in no mood to entertain misgivings from the regiment's officers. So neither the promised six weeks nor three days of training materialized. Instead, the two battalions were dumped at the front lines, with rifles and mortars that had not been test-fired and with .50 caliber machine guns still coated with the heavy grease Cosmoline.

Through cable traffic from Tokyo, the Joint Chiefs of Staff knew what was happening, yet did nothing to halt a troop movement which gave every sign of a disaster in the making.

On July 26, a few hours after coming onto the line, the 3rd Battalion walked into a North Korean ambush near Hadong. Machine guns emplaced on either side of a deep draw swept the American column. Officers frantically tried to call in air strikes from American planes visible overhead; the radios would not work, and the planes flew off, oblivious to the tragedy below. American infantrymen tried to flee across a deep twenty-foot-wide stream, shedding combat boots, clothing, even their weapons as they tried to swim. North Korean soldiers rushed to the banks and methodically shot down Americans by the score. In the words of one survivor, "They hunted us down like they were shooting rabbits fleeing a brush fire."

The 3rd Battalion had gone into battle with some 757 men on its rolls. When American troops retook the Hadong area two months later, graves registration teams found the bodies of 313 slain Americans, most along the rivers and in the rice paddies. A North Korea POW reported that his comrades took about 100 more Americans captive.

MacArthur had told the JCS, in effect, that he intended to buy time —and space—with blood and bodies. In this instance, he spent the cruelest blood available, that of inexperienced men thrust into combat with weapons still gummed with Cosmoline and without the slightest cohesion as a military unit. But the Hadong massacre, which cost more than 300 American lives, was so insignificant in the grand scale of the war that MacArthur did not even mention it in his memoirs. Thus did the United States pay part of the price for the military budget cutting of the late 1940's.

A Bare Military Cupboard

The same lack of military readiness tormented officers responsible for preparing the American divisions in Japan for shipment to Korea. The units lacked heavy weapons, ammunition, mortar tubes and tripods, trip flares, hand grenades, even cleaning rods for rifles. The 1st Battalion of the 35th Infantry Regiment, to cite a not-untypical unit, had only one recoilless rifle, the basic antitank weapon supplied to foot soldiers; it had not a single spare machine-gun barrel, although these tended to burn out quickly during heavy fighting. Most of the M-1 rifles and M-2 carbines carried by soldiers in the battalion were not combat-serviceable.

The vehicle situation was even worse. All dated to at least the Second World War. Some trucks were so ramshackle they had to be towed to transport ships; they would not start on their own. Radiators were clogged; run a motor a few moments, and it would overheat and explode. Worn tires and inner tubes would not long survive the rough Korean roads. Although Korean maps showed "highways" linking major cities, the description was overly generous. Korean roads were designed for oxcarts, not modern military equipment. Even the main highway connecting Pusan and Seoul—which would have to be used in any American attempt to retake the capital—was an unpaved, rock-strewn, chuck-holed lane with steep shoulders on either side.

General Walton Walker's troops were not in much better shape than the Korean roads. No men had been drafted the past eighteen months, and with the postwar economy booming the army had been forced to take whatever recruits it could find, relying on shorter enlistment terms and lower mental and physical standards. When the Korean War began, 43 percent of the army enlisted men in the Far Eastern Command were rated in Class IV or V, lowest on the Army General Qualification Tests —the stumbling dullards drill sergeants called yo-yos or bolos. Although Walker had made sincere efforts to toughen soldiers grown soft during occupation duty, by July 1950 there had been no field exercises larger than battalion size. Thus regiments and divisions went into combat without any training in how to coordinate their activities in the field.

The army's official explanations were many: rapid turnovers of officers and men in a peacetime army; lack of space for field maneuvers in congested Japan, the medieval road system of which would collapse if the army started moving around tanks and other heavy vehicles; a feeling among commanders and troops alike that the atomic bomb made infantrymen obsolete—America had the ultimate weapon, so why bother to go into the field to shoot a rifle on a rainy day?

The attitudes of these fighting men were not encouraging either. A veteran Associated Press correspondent serving in Japan, O. H. P. King, was appalled when he interviewed the first troops of the 24th Division to arrive in Korea. The younger GIs almost to a man admitted they cared more about the fleshpots and comforts of Japan than war in Korea. One of these youngsters told King:

> I just want to get back to Japan to my little Sasebo Sadie. I have been shacked up there now for more than two years with the prettiest little moose* you ever did see. I got a place to live that beats the dump I lived in for fifteen years in Enid, Oklahoma. I get my meals cooked, my washing done, my socks mended, my orders obeyed like I was MacArthur myself, with no back talk, and all of everything a fellow wants, you know, and it all comes to $37 a month. I never had it so good.[10]

Until, of course, the young Oklahoman found himself, ill-trained and out of shape, engaged in battle with an enemy less obsessed with creature comfort.

A good deal of the blame for the poor training must be assigned to General MacArthur. In his memoirs MacArthur was to decry the State Department for blocking development of a strong South Korean Army, yet he remained silent about the ragtag quality of the American troops in Japan (which he referred to as "my forces"). For all his attention to diplomatic and political detail, his constant carping about how the State Department and an unspecified force called "Washington" discomfited his life, and his preoccupation with the strength of such distant armies as Chiang Kai-shek's Nationalist Chinese, MacArthur never stirred himself to perform the military commander's fundamental duty of checking the status of his troops. For this omission, thousands of young Americans—undirected innocents who deserved better of the professional officers charged with their training—were to pay dearly on the battlefields of Korea.

Relman Morin of the Associated Press early in the war met hospital planes flying into Japan with American wounded.

> A Negro infantryman lay in the stretcher, softly humming. A bearded GI, both legs in splints, called gruffly for water. A slight blond boy, unnaturally pale, stared at nothing, whispering: "He was covered with

*A corruption of the Japanese word for woman, moose was the name American soldiers commonly gave their girl friends.

worms. He was just laying there, all covered with worms. Oh, Jesus, the worms were—."[11]

In Tokyo, Morin noted, there was much talk about the occupation troops being "blooded" in combat, the military term that means they were receiving battle experience. But as Morin wrote, "The word is used more often by officers at headquarters than men in the field."

The Far Eastern Command scratched in every conceivable corner for men and equipment. Clerks, cooks, motor pool mechanics, chaplains' assistants, aides to officers—all were rousted from their jobs, given rifles and field equipment, and marched away to planes and ships. MacArthur also ordered a general scouring of stockades, the prisoners of which were "restored" to service and sent away to battle. Soldiers awaiting trial were released in many instances because the witnesses against them had suddenly gone to war. The Department of the Army, to speed things along, authorized the EUSAK provost marshal to release prisoners at his discretion without following the formalities prescribed by army regulations. The search, formally Operation Flushout, produced a total of 2,430 soldiers for Korea.

Outfitting the Eighth Army for transport into war proved not unlike assembling a checklist for a prolonged family picnic.[12] Some obscure units appeared on the transport lists: the 95th Veterinary Food Inspection Detachment, the 55th Engineer Treadway Bridge Company, the 8080th Army Postal Unit, the 56th Army Band, each to make its own contribution to the war. The supply requirements were as varied. The EUSAK finance section asked that fifteen field safes be procured for its 179th Finance Disbursing Section "so that Major Clynes could use them for transporting his money" (to pay troops). The Graves Registration Service wanted four fingerprint kits and 100 locks. The quartermaster section wanted 25 locks for its warehouse; the Signal Corps, 44.4 tons of dry batteries.

A message from units already in the field sought to ensure that creature comforts were not ignored in the scurrying: "Quartermaster requires 25,000 cases of beer for shipment to Korea, 10,000 cases to be shipped immediately," a requirement based on one man, one can per day. (Tokyo supply officers shopped around and found a brewery that could "supply up to 100,000 cases on short notice, price $2.15 per case.") Special Services, the military's entertainment arm, in one day packed seven crates of "expendable reading materials" for shipment to Korea, each containing a "kit" of twenty-five paperbound books, twenty-two kits of fifty magazines each, and ten kits of twenty-five phonograph records. In Tokyo a supply officer arranged to buy 1 million bags of Korea crackers, each weighing 250 grams. And the quartermaster officers, after consultation with EUSAK's medical section, concluded that one teaspoon of calcium hypochlorite was sufficient to chlorinate each 300-pound block of ice produced at a portable ice-making facility to be set up at Taegu.

Ill-prepared though it was for war, the U.S. Army now began moving with the crushing efficiency of a trained bureaucracy. The question was whether America's overwhelming material superiority could be brought into play before South Korea totally collapsed.

Some Military Arrogance

In Pusan, meanwhile, callous disregard of ROK sensitivities by American military commanders brought relations with President Rhee to the breaking point.[13] The old man's pride was hurt; he had been forced to surrender tacit control of his country to the Americans, and he lived in a small house in Pusan, ignored now even by his own people. But as a gesture, Rhee wished to send cables to the UN members that had promised help in the war. For convenience, he wanted the messages to be routed through his embassy in Washington. However, the U.S. Army had taken control of all Korean telegraph and cable facilities, even the commercial cable between Pusan and Tokyo. Messages could be sent only with army permission.

Rhee called Harold Noble of the American embassy to his makeshift office and explained his idea. Would Noble be so kind as to send the cable to the ROK embassy in Washington via the army facilities?

Noble thought the request proper, and he took the messages to the 24th Division signal office. The sergeant told him that the messages would be dispatched as soon as military traffic lessened. The next day Noble checked to ensure that the messages had gone out as promised. They had not. The division's public information officer had killed them because some of Rhee's messages to other chiefs of state criticized the Soviet Union, "contrary to command policy and the express orders of the 24th Division."

Noble bit his lip and worked his way through the army chain of command. The chief of staff was in the north at the battlefront. The G-2 repeated that the division had orders to say nothing in public statements about the Soviet Union.

Look, retorted Noble, this isn't a press release; this is a statement by the president of the Republic of Korea, and the statement is being issued in *his* name, not that of the United States Army.

The G-2 grunted. The 24th Division had its orders, and the 24th Division controlled the cables. If Rhee wished to issue inflammatory statements, he must find another way. A subordinate G-2 officer even pointedly asked Noble to show his credentials.

After two frustrating days of battle with the military bureaucracy Noble finally managed to put his case directly to General William Dean, an old friend. For God's sake, send the messages, Dean told the signal office.

This needless slight intensified Rhee's sporadic tendency to issue irrational statements about "going it alone" in the war without American support, comments which Ambassador Muccio managed to keep away from the press. The only calming influence over Rhee was his patient European-born wife, a woman with a keen sense of political reality. As Muccio recounted, he and Mrs. Rhee developed a "little procedural understanding." If she sensed that "he [Rhee] was about to do something that she thought was not advisable," she would telephone Muccio and suggest that he come in for a visit. She would say nothing of substance on the phone; the "call itself was a tip-off to me." So Muccio would then "find some excuse for dropping in on the old man. And if I sat there long enough, he'd come out with what he had in mind. She did this repeatedly during those very crucial days."

Muccio could sympathize with Rhee in the cable incident because of his own ongoing problems with the American military. Several times sentries at Eighth Army headquarters stopped his car when he drove up to the front entrance. Using this gate, they said, was a privilege reserved for colonels and higher-ranking officers. Even Muccio's credentials as ambassador did not satisfy certain of the guards.

Muccio had been around the military long enough to realize that shouting and stomping one's feet, especially by a civilian, have no effect upon uniformed sluggards. So he fashioned a device calculated to make the proper impression upon the slowest of military minds. The standard on one front bumper of his auto flew the American flag; on the opposite he displayed a blue flag with forty-eight white stars, or forty-five more than General Walker.

The puzzled Harold Noble asked Muccio just how many stars he was entitled to fly as an ambassador. "Forty-eight," replied Muccio. "I represent the whole United States." The sentries gave him no more trouble.

But Muccio was powerless to do anything about the disdain the American military felt toward the ROK Army. Although the ROKs held half the battle line, they had trouble getting anything approaching a fair share of the equipment shipped over from Japan. EUSAK quartermasters wanted to accumulate supplies for their own units, and they ignored the Koreans. Flouting direct orders of General Walker, underequipped Americans in the rear areas hijacked supplies intended for the ROKs. EUSAK's aloofness extended even to American military advisers, whose officers lost not only their quarters but also their mess to the newcomers.

To Muccio's distress the newly arrived Americans made no attempt to conceal their contempt for the ROKs. Major General Hobart R. Gay, commanding general of the 1st Cavalry Division, told a press conference he did not intend to take the ROK Army into consideration "at all" in deciding how to deploy his troops. (A few days later, when a ROK unit saved his right flank from a severe beating, he reconsidered.) Gay also forced Korean farmers out of his division area, oblivious to the suffering this caused them and their families. He told the Korean national police to leave the area, thus undermining his own security. (Walker forced him to rescind this absurd order.) The Americans were so chary of telling the Koreans anything of significance that the ROK foreign minister was forced to attend press briefings to find out what was happening in the war.

The South Koreans could do nothing about the American arrogance for the moment. But a year later, when they had their opportunity for vengeance during a crucial period of peace negotiations, the ROKs repaid the Americans many times over for their unkindness.

Water Through a Fishnet

Throughout July General William Dean threw battalion after battalion into the path of the advancing North Koreans, a piecemeal commitment that slowed but never really stopped the invaders. The war was a series of skirmishes large and small, with the American forces being steadily pushed southward, under conditions approaching chaos. "Stopping the gooks," Dean said at one point, "is like trying to keep water from coming through a fishnet."

But in instance after instance what the U.S. Army lacked in equipment and strength was overcome by heroism by individual officers and enlisted men. In a confused engagement at the squalid little hamlet of Chonan, Colonel Robert R. Martin, the commander of the 34th Infantry Regiment, found himself the only man present who knew how to fire a 2.36-inch rocket launcher. A convoy of tanks was rumbling into the city. Martin had a sergeant, Jerry C. Christensen, load the bazooka. Then Martin stepped out of a hut and aimed the rocket at a tank at point-blank range. Both fired simultaneously. The North Korean shell cut Martin's body in half. The concussion caused one of Christensen's eyes to pop from its socket. Painfully, bloodily, he worked it back into place, his consolation being the sight of the North Korean tank in flames. (Christensen was captured later that day; he died of his wound in a POW camp in December.)

The 21st Infantry Regiment—2,000-odd men fighting against two

North Korean divisions of 17,000 men augmented by tanks—was told by Dean to "fight like hell" to hold the city of Chochiwon, just north of Taejon. Air support helped the first day. Then came a night and day of heavy fog that made enemy targets invisible from the air. The regiment's 3rd Battalion, commanded by Lieutenant Colonel Carl C. Jensen, caught the brunt of a tightly coordinated attack: tanks that crossed a minefield with impunity because the antiquated American mines did not detonate; skillfully aimed mortar barrages that destroyed the battalion command post, communications center, and ammunition dump the first few minutes of the fighting; and infantrymen who crept past the American lines under cover of the dense fog. But courage coexisted with panic. Private Paul R. Spear was among men pinned down by a machine gun firing at his company's command post. Spear snatched up a pistol, the only weapon he could find, and charged the gun emplacement alone. His pistol was empty by the time he reached his goal, but he barged in anyway, swinging the handgun as a club. The ferocity of his attack routed the gunners. (The gravely wounded Spear was to receive a Distinguished Service Cross.)

The raw power of the North Korean attack—the combination of tanks and superior firepower—unnerved many of the battalion's soldiers. When the order to withdraw finally came, they ignored it. One officer talked to a group of uninjured men huddled by the side of a road. They refused to move. One noncom said, "Lieutenant, you will have to go on. I'm too beat up. They'll just have to take me." Altogether the 3rd Battalion lost about 60 percent of its 800-odd men during the engagement. Of those who made their way to the rear, 90 percent had lost their rifles, their ammunition, their canteens; one hapless soldier appeared with neither helmet nor shoes.

But to Dean, the important point is that a relative handful of American soldiers had slowed the advance of two crack North Korean divisions for three days, giving General MacArthur the time he so desperately needed.

General Dean Is Captured

Nonetheless, the overall tide of battle definitely favored the North Koreans, and by the night of July 19 the front was so fluid around Taejon —the linchpin of the UN defensive line—that General Dean confessed, "I could not even be certain we still held a solid line northwest of the city, and very few important command decisions were made at that time." A career sergeant could have functioned in his stead during those confused days, Dean said. The general, away from his own headquarters, crept into an abandoned house with aides and fell into fretful sleep, inhaling the "odors which no one ever escapes in Korea, of rice-paddy muck and mud walls, fertilizer and filth," now mixed with the acrid afterodor of cordite from artillery shells.

He awoke before dawn to the crack of small-arms fire at close range.[14] Enemy tanks were entering the city, and infiltrators and turncoats crouched in shattered houses and fired at ROK and American troops and fleeing refugees. The doom of Taejon was evident to everyone—to the ROKs, to the lost and weary American soldiers straggling through the town, men who, Dean noted, "less than a month before had been fat and happy in occupation billets, complete with Japanese girl friends, plenty of beer, and servants to shine their shoes."

Lacking any communications between units, the 34th Infantry command structure collapsed. No officer knew the location of other American forces; no one could direct the few HEAT antitank weapons against the North Korean tanks roaming the city. Any contacts were happenstance and at the North Koreans' choosing. In one especially grisly episode North Korean tanks roared into a compound manned only by American service troops—truck drivers, mechanics, cooks, and clerks. With savage cannon fire the tanks razed the compound, killing many of the 150 men there and destroying much of their equipment. Not until the tanks had rumbled away for attacks elsewhere did someone find a 3.5-inch bazooka. The only targets seen were snipers lurking in nearby houses. One of the first bazooka rounds ignited a house. The fire spread to other thatched-roof houses, and soon much of Taejon was burning.

Dean, sick at heart, at this point saw no poetic beauty in the phrase "fight and fall back." He and his troops had endured twenty wearying and bloody days, and time and again he had had to tell soldiers when to withdraw and when to turn and fight again. "Any infantry officer must at times be ruthless," he wrote later in his memoirs of the war. "Part of the job is to send men into places from which you know they are not likely to come out again. This is never easy, but it's an especially soul-searing business when the only thing you can buy with other men's lives is a little more time."

At six-thirty in the morning Dean found himself in a situation in which he felt there was "no general officer's duty to be done." The 34th Infantry Regiment headquarters had lost contact with two of its leading battalions; it did not know the location of its flanks or much about the war in general. Dean brought the battle down to a personal, primitive level. He could do nothing about the overall war, but "perhaps we could do something about a couple of tanks." He, an aide, and a Korean interpreter set out to go tank hunting.

Even this low-level mission failed. Dean commandeered a truck mounting a 75 mm recoilless rifle and directed it to fire at two tanks stalled at an intersection. None of the four or five shots fired hit. Later that morning Dean's *ad hoc* antitank group had one round of bazooka ammunition remaining. The bazookaman, nervous, missed at a range of 100 yards. The tank turned and rumbled right past Dean and party, at a distance of 20 yards. Infuriated, General Dean stood in the street and fired at the tank with the only weapon he had: a .45 caliber pistol. He did not think he could harm the tank; "it was plain rage and frustration—just Dean losing his temper," he said later.

The third encounter was more successful, although the price included a bone-chilling scare for Dean. This time his party traced a sole tank to an intersection. They crept through vacant stores and houses and across a courtyard. Dean and the bazookaman chinned themselves up to a window ledge overlooking the street where the tank was parked.

The general cautiously peered around the corner of the window—"directly into the muzzle of the tank's cannon, no more than a dozen feet away. I could have spat down the barrel." Three bazooka shots later, the tank was destroyed.*

Dean remained on the streets, hunting tanks, from dawn to late afternoon. The "larger issue," when he finally returned to his chaotic headquarters, was conducting an organized withdrawal from Taejon. The remnants of the 34th Regiment, with light tank escort, set out for the south in two columns, Dean in a jeep in the last contingent.

The lead column ran into a strong enemy ambush before it reached the southern limits of the city. Trucks caught fire and blocked the narrow streets; infantrymen tried to fight back Communist soldiers firing down from the rooftops.

Through this shot-torn melee raced the jeep carrying Dean, "careening between the stalled trucks . . . a solid line of fire, an inferno that seared us in spite of our speed." The driver missed a turn. But with rifle fire pouring down from buildings on both sides of the street, turning around was out of the question. They would press on, in hopes of finding an alternate, safer route.

The next hours became even more hectic. Dean began picking up walking wounded in his jeep. He paused at an overturned truck. The driver was dead, and one of the two men trapped underneath told the general, "We might as well surrender. There isn't any use in this." Dean squatted to talk with them. The silhouette of a Communist sniper was suddenly visible on a ridge. Dean snatched up an M-1 and fired. The sniper vanished.

Dean then told drivers of his jeep and an escort vehicle to continue

---

*While superiors later recognized Dean's heroism in personally leading his men against the feared T-34 tanks, General Lawton Collins, the army chief of staff, commented, "The personal involvement of a senior commander in the combat of small units or in one small segment of an action tends to divert his mind from larger issues."

south; he stayed by the truck and persuaded the two "cowering" men to join him. He next caught a ride on an artillery half-track "so crammed with men that we couldn't get in—we just got on, hanging by precarious toe- and hand-holds."

Another ambush, and everyone jumped from the truck and tumbled into a roadside ditch for protection. They survived and talked about a route south, finally deciding to ford the Kum River, cross over steep ridges of the mountains on the other side, and make their way south.

Abandoning the jeep, they walked in loose, sandy soil, carrying a gravely wounded man. The night was pitch-dark, yet they tried to move in silence to avoid alerting the North Koreans. The wounded man became delirious; he drank all the available water and cried out for more.

During a rest stop Dean thought he heard water running off to the side of the ridge on which they were walking. He started in that direction, but the slope was so steep he broke into a run and could not stop. He plunged forward and fell.

Dean awoke sometime later in agony. His shoulder was broken; his head was gashed; "my abdomen where I'd had an operation a year before hurt fearfully." Further, the party with which he had been traveling was gone. Dean lapsed into unconsciousness; he awoke to see a North Korean patrol passing by only a few yards away, oblivious to him. At dawn he started trying to make his way south. He met up with another straggler, Lieutenant Stanley Tabor, and they walked together for one, two, four days—Dean, in his pain, lost track of time—and finally took shelter with a South Korean family. Dean offered the family 1 million won (about $110) to lead them to Taegu. Instead, the people brought in a North Korean patrol.

Dean and Tabor heard the patrol, bolted out the door into a rice paddy, and hid. Dean, flat on his belly in the mud, used his elbows to crawl to a dike and scrambled across it to another rice field. Tabor was not with him. (Tabor was apparently caught several days later. Having been brought into a POW camp suffering from malnutrition, he died within weeks.)

For the next thirty-five days Dean wandered the hills of South Korea, sometimes begging food from civilians, more often refused and reported to the North Koreans; he escaped capture half a dozen times through sheer bluff.

His luck ran out on August 25. Two men offered to help him through the lines. Instead, they turned him into the North Koreans for a bounty of $5 each.

Dean was to be held as a prisoner for three years. For his bravery both before and after capture, he was awarded the Medal of Honor after his release in September 1953. But the loss of his key battlefield commander was only one of the problems besetting General Walton Walker's Eighth Army as the war entered its second month.

The Chinese Problem

In addition to the continuing battlefield rout, President Truman had to deal with two other major related problems the first week of the war: a controversy over policy toward Nationalist China, stirred by General MacArthur, and a nasty squabble that ended with the firing of Defense Secretary Louis Johnson. The former proved the most significant, for it marked the first round of a months-long struggle between the general and his superiors in Washington.

Here some background is in order. After Chiang Kai-shek fled the mainland for Formosa, the Truman administration tried to keep a comfortable distance from his Nationalist government. The U.S. had given Chiang billions of dollars in military and economic aid during the 1940's, to no avail; Dean Acheson told *Time* off the record in December 1949, "What we must do now is shake loose from the Chinese Nationalists. It will be harder to make that necessary break if we go to Formosa" (i.e., continue support of Chiang).[15] At a National Security Council meeting on December 29, 1949, Truman decided to give no further material aid to Formosa and to maintain a "hands-off" attitude should the Communists try to seize the island.

The decision disturbed MacArthur, for several reasons. He saw Formosa as necessary to defense of Japan, a lesson he had learned during the Pacific war; he admired Chiang; and he did not wish to see the Communists conquer any more real estate in Asia. Through comments to visitors, MacArthur let it be known that he considered Formosa "an unsinkable aircraft carrier" that the U.S. could ill afford to lose.[16]

At the outset of the Korean War, Truman revised Formosan policy, but on a cautious double track. The June 28 directive to MacArthur authorizing the use of force in Korea also called for the Seventh Fleet to protect Formosa against a Communist invasion. But the same order told the fleet to prevent Chiang from attacking the mainland. Militarily the order meant little, for the Seventh Fleet the summer of 1950 consisted of one carrier, one heavy cruiser, one light cruiser, and twelve destroyers—a "fleet" responsible for all of East Asia. As Acheson was to admit in Senate hearings the following May, given its duties in the Korean War, the fleet could not have stopped the Chinese Communists from taking Formosa.

But the deployment of a shadow force had symbolic significance. The diplomatic historian Foster Rhea Dulles felt Truman's drawing of a defensive line around Formosa was a necessary sop to Republicans who had long advocated such a shield; Dulles called the decision "a key factor in winning the bipartisan support necessary" for intervention in Korea.[17] The Communist Chinese, however, felt the move to Formosa "was a . . . direct threat" to their safety, according to K. M. Panikkar, the Indian ambassador in Peking.[18]

MacArthur, however, thought Truman's order gave a "tremendous advantage" to the Chinese Communists, who no longer had to tie down armies opposite Formosa to prevent an invasion by Chiang.[19] MacArthur would rather keep the Chinese Communists off-balance by not publicizing U.S. policy.

But MacArthur did support another Truman decision concerning Chiang. The first days of the war Chiang offered three divisions for use in Korea, an offer Truman politely refused. Truman wished to keep Formosa separate from the Korean War; he knew use of Nationalists would cause problems for the British, who retained their crown colony of Hong Kong only by Communist sufferance; finally, he did not think Chiang's troops would be of military value. MacArthur agreed with the latter point: Outfitting the Nationalists, and transporting them thousands of miles, would be costly and time-consuming, and there was no reason to think they would fight any better in Korea than they had in mainland China. Also, withdrawing 33,000 men—the number Chiang offered—would leave Formosa vulnerable to attack. And Truman tried to make plain that any interim actions concerning Formosa would not necessarily affect long-range policy. In a statement on July 19, the President said:

> The present military neutralization of Formosa is without prejudice to political questions affecting that island. Our desire is that Formosa not become embroiled in hostilities disturbing to the peace of the Pacific and that all questions affecting Formosa are to be settled by peaceful means as envisaged in the Charter of the United Nations.
>
> With peace reestablished, even the most complex political questions are susceptible of solution. In the presence of brutal and unprovoked aggression, however, some of these questions may have to be held in abeyance in the interest of the essential security of all.

Nonetheless, Truman remained wary that the Chinese Communists might strike at Formosa at any time (both the CIA and General Willoughby's G-2 section in Tokyo had been predicting an invasion for months). In late July intelligence reports stated some 200,000 Communist troops were massed opposite Formosa, enough to attack successfully despite the U.S. shield. On July 28 Secretary Johnson and the JCS proposed permitting Chiang to mine waters between Formosa and the mainland and to bomb the Communist troop concentrations. Acheson successfully argued down both ideas, calling them "out of the question."

Truman's ultimate decision was that a survey team be sent to Formosa to work out details of an enhanced military aid program.

On July 29 the JCS asked MacArthur's opinion of the "defensive measures" that might be taken for Formosa, mentioning, inexplicably, the mining and bombing operations vetoed at the NSC meeting two days earlier. The JCS also told MacArthur of the proposed survey team. MacArthur replied with a rousing endorsement of bombing and mining, saying they would end the "deep resentment" of many Nationalist officers toward the United States and end the "distinct military advantage" the strictures on Chiang gave to the enemy. He also announced he intended to go to Formosa personally on July 31 for a look at its defenses and to explain to Chiang personally why his troop offer was being refused. The JCS suggested MacArthur consider sending another senior officer, but the message concluded: "Please feel free to go, since the responsibility is yours." (According to General Courtney Whitney of MacArthur's staff, MacArthur saw a double meaning in this sentence: that the State Department, not the JCS, had reservations about making the trip and that the JCS were subtly telling him, "Go ahead.")

So MacArthur went as scheduled. Conspicuously absent from his entourage was William Sebald, the senior U.S. diplomat in Tokyo. MacArthur told Sebald he could not go because only military matters would be discussed and his presence would suggest "political implications."[20] (The suspicious Acheson thought this a transparent subterfuge to keep the State Department in the dark about the talks.)

The Chinese gave MacArthur a warm airport welcome. He bussed Madame Chiang and called her husband "my old comrade-in-arms of the last war." Whitney was "struck by the fact" that the two men had never met, despite their years of fighting common foes. But they talked as if they were old friends.

The record, unfortunately, is scanty as to the exact business MacArthur and Chiang discussed. They pored over maps and tramped along the beach, Chiang gesturing in the direction of the mainland. MacArthur did have to emphasize a bit of bad news: If Chiang tried to attack, the Seventh Fleet was under presidential order to stop him. Whitney wrote later that a prime result of the talks was that MacArthur received a "general feel" not only of the local military situation but also of mainland intelligence gathered by the Nationalists. The visit ended with a lavish banquet and the exchange of fulsome toasts.

From his Tokyo office the next day MacArthur expanded considerably upon Truman's earlier statement (which was deliberately terse) about U.S. intentions to protect Formosa against Communist attack. MacArthur artfully noted at the beginning that "this island, including the [offshore] Pescadores, is not under the present circumstances subject to military invasion." He continued that he and Chiang had discussed the "prompt and generous offer" of Nationalist troops for Korea but agreed their dispatch "might seriously jeopardize the defense of Formosa. Arrangements were completed for effective coordination between the American forces under my command and those of the Chinese Nationalists, the better to meet any attack which a hostile force might be foolish enough to attempt." MacArthur concluded with praise of Chiang: "His indomitable determination to resist Communist domination arouses my sincere admiration. His determination parallels the common interest and purpose of Americans, that all peoples in the Pacific shall be free—not slave."

Truman and Acheson sensed an underlying mischief in MacArthur's mission, especially when "background sources"* in Tokyo began offering elaborations. *Time* found one "reliable source" there who said with authority that MacArthur "believed" the Korean War would be useless unless the United States was willing to fight communism "wherever it arose in Asia,"[24] even if it meant backing Chiang, the British in Hong Kong, and the anti-Communists in Indochina, Siam, and Burma, and that "anything less than this firm, determined action would invite Communism to sweep over all of Asia." The NSC had decided on just such a course of action the previous April (except for support of Chiang's collapsed regime), but a casual reader would conclude Asia was another instance of the Truman administration's being "soft on Communism."

MacArthur professed "astonishment" at the turmoil, blaming it on his "habitual critics" in the UN and elsewhere "who advocated appeasement of the Soviet Union and Red China" and on "certain groups within the United States itself."[25] After listening to these criticisms for a few days, he issued a "conciliatory" statement that was in fact a vicious attack against those who questioned him. The Formosa visit, he said,

has been maliciously misrepresented to the public by those who invariably in the past have propagandized a policy of defeatism and appeasement in the Pacific. I hope the American people will not be misled by sly insinua-

*General Whitney was the "official leak" in MacArthur's headquarters. When he spoke, correspondents recognized that although they were hearing Whitney's voice, the words came directly from the general.

Press reaction—especially abroad—was that MacArthur unilaterally had decided to align the U.S. with Chiang in his continuing war with Communist China and that he was flouting administration policy. Truman commented, "The implication was—and quite a few of our newspapers said so—that MacArthur rejected my policy of neutralizing Formosa and that he favored a more aggressive method."[21] Even some steadfast supporters thought MacArthur had overreached. David Lawrence asked in a *U.S. News & World Report* editorial whether a "general disposed to brusqueness, independence and personal decisiveness is the best of diplomatic material."[22] Truman was even more irritated when MacArthur refused anything other than a *pro forma* report to William Sebald. When Sebald insisted that military agreements had a bearing on foreign policy, MacArthur airily replied, "Bill, I don't know what you're talking about."[23] He cited Truman's order to protect Formosa from attack and said he had sent a full report to the Defense Department. The apprehensive Sebald foresaw "a growing rift between the American authorities in Tokyo and Washington which, if uncorrected, could only lead to disaster."

tions, brash speculations and bold misstatements invariably attributed to anonymous sources, so insidiously fed them both nationally and internationally by persons 10,000 miles away from the actual events. . . .

MacArthur's statement, loaded with scare words and insinuation, was itself a propagandistic masterpiece—one impossible for the administration to answer without dismissing MacArthur.

MacArthur's sense of estrangement from Truman was deepened on August 5, when the JCS told him that Truman had rejected their proposals for defensive raids against the mainland. If the Nationalists attempted any such attacks, MacArthur should stop them. "No one other than the President . . . has the authority" to permit such raids, the message said. "The most vital national interest requires that no action of ours precipitates general war or gives excuse to others to do so."[26]

When MacArthur read this message, Whitney notes, he "might have been insulted had he not been so surprised."[27] The JCS had made the original recommendation on the raids, and he had concurred when asked for an opinion; he had not implied the recommendation would be carried out without the President's approval. The view of the MacArthur camp, as expressed by Whitney, was that the general "must be wary hereafter of giving an honest opinion, even on military matters, when it was requested by his superiors in Washington," for if he recommended any other course of action, he could be "accused of threatening to put his recommendations into actual practice." MacArthur's irritation showed in his reply: He said he fully understood the presidential determination "to protect the Communist mainland."

Averell Harriman's Mission

As Truman confided to his diary, the entire episode so disturbed him that he briefly considered dismissing MacArthur. But with the war at a critical stage, he decided to leave him in place. As an alternative, he dispatched Averell Harriman, the veteran and trusted diplomat and adviser, to Tokyo to talk with the general.[28] Harriman relates, "I asked the President what he wanted me to tell MacArthur. He said, 'Tell him two things. One, I'm going to do everything I can to give him what he wants in the way of support; and secondly, I want you to tell him that I don't want him to get us into a war with the Chinese Communists.'" Truman also wanted Harriman to ascertain exactly what MacArthur had promised Chiang.

Harriman flew to Tokyo on August 6 and spent some eight hours alone with MacArthur, in addition to their talks over meals.[29] He was perhaps the first visitor to MacArthur's table in more than a decade who did not approach the general in awe. A man of immense wealth and long diplomatic background, uncowed even during his wartime dealings with Joseph Stalin, Harriman commanded the presence that enabled him to speak with MacArthur as an equal—a polite equal, to be sure, but one who did not quake at asking probing questions. MacArthur had the judgment to recognize that he was not dealing with a run-of-the-mill presidential messenger, that Harriman's appearance demonstrated a presidential pique that should not be ignored.

On the surface, things went smoothly. MacArthur praised Truman's decision to intervene. He spoke at length about his strategy. The North Korean forces "must be destroyed as early as possible" lest the Russians and Chinese Communists decide to "greatly strengthen" their forces. Time "was of the essence, or grave difficulties, if not disaster, were ahead." He did not believe either the Chinese or the Russians wished to get into a general war, although both had a role in encouraging and equipping the North Koreans in their venture.

Then Harriman got down to serious business. He told the general that Truman "wanted me to tell him that he must not permit Chiang to be the cause of starting a war with the Chinese Communists on the mainland, the effect of which might drag us into a world war." MacArthur replied that he would, "as a soldier, obey any orders that he received from the President." He and Chiang had talked only about military matters; when Chiang attempted to talk political issues, he declined. Chiang had offered him command of the Chinese Nationalist troops; he said this was "not appropriate," although he was willing to give military advice if requested to do so.

Harriman found MacArthur's statements unconvincing:

> I did not feel that we came to a full agreement on the way we believed things should be handled on Formosa and with the Generalissimo. He accepted the President's position and will act accordingly, but without full conviction. He has a strange idea that we should back anybody who will fight Communism, even though he could not give an argument why the Generalissimo's fighting communists would be a contribution towards the effective dealing with the communists in China.

Harriman tried to point out the essential conflict between the United States and Chiang. The generalissimo "had only the burning ambition" to use Formosa as a stepping-stone back to the mainland. The United States wanted to work through the UN to establish an independent government on Formosa.

MacArthur countered with a proposal that was cold-blooded even when measured against the standards that Harriman had witnessed in Stalinist Russia. MacArthur recognized that Chiang could never retake the mainland. Yet he "thought it might be a good idea to let him land and get rid of him that way." Harriman listened to this proposal in silence.

One delicate feature of his mission Harriman chose to keep out of his written report. As he left for Tokyo, Truman had said to him, in effect, I want you to watch and listen to MacArthur carefully and let me know whether you think he is mentally and physically capable of continuing in his command. Harriman did so, although his conclusion is not a matter of record. One snippet of evidence suggests that he gave the President cause for alarm. A few days after Harriman's return Truman sent a trusted military physician and friend, Major General Frank Lowe, to Tokyo "to report on General MacArthur's physical condition and ability to withstand the tremendous stresses incident to his duty." Lowe reported MacArthur "hale and hearty," and the White House apparently let the matter drop.[30]

Truman "assumed . . . that General MacArthur would accept the Formosa policy laid down by his commander in chief."[31] After hearing Harriman's report, he told a press conference on August 10 that "General MacArthur and I are in perfect agreement, and have been ever since he has been in the job he is now. . . . I am satisfied with what he is doing." Although untrue, Truman's remarks were a signal to MacArthur that he was willing to forget the episode. Had the general been more politically discerning, he would have realized that Truman, in effect, had put him on probation. But MacArthur saw the situation entirely differently. He had dared goad Truman and the JCS, and they had backed away from him. Defense Secretary Johnson, he knew, supported him on the issue of freeing Chiang to harass the mainland Communists. MacArthur would be silent for the moment, yet he knew another opportunity would arise for him to speak out on Formosa. And as an official JCS history aptly stated, he succeeded in widening a "hairline crack . . . into an unbridgeable gulf."[32]

Mutiny in the Cabinet

After the very first days of the war President Truman knew he must face up to an unpleasant piece of business: the firing of Defense Secretary Louis Johnson. The task would be hard, for Truman had known Johnson well from the years after the First World War, when both men were active in veterans' affairs. Johnson went on to become a prosperous lawyer, with a practice divided between his native West Virginia and Washington, and national commander of the American Legion. He served the War Department as a civilian executive during the Second

World War, and Truman (by then a senator) found him helpful on industrial mobilization matters. Truman was so impressed with Johnson, in fact, that he asked him to run the financial end of his 1948 campaign. Johnson performed well under the worst of circumstances, for few people wished to contribute to an apparently hopeless campaign.

In 1949 James Forrestal, the first secretary of the new Defense Department, began the mental deterioration that ultimately ended in suicide. Truman wished to reward Johnson for his campaign service, so he chose him for the secretaryship. The appointment worried such observers as Hanson Baldwin, military correspondent for *The New York Times*.[33] "I think most of us who had known him before . . . thought that this would be disastrous. He was such a complete politician that he would sacrifice any defense . . . or combat effectiveness in the interests of political achievement." To Baldwin, Johnson was "completely Truman's creature."

Johnson satisfied Truman initially. He cut the military budget with a vengeance. He ended a noisy air force-navy dispute by canceling orders for an aircraft carrier desired by the admirals. He was not cowed by high-ranking brass. Then Truman began noticing flaws in his old friend. The President said:

> Something happened. I am of the opinion that Potomac fever and a pathological condition are to blame for the fiasco at the end.
> Louis began to show an inordinate egotistical desire to run the whole government. He offended every member of the Cabinet. We never had a Cabinet meeting that he did not show plainly that he knew more about the problems of the Treasury, Commerce, Labor, Agriculture, than did the secretaries of these departments. He played no favorites—all of them were included. He never missed an opportunity to say mean things about my personal staff.[34]

Next, Johnson "tried to use the White House pressmen for blowing himself up and everyone else down, particularly the Secretary of State" to Truman's chagrin. Johnson also bad-mouthed the administration in talks with the President's hard-core enemies in the Senate: Kenneth Wherry, Joseph McCarthy, Owen Brewster, Robert Taft, Bourke Hickenlooper, and others, making what the President called "terrible statements."

Johnson's sniping at Acheson became especially annoying during the early days of the war. Press stories that smacked of Johnsonian inspiration claimed that the United States had got off to a slow start because of Acheson's ineffectiveness and that he might be forced out of office as a result. Eben Ayers, a deputy press secretary whom the President often used as a conversational sounding board, quoted Truman as storming in private that "the fact was that they had had trouble getting the defense establishment to move. If this keeps up," the President commented, "we're going to have a new secretary of defense."[35]

Nonetheless, Johnson kept getting underfoot. On July 1, a Saturday, Truman slipped away from the White House for a cruise on the presidential yacht the *Williamsburg,* forgetting the war for a few refreshing hours. When the *Williamsburg* came into the Washington Navy Yard, Johnson arrived, unannounced and uninvited, and came aboard. Ayers wrote in his diary: "It was apparent to all of us that it was simply a grandstand play, knowing as he did that the newspapermen would be there and would see him."

The next afternoon—Sunday, July 2—Truman and daughter Margaret drove through the Virginia countryside to the Leesburg home of General George C. Marshall. Truman admired Marshall, who had served as chief of staff during the Second World War and then as secretary of state. But Marshall had had to retire in early 1949 after removal of a kidney, and now he held the mostly honorific post as head of the American Red Cross. Marshall was content in retirement and told Truman so. But he also said, I am a soldier, and you are my Commander in Chief; if you want me at the Defense Department, I'll serve. Truman said that he was not yet ready to move against Johnson but that he wished Marshall to think about returning to government.

A day or so later Johnson managed to get himself into the most serious sort of trouble possible for a subordinate of Harry Truman: disloyalty to the President. Averell Harriman, "whitefaced and upset,"[36] came to the White House to tell the President of an extraordinary happening. He had been in Johnson's office when the secretary spoke with Senator Taft by telephone. As Harriman listened, Johnson congratulated Taft for a speech of a few days earlier in which he had criticized Truman for not consulting Congress before acting in the Korean crisis. Taft had also called for the resignation of Acheson. Johnson told Taft the speech was "something that needed to be said." After Johnson finished his talk with Taft, he told Harriman that if they "could get Acheson out," he would "see that Harriman was made secretary of state."

Harriman walked out and reported the conversation immediately to Truman, saying he (Harriman) "could not be bought that easily."

Other disquieting bits of information reached Truman. One friend told him that Johnson declared to a group of West Virginia Republicans that he would be willing to be a "Republican presidential conservative candidate . . . under certain conditions involving the possible candidacy of General Eisenhower." Johnson constantly leaked administration secrets to the columnist Drew Pearson—usually items that put Acheson and other Cabinet members in a poor light. In a talk with Ayers in late August Truman said Johnson's situation "has become impossible," yet there "seems no way, at this time," for the President to fire him. Ayers wrote in his diary: "The President . . . realizes that were he to dismiss Johnson at this time, it would arouse a storm and provide further ammunition for the critics and opponents. . . ."

Acheson, however, refused to fight Johnson in the dirty back alleys of Washington politics. Whereas the Alsop brothers, in their newspaper column, cited "a total absence of principle" as a "major Johnson asset," Acheson enjoined State Department subordinates not to criticize or demean the defense secretary in any fashion. He knew that he enjoyed the confidence of the President and that Truman would not long tolerate an insubordinate Cabinet member. Johnson would commit a fatal blunder on his own in due course. And this Johnson did, in an issue involving General MacArthur.

On Friday night, August 25, Michael McDermott, a deputy press officer in the State Department, stood sipping a drink and reading wire service copy at the ticker in the National Press Building. He saw a story about a statement MacArthur had sent to the United States for delivery to the Veterans of Foreign Wars convention the following week. MacArthur's public relations staff sent advance copies to many publications, including *U.S. News & World Report,* editors of which decided to publish the text. It was from this copy that the Associated Press story was written. McDermott sensed policy troubles. He tore the story off the machine and telephoned Acheson. Come on out to my country place, Acheson replied.

Acheson's mustache quivered as he read MacArthur's pronouncement, which was a broad swipe at administration policy in the Far East.[37] He took special exception to one paragraph: "Nothing could be more fallacious than the threadbare argument by those who advocate appeasement and defeatism in the Pacific that if we defend Formosa we alienate continental Asia." It was the Oriental psychology, MacArthur declared, to respect "aggressive, resolute and dynamic leadership" and to turn on a leadership "characterized by timidity or vacillation." The American determination to "preserve the bulwarks" of the U.S. strategic position in the Pacific had inspired the Far East, he concluded, and to "pursue any other course would . . . shift any future battle area five thousand miles eastward to the coasts of the American continents."

In Acheson's words, "Well, we *were* defending Formosa; nobody was saying we shouldn't defend Formosa. The Seventh Fleet was there to defend it, and this seemed a very gratuitous crack at what had been the policies of the Administration before the Korean War."

Early the next morning Acheson talked over the message with Harriman and Dean Rusk, and all agreed it should be put before the President. Johnson joined them at the White House.[38] As Truman skimmed the statement, "he was obviously very mad indeed." He turned to Johnson and said, "I want this letter withdrawn, and I want you to send an order to MacArthur to withdraw this letter, and that is an order from me. Do you understand that?"

Johnson replied, "Yes, sir, I do."

Truman continued, "Go and do it, that's all."

Incredibly Johnson no sooner reached his Pentagon office than he sought to reopen the discussion about what should be done.[39] He telephoned Acheson and said he had "been thinking over" the order to MacArthur to withdraw the statement, for doing so would cause a "great deal of embarrassment." He and the JCS had a different idea: They would tell MacArthur that if he issued the statement, "we" [apparently Johnson and the JCS] would issue a disclaimer "stating that it is one man's opinion and is not the official policy of the government."

Acheson strongly disagreed. The matter "raised the issue as to who is the President of the United States"; MacArthur had said something contrary to what both Truman and UN Ambassador Warren Austin had stated to be U.S. policy toward Formosa. Simply saying the statement was one man's views would get the President and the government into "complete confusion" as to what parts of the statements were not official policy and what the administration knew of the letter before it became public. "There was nothing to do but for the President to assert his authority."

Johnson asked Acheson if he thought "we dare send him a message that the President directs him to withdraw his statement." Acheson "saw nothing else to do."

Johnson continued to argue. Acheson related:

He didn't see that this order of the President's made any sense. You couldn't withdraw a letter which was already on the ticker. I said, "Louis, don't argue with me as to whether the President's order makes any sense or not. I heard him give it, and you accepted it; and whether it can be done or not, you'd better do it. He wants that order sent to MacArthur."

When Johnson persisted, Acheson rang off.

The wrangling continued by telephone the rest of the day, with calls between Acheson, Johnson, and Harriman, with Johnson's deputy, Stephen Early, occasionally joining in. In Acheson's words, "Everyone knew that this was going to cause a bad mess at the best."

Harriman recognized the consequences that Johnson and the JCS apparently were wary of stating outright: "the possibility that it might mean MacArthur's resignation. But to do less would mean that there would be repercussions which could never be caught up with."

Word of Johnson's rebellion reached the White House as the dispute continued, for the President in midafternoon telephoned Johnson and dictated the precise language he wished sent to MacArthur:

The President of the United States directs that you withdraw your message for National Encampment [convention] of Veterans of Foreign Wars because various features with respect to Formosa are in conflict with the policy of the U.S. and its position in the UN.

Johnson persisted. In yet another talk with Acheson, he said he, Early, and the JCS preferred other language, under Johnson's signature, which would disavow "several features" (unspecified) of the statement and dismiss it as the "statement of one individual only," not of the U.S. government. Early cited the mechanical impossibility of "withdrawing" a statement that had already been distributed by the news services and that would appear in a national magazine already on the presses. He suggested that "perhaps the President might talk on the telephone to MacArthur." Acheson knocked down this idea: "This would put the President in the position of supplication, which he did not think was wise." Acheson said a written order should be sent, that the decision "should not be left to a telephone call."

Harriman by this point was so frustrated with Johnson's obstructionism that he suggested they "go back to the President" for further discussion. But MacArthur cut off the debate. In a cable received Saturday evening, MacArthur said that if the President wished him to withdraw the letter, he would do so. But, in Acheson's paraphrase, he "didn't see what he'd done wrong. He thought he had stated government policy and he didn't understand all this commotion."

In retrospect, Harriman felt the episode set an important precedent vis-à-vis MacArthur. He was forced to follow a presidential order, "an experience that MacArthur had never had."

The squabble proved Johnson's downfall. Truman's first impulse was to fire him immediately and name General Marshall as the replacement. But he found that Marshall was on vacation in upstate Michigan. When he reached him by phone, the general's half of the conversation was overheard by curious farmers in a country store. So Marshall could speak only in noncommittal grunts when Truman asked him to come to the White House.

The actual execution of Louis Johnson was as messy an affair as the events leading up to it. Truman's intention to replace him with Marshall leaked to *The New York Times,* and the secretary called the White House to ask about it. Drop in around four o'clock, and let's talk, Truman told him.

"Lou came in full of pep and energy," Truman said later that evening.[40] "He didn't know anything was wrong. I told him to sit down and I said, 'Lou, I've got to ask you to quit.'

"He just folded up and quit. He leaned over in his chair and I thought he was going to faint. He said, 'Mr. President, I can't talk.' "

Truman did what he could to salve Johnson's pride. Instead of telling him the truth—that he was being fired for incompetence and disloyalty —Truman said the pressure on him to get rid of Johnson had become so great he "could not withstand it any longer."

Johnson sought to argue his case, but Truman told him, "I have made up my mind, Lou, and it has to be this way."

Johnson asked for a "couple of days to think it over," to which Truman agreed (although he had no intention of changing his mind). When Johnson finally left, he was "really beaten down," Truman told Charles Ross, his press secretary.

"I feel pretty bad myself," the President said. "This is the toughest job I have ever had to do. I feel as if I had just whipped my daughter, Margaret."

But the absurdly obtuse Johnson still clung to office. When he came to the White House the next day, Tuesday, September 12, for his regular weekly appointment, he brought Thomas Finletter, the air force secretary, with him. Truman chose not to raise the subject of resignation. But as soon as Johnson and Finletter left, Truman telephoned Stephen Early and urged him to "try and bring the matter to a head." Early and other advisers wrote Johnson's letter of resignation for him to bring to a Cabinet meeting at four o'clock that afternoon.

Again a snag. Johnson handed the letter to Truman after the meeting ended. It was not signed.

"Louis," the President said, "you haven't signed this—sign it."

Johnson wept as he scrawled his signature. "I didn't think you'd make me do it."

The same day Truman telephoned General Marshall and asked the old soldier to return to duty as Johnson's replacement. Truman noted in his diary that night that thirty-two years before, he had been a captain of infantry, while Marshall served General John J. Pershing as a staff officer. "On September 12, 1950 . . . Gen. Marshall and I with positions reversed are still working to save the country and our way of life," Truman wrote.

A New Chief Spook

Truman took advantage of Johnson's departure to perform another long-overdue chore, the replacement of Admiral R. H. Hillenkoetter as director of central intelligence.[41] The CIA's performance in its first three years of existence had suffered because of a lack of strong leadership. At General Marshall's urging, Truman selected as the new director General Walter Bedell Smith, who had been General Eisenhower's chief of staff in the Second World War and later ambassador to Moscow.

A gaunt, ulcer-ridden man of incisive intellect and superb managerial qualities, Smith was one of the more admired—if not popular—men in the professional military. As Ray Cline, one of his CIA subordinates, was to say of Smith years later, "Beetle [his nickname] was a very even-tempered man. He was always in a rage." But Smith's presence at the CIA meant the spook agency would no longer be treated as an orphan child by the military services and State Department.

CHAPTER SIX

"No Korean Dunkirk"

Throughout July the North Korean People's Army continued pounding General Walton Walker's Eighth Army down the Korean peninsula toward the tip of the boot in what to outward appearances was a continued rout of his command. War correspondents wrote of "human wave attacks" of the North Koreans and of the enemy's four-to-one battlefield advantage. Each day the black line marking the battlefront slipped farther south on the newspaper situation maps. "Enough of this nonsense," stormed the British newspaper the *Statesman,* protesting the dispatch of a brigade of 1,800 men to Korea. "The United States should recognize a lost cause and stop pouring men into this Asian sinkhole." The Communist world exuded confidence over what seemed to be a sure North Korean victory—so much so, in fact, that the Soviet Union clucked sympathetically about the "futile attempts of the American imperialists to halt the aspirations of the Korean peoples for unity, independence and freedom."

Beneath these surface signs of confusion, however, were some distinct trends that boded well for Walker's command. The most important was the swift buildup of UN manpower to a point that by July 22 made it equal in numerical strength to that of the North Koreans— roughly 95,000 men each. EUSAK had three U.S. divisions committed to the line—the 24th, battered the first days of combat, but still viable; the 25th; and the 1st Cavalry. A brigade of U.S. marines, some 2,200 more men, was en route, as was a British brigade. Through forced conscription the ROKs had rebuilt their army to some 45,000 men. Many of the latter, however, were of questionable value—men and young boys gathered up in farm villages by press gangs and thrust into combat without training.

Concurrent with the arrival of these fresh troops came the heavy equipment Walker needed to fight the NKPA on an equal basis—the first tanks, dragged from mothballs in Japan; self-propelled guns; heavy mortars; radio equipment that actually worked. Given the state of training of his new men, Walker was by no means ready to take to the offensive. But even as he retreated, he knew exactly where he was going and what he intended to do when he got there.

Walker's objective was to establish a line around the southernmost port of Pusan, hold it, and use it as the conduit through which his army could continue to receive men and equipment.[1] He would give the NKPA all of Korea other than what came to be called the Pusan Perimeter, 5,000 square miles which the Eighth Army was to hold during forty-five savage days of fighting that cost both sides some of the heaviest casualties of the war. Defense of the Pusan Perimeter began on the night of July 31–August 1, when the last EUSAK troops crossed the Naktong River and took up positions on its south banks; the siege was to last until mid-September, when General MacArthur's behind-the-lines landing at Inchon turned the war around.

Since Walker's main objective was to hold Pusan and the space immediately around it, terrain dictated the logical line on which to stand: a rectangular area roughly 50 miles in width, stretching from the Naktong River east to the Sea of Japan, roughly 100 miles in depth. The Naktong sprawled across the peninsula like a snake contracting its length before coiling. In the lower course, the area of interest to Walker, it ranged from a quarter to a half mile in width, with depths of from 6 to 8 feet. The river's shores are punctuated by sandy banks and valleys containing rice paddies. Looming on both shores are commanding hills: 1,200 feet on the east side toward Taegu, rising to 2,500 feet a few miles inland; and on the west bank, from which the North Koreans would be attacking, about 2,000 feet.

Walker had his pilot, Captain Mike Lynch, fly him over the Naktong repeatedly in late July and early August. "General Walker got to know every nook and cranny of the river," Lynch related. "When the fighting began, and Hill So-and-so was the scene, Walker could immediately envision the terrain. This helped him immensely in his defense."[2] To Walker, the Naktong was a huge natural moat protecting about three-fourths of his perimeter.

The defense mounted by Walker came out of the basic doctrinal books that West Point cadets begin learning in their first year. He would fight with the river at his front, not his rear. He stationed men on the hills overlooking the river crossings and their approaches. During daylight hours (when the North Koreans disliked moving around in the open because of American air superiority) these defensive points were little more than observation posts. When dusk fell, they tightened into listening posts and self-contained defensive points, often manned by half a squad—that is to say, six or so soldiers. These men were not expected to stand and fight when superior forces approached; they were an early-warning line charged with reporting on enemy movements. When hit in force, they would fade back to the main American lines.

There stood the main American force, a fire brigade army poised to answer any alarm sounded along the front. Artillery and mortar crews, also to the rear, spent hours positioning their weapons to fire on known ferry and other probable crossing sites as well as on hills the NKPA might try to seize. The overall goal was to coordinate infantry and artillery so as to hold the commanding high ground and control the crude roads winnowing between the hills and rice paddies.

The grand scheme read better on paper than it appeared in reality. American and ROK intelligence gathered grim estimates from across the Naktong in early August: The NKPA force massing for the attack numbered no less than ten divisions, almost 100,000 men.[3] Watching preparations for the battle from Washington, General J. Lawton Collins, the army chief of staff, recognized that "the enemy was bound to be able to get across the river wherever he decided to concentrate his efforts. The big job of the Americans and the South Koreans would be to counterattack and drive the North Koreans back into the river with heavy losses of men and equipment." Whether the Naktong defense line worked depended on Walker's ability to shuffle his outmanned reserves and to have them in the right place at the right time.

A Disgraced Regiment

Walker's first concern was to block enemy access to Taegu, fifty-five miles north of Pusan, a highway and rail center which also had the only operative airfield north of Pusan.[4] Walker did not want the added hazard of North Korean air attacks. The defense of Taegu fell to the 25th Infantry Division, commanded by Major General William B. Kean. General Collins described Kean as a "sound, steady soldier with a quiet personality." He had served under General Omar Bradley as a chief of staff during the Second World War. He had seen fighting in North Africa and Europe. But despite his thirty-one years as a commissioned officer (he was graduated from West Point in 1919), the 25th Division was Kean's first experience in command of a unit in action.

Walker ordered Kean to take up positions to the north of Taegu to keep the North Koreans from sweeping down into the Naktong Valley. Kean moved his troops to the area commanding the town of Sangju, a crossroads center for the mountain roads in that part of Korea and forty-five miles up the Naktong Valley from Taegu. There the American troops found a swirl of confusion, with refugees and fleeing ROK soldiers mingling in dusty columns.

On July 20 the 25th Infantry Division entered the battle. The first assignment, to defend the small town of Yechon, fell to the 24th Infantry Regiment—an all-black unit preserved as such by an act of Congress in 1878. The 24th Regiment had made a distinguished record for itself in the Indian wars of the 1870's and 1880's but had thereafter fallen victim to the racism that permeated the American military. Its men were used as service troops, shunned and scorned by other units, treated as "second-class soldiers" regardless of how well they performed. Thus the prevalent attitude through much of the regiment was in effect: Why should we get our asses shot off fighting for a bunch of people who don't give a damn about us as human beings? And what happened to the 24th Regiment in its first months in Korea pointed up the absurdity of a segregated army and hastened the integration of black troops into units where they were treated the same as other soldiers.

The 24th's ordeal began its very first day in the line, at Yechon, when its troops broke ranks and fled after only a few hours' fighting, its officers claiming they had encountered a vastly superior NKPA force. But a scouting party the next day found no evidence North Koreans had been in the town, which appeared to have been set ablaze by American artillery. An inquiring commander of the 35th Infantry Regiment, on the flanks of the 24th Regiment, complained he "could get no information of value" from a battalion commander of the 24th about what had happened.

In ensuing days the 24th Regiment and its officers did not gain any confidence. One battalion, the 2nd, was advancing up a mountain road when it was hit by fire from a light mortar and one or two automatic weapons. ROK officers with the company suggested an enveloping movement to bypass what appeared to be a minor roadblock, but the commander apparently did not understand him. The American troops withdrew in a "disorderly manner," and only the appearance of the battalion commander brought the men out of a "state of panic." (The next day a ROK unit stormed the roadblock and captured two light machine guns, a mortar, and thirty guerrillas.)

Two days later the ROKs withdrew to the east to try to flank North Koreans advancing down the coast, leaving the 24th Regiment as the sole guard of the western approach to Sangju. By any criteria, the 24th Regiment again disgraced itself. The official U.S. Army history, reluctant as it is to criticize units or individuals, states:

> The tendency to panic continued in nearly all the 24th Infantry operations west of Sangju. Men left their positions and straggled to the rear. They abandoned weapons on positions. On one occasion the 3d Battalion

withdrew from a hill and left behind twelve .30-caliber and three .50-caliber machine guns, eight 60-mm mortars, three 81-mm mortars, four 3.5-inch rocket launchers and 102 rifles.

On another occasion, L Company took into position [i.e., on the battle line] four officers and 105 enlisted men; a few days later, when the company was relieved in its position, there were only seventeen men in the foxholes. The number of casualties and men evacuated for other reasons in the interval had been one officer and seventeen enlisted men, leaving three officers and 88 enlisted men unaccounted for.

As the relieved unit of seventeen men moved down the mountain it swelled in numbers to one officer and thirty-five enlisted men by the time it reached the bottom.

The 24th Infantry's fighting pattern was to hold by day and run by night. On July 29, after a daylong mortar barrage from the North Koreans, "an inexplicable panic" seized men of the 1st Battalion, who fled into the night. A field artillery battalion and one combat engineer company were left to hold the line—which they did, thanks chiefly to an incredible 3,000 rounds of howitzer shells, much of it direct fire at the North Koreans. They held for the night.

Disgusted regimental officers finally set up checkpoints to the rear of the fighting lines. Major John Woolridge, the regimental S-1 (or personnel officer) stopped every vehicle leaving Sangju. He averaged 75 stragglers a day; one day he caught 150.

By July 30 the 24th Infantry had withdrawn to the last defensible ground, three miles west of Sangju. Kean knew the regiment was finished. He moved a battalion of the 35th Infantry into position behind it. The next day the North Koreans hit again, aiming at an outpost line just in front of the main line of resistance.

First Lieutenant Leon A. Gilbert, of York, Pennsylvania, commander of a company on the outpost line, walked away, fifteen enlisted men behind him. Colonel Horton White, the regiment commander, and other officers ordered Gilbert back into the line. He refused. He said he was scared. A noncommissioned officer took the men back to their positions.*

The 24th Regiment never overcame its reputation as a "bugout" unit —a derisive name GIs gave to troops who broke under fire. A year later the appearance of a 24th Regiment patch on a uniform would bring jeers from other units, and sometimes the derisive lyrics of "Bugout Boogie":

---

*A court-martial sentenced Lieutenant Gilbert to death for refusing to obey a combat order.[5] Gilbert's defense was that compliance with the order to "move up" would "have led me and twelve other men to certain death." The judge advocate general of the army recommended commutation of the sentence to twenty years at hard labor. President Truman did so on November 27, 1950.

When the Chinese mortars begin to chug,
The ol' deuce-four begin to bug. . . .

The 24th's performance gave impetus to the drive for an integrated
army. General Lawton Collins argued that "Negro soldiers, when properly trained and fully integrated with their white comrades, would fight
as well and would readily be accepted as equals." And many individual
soldiers of the 24th Regiment distinguished themselves by bravery
under fire.

Consider William "Willie" Thompson, of New York City, a private
first class in a heavy weapons company of the regiment's 3rd Battalion.
During an operation in early August in the mountain mass north of
Pusan, two other companies in the battalion panicked under fire and
fled; one officer stated later his own stampeding soldiers had knocked
him to the ground three times. Not so with Thompson. When an enemy
ambush caught his company in an assembly area, he set up a machine
gun and directed a deadly rain of fire at the attackers. The platoon
leader ordered withdrawal to more tenable positions. Thompson kept
firing; he intended to cover the withdrawal. A corporal tried to pull him
away from the machine gun. Thompson shook him off.

"Maybe I won't get out," he said, "but then I'm gonn' take lot of them
with me."

As other members of the platoon sprinted for safety, they heard the
continued clatter of Thompson's machine gun, then the thud of exploding North Korean grenades. After a bit his gun fell silent. A year later
the Department of the Army awarded a posthumous Medal of Honor
to Private William Thompson, M Company, 24th Infantry.

North Korean Brutality

After a month of battle the raw American troops had learned quite a
bit about the unorthodox combat techniques of the North Koreans.[6]
Some of the tactics made callous use of civilians. In one instance, about
200 women, children, and old men walked into a battle area from the
direction of the North Korean lines, "creating some confusion as they
were . . . rounded up and processed," in the words of an army intelligence report. The North Koreans took advantage of the chaos to launch
an attack. Some of the refugees said later the North Koreans forced
them to walk toward the American lines. The North Koreans had an
entire bag of tricks:

—Enemy soldiers stripped off their clothing, camouflaged their bodies with mud, and tried to slip through U.S. lines.

—A group of eight or ten soldiers would attack, then raise their hands as if to surrender. When American fire stopped, and men moved out to accept their surrender, "a company-sized North Korea force launches attack from concealed position."

—Groups of fifty or more North Koreans would launch suicidal banzai charges. While U.S. soldiers concentrated their fire on this group, other forces would slip around the flanks and attack.

—Many of the North Korean soldiers carried civilian clothing (the white pajama type of garb traditional in the South) and slipped out of their military uniforms when they wished to avoid detection, or to hide in a supposedly friendly village.

The North Koreans took advantage of the turmoil to slip psychological warfare experts into the South. The propaganda message varied depending upon the battlefield situation. In early August, for instance, three themes were stressed: that the North Koreans had captured Pusan; that South Koreans should remain in their homes even if their cities were overrun by the invaders or they would be shot; and that South Koreans should "not be afraid of the North Korean People's Army as they will release you and give you freedom."[7] The North Koreans devised a crude system of visual identification to enable undercover agents to recognize one another. Around Chungchong, for instance, male agents were to wear a white bandage on the little finger of the left hand, spotted with blue ink. Female spies were to wear a black jacket and a black shirt and to carry a piece of white cloth and two apples.

To the veteran war correspondent John Osborne, in Korea for *Time* and *Life* magazines, the North Korean tactics—especially the use of civilians as shields—had a brutalizing effect on American soldiers.[8] These tactics began to "force upon our men in the field acts and attitudes of the utmost savagery. This means not the usual inevitable savagery of combat in the field, but savagery in details—the blotting out of villages where the enemy *might* be hiding; the shooting and shelling of refugees who *may* include North Koreans." Every U.S. soldier had heard stories of North Korean troops hiding in refugee columns, waiting for a chance to pull a weapon from a ragbag and fire at unsuspecting GIs. Osborne described an episode when several hundred refugees stumbled down a dirt road toward an American regiment. "Don't let them through," the commanding colonel said. "But try to talk to them, try to tell them to go back."

"Yeah, but what if they don't go back?"

"Well, then, fire over their heads."

"OK, we fire over their heads. Then what?"

"Well, then," the colonel said with sigh, "fire into them if you have to. *If you have to, I said.*"

Because of their superior armor, the North Koreans slowly shoved the American and ROK defenders tighter and tighter into the Pusan Perimeter. But by mid-August intelligence analysts reviewing interrogations of North Korean prisoners found serious weaknesses in the enemy— flaws that would become more obvious when the United States mustered the strength for a counterstrike.

Some prisoners were as young as sixteen years of age. "Large numbers" had been conscripted in early 1950 and received only four to six weeks of basic training before being assigned to a combat company. Those with skills suitable for direct military service bypassed basic training altogether. Marksmanship training was "extremely limited."

The quality of training varied widely between units. The dominant figure seemed to be the "cultural officer," who conducted "political education" at the company level. In the words of an army intelligence summary, the North Korean soldier lacked "the ability to think and act with initiative." He was "poorly informed and obedient through fear of . . . superiors. . . ." But the cultural officer had inculcated "a belief that he must do his job for the benefit of the masses and that individualism is a secondary and undesirable factor." Signs of any political ideology were "so minute as to be undetectable."

But the North Korean foot soldier fought without expectations of such PX comforts as paperback books or canned beer. Army intelligence stated:

> The North Korean infantry man is . . . a rugged individual accustomed in his ordinary daily life to hardship. His equipment is scant and light; he has one uniform, a hand weapon, and ammunition plus a few personal effects in his pockets. He wears light canvas and rubber shoes in which he can negotiate difficult terrain (mountains, rice paddies, etc.) with more speed and endurance than a soldier equipped by our concepts. He subsists on a relatively small amount of food, which he obtains largely by foraging; when he is tired he rests in the nearest shelter or in the open. A straw mat is his accustomed bed.[9]

Even when his unit was disrupted by casualties, losses, the North Korean soldier continued fighting, individually or as an *ad hoc* guerrilla, discarding his uniform and taking whatever clothing he could find in the nearest house.

> This persistence in combat appears to be a result of training bolstered by fear rather than personal belief in the cause for which he is fighting. . . . In general, the North Korean soldier lives in a state of fear. He has been beaten, slapped and kicked whenever he failed his superiors. He fights to avoid punishment and he expects brutal treatment if captured. . . . It should not be believed that the North Korean soldier will stop fighting but it appears that he will surrender if he is out of contact with his leaders.

By late July General Walker was outspokenly disappointed by the inability of the 1st Cavalry and 25th Infantry divisions to stop the North Koreans. They often withdrew "in circumstances that seemed not to justify it, and with troops in panic and out of control."[10]

Walker recognized the necessity to hold a beachhead; he also recognized the danger of his army's being flanked and decimated. The North Koreans now realized they did not have to hit the Americans head-on. They simply slid around the flanks and attacked from the rear.

"Stand or Die"—Walker

On July 26 Walker decided to try to withdraw his forces into "prepared positions" which could be held until the United States and ROKs could turn to the offensive. The time of the withdrawal was to be set later. The same day Walker telephoned MacArthur's Tokyo headquarters and spoke with General Edward Almond, the FEC chief of staff. Details of their conversation have been heard from one side only, Almond's, for Walker was to be dead within six months. But the outcome permanently soured each general on the other.

According to the account Almond later gave to army historian Roy Appleman, Walker wanted authority to move his Eighth Army headquarters from Taegu to Pusan, and immediately. He feared loss of his communications equipment, virtually irreplaceable if destroyed or captured. He felt the enemy was thrusting so close to Taegu that the equipment was endangered. The "planned withdrawal" positions would leave EUSAK along the Naktong River.

Two of Walker's ranking staff officers dispute that he said any such thing. Neither the EUSAK staff nor its signal section heard any such plan for withdrawal until nearly a month later, and the new command post was to be Ulsan, on the east coast, rather than Pusan. Even when a danger arose in late August that the communications equipment might be lost, "no responsible member of the [Eighth] Army staff . . . proposed a move to the command post to Pusan."

Almond said he would pass the request to MacArthur, but he "personally" thought a move to Pusan would have a bad effect on both EUSAK units and the ROKs. Withdrawal could cause the latter to conclude EUSAK did not intend to stay in Korea and "might be the forerunner of a general debacle."

After the talk with Walker, Almond told MacArthur the situation in Korea was "critical" and required his personal attention. He urged MacArthur to go there "at once" to talk with Walker. The suggestion is strong that Almond felt Walker was wavering and needed a personal pep talk—or ultimatum—from his supreme commander. So the next morning MacArthur and Almond flew to Taegu and closeted themselves for ninety minutes with Walker.

By Almond's account, MacArthur never mentioned Walker's request of the day before, nor did he criticize his field commander directly. He simply said that EUSAK must cease its withdrawals and stand its ground. There would be "no Korean Dunkirk."

In his memoirs MacArthur does not mention this crucial meeting with Walker. However circumspect his language, MacArthur gave Walker a message: The Eighth Army was expendable. Regardless of how many men perished, and under what circumstances, it must stand or die—or *stand and die.* Old Army man Walker understood. In a talk two days later to General Kean and 25th Division staff, he laid out what he (and MacArthur) expected:

> We are fighting a battle against time. There will be no more retreating, withdrawal, or readjustment of the lines or any other term you choose. There is no line behind us to which we can retreat.
>
> Every unit must counterattack to keep the enemy in a state of confusion. There will be no Dunkirk, there will be no Bataan; a retreat to Pusan would be one of the greatest butcheries in history.
>
> We must fight until the end. Capture by these people is worse than death itself. We will fight as a team. If some of us die, we will die fighting together.
>
> Any man who gives ground may be personally responsible for the death of thousands of his comrades.
>
> I want you to put this out to all the men in the Division. I want everybody to understand that we are going to hold this time. We are going to win.[11]

Walker's ultimatum was relayed to every soldier in the field, with varying interpretations. One field officer said his men heard the order as meaning, "Stay and die where you are"—an unfair demand, in a battle where no friendly units protected their flanks. But a regimental commander said he and his men received the order with a "great sense of relief." As the officer said, "a greater amount of earth came out with each shovelful" when the troops dug in their positions.

Hanson W. Baldwin, the military critic of *The New York Times,* wrote a few days later that Walker's "stand or die" order was a "well-merited rebuke to the Pentagon, which has too often disseminated a soothing syrup of cheer and sweetness and light since the fighting began."[12]

Figures from past wars highlight Walker's dilemma.[13] During the First World War, fought on the flat battlefields of western Europe, American divisions of from 12,000- to 13,000-man strength held frontline positions ranging from 11,500 to 18,500 yards. Yet the ROK and U.S. Army divisions in Korea, half the strength of the 1918 divisions, had frontages ranging up to an incredible 103,600 yards (the 1st Division opposite Waegwan, August 1950).

"These are terrific distances to defend, or hold, or even keep under patrol surveillance," an FEC staff commentary said. "The density per yard factor represents an average of one or two men every ten yards and nothing behind them; of course, there is no such rubber-band distribution; there were miles of gaps through which the enemy penetrated. . . ." All General Walker could do was shuttle "his weary reserves from one crisis to the next."

The Marines Arrive

But there was one bright spot in General Walton Walker's defenses in August—the performance of the 1st Marine Brigade, sent to Korea as an advance party of the 1st Marine Division. The marines had several inherent advantages over the army. They had been in combat training in the United States; they arrived in cohesive units in which officers and men had served together for months (not hours, as was the case with many jerry-built army "companies"); they insisted on controlling their own air support, in coordinated actions based upon years of experience. Further, given the corps's stress on arduous physical training for every man, regardless of his assignment, the marines arrived in Korea in far better condition than their army counterparts.

Walker gave the marines responsibility for defense of the western portion of the Pusan Perimeter—roughly, the area around Chinju and Masan, cities just west of Pusan. The brigade faced a formidable foe, the North Korean 6th Infantry Division, which had played a large part in the capture of Seoul and then swept down the west coast relatively untouched (of a strength of some 8,000 men, the division suffered only 400 killed or wounded). The commander, Major General Wae Pang, had reason for confidence when he told his troops on July 28: "Comrades, the enemy is demoralized. . . . The task given to us is . . . the annihilation of the remnants of the enemy. . . . [T]he liberation of Chinju and Masan means the final battle to cut off the windpipe of the enemy. . . . Men of the 6th Division, let us annihilate the enemy and distinguish ourselves."[14]

But the marines brought the North Koreans to an abrupt halt, fiercely contesting them for control of obscure hills known only by their highest peak in meters. Thus it was that the marines' first combat was on the slopes of something called Hill 342, which one officer likened to a huge molar rising from the flatlands west of Chindong-ni.[15] Reaching the crest required extraordinary will in the late-summer heat. Stumbling and gasping for breath, "every Marine reached the point where he barely managed to drag himself up the steep incline." Men gained a few feet, slipped and fell back, and cursed. Some dropped unconscious along the trail; others bent double, retching. But NCOs and officers kept the column intact and moving. At the summit they were fired upon: The North Koreans and the U.S. Marine Corps had joined battle.

For the next weeks the marines fought their private war with the North Koreans along the western side of the Pusan Perimeter—probing, contracting, lunging at each other's positions. During their first days the marines even managed advances, seizing the towns of Kosong and Sachon and setting up the first major American victory of the war —the Kosong Turkey Shoot. It happened this way.

Aggressively pushing through roadblocks and attempted ambushes, advancing marines broke into the small town of Kosong, panicking the Korean defenders. A column of enemy vehicles dashed for safety, only to come under fire from marine artillery.

Given the relative speed of the vehicles and the loading and re-aiming time of the cannon, the North Koreans might have escaped. But by happenstance, the carrier USS *Badoeng Strait* had just launched a division of fighter attack planes on a search and attack mission, to seek targets north of Kosong. Major Arnold A. Lund, the division commander, and his pilots swept down on a trigger-tingling array of targets: some 100 vehicles of a North Korean motorcycle regiment, including jeeps, motorcycles, and troop-carrying trucks.

Corsairs screamed the length of column at low level, blazing rockets and machine-gun bullets. Vehicles smashed into one another or skidded into ditches as North Koreans scurried for cover. Once the convoy was halted, the Corsairs methodically swept up and down the line, directing fierce fire at individual vehicles; plumes of smoke rose from more than twoscore of them.

Several hours later, the attack over, advancing marines came upon the mangled column. Officers and NCOs looked the other way while infantrymen tried out sleek black Soviet Army jeeps and motorcycles with sidecars, most of which had gone into battle in mint condition. Looking under the hoods, the marines found the jeeps powered by familiar Ford Motor Company engines—apparent relics of American lend-lease aid to the Soviet Union during the Second World War.

For several days the marines enjoyed a fleeting euphoria; through adroit use of close air support, they methodically smashed back the North Koreans. In close ground encounters their superior discipline and firepower brought them victory time and again. The North Koreans took ferocious losses. One example among many: Observers spotted a group of enemy soldiers creeping up a hill near Sachon. A squad led by Technical Sergeant F. J. Lischeski formed a line along the ridge and coolly waited until the enemy approached within seventy-five feet.

In a matter of seconds the marine fire killed all but one of the thirty-nine oncoming enemy; the sole survivor, an officer, died of wounds before he could be taken to the command post.

But before the marines could exploit their gains, the order came to withdraw to the south; enemy troops had broken across the Naktong River, the last natural barrier protecting the Pusan Perimeter. The marines were needed for a counterattack.

Battlefield Atrocities

The North Korean breakthrough came at a point opposite the town of Tugok, where the Naktong made a wide swing to the west, dropped southward, and then curved back west in a horseshoe, leaving a nub of land shaped like a toppled *U,* roughly three by five miles in area, broken by jumbled masses of ridges.

The dominant landscape feature facing the marine position was Obong-ni Ridge, which marine historian Lynn Montross wrote looked like "some huge pre-historic reptile," with its head overlooking Tugok and its elongated body stretching southeast more than 2,000 yards before losing its identity in a complex of swamps and hills. Individual hillocks dotted the spine of the reptile, separated by alternating spurs and deep gullies which ran down into rice paddies. To shove the North Koreans back across the Naktong, the marines had first to drive them off this wretched patch of land.

The assault fell to the 2nd Battalion of the 5th Marine Regiment, which jumped off at eight o'clock in the morning of August 17 after an abortive artillery and air barrage that failed to soften the enemy positions materially. *Time* correspondent James Bell watched the marines move up what came to be known as No Name Ridge:

> Hell burst around the leathernecks as they moved up the barren face of the ridge. Everywhere along the assault line, men dropped. To continue looked impossible. But, all glory forever to the bravest men I ever saw, the line did not break. The casualties were unthinkable, but the assault force never turned back. It moved, fell down, got up and moved again.[16]

General Edward Craig, the brigade commander, watched from a roadway in the valley. His hands trembled as he held binoculars to his face. "I never saw men with so much guts," he said.

Red machine guns and mortars beat down on the assault force for more than an hour. The marines pulled back, struck again, pulled back once more as grenades rolled down the hill through their ranks. Medical corpsmen led South Korean litter bearers through the rear fringes of the battle to pick up the wounded. *Time*'s Bell asked one marine if he had been in the last war. "No, and I wish I wasn't in this one, either," he replied.

A platoon led by Second Lieutenant Michael J. Shinka had as its objective Hill 109, one of the many subsummits on No Name Ridge. But machine-gun fire from two adjoining hills caught his troops in a deadly bracket. Despite supporting artillery fire and another air strike, by late morning only fifteen men remained alive in his platoon. Nonetheless, he managed to beat off a counterattack. Shinka told what happened next:

> Running short of ammo and taking casualties, with the shallow enemy slit trenches for cover, I decided to fall back until some of the fire on my left flank could be silenced. I gave the word to withdraw and take all wounded and weapons. About three-quarters of the way down, I had the men set up where cover was available. I had six men who were able to fight.
>
> I decided to go forward to find out if we had left any of our wounded. As I crawled along our former position (on the crest of Hill 109), I came across a wounded Marine between two dead. As I grabbed him under the arms and pulled him from the foxhole, a bullet shattered my chin. Blood ran into my throat and I couldn't breathe.
>
> I tossed a grenade at a gook crawling up the slope, didn't wait for it to explode, turned and reached under the Marine's arms and dragged him as far as the crest.
>
> Another bullet hit my right arm, and the force spun me around. I rolled down the hill for a considerable distance before I could stop myself.[17]

Shinka managed to walk to a command post, where he had supplies of ammunition rushed to his remaining men. Only then did he seek medical attention. Shinka won the Bronze Star for his bravery.

By midafternoon marine air artillery hit No Name Ridge in force, leaving the entire crest strewn with bodies, weapons, and wreckage. The Corsairs then moved to the rear of enemy lines, where they strafed and bombed troop reinforcements being brought across the Naktong. Other companies moved up from marine reserves in an attempt to exploit a seeming slackening of enthusiasm for battle among the North Koreans.

In the valley below, meanwhile, marine M-26 tanks fired at North Korean armor and antitank and machine guns on the line of the crest. Late in the evening North Korean tanks, four of the feared T-34's, rumbled out to meet the challenge—the first direct confrontation between marine and Communist armor. In five flaming minutes the marines dashed forever the myth of the invincibility of the T-34. Antitank guns knocked the track off the lead tank; a salvo from the 90 mm guns on the first M-26 in line reduced it to a blazing hulk. The second T-34 died even more spectacularly: A 3.5-inch rocket damaged the right track; then another rocket erupted the gas tank. It slithered off the road, and two marine tanks methodically blasted it with shell after shell of 9 mm cannon fire, ripping through the turret and exploding the hull. An enemy tanker somehow managed to throw open the turret hatch. Just as he did, a 2.36-inch white phosphorus round glanced off the open lid and ricocheted into the tank. The enemy soldier fell back inside, and the interior turned into a furnace. The third enemy tank in line came around the bend in the road and could not move past the burning hulks of the first tanks. The marines directed the full ferocity of their fire at it—rockets, bazookas, cannon. Within seconds it exploded. The marines' first tank battle ended in total victory for the American forces.

The marines and the North Koreans fought on and around Obong-ni Ridge for days afterward, with U.S. air and artillery superiority slowly, inexorably seizing the upper hand. No longer could the North Koreans stand and fight for any extended periods; pounded into submission by bombs and cannon fire, major units broke formation and ran like a "routed mob" when attacked. On August 17, in a slaughter reminiscent of the Kosong Turkey Shoot, hundreds of fleeting enemy soldiers fled in daylight to the banks of the Naktong and tried to ford the river to escape a beachhead that the marines had transformed into a deathtrap. Marine Corsairs strafed and bombed hundreds of enemy troops massed on the riverbanks; napalm and artillery fire scoured the slopes on both sides of the Naktong.

In the aftermath of battle the marines came upon an abandoned American Army medical aid station near the tip of Finger Ridge. The Communists had overrun the hospital during army reverses a week earlier.[18] Wounded men had been bayoneted and shot in their beds, and their bodies mutilated. Corpsmen who had stayed behind to tend to them had had their hands wired behind their backs; they had then been murdered with a shot in the back of the head.

Other such atrocities were uncovered all along the front. The afternoon of August 17, just below the Waegwan Bridge to the east of the marine sector, troops of the army's 5th Cavalry Regiment came across an eighteen-year-old American private from Chicago, Roy Manring, crawling down a hill toward the advancing forces. Manring had burpgun wounds in both legs and one arm, and he told a horrible tale.

Two mornings previously his unit, H Company, had received word that a platoon of ROKs was en route to reinforce the company's mortar platoon. About breakfasttime they saw a group of Koreans moving through an apple orchard. Not until the Koreans stood alongside the Americans' foxholes did anyone realize they were Communist troops. (As one of the North Koreans said a few days later, after his capture, "the American soldiers looked dazed.") Outnumbered ten to one or so, the platoon surrendered. Manring said:

> They come up and stuck their burp guns in our stomachs with one hand and with the other they reached out like to shake hands, but they grabbed our rifles. One jerked on mine and I jerked back. Then he jerked again. I said to myself, "This ain't no time to argue," and let go. They stripped us down and took our helmets. They took my watch and billfold that had $11.81 in it. My girl's picture was in it, too. They took that out and looked at it and kept it. They like girls' pictures. . . .

The apparent North Korean commander told the prisoners they would be sent to a POW camp near Seoul if they behaved. The captors tied their hands behind their backs and moved them several times that night and the following day; heavy American fire kept them from fording the Naktong under cover of darkness. An incident that night indicated that the North Koreans initially intended no mistreatment of the Americans. Two of the prisoners succeeded in loosening the shoelaces binding their wrists. When a North Korean soldier threatened to shoot them for this transgression, he himself was shot down by a Communist officer. But the next day one of the Americans who understood enough Japanese to converse with the North Koreans overheard a lieutenant say that if the Americans got too close, the prisoners would be killed.

That is exactly what happened on the morning of August 17. Around noon the Americans were marched into a gully and left there with a light guard. Then came artillery and air strikes, the obvious prelude to a U.S. attempt to take the position. Around three or four in the afternoon North Korean troops took up positions on either side of the gully. Manring again:

> I heard the Reds' weapons going off and I heard our boys groaning and grunting. I said to myself, "Please, Lord, don't let them get us with these burp guns."
> The Reds walked up and down the line of prisoners, shooting. I was hit in the leg. I reached down to my leg and got some blood and smeared it on my head and laid down under a dead man. I didn't move a muscle. When they came back along the line I got shot in the arm but I didn't yell.

Another prisoner, Corporal James M. Rudd, of Salyersville, Kentucky, although hit three times in the arms and legs, escaped death by burrowing under the bodies of fallen comrades. So did four other men. All managed to make their way back to American lines. One of the 5th Cavalry troopers who went to the scene of the tragedy described it:

> The boys lay packed tightly, shoulder to shoulder, lying on their sides, curled like babies sleeping in the sun. Their feet, bloodied and bare, from

walking on the rocks, stuck out stiffly. . . . All hands were tied behind their backs, some with cord, others with regular issue army communications wire.[19]

Later the same afternoon the same troops who had found Manring captured a group of North Koreans and took them before the survivors. Lying on a litter at an aide station, Manring pointed out one North Korean enlisted man as the soldier who had helped kill his buddies. Another prisoner didn't want to look at Manring. "Turn your head," snarled an American corporal. Manring said quietly, "I'm almost positive this one is the guy who gave the firing order."

The official army history does not record the disposition of the North Koreans fingered by Manring. Nor, for that matter, does it blame the North Koreans for any systematic mistreatment of American prisoners. Indeed, it quotes an order issued on July 28 by the North Korean Army advanced general headquarters which forbade "the unnecessary killing of enemy personnel when they could be taken as prisoners of war. . . . Those who surrender will be taken as prisoners of war, and all efforts will be made to destroy the enemy in thought and politically."[20] Another order, this one from the North Korean 2nd Division on August 16 (ironically the day before the massacre near Waegwan), said in part, "Some of us are still slaughtering enemy troops that come to surrender. Therefore, the responsibility of teaching the soldiers to take prisoners of war and to treat them kindly rests on the Political Section of each unit."

American correspondents with the ROK and the American armies were not oblivious to gross misbehavior on their side of the lines. The veteran correspondent John Osborne, in fact, was so disturbed that he complained in *Time* in late August of what he called "savagery by proxy."[21] Osborne did not presume to issue any "righteous indictments" or to condone "the even greater savagery of the North Korean army." But he did state "the elementary facts of war in Korea"—to wit:

> The South Korean police and the South Korean marines who [sic] I observed in front line areas are brutal. They murder to save themselves the trouble of escorting prisoners to the rear; they murder civilians to get them out of the way or to avoid the trouble of searching and cross-examining them. And they extort information—information our forces need and require of the South Korean interrogators—by means so brutal that they cannot be described.

Americans came to accept cruelty to prisoners and suspected Communists as an ineradicable Korean characteristic.[22] Keyes Beech of the Chicago *Daily News* admitted his indifference had reached the point where he could watch, without interfering, as "Korean soldiers beat suspected Communists into a bloody pulp." Another time he came upon a group of women who had been forced to kneel with their knees on sharp rocks, hands flat on their heads, guarded by bayonet-wielding soldiers. A baby scrambled in front of one of the women, trying to reach her breast so he could suckle. She dared not move. Carl Mydans, the *Life* photographer, could not resist: He picked up the baby and held him to his mother's breast. Korean torture was cruelly inventive: In battlefield interrogations soldiers relied upon such timeless techniques as beating the soles of the feet with sharp sticks, driving splinters under fingernails, and tying knees and ankles together so that bones could be broken with a simple lever. Keyes Beech noted a local innovation: wrapping a man's testicles in kerosene-soaked cotton and setting it afire.

A Brief Pause

In late August there came an uneasy lull in the fighting, as if both sides had tacitly agreed to take a breathing spell. The 1st Marine Brigade moved its headquarters to a new bivouac area near Masan that came to be known in marine lore as the Bean Patch. The area in calmer times had been exactly that. For the first time the marines had a chance to repair and test-fire their weaponry and to replenish the personal supplies that had been abandoned during the exhausting days of combat. Even patrols in rugged country to the north of the rest area could now enjoy hot meals thanks to helicopters. President Syngman Rhee came down to pass out Purple Hearts and other medals, and there was even a songfest by a group of South Korean girls.

The immediate crisis seemed to have passed, but one puzzling occurrence could not help being noted by the dumbest of privates: At the same time truckloads of supplies were being brought into the Pusan beachhead, presumably for use by troops already in the country, logistics officers of the 1st Marine Brigade were quietly readying equipment for shipment *out* of the country. The Bean Patch most obviously was not to be the brigade's home for much longer.

But where were they going? Surely not home, even though some optimist in MacArthur's headquarters in Tokyo—a comfortable distance from the roar of a war that had by no means ended—suggested to a *Time* correspondent in early September that the war might be over by Thanksgiving.

Intelligence reports stated one reason for the lull was that the North Korean People's Army had lost so many experienced soldiers and that many of its 133,000 men were ill-trained replacements. Thus Premier Kim Il Sung had not been able to meet his announced goal of ending the war by August 15, the anniversary of Korean independence from the Japanese. When this deadline passed, Kim issued another order over Pyongyang Radio: His troops must drive the UN forces out of Korea by the end of August since "the longer this is delayed the stronger UN defenses will become." The CIA warned on August 15 that "this type of broadcast may forecast an all-out troop and guerrilla offensive."[23]

Kim needed no inside information on U.S. strategy, for MacArthur had a seemingly uncontrollable compulsion to reveal his grand design in countless interviews with the American and world press. He would "buy time with space" while building up his forces, then break out of the Pusan Perimeter and perhaps even surprise the North Koreans with a flanking attack. The only way a "flanking attack" could be launched under existing circumstances, of course, was by an amphibious landing farther up the peninsula.

Thus Kim had every incentive for an all-out offensive to force MacArthur's command out of Korea before he could strike elsewhere. The lull ended with an explosion early on the morning of September 1, with the North Koreans launching no less than five major assaults against the tight Pusan Perimeter. Walker frantically shifted units along the line, trying to plug weak points. The Eighth Army defenses sagged and occasionally broke. But Walker knew that the NKPA lacked the logistical stamina to continue the offensive for more than three or four days; hold, and the shortages of supplies would force the enemy to pull back.

Perhaps. But in the interim American forces took some of their heaviest losses of the war. On September 5 alone the army lost 102 men killed, 420 wounded, 587 missing; the marines 35 killed, 91 wounded, for a total of 1,245 casualties. The NKPA suffered grave losses as well: 1,000 against a single American battalion on September 2–3 near Haman; 2,000 more the first week of the month near the juncture of the Nam and Naktong rivers. But despite the carnage, the NKPA continued attacking, in almost fanatical fashion.

By now, however, knowledge that the Korean War was about to enter a new phase was common. During the middle days of September marines of the 1st Brigade slipped out of line and away to Pusan. A counterstroke that would mean the end of the isolation of the troops in the Pusan Perimeter was in the offing.

General Walker had succeeded in his mission. There would be "no Korean Dunkirk."

CHAPTER SEVEN

A Winning Gamble at Inchon

General Douglas MacArthur's strategic success in the Second World War rested squarely on his island-hopping campaign, with marine and army units mounting surprise amphibious operations to seize islands in the enemy rear, bypassing more obvious points of attack. As noted earlier, on his first battlefield trip to Korea, five days after the war began, MacArthur immediately seized upon the same concept as a means of defeating his new enemy. By his later testimony the concept flashed upon him during a twenty-minute period as he stood on a hill watching the broken ROK Army fleeing south across the Han River. As the North Koreans thrust down the peninsula, their supply routes would stretch dangerously taut. Striking the North Koreans behind the front would enable the United States to "envelop and destroy his main force with only a handful of troops."[1]

MacArthur was so taken by his own idea that as soon as he returned to Tokyo, he ordered his staff to prepare plans for an amphibious landing "near Seoul," the exact location unspecified. This was on July 4. By July 10 the staff had laid out plans for Operation Bluehearts which would put U.S. troops into the port of Inchon, to the west of Seoul by about two dozen miles, on July 22. The army's 1st Cavalry Division would launch the attack.

Bluehearts was absurd on its face.[2] The few American troops then in Korea were fighting for survival; pulling a landing force from their meager ranks was impossible. So, too, were the logistics of mounting such an operation in eighteen days. The navy would have to find and reactivate rusting landing craft and convert Military Sea Transportation

Service (MSTS) transports into vessels capable of mounting an amphibious landing. Few of the army troops then in Korea had any amphibious experience. As a marine officer explained to MacArthur's staff, "An amphibious landing is not quite the same as sailing some boats into a harbor and stepping out onto a pier. Lacking proper preparation, we could end up with a hell of a lot of bodies on the beach."

True, the 1st Marine Brigade was en route to Asia, and its officers and men knew amphibious tactics. But marine officers ticked off the Bluehearts questions. What was actually known about the tides and beaches at Inchon? The cursory data in hand showed ferocious tides of up to thirty-five feet, with high stone walls at water's edge. The marines made it plain that they thought little of Bluehearts.

His dream dashed by realities, MacArthur abandoned Bluehearts—but not the idea of an amphibious landing. Keep planning, he told his staff, but shove the date back several months. On July 23 the staff proposed an alternative called Operation Chromite, with several variants: a landing at Inchon, coupled with a simultaneous attack north out of the Pusan Perimeter by EUSAK; a landing at Kunsan, also on the west coast; or a landing near Chumunjin, on the east coast. Both the FEC staff and MacArthur favored the Inchon option, although navy and marine officers expressed doubts. MacArthur cabled Washington on July 23:

> Operation planned mid-September is amphibious landing of a two division corps in rear of enemy lines for purpose of enveloping and destroying enemy forces in conjunction with attack from south by Eighth Army. I am firmly convinced that early and strong effort behind his front will sever his main line of communication and enable us to deliver a decisive and crushing blow. The alternative is a frontal attack which can only result in a protracted and expensive campaign.[3]

MacArthur had defined his strategy. Now he needed troops to implement it.

Assignment for the Marines

One morning in early July General MacArthur strode across his office and gestured to a large wall map of Korea.[4] He turned to his visitor, Lieutenant General Lemuel C. Shepherd, Jr., commander of the Fleet Marine Force, Pacific, the corps's force in readiness for amphibious operations.

"Lem," MacArthur said, "if I had that First Marine Division, I'd land it here at Inchon."

Shepherd moved a few steps closer and looked at the map. He thought over what MacArthur had asked. A brigade of the 1st Marine Division was already en route to Korea, and Shepherd had hurried to Japan to see what its assignment might be. As Shepherd put it, "We didn't want to go over there with a bobtail brigade attached to an army division."

Shepherd liked MacArthur's idea for an end-run invasion around the North Koreans. He had served under MacArthur during the Second World War and shared his appreciation of amphibious operations. Shepherd saw a chance for the marines to grab themselves a significant role in the Korean War.

"General, why don't you ask for them?" Shepherd said, meaning the 1st Marine Division.

MacArthur waved his hand at the marine. "You sit down," he said, "and write me up a dispatch to the JCS requesting that the First Marine Division be sent out to my theater of command."

This request shook Shepherd. "I looked at MacArthur's desk—it was a great big desk—and to the large chair he wanted me to sit down in while writing a dispatch which would be difficult to compose, to the Joint Chiefs." Shepherd needed privacy. "It was a delicate dispatch to compose. Here I was, recommending that a marine division be sent to Korea, and the [Marine Corps] commandant didn't know anything about what I was doing. This was a hell of a spot to be in, but the ball had been dropped in my hands, and I felt I must run with it."

MacArthur had one more question. He wanted to conduct the Inchon operation on September 15—sixty-seven days away. Could Shepherd put the division together and ship it to Korea by that time?

Shepherd mulled the request. He knew that the activation of the 1st Marine Brigade, mustered chiefly from 1st Division marines at Camp Pendleton, had left the division at less than regimental strength. To flesh it to full strength would mean activation of hundreds of men from factories, fields, cities, and college campuses, outfitted and shipped 6,000 miles.

Yes, Shepherd replied, he could deliver the division in time for the invasion.

But other visitors to MacArthur several days later were not as optimistic about the Inchon plan. General Collins, the army chief of staff, and General Vandenberg of the air force had come to Tokyo specifically to hear MacArthur's idea. Collins was openly dubious. He shook his head when he heard that MacArthur wanted two additional divisions beyond the troops already promised.

"General," he said, "you are going to have to win the war out here with the troops available to you in Japan and Korea."[5]

MacArthur smiled and shook his head. "Joe," he said, "you are going to have to change your mind."

At a staff meeting the next day Collins warned MacArthur's aides once again that American resources were scarce. "Don't get too grandiose," he said.[6]

Collins found Admiral James Doyle, the naval commander, unenthusiastic about the Inchon invasion. When Collins questioned landing in an area with thirty-five-foot tides, Doyle replied, "It will be extremely difficult and will take considerable preliminary destruction ashore, but it can be done."

Collins had been in the military long enough to recognize a hedge when he heard one; what Doyle was saying was that although he was not prepared to argue against MacArthur—at this stage, at any rate—Chromite was a foolhardy scheme, but one which he would undertake if ordered.

After a hurried visit to the battlefield Collins met again with MacArthur, this time privately. He felt a full marine division could be sent to the Far East. But he remained skeptical about a landing at Inchon mainly because of the high tides.

MacArthur did not press the issue for the moment. He had the implied promise of his marines. Once he got them into the theater, he would deal with the JCS on Inchon.

The JCS Are Dubious

But MacArthur's request for the 1st Marine Division received a cool reception at the JCS. The animosity was as much toward the Marine Corps as the plan. The chairman, General Bradley, an old soldier of the foot-slogging school, actively disliked the marines. The previous October, at congressional budget hearings, he said flatly that the day of the marines had passed; that "large-scale amphibious operations . . . will never occur again." Referring back to the interservices rivalries left unresolved by the unification provisions of the National Security Act, Bradley tartly said that "this is no time for 'fancy-dans' who won't hit the line with all they have on every play, unless they can call the signals."[7] *New York Times* correspondent William L. White wrote that senior navy and marine officers, the targets of Bradley's harsh comments, "sat in white, silent anger,"[8] as they listened to "one of the most extraordinary tongue-lashings ever given to high military officers in such a forum."*(MacArthur, in turn, did not care for Bradley, a car-

*Truman shared Bradley's low opinion of the two services. In a letter to a congressman some weeks after the war began, the President wrote, "The Marine Corps is the Navy's police force and as long as I am President that is what it will remain. They have a propaganda machine that is almost equal to Stalin's." Unfortunately for Truman a marine

ryover from the rivalry between the European and Pacific theaters of the Second World War. To one visitor, he called the JCS chairman "a dirt farmer." Nor did he think much of General Marshall, saying that "his fine patrician Virginia nose does not tolerate the daily smells of Asia.")

In any event, Bradley and another marine-navy foe on the JCS, General Vandenberg, now had the opportunity to fulfill their own prophecy about the buggy-whip standing of the rival services. Surprisingly even Admiral Sherman, the navy representative, was skeptical. Stripping the entire corps to bring the 1st Marines to battle strength would seriously deplete the service's capability to meet other responsibilities. He referred specifically to the Fleet Marine Force, Atlantic, based at Camp LeJeune, North Carolina. So the JCS told MacArthur, on July 20, that he would not have the 1st Marines before November.

MacArthur would have none of this. In an angry cable on July 21 he repeated his plea for immediate dispatch of the division in strong terms. "There can be no demand for its potential use elsewhere," he argued, "that can equal the urgency of the immediate battle mission contemplated for it."[9]

After several more exchanges of messages the JCS effectively capitulated. They would give MacArthur the marine division, less, however, the brigade already en route to Korea—in effect, two-thirds of a division. Now MacArthur could start planning in earnest for an Inchon landing. First, however, the marines had to put together the promised division.

Reservists Are Mobilized

Raymond G. Davis, a lieutenant colonel when the war began, but later commandant of the Marine Corps, was typical of the cadre of regular officers charged with molding disparate reservists into a fighting division in quickstep time.[10] Davis had been working with reservists in the Chicago area, and the first major problem he encountered was that many of them did not wish to leave civilian life to go fight in Asia. Examining physicians listened sympathetically to these reluctant soldiers:

> I forgot how the doctors were expressing it, but they were finding all these people unqualified to go. I looked over a lot of them [rejected reser-

veterans' association was meeting in Washington when the congressman received—and leaked—the letter. The clamor was so great that Truman had to appear in person at the convention and apologize for his intemperate language.

vists] and I knew some of them, and I couldn't believe the findings.

The two doctors worked out at Hines Veterans Administration Hospital, full-time, and the next thing I knew, the doctors' reports came in and they weren't qualified to go either. It turned out that they had examined one another and found one another not qualified to go.

With that, I took all these unqualified people, got me another doctor, and had him examine them, and they were all qualified to go. We got rid of those two doctors.

Davis felt fortunate that his unit, the 9th Battalion, a Chicago unit, had finished its annual summer training only a few weeks earlier; hence it arrived at Camp Pendleton as an armed, trained unit, ready for combat. But to Davis's dismay, his troops got off the train in the dark, were assembled into groups of seventy-five men by staff officers, and marched away into the night, to be assigned piecemeal to other units. Another battalion officer told Davis, "I saw them walk off into the dark, I've never seen them since." Men, records, and equipment were scattered over the vast expanse of Camp Pendleton.

Davis thus was left with the task of rebuilding his battalion as best he could. Conventional channels having failed, he and officers procured trucks and drove around the base, asking for volunteers. "At times they got a whole working party off a job somewhere," Davis said. "They'd drive up and say, 'Anybody want to go?' and in less than a day they got our entire complement of marines, just like that."

At Camp Pendleton, California, meanwhile, the 1st Division's acting commander, Colonel Alpha L. Bowser, scoured area military posts for equipment. The main assembly area, a portion of Pendleton known as Camp Pulgas, had not been used for years; "it was just sitting there in tumbleweed."[11] The landing vehicles to be used in the invasion had been parked since 1945 on the dry desert near Barstow, California; now they were trucked to ports in Southern California without time for even rudimentary test drives. The marines felt—indeed, they had been promised—they would have time for such checks once the division paused in Japan. Such was not to be. As Major General Oliver P. Smith, the division commander, recalls, "When they got to Kobe, they were gassed up, lifted out of the hold, dropped into the water, and [they] swam ashore—that was it. There was no rehearsal for Inchon. The next time these amtracs were run was when they were launched from LSTs [landing ships, tanks] in the water to make the run to the beach."[12] Andrew Geer, the marine historian, commented, "There were more veterans of Iwo and Okinawa among the vehicles than among the men who would drive them."[13]

But from all the turmoil, General Smith and Colonel Bowser managed to create a division which set sail between August 14 and 18 in what Bowser called the "damnedest hodgepodge of shipping you've ever seen." Only one thing was lacking: any idea whatsoever as to where the division would go into combat. The JCS knew MacArthur still insisted on going ashore at Inchon; but Washington had been told nothing more than the anticipated date, and even that had not been given final approval. Somewhat curious as to exactly what he was to accomplish once he arrived in the Far East, General Smith sent Bowser to Japan by air in early August, then followed once the division embarked. Smith realized he could not give himself the luxury of sitting aboard ship for three weeks.

Colonel Davis also hated to see the time go to waste, for he, too, knew the 1st Division was by no means a polished outfit. Training commenced as soon as the ships cleared harbor. "We took sandbags along and set up mortars on the fantail of the ship and fired. It was the first time the boys had ever fired their mortars." The commodore in charge of the fleet "was pretty much startled by all this racket." So the marines sailed off for the war, lobbing practice mortar shells at boxes dropped over the fantail.

MacArthur's Plan Challenged

Colonel Alpha Bowser's flight across the Pacific from California to Japan took three mostly sleepless days; nonetheless, a Far East Command staff car met him at the airport and whisked him directly to the Dai Ichi Building for the first briefing a marine officer heard on Inchon. At two in the morning Bowser then went to a planning command post set up on the USS *McKinley* and worked for several more hours until falling asleep "with a trillion questions totally unanswered . . . as far as I was concerned."[14] MacArthur's projected landing date was less than a month away, yet his staff could not answer a host of queries posed by Bowser: "What was on the bottom of the mud flats when the tide was out? Could you get across it? Would it bog down an amtrac? Would a boat just be totally stuck in it when the next tide came in? How high was the seawall over the high-tide mark? Was it two feet; was it twenty? Nobody would answer these questions."

After a troubled sleep Bowser set about trying to obtain hard information about Inchon. He was disappointed. "The army staff should have had it; we were in Inchon for years." Fortunately the army soon produced a warrant officer from the Transportation Corps who had actually worked on the Inchon docks. "This guy was," Bowser said, "as far as I am concerned, a real encyclopedia." The air force and navy began aerial reconnaissance.

Thus Bowser had a smidgeon of information in hand when General

Smith flew into Tokyo on August 22. He spoke with Bowser and then at length with Admiral Doyle. Doyle's reaction, Smith said, "was that it was a terrible place to land, but he couldn't say it couldn't be done. I wasn't very happy with it, but we went to work."

MacArthur Stonewalls the JCS

Nor were the Joint Chiefs of Staff happy either with MacArthur's incessant demands for more manpower or with an invasion scheme that seemed increasingly implausible. All summer MacArthur hammered at the Pentagon for more men, finally wearing down the JCS through nagging persistence. To the chiefs' distress he put the most liberal interpretation possible on what they intended to be restrictions.

One such instance was the decision—at White House level—on August 10 to give him the 3rd Army Division, one of the few units left in the nations' General Reserve—that is, the troops maintained in the continental United States for use in the event of all-out war. General Collins, in transmitting the order, warned of the gravity of the risk involved:

> In withdrawing this division from the general reserve, the JCS have accepted for the next few months a further serious reduction in US capabilities to meet other possible demands for combat ground forces, as well as a further serious reduction . . . in the army's capability to train additional forces for your theater.
> It is the understanding of the JCS that this division is furnished you as a theater reserve, because of your reported intention of committing all remaining combat reserves now in or en route to your theater in your planned offensive operation, and further that it is your intention that this division, which will arrive in your theater at a very low combat effective level, will, *except for the most compelling reasons* [emphasis added], be permitted sufficient training time to reach a minimum acceptable training level before commitment to battle.[15]

Through July and early August the JCS became more and more uneasy about MacArthur's overall conduct, especially the lack of any specific information about the Inchon invasion other than date and location. Collins and Vandenberg surmised following their July 13–14 visit to Tokyo that MacArthur was deliberately close-mouthed because he feared a security leak in Washington.* Even after the visit, when he

*If this in fact was true, MacArthur was absolutely correct, for the Soviets had a nest of highly placed espionage agents in the British embassy in Washington, men with access

tried to persuade the JCS to give him the 1st Marine Division, MacArthur continued to hold his cards close to his vest, advising Washington in one cable that it would be "unwise" to describe fully in a message his plans for the use of this unit.[16]

Pressed on July 24 in a teleconference on whether he still thought it possible to land by mid-September, MacArthur replied that his chances were "excellent"—provided he received the marine division.[17] Once again MacArthur stressed security. "The spokesman for the Department of the Army should not reveal our grand strategy in the slightest degree," he cautioned Washington.

By early August discussion of MacArthur's strategy had reached into the White House.[18] At a meeting on August 10 Admiral Sherman was "confident that General MacArthur would make good use of the forces, but that the JCS would have to pass on his plans for amphibious landings." Pentagon G-3 (operations) as late as August 7 did not think the invasion could be mounted until mid-March 1951 because "a campaign plan for the Korean operation has not yet been received" from MacArthur.[19] What G-3 did not realize was that MacArthur had no intention of making the Pentagon privy to his strategic planning.

In his memoirs MacArthur faults Washington for a "silence of three weeks" lapsing after he told Collins and Vandenberg in general terms what he intended to do. The view from Washington was 180 degrees different; the JCS felt they were the party being ignored. In exasperation, the chiefs decided to send General Collins and Admiral Sherman across the Pacific once again. They left on August 19, and MacArthur growled at the news. "It was evident immediately upon their arrival," he said, "that the actual purpose of their trip was not so much as to discuss as to dissuade."[20] Collins disagreed. As he told Senate hearings the next spring, the Tokyo visit was made "to find out exactly what the plans were. Frankly, we were somewhat in the dark. . . ."

MacArthur's "Masterful Exposition"

They met at five-thirty in the afternoon of August 23 in a paneled six-floor conference room in the Dai Ichi Building, the most impressive assemblage of brass since the war began.[21] Admiral Sherman and Generals Collins and Idwal Edwards, the air deputy, represented the JCS; Admirals Arthur Radford, C. Turner Joy, and Doyle, the Navy; Generals Almond, Doyle Hickey, Clark Ruffner, and Edwin K. Wright, from

to the most intimate details of planning for the war. See Chapter Eight below on Messrs. Philby, Burgess, and Maclean.

MacArthur's staff. The strains between Almond and the marine generals, Shepherd and Smith, were reflected in the absence of the latter officers. The marines would do the actual landing, the most dangerous and intricate part of the operation, yet they were represented by a mere lieutenant colonel, who attended as one of Doyle's briefing officers. The omission was petty; Shepherd noted in his diary later: "Marines weren't *persona grata* in Tokyo in those days."

The navy briefers led off, filing into the conference room one by one, at eight-minute intervals, eight of them in all. They did not address themselves to MacArthur's grand strategic scheme but confined themselves to the immediate logistics of the operation. "We drew up a list of every conceivable and natural handicap—and Inchon had 'em all," said Lieutenant Commander Arlie G. Capps, the gunfire support officer. "Make up a list of amphibious 'don'ts,'" said Commander Monroe Kelley, the communications officer, "and you have an exact description of the Inchon operation. A lot of us planners felt that if the Inchon operation worked, we'd have to rewrite the textbook."

The navy's major problems with Inchon were tide and terrain. The average rise and fall of tides there were 20.7 feet, one of the greatest in the world. But on the invasion target day, the moon's position would cause a rise and fall of about 32 feet. When the tides were at low ebb, mud flats that had accumulated over the centuries jutted more than two miles into the harbor. During ebb and flow the tide gushed through narrow, serpentine Flying Fish Channel, the best approach to land, at up to six knots an hour. The navy's mine expert said that Flying Fish Channel was a natural location for mines and that any ship sunk there would clog the passage. There were "dead-end" points on the approach where a disabled vessel would halt the entire column, for the channels had no space for turns.

The first high tide would peak at 6:59 A.M.; within two hours, however, it would have so receded that assault craft would be stranded on Inchon's sticky mudbanks, easy targets for Communist shore batteries. There they would remain until the next high tide, at 7:19 P.M., about half an hour after sunset. Thus the amphibious force had only two hours to force a passage of the channel, neutralize and occupy foreboding Wolmi-do Island, the heavy fortifications of which commanded the harbor, and bring enough supplies to last the remainder of the day.

The evening landing force would have two hours to put troops ashore, secure a beachhead, land supplies, and build defensive positions to withstand counterattacks until the tides returned just after dawn.

The navy disliked trying to put forces ashore in the heart of a city in which every wharf, warehouse, and building were potential strongpoints. Because of the necessity of leveling Wolmi-do, there would be no chance of a tactical surprise.

The primary landing point on Wolmi-do, Green Beach, was a 200-

yard stretch of intermittent patches of sand and rock. On the mainland, Red Beach and Blue Beach were four miles apart, at opposite ends of the city, separated by a dismal industrial and wharf area, the harbor front lined with sagging piers and a high seawall. At low tide, Red Beach looked onto 1,000 feet of gooey, semiliquid mud flat; the consistency, wrote marine historian Robert Debs Heinl, was "of solidifying chocolate fudge, but the smell is different." At the opposite end of town, Blue Beach faced 4,500 yards of mud flats, with a 14-foot seawall.

Months later even General Almond was to agree that Inchon was "the worst possible place we could bring in an amphibious assault." But *because* it was the worst place possible, it was, militarily, the best possible place, if MacArthur could turn the seeming disadvantage to his own advantage.

Doyle, who would command the naval force, noted the dangers of taking ships into the narrow approach channels. Sherman snorted, "*I* wouldn't hesitate to take a ship up there."

"Spoken like a Farragut!" MacArthur approvingly exclaimed.

Speaking after the navy presentation, General Collins worried about the ability of EUSAK to break out of the Pusan Perimeter. Collins had made a hurried visit to General Walton Walker, the EUSAK commander, before the conference. Walker was "too busy plugging holes in his leaky front to give much thought to a later breakout." Further, Walker was about to be weakened by withdrawal of the 1st Marine Brigade, to be taken from his command and attached to the invading force.

Collins warned that failure of EUSAK to strike north "might result in disaster" to the Inchon invading force. As an alternate, he suggested Kunsan. This port, 100 miles to the south, lacked Inchon's physical disadvantages, was close to NKPA supply routes running through Nonsan and Taejon, and was closer to the Eighth Army lines, thus making a juncture of the two UN armies easier. Sherman agreed. He asked MacArthur to forget Inchon and strike for Kunsan.

MacArthur sat silently, impassively, puffing on his pipe as he listened to the navy staff and Collins and Sherman. When they finished, he remained dormant a few more moments, as if striving for maximum dramatic effect. Many of the men in the room had seen MacArthur in full oratorical bloom before; they knew his penchant for the theatrical; nonetheless, they could not help being moved.

MacArthur enjoyed the suspense. He wrote later: "Almond shifted uneasily in his chair. If ever a silence was pregnant, this one was. I could almost hear my father's voice telling me as he had so many years ago, 'Doug, councils of war breed timidity and defeatism.'" Then MacArthur spoke for forty-five minutes, quietly at first, then gradually "building up emphasis with consummate skill." Collins commented later: "Even discounting the obvious dramatics, this was a masterly exposition of the argument for the daring risk he was determined to take by a landing at Inchon."

Save for MacArthur's voice, the room was completely silent. Wisps of cigarette smoke drifted across the huge battle maps along the walls. MacArthur spoke without notes. No one at the conference challenged the accuracy of the account given in his memoirs.

With the bulk of the NKPA concentrated at the Pusan Perimeter, MacArthur was convinced "the enemy . . . has failed to prepare Inchon properly for defense." The very arguments raised against a landing at Inchon "will tend to ensure for me the element of surprise." No enemy commander would reason that the Americans would be so "brash" as to risk such an attack. As a parallel he cited the surprise British raid on Quebec in 1759, when a small force scaled supposedly impossible heights and caught the French by surprise.

MacArthur recognized the navy's objections were "substantial and pertinent" but "not insuperable." He had confidence in the navy—more so, perhaps, "than the navy has in itself." The navy had overcome similar difficulties in Second World War amphibious operations; it could do the same at Inchon.

The proposed alternate landing site, Kunsan, would be less risky, MacArthur continued, but also less valuable. A strike there would not disturb enemy logistics lines. "Better no flank movement than one such as this." Nor did he see any logic in a "bloody and indecisive" attempt to try to break Walker's Eighth Army free from Pusan. "The enemy will merely roll back on his lines of supply and communication."

Capturing Inchon and Seoul, however, would cut the enemy's supply lines and seal off the entire peninsula. The farther south the NKPA went, the more tenuous its supply routes, all of which converged at Seoul. "By seizing Seoul I would completely paralyze the enemy's supply system," MacArthur said. "Without munitions and food [the enemy troops] will soon be helpless and disorganized, and can easily be overpowered. . . ."

The only other alternative MacArthur saw was continued attritional warfare at Pusan. "Are you content to let our troops stay in that bloody perimeter like beef cattle in the slaughterhouse?" he said. "Who will take the responsibility for such a tragedy? Certainly, I will not."

MacArthur built toward his climax. "I can almost hear the ticking of the second hand of destiny. We must act now or we will die." He concluded:

> If my estimate is inaccurate and should I run into a defense with which I cannot cope, I will . . . personally withdraw our forces before they are committed to a bloody setback. The only loss then will be my professional reputation. But Inchon will not fail. Inchon will succeed. And it will save 100,000 lives.

Even the skeptical Collins went away impressed but with reservations. The next day Admirals Sherman and Radford talked with the two marine generals, Oliver P. Smith and Lemuel Shepherd, who had been excluded from the conference. On the basis of naval reconnaissance they had received over the past several days, the marines argued that a better landing site would be Posung-Myon, thirty miles south of Inchon, where the water was deep enough for a landing at any time.

Almond would hear no argument about an alternative to Inchon, and the longer he talked, the more he infuriated Smith and Shepherd.[22] Almond told them, "All this amphibious stuff is just a mechanical operation."

Smith knew better. "I tried to tell him a few of the facts of life, and he was rather supercilious, and he called me 'son,' which kind of annoyed me."

The marine generals demanded, and finally received, an audience with MacArthur, who was in no mood to entertain further dissent; he had argued down the larger group the previous day, and now he wanted the marines to shut up and carry out their orders. Seizing Inchon and then Seoul, MacArthur said, would quickly end the war. "For a five-dollar ante," he said, "I have an opportunity to win fifty thousand dollars, and I have decided that is what I'm going to do."

Sherman had a final meeting with MacArthur. What they discussed is not a matter of record, but Sherman did say afterward, "I wish I could share that man's confidence."

A Presidential Endorsement

By supreme irony, the Formosan controversy that had so enraged President Truman in early August (see Chapter Five)[23] now provided General MacArthur with a conduit through which he could argue his case for Chromite directly with a White House emissary, effectively bypassing the Joint Chiefs. As will be recalled, Truman had sent adviser W. Averell Harriman to Tokyo to remonstrate with MacArthur about his statements in support of Chiang Kai-shek.

Harriman at the time had heard of the Inchon plans only in cursory form. During his long conversations with MacArthur he asked for more detail, and he liked what he heard. Although MacArthur's meddling with national policy irritated Harriman, he felt that on military matters "political and personal considerations should be put to one side, and our government [should] deal with General MacArthur on the lofty level of the great national asset which he is."

Harriman's enthusiasm was not lost upon the President. And fortunately for Chromite, Harriman had Truman's ear for several days before Generals Collins and Vandenberg returned from their Tokyo briefing by MacArthur. Truman emphatically told Defense Secretary Johnson that MacArthur should be permitted to proceed with the invasion plans.[24]

The JCS judiciously chose not to argue with Truman, although they continued to have deep reservations about Chromite. On August 28 the Joint Chiefs sent MacArthur a highly hedged "approval." They took care not to approve any specific site, and they made plain MacArthur should consider landing elsewhere than Inchon. Indeed, the order could be interpreted as a strong suggestion that MacArthur change his plans:

> After reviewing the information brought back by General Collins and Admiral Sherman we concur in making preparations and executing a turning movement by amphibious forces on the west coast of Korea either at Inchon in the event that enemy defenses in vicinity of Inchon prove ineffective or at a favorable beach south of Inchon if one can be located. We further concur in preparation, if desired by CINCFE,* for an envelopment by amphibious forces in the vicinity of Kunsan. We understand that alternative plans are being prepared in order best to exploit the situation as it develops.
>
> We desire such information as becomes available with respect to conditions in the possible objective areas and timely information as to your intentions and plans for offensive operations.[25]

The JCS did not act on another recommendation brought back by Harriman and Ridgway and General Lauris Norstad of the air force, who accompanied them as an observer. They urged that General Walton Walker be replaced as Eighth Army commanding general.[26] The consensus was that Walker was worn-out and lacked the finesse to keep grips on the myriad problems facing an army in the field. No one challenged Walker's bravery; if anything, they faulted him for taking too many risks by his frequent trips into combat areas. Two months of war had ground down the man. "It seemed very clear to us, the three of us," Harriman remarked years later, "that Walker wasn't up to the job." But the JCS let the issue ride for the moment. Besides, according to Harriman, the JCS feared "adverse reaction" by MacArthur if it dared fire his most prominent field general.

*Commander in chief, Far East Command, pronounced "sink-fee" by the military.

JCS Doubts Deepen

On August 30 MacArthur issued the bulky operations plan for the Inchon landing, which was distributed widely through the Far East Command. But despite the specific order given him by the JCS directive of
August 28, he did not send a copy to Washington.

On September 1, as noted previously, events took a dangerous turn
around the Pusan Perimeter. A general North Korean offensive
punched holes in the allied lines. The 1st Marine Brigade, already disen-
gaging for Inchon, was hurriedly thrown back into the line, and General
Walker considered further tightening of his already crowded positions.

Worried, the JCS sent another message to MacArthur on September
5, inquiring about Chromite and reminding him of their "desire to be
informed of any modification which may have been made in your plans
for a mid-September amphibious operation."[27]

MacArthur replied blithely that "the general outline of plan remains
as described to you"[28] and that he was sending copies of the operations
order and other relevant documents by a courier, who would arrive in
Washington about September 11.

The JCS now feared that MacArthur was on the brink of an operation with disastrous potential. Should the Eighth Army be pushed out
of the Pusan Perimeter, a grim possibility, MacArthur's invasion force
could be isolated and destroyed. In a September 7 cable the chiefs
repeated their support for a counteroffensive "as early as is feasible."[29] But given the commitment of virtually all his reserves available to EUSAK, did he think Chromite would succeed if launched as
scheduled? The JCS reminded him that the 82nd Airborne Division
was the only remaining division in the United States and that recently
mobilized National Guard units would require four months for training and transport.

MacArthur later wrote that this message "chilled me to the marrow
of my bones" by implying that the "whole movement should be abandoned."[30] So he changed the stated purpose of Chromite.[31] No longer
was it a hammer-and-anvil maneuver, with EUSAK driving north to
pound the North Koreans against the blockade positions around Seoul.
Success did not depend upon rapid juncture of the two armies. What
he wanted was seizure of the supply lines around Seoul; once this was
done, "the enemy cannot fail to be ultimately shattered through disruption of his logistical support and our combined combat operations. *The
prompt junction of our two forces, while it would be dramatically
symbolic of the complete collapse of the enemy, is not a vital part of
the operation* [emphasis added]."

Embarkation of the invasion force and preparations for air and sea
bombardments "are proceeding according to schedule." He repeated
his total confidence of success.

The JCS now had no choice. Later the same day they sent yet another cable to MacArthur. "We approve your plan and President has been so informed," it said.[32]

Only then did MacArthur do anything about sending the courier to Washington, as he had promised several days earlier.[33] The JCS had requested a senior staff officer. MacArthur looked deep into the ranks of his headquarters and selected a young lieutenant colonel, Lynn D. Smith, from his planning staff.

MacArthur called Smith to the Dai Ichi Building late the night of September 9. Marines were already boarding boats at Pusan, and the support bombardment was under way.

"Do you personally believe in the plan we are going to execute?" MacArthur asked Smith.

"Yes, sir," Smith replied.

"Good. Start for Washington tomorrow—but don't get there too soon."

MacArthur told Smith to take the operations plan and other documents—eleven volumes weighing thirty-five pounds—to the Pentagon and personally deliver them to the Joint Chiefs. Then he should answer their questions.

The general added, "If they say it is too big a gamble, tell them I said this is throwing a nickel in the pot after it has been opened for a dollar. The big gamble was Washington's decision to put American troops on the Asiatic mainland."

MacArthur did nothing to make Smith's journey comfortable or fast. Instead of being put on a courier aircraft, Smith waited around Tokyo all night and then boarded a weather-beaten old DC-4 for the long flight across the Pacific, satchels of the documents at his feet. Wake Island: a stopover for fuel, food, and minor repairs. Then on across more ocean to Oahu and another stop. Then on to Travis Air Force Base in California.

Meanwhile, the JCS fretted over the whereabouts of the promised plans, and MacArthur's invasion armada gathered its full force.

The Invasion Format

Although paper work was kept to a minimum, by necessity and design, by the first week of September the joint planning staff of the army, navy, and marines had worked out the basic landing plan. The invasion would progress by stages.

First would come saturation bombing and naval barrages of Inchon and environs, concentrating on the menacing island fortress of

Wolmi-do. The barrages would continue until seconds before the assault marines landed.

Because of its controlling position, Wolmi-do would be seized first, by an invasion force using the morning tide. In battalion strength, with supporting engineers and tanks, the first force would come into the harbor on high-speed APDs (auxiliary patrol destroyers), escorts rebuilt for raiding and landing light forces.

It was hoped that Wolmi-do would be secured within a matter of hours and the first battalion could protect itself from the NKPA until the bulk of the landing force swept into Inchon on the high evening tide —one segment bound for Red Beach, the other for Blue Beach. The two evening forces would join up in Inchon with marines coming over the causeway from Wolmi-do and then attack east toward Yongdungpo.

The navy anticipated problems. Because of the narrowness of the channels, the cumbersome landing craft, some capable of carrying 500 tons each, would have to sidle onto the beach and park parallel to one another, noses dug into the sand like giant sea turtles, while the battle raged just over the seawall.

The landing force would be two regiments of the 1st Marine Division, with a regiment of the Korean Marine Corps in reserve. After mopping-up operations around Inchon, the force would advance and seize Kimpo Airport, cross the Han River, occupy Seoul, and then set up blocking positions in an arc above Seoul.

The 7th Infantry Division would follow the marines ashore, advance on their south flank, and eventually wheel and link up with the Eighth Army, advancing, it was hoped, from the south, out of the Pusan Perimeter.

Such was the plan. Now the pieces must be brought into place. The 1st Marine Brigade pulled out of Pusan the night of September 5–6; the 7th Infantry Division, commanded by a practical-minded Alabaman, Major General David G. Barr, filled by levies from stateside service schools and the streets of Pusan, began boarding transports in Kobe.

But as planning progressed, and D-Day neared, the acrimony between General Shepherd of the marines and General Almond of the army daily became more bitter.[34] Shepherd in later years said candidly that he "very shortly lost confidence in the higher command out there." Almond, fifty-eight years old at the time, was a much-decorated combat veteran of two wars who had served MacArthur since 1946, becoming chief of staff in 1949. He was not a popular man in the Far East Command; in the careful words of army historian Roy Appleman, he was "both feared and obeyed" throughout MacArthur's realm.[35] Almond had ample stores of both energy and impatience, and more than one officer quaked at the sight of his chill eyes flickering in anger.

The first interservice dispute arose in mid-August, when MacArthur offhandedly told Almond he intended to create a new command, X

Corps, as the invasion force, with Almond as commander. Walton Walker's Eighth Army would continue as a separate organization, and both EUSAK and X Corps would report directly to Tokyo. Who would become chief of staff of the Far East Command? Almond inquired. Oh, you keep both jobs, MacArthur said; the Inchon and Seoul thing will be wound up in a hurry, and you can return to Tokyo. The FEC would provide most of the staff officers for the landing operation as well. (MacArthur's decision on a divided command stung General Walker, who remarked to a visitor, "I'm just a defeated Confederate general."[36] Walker now knew beyond a doubt his days under MacArthur were numbered.)

The divided command proved to be one of MacArthur's worst blunders (among many) of the war. The immediate effect was to put Almond onto a certain collision course with General Oliver P. Smith, who would be leading the 1st Marine Division.

The two generals were physical and psychological opposites. Smith, a native of Texas, fifty-seven years old that late summer, had had distinguished careers in two wars and enjoyed a reputation as somewhat of an intellectual. During a tour with the American embassy in Paris during the 1930's he took the full two-year course at the École Supérieure de Guerre and after the war commanded the Marine Corps's schools. Mild of speech and manner, Smith was lithe and tall, with a finely chiseled face and a shock of prematurely white hair. Some rougher marines occasionally mistook Smith's outwardly gentle nature for weakness. Weak Oliver Prince Smith was definitely not.

Smith agreed with Admiral Doyle that Inchon was a "terrible place to land," and he admitted, "I wasn't very happy with it. But we went to work."[37] Almost immediately he and Almond got into a tug-of-war over use of the 1st Marine Brigade as part of the Inchon force.

Smith could see the army's point. General Walker wished to keep the brigade in his Pusan Perimeter defense; the marines fought well, and the NKPA seemed determined to shove EUSAK off the peninsula with its September offensive. Walker even offered Smith a trade: Give me the 1st Brigade, he said, and I'll swap you a regiment of the 7th Division.

"I protested bitterly," Smith said, "because this regiment was made up forty percent of South Koreans who couldn't speak English; they'd had only a minimum of amphibious training. Logistically, they couldn't have made it [to Korea in time for the invasion] because they were up at Yokohama."

Also, Smith and other marine officers had seen some of the South Koreans routed off the street and sent to Japan to augment the 7th Infantry Division before it embarked for Inchon. More than 8,000 men and boys were grabbed by ROK Army press gangs and piled into ships and sent across the Sea of Japan. On arrival at the wharves their clothing ranged from business suits to shirts and shorts or only shorts. The majority wore sandals or cloth shoes. They were a pitiable mob of tired, confused civilians, only a few of whom could speak English. Smith sympathized with them, but he would not rely upon such people to storm an enemy beach with his marines.

Admiral C. Turner Joy was one person in the FEC who did not quake before Almond, and in this instance he sided with Smith.* At a meeting at the FEC headquarters to discuss the control of the marine brigade "Admiral Joy really read off General Almond." Then Joy asked Smith what he thought. "I told him frankly that if they did make that substitution, I would call off the Blue Beach landing and land only with the First Marines on Red Beach. If I [landed on both] I was going beyond the point of a considered risk." But Almond would not yield.

At Smith's insistence Almond gave him and Admiral Doyle an audience with MacArthur for a final decision. The marine staff neared open revolt over the issue, some fifteen officers cramming into a shipboard cabin for a strategy meeting. Colonel Bowser, Smith's deputy, was to marvel later that Doyle and Smith "pretty much laid their careers on the line that night" by making such a personal appeal over Almond to MacArthur. They told him, in effect, "Either you do this [give us the brigade] or you find yourself another couple of boys to do the operation."

Admiral Arthur Struble, the Seventh Fleet commander, finally hit on a solution that both satisfied the marines and gave Almond an opportunity to save face. The 7th Division regiment packed with ROK replacements would be put ashore at Pusan to replace the marine brigade, which would join the 1st Division for the Inchon assault.

Nonetheless, the episode "kind of shook my confidence," Smith said later, "that anybody would think you could take an untrained regiment like that and at the last minute substitute it for a veteran regiment."

No sooner had the brigade issue been resolved than the enterprising Almond produced what Smith called "another brainstorm." He wanted to form a "special action company" for commando operations, and the marines must give him 100 select men to add to it. "I wanted no part of that," Smith said, "because I needed all the marines I had." Only a few days earlier the secretary of the navy had ordered the marines to leave any men under eighteen years of age in Japan and keep them out of combat. This decision, the result of domestic political pressures, cleaved some 500 men from the 1st Division, and Smith felt he could spare no more losses.

Smith thought the commando scheme a "wild idea. They were going to embark in a British frigate and go around to Inchon and transfer to

*Turner Joy was such a ferocious, tenacious man in an argument that the Far East Command eventually selected him as the chief UN negotiator when peace talks began with the Communists. He did not give away anything at the bargaining table.

a small boat, go in, and row ashore in rubber boats and capture the Kimpo Airport." He pointed out obvious flaws. The unit would be carrying radios with ranges of only four miles; thus the navy would not know where it would safely put down essential supporting gunfire for the main body. "Anyway," Smith said, "according to the intelligence reports, there were more people at the Kimpo Airport than these people could handle, and if they'd just leave us alone, we'd go in and capture the airfield for them, and in a very short time."

Although Smith succeeded in getting the marines dropped from the unit, Almond doggedly kept the idea alive through D-Day. "It never occurred to these jokers to figure out what would happen when the tide was going out, and they tried to row ashore against the [six- to eight-knot] tide. It was just foolishness." (Almond dropped the plan at the last minute.)

When not fighting with each other, the marines and army improvised equipment needed for the invasion. One problem that worried Bowser was the seawalls.[38] Built to turn back unusually high tides, they were sixteen feet above the mud flats. But even at the height of the tidal surge "we still had the problem of getting individual marines over the seawall. . . . A man standing on the top of the ramp of a [landing ship] could, conceivably, if he was very agile . . . jump far enough to get a leg over the seawall." But the men would be carrying weapons and heavy packs. So Japanese workers and ship crews were put to work fashioning scaling ladders from wood and aluminum.

The marines had brought their own landing craft with them, small Second World War vessels plucked from desert storage in California. But all the navy could find for the 7th Division were thirty or so old LSTs which MacArthur had turned over to the Japanese for coastal and commercial shipping. The crews were entirely Japanese, and few spoke any English. So the army had to put a communications detail with a radio on each ship—an army Nisei interpreter, two navy signalmen, and an ensign who might or might not be able to convince the Japanese captain he was in command for the duration of the invasion.

Another matter was intelligence.[39] Just how many troops did the NKPA have in the Inchon area? MacArthur and his intelligence officer, General Charles Willoughby, were convinced the vast majority were concentrated around Pusan. One Willoughby report estimated NKPA strength in the area as of September 1 as 1,000 men in Inchon, 5,000 in Seoul, and about 500 in Kimpo Airport. North Korean artillery was considered insignificant. Because of American air superiority, intelligence analysts estimated the North Korean "Air Force" possessed only nineteen obsolete Soviet-made planes.

But aerial photography and nighttime reconnaissance runs by small naval craft could produce only a limited amount of intelligence. Planners needed hard, verifiable intelligence, the sort of information that can come only from a person on the scene. None existed from ROK sources. An American involved in intelligence activities during the war stated, "By this time the ROKs were having trouble getting people to go to the front lines, much less behind them. Agent material dried up a few weeks after the war began. You can't blame the ROKs. Anyone who went behind the lines was likely to be thrown in the North Korean Army anyway."

A "Nerves of a Burglar" Mission

For more solid intelligence,[40] the military turned to a navy lieutenant named Eugene F. Clark, a onetime chief petty officer who had served in the Orient for almost two decades. In addition to maritime skills, Clark "had the nerves of a burglar and the flair of a Barbary Coast pirate," according to one intelligence operative who had known him during the Pacific war.

In a joint CIA-military operation code-named Trudy Jackson, Clark led a landing party onto the minute island of Yonghung-do, some fourteen miles south of Inchon. His mission was to scout the physical terrain over which the invasion would be launched—the tides; the mud flats; the seawalls; the defenses on Wolmi-do. Accompanied by an army captain, three U.S. enlisted men, and two ROK interpreters, Clark mobilized friendly Koreans on the island into what he called the Young Men's Association and sent them on audacious patrols into the Inchon area; one youth even crept onto tightly guarded Wolmi-do.

When the North Koreans tried to dislodge the Clark party, the spunky officer mounted a .50 caliber machine gun on a sampan and roared out to do battle with an enemy patrol boat. A sustained burst shattered the boat; it sank with eighteen Communist soldiers aboard.

A few nights later, on September 11, Clark personally scouted an abandoned lighthouse on Palmi-do, an island at the mouth of Flying Fish Channel, through which the invasion flotilla would sail. He found the light dismantled but operative. Could the navy use a guidelight the morning of the invasion? he radioed. Yes, indeed, was the reply. So he put the light into working order.

The night before the invasion Clark and his infiltrators silently stole away to Palmi-do. No sooner had they left Yonghung-do than North Korean soldiers came to the island, lined up some fifty Koreans who had helped the Americans, and shot them down.

Clark was worried about his own safety during the mission, for he knew many details of Chromite that would have been of immense value to the enemy were he to be captured. So he made sure he kept a grenade on his body at all times. He told another intelligence officer, "A grenade is a lot more certain than trying to shoot yourself with a pistol."

First Fire at Inchon

Given the congested geography of Japan, Chromite planners made no attempt to conceal what journalists in the Tokyo Press Club called Operation Common Knowledge. Instead, they relied upon systematic deception. Air strikes hit both coasts of Korea, seemingly indiscriminately. But suggestive hints pointed at Kunsan, the port to the south of Inchon. For nine days running the Far East Air Force rained bombs and shells on highways, bridges, and railways within a thirty-mile radius of Kunsan. The British cruiser HMS *Triumph* made run after run at Kunsan, its guns spurting explosive fire. On September 11 Kunsan itself suffered a major bombing strike. And, finally, the 1st Marine Brigade, while waiting to board ships on the Pusan docks, was brought into formation for a loud lecture by briefing officers on the defenses, beach, and terrain they were apt to encounter in Kunsan.

Korean dockworkers also enjoyed the lecture, for it was amplified over a public address system. By the time the armada sailed, *The New York Times,* despite the strictures of voluntary censorship, felt free to publish (on September 14) an article stating: "An amphibious landing on the Korean coast well behind the enemy's lines is an obvious and possible strategy."

Then, two days before the invasion, the emphasis abruptly shifted. Loaded with 95,000 pounds of napalm, packed into 150-pound containers, marine Corsairs blitzed the seaward sides of Wolmi-do, scorching its faces with molten fire. The next day, September 14, was the navy's turn, and carrier-mounted attack planes dropped bomb after bomb onto the smoldering debris left by the Corsairs.

Now the invasion force was ready.[41] At dawn a formidable fleet of four cruisers (two of them British) and six destroyers arrogantly sailed to the neck of Flying Fish Channel leading to Inchon, riding the surge of the high tide. The cruisers took up positions there; the destroyers formed a column and picked their way down the narrow channel, hoping to draw fire from enemy coast artillery and then destroy the gun positions. The sun broke through a haze of mist and smoke from cooking fires as the ships entered the channel; a Los Angeles *Times* correspondent, watching from the cruiser USS *Rochester,* thought Wolmi-do "looked like a picnickers' paradise, green-wooded and serene."

But for only a few minutes. The Communists ran out a gun on the northern tip of the island, and the crew frantically prepared it for firing. But the gunnery section of the destroyer USS *DeHaven* acted first, blowing away the gun with a salvo from its battery of five-inch guns. The remainder of the fleet joined in, firing at 1,300-yard range into the island, probing for gun positions.

For almost ten minutes the North Koreans' guns remained silent, either because crews were slow to react or because commanders did not wish to give away their positions. Then they opened return fire, and with a vengeance. "A necklace of gun-flashes sparkled around the waist of the island," reported the Associated Press's Relman Morin. "The flashes were reddish gold and they came so fast that soon the entire slope was sparkling with pinpoints of fire."

The ferocity of the counterfire resolved any lingering questions about whether the NKPA had heavily fortified the island. Five armor-piercing shells hit the destroyer USS *Collett* alone.

But in less than an hour the six destroyers hurled 998 five-inch shells at Wolmi-do; the cruisers, hanging at the entrance to the channel, threw salvos at both the island and Inchon proper. As the vessels finally withdrew, carrier-based planes swept over Wolmi-do for parting blasts.

The attack shook the confidence of the Inchon defense commander, who warned his higher headquarters of the air and naval bombardment. "Every indication enemy will carry out a landing," he cabled. "All units in my command are directed to be ready for battle; all units will be stationed in their assigned positions so they may throw back enemy forces when they attempt their landing operation." American forces found the message in captured NKPA files weeks later; there was no indication the higher command had heeded it.

The next day the force hit Wolmi-do again, in a repetition of the previous day's bombardment. This time the guns roared for seventy-five minutes, hurling 1,732 rounds at the island—just about the same number that hit Omaha Beach before the Normandy landing in 1944. A pilot from the carrier USS *Valley Forge* reported, "The whole island looked like it had been shaved."

Nonetheless, qualms remained. The close-range battle revealed that the North Koreans had concealed many of their guns deep in caves. Had enough survived to destroy the relatively fragile fleet of small landing craft that would be approaching the next morning? During the Pacific campaign the marines learned time and again the ability of Japanese infantry to burrow deep into the ground and emerge fighting once the barrage lifted. Wolmi-do might look like "one worthless piece of real estate" to a *Valley Forge* pilot viewing the island from the air. From beach level, the view could be entirely different.

* * *

The Joint Chiefs of Staff, it will be remembered, still awaited receipt of MacArthur's invasion plan, which had been repeatedly requested since mid-August. At eleven o'clock the night of September 13, a grimy Lieutenant Colonel Lynn Smith walked into the Pentagon and reported to a night duty officer. Three days had passed since he left Tokyo, charged by MacArthur with delivering the invasion plans. A security officer gave him a receipt for his thirty-five pounds of documents.

Someone asked Smith where he had been. Many places, the colonel replied. Despite the supposed urgency of his mission, no special plane had awaited him when he arrived at Travis Air Force Base in California on his flight across the Pacific. So he hitched a ride into San Francisco and took a commercial flight toward Washington. The flight terminated in Chicago, so Smith changed to a feeder line that hopped and skipped to the capital.

Now he was exhausted, and all he wanted was a chance to change clothes, shave, and perhaps sleep for a few hours. Someone pointed him to an office couch. The JCS would have their first look at the long-awaited Chromite plans in the morning.

MacArthur Embarks

Titan though he was, even Douglas Arthur MacArthur had to take note of the weather.[42] On September 3 Typhoon Jane had formally opened the Asian typhoon season by howling through the assembled invasion force with 100-knot winds and forty-foot waves. For all the fury, however, the damage was slight: lost moorings from half a dozen ships; a temporarily adrift crane; much fear about the floatability of a ship carrying the major communications gear. But the blow passed, and within a day ships' crews had the fleet tidy again and ready for sail.

Seawise Japanese, however, gave the Americans an admonition: In these waters, they said, experience was that one typhoon follows on the tossed white caps of another within ten days. So Admiral Doyle hastened his schedule by a day, and on September 11 his flagship, the *Mount McKinley,* followed the last of the transports out of Kobe Harbor into the smashing waves and high winds of the Sea of Japan.

MacArthur was aboard. A few days previously he had called in a group of newsmen, many of whom had been with him since his Pacific campaigns of the Second World War. MacArthur greeted the newsmen as if he were embarking on a pleasant Sunday outing, rather than a dangerous military campaign. With subordinates and prominent visitors he could exude aloofness; but with a press audience he almost invariably was jovial, permitting the small jokes that staff officers seldom heard.

"I'm going on a little operation, and I'd like to have you boys with me if you'd like to go," he said.* "I say a little operation—it's a big operation." The party would fly south the next morning. "I've got a new plane," he said, "and I'll follow you in that." He gestured at the newsmen with his black pipe and laughed. "But you bums will go in my old plane, the *Bataan.*"

At Sasebo, the port on the point of Japan that juts nearest to the Korean peninsula, MacArthur invited the press party to accompany him aboard the *Mount McKinley* and then to a briefing in the cabin of the task force commander, Admiral Doyle. Although worn by the buffeting of seas still torn by the departed typhoon, MacArthur talked at length of the strategy behind Chromite. As quoted by Carl Mydans of *Time,* much of his lecture was a popularized version of the spiel he had given on August 23 to the JCS skeptics General Collins and Admiral Sherman. Now MacArthur spoke to men whose reportage in the next few days would describe either his brilliance—or his failure.

"The history of war," MacArthur said, "proves that nine times out of ten an army has been destroyed because its supply lines have been cut off. That's what we are trying to do." Seizure of Seoul would cut off supplies to the NKPA forces fighting around Pusan, causing their disintegration. MacArthur concluded:

> We could commit 150 million Americans, and they could still put in four Asiatics for every American. I therefore made the decision I would not fight war to the enemy's strength, but would fight a war to my strength. We have devised a plan where we can get away from his advantages and use our advantages. . . .

Doyle admitted the landing would be technically difficult. He called Inchon "the worst possible place we could bring in an amphibious assault along the coast of Korea but . . . also the only possible place where our assault will carry out its purpose: to land, cut off and destroy the enemy."

Someone inquired whether MacArthur feared Chinese Communist intervention. "If the Chinese do intervene," MacArthur replied, "our air will turn the Yalu River into the bloodiest stream in all history."[43]

---

*MacArthur here employed the same quasi dare he tossed at correspondents before his visit to the Korea battle line in late June. What choice did the correspondents have? And why imply they might wish to choose otherwise? MacArthur uttered such insults without challenge, to both newsmen and fellow officers.

MacArthur's "Courier" Finally Reports

Lieutenant Colonel Lynn Smith, after a restless night on his couch, shaved and changed clothes in a washroom on the E ring of the Pentagon, then sought out the deputy chief of staff for operations, per orders.

The officer looked surprised when he discovered that the long-awaited "senior staff officer" from Tokyo was a mere light colonel. Then he grinned. "I'll get you down to Al right now," he said.

"Al" turned out to be Major General Alfred Gruenther, director of the Joint Staff. Gruenther, too, seemed amused. "The chiefs have a meeting at 1100," he told Smith. "That's an hour and a half from now. Can you be ready by then?"

All Smith could do was answer yes. He looked at his watch and computed the time in Korea. Inchon time is thirteen hours later (and a calendar day earlier) than Washington time. H-Hour on Wolmi-do Island was only eight hours away.

Smith enlisted the help of cartographers and artists to help him fill the panel space on five walls of the briefing room. The nervous Smith wondered how he would be treated when the members of the JCS filed in; he did not desire to bear the brunt of anger that might be directed toward General MacArthur because of his little prank. But everyone was polite.

As Smith picked up his pointer to begin the briefing, General Collins interrupted him. "This is D-Day, isn't it, Colonel?"

"Yes, sir," Smith replied.

"When is H-Hour?"

Smith consulted one of the time-zone clocks on the wall and did some mental calculations. "The landing at Wolmi-do will begin in six hours and twenty minutes—1730 your time," he replied.

"Thank you," Collins said, "you'd best get on with your briefing."

Smith talked for two hours, and not a single member of the JCS interrupted him with a substantive question. Nor did he get a chance to use the "nickel after a dollar" line MacArthur had given him in the event any of the chiefs suggested Inchon was too big a gamble. After he finished, each of the chiefs thanked him and shook his hand.

Smith glanced at the wall clock when they had left. If everything were on schedule in Flying Fish Channel, the invasion would commence in four hours.

MacArthur's ploy—a deliberate and naked violation of the gentleman's code by which the military officer corps lived and worked—had succeeded. By the time the young colonel finished his presentation the invasion was too far along to be canceled.

MacArthur won his point, but he paid a costly price. The JCS now had personal evidence of the deceit and underhanded tactics he had long used in his fights with Washington. This time, however, the foul punch struck not a political enemy or a diplomat but fellow officers. When Truman finally decided to fire MacArthur the following spring, not a single member of the JCS raised a voice in his defense.

The Marines Hit the Beaches

Early on the morning of September 15 the invasion armada, a total of nineteen ships—ranging from the *Mount McKinley,* the control ship, through cruisers, destroyers, and three bristling rocket vessels—snaked their way into the approaches to Flying Fish Channel under cover of darkness. The cruisers set up station and trained their big guns on Wolmi-do and targets beyond. As they had done the two previous days, the destroyers cautiously moved into the main channel, trailed closely by the rocket ships. MacArthur came onto the flag bridge of the *McKinley* to watch the show, picking his way through a star-studded confusion of generals and admirals in helmets and life jackets. As usual MacArthur wore his battered, salt-stained garrison cap. Out of deference to his senior status, he was given the admiral's bridge chair.

As the *McKinley* steamed through the predawn darkness, MacArthur gestured at the blinking navigational light on Palmi-do and said, "That's courtesy." He wrote in his memoirs, "We were taking the enemy by surprise. The lights were not even turned off." So tightly held was the secret of Lieutenant Clark's intelligence mission—and his lighting of the beacon—that no one on the bridge was in a position to correct MacArthur.

The navy and air force had prepared an awesome final bombardment. The four cruisers were to stand offshore 13,000 to 15,000 yards; the more mobile destroyers would dart within 800 yards of the beach. Forty-five minutes before the landing (L-minus-45) they would begin firing and dump a total of 2,845 shells on Wolmi-do and Inchon before ceasing at L-minus-2.

The rocket ships would add their especially deadly thunder beginning at L-minus-15. "Floating shotguns," someone in the invasion fleet called these vessels (LSMRs, for landing ships, medium, rocket). During a hellish thirteen-minute span, each of these ships would fire 1,000 five-inch rockets into Wolmi-do at a range of less than 1,000 yards. Then two of the LSMRs would cease fire and break away; the third, however, would dash in front of the first line of invasion craft, sail parallel to the shore, and give a final slap at the defenders, firing directly at the slopes in front of the attacking troops.

Meanwhile, marine and navy planes would be inundating Wolmi-do

with cannon and rocket fire and bombs. The plan called for tight coordination between the ship and air phases; marine and navy gunners
would fire only below a maximum trajectory of 1,100 feet, while the
minimum altitude of the planes was set for 1,500 feet.

At daybreak Inchon and Wolmi-do lay invisible in the shadow of the
black saw-toothed hills behind them. There was an occasional flicker
from fires of the previous's day's bombardment, but the coast seemed
eerily quiet. At 5:45 A.M. Admiral Doyle gave the order: Open fire. The
six- and eight-inch guns of the cruisers belched sheets of orange flame
toward the gray shoreline. Next came the smaller guns of the destroyers. Next, the whine of navy and marine planes and the dull thumps of
the bombs they dropped on the island. Radio Hill, most prominent
promontory on the tiny island, was an indistinct mass behind shrouds
of smoke.

So savage was the destruction that navy pilots had trouble finding
specific targets.[44] Lieutenant Edward H. Albright, of Herington, Kansas
(speaking through the medium of a navy press release later that day),
said, "There was a slope leading down to a cove that I happened to
notice yesterday. It was covered with grass and shrubbery. Today, when
I was directed to work the area over again, every bit of grass was gone,
and only a few trees remained." Another navy flier, Lieutenant Commander Marvin L. Ramsey, of Kansas City, said, "There's just not much
left of the island." First Lieutenant Sidney Fisher, of Los Angeles, marveled, "Boy, that island was really quivering, I thought it would roll over
and sink."

At six o'clock nervous young marines of the 3rd Battalion, 5th Marine
Regiment, squatted on the decks of a 457-foot LSD (landing ship, dock)
and watched in quiet awe the fury being directed at Wolmi-do. Most
of these men were youngsters of eighteen to twenty-one years of age,
and some seemed to wish to be elsewhere. One of them told *Time*
correspondent Frank Gibney, "Three months ago I was so happy." But
they did take solace from the sight of the destroyers between them and
the Wolmi-do beach and of the bulky rocket ships.

A metallic voice over the public address system: "Lower the stern
gate." The next order was for the marines to board their smaller LSUs
(landing ships, utility), the 120-foot craft that would take them ashore.
They crouched among tanks and cargo.

The LSD came to a halt in the water, and the low barrier separating
its well deck from the sea lowered. The LSUs backed down a ramp into
a calm sea, did awkward U-turns, and headed toward the shore.

At this moment the rocket ships unleashed their barrage. Squat and clumsy, in contrast with the sleek lines of the destroyers and aircraft carriers, the LSMRs looked like stray tugboats as they edged within a few hundred yards of the shore. Then came the fire order. Clusters of rockets surged from each ship, arched steeply and briefly, and crashed down on the surviving defenders of Wolmi-do.

As the LSUs churned toward the shore, marine Corsair planes flashed down over the island again, dropping bombs.[45] The LSUs now were only a few hundred yards from the beach, and one marine shouted, "Save us a little of that island." The last bombs hit at 6:29 A.M.; four minutes later seven landing craft touched Green Beach, at the upper end of the island. They shuddered as they hit the sand, then steadied. Down went the ramps; off went the tanks, followed by sprinting marines.

The first men off the boats sprawled onto the beach, rifles in firing position, wary of opposition. None existed. They landed in a scene of total devastation. As the marines raced across the beach and up the north point of the island, they were greeted by only a few scattered rifle shots. The close air support continued: F4Us hosed the lines of advance with machine-gun bullets that kicked up dirt no more than fifty yards in front of the marines.

The marines' first objective was the northern slope of Radio Hill, the highest ground on the island. The scattered, numb North Koreans encountered along the way preferred to surrender rather than fight. At 6:55 A.M., a scant twenty-five minutes after the first marines stepped ashore, Sergeant Alvin E. Smith tied an American flag on a shell-torn tree on the crest of Radio Hill.

MacArthur, binoculars focused on the island, nodded approval. He arose. "That's it," he said, "let's get a cup of coffee."

The marines' Colonel Alpha Bowser, reconstructing the Wolmi-do assault later, credited the air and naval bombardment for the relative ease with which the assault troops went ashore.[46] "Many of these people [NKPA soldiers] staggered out of bunkers and holes in a total state of shock. . . . If they weren't dead or badly wounded, they were in such a state of shock that they were just staggering around."

Time's Frank Gibney saw the disintegration of the defenders the moment he stepped ashore:

> Three or four half-naked North Korean soldiers, hands held rigid over their pinched, scared faces, stumbled into one of their old shallow trenches at the command of a Marine. I talked to them in Japanese. "Are you going to kill us?" stammered one. When I said we wouldn't, he chattered to the others and a little of the fear went out of their eyes.

Surprisingly the third wave of Marines to land caught the stiffest resistance. H Company of the battalion, from the first wave, supposedly had cleared the north point of the island. But I Company, in the third wave, was attacked by a flurry of hand grenades. Regaining their composure, they saw a bypassed emplacement dug into the base of a cliff. North Koreans rose sporadically, hurled grenades, then ducked for shelter.

I Company decided to give the twenty or so defenders the chance to abandon a hopeless battle. An interpreter crept to the edge of the cliff, told the soldiers their situation was hopeless, and begged them to surrender. They responded by throwing more hand grenades.

The company commander, Captain Robert A. McMullen, waved to tanks following the marines up the slope. One of them—actually a modified bulldozer—rumbled up to the troublesome pocket and systematically sealed it with rubble, permanently silencing the North Koreans.

Elsewhere North Koreans threw down their arms and quit. Some begged for mercy. *"Salyo chu sio* [Please help me]," one critically wounded man pleaded to Frank Gibney. All his clothes save his boots had been blown off. He died in a minute. The marines ordered the prisoners to strip naked, so they could not conceal weapons, and marched them to the beach. The vanquished Communists expected death. One knelt on the roadway with hands folded. "Don't shoot me, I'm a Christian," he begged.

At eight o'clock all resistance on Wolmi-do ceased. The marines now held the approaches to Inchon Harbor, news relayed to the *Mount McKinley.* MacArthur stepped to his cabin and handwrote a message for Vice Admiral Struble, aboard the *Rochester:* "The navy and the marines have never shone more brightly than this morning."

The first phase of MacArthur's "nickel after a dollar" gamble had succeeded even beyond his expectations. Only 17 marines had been wounded, none seriously. The NKPA lost 108 dead and 136 captured, with an estimated 150 more fatalities entombed in rubble.

Now would come the assault on Inchon proper.

The Main Assault

The rest of the morning the marine assault troops uneasily watched the tide recede. At one in the afternoon the marines realized that although they controlled the island, they sat surrounded by a sea of mud. The commanding lieutenant colonel, Robert D. Taplett, ran through a number of possibilities. An NKPA force would materialize in the seemingly dead streets of Inchon and attack en masse. Or Communist tank columns would streak across the causeway and overwhelm his forces.

But the afternoon remained silent. One of the few signs of life in Inchon was that of civilians raiding stores of rice. One group of NKPA soldiers was seen briefly in a trench; a barrage of thirty five-inch shells from the destroyer USS *Mansfield* buried them. Taplett felt so confident that in midafternoon he asked permission to move a tank-infantry force across the causeway and strike at Inchon proper. Such a risk his seniors were not prepared to take. "Negative," said the *McKinley*.

Late in the afternoon Taplett's men prepared to move again, this time to Inchon. Despite orders to hit only military targets, enough bombs and shells had gone astray to set the entire city ablaze, and fumes and cinders choked the sky. But to the west the setting sun painted one small patch of sky a subdued yellow. A chaplain standing alongside Frank Gibney of *Time* looked first at the hell of Inchon, then at the sky. "Heaven on one side," he said, "and hell on the other." Interrogations of the captured NKPA soldiers did bring encouraging news: Only 1,600 NKPA troops remained in the Inchon area, most of them recent conscripts with sketchy training, no experience, and poor morale. Now their first taste of battle would be the awesome firepower of modern combined arms.

As the tides returned in late afternoon, once again marine assault craft crept through Flying Fish Channel toward land. The men were at once apprehensive, sea-weary, and uncomfortable. For the 1st Regiment's 3rd Battalion, even battle seemed a more comfortable prospect than the rolling old tub they had ridden across the Sea of Japan. Reclaimed from the Japanese coastal trade only two weeks previously, it "stank of fish," recalled Technical Sergeant Allen G. Mainard,[47] and cat-size rats scurried around the decks. The craft encountered boats crammed with fleeing Koreans and their few pitiful possessions. One mother stood in a tiny junk and raised her child. "Her words were unintelligible, but her meaning was plain," Mainard recollected. Behind them a towering smoke pall marked their city; the air and naval bombardment was resuming again. With the guns of Wolmi-do now silent, the destroyers crept close to the port.

On the bridge of the *Mount McKinley,* General MacArthur sat in his swivel chair again, raised his binoculars, and watched the concluding salvo from the rocket ships, 6,000 missiles erupting into the port in twenty minutes. The barrage further numbed the defenders, but it also increased the density of the overcast. What awaited the two marine regiments (less the Wolmi-do battalion) when they finally stepped onto the smoke-shrouded mainland—the spiritless opposition of the morning or a Tarawa-style bloodbath in the mud patches and dark, crooked streets of the strange port city? Sudden rainsqualls added to the confusion. The marines now clambered off the transports onto the smaller landing craft, which this time included a host of amphibious tractors that they hoped could slosh through the mud if the tide level proved insufficient.

The strafing planes continued their runs until the boats were a mere thirty yards shy of the landing points, then waggled their wings at the marines below and swept away to strike at reinforcement convoys on the Seoul–Inchon road. The NKPA command had finally decided the thunder and lightning of the past days were no diversionary feint.

Marguerite Higgins of the New York *Herald Tribune,* riding toward Red Beach with the 1st Battalion of the 5th Marines, glanced at Wolmi-do as they rode past. It "looked as if a giant forest fire had just swept over it," she wrote. "Beyond was Red Beach. As we strained to see it more clearly, a rocket hit a round oil tower and big, ugly smoke rings billowed up. The dockside buildings were brilliant with flames. Through the haze it looked as if the whole city was burning. . . ."[48]

Now the marines switched to the smaller craft, twenty men and two ladders to each LCVP (landing craft, vehicles, personnel). To James Bell of *Time,* riding in the third wave, the 1,000-foot-long seawall that was Red Beach "seemed as high as the RCA Building."[49]

The first wave of boats, a row of four of them, touched the wall at around 5:30 P.M. and came to a grinding halt with their prows hard pressed against the rugged stone. Despite the surging tides, the wall nonetheless loomed four feet above the landing ramps. So up went the scaling ladders as marines hurled hand grenades indiscriminately over the revetment, at enemies who might or might not exist. The ladders swayed and slipped along the wall as the craft bobbed in the churning water. "Up and over!" shouted Second Lieutenant Edwin A. Deptula, and at 5:31 P.M. the first marine stepped onto solid ground at Inchon.

The others followed in a rush, some risking the increasingly wobbly ladders, others simply hurling their field packs into the blackness, catching outstretched arms of the few already ashore, and pulling themselves up. Only sporadic stray bullets crackled through the air, and Deptula's platoon quickly secured its first objective, a hill a few hundred yards inland.

Deptula's company commander, Captain Sam Jaskilka, rode in the third wave. A few minutes before his LCVP hit the wall he gave orders in a quiet, calm voice: "You people know what to do. Keep your god-damned heads down. There's a ditch on the other side of the wall. Roll over the wall into the ditch, then get up fast and make for the right side of the beach. Good luck to all of you."

But now the opposition heated up. Back away from the seawall, to the north, machine guns opened fire from a bunker; other fire, from rifle and machine guns, came from scores of yards to the rear. Some marines clambering over the wall walked right into it.

First Lieutenant Baldomero Lopez, an Annapolis graduate and Second World War veteran, crawled to the enemy bunkers housing the machine guns. Baldy Lopez was in Inchon by choice. When marines at Camp Pendleton were alerted for their move to Korea, Lopez was under orders to report to the Marine Corps school at Quantico, Virginia, for advanced training. Lopez protested to his commanding officer. The Quantico orders were rescinded, and now, two months later, he was face-to-face with the enemy. He took out one of the bunkers with a grenade, then pulled the pin from another and prepared to throw it into a second bunker. A spurt of machine-gun fire wounded him in the right arm and shoulder, and he fell, the sputtering grenade beyond reach of his shattered arm. "Grenade!" he cried, and lurched for it, cradled it under his body with his elbow, and died.*[50]

But despite eight dead in the first ten minutes of the assault the advance on objectives beyond Red Beach went well. Marines drove up Cemetery Hill, the highest ground in the center of Inchon. They seized the hulking building containing the Ashai Brewery. Take it intact, an officer had promised, and we'll have a beer bust to end all beer busts. Alas, the rocket bombardment had been too efficient. Not a single bottle remained unbroken, and the brewery tanks were debris.

Meanwhile, the scene in the few hundred yards of water leading to the landing areas approached chaos. For an amphibious operation the size of Inchon, navy doctrine called for thirty-two guide ships with range finders, radios, and other sophisticated guidance gear to ensure that the cumbersome landing craft kept in line and touched land where directed. But for Inchon the navy could find only eight guide ships. Thus subsequent waves of invaders wandered around in confusion, trying to find their way through the darkening evening onto a shore cloaked with smoke and fire. One officer, Major Edwin H. Simmons, waiting in vain for one of the guide ships, yelled to a nearby LCVP for assistance.[51] It happened to be filled with Korean interpreters, and two hastily came aboard. They spoke Korean and Japanese—but no English. He shouted to a naval officer in another nearby boat for direction to Sector Two of Blue Beach. The navy man waved vaguely through the smoke. Simmons broke out a map and asked the sailor piloting his amtrac if he had a map. The sailor looked sadly at his instrument panel. "Search me," he said. "Six weeks ago I was driving a truck in San Francisco." One battalion missed its target on Blue Beach by two miles.

Even Admiral Struble unwittingly added to the confusion.[52] Desiring to see what was happening on Blue Beach, he invited Generals Shep-

*For his bravery, Lopez was awarded the Medal of Honor.

herd and Almond to take a ride in his barge. Almond was witnessing his first amphibious operation, and both Struble and Shepherd wanted him to see firsthand it was not a "mechanical operation," as he had derisively commented several weeks earlier.

The party arrived along the seawall just as marine engineers prepared to blow a hole in it so that tracked vehicles could get ashore.

"Lay off, you stupid bastards," a marine NCO shouted at the barge. "We're going to blast a hole in the wall!"

The coxswain of the barge called back, "*This* is Admiral Struble's barge."

"I don't give a shit whose barge it is," the marine yelled. "Get it clear before I blow the seawall." Struble quietly told the coxswain to do as told, and less than a minute later a tremendous explosion ripped the wall apart.

Less than an hour after H-Hour, Communist gunners finally opened up on naval targets—a string of eight LSTs (landing ship, tanks) carrying ammunition, gasoline, and napalm toward the shore. Bulky, slow, and in perfect formation, the LSTs lumbered into a hail of machine-gun and mortar fire. Fires broke out near ammunition trucks on one vessel, but crewmen and marines quickly controlled them. (Ashore a few hours later, marines found machine-gun bullet holes in gasoline drums; miraculously, none of the drums had exploded.)

Seven of the eight ships immediately returned fire with 40 mm and 20 mm cannon, aimed at Cemetery and Observation hills and the right flank of the beach—right into marine positions. One battalion took more casualties from the navy fire—one killed, twenty-three wounded —than it did from the NKPA that evening.

Correspondent Marguerite Higgins, arriving ashore at the same time the "friendly" fire began, found bullets

spattering the water around us. We clambered over the high, steel sides of the boat, dropped into the water, and, taking shelter beside the boat, as long as we could, snaked on our stomachs up to a rockstrewn dip in the seawall. Whatever the luck of the first four waves, we were relentlessly pinned down by rifle and automatic weapon fire coming down on us from another rise on the right. . . .

A sudden rush of water came up into the dip and we saw a huge LST rushing at us with the great door half down. Six more yards and the ship would have crushed twenty men.* Warning shouts sent everyone speeding from the seawall, searching for escape from the LST and cover from the gunfire.

Shouted commands finally broke off the LST fire when the craft reached the shore.

*And presumably the adventurous Miss Higgins as well.

Nonetheless, two young sailors were so infuriated that they told Marine Master Sergeant Robert Tallent, a combat correspondent for *Leatherneck* magazine, they intended to "do a bit of Commie hunting" on their own.[53] They fitted themselves with M-16 rifles, bandoliers of ammunition, and some grenades and ignored Tallent's warning and trudged off up the beach. "They returned a short time later, sans weapons, mud-stained and shaken, and informed all hands that some misguided soul had been using them for target practice."

At Blue Beach the chief problem was mud. Some of the LVTs (landing vehicles, tanks) managed to reach the beach; others ground to a halt in mud 300 yards offshore, and cursing marines had to trudge through the muck to dry ground. The Blue Beach battalions also suffered poor guidance from the navy, with several waves landing out of sequence and many yards from their assigned destinations. Once ashore the heavy armored tractors had trouble with the terrain, bogging down in mud and sand.

Despite these delays and mishaps, the first waves cleared the beach swiftly, taking a few casualties from a concealed machine-gun nest in a tower 500 yards inland before silencing it and moving into a labyrinth of burning buildings and smoke-filled streets.

The NKPA fire gradually quieted, and the marines took stock. As planned, they had seized the heart of the city, the western approaches, and all relevant high points and buildings. Their casualties totaled 196: 20 dead, 1 dead or wounded, 1 missing in action, 174 wounded in action. The NKPA lost an estimated 1,350 men dead, wounded, and captured.

MacArthur's gamble had worked. By the time the night ended some 18,000 American troops were ashore, along with tons of supplies and scores of tanks and other vehicles. Now the invasion force could strike for the second objective: to seize Seoul and the communications lines running through it. MacArthur now had the opportunity not only to recapture the South Korean capital but to drive east across the entire Korean peninsula, trapping the North Korean Army to the south.

MacArthur's masterstroke had seemingly changed the course of the war. But the praise that poured upon him from all quarters—including the Joint Chiefs—tended to skip over two facts that made the successful landing possible. The hellish barrage of naval gunfire, the hail of bombs and rockets that preceded the landing, had transformed Wolmi-do and Inchon into a smoking rubble. Furthermore, the North Koreans had left only a corporal's guard to defend the city. The NKPA's determination to push the Eighth Army out of the Pusan Perimeter clearly had taken precedence over defending Inchon. Now the North Koreans faced a two-front war, with a vastly superior American force sweeping across Korea to the rear.

The Marines Drive Inland

Marine strategy on D-Day-plus-1 was to move out of Inchon as swiftly as possible, leaving control of the city to the Korean Marine Corps, which began arriving by boat on the morning of September 15.

As so often was true in Korea, terrain dictated tactics. Inchon occupies a wart-shaped peninsula. Go inland three miles, and the wart narrows, pinched on north and south by tidal estuaries, gummy mud flats, and salt pans. The land solid enough to walk on is barely a mile wide. The road reaching on to Seoul, twenty-five miles from Inchon, is narrow, of macadam, and paralleled by a railway. Both road and railway lead, first, to Ascom City, the American-built "new town" of Quonset huts and warehouses long used by the military as a logistical base; next, to Kimpo Airport, the main aerodrome serving Seoul. The marine goal was to strike across this twenty-five-mile stretch and seize Seoul before the NKPA brought up reserves to break the beachhead.

Incredibly the NKPA command still did not seem to have realized the immensity of the calamity that had befallen the Inchon defenders. A flight of eight Corsairs left the carrier USS *Sicily* just after dawn and cruised the Seoul–Inchon highway in search of targets of opportunity. They found them easily, a column of six T-34 tanks, nonchalantly clanking down the highway toward Inchon. Major Robert Floeck, the flight commander, led the attack: a roll, a dive, a level-out, followed by his wingman and the other fliers. His napalm container hit the lead tank dead center, and it burst into orange flames. Following Corsairs ripped up the next two tanks in line, one stray NKPA shot sending a U.S. plane crashing to earth in flames. Another Corsair flight took over and demolished two other tanks and then NKPA soldiers and vehicles concealed in huts. Napalm fires added their own pall to the smoke around Inchon.

The first day's advance took the marines some ten miles east on the Seoul highway. That night Dog Company of the 2nd Battalion of the 5th Marine Regiment—the lead unit in line—dug in alongside the roadway on a bald hillock abutting an abandoned quarry.[54] Ahead of the marines, the narrow road twisted to the right around a large hill.

Throughout the night the men of Dog Company grumbled about the bright flash of enemy flares in the distance that made sleep uncomfortable, if not impossible. The marines were to continue their advance the next day, September 17, supported by five new Pershing tanks. But their commanding officer, First Lieutenant H. J. Smith, insisted they dig in tightly for the night. Smith, a prudent officer, expected a North Korean counterattack at any hour. He sent a machine-gun crew and a 2.36-inch bazooka forward to a slight hill overlooking the turn in the road. In the main defile, a few hundred yards behind Dog Company, were 75 mm recoilless rifles and heavy 3.5-inch rocket launchers. Dog Company was ready for what might come.

Just before dawn the men of Dog Company heard a distant clanking of machinery not unlike farm tractors rattling down a midwestern highway. Word was quickly flashed back to battalion headquarters, which first refused to believe that the NKPA would be audacious enough—or stupid enough—to drive tanks directly at marine lines with patrols moving in advance.

But then the first of the Soviet-made T-34 tanks nosed around the curve, and according to one observer, "it brought the quasidawn with it." Another tank followed. Their turrets rotated, probing the still morning air like antennae of the large black ants they resembled in the morning light. Then another, and another, until six tanks had come into full view under the marine guns.

Infantry came with them, some men marching in ragtag formation, laughing and jabbering; others sitting on the sides of the tanks, finishing breakfast.

The lead platoon commander, Second Lieutenant Lee R. Howard, let the head of the column slip by until the tanks began to round the turn toward Dog Company's main position. Then he shouted an order, and his men opened up with machine guns, rifles, and BARs (Browning automatic rifles). The Red infantry fell like grass under a sickle. Soldiers on the tanks were knocked sprawling to the ground, and many were crushed as the heavy vehicles wheeled and tried to turn out of the ambush.

A corporal, Okey J. Douglas, crept partway down the hill and fired at the lead T-34 with his 2.36-inch rocket launcher, at a range of seventy yards. The vehicle burst into flames. Douglas then turned on the second tank and damaged it just as the main U.S. guns opened up.

The fury of fire lasted only a few minutes. Some of the tanks turned off the road and tried to flee through adjacent rice paddies. In doing so, they ran headlong into the marines' M-26 Pershing tanks, the commander of which, First Lieutenant William D. Pomeroy, took them under fire at 600-yard range. The recoilless rifles also roared.

All six T-34's were left burning hulks; scattered among them were some 200 enemy dead. So successful was the ambush that only one marine suffered a slight wound.

MacArthur Comes Ashore

By incredible coincidence, Dog Company was scarcely out of sight when a caravan of jeeps roared into the battle area and parked next to the still-burning North Korean tanks. Dead Communist troops lay all about, some "half-cooked on top of several of the tanks," according to the marines' General Lem Shepherd, in the jeep party. The acrid odor of cordite and high explosives permeated the air, and General Douglas MacArthur stepped down from his jeep and sniffed.

The general had come ashore shortly after dawn to gloat over his work, and he pressed inland after looking at shattered NKPA positions and corpses in the beach area ("There's a patient you'll never have to work on," he joshed to his personal physician as he pointed to one Communist body).

The "tour" was staged as much to afford MacArthur a chance to appear before the assembled media as to give him a look at the battlefield. Reporters and photographers scrambled for seats in the caravan of jeeps, and the triumphant general was the very picture of cordiality. At the 1st Marine Division command post he even stopped for a friendly chat with Colonel Alpha Bowser—an officer he had never met, although he knew the marine as an archfoe of Chromite. MacArthur could not resist a gentle jibe. "He [MacArthur] said that he still felt that his concept was right," Bowser said, "and that our presence there was ample proof of the fact that what he thought could be done was done."

MacArthur gathered up varied generals and other brass and announced he wanted to find Colonel Lewis "Chesty" Puller, a marine regimental commander, and give him a Silver Star for heroism during the landing.[55] (Just what Puller had done the previous two days to warrant the medal is not mentioned even in the colonel's biography.) Sentimentality perhaps was involved, for MacArthur had admired the crusty Puller since the Second World War, when he repeatedly distinguished himself in combat. But when a radio message summoned Puller to come meet the general, he was busy attacking a ridge.

"Signal them that we're fighting our way for every foot of ground," Puller snapped to a subordinate. "I can't leave here. If he wants to decorate, he'll have to come up here."

Puller's impertinence seemed to delight MacArthur. Everyone into the jeeps, he said; we'll visit Puller in the field.

In due course the entourage reached a farmhouse near the battle line identified as Puller's command post. There was much bustle, and a plethora of communications wires indicated the house was of importance. But there was no sign of Puller. Enlisted marines pointed up the ridge, where brisk gunfire could be heard. MacArthur waved his arm; the jeeps roared on.

From the ridge Puller's aide looked down and saw the vehicles speeding through the dust. "General MacArthur's coming!" he called to Puller.

"How do you know?" the colonel asked.

"Who the hell else in Korea could have enough jeeps for a funeral and have a light colonel dogtrotting out in front?"

Near the top of the ridge the grade became so steep the jeeps stalled, so everyone got out and walked, MacArthur huffing but smiling broadly for the photographers running ahead of him. He and Puller exchanged brisk salutes. One of MacArthur's staff officers told Puller they had expected to find him in the command post (CP), an oblique suggestion that Puller should have come down the mountain.

Puller grinned and patted a folded map in his hip pocket. "This is my CP," he replied.

After all the bother MacArthur searched his pockets and could not find a Silver Star. "Make a note of that," he told the reporters pressing around him. The medal would be sent along later.

Back down on the road the party came upon the North Korean tanks destroyed the previous day by the Corsair fighters. "Considering they are Russian-made"—MacArthur laughed—"these tanks are in the condition I desire them to be."

Lieutenant Colonel Raymond Murray, a marine battalion commander, spoke up. "Oh," he said, "these are yesterday's kills. If you want to see some fresh-killed tanks, we have some just up the road." He pointed down the road toward the site Dog Company had occupied a few hours earlier.

General Oliver Smith, the ranking marine in the party, flinched. Small-arms fire still crackled in the area, and he did not want his Commander in Chief killed—especially in a marine area. MacArthur, of course, thought the idea splendid, and he waved the jeeps forward. They had proceeded only a few yards when a much agitated marine officer ran up waving his arms. "General," he exclaimed, "you can't come up here!"

MacArthur looked at the young officer, a smile flickering across his face. "And why not?" he asked.

"We've just knocked out six Red tanks over the top of this hill," the marine said.

"That was the proper thing to do," MacArthur said, and the jeeps rolled on. At the ambush site he got out of the jeep and stood on a culvert for a better view of the burning wreckage, turning toward the photographers. He studied the North Korea corpses with detachment and poked his finger through a shell hole in one of the tanks.

General Almond, also in the party, seethed; he felt the spectacle was too good to be authentic. And even if it were, he suspected the marines' famed public relations machine had arranged it. He said to General Lemuel Shepherd, only half in jest, "You damned marines! You always seem to be in the right spot at the right time. Hell, we've been fighting this battle with army troops [he meant the pre-Inchon war] but MacArthur would arrive just as the marines had knocked out six enemy tanks." Shepherd smiled and said nothing.

A few minutes after MacArthur's party left the ambush site, a lieutenant noticed suspicious noises coming from beneath the culvert where the general had stood to look at the smashed tanks. He summoned a squad. A few shots flushed out seven armed NKPA soldiers, who resisted briefly before surrendering. Questioned, they proved to be survivors of the infantry hit in the morning strike. And yes, they had been under the culvert since the battle ended.

Back in Inchon proper, MacArthur next wanted a boat tour of the landing areas. He looked at the approaches to Wolmi-do and Blue Beach, then pointed to another area to the south where considerable rifle fire could still be heard. General Shepherd finally spoke up. "I don't think it's safe to take the commander in chief of the theater in here and expose him to this occasional rifle and mortar fire," he said. "I think we should get the general's boat out of danger."

Admiral Struble ("Damned old Struble," Shepherd called him[56]) made a remark about Shepherd's being "scared of getting into the beach." Shepherd shot back a remark of his own. But his decision held, and the party returned to the *Mount McKinley* in strained silence. For MacArthur, however, the day had served his purpose. He had now seen at first hand his magnificent victory.*

Eighth Army Breaks Out at Pusan

The battle line in the south was approximately 180 air miles at its closest point from the Seoul-Inchon line—and considerably farther via winding mountain roads.[57] General Walton Walker's planned breakout called for a thrust up the same central axis the North Koreans had used in their move to the south—the highway linking Taegu-Kumchon-Taejon-Suwon. Walker anticipated that once the North Koreans learned of the Inchon invasion, they would become demoralized and easy prey. So he set his own jump-off date at September 16, one day after the landing.

Eighth Army staff officers were not so optimistic at MacArthur's anvil-and-hammer strategy. Despite the continued buildup of men and material in the perimeter, EUSAK forces could do little more than blunt North Korean attacks and launch limited counterattacks of their own. Ammunition shortages were a serious factor. Artillery units were limited to fifty rounds daily per gun for primary attacks. Further, although the advance would carry EUSAK across a succession of rivers, engineers lacked the equipment to put up spans rapidly. Intelligence estimates put the North Korean strength around the Pusan beachhead at 101,147

*Shepherd still seethed over the episode a quarter of a century later, saying Struble mistook his sense of responsibility for MacArthur's safety for cowardice. "I never had a damn bit of use for Struble after that," he said. He demanded that Struble write him an apology; none ever came.

troops. Although the combined American and ROK forces totaled some 140,000 men, some of the South Koreans were ineffective because of lack of leadership and training. The EUSAK battle plan pessimistically stated: "Currently the enemy is on the offensive and retains this capability in all general sectors of the Perimeter. It is not expected that this capability will decline in the immediate future."

EUSAK began the offensive on schedule, at nine o'clock the rainy, overcast morning of September 16, in weather so foul that the air force had to cancel planned saturation bombings of the first target areas, around Waegwan. Things did not proceed as planned, for the North Koreans chose the same day for a new offensive of their own. So instead of moving to the attack, the U.S. troops found themselves once again in the uncomfortable position of defending their positions. (Scattered North Korean prisoners had not even heard of the Inchon landing; so much for "demoralization.")

In addition to stiff enemy resistance, equipment shortages prevented Walker from a rapid break from the perimeter. Harried by MacArthur to get moving, he retorted on September 21 that he was "ready to break loose if it weren't for the physical trouble."[58] He had no means of moving his heavy tanks across the Naktong River because most logistical support was going to X Corps. "We have been bastard children lately, and as far as our engineering equipment is concerned we are in pretty bad shape." Walker recognized MacArthur's impatience with officers unable to carry out assignments promptly, regardless of the obstacles. "I don't want you to think that I am dragging my heels," he told Tokyo, "but I have a river across my whole front . . ." with only two bridges intact.

After several days of indecisive struggle MacArthur decided that a second amphibious assault was required to break EUSAK out of the Pusan Perimeter. He told General Doyle Hickey, his deputy chief of staff, to prepare a plan that would pull two of Walker's American divisions and one ROK division out of line and land them at Kunsan, on the west coast about 100 miles south of Inchon. Walker protested. If he pulled three divisions out of the Pusan area, the North Koreans would quickly mop up the remaining UN troops there and be free to move to counter any attempted invasion to the north.

As it happened, events overtook MacArthur's idea. Before anything was done to implement the planned invasion, the clearing skies permitted the air force to fly again. Bombs and napalm gradually broke the enemy's will to fight. The North Koreans began abandoning their equipment and running. A few stayed and died in their foxholes in futile rearguard actions; others fled so fast they left wet laundry hanging on bushes and hot food in headquarters buildings. Uncountable thousands simply shucked their uniforms and tried to meld into the general population or marched into remote areas to continue fighting as guerrillas.

In one sprint the 1st Cavalry Division raced fifty-five miles in three days.

One unit of the 1st Cav., a reconnaissance company commanded by Lieutenant Robert W. Baker, went even faster, under orders to link up with the 7th Division. In a flotilla of three Sherman tanks and three jeeps, Baker's task force raced up the highway through Osan, bound for Suwon. His gunners popped away at North Korean soldiers on the roadway, one of them keeping a lively log: "9:05 P.M.—two more; two more; seven more; 9:35 P.M.—3 Reds, two carts; two more; two mule carts full of Reds; one jeep; six more. . . ." In eleven hours Baker covered 106.4 miles.

Outside Taejon a machine gunner composed a little ditty about the town he and comrades had been forced to abandon in July:[59]

> The last time I saw Taejon it was not
> bright and gay;
> Today I'm going to Taejon and blow
> the place away.

When the pressure from the UN and ROK forces became so great that the enemy had no recourse but to retreat in daylight, the air force swooped down at them with strafing runs and deadly napalm. The Counter Intelligence Corps's Robert Edson, moving north with EUSAK headquarters, noticed a charred object a few yards off the road. He looked more closely. "Napalm had literally incinerated a North Korean soldier on his feet. He was still standing there, rifle at his feet. 'Old Charlie,' we called him."[60]

By the last week of September the enemy was in full rout. On September twenty-seven soldiers of the 7th Cavalry Regiment of EUSAK linked up with the 31st Infantry Regiment of the 7th Division near Suwon; meanwhile, ROK troops steamed up the east coast, while other American units moved up the coastal plain in the west of the country.

The day before the landing MacArthur had told reporters aboard the *Mount McKinley* that the North Koreans could not both defend Inchon-Seoul and keep the Eighth Army pinned down in Pusan. "They'll have to take their choice," MacArthur said. The North Koreans chose Seoul.

MacArthur Pushes the Marines

The UN advance on Seoul was what General Oliver Smith called "one of those routine operations that read easier in the newspapers than on the ground."[61] What MacArthur wanted—as General Almond told

Smith—was the capture of Seoul by September 25, "exactly three months after the date that the North Koreans invaded South Korea." Almond mentioned that MacArthur strongly desired a "communiqué" to that effect and that the marines should adhere to his timetable.

Smith did not desire to put his troops on a schedule dictated by public relations. "I told [Almond] that I couldn't guarantee anything; that was up to the enemy. We'd do the best we could and go as fast as we could."

Almond, however, was not to be distracted; he intended to meet MacArthur's schedule, the marine protests notwithstanding. On September 19, when the UN force was on the south bank of the Han River, Almond told Smith he was "in a hurry" to get across the river, apparently to meet MacArthur's timetable.

The marines would have been far more comfortable had they been permitted to clear out pockets of the enemy as they advanced, rather than make the rapid strike toward Seoul. To Colonel Alpha Bowser, the army generals "were still suffering from the phase of the grand sweeps in the broad arrow operations of Europe."[62] The army "failed to appreciate the fact that an Oriental who is bypassed is not out of the ball game. He is not a German or an Italian, and he doesn't get out on the road and hold up his hand. He gets in a hole with a sackful of rice and a few rounds of ammunition and he'll kill anyone that he has a chance to kill." The marines and the army exchanged "a great deal of unkind words" about problems to the rear and on both flanks caused by North Korean guerrilla bands.

Almond and the X Corps staff, however, would not tolerate any delays or any modification of the "broad arrow" strategy. The marines, for instance, wanted to move west around Seoul, then strike down from the north. This move had the advantage of cutting off reinforcements from North Korea. Furthermore, the marines calculated it would be easier to cross the Han River—the bridges of which had been blown— a few miles distant from Seoul, rather than under the direct guns of the forces defending the capital. Almond, however, ordered a frontal assault. There was also constant squabbling between Almond and Smith over the availability of bridging materials. Almond "had a habit of treating the Han River like it had five or six intact bridges across it, and of course it had none," Bowser said. Smith flatly refused to cross the river without the support of tanks. On this point he prevailed: The marines contrived makeshift ferries from bridge sections and managed to get the tanks across the river, despite heavy enemy opposition.

The marines fought into the southern outskirts of Seoul against fierce Communist opposition, some 10,000 fresh, well-armed troops rushed down from the north, entrenched on strong terrain, and prepared for a last-ditch defense. The main marine force, the 5th Regiment, numbered some 2,500 men, all of whom had been fighting constantly since landing at Inchon. Watching the deadline tick closer, Almond gave a blunt threat to Smith: If the Marines did not move decisively within twenty-four hours, he was turning the Seoul assault over to the army's 7th Division, under General David Barr, which was moving north from the old Eighth Army area. The irritated Smith wrote in his diary that if Almond thought it was necessary to goad marines into fighting, "he displayed a complete ignorance of the fighting qualities of marines."

Early in the evening of September 25—MacArthur's deadline for the retaking of Seoul—the South Korean capital was a shattered city, its buildings and streets pounded by incessant UN artillery fire and air strikes, attacks necessary to destroy strong defensive positions. (Had the marines been permitted to attack from the north, as they wished, Bowser believed "that we could have captured Seoul with hardly a brick out of place.") As it was, the frontal assault demolished much of the city. Then, a few minutes after eight o'clock, Bowser received an order from Almond by field telephone.

UN pilots, the order said, reported "enemy fleeing city of Seoul on road north of Uijongbu" and gave the map coordinates of the location of the sighting. "You will attack now repeat now to the limit of your objectives in order to insure maximum destruction of enemy forces. Signed, Almond."

The message puzzled Bowser. He quickly checked his map, peering at it under the flickering light of a pressure lantern. The text referred to movements *north* of a town sixteen miles above Seoul; his units still fighting in the streets of Seoul reported no such retreat by the North Koreans. To the contrary, they seemed determined to fight to the death. Nor did the coordinates make any sense; they referred to a point on the Seoul–Kaesong road where the 7th Marine Regiment had reported only a few hours earlier it was still meeting stiff resistance. As marine historian Colonel Robert Debs Heinl pointed out in his account of the battle for Seoul, "it suggests much as to the functioning of Corps headquarters that an attack order of this importance could have been sent out with so gross an error undetected."

Bowser, experienced combat officer that he was, thought the order incredible. A night attack is an operation requiring delicate coordination and planning. This particular foray would be into the twisted, dark streets of a strange city where concrete roadblocks guarded virtually every intersection.

Bowser telephoned Colonel John H. Chiles, the X Corps operations officer and a devout Almond loyalist. They quickly resolved the error in citing coordinates, but when Bowser asked that the attack-now order be reconsidered, Chiles refused. The order was Almond's; it must be carried out; the marines must attack now.

Bowser next hurried to General Smith's command tent and interrupted his C ration dinner. Smith shook his head in disbelief and called Major General Clark Ruffner, Almond's chief of staff. He told Ruffner

his line troops saw no evidence of a North Korean advance and reminded him of the inadvisability of plunging blindly into a nighttime
fight. Ruffner was sympathetic, but he had no choice: Almond
had personally dictated the order, and it was to be executed without
delay.

At that very moment Smith's men were under counterattack by
North Korean tanks and troops. He looked at Bowser and shook his
head. "I had no alternative but to pass this order on to the First and
Fifth Marines [regiments]," Smith said. But he did so with a cautionary
note. "I directed that the attack be coordinated carefully and that no
effort be made to make a rapid advance."

The attack began at about 1:45 A.M. on September 26 and, despite a
fifteen-minute artillery "preparation" barrage, ran immediately into a
strong North Korean counterattack—300 infantrymen backed by ten
tanks. One marine likened the ferocity of the charge to the suicidal
Japanese banzai attacks of the Pacific war. All the marines could do was
pour a deadly barrage of howitzer and machine-gun fire into the dark-
ened city; one machine-gun section alone fired 30,000 rounds during
the night.

At about dawn the North Koreans yielded and broke off the attack,
leaving hundreds of men dead in the Seoul streets. Colonel Chesty
Puller came up to inspect the carnage. A war correspondent asked
Puller what he thought about the "fleeing enemy" report of the previous evening.[63] "All I know about a fleeing enemy," he said, "is that
there's two or three hundred out there that won't be fleeing anywhere.
They're dead."

Later that day the marine high command heard—with disgust—of a
communiqué that Almond had issued to the press at midnight several
hours before the night fight had begun, stating that Seoul had been
"liberated." MacArthur issued his own statement later that day:

> Three months to the day after the North Koreans launched their sur-
> prise attack . . . the combat troops of X Corps recaptured the capital city
> of Seoul. . . . The liberation of Seoul was accomplished by a coordinated
> attack of X Corps troops. . . . By 1400 hours 25 September [2 P.M.] the
> military defenses of Seoul were broken. . . . The enemy is fleeing the city
> to the northeast.

The same day, however, troops in Seoul fought house to house against
diehard defenders. "If the city had been liberated, the remaining North
Koreans did not know it," an Associated Press correspondent wrote.
The fighting continued for three more days.

MacArthur, however, had not let reality deter him from public pos-
turing. To him, the "truth" was what he stated in Tokyo press releases,
not what fighting men actually encountered on the battlefield.

THE X CORPS
CAPTURES SEOUL
Sept. 17-30, 1950

10 MILES

SEOUL

SUWON

KIMPO
AIRFIELD

SUWON
AIRFIELD

U.S.
1ST MARINE
DIVISION

U.S.
7TH INF.
DIVISION

ASCOM CITY

INCHON

FLYING FISH CHANNEL

MUD FLATS

MUD FLATS

MUD FLATS

YELLOW SEA

Ascom City

INCHON

Cemetery Hill

Observatory
Hill

WOLMI-do

U.S. 3rd
Marine
Reg.

U.S. 1st
Marine
Reg.

Night
Sept. 15

Night
Sept. 16

THE
INCHON LANDING
Sept. 15-16, 1950

Recapture of Seoul

By September 28 fighting in Seoul had calmed sufficiently for General MacArthur to make a triumphant return to the city. But he wished to do so with customary flair. He wanted to ride into Seoul from Kimpo Airport in a limousine, President Syngman Rhee at his side. But doing so required that he pass over the Han River, which separated Kimpo from the city, and no bridge existed. The marines had moved an entire division across the Han on rafts and amphibious landing craft, as had the army. All the bridging material brought in from Inchon had been converted into rafts. Would not a helicopter suffice for the ride from Kimpo to Seoul? someone queried MacArthur's headquarters. No, the general wanted to travel by auto. If no bridge existed, build one.

An exasperated General Oliver P. Smith was still busy with mopping-up operations in outlying areas of Seoul. "Nonetheless it fell the lot of the marines to build MacArthur's bridge," he said. "They did some sweating. They [the marine engineers] were flying in pontoons from all over the Far East. We broke up a couple of our rafts and sent those pontoons down to help them out."[64] At midnight before MacArthur's morning arrival, the bridge was finished.

MacArthur arrived in style. Emerging from his aircraft at Kimpo Airport, he stretched expansively and remarked, "It's just like old times." Then he got into a Chevrolet sedan and set out for Seoul, trailed by four other staff cars and twoscore of jeeps loaded with reporters and lesser brass.

Understandably for a city that had been captured twice in the space of three months, Seoul looked a mess, worse even than Tokyo or Yokohama in 1945, thought Harold Noble, returning with other former embassy people. "The sight of the wreckage sickened me," he said.[65]

Bombs had crashed through the sides of the U.S. Embassy building at ground level, and a corpse floated in the water in the basement. (Later, during renovation, workmen found six more bodies elsewhere in the building; there were perhaps a dozen others, hands bound behind their backs with wire, in a water-filled ditch near the chancery.) Artillery fire had blown away part of the roof of Ambassador Muccio's former residence, and looters had carried away every stick of furniture.

Despite the havoc, the Seoul citizenry—what survived of it, at any rate—turned out en masse to greet MacArthur and Rhee. Noble's careful eye noted that military-age men were not in the crowds, which were predominantly composed of small children and old men and women. But they waved miniature Korean flags and shouted greetings. Noble looked at their gaunt faces and, despite his skepticism about the ROK government, decided that no one could have arranged the demonstration. "They were cheering and crying because they were so happy to have Seoul free again."

MacArthur and Rhee drove to the shattered National Capitol, now a fire-blackened shell of masonry, its walls pockmarked with bullet holes. MacArthur's nose wrinkled imperceptibly: Although details of soldiers and marines had spent hours hauling corpses away from the building, the general detected "the smell of death" wafting through the broken windows.

The audience was almost totally military—U.S. and ROK officers in fatigue and olive drabs; a few British naval officers in white shorts, long white stockings, and white shoes. The marines' General Smith deliberately attended in battlefield dress, as did his subordinates, Colonels Edward Craig and Lewis Puller. "The order was that two officers from the division and one officer from each regiment could attend," Smith said.[66] "As far as the [marine] troops were concerned, we were directed to keep them out of sight. They were not to be visible." Craig was especially irked that the honor guard did not include any marines, who "did the bulk of the fighting to take Seoul." The army military policemen, although "very nicely dressed and shined up . . . looked more or less out of place." The snub did not go unnoted by men in the ranks. "The marines were a little caustic about it," said Smith. "But that was politics, I guess."

MacArthur was at his oratorical best. He said:

By the grace of merciful Providence, our forces fighting under the standard of that greatest hope and inspiration of mankind, the United Nations,* have liberated this ancient capital city of Korea. It has been freed from the despotism of Communist rule and its citizens once more have the opportunity for that immutable concept of life which holds invincibly to the primacy of individual liberty and personal dignity. . . .

And so forth, for several hundred more words.

Then MacArthur called on all present to join him in the Lord's Prayer. As they did, fire-weakened chunks of the glass dome of the building broke away and crashed to the floor 100 feet below. Miraculously no one was hurt (MacArthur, characteristically, did not flinch).

Then the general turned to Rhee. "Mr. President, my officers and I will now resume our military duties and leave you and your government to the discharge of the civil responsibility."

Rhee, moist-eyed, grasped MacArthur's hand. "We admire you," he said. "We love you as the savior of our race."

Within the hour MacArthur was en route back to Tokyo, confident that the war had been won. *Time* agreed. Its cover story on October 9 spoke of the "victory in South Korea" and "Stalin's defeat in Korea."

---

*Privately MacArthur considered the UN a nuisance, and he resented having to fly its flag.

An Aftermath of Problems

The Inchon victory, in an operation undertaken against the advice of almost every other officer involved, stands as MacArthur's finest hour of the Korean War. General Matthew Ridgway, then of the JCS staff, lauded MacArthur's military genius. He wrote later:[67] "for boldness in concept, for competence in professional planning, and for courage, dash, and skill in execution, this operation ranks high in military annals." But at the same time he recognized that Inchon, through its very success, created problems. Because of MacArthur's hurry-up planning, no detailed thought had been given to the follow-up in the event of stunning victory—that is, how to reap maximum advantage from success. As a consequence (as shall be seen), major portions of the North Korean People's Army managed to escape to the north or melt into the South Korean countryside in guerrilla bands.

Nor had Washington had the time to resolve major mysteries about the Chinese and Russian reaction to a major victory: Would they remain dormant, or would they openly intervene and attempt to save the North Korean Army? Answering these questions consumed precious weeks *after* Inchon.

The long-range effect was also important in an area not recognized at the time. As Ridgway put it:

> A more subtle result of the Inchon triumph was the development of an almost superstitious regard for General MacArthur's infallibility. Even his superiors, it seemed, began to doubt if they should question *any* of MacArthur's decisions and as a result he was deprived of the advantage of forthright and informed criticism, such as every commander should have—particularly when he is trying to "run a war" from 700 miles away.

Telling a superior officer that he is wrong is an act that requires enormous moral courage ("laying your commission on the line" was the phrase often used by General George Marshall). But a good officer does so, nonetheless, when he feels that a serious mistake is about to be made, and lives lost as a result.

MacArthur escaped such hard-eyed scrutiny within the next few days when he proposed pulling half his victorious army out of the battle and transporting them around the boot of the Korean peninsula for yet another behind-the-lines amphibious assault, this one at the port of Wonsan. Both naval authorities and division commanders opposed the scheme, but few were willing to question out loud the sagacity of a general who had just performed a military miracle. (See Chapter Eight.)

General Ridgway put it this way: "Had he [MacArthur] suggested that one battalion walk on water to reach the port, there might have been somebody ready to give it a try."

CHAPTER EIGHT

"Feel Unhampered Tactically and Strategically"

With the North Korean People's Army on the run, the United States in late September faced the political question of whether UN troops should pursue them across the 38th parallel. On this issue Dean Acheson and Douglas MacArthur were in full agreement. To require commanders to break contact and revert to the defensive once they reached the frontier would be a military absurdity. As Acheson put it, troops could not be expected "to march up to a surveyor's line and stop."[1]

But authorizing hot pursuit to permit the UN Army to complete the destruction of the North Korean People's Army would not solve the larger question of Korea's political future. If the UN Command withdrew after winning militarily, what would prevent the Soviets and the Communist Chinese from outfitting the North Koreans for another invasion a few years hence? To MacArthur, the only solution was to destroy the North Korean regime and unite the entire country under a single government, as various UN resolutions had asked during the past several years.

The UN Security Council resolutions in the first days of the war were ambiguous on specific war aims. The first, on June 25, condemned North Korea's attack, demanded withdrawal of its forces beyond the parallel, and called on member states to assist in repelling the aggression. On June 27 the council asked that members "furnish such assistance to the Republic of Korea as may be necessary to *repel the armed attack and to restore international peace and security in the area* [emphasis added]." The resolution of July 7 simply provided for a unified command under the United States and reiterated the objective stated on June 27.

In both private and public declarations the administration showed no desire to take the war beyond South Korea. Truman told the National Security Council on June 29 that he "wanted it clearly understood that our operations in Korea were designed to restore peace there and to restore the border."[2] In a speech the same day Acheson declared that U.S. air and naval forces were fighting "solely for the purpose of restoring the Republic of Korea to its status prior to the invasion."

But as the American commitment deepened, debate began on whether the United States could use defeat of the NKPA as an opportunity to enforce UN resolutions on Korean unification. In late July and early August staff-level memos in the Defense Department advocated that the UN Command "seek to occupy Korea and to defeat North Korean armed forces wherever located north or south of the 38th Parallel."[3] The State Department was divided on the issue. The Far Eastern Division, under the hawkish leadership of Dean Rusk and John Allison, urged that breaching the parallel not be precluded. The Policy Planning Staff (PPS), heavily influenced by George Kennan, urged that Acheson recognize that the balance of forces in the area precluded unification. "There is ample evidence of the strategic importance to Russia of the Korean peninsula," the PPS stated in a July 25 memorandum.[4] "It is unlikely that the Kremlin at present would accept the establishment in North Korea of a regime which it could not dominate and control." It warned that UN actions above the parallel might "result in conflict with the USSR or Communist China" and foresaw a reluctance of UN members to attempt unification. But after citing these drawbacks, the PPS fudged by recommending that no unification decision be made until the military and political situations clarified.

Given such bureaucratic timidity and inertia, MacArthur proved quite willing to make the decision on his own. When Generals Collins and Vandenberg visited Tokyo in mid-July, he emphatically stated, "I intend to destroy and not to drive back the North Korean forces. I may need to occupy all of North Korea."[5] MacArthur had authority to do no such thing, and both generals knew the issue was under intense study at that very moment in Washington. But the record does not reflect that they argued with MacArthur. And when General Collins returned to Tokyo in mid-August, to review Chromite plans, he told MacArthur he personally felt he should be permitted to attack across the 38th parallel to destroy the North Korean forces. But he cautioned MacArthur that the President had made no decision.

The National Security Council tried to resolve these conflicting views in a study (NSC 81), issued on September 1, which General Collins rightly called a "long, somewhat rambling paper," laden with on-the-other-hand arguments. The military thought NSC 81 overly timid; although the study conceded that Security Council resolutions gave a sound legal basis for crossing the parallel, it felt any breach of the line should be for local tactical reasons, and only by ROK forces. Even if the enemy collapsed and rejected surrender terms, MacArthur should "request new instructions before continuing operations north of the 38th Parallel with major forces for the purpose of occupying North Korea."

NSC 81 recognized that operations above the parallel risked provoking a Soviet response. "It is unlikely that the Soviet Union will passively accept the emergence of a situation in which all or most of North Korea would pass from its control, unless it believes that it can take action which would prevent this *and* [emphasis in original] which would not involve a substantial risk of general war or unless it is now prepared to accept such a risk." The NSC felt the Soviets were not so prepared.

The JCS called NSC 81 "unrealistic" because it "envisages the stabilization of a front on the 38th Parallel." Led by Collins and Sherman, the JCS argued that the main objective should be destruction of the NKPA. Most of the enemy troops could be destroyed south of the parallel, but subsequent mopping-up operations north of the line would be necessary. The JCS believed that only major northern cities should be occupied and that elections should be held in the name of the Republic of Korea as soon as feasible. (No one in the military wanted to stay in Korea a day longer than absolutely necessary.)

The final version of NSC 81—NSC 81/1*— adopted after negotiations between Acheson and the JCS at the National Security Council on September 9 gave the military its desired flexibility in operations in northern Korea. The original statement that UN operations "should not be permitted to extend into areas *close* [emphasis added] to the Manchurian and USSR borders of Korea" was amended to say that such operations should not be permitted *across* those borders. Where NSC 81 stated that forces other than ROKs should "in no circumstances" be used along the northern frontiers, NSC 81/1 stated "it should be the policy" not to employ non-ROK troops there. A JCS paper commented later: "These innocuous-sounding changes in phraseology contained the seeds of future difficulty."[6] Acheson, for his part, retained the requirement of presidential approval before UN forces crossed the 38th parallel.

In another section, NSC 81/1 dealt with the possibility of "the open

*Under NSC procedures, an original working paper bore a single number. Subsequent revisions were indicated by a slash mark and a new sequential number. For example, the seventh revision of NSC 65 would be designated NSC 65/7.

or covert employment of major Chinese Communist units south of the 38th parallel." (Oddly the paper was silent on intervention north of the parallel.) The NSC concluded that the United States "should not permit itself to become engaged in a general war" with China. But it gave MacArthur considerable leeway in retaliating: "As long as action by UN military forces offers a reasonable chance of successful resistance, the UN Commander should continue such action and be authorized to take appropriate air and naval action outside Korea against Communist China." Here the NSC was consistent with its very first war planning document, NSC 73, drafted on July 1, only four days after the North Korean invasion. NSC 73 stated that if the Chinese "become engaged in the theater we would have adequate grounds for air and sea attacks on targets in Communist China directly related to the enemy effort in Korea." Thus in both these key papers the National Security Council displayed a willingness to bomb China if it entered the war.

NSC 81/1 ignored the political disposition of North Korea—a meaningless omission, for Truman declared on September 1 that the Koreans "have a right to be free, independent and united" and that "under the guidance of the United Nations, we, with others, will do our part to help them enjoy that right." But in a private meeting on September 8 with Dr. John M. Chang, the Korean ambassador, Dean Rusk refused to make any commitments on reunification pending United Nations discussion.[7] Chang was explicit about his own government's goals: It wanted the complete destruction of the NKPA and unification of Korea under the existing southern government. He pointedly reminded Rusk that Rhee had won elections held under UN auspices and that his authority "should not be prejudiced" by any further elections.

Rhee: "To the North"

In Seoul President Syngman Rhee thought the discussion about the inviolability of the parallel senseless. Speaking at a mass meeting in Pusan on September 19, he declared, "We have to advance as far as the Manchurian border until not a single enemy soldier is left in our country."[8] Regardless of what the UN Command decided, "we will not allow ourselves to stop."

MacArthur outspokenly supported Rhee as president of a united Korea. The State Department, however, was not as certain; in early September it asked MacArthur to explain what he intended to do about Rhee when Seoul was recaptured.

One must sympathize with MacArthur at this juncture. His direc-tives, both from the UN and from Washington, spoke of the "restora-tion" of peace and security; even Acheson had said publicly that Amer-ica fought "solely for the purpose of restoring the Republic of Korea to its status prior to the invasion."[9] With understandable peevishness, MacArthur replied, "I do not know precisely to what your message refers, but I have no plans whatsoever except scrupulously to imple-ment the directives which I have received."[10] He intended—and Am-bassador Muccio agreed—to return Rhee to Seoul as soon as possible. He did not think that restoration of a lawful government that had continued to function even when driven from its capital could be characterized as a "reestablishment."

Still unsatisfied, State said that it would agree to restoration of ROK authority only in the South and that the future of the North should await UN action. This addition, approved by Truman, was incorporated into the formal directive based on NSC 81/1 that the JCS sent to MacArthur on September 27.* The most important parts of the messages came in the two opening paragraphs:

> This directive . . . is furnished . . . to provide amplifying instructions as to further military actions to be taken by you in Korea. These instructions, however, cannot be considered to be final since they may require modifica-tion in accordance with developments. In this connection, you will con-tinue to make special efforts to determine whether there is a Chinese Communist or Soviet threat to the attainment of your objective, which will be reported to JCS as a matter of urgency.
>
> Your military objective is the destruction of the North Korean armed forces. In attaining this objective you are authorized to conduct military operations, including amphibious and airborne landings or ground opera-tions north of the 38th Parallel in Korea, provided that at the time of such operation there has been no entry into North Korea by major Soviet or Chinese Communist Forces, no announcement of intended entry, nor a threat to counter our operations militarily in North Korea. Under no cir-cumstances, however, will your forces cross the Manchurian or USSR bor-ders of Korea and, *as a matter of policy, no non-Korean ground forces will be used in the northeast provinces bordering the Soviet Union or in the area along the Manchurian border* [emphasis added]. Furthermore, sup-port of your operations north or south of the 38th Parallel will not include air or naval action against Manchuria or against USSR territory.[11]

The directive continued that in the event "major" Soviet forces in-tervened in the North, or either Soviet or Communist Chinese troops

*The three-week delay between approval of NSC 81/1 and dispatch of the formal orders was caused by the bureaucratic confusion stemming from the firing of Defense Secretary Johnson and his replacement by General George Marshall.

in the South, MacArthur was to assume the defensive and consult Washington. (The word "major" applied only to the Soviets. As noted, the North Korean Army contained many soldiers who had previously served the Chinese Communists, and many were of uncertain ethnic origin. In all probability enemy soldiers who had come from the Chinese Army would be captured. Although open JCS files are silent on the point, the Pentagon did not wish the presence of these strays to halt the advance to the north.) The order, finally, authorized MacArthur to "facilitate the restoration" of the ROK government but told him to avoid involvement in the political future of the North.

The same day the JCS dispatched its secret orders (September 28), confusing press reports from the Far East quoted General Walton Walker to the effect that the Eighth Army would pause at the 38th parallel to await permission to pursue the fleeing North Koreans. Queried, MacArthur denied Walker said any such thing. But the report touched off a brief storm of political controversy. Senator William Knowland, Republican leader in the Senate, charged that failure to pursue the invaders would be "appeasement of the Communists." Newspaper editorials strongly favored destroying the Communist satellite state to prevent a reopening of the war.

But the 38th parallel issue posed international problems for the United States. Allied ambassadors who had been briefed secretly on restrictions contained in NSC 81/1 supported taking the war to the North and unifying Korea. The British foreign secretary, Ernest Bevin, had called publicly for an end to the "artificial division" of the country.[12] Nonetheless, the United States did not wish to risk a UN vote on the direct question of whether the 38th parallel should be breached. The Soviets had returned to the Security Council, and surely they would cast a veto. The thinking in the State Department was that a veto would strip legitimacy from any move above the 38th parallel. So the Truman administration decided to avoid the issue, to do what must be done without any public proclamation. On September 29 General Marshall sent a personal-eyes-only message to MacArthur:

> We want you to feel unhampered tactically and strategically to proceed north of 38th Parallel. Announcement above referred to [that ROK divisions might pause for "regrouping"] may precipitate embarrassment in UN with necessity of a vote on passage of 38th Parallel, rather to find you have found it militarily necessary to do so.[13]

MacArthur replied the next day that he was "cautioning Walker against any involvement connected with the nomenclature of the 38th Parallel" and continued in words that put the broadest interpretation possible on his authority:

Parallel 38 is not a factor in the military employment of our forces. The logistical supply of our units is the main problem which limits our immediate advance. In exploiting the defeat of the enemy forces, our own troops may cross the parallel at any time in exploratory probing or exploiting local tactical conditions. My overall strategic plan for North Korea [using EUSAK and X Corps in separate columns] is known to you. Unless and until the enemy capitulates, I regard *all of Korea open for our military operations.* [emphasis added].[14]

MacArthur Spots a Loophole

MacArthur's last sentence slid around the JCS directive that only ROK troops be used in the northernmost areas of Korea, and he was later to cite Marshall's message as justification for continuing operations even after massive Chinese intervention. Acheson (who claimed not to have seen the message before it was dispatched) agreed that Marshall's language was dangerously vague. "To me," he wrote in his memoirs, "the message seems directed toward soothing MacArthur's irritation at being required to submit his plan of operations. He was assured that Washington wanted him to feel unhampered in proceeding north, *except as his orders confined him* [emphasis added]."[15] Unfortunately for Acheson's position, Marshall's words were easier to read than MacArthur's mind.

But the JCS did not challenge the broad interpretation MacArthur put on his orders in his September 30 message calling "all of Korea open for our military operations." It took issue with only a single minor point. For MacArthur to state his plans publicly, as he said he intended to do, would be "unwise." Instead, the Joint Chiefs preferred that he proceed "without any further explanation or announcement and let action determine the matter. Our government desires to avoid having to make an issue of the 38th Parallel until we have accomplished our mission of defeating the Korean forces."[16]

At one point in these semantical skirmishes the State Department tried to render the issue moot by asking MacArthur to make a broadcast asking the North Koreans to lay down their arms in view of their inevitable "early and total defeat." MacArthur did not expect the North Korean Command to accept the demand; indeed, there was no response whatsoever when it was broadcast on October 2. He already was planning an invasion of the North. Characteristically he gave a broad outline to the JCS on September 28, with a promise of "complete details" later; as usual MacArthur did not intend to give Washington a chance to kibitz his strategy.

A Dubious Strategy

Even in outline form MacArthur's planned offensive gave pause to Pentagon planners. MacArthur intended for the Eighth Army, under General Walker, to attack northwest from Seoul across the 38th parallel and capture Pyongyang, the North Korean capital. X Corps, under General Almond, would be pulled back through Inchon and be transported by sea around the peninsula for an amphibious landing at Wonsan. X Corps would drive westward to join the Eighth Army. Then both forces would move north to a line crossing northern Korea at its narrowest point, from Hungnam on the east coast through Yangwon to Chongju on the west. Only ROK troops would operate beyond this line, roughly 100 miles north of the 38th parallel.

MacArthur had a rationale for splitting his forces. Despite its swift seizure of Seoul, X Corps had been unable to block all escape routes of the fleeing NKPA. Even though three-quarters of the enemy army was destroyed, many senior officers had slipped away through the mountains or along the coast. MacArthur was "galled" that thousands of enemy troops were getting across the border unscathed.[17] A landing at Wonsan, he felt, would cut off these troops and also provide a good east coast port for future operations in the North.

Terrain was also an important factor. The Taebaek mountain range rises to rugged heights above the Seoul–Wonsan corridor, forming what an army historian called "an almost trackless mountainous waste in the direction of the Manchurian frontier." The principal rail and land routes follow the north-south valleys. Virtually the only passable east-west road and rail lines in all of the north are those connecting Wonsan and Pyongyang, and this route MacArthur intended to follow. Without a supply base on the east coast (i.e., Wonsan) the UN Command would find it difficult to operate in the interior of North Korea.

MacArthur thought Wonsan would be a more efficient supply base than Pusan. The U.S. Air Force, with destructive efficiency, had blasted away virtually every rail and highway bridge north of the Pusan Perimeter. Their restoration would require weeks; hence Pusan could not be relied upon as a major port of entry. Nor was Inchon large enough to supply both the Eighth Army and X Corps for the lightning advance MacArthur wanted.

One ineffective protest was made against the plan.[18] Colonel John A. Dabney, the EUSAK G-3, voicing the reservations of many fellow staff members, argued that the logistics of pulling X Corps out of the country would unnecessarily delay pursuit of the defeated NKPA and impede the Eighth Army's advance. He and other staff officers felt that the ROK advance up the east coast would seize Wonsan long before X Corps could be landed there. The EUSAK staff recommended an alternate plan: assigning X Corps to the Eighth Army and moving against both Pyongyang and Wonsan overland.

These thoughts were put into a memorandum which Colonel Dabney took to General Walker. Walker read it and said he agreed; nonetheless, he did not intend to pass it along to MacArthur. He told Dabney that he had "made his views known" and had received contrary orders. He would not push the argument. Further, MacArthur was firm in his intention of retaining two separate commands in Korea, despite urgings by his own staff officers (chiefly Generals Hickey and Wright) that X Corps and EUSAK be combined once Seoul fell.

The split command offended Walker, according to officers who served with him.[19] He had done the bloody scutwork of the first months of the war, preserving the shattered ROK Army with equal parts of legerdemain and military skill. With only a corporal's guard of American troops he had managed to win the desperate battle of the Pusan Perimeter and prevent a feared Dunkirk. According to Melvin Voorhees, his public information officer, Walker was "hurt and offended" when X Corps carried out the Inchon invasion as a separate command. When MacArthur then left X Corps as a separate entity, Walker's hurt deepened. He scathingly called Almond's corps "the public relations brigade" and felt MacArthur misused it after Inchon. In his view, reports Voorhees, MacArthur should have ordered Almond to strike directly across the neck of South Korea after capturing Inchon to cut the escape route of the NKPA. Instead, MacArthur opted for the symbolic target of Seoul.*

Now Walker fretted once more as his command was disrupted by the withdrawal of X Corps through the clogged Inchon port. The decision infuriated leaders of the 1st Marine Division, who wanted to continue in hot pursuit of the NKPA. "Logistically it was pretty rough," lamented General Oliver P. Smith.[21] But the marines followed orders; on October 3 the 1st Division turned over to EUSAK its positions outside Seoul and moved back to Inchon.

The marine commanders could not resist glances at their situation maps. The ROK Army had burst past the 38th parallel on the east coast and was rushing toward Wonsan. Were the marines embarking upon a futile expedition that would find them "invading" a North Korean port that had already fallen to the ROK Army? Smith felt that military wisdom dictated that his division pursue the NKPA on the ground, rather than break contact for almost two weeks.

A split command. A two-pronged advance through treacherous mountains, with only hopes of a linkup. Thus did MacArthur jerry-build the foundation for a military disaster.

---

*One officer close to Walker told me that "Tokyo palace politics" also contributed to the split command; that MacArthur did not wish to put his favored General Almond under General Walker, a commander he did not trust.[20]

* * *

To soften enemy resistance along the advance route, the UN Command once again called upon Eugene F. Clark, the young naval lieutenant who had done invaluable intelligence work before the Inchon invasion.[22] This time Clark's mission was threefold: to locate and pinpoint the center of minelaying activity off the west coast of North Korea; to gather positive intelligence on what was happening in the Yalu River area, with special emphasis on Chinese activities; and to capture any equipment helpful to UN operations.

Clark left Inchon on October 15 with some 150 South Korean guerrillas, 4 of them women, in small boats. One group of 5 agents went ashore the first night and scouted Paengnyong to sample NKPA strength and to chart strongpoints of resistance. The next night the mission was even more daring. Twenty guerrillas, armed only with grenades, slipped ashore under cover of darkness and circulated through villages under the very nose of the NKPA. They told residents that a major invasion of Paengnyong would be launched at sunrise. It was likely that all North Korean troops would be killed if they were to oppose the landing, because of the overwhelming superiority of the forces of the United Nations Command. They described the great havoc and loss of life at Inchon and suggested these villagers might meet the same fate. Thus the North Korean civilians would do the NKPA a big favor by urging an immediate evacuation. The women agents were especially useful because they could talk to peasant women. (In Korean village society women are wary of speaking with strange males.) The civilians left.

Within hours North Korean intelligence heard of the incident and shifted troops to the village. The U.S./UN advance slid around the village, through the depleted NKPA lines.

The British Are Nervous

Meanwhile, Washington worked to quell jitters among the British, heretofore strong supporters.[23] On October 4 the British ambassador, Sir Oliver Franks, asked many questions of Dean Rusk about operations north of the 38th parallel. Franks was concerned whether the United States felt existing UN resolutions authorized such operations.

Yes, Rusk replied; MacArthur was in hot pursuit of a viable enemy, and although only ROK troops had crossed the border at the time, "there is a hostile army in the field which is still shooting at United Nations forces," and the United States considered it a "military necessity" for MacArthur to "continue the fight in whatever way seems appropriate to him."

The next day Air Marshal Lord Tedder, the ranking British military representative in America, met with General Bradley and told him the British military command—as well as the Foreign Office—questioned the wisdom of crossing the 38th parallel.[24] The view in London was that the principal objective should be to localize the war in Korea and avoid any risk of a protracted conflict. The British felt that sending UN troops into North Korea might extend the conflict. The British Chiefs of Staff recommended that UN forces stop at the 38th parallel for a week or so and warn North Korea it would be invaded unless its army surrendered. Recognizing reality, the British plan would put no strictures on the ROKs (who had crossed the 38th parallel on September 28).

Bradley chose to ignore the British request, telling Tedder that what he asked was "just about what we are doing."[25] Pacified, at least temporarily, the British agreed to work on Washington's behalf to obtain a General Assembly resolution providing political guidance for the continuing military operations.* With seven other friendly nations, Britain presented a resolution calling for "all appropriate steps . . . to ensure conditions of stability throughout Korea," with a unified government elected under UN auspices and prompt withdrawal of troops. The resolution passed on October 7 by a vote of 47 to 5, with 7 abstentions.

In this instance, Acheson's zeal overcame his lawyer's common sense. Determined to gain the UN imprimatur for operations beyond the 38th parallel, Acheson (and his staff) produced wondrously loose language— a fault that was to cause the United States grave problems within the next two months. The resolution spoke of establishing "conditions of stability." But did not such "conditions" already exist in North Korea, docilely under Communist control since 1945? The North Korean government had ignored the United Nations in the past, refusing even to permit its representatives to enter the country. Why should the UN expect cooperation now? If North Korea did refuse, just what were the "all appropriate steps" the UN was willing to take to ensure "conditions of stability"? The resolution did not say.

Acheson had explanations later, although lame ones.[27] He felt that the 1947 UN resolution on unification elections had been blocked by Soviet military power. "Only scattered remnants remained of the NKPA. Our hope was that the rounding up, or surrender of the forces which started this aggression, would result in the carrying out of the UN resolution . . . and . . . try and bring that whole country together." Chances were "believed good" that neither the Russians nor the Chi-

*Washington worked through the General Assembly rather than the Security Council to avoid a certain Soviet veto.[26] A majority vote is sufficient to pass an Assembly resolution.

nese would intervene *"if only Korean soldiery* [emphasis added] attempted to establish whatever degree of order was possible in the rugged country of the extreme north."[28]

To Acheson's claimed dismay, MacArthur "at once stripped from the resolution . . . its husk of ambivalence and gave it an interpretation that the enacting majority in the General Assembly would not have accepted." Acheson took particular issue with a surrender demand which MacArthur broadcast on October 9. The general quoted the UN resolution and declared:

> In order that the decisions of the United Nations may be carried out . . . I . . . for the last time, call upon you and the forces under your command . . . forthwith to lay down your arms and cease hostilities. . . . Unless immediate response is made by you . . . I shall at once proceed to take such military action as may be necessary to enforce the decrees of the United Nations.

Acheson said this statement removed any doubt that MacArthur was ready to use his "terrible, swift sword" to create a "unified, independent and democratic government" of all Korea. In Senate testimony the following spring, after his dismissal, MacArthur succinctly defined his mission: "to clear out all North Korea, to unify it and to liberalize it." Acheson's distress notwithstanding, MacArthur's interpretation was by no means outlandish. The preamble to the October 7 resolution cited three earlier ones (in 1947, 1948, and 1949) calling for unification of Korea and noted that the goal had not been achieved. Coupling these provisions with the loosely phrased operative portions of the resolution, MacArthur understandably could conclude that the UN indeed intended him to bring unity to Korea. Nonetheless, as General Collins has pointed out, "no directive to unify Korea was ever included in the missions" assigned to MacArthur.[29]

Collins's statement was true—but also grossly incomplete. President Truman and the Joint Chiefs of Staff watched MacArthur prepare for his march to the north, and they had at least a month in which to countermand his orders if they chose to do so. They did not. As shall be seen (in Chapter Eleven), China repeatedly warned it would intervene in the war if U.S. forces crossed the 38th parallel. All parties concerned arrogantly dismissed these warnings—Truman, Acheson, and MacArthur. Even a small-scale entry of Chinese "volunteers" in late October did not bring any change in MacArthur's orders. Truman and Acheson had convinced themselves that since the United States had no designs on Chinese territory, the Chinese should trust their motives. The Chinese did not. In sum, the Truman administration (the President, Acheson, and the JCS) made errors of a magnitude comparable to those of MacArthur. Truman apologists unfairly condemn MacArthur for the debacle that was to follow. But a share of the blame must be assigned to Washington.

Buoyed by his success at Inchon, undeterred by General Almond's inability to provide the "anvil" against which the NKPA could be smashed by General Walker's "hammer," opposed now only by a broken and demoralized enemy, General Douglas MacArthur in early October prepared to strike north.

Red Spies in Washington

MacArthur's planned march north, unfortunately, was handicapped by the fact that the Communists knew exactly the strictures placed upon his command (particularly the ban on any UN troops other than South Koreans approaching the Yalu border regions) and the uneasiness in Washington about the wisdom of any moves north of the 38th parallel.[30] The conduits for this intelligence were three deep-cover Soviet agents who held high positions in the British government: H. A. R. "Kim" Philby, an intelligence officer assigned to the embassy in Washington; Guy Burgess, the second secretary there; and Donald Maclean, of the American desk in the Foreign Office in London. All products of the British establishment, the men had converted to communism during their university days in the 1930's and agreed to serve as Soviet intelligence agents as their careers took them toward the upper echelons of the government. Philby especially was well placed. His myriad duties in Washington included liaison with the Central Intelligence Agency, and he frequently socialized with high officials of the Defense and State departments as well.

Despite his position, Philby did not carry the full trust of American counterintelligence. During the Second World War several grave leaks of Anglo-American security information had been traced to the British embassy—where Philby had then served also—and he was on the list of suspected sources. Thus, when he returned to Washington in mid-1949, the FBI put him under loose surveillance. Nonetheless, Philby still enjoyed *ex officio* access to all information that went through the embassy, including details of American military and strategic planning on Korea.

What Philby missed would go across the desk of Guy Burgess, a security officer's nightmare. An alcoholic and a homosexual (and discreet about neither characteristic), Burgess had been assigned to America as a "last chance" after disgracing himself in other foreign posts. Many in the embassy would have nothing to do with the drunken boor, whose anti-American outbursts (on Korea and other subjects) caused them frequent embarrassment. Both British and American counterintelligence suspected Burgess as a glaring security risk; oddly, however, no one challenged him when he asked about Korean matters, which were none of his professional concern. Burgess's excuse—and a thin one —was that he wanted all the information he could find about the Korean scandal and "how the big fool MacArthur is taking us into war."

One person whom Burgess attempted to use as an inside source was a Washington official of the Foreign Policy Association, a private research group.*[31] Burgess asserted to this person that his job at the British embassy was to analyze the motivations and tendencies of the American attitude toward the Far East, not only in regard to the official government opinion, but also in regard to the opinion of the general American public." To this person, Burgess seemed "very restless and agitated" and obsessed with the notion that the United States "was headed for doom because of having gotten . . . bogged down with regard to Oriental affairs." Burgess seemed "very tolerant of Russia's role in world affairs."

Burgess was a sloppy spy—a man who could gulp down six highballs with no visible effect, but who went about with tousled hair and dirty fingernails, declining to raise the top of his convertible even in winter. He considered the congressional investigations of homosexuals in the State Department "a personal affront" and indeed was so vociferous on the subject the Foreign Policy Association person concluded (accurately) that Burgess himself was homosexual. But Burgess did covet some amenities of capitalism: At one point he inquired about joining the extra-exclusive Metropolitan Club in Washington.

As a backstop to Burgess and Philby, there was Donald Maclean in London, who read all cable traffic from the Washington embassy. Like his longtime friend Burgess, Maclean was a drunken homosexual who had spent the past several years under intensive psychiatric treatment. But he was unsuspected by either American or British security services, and daily he copied vital documents that came across his desk.

According to a former CIA counterintelligence specialist, "Because of the British problems during and after the Second World War in security areas, we had to deal with them on the assumption that Soviet agents were still in place in their Foreign Office and Secret Intelligence Service. However, the United States government had no alternative but to share a good deal of secret information with a nation that was our ally in the war and in fact had men fighting in the war." But the CIA did impose one stricture. It did not inform Philby of secret covert

*The name of the FPA official is deleted from the FBI account of his interview, but it was readily obtained elsewhere. The FBI report gives no indication whatsoever that Burgess received information from this person other than what would have been supplied to any inquiring citizen. But to avoid any possible embarrassment, I am not using the person's name.

operations against Communist China, even though he was made privy to most other intelligence CIA gathered from around the world.

How important was the information that Philby *et al.* passed to their Soviet overseers? "The most important governmental conclusion," one State Department official said years later, "was that the United States truly intended to contain the war, and that we would not be ready to take on the Soviets for another thirty months. However, decisions have a way of signaling themselves via events. Anyone who read the public press, and watched MacArthur's actual progress, could have concluded what Washington intended to do. At the same time, however, I'd have given my left arm to have had three comparable spies working for *me.*"

Nonetheless, the circumstances point to a significant mystery. The United States was telling the British embassy—as well as the general public—that it did not intend to move against Communist China. Nonetheless, in October and November 1950, the Chinese responded to MacArthur's march to the north as if in fact they were faced with an American invasion. Several possibilities—they can be called only that—are present. First, the Soviets did not trust the information turned up by its spies and gave it no credence. Secondly, the Soviets chose not to pass the intelligence to their ostensible friend the Communist Chinese. Or thirdly, the Chinese received the information and decided to ignore it.

Of these possibilities, the second is the most credible. The Soviet Union was happy to tie the United States down in a proxy war in Korea, with the Chinese and the North Koreans suffering the casualties. The war increased China's reliance upon the Soviet Union; it prevented China's growth into a significant world power, and the Soviets could sit back and watch with assurance that the United States did not wish global conflict. Thus the value of the material gathered by the Philby-Burgess-Maclean ring.

CHAPTER NINE

"Operation Yo-Yo"

During the diplomatic wrangling over the 38th parallel the Eighth Army paused to regroup after its capture of Seoul and to prepare for whatever further fighting would be required. Following orders from Washington, General MacArthur in early October broadcast a demand that North Korea surrender. Premier Kim Il Sung replied on October 7 with an order to his troops to "fight to the end."

The Eighth Army had already sent units across the parallel to probe North Korean defenses, and on October 9 the full invasion force moved —the 1st Cavalry, the 24th Infantry Division, the ROK 1st Division, and the British 27th Brigade. The North Koreans managed stiff resistance for some five days, then the 1st Cavalry broke through to seize Kumchon, the first major town on the Seoul–Pyongyang corridor.

The next days saw a total rout of the NKPA, with the 1st Cavalry and 24th Infantry racing to see which would be the first to reach Sariwon, the halfway point on the highway to Pyongyang.[1] The advance was so rapid that large pockets of enemy troops were overrun and bypassed. North Koreans surrendered in wholesale lots, one UN battalion taking 1,700 prisoners in a single evening. An air force pilot even succeeded in capturing an NKPA company from the air. He noticed a group of North Korean soldiers on a hill northeast of Kunsan and dropped a note ordering them to lay down their arms. They obeyed, and the pilot guided a patrol to 200 waiting prisoners. The UN forces captured tons of artillery and tanks and munitions, including three entire trains laden with supplies, which the retreating enemy had concealed in tunnels. High-ranking officers began to surrender (they included Senior Colonel Lee Hak Ku, chief of staff of the NKPA 13th Division, who slipped away from his unit, shook awake two American soldiers he found in a foxhole, and turned over his weapon). One large group of prisoners was captured near an encampment of Australians of the 3rd Battalion. The American commander, Lieutenant Colonel Peter D. Clainos, radioed the Australians he was approaching with the column of prisoners, escorted by trucks with headlights ablaze. As Colonel Clainos approached, he heard an Aussie on an outpost exclaim, "Now what do you make of this? Here we are, all set for a coordinated attack in the morning, and the bloody Yanks come in at midnight from the north, with their lights burning and bringing the whole damned North Korean army as prisoners."

Still, General Walton Walker had cause to worry. EUSAK remained critically short of ammunition and other supplies, a condition that worsened as the rapid advance continued. EUSAK's closest railhead was at Waegwan, 200 miles distant on the Naktong River. Inchon remained clogged with the remnants of X Corps, in the final stages of withdrawal under MacArthur's plan for an invasion on the east coast.

In the east the ROK advance was even swifter. The ROKs were not encumbered by the grand strategic planning of a Douglas MacArthur. The enemy was on the run, and they pursued. By one army intelligence estimate, only about 25,000 members of the NKPA managed to stagger across the 38th parallel in this sector. The ROKs, still smarting from their disgrace of three months earlier, gave the enemy little breathing room.

The pursuit up the east coast was a remarkable feat in an era of "modern" warfare. The ROK 3rd Division traveled by day and by night, on foot and by vehicle, more often than not out of communication with any headquarters. The commanders ignored such fundamentals as flank security; whatever counterattacks the NKPA might launch from the west the ROKs felt they could ignore or contain. The ROKs did not pause to clean up every pocket of resistance. Stragglers could be rooted out and shot or captured later.

This is not to suggest that the ROK advance was easy. The NKPA 5th Division had only about 2,400 survivors, but it did retain mortars and 76 mm antitank weapons, which were used with deadly effect on the narrow coastal roads. The NKPA also had fortified caves and gun positions. Still, the ROKs pounded on, often gaining fifteen miles a day, even though many shoeless soldiers walked northward on bloody feet.

Troops of the ROK 3rd and Capital divisions entered Wonsan on October 10, less than two weeks after crossing the 38th parallel; the city was in UN hands by the next evening. The 3rd Division remained there to prepare for the arrival of MacArthur's "invasion" force; the Capital Division surged another fifty miles up the coast.

To officers' profound disgust, the 1st Marine Division was still boarding ships at Inchon for its long voyage for the Wonsan "invasion" when word came the ROKs had already captured their target by an overland march. Would MacArthur rescind his foolish order and permit the 1st Marines to return to battle without a nonsensical sea voyage of a week's duration? No, the marines would still be shipped to Wonsan.

A colonel sat in the wardroom of the USS *Mount McKinley*—once again serving as an invasion flagship/command post—and wrote a letter to an army friend in MacArthur's headquarters. "I hate to use that old canard, 'We told you so,' but, buddy, we damned well sure did. So now we're sitting on our asses in a boat in the harbor while we could be out in the field killing Commies. Your 'Great God MacArthur' is not infallible, you know. And this time he really screwed up!"

The colonel addressed the envelope but the next day decided not to mail it. The letter could be interpreted as sour grapes. MacArthur, after all, had pulled off Inchon over marine opposition. So permit the general one mistake. The colonel stuffed the letter away in his seabag.

Pyongyang Captured

The fall of Pyongyang, the North Korean capital, was almost anticlimactic, with defenders finding little apparent inspiration in Premier Kim Il Sung's order of October 14: "Do not retreat one step farther. Now we have no space in which to fall back." To enforce his order, Kim set up a "supervising army"—a summary execution squad—to shoot deserters on the spot.

Kim's exhortation came too late. On October 14 the UN forces broke Pyongyang's defensive lines, throwing the NKPA into utter confusion. A British battalion, the Argyll 1st, found haggard North Koreans milling around the roadside, waiting for a chance to surrender. North Koreans several times mistook the British, in their unfamiliar garb, for Russians. One group ran up to a platoon of Argylls, shouting, "Comrade! Comrade!" as if the Russians had intervened to save them.[2] They offered cigarettes and the red stars from their caps as souvenirs. The Argylls accepted the cigarettes and the stars and the slaps on the back. Then they stepped back and shot down the North Koreans.

On October 17 EUSAK intelligence estimated that fewer than 8,000 North Korean soldiers remained to defend Pyongyang and that the beaten NKPA would attempt only delaying actions. The UN came at the Communists from seemingly every direction—the 1st Cavalry from the south, the ROK 1st Division from the southeast. The ROK commander, Brigadier Paik Sun Yup, had a grim ambition to be the first into Pyongyang. Five years earlier, when the Communists took control of North Korea, the city's rulers had killed several members of Paik's family. Paik told an American correspondent during the 1950 advance that the Communists "sawed off the head" of his baby.[3]

The final assault began on October 19. The NKPA put up one last counterattack, sending three tanks out to challenge an advance column of the 5th Cavalry Regiment. A team led by a young American soldier knocked out the tanks with a bazooka.

By midday the 1st Cavalry and the ROK 1st division had punched into the city, blasting away the last diehard defenders. Brigadier Paik wanted blood. When one NKPA contingent fought back from entrenchments, he simply directed his tanks to run over them. Some 300 North Koreans were crushed or otherwise killed.

The relative ease of the battle meant that Pyongyang escaped the devastation suffered by Seoul. For this or other reasons, residents received the UN armies with "South Korean flags, British flags, Chinese Nationalist flags, and improvised UN flags which had been designed from hearsay," according to Dwight Martin of *Time*. The American troops marveled at Russian trappings in the city: the concentration of houses for Russian officials around the USSR embassy; the Russian commissary crammed with wine, vodka, caviar, and cosmetics; the expensive radios and photographic equipment in the Soviet embassy itself. Kim Il Sung's office was entered through four anterooms, each with a portrait of Joseph Stalin; the inner sanctum was "rich with gaudy rugs and expensive furnishings . . . [and] dominated by an enormous mahogany desk which is flanked on the left by a foot-high plaster bust of Kim, on the right by a bust of Stalin." In his air-raid shelter Kim had a music room with an organ and a one-chair barbershop.

The Americans moved quickly to install a new government in the captured capital. Colonel Archibald W. Melchoir, a civil affairs officer, chose a council of what he hoped were Pyongyang's leading non-Communist citizens. Explained Melchoir: "We were sitting on some logs by a foot bridge when we saw a Korean walking toward us. Since he was well-dressed, we collared him and told him to round up some substantial citizens." The citizen, an innkeeper, happily obliged and gave the Americans a cadre of high school teachers and low-level county officials. The five-year Soviet domination of North Korea had ended.

Willoughby Declares Victory

On October 20 General Charles Willoughby effectively announced the end of the war.[4] In an intelligence summary distributed throughout the Far East Command, Willoughby stated:

Organized resistance on any large scale has ceased to be an enemy
capability. Indications are that the North Korean military and political
headquarters may have fled to Manchuria. Communications with, and
consequent control of, the enemy's field units have dissipated to a point
of ineffectiveness. . . .

In spite of these indications of disorganization, there are no signs, at
the moment, that the enemy intends to surrender. He continues to retain the capability of fighting small scale delaying actions against
UN pressure. . . .

The frustrated X Corps wallowed helplessly at sea as the war swept
around it. The North Koreans—probably with Soviet assistance—had
sprinkled approaches to Wonsan with more than 3,000 mines, and navy
efforts to remove them proved disastrous.

A flotilla of twenty-one minesweepers began operations on October
10 and managed to clear a channel to within ten miles of the coastline.
Then some officer unidentified in naval histories conceived the idea of
exploding mines along a narrow passageway by aerial bombardment to
permit the lead sweeps to pass. On October 12 thirty-nine planes from
the carriers *Leyte* and *Philippine Sea* dropped 50 tons of 1,000-pound
bombs. The scheme didn't work; the concussion would not detonate the
mines. Then three minesweepers entered the channel. Within minutes
the *Pirate* struck a mine; the *Pledge,* following closely, hit another. Both
vessels quickly sank. The third sweeper, the *Incredible,* picked up more
than two dozen survivors. But twelve men went down with their ships,
and another died later of wounds; thirty-three others were wounded.
The operation continued for two weeks, with the loss of three more
vessels, two South Korean, one Japanese. The Russian-made mines
proved devilishly complex; one magnetic variety could be set to allow
as many as twelve ships to pass before it exploded. So the sweepers had
to make at least thirteen passes over an area before it could be considered safe.

The 1st Marine Division—one of the best fighting units committed to
the war—thus remained in idle frustration as its transport ships steamed
slowly back and forth from October 19 to 25 in the Sea of Japan just
outside the Wonsan Channel. The derisive marines spoke caustically of
Operation Yo-Yo, and each time the vessels turned to the south they
started rumors about returning to Pusan—and then home. But the
joking soon stopped, especially on the LSTs and small transports which
were not prepared for a voyage that was taking nearly as long as a
crossing of the Pacific. Gastroenteritis and dysentery swept the transports; one vessel, the *Marine Phoenix,* had a sick list of 750 men. Food
supplies ran dangerously low. As marine historian Lynn Montross
wrote, "Never did time die a harder death, and never did the grumblers
have so much to grouse about. Letters to wives and sweethearts took

on more bulk daily, and paper-backed murder mysteries were worn to tatters by bored readers."[5]

The evening of October 24 entertainers Bob Hope and Marilyn Maxwell presented a USO show at Wonsan heavily laden with quips about the unhappy seabound marines. The next day, to the jeers and catcalls of advance parties who had arrived by land and air (air maintenance crews had been in Wonsan a full twelve days), the 1st Marine Division finally put ashore. MacArthur's "strategy" had kept the most effective fighting men in his command out of the war for four full weeks.

The 7th Army Division, meanwhile, endured its own version of Operation Yo-Yo. In a sense its situation was even more frustrating than that of the marines. The original plan had been for the 7th Division to follow the marines ashore at Wonsan; hence they loaded at Pusan as if for an unopposed landing. But before the boats could leave Pusan, the ROKs had seized Wonsan, so the Tokyo command decided on a change in the 7th's mission: It would land as far north as possible to link up with troops already in North Korea. General Almond chose Iwon, where the 7th would be positioned to move northward on the road Pukchong–Pungsan–Hyesanjin toward the Yalu.

But a complicating factor: Would Iwon be cleared of NKPA troops when the 7th Division arrived? For ten days the forlorn, seasick soldiers sat in transport ships in Pusan Harbor while Tokyo staff officers tried to make decisions. Then the order: Everybody off the boats, we must do it over, and this time "combat load"—that is, the men who would assault the beach and the equipment and supplies they would need immediately after landing must be on the same ships. As General Collins noted, combat loading takes an inordinate amount of time, for there is little margin for error; once troops hit a hostile beach, they must have enough supplies to operate on their own until a perimeter is secured. So not until October 27 did vessels bearing the 7th Division finally leave Pusan. Luckily the Communists had not got around to mining the waters off Iwon, and the ROK Capital Division had chased defenders out of the town. Hence the landing was unopposed and went off without a hitch.

But the men and equipment of the 7th Division did not finish unloading until November 9.

A Misguided "Masterstroke"

By any reckoning, MacArthur's decision to take half his army out of the battle when the enemy was on the run ranks as one of the more glaring blunders of American military history—one that well cost his command victory. Out of professional courtesy, perhaps, his fellow generals for the most part glossed over the miscalculation in their accounts of the war. General J. Lawton Collins noted that "it is easy to 'Monday-morning-quarterback' an operation long after its completion."[6] Although the movement of X Corps proved unnecessary, it did wind up exactly where MacArthur wanted it—that is, on the east flank of the Eighth Army. Wonsan and Hungnam were essential ports, and the mines blocking the harbors would have had to be cleared eventually anyway. So Collins wrote. But he also recognized the logistical disruptions caused by the withdrawal of X Corps through Inchon at the very time the Eighth Army was pursuing the North Koreans. Still, Collins was Old Army, and he criticized MacArthur in gently indirect language:

> It is impossible to assess with any certainty the effect of the lull in the pursuit of the North Koreans in the west. It is an axiom of military tactics to press relentlessly on the heels of a defeated enemy. This was not done after the fall of Seoul. Only the X Corps was in a position to do so, in conjunction with the smashing drive of the ROK army in the east.

What Collins was saying, in his own polite roundabout fashion, was that simple military sense dictated that MacArthur allow X Corps to chase the NKPA and destroy it. But MacArthur was so obsessed with "strategic masterstroke" that he permitted his fantasies in Tokyo to overshadow the realities on the battlefield in Korea. He bungled a chance to win the war in October. Now he proceeded to compound his error. He decided to permit X Corps and Eighth Army to continue operating as separate commands, both reporting to Far East Command headquarters in Tokyo.

Long after the war ended, some of MacArthur's ranking staff officers told army historians that they felt X Corps should have been integrated into the Eighth Army once the Inchon landing was complete. These included Major General Doyle Hickey, the acting chief of staff; Brigadier General Edward Wright, the chief planner; and Major General George L. Eberle, the logistical chief. But in his memoirs MacArthur professed ignorance of any such dissent. So, too, did General Almond, who also stated: "It should be noted, however, that General MacArthur was at all times fully capable of making up his own mind without benefit of advice."

* * *

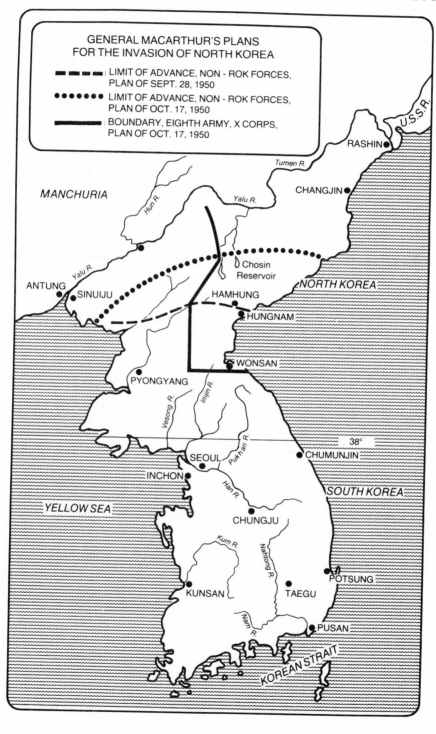

GENERAL MACARTHUR'S PLANS
FOR THE INVASION OF NORTH KOREA

- - - - LIMIT OF ADVANCE, NON - ROK FORCES,
PLAN OF SEPT. 28, 1950
•••••• LIMIT OF ADVANCE, NON - ROK FORCES,
PLAN OF OCT. 17, 1950
BOUNDARY, EIGHTH ARMY, X CORPS,
PLAN OF OCT. 17, 1950

U.S.S.R.

RASHIN

Tumen R.

CHANGJIN

MANCHURIA

Hun R.

Yalu R.

Chosin
Reservoir

NORTH KOREA

Yalu R.

ANTUNG

SINUIJU

HAMHUNG

HUNGNAM

WONSAN

PYONGYANG

Vesong R.

Imjin R.

38°

SEOUL

Pukhan R.

CHUMUNJIN

INCHON

Han R.

SOUTH KOREA

YELLOW SEA

CHUNGJU

Kum R.

Nahtong R.

POTSUNG

KUNSAN

TAEGU

Nam R.

PUSAN

KOREAN STRAIT

MacArthur Stretches Orders

With Pyongyang in UN hands, MacArthur now pressed for a swift end to the war. On October 17 he assigned a new objective line that went 50 to 100 miles beyond the September 27 line approved by the JCS on September 28. The new line ran roughly from Sonchon on the west coast to Pyongwon, northwest of the Changjin Reservoir, then eastward via Pongsan to Songjin on the Sea of Japan. The northeastward arc roughly paralleled the North Korean frontier, some 45 miles distant. All UN forces could advance freely to the new objective line; beyond it, however, non-ROK forces could not operate "except on direct orders" of MacArthur. X Corps and the Eighth Army were to continue operating as separate commands. In Washington nervous staff officers noted the commands would be divided by peaks of up to 7,400 feet in the rugged Taebaek Range, with communications possible only between their respective headquarters, not between field commands.

MacArthur's new operations order perhaps followed the letter of his instructions to restrict operations of non-Korean forces near the northernmost borders. But it damaged the spirit of the UN resolution of October 7, under which the task of pacifying the far north, beyond the narrow "waist" of Korea, was to be left to ROK troops. General Collins wrote later: "This was the first, but not the last, stretching of MacArthur's orders beyond JCS instructions. If the Chiefs noted this—and I have no recollection that we did—we offered no objection."[7]

Two days later MacArthur stretched his authorization even tauter. On October 20 he directed that *"all concerned"* make a "maximum effort" to seize the new objective line rapidly and be "prepared for continued rapid advance to the border of North Korea."[8] Here MacArthur made artful use of ambiguity: Did *"all concerned"* mean his entire command, Americans as well as ROKs, or was he talking to the ROKs alone, the only force authorized to approach the frontier? The implication was that U.S. troops were now free to go to the Yalu River. Nonetheless, the Joint Chiefs remained silent.

MacArthur's new offensive moved with dispatch. By October 23 Eighth Army and ROK units had reached the Chongchon River, which parallels the Yalu at a distance of about sixty miles to the south. North of the Chongchon Valley is a narrow ridge line that curves back and forth from the Yalu. At its nearest point to the Yalu, the ridge line looks down upon the vast Suiho hydroelectric dam and reservoir, which branches into uncountable fjordlike valleys in the rugged hills on both sides of the river. If the UN were to dominate the Yalu River crossings, it must first dominate the divide. And to do so, it must take the villages of Taechon, Unsan, and Onjong, which lie at the southern entrances to three of the larger valleys.

*   *   *

Colonel Paul Freeman, commanding the 23rd Infantry Regiment of the 2nd Division, came to hate the North Koreans during the drive north.[9] "This was the first time we had really encountered Communist cruelty," he said. "When we first met some of these North Korean attacks, they were driving civilians, elderly people, in front of them as a shield. We had a very difficult time making our men fire into them because if we didn't, we were dead. This was a very hard thing to do."

North of Pyongyang, men of the 187th Airborne Regiment heard reports from Korean civilians of American POWs massacred in a railroad tunnel. The commander, Brigadier General Frank A. Allen, Jr., took correspondents Don Whitehead of the Associated Press and Richard Tucker of the Baltimore *Sun* with him in his jeep to check the rumor. With a ROK colonel as a guide, they entered a tunnel near Sunchon and found the emaciated bodies of five Americans lying on grass mats.[10] They had either starved to death or died of wounds. Outside, a wounded thin young American private staggered from the bushes with a horrible story. "They are over there," he said, pointing to a gully. There were found seventeen more Americans, shot to death; the private, Valdor John, had escaped by feigning death. Allen placed his coat around the shivering youth, who rejected it, saying, "I'm too dirty."

The search continued. The AP's Whitehead, walking ahead of the others, came to a cornfield. There he found a semicircle of fifteen more dead Americans—shot as they sat on the ground with rice bowls in hand, apparently expecting to receive food.

About fifteen more survivors appeared with the same story. A month earlier the North Koreans had marched 370 American POWs north from Seoul to escape the Inchon invasion. Only 150 or so survived as the Americans began approaching Pyongyang. They were put onto rail cars, which moved slowly north, more of them dying en route of dysentery, other illnesses, and wounds. Finally, the North Koreans herded them from the train and told them to prepare for their evening meal. Instead, death squads appeared and began shooting the POWs. Allen and his party searched further and found thirty-four more bodies under a thin layer of dirt. Altogether, sixty-six men had died (not counting the seven found in the tunnel); of the twenty-three survivors, two more died during the night.

Atrocities are often the mark of a panicked army, and such proved the case with the North Koreans. The UN advance was so rapid, the NKPA rout so complete, that on October 24 MacArthur issued another directive effectively making the Yalu River itself his new—and he hoped final—objective line. He removed the remaining restrictions on the advance of American troops. The Eighth Army and X Corps were "authorized to use any and all ground forces . . . as necessary to secure all of North Korea."[11]

This time the JCS balked.[12] In a message the same day they reminded MacArthur of their September 27 directive that only ROK forces would operate "in the northeast province bordering the Soviet Union or in the area along the Manchurian frontier." Although expressing confidence that MacArthur had "sound reasons" for his new order, they asked to be told what these were inasmuch as his action was "a matter of some concern here."

MacArthur was not about to permit Washington to interfere with his offensive. He replied that his orders had been a "matter of military necessity"[13] because the ROK forces acting alone were not strong enough to seize North Korea. Besides, the ROK commanders were often highly emotional and unreliable. Then MacArthur went into dizzily illogical language to support his contention that he was not violating the JCS directive of September 27. The portion of this directive keeping non-ROKs away from the Yalu was merely a "matter of policy." He continued that the directive itself specified that its provisions "cannot be considered final since they may require modification." (The JCS might have found it odd that the recipient of the directive, rather than the originator, had taken the initiative in modifying it.) As further justification, MacArthur cited Secretary Marshall's message of September 29 that he was to "feel unhampered tactically and strategically to proceed north of 38th Parallel." In fact, of course, Marshall had intended this eyes-only message as a means of inducing MacArthur to cross the 38th parallel with as little fanfare as possible, so as to avoid unnerving American supporters in the UN. Subsequent directives on keeping non-ROKs out of the far north were letter-clear.

Next, MacArthur took a trust-me-or-else tack. He was aware of the purpose and intent of the September 27 directive. Nonetheless, any alternative course might produce "tactical hazards." Almost as an afterthought, MacArthur added, "This entire subject was covered in my conference at Wake Island."*

The JCS did not challenge MacArthur. Nonetheless, his labored explanation, one which at least General Collins felt was intellectually dishonest, put the general's military superiors on guard. In Collins's view, the incident was the first instance in which MacArthur stood in clear violation of orders. Testifying in Senate hearings six months later, Collins stated:

> I think this was one indication among many others which certainly have been clear, that General MacArthur was not in consonance with . . . basic

---

*Nothing in the Wake record (see the next chapter) or in the memoirs or papers of participants—including MacArthur's—shows any discussion of the issue of using non-ROK troops near the Yalu.

policies. . . . [It] led us gradually to fear that just as he violated a policy in this case without consulting us, perhaps the thing might be done in some other instance of a more serious nature.[14]

The same week MacArthur thumbed his nose at the JCS in another, more indirect fashion. The episode began with a CIA warning that the Chinese might send forces across the Yalu to protect the Suiho hydro-electric plant, which supplied much of the electrical power for Manchuria. Through the JCS, the State Department asked that MacArthur assure the UN Security Council that he did not intend to disturb Suiho.[15] The JCS on October 21 "authorized" MacArthur to do what State requested—a military euphemism for telling him to do so.[16] MacArthur refused.[17] He did not intend to bomb Suiho, but he did not wish to commit the UN Command until he could assure himself the hydroelectric plant was not being used to manufacture Communist munitions.

The JCS did not press the matter. Once again, however, MacArthur had subtly ignored superiors—and gotten away with it.

"Let's Go Home"

The U.S. military had spent the summer and early autumn bringing itself to fighting strength; now, with victory apparently in sight, what army historian Roy Appleman called "cutback fever" was found everywhere. The Department of the Army talked with MacArthur about returning some Eighth Army troops to the United States or to Europe. On October 25 the Pentagon told MacArthur it was canceling shipment of troops to the Far East scheduled for October and November, save for 17,000 noncommissioned officers. MacArthur did not object. In the Far East Command itself, General Walker, only a few weeks earlier desperately pleading for ammunition, told MacArthur he had enough; henceforth munitions ships arriving from the United States should be diverted to Japan. Major General Walter L. Weible, commanding the Japan Logistical Command, told his counterpart in San Francisco to cancel any outstanding requisitions for ground ammunition and to unload any ships still in port. X Corps circulated a planning document calling for a single American division, the 3rd Infantry, to remain in Korea; everyone else would leave.

Troops of the 1st Cavalry Division were the most optimistic of all. They talked of parading on Thanksgiving Day in Tokyo wearing their favored yellow scarves. Some units even began turning in equipment in preparation for the trip home. When clerks distributed handbills listing prices for Christmas gifts at Korean post exchanges, many troops threw them away; they intended to do their shopping in Tokyo.

Yet pockets of unease persisted. One of these was the 1st Marine Division, which after its unopposed landing at Wonsan had gone inland about thirty-five miles to Kojo and ran headlong into NKPA units that had regrouped as guerrillas. Superior strength and firepower eventually quashed the irregular forces, but only after casualties approaching what the marines had suffered in Inchon and environs.

Despite scattered resistance—notably in the eastern part of Korea, south of Soviet Manchuria—the advance continued smoothly. With MacArthur's approval separate columns raced northward with little or no physical contact between them. The object was for each column to advance as fast and far as possible, without respect to gains by others —or to dangers left by gaps in the line. "Everything is going fine—just fine," General Walton Walker told newsmen with his headquarters on October 25.

The ROK 6th Division moved most swiftly of all. Rushing up the main Chongchon Valley without significant opposition, it swept through town after town until, on the morning of October 26, the Reconnaissance Platoon of the 7th Regiment marched into Chosan—a town square on the Yalu River. With the platoon was an American army adviser, Major Harry Fleming.

From a river bluff Fleming and the ROKs could see NKPA soldiers fleeing into Manchuria on a footbridge. They set up a machine gun— positioned so that the impact area would not be in China—and shot down a number of the North Koreans. After a few hours of reconnaissance the platoon pulled back to its main units.

The Reconnaissance Platoon therefore became the first—and the only—Eighth Army element to reach the Yalu during the entire war.

Thus the situation in mid-October: the Eighth Army pounding away in the western regions of North Korea; ROK divisions storming up the east coast; the international community united in its desire for a swift victory and peace. But skeptical eyes kept flicking to the north. Would the Soviets permit the destruction of a satellite state? Would the Chinese sit idly as a hostile state came into being on its very borders? The marine landing at Iwon brought the UN a quantum jump closer to the Chinese frontier. To the Chinese, this move well could forebode preparations for a thrust across the Yalu.

MacArthur's bungling deployment of X Corps had already cost him any chance of a swift victory. Now fall was turning into winter, and his troops were deep into Asian mountains soon to be gripped by sub-zero temperatures and snow. President Truman and his chief advisers thought the time appropriate to meet with General MacArthur and plan for the peace that they felt was at hand.

CHAPTER TEN

"Summoned for Political Reasons"

As a veteran diplomat Ambassador John Muccio was accustomed to receiving cryptic messages in the middle of the night.[1] This one, however, had him stumped. It arrived from the State Department around 8:30 P.M. on October 14, and it read enigmatically: "If invited, take the trip." Muccio read the cable several times and tried to remember if anything in the massive flow of message traffic he received daily from Washington had mentioned any travel. He could recall none.

About two hours later another puzzling cable arrived, this one from General MacArthur in Tokyo: "I have been instructed to invite you, and if at Haneda [an airport outside Tokyo] before 11:00 in the morning, should be glad to have your company."

Still baffled, Muccio packed an overnight bag and at four-thirty in the morning flew off on a military courier plane to Haneda, wondering, as he sped through the Asian night, just where he might be when he next slept. He found MacArthur's plane, the *SCAP*, at Haneda, and made idle chatter with Colonel Story, the pilot, for forty-five minutes. "He threw no light on destination, or why." Then MacArthur boarded, and the *SCAP* took off at eleven o'clock. All right, Muccio thought, if they want to be stubborn, I can be, too. He settled into his seat, determined not to ask a question of MacArthur or anyone else.

"About fifteen minutes [after takeoff] General MacArthur sat down beside me and very clearly reflected his disgust of 'being summoned for political reasons' when the front and active military operations had so many calls on his times," Muccio recollected.

"And that's the first time I . . . knew that a meeting was to be held

at Wake Island between General MacArthur and President Truman.
. . . [MacArthur] . . . was mad as hell."

With relations with MacArthur once again on a civil basis, even if
guardedly so, Truman decided in early autumn the time had come to
meet his field commander in the flesh. "The first and simplest reason,"
Truman wrote in his memoirs, "was that we had never had any personal
contacts at all, and I thought that he ought to know his Commander in
Chief and that I ought to know the senior field commander in the Far
East."[2] Truman regretted that MacArthur had declined the many invitations to visit the United States during his years in Japan. MacArthur
should have returned if only "to familiarize himself with the situation
at home." The events since June showed that MacArthur had "all his
thoughts wrapped up on the East" and had lost some of his feel for
America. Although Averell Harriman and others had sought to explain
U.S. policy during personal visits, "I felt that we had had little success.
I thought he might adjust more easily if he heard it from me directly."

Such was the official explanation for the President's decision to fly
halfway around the world to spend a handful of hours with MacArthur.
"I would suppose I would have to say candidly," presidential adviser
Charles Murphy admitted years later, "that among us on the White
House staff, at any rate, was the feeling that this would be good public
relations."[3]

The White House certainly needed a political boost the autumn of
1950, for Republicans were making the Korean War the major and
bitter issue in congressional campaigns then in progress. In August four
Republican members of the Senate Foreign Relations Committee
charged that Truman had "sold out" Chiang Kai-shek at the Potsdam
Conference and that the collapse of the Nationalist Chinese government had led directly to the North Korean invasion. Even Republican
moderates such as Senator Arthur Vandenberg expressed "general
agreement" with this statement. Nor would the Republicans accept
rebuttals that the Truman administration had taken a risky anti-Communist stand by sending troops around the world. Former Congressman Everett Dirksen, running against Democratic Senate leader Scott
W. Lucas in Illinois, charged, "All the piety of the Administration will
not put any life into the bodies of the young men coming back in
wooden boxes." Senator Kenneth Wherry of Nebraska declared that
the "blood of our boys in Korea" was on Dean Acheson's hands.

The first plan discussed was to bring MacArthur to Washington, an
idea rejected because of the time the general would be absent from his
command. Next was a proposal that MacArthur fly to Hawaii, as he had
done to meet President Roosevelt on the eve of the 1944 presidential
election to discuss final strategy for the Pacific war. The consensus

pointed to Hawaii, about equidistant between Tokyo and Washington. But after discussions with Pentagon officials, the President offered MacArthur an alternative: "If the situation in Korea is such that you feel you should not absent yourself for the time involved in such a long trip," Wake would suffice as a substitute. MacArthur replied tersely, "I would be delighted to meet the President on the morning of the 15th at Wake Island." Truman agreed, although some on his staff continued to advocate Hawaii. They knew MacArthur's obsession with "face"[4] and questioned whether Truman's submission on the site would give the general a psychological advantage. Truman cut off such talk. According to Army Secretary Frank Pace, "He felt that under the circumstances that it was fitting that he should go out into the area where General MacArthur had the responsibility. . . . There's no lack of sense that he had the right to order General MacArthur back; it was just that General MacArthur had the responsibility for the day-to-day management of the war." Thus Truman would fly 4,700 miles, and MacArthur 1,900, for the meeting.

The White House sent no advance agenda to Tokyo, puzzling MacArthur. According to General Courtney Whitney, MacArthur wondered whether the United States planned a diplomatic or military move "so important that the President felt that he had to make so long and arduous a journey."[5] Truman had MacArthur's views "in fullest detail," and any clarification desired would be forthcoming. Whitney maintains —untruthfully, as the conversation aboard *SCAP* with Muccio made plain—that MacArthur "refused to accept" suggestions that the conference was intended to "establish in the eye of the voter a closer relationship between the administration and the victory just won [at Inchon]. . . . He would countenance no slightest criticism of the President," Whitney wrote. Nonetheless, MacArthur found time to tell William Sebald of the Tokyo embassy the trip was a "political junket" and refused to permit him to join his party, counseling that he should "escape the implications of the meeting."

MacArthur did have reason to focus his attention on the battlefield. X Corps was preparing its "invasion" at Wonsan. The pell-mell advance north of the 38th parallel continued, with American and ROK forces racing closer daily to the foreboding terrain near the Yalu River. Because of the decision to place X Corps and the Eighth Army under separate commands, control of the former was from Tokyo. MacArthur clearly did not wish to step away from the battle, even temporarily, at the brink of victory.

The planning details also annoyed him. A planning cable stressed that any publicity about the meeting was to be controlled by Charles Ross, the White House press secretary. The White House press corps would travel with the President. MacArthur, through underlings, asked that correspondents covering his headquarters also be invited to attend. Some of these men had been around the general so long they practically considered themselves members of his official family. By having them at hand, MacArthur could assure that some of the coverage would not come from what he considered a "hostile" press corps from Washington. MacArthur was "surprised"—and also angered—when his request was "promptly and curtly disapproved."[6] He now recognized the political nature of Harry Truman's journey.

Truman's Misgivings

Although Truman kept his own counsel at the time, he confessed later to Acheson he had misgivings of his own as he prepared for the journey.[7] He was "aware of the possibility of things going wrong," and he saw the danger of unspecified "pitfalls." Acheson begged off attending. "I said that as I understood my duties, it was dealing with foreign powers, and although MacArthur seemed often to be such, I didn't think he ought to be recognized as that," Acheson said.[8] The secretary of state thought the meeting ill-conceived. Private talks are

> the sort of lethal things which chiefs of state get into. MacArthur was practically a chief of state at this time—he was the Mikado of Japan and Korea. . . . This is just sheer murder and never ought to occur to a dog. You have no idea of what is said, and the President can tell you what he thinks was said; the other fellow is quite as sure that something different was said, and there is no way of resolving this thing. . . .

General Marshall also declined the trip; with MacArthur away from FEC headquarters, someone of authority should be around the Pentagon in case of military emergency. Another reason, according to Secretary of the Army Frank Pace, was that "General Marshall didn't think very much of General MacArthur . . . and vice versa."[9]

Because of the time differences involved in traveling to the mid-Pacific, Truman proceeded to Wake in stages. He stopped overnight at his home in Independence, Missouri, then flew to Hawaii, where the navy gave him a requested low-key schedule. When Truman left Hawaii that night for the last leg, a 2,300-mile flight to Wake, his retinue had swelled to three planes of aides and press (the press party roster listed thirty-eight persons). Robert Sherrod of *Time* likened him and MacArthur to "the sovereign rulers of separate states, approaching a neutral field with panoplied retainers to make talk and watch each other's eyes."[10]

MacArthur, meanwhile, was angry. During the eight-hour flight from Tokyo he restlessly paced the aisle of the *SCAP.* He felt the entire trip "most distasteful,"[11] and he wondered about how to deal with "Mr. Truman's quick and violent temper and prejudices."[12] Because of the time difference of three hours, it was almost midnight local time when he landed in Wake, but only about nine o'clock Tokyo time. And a crowning breach of protocol: The Pan American Airlines local manager, in intended graciousness, turned his bungalow over to the men he considered the ranking members of the Tokyo party—MacArthur and Muccio. To Muccio's silent amusement, the arrangement "outraged" General Whitney, who did not like his idol's sharing a shower and bath with another person.[13] MacArthur sat and puffed on his pipe until two in the morning, when Whitney persuaded him to go to bed. For the first time in six years MacArthur must sit across a conference table from a superior. It was not a happy prospect.

The drama of the confrontation was heightened by the hour and setting: The *Independence* approached Wake just before dawn and made leisurely circles against the backdrop of a huge black thundercloud looming over the ocean. Showered, shaved, and having had breakfast, MacArthur waited in an airport shack for half an hour for the President. Truman peered down at dozens of Japanese tanks and landing craft rusting into oblivion on the barren beaches below, remnants of the battle in December 1941, when outnumbered marines were beaten into surrender in the first loss of U.S. soil to a foreign invader.

MacArthur rode out to the *Independence* in a battered 1948 Chevrolet sedan and walked toward the plane as Truman descended the ramp. The President noted that the general was "with shirt unbuttoned, wearing a greasy ham and eggs cap that evidently had been in use for twenty years."[14] (Truman wore his usual haberdasher-proper business suit and hat, the tropical setting notwithstanding.) Edward T. Folliard of the Washington *Post* noted that MacArthur did not salute the President, although they did shake hands. "I've been a long time meeting you," Truman said with a grin. "I hope," replied MacArthur, "it won't be so long next time."

The sky now tinged by light from the approaching sun, the two men clambered into the derelict Chevrolet, climbing over the front seat into the back because the rear doors were jammed. Some 200 airfield laborers—Guamanians, Filipinos, and Marshallese—clapped and cheered. Led by four GIs in a jeep, they drove to a Quonset hut on the perimeter of the airstrip and went inside for an hour.

No one else was present. Peering journalists could record only that the general sat on a rattan settee, the President on a wicker chair. MacArthur did not even mention the interlude in his memoirs, and afterward he told Whitney that the meeting was a "relatively unimportant conversation." When he expressed regrets at the misunderstanding over the VFW message on Formosa, he told Whitney, Truman brushed the subject aside. "Oh, think nothing more on that."[15]

Truman's account was also terse. According to a memo Truman wrote at State Department request the following April, MacArthur assured the President that the victory was won in Korea, that Japan was ready for a peace treaty, and that the Chinese Communists would not attack.

> A general discussion was carried on about Formosa. The General brought up his statement to the Veterans of Foreign Wars. . . . The General said that he was sorry for any embarrassment he'd caused, that he was not in politics at the time, that the politicians had made a "chump" (his word) of him in 1948 and that it would not happen again. He assured the President that he had no political ambitions.
>
> He again said the Chinese Commies would not attack, that we had won the war and that we could send a Division from Korea to Europe in January 1951.*[16]

As MacArthur and Truman emerged, the sun soared hotly into the sky. The creaky Chevrolet took them to a low pinkish building, faced with coral, built as an office for the Civil Aeronautics Authority. A wind sock, but no American flag, flapped in the steady breeze. There was a marked disparity in the two entourages. Flanking Truman were General Omar Bradley, the army chief of staff; Army Secretary Frank Pace; Admiral Arthur W. Radford, commander of the Pacific Fleet; Ambassador at large Philip C. Jessup; Assistant Secretary of State Dean Rusk; Averell Harriman; and press secretary Charles Ross. MacArthur had only Muccio, Courtney Whitney, and Colonel Laurence E. Bunker, his aide-de-camp.**

The meeting began at 7:36 A.M. with open good humor. With a bow toward Wake's pervasive heat Truman suggested "this is no weather for coats" and doffed his suit jacket; others followed. A steward put a bowl of freshly sliced pineapple in front of each participant. MacArthur pulled out one of his famed corncob pipes and asked, "Do you mind if I smoke, Mr. President?" "No," said Truman, a nonsmoker. "I suppose I have had more smoke blown at me than any other man alive."

Colonel Bunker, MacArthur's aide, put pad and pencil on the table and started to scrawl notes, but Charles Ross objected (with "anxiety," in Whitney's words), saying that no notes were to be taken on either side. The account is Whitney's, and it is suspect: General Bradley told Senate hearings the following May that he took notes openly, as did two aides. MacArthur told the same hearings that he asked Ross, "who was in charge of public relations, whether there should be stenographic

*Truman dictated this memorandum of conversation on April 4, 1951, a week before he fired MacArthur. Thus it should be read as an after-the-fact account intended to put Truman in the best possible light.

**Rosters vary. One account includes Story, MacArthur's pilot, on his side of the table. Whitney cited "numerous other Truman aides and aides' aides."

notes taken, because I wished to take them myself. But he told me that no notes would be taken, and there was no stenographer present."

Another note taker was present, but out of sight of most participants. Vernice Anderson, longtime personal secretary to Ambassador Jessup, had accompanied the party to do stenographic odd jobs. A svelte government career woman with large blue eyes and an olive complexion,[17] Miss Anderson had bounced around the world's capitals at Jessup's side. She was good; she could bat out diplomatic letters and communiqués on a portable typewriter regardless of the hour or locale, and she could take dictation when air travel was so rough she often had trouble reading her shorthand notes the next day. Important personages impressed Vernice Anderson, but did not awe her; she had staffed foreign ministers' meetings, North Atlantic Treaty Organization conferences, summits throughout Europe and Asia. Because of Jessup's fireman assignment in the State Department, she always kept a bag packed. She had no specific assignment at Wake, but experience taught her not to wander too far from where things were happening. So she reflexively followed the group into the cinder-block shack and found a seat in an anteroom off the main conference area. Strong prevailing winds blew from the main room into Ms. Anderson's cubbyhole, keeping ajar the louvered door separating them. She heard what people were saying, and she "automatically" took stenographic notes,[18] for she knew she would likely be called upon to help Jessup prepare a formal report. "I hadn't even gone there with a regular notebook. I just happened to have a pad of lined paper, and I just began notes."

Memories of whether anyone knew of Ms. Anderson's presence differed later. Charles Murphy and Dean Rusk expressed surprise, Murphy saying, "None of us knew that she was taking notes."[19] Whitney's account had the stenographer "lurking behind the door" and able to "record only what she could hear through the small opening and what she could see by peeping through the keyhole." He called the Anderson account "sadly inadequate."[20] Ambassador Muccio disagreed. "There was very, very little mystery about her presence because the door was wide open and all—at least all one side of the conference table could see her at all times."[21] Muccio presumably referred to Truman's side of the table, for the MacArthur entourage was emphatically unanimous that they did not see her. Muccio also recalls Whitney's roaming around the room "quite a bit" during the talks and felt sure he could have spotted Ms. Anderson. But the circumstances were to prompt a nasty dispute the next spring (see Chapter Twenty).

Most of the words Ms. Anderson recorded came from MacArthur, for he did the bulk of the talking, and his performance dazzled even those who had come to Wake prepared to dislike him. MacArthur spoke in polished, confident sentences; after a few minutes Frank Pace was convinced he "was indeed a military genius." To MacArthur, all that was left of the Korean War were a few loose ends that must be tied down. He said flatly that "formal resistance will end throughout North and South Korea by Thanksgiving."*

Minimal resistance remained in the South—only about 15,000 men, MacArthur estimated—"and those we do not destroy, the winter will."

In North Korea, the enemy pursued a "forlorn hope," with only about 100,000 men "who were trained as replacements. They are poorly trained, led and equipped, but they are obstinate and it goes against my grain to have to destroy them. They are only fighting to save face. Orientals prefer to die rather than to lose face."

MacArthur expressed his "hope to be able to withdraw the Eighth Army to Japan by Christmas," leaving only X Corps in Korea. He would try to hold elections by the first of the year and to end the military occupation of the North as soon as feasible. "Nothing is gained by military occupation. All occupations are failures." MacArthur would leave the Koreans with about ten U.S.-equipped army divisions, plus a "small but competent" air force and navy. Such a force "will not only secure Korea but . . . will be a tremendous deterrent to the Chinese Communists moving south. This is a threat that cannot be laughed off," the general said.

MacArthur emphasized that "the military should get out the minute the guns stop shooting and civilians take over." Korea "has been knocked down for a long time," and minimal recovery money "goes a long way." He thought that a "billion dollars spread over three to five years will more than make up the destruction." After all, MacArthur noted, "Houses are made of mud and bamboo. When knocked down they can be put up in two weeks."

Moving down the agenda, Truman then asked, "What are the chances for Chinese or Soviet interference?" MacArthur confidently replied:

> Very little. Had they interfered in the first or second months it would have been decisive. We are no longer fearful of their intervention. We no longer stand hat in hand. The Chinese have 300,000 men in Manchuria. Of these probably not more than 100,000 to 125,000 are distributed along the Yalu River. Only 50,000 to 60,000 could be gotten across the Yalu River. They have no air force. Now that we have bases for our air force in Korea, if the Chinese tried to get down to Pyongyang there would be the greatest slaughter.

*This account is based upon notes the Joint Chiefs of Staff submitted to two Senate committees in May 1951.[22] As shall be detailed in Chapter Twenty, the submission was an amalgam of a partial stenographic transcript made by Vernice Anderson and notes taken by Washington participants. Copies were furnished MacArthur's headquarters within a week after the conference ended; according to General Omar N. Bradley, the JCS Chairman, nothing was received from the general or his aides "that would indicate any nonconcurrence with the record of the conference." The direct quotations in this section are taken from the JCS document.

MacArthur's chief fear of the Russians was air support of Chinese ground troops. But coordination "would be so flimsy that I believe the Russian air would bomb the Chinese as often as they would bomb us."

MacArthur promised Bradley a division for diversion to the European theater by January. Discussing the Japanese peace treaty, still being negotiated by John Foster Dulles, Assistant Secretary of State Dean Rusk marveled, "Your operations in Korea are going faster than the diplomats can in getting a treaty."

The compliment pleased MacArthur, and he repeated, "I hope to get the Eighth Army back by Christmas."

Much of the rest of the conference dealt with the Japanese peace treaty, prospects for an Asian defensive alliance, and the growing war in Indochina.

At the end there was tough political talk about President Syngman Rhee. MacArthur decried a UN General Assembly draft resolution that equated the South Koreans with the North Koreans in terms of a postwar settlement. The resolution ignored the elections the South Koreans held in 1948 and called for a new vote in both parts of the country. "It would be bad to turn out of office a government which had stood up so well and taken such a beating, and to treat them just like the North Koreans," he said.

Truman agreed. "This cannot be done and must not be done. . . . We must make it plain that we are supporting the Rhee government and propaganda can go to hell."

Thus ended the formal talks, Truman saying, "No one who was not here would believe we have covered so much ground as we have." He suggested a break for lunch—the time was a few minutes past nine in the morning—during which the staff could write a communiqué for the press. MacArthur, however, did not wish to tarry. "If it's all right," he said, "I am anxious to get back as soon as possible and would like to leave before luncheon if that is convenient." Truman did not object, and the conference ended at 9:12 A.M.—ninety-six minutes after it began.

Charles Ross, Truman's press secretary, Ambassador Jessup, and Charles Murphy retreated to an adjacent office to prepare the communiqué (to the unspoken chagrin of the MacArthur staff, who fidgeted in the main conference room during the delay).

Truman relieved the tension by inviting MacArthur back into the Quonset hut for small talk, which eventually got around to politics.[23] According to what MacArthur told Whitney later, the general asked if the President intended to seek reelection in 1952. Truman countered by asking whether MacArthur had any political ambitions. MacArthur replied, "None whatsoever. If you have any general running against you, his name will be Eisenhower, not MacArthur."

Truman chuckled; in 1948 he had withstood draft Ike movements by segments of both parties, and he was well aware of Eisenhower's ambitions. He admired Eisenhower as a military man, "but he doesn't know the first thing about politics," Truman said. "Why, if Eisenhower should become president, his administration would make Grant's look like a model of perfection." At this point, says Whitney, MacArthur "quickly swerved the conversation into other channels."

Truman seemed disappointed at MacArthur's hasty departure. To MacArthur's surprise, there was a small awards ceremony, a Distinguished Service Medal (his fifth) with a laudatory citation. As Whitney tartly commented, no one who heard Truman's words could suspect that the President four years later would answer the question "Have you repented the firing of General MacArthur during your term of office?" with the statement "The only thing I repent is that I didn't do it two years sooner." The formal communiqué was innocuous. One reporter observed it was initialed by both men "as if they were heads of different governments." The restless MacArthur did not conceal his eagerness to be gone. He took out a gold pocket watch, looked at it, rubbed a finger slowly over its crystal, and returned it to his pocket. At an impromptu news conference Truman told reporters, "I've never had a more satisfactory conference since I've been President." MacArthur brushed away questions, saying, "All comments will have to come from the publicity man of the President."

As Anthony Leviero of *The New York Times* watched the two men, he was reminded of "an insurance salesman who has at last signed up an important prospect . . . while the later appeared dubious over the extent of coverage." Truman seemed fawningly eager to show his goodwill toward MacArthur and the men around him. As he was about to board the *Independence,* he called back to Courtney Whitney, who then wore the single star of a brigadier general. "General Whitney," the President said, "you should have been a major general long ago. As soon as I get back to Washington I am going to see what I can do about having you made one." Truman kept his promise; shortly after he returned to Washington Whitney received his second star. MacArthur remained on the ground until the *Independence* cleared the end of the runway and then strode rapidly to the *SCAP;* within minutes he was away for Tokyo, seething at the intrusion of the President into his war and at the fact that conferees other than Truman had dared attempt to deal with him as an equal. He demanded of William Sebald, "Who was that young whipper-snapper who was asking questions?"[24] Sebald finally deduced that he meant Dean Rusk, an assistant secretary of state. MacArthur made clear he was "indignant" that a person of such rank would question him. He wrote years later: "The conference . . . made me realize that a curious, and sinister, change was taking place in Washington. The defiant, rallying figure that had been Franklin Roosevelt was gone. Instead, there was a tendency toward temporizing rather than fighting it through."[25] Truman's "original courageous decision . . . was apparently being chipped away by the constant pounding whispers of timidity and cynicism. The President seemed to be swayed by the blandishments of some of the more selfish politicians of the United Nations. . . ."

MacArthur's summation means that he never caught an essential point of the entire conference. As he had been told repeatedly—by cables, by Harriman during his mid-August mission, now by President Truman directly, in clear language—the United States was in no military position to fight total war and must avoid direct conflict with the Soviets and the Chinese. The legitimacy of the U.S. presence in Korea relied upon the UN, and Washington's support there was fragile. Whether MacArthur (or Truman, for that matter) liked these circumstances was of no consequence; they were political realities. When MacArthur groused about the "deliberate under-estimating of the importance of the conflict to which the government [was] committed," he tiresomely continued in a debate he had already lost; no matter how many times he was told, and by whom—be it the Joint Chiefs of Staff or the President—that the United States could not strip Europe for troops to fight in Korea, MacArthur returned to the petulant refrain that anyone who denied him everything he wanted was either timid or traitorous. Thus Wake was a failure, a waste of time for everyone concerned.

Nonetheless, the Wake meeting fleetingly allayed White House suspicions about MacArthur. To the Washington participants, MacArthur projected himself as a man of godlike infallibility, someone so wreathed in confidence that he could not possibly fail in his mission or err in his predictions of what was to happen on the battlefield. MacArthur's claims of imminent victory were so persuasive that Dean Rusk approached Ambassador Muccio after the meeting and said, "John, I think you'd better come home with me to discuss the post-hostility setup in Korea."[26] Muccio pleaded immediate business and said he would return as soon as feasible. (When he did visit Washington, in late October, the subject was not victory, but the consequences of Chinese intervention.) Charles Murphy, seeing the general in person for the first time (as did everyone else in the Washington party save Harriman and some of the generals), said MacArthur "spoke very persuasively, very plainly, very understandably. He just laid it out cold. And when he explained why and how it was *impossible* [Murphy's emphasis] for the other side to do anything about it, why, I understood precisely what he was saying, and I was convinced completely."[27]

One Murphy recollection not contained in the JCS notes dealt with MacArthur and intelligence. MacArthur professed to have "an intelligence operation which was bringing in reports somewhat different from the intelligence reports that the departments were receiving

. . . in Washington and . . . he believed his and not those of the departments."

After leaving Wake, Truman flew to San Francisco for a foreign policy speech; there he said he had "felt that there was pressing need to make it perfectly clear—by my talk with General MacArthur—that there is complete unity in the aims and conduct of our foreign policy." Press accounts interpreted these comments to mean that the President had either brought MacArthur around to his way of thinking or muzzled him. Ever hypersensitive to slights to his infallibility, either real or imagined, MacArthur exploded. Speaking through a Dai Ichi spokesman, he said, "There has been absolutely no change on General MacArthur's part in any views he has held as to the strategic value of Formosa." He also said that "no policy discussion whatsoever was held at Wake Island with reference to Formosa."

By strictest technical interpretation, both MacArthur statements are correct. Truman recognized Formosa's strategic value; he also recognized the political price of long-term involvement with Chiang Kaishek. And they did not "discuss" Formosa in a formal sense: Truman simply laid down the law, and the general apologized for his past indiscretions. (After returning to Washington, Truman told Ross and Eben Ayers, his deputy press secretary, the reason he did not discuss Formosa at the main conference was that he and MacArthur had threshed out the issue privately, and he wanted to "avoid any possibility of humiliating MacArthur before the others."[28] But the net effect of the postconference pronouncements again put the President and the general at public odds. Distance apparently gave MacArthur courage; he would say (through a spokesman) in Tokyo what he dared not tell Truman to his face.

Another episode, in mid-November, should have alerted Truman that the "MacArthur problem" was by no means solved. The columnist Stewart Alsop began to pick up snippets of what transpired at Wake. He reported that MacArthur had assured Truman the danger of Chinese intervention had passed. The *Freeman,* a conservative publication, asked MacArthur to confirm or deny the report. The reply: "The statement [from Alsop] quoted in your message of the 13th is entirely without foundation in fact. MacArthur. Tokyo, Japan." The White House knew otherwise, but MacArthur by this time had face-saving reasons to disavow his bland assurances at Wake: On October 26, eleven days after the conference ended, his troops captured a Chinese prisoner. The war was about to take on a savage new dimension.

General George C. Marshall had his own worries about the Wake Conference, ones that Army Secretary Frank Pace found hard to understand at the time. Soon after his return to Washington, Pace visited Marshall to report what had happened.[29] Pace reconstructed the conversation:

PACE. General Marshall, General MacArthur says the war will be over by Thanksgiving and the troops home by Christmas.

MARSHALL. Pace, that's troublesome.

PACE. Sir, you must not have heard me. I said, "The war will be over by Thanksgiving and the troops home by Christmas."

MARSHALL. I heard you, but too precipitate an end to the war would not permit us to have a full understanding of the problems that we face ahead of us.

PACE. Do you mean by that that the American people would not have fully had an opportunity to grasp the implications of the Cold War?

MARSHALL. I certainly do.

PACE. General Marshall, this has been a very difficult and extensive war from the American people's point of view.

MARSHALL. Yes, I know, Pace, but you didn't live through the end of World War Two the way I did and watch people rush back to their civilian jobs and leave the tanks to rot in the Pacific and the military strength that was built up to fade away.

PACE. I know, General Marshall, but a great deal of water has passed under the bridge since then. Would you say I was naïve if I said that the American people had learned their lesson?

MARSHALL. No, Pace. I wouldn't say you were naïve. I'd say you were *incredibly* naïve.

The post-Wake euphoria, however, rested upon a most uneasy foundation: the belief that the Chinese Communists would not enter the Korean War. The conference was held on October 15. And even as the two parties headed back for Washington and Tokyo, Chinese troops were also moving.

CHAPTER ELEVEN

"The Idle Armed Millions of Communist China"

From the very first days of the war American intelligence had pondered whether the Soviets or the Chinese—or both—would enter the war as active combatants. And from the very beginning the analysts consistently reached much the same conclusion: Both nations had the capacity to do so but probably would not, for international political reasons.

The CIA's first emphasis was on Soviet intentions, for Washington accepted without reservation the thesis that the Kremlin had inspired its North Korean "puppet" to launch the invasion. A CIA memorandum on June 28 suggested that the Soviets would support the North Koreans sufficiently "to perpetuate the civil war and maintain North Korean positions south of the 38th Parallel."[1] But the CIA did not expect any direct Soviet involvement. Although the agency believed the Soviets could land ten to eleven divisions in Japan (upward of 121,000 men) by waterborne assault and launch large-scale air attacks,[2] it expected no moves there either. Another CIA estimate, this one on July 8, suggested the possibility of the Soviets' "employing Chinese Communist troops, either covertly or overtly,"[3] while remaining aloof from the actual fighting. The CIA entertained no doubts that the Chinese would do as told; in another July estimate, agency analysts stated:

It is not yet clear whether the USSR will force the Chinese Communists to give open support to the Korean operations or to start a new operation elsewhere in the area. The Peiping regime is unlikely to commit military forces to operations outside China on its own initiative, but almost certainly would comply with a Soviet request for military action. Chinese

Communist troop strength and dispositions would permit intervention in Korea . . . with little or no warning. . . .[4]

On August 1, Rear Admiral R. H. Hillenkoetter, the director of central intelligence, sent President Truman a report which he tacitly admitted the CIA could not evaluate. The intelligence memorandum stated:

A possible but inconclusive indication of preparations for the movement of foreign troops into North Korea is contained in a recent field report that a "Supreme Military Committee" consisting of forty Russians, twenty Chinese, and fifty North Korean Army personnel was established in Seoul on 1 July 1950.

Because a Chinese Communist Army liaison office has existed in North Korea since 1946 and Soviet advisors have been attached to North Korean GHQ since the People's Army was formed, the report, even if true, does not necessarily indicate any increase in cooperation among Chinese, Russians, and North Koreans.[5]

Later the same month a highly sensitive CIA report circulated in the upper echelons of government found the Soviet Union "accelerating its war readiness program, notably regarding petroleum processing, completion of a plant conversion program, aircraft production, airfield construction, and the stockpiling of reserves."[6] Analysts concluded that "the Soviet leaders would be justified in assuming a substantial risk of general war during the remainder of 1950, arising either out of the prosecution of the Korean incident or out of the initiation of new local operations." One major deterrent, in the CIA's view, was the Soviet lack of capability for a "large scale atomic bombardment campaign in 1950," even though the Soviets "are capable of employing against the continental U.S. the twenty-five bombs estimated to be currently available." It suggested a possible Soviet use of TU-4 bombers, "possibly disguised with U.S. markings on one-way missions, and clandestine introduction of nuclear weapons into key harbors by merchant ships."

For reasons unexplained in the CIA archives available as of early 1980, this gloomy estimate never reached the level of an official "National Intelligence Estimate." One person familiar with the intelligence community at the time notes, "You've got to realize that CIA was a diverse organization in those days, with many people peddling their pet ideas. You could take scattered field reports and build a case for almost any scenario you wished to push."

The CIA reports in early autumn were so contradictory as to be meaningless. On September 1, for instance, the agency told the White House in a daily intelligence summary it had received "many unconfirmed reports"[7] of a summit conference between Mao Tse-tung, the Chinese leader, and V. M. Molotov, the Soviet foreign minister, in Peking in early August. Chinese propaganda mediums thereafter intensified attacks on the United States as the "aggressor" in Korea. This particular CIA report concluded:

> Thus the stage has been set for some form of Chinese Communist intervention or participation in the Korean war. Overt participation by regular forces would preclude admission of Communist China to the UN, while covert participation of Manchurian "volunteers" might ensure continued localization of the conflict.
>
> Intervention could be launched to restore peace by preventing further U.S. "aggression" and could be linked with the USSR-sponsored peace campaign. It is impossible to determine at this time whether a decision has been made.
>
> *In any case, some form of armed assistance to the North Koreans appears imminent* [emphasis added].

But other reports later in September kept to a common theme: There was no "indication" or "evidence"[8] of any Soviet or Chinese intent to intervene. Indeed, the CIA seemed more concerned about the possibility of Soviet moves in Eastern Europe, Iran, or elsewhere. On September 22, for instance, the CIA noted these happenings in Eastern Europe alone: Bulgarian citizens were being evacuated from areas along the border with Yugoslavia; a bridge with "little commercial justification" was being constructed across the Danube River linking the city of Calafat, Rumania, with the city of Vidin, Bulgaria; the Rumanian government was extending the term of military service; Albanian-based guerrillas were returning to Greece; and cargoes arriving in Albanian ports from other Soviet-satellite countries "are believed in excess of normal Albanian requirements." The Soviets started a Russian-language course for the Czech armed forces. Budapest propaganda broadcasts, "made slowly enough to be copied," outlined detailed instructions for industrial and agricultural sabotage in Yugoslavia. (The Yugoslav prime minister, Josip Broz Tito, although a Communist, was asserting his independence of Moscow.) The CIA concluded:

> Throughout the Soviet orbit, the trend toward military, economic and psychological preparedness for war has continued. There is, moreover, evidence that certain phases of this program are being accelerated with some urgency, and that completion of several of the projects, especially in the Balkans and the China area, is to be accomplished this fall.
>
> There is not sufficient evidence at this time, however, to support specific conclusions concerning Soviet intentions in the near future.[9]

On October 12, in an estimate that bore the concurrences of both Defense and State Department intelligence units, the CIA reaffirmed its earlier estimates that China probably would not intervene because disadvantages of participation in the war appeared to outweigh the advantages.[10] The CIA concluded:

While full-scale Chinese Communist intervention in Korea must be re-garded as a continuing possibility, a consideration of all known factors leads to the conclusion that barring a Soviet decision for global war, such action is not probable in 1950. During this period, intervention will probably be confined to continued covert assistance to the North Koreans.

In late October the CIA felt the North Koreans were moving toward a period of protracted guerrilla warfare, with no indication of Chinese or Soviet intervention. By U.S. estimate, only 20,000 North Korean troops, the remnants of seven divisions, continued in combat.[11] An additional 15,000 were north of the 38th parallel but cut off behind UN lines. Some 10,000 others remained in the South as guerrillas, although "apparently not centrally organized or coordinated." The CIA did offer one cautionary note: "Large Chicom [Chinese Communist] purchases of drugs and medicines abroad during past months could represent an attempt to satisfy huge normal requirements, but a sharp increase in the rate of acquisition since the start of the Korean War may indicate military stockpiling."

The most sensitive—and accurate, as it proved—intelligence gath-ered by the CIA came from a daring former Chinese Nationalist officer who volunteered to sneak onto the mainland in late summer 1950 to survey the military situation in Manchuria.[12] In the pre-Communist days, the officer had served with Nationalist forces in the northern provinces, and many of his former colleagues now served in the Peo-ple's Liberation Army. "From his conversations with them, and from his close observations," reported Harry Rositzke of the CIA, "he was able to establish with some precision the number and distribution of Chinese Communist troops along the Manchurian-North Korean bor-der." These reports, coupled with others, "gave fair warning to the UN Command of the imminent Communist crossing of the Yalu. . . ."

Nonetheless, no intelligence agency—the CIA, the military, the State Department—provided an answer to the core question: Granted the Chinese had the power to intervene, *would* they do so? And the United States had no meaningful contingency plan to follow in the event the Chinese did come into the war. To the JCS, the course was clear. "We all agree, that if the Communist Chinese come into Korea, we get out," General Bradley said at a meeting of the U.S. and British chiefs of staff in Washington on October 23.[13]

* * *

Willoughby Counts Chinese

Reports from the Far East Command intelligence apparat headed by General Willoughby were equally deficient. As was true in Willoughby's failure to predict the June invasion, in the summer and early fall his analysts managed to see many single trees* but never an entire forest —that is, they detected many signs pointing to possible Chinese intervention, but never to the point at which they could convince MacArthur or Willoughby that such was about to occur.

The most significant continuing trend detected by the FEC during late summer was the gradual shift of Chinese military units from the southern and central provinces north to Manchuria. An FEC *Daily Intelligence Summary* circulated on July 6 fixed Chinese strength at 189,000 in Manchuria (115,000 regulars, the remainder militia) and 176,000 regulars in North China. By August the number of regular troops in Manchuria was up to 246,000, and to 450,000 by September 21. However, much of this movement was believed to be the return of the Fourth Field Army to its normal stations following the successful campaign against the Nationalists, fought chiefly in central China. None of Willoughby's estimates for the period raised the possibility that these troops were being brought north to enter the war.

But Willoughby's daily intelligence summaries did contain an inordinate amount of odd information. For instance, on October 1 he circulated a report that as of September 10, twenty divisions of Chinese Communist troops were located in North Korea, six of them in the northwest border area, the remainder in unknown locations. The next day another report hedged: The FEC could not decide whether men in these "Chinese Communist troops" were in fact Chinese or Koreans serving in the Chinese Army.

On October 18 American reconnaissance aircraft flying along the Yalu spotted 75 to 100 aircraft on the ground at the airfield near Antung, Manchuria, just across the Yalu from North Korea. The report apparently startled both Willoughby and the Far East air commander, Lieutenant General George E. Stratemeyer, for additional reconnaissance craft were sent to the Antung area the following day. The presence of such an air armada certainly did not jibe with what MacArthur had told President Truman on Wake Island only three days earlier—that the Chinese emphatically would not enter the war. To Willoughby's relief,

---

*Seemingly no item, however trivial, escaped the far-flung nets of Willoughby's operatives. In July, for instance, crew members of smuggling craft plying between Macao and other ports reported "that the combined military strength of the USSR and Communist China will be used to attack the US via Alaska, bypassing Japan." Someone in Willoughby's headquarters apparently consulted the map, for the item was written off as a "plant." Nonetheless, it occupied a paragraph of Willoughby's daily summary.

the planes were no longer at Antung; the second reconnaissance mission saw "no evidence of aircraft," only a motor vehicle on one of the runways. Further, rail and highway traffic was lighter than the previous four days.

Willoughby permitted himself a sigh of relief. He did accept as "factual" the sighting of the planes on October 18, but he had an explanation: "It would be a sound, reasonable tactic for the Chinese Communist air forces to conduct mass long distance flights, stepping briefly at selected air fields, as an integral part of their training program. . . ." Another possibility was that the sudden massing of aircraft was part of the "saber-rattling" then being pursued by Chinese Premier Chou En-lai.

Nor did Stratemeyer put any significance on this discovery of Russian-built fighter planes. In a cable to General Hoyt Vandenberg, the air chief of staff, he said the planes were probably brought to Antung to lend "color and credence to menacing statements and threats of Chinese Communist leaders, who probably felt that display of strength involved no risk in view of our apparent desire to avoid border incidents."[14] If the Chinese wished to fight with the planes, Stratemeyer said, they would have attacked the observation craft, easy targets. And if they were intended for use later, "it would be highly unlikely aircraft would have been positioned to attract attention from south of the border."

One of Willoughby's major sources of information was the American military and diplomatic establishment on Formosa, which in turn drew heavily from Chinese Nationalist intelligence.[15] (Willoughby's daily intelligence summaries conceded occasionally that some of the Taiwan reporting was "open to question.") In the course of a single page the FEC would cite reports that (a) Chinese troops *would* fight in Korea, an item relayed by U.S. Seventh Fleet intelligence, or (b) that Chou En-lai had "privately stated" in mid-August the Chinese *would not* fight in Korea or in any area outside China "unless they were attacked," to avoid prejudicing their desired entrance into the United Nations. Two days later the FEC told of a Peking conference attended by Chinese, Soviets, "two Czechoslovakians, one German, one Pole, one Frenchman and one North Korean" to discuss a wide array of aid, including the dispatch of 250,000 Chinese troops to battle. (Willoughby discounted the report.)

Yet another item: "The question of Chinese Communist entrance into the Korean War was the subject of a heated debate at a conference in Peking during September." Mao Tse-tung, the premier, led a faction which opposed active intervention; Chou En-lai and others "insisted on intervention. The final decision allegedly calls for Chinese Communist intervention, if UN forces cross the 38th Parallel." The FEC added a comment: "An independent source, evaluated as C-3,* believes that the Chinese Communists will take no action in *spite of the foregoing decision,* because of negotiations for a seat in the UN [emphasis added]."

Two days later:

> With the collapse of the North Korean armies, the immediate problem facing the UN forces involves the attitude of Communist China and the Soviets. Both are already committed indirectly in supply activities. Will they intervene openly or surreptitiously to salvage their neighbor? It is accepted at present that Russia would find it both convenient and economical to stay out of the conflict and let the idle armed millions of Communist China perform the task as part of the master plan to drain United States resources into the geographical rat-holes of the Orient. The interest of all intelligence agencies, consequently, is focused on the Yalu River and the movements of the elusive Lin-Piao [a military hero of the Chinese Civil War, widely identified as the commander of the forces mobilizing in Manchuria]. . . . Recent declarations by CCF** leaders, threatening to enter North Korea if American forces were to cross the 38th Parallel, were probably in a category of diplomatic blackmail. The decision, if any, is beyond the purview of collective intelligence; it is a decision for war, on the highest level; i.e., the Kremlin and Peiping.

A Chinese Warning

In embarassed hindsight, intelligence analysts came to recognize that the major warnings they dismissed as "diplomatic blackmail" were exactly what they purported to be: a clear statement to the United States of the course of action China intended to follow if American troops crossed the 38th parallel.[16] The warnings came through the conduit of the Indian ambassador in Peking, K. M. Pannikar, vociferously pro-Communist and anti-American. Pannikar was a frequent (albeit sometimes untrustworthy) source of diplomatic signals from the first days of the war.

The Chinese leadership treated Pannikar as a useful tool; high officials dined him, and praised him, and puffed his self-importance, knowing full well that the messages they planted with him would swiftly pass

*The reliability of sources or informants is rated with letters from *A* to *D*. The letter *A* indicates the source is highly reliable; *D* that it is unreliable or untested. The probability of the information's being accurate is rated with numerals from 1 to 4, with 1 indicating it is highly probable, accurate, and corroborated, and 4 that it is considered improbable or inaccurate. C-3 means respected but not necessarily accepted.

**In American military abbreviation, CCF means Chinese Communist Forces, a designation that will be used hereafter, as well as the PLA, or "People's Liberation Army," the Chinese name for their forces.

through his foreign office to London and then to the United States.

Nonetheless, the Chinese gave the Ambassador what proved to be valid warnings. On September 25 Pannikar dined with General Nieh Jung-chen, acting chief of the Chinese military. Pannikar thought that Nieh, "whose round face and shaven head gives one the impression of a Prussian officer," was friendly and frank. They dined. Then the general told Pannikar that his people "did not intend to sit back with folded hands and let the Americans come up to their border." When Pannikar protested how destructive total war would be, Nieh replied with a laugh. "We have calculated all that. They may even drop atomic bombs on us. What then? They may kill a few million people. Without sacrifice a nation's independence cannot be upheld." Nieh did not feel a war could be won by air bombardment alone, and he did not believe the United States could spare combat troops to fight in China.

Pannikar immediately reported the conversation to the Indian Foreign Office, whence it immediately fell into British hands for relay to London and then to the British embassy in Washington, where it arrived on the afternoon of September 27. Hubert A. Graves, counselor to the embassy, rushed to the State Department with what he told Livingston Merchant, the deputy assistant secretary for Far Eastern affairs, was an "urgent matter."[17] What did Graves think of the reports? Merchant asked. Graves said British diplomats "do not take seriously Pannikar's fears, believing him volatile and an unreliable reporter." But they were alarmed that the reports might upset the Indians so much that they would no longer support the war in the UN.

The State Department consensus was that it was propagandistic bluster.

A week later Pannikar was heard from again, and this time he conveyed a warning from an even higher source.[18] The Chinese Foreign Ministry summoned him from his bed shortly after midnight on October 2 and directed that he come to the residence of Prime Minister Chou En-lai immediately. Chou greeted the Indian with tea and polite small talk and apologies for arousing him at such an hour. Then he delivered his message: If the Americans crossed the 38th parallel, China would be forced to intervene in Korea. Otherwise, Chou was anxious for a peaceful settlement.

Had Chou heard of any actual border crossings by the Americans? Pannikar asked.

Yes, Chou replied, he had heard they had crossed, but he did not know where. (At this time only U.S. patrols had crossed the parallel.)

What if only South Koreans crossed the parallel?

Chou's reply was emphatic: "The South Koreans did not matter, but American intrusion into North Korea would encounter Chinese resistance."

This time Pannikar's warning received considerably more attention, but again widely varying interpretations. Administration officials were clearly nervous on the morning of October 3. The Associated Press was carrying a story about a nine-mile Chinese column, including artillery, stretching from Manchuria across the Yalu River into North Korea. MacArthur was poised on the 38th parallel while ROK units probed what was left of enemy defensive positions. Now the Chinese premier was sounding what appeared to be a clear warning that the Americans should go no farther.

Threat or Bluff?

Nonetheless, once again the majority of the State hierarchy wrote off the threat as a "bluff" (although Livingston Merchant, for one, felt that "we should treat it with extreme seriousness"). So, too, did U. Alexis Johnson, deputy director of the Office of Northeast Asian Affairs, who suggested to his superior, Dean Rusk, that it would be "well worthwhile further to explore the possiblity of using entirely ROK forces for the subjugation of North Korea."[19] Secretary Acheson, in congressional testimony seven months later, admitted that he and other persons in Washington with access to all available intelligence "all came to the conclusion that it was more likely that they [the Chinese Communists] would not come in than that they would." General Bradley, speaking for the military establishment, agreed with Acheson.

Embassies added their own assessments. From Moscow, Ambassador Alan Kirk expressed surprise that a "message of such serious nature" was not conveyed more directly to the UN or the United States.[20] James R. Wilkinson, the American consul general in Hong Kong, the chief China watch station for the United States, spoke of "saber-rattling."[21] Selden Chapin, the American ambassador in the Netherlands, reported some other tidbits gleaned from Dutch diplomats.[22] The chief of staff of the Chinese Army had said in a private conversation with a Dutch diplomat in Peking that China had "no choice but fight" if the 38th parallel was crossed; although war with the United States would set back China's development fifty years, if China did not resist, it would "forever be under American control." Also, the Dutch said, Nehru had cabled Mao Tse-tung that the United States, Britain, and France had decided that the 38th parallel would not be crossed without specific UN authorization (a misstatement) and that India was working to block such authorization.

Great Britain reacted much less ambivalently. Its foreign minister, Ernest Bevin, was terror-stricken. From his stateroom on the *Queen*

Mary (he had been on a visit to Commonwealth nations) he cabled the Foreign Office to work with the Americans on a UN statement that would discourage China from intervention and also offer China a prospect of being heard in the UN on the Korean resolution then pending. (The United States, it will be recalled, did not wish to have China involved in any UN talks on the grounds it was not a member and thus had no legal standing in the Korean debate.)

The afternoon of October 4, at a meeting at the American delegation offices in New York, Secretary Acheson tried to stiffen the British.[23] It was too late to bring the Chinese into the debate; doing so would only confuse the issue. He agreed there was a risk in proceeding across the 38th parallel; nonetheless, "at present he believed a greater risk would be incurred by showing hesitation and timidity." Acheson put little value in Chou En-lai's private statements to Pannikar, which the Chinese could always disavow. If the Chinese "wanted to take part in the poker game," Acheson said, "they would have to put more on the table than they had up to the present." He concluded by saying that "we should not be unduly frightened at what was probably a Chinese Communist bluff."

The British seemed satisfied when the meeting ended.

In any event, the Chinese threats did cause the JCS to hasten to fill a gap in the instructions they had given MacArthur. Through apparent oversight, no previous directives had specified what action should be taken should the Chinese intervene in Korea without first announcing their intention to do so. With Truman's approval, the JCS sent MacArthur a cable on October 9 directing:

> Hereafter in the event of the open or covert employment anywhere in Korea of major Chinese Communist units, without prior announcement, you should continue the action as long as, in your judgment, action by forces now under your control offers a reasonable chance of success.
>
> In any case, you will obtain authorization from Washington prior to taking any military action against objectives in Chinese territory.[24]

The final sentence was not intended to handcuff MacArthur or to suggest he would be denied the opportunity to strike at Chinese home bases. In fact, the JCS and the National Security Council had agreed in August that should the Chinese attack, the United States should not only resist with the forces in Korea but "take appropriate air and naval action outside Korea against Communist China."[25] The President had not given his final approval to the decision. But by requiring MacArthur to consult Washington before bombing airfields in Manchuria or blockading the China coast, the JCS thought they were ensuring that decisions of great political significance would not be made in Tokyo.

* * *

The Pannikar signals were part of the intelligence studied by the CIA in preparing a briefing book for President Truman for use at his Wake Island Conference in mid-October. The CIA stuck to its themes of previous months: The Chinese ground forces "are capable of intervening effectively, but not necessarily decisively," in the war. But it concluded: "Despite statements by Chou En-lai, troop movements to Manchuria, and propaganda charges of atrocities and border violations, there are no convincing indications of an actual Chinese Communist intention to resort to full-scale intervention in Korea."[26] Although intervention gave China a chance for a "major gain in prestige" were it to defeat the United States, the CIA ticked off a host of reasons it would not do so. The major reason: "The Chinese Communists undoubtedly fear the consequences of war with the United States. Their domestic programs are of such magnitude that the regime's entire domestic program and economy would be jeopardized by the strains."

The CIA estimate was written on October 12. A week later, on October 20, Willoughby's G-2 section took much the same view from its vantage point in Tokyo. However, throughout the month the Far East Command had continued to pick up bits of information about stirrings of Communist troops in Manchuria. The October 20 "Daily Intelligence Summary" repeated that the presence of a vast Chinese army in Manchuria was a *fait accompli.* So, too, was its "capacity for crossing" the Yalu at Antung or elsewhere. But Willoughby concluded: "The decision, however, is not within the purview of local intelligence; it will be based on the high-level readiness of the Kremlin to go to war through utilizing the CCF-Manchuria on orders."

One officer in Tokyo did not agree with Willoughby's estimates and told him so, but to no avail.[27] Rear Admiral Arleigh A. Burke, deputy chief of staff to the FEC naval commander, talked with intelligence officers on his staff one morning in mid-October. One of them reviewed the raw intelligence data they had been receiving and said, "It looks to us like the Chinese are in North Korea."

Burke raised the question with Willoughby, who brought in his analysts to go through the material. Their interpretation was exactly the opposite of that of the navy, and Willoughby agreed with them. "I don't think they're in there either," he said, "and I don't think they will come in."

Two or three days later the naval intelligence officers again concluded the Chinese were in Korea, and again Burke approached Willoughby. This time, however, Burke did not find Willoughby's case convincing. Upon return to his office he told his superior, Admiral C. Turner Joy, that he intended to retain in the Far East one of every five transports that came in with supplies, so that he would have evacuation craft ready in event of an emergency. Joy (and the Navy Department) agreed, and over the next several weeks Burke managed to stockpile some ninety transports.

Stalin Takes a Hand

But the seminal event in determining Chinese intervention took place far beyond the view of any Western intelligence agency.[28] In early autumn Joseph Stalin received Chinese Foreign Minister Chou En-lai at the Soviet premier's vacation retreat in Sochi. Chou approached Stalin by direction of Mao Tse-tung. According to Nikita Khrushchev, "Chou asked Stalin whether Chinese troops ought to be moved into North Korean territory in order to block the path of the Americans and South Koreans." Stalin and Chou at first "seemed to conclude that it was fruitless for China to intervene." But after lengthy discussion they reached a decision: China would give "active support" to North Korea. Both Chou and Stalin, according to Khrushchev, "believed these troops could manage the situation completely." Chou flew back to Peking with Stalin's support.

By Khrushchev's account, there was no mention of Stalin's expressing any willingness to have Soviet troops enter the war. As had been the case the previous spring, when Stalin approved Kim Il Sung's invasion, the Soviets were to act through a surrogate state, this time Communist China.

CHAPTER TWELVE

Enter the Chinese

The morning of October 25 a battalion of the ROK 6th Division moved northwest from the tiny crossroads village of Onjong, the first move in a planned forty-mile push to Pyoktong, on the Yalu River. The morning began smoothly; within a few hours the advance had carried some eight miles. Then enemy fire was encountered.

The ROKs unworriedly dismounted from their trucks and fanned out to displace what their commanders assumed was a small delaying force of North Koreans. Disaster: The enemy proved to be a large group of Communist Chinese, who in the ensuing fire fight put the ROK battalion to rout. Within a few minutes the battalion was decimated; of its 750-man strength, 350 were killed, wounded, or captured.

Another ROK battalion hurriedly moved up the same road. It could not dislodge the Chinese, but it did take two prisoners. One of them said Chinese forces had been waiting in the mountains since October 17 to ambush the advancing ROKs.

Early the next morning the Chinese struck down the road to Onjong, dislodging and smashing remnants of the ROK defenders. When another regiment came out in attempted rescue, it, too, ran into heavy concentrations of Chinese and lost all its vehicles and three batteries of artillery.

On October 28 the ROKs committed yet another regiment in the same area. It ran into a Chinese roadblock near Kojang and survived only with the aid of close American air support. At nightfall, however, the air cover ended, and the Chinese killed or captured the few men who did not flee to the mountains. Of the 3,552 officers and men in the regiment, only 875 escaped. By October 29 the ROK portion of the advance had ended, and an entire corps had been driven back forty miles, to the Chongchon River.

To the west, in the area above the Chongchon toward Unsan, the ROK 1st Division also began encountering Chinese on October 25. These ROKs began their day with several miles of easy advance, only to encounter a roadblock and heavy mortar fire. Tankers blasted through the roadblock, and that afternoon a prisoner was taken. The man wore a North Korean uniform, but interrogation quickly established his true identify: Shien Chung San, thirty years old, a private in the Chinese Communist Army.[1] He told the following story:

Shien's unit, consisting of some 2,000 men, left Tangshan, Manchuria, about eighteen miles north of the frontier, on October 19 and traveled to Antung, on the Yalu, by train. They were issued North Korean uniforms and instructed to remain silent if captured unless they could speak Korean. They then marched across the Yalu on a newly constructed wooden bridge and into the mountains. Officers told them the United States had 100,000 troops in Korea and that China was going to send "600,000 men to defeat the U.S."

At first blush Shien's unit did not appear to be a dangerous adversary. It had no weapons heavier than machine guns and light mortars; 300 of the men carried no firearms at all. Training was minimal, and Shien said morale was poor because of UN air strikes and because many of the old CCF weapons they carried did not work properly.

But Shien had some discomforting estimates of Chinese strength. He said there were 10,000 CCF troops in the hills around Unsan and another 10,000 eastward toward Huichon.

The next day, October 26, even more Chinese prisoners were brought to Pyongyang for interrogation. There could be no doubt of their nationality; as one interrogation report stated, they "looked Chinese, spoke Chinese, and understood neither Korean nor Japanese." Reports swiftly spread along the line; unit after unit reported confirmed contacts with Chinese, in up to division strength. Eighth Army intelligence officers collected these reports and dispatched them to Tokyo with an admonition that a new enemy was definitely in the war. Tokyo did not believe it.*

MacArthur's headquarters airily dismissed the reports. Since the information about a Chinese presence came from POW interrogations, the information was "unconfirmed and thereby unaccepted."[2] In a supplemental analysis the next day, with even more Chinese POWs in hand, General Charles Willoughby still spoke of the "potential" of Chinese intervention, rather than its reality. Even if the Chinese were in Korea, they should not be taken seriously. He wrote:

*Neither did the CIA's Tokyo office. Although it had the Eighth Army's interrogation reports on the first Unsan prisoner, it sent the information to Washington with an evaluation of F-6, the lowest possible appraisal of both source and content.

It is to be recognized that most of the CCF troops have had no significant experience in combat operations against a major combat power. In addition, their training, like that of the original North Korean forces, has been greatly handicapped by the lack of uniform equipment and assured stocks of munitions.

Willoughby concluded:

From a tactical standpoint, with victorious United States divisions in full deployment, it would appear that the auspicious time for intervention has long since passed; it is difficult to believe that such a move, if planned, would have been postponed to a time when remnant North Korean forces have been reduced to a low point of effectiveness.

The Evidence Mounts

As evidence of Chinese intervention continued to amass the next few days, and in such quantity it could no longer be dismissed, MacArthur reacted with a statement to the effect that it was unsporting of the Chinese to take away his seemingly sure victory. He accused "the Communists" of sending "alien Communist forces" across the Yalu and of concentrating possible reinforcements behind the "privileged sanctuary" of the Manchurian border. (MacArthur seemed truly unable to resist digs at Washington officials who had ordered him to keep the war out of China.) He continued:

While the North Korean forces with which we were initially engaged have been destroyed or rendered impotent . . . a new and fresh army now faces us, backed up by a possibility of large alien reserves and adequate supply *within easy reach to the enemy but beyond the limits of our present sphere of military action* [emphasis added].

On October 29, with an entire ROK Army corps now totally routed on the battlefield, opposed by what appeared to be three full field armies of Chinese Communists, all Willoughby would concede was that it

appears likely that an unknown number of Chinese were incorporated . . . into North Korean units to assist in the defense of border areas. However, because of the few prisoners taken and the conflicting statements it is not believed that further conclusions can be made at this time. There has been no indication of open intervention on the part of Chinese Communist forces.

On October 31, Willoughby began to backtrack. In a long "comment" paragraph in his "Daily Intelligence Summary" he quoted a highly selective series of earlier warnings he had made about reports of Chinese intervention (not bothering to mention that he had discounted them at the time as unlikely or unconfirmable) and said current reports "probably are exaggerated." Nonetheless, for the first time he said that "greater credence must be given" to reports that the Chinese had arrived.*

On the battlefront the Chinese Communists cut ROK and American supply lines at will and launched surprise attacks from the rear, cutting off unit after unit. Only an emergency airdrop of supplies by ten C-119 planes saved the ROK 1st Division and two tank companies from being overrun. When the ROKs tried counterattacks, they found the Chinese well dug in, well camouflaged, and hard to locate.

General Walton Walker for several days had shared Tokyo's skepticism. The first prisoners taken were foot soldiers, unlikely to know about high strategy. But Major General Paik Sun Yup, commander of the ROK 1st Division, entertained no doubts. He had fought with the Japanese Army in Manchuria, and he knew the Chinese intimately. He looked at the dead on the battlefield in front of his troops and said they were "all Chinese." He told Major General Frank W. Milburn, the I Corps commander, there were "many, many Chinese,"[4] at least a division of 10,000 soldiers. By October 28 Walker was sufficiently alarmed to pull the 1st Cavalry Division out of reserve at Pyongyang and throw it into the fight.

The prisoners taken did seem at first glance a scraggly, ill-trained lot.[5] None carried any official identification, although a few had written their names and units in ink on the inside of their blouses. The basic uniform was heavily quilted cotton, usually of a mustard brown hue that blended with the bleak Korean landscape. The officers' uniforms differed only by the presence of vertical red piping on the trousers, on the left side of the jacket, around the collar, and a diagonal across the sleeve cuff. Warm in dry weather, the quilted uniforms were impossible to dry when soaked. Beneath them the Chinese wore summer uniforms and any other clothing they happened to own. The cloth shoes were laceless and with rubber soles.

Most of the foot soldiers carried Japanese rifles apparently confiscated

*Willoughby was to claim later, to Paul Nitze of the State Department, that he "had correctly estimated the extent of the Chinese intervention at that time and that he was unable to persuade MacArthur of the fact that this was to be taken seriously.[3] Willoughby claims that he knew what the size of this force was." In his memoirs, Willoughby makes no such claim. MacArthur was still alive when it was published.

in Manchuria at the end of the Second World War. Mortars and submachine guns, however, were American, spoils seized from the Chinese
Nationalists. Indeed, at least 70 percent of the prisoners captured from
one division, the 124th, said they had fought for Chiang Kai-shek. The
CCF carried no artillery because of the mountains.

The new enemy was so effective that by November 1 the Americans
and ROKs were on the defensive all along the line in the east. The main
Chinese thrusts were against ROK units holding the three main roadways leading south from the Yalu. Major John Millikin, Jr., a battalion
commander in the 5th Cavalry Regiment, watched Chinese move
through a demoralized ROK unit and remarked later, "The hillside
seemed alive as waves of enemy troops moved along the ridge leading
into the ROK lines."

Refugees brought stories of large forces of Chinese coming down
from the north, accounts of which further shook the battered ROK
soldiers. Colonel Harold K. Johnson,* commander of the 5th Cavalry
Regiment, tried to set up a defensive position; then he saw the retreating ROK II Corps. "They were a solid mass of soldiers on the road—
indifferent to vehicles moving, indifferent to all that was around them.
They were a thoroughly defeated outfit. . . ."[6] Johnson thought back to
the Philippines, where he had served early during the Second World
War, and he likened the behavior and appearance of the dazed South
Koreans to what he had seen on Bataan just before the American surrender there.

On the western flank, ironically, the rapid UN advance continued.
The opposition continued to be the NKPA; no Chinese were to be
found.

At noon on November 1, a battalion of the 24th Infantry Division
reached the outskirts of Chonggodong, eighteen air miles south of the
Yalu. It prepared a defense in depth and in midafternoon fought an
estimated 500 enemy infantrymen supported by seven tanks. The blazing battle lasted half an hour. The NKPA lost all its tanks; two of the
American tanks were slightly damaged. The North Koreans also lost 100
men killed. The commanding officer was Lieutenant Colonel Charles B.
Smith, the same officer who had led Task Force Smith in the first
American engagement of the war, near Osan, nearly four months earlier. At Chonggodong the advance ended—it was to be the northernmost action fought in the war by an Eighth Army unit. (The penetration
to the Yalu several days earlier was by the ROK Army; the sole American along had been an adviser.)

But General Walton Walker realized his units had advanced beyond
the bounds of prudence. The ROK II Corps had disintegrated in the
area around Unsan, leaving the U.S. I Corps's right (east) flank totally

---

*Johnson ended his career as chief of staff of the army.

unprotected. Walker began pulling the 24th Division to the south to avoid entrapment of the entire Eighth Army.

The Chinese intention seemed clear when Walker studied the battle maps. By seizing Unsan, the Chinese would position themselves for a strike westward to the coast of the Yellow Sea, cutting off all UN forces in northwestern Korea. With several hundred thousands of troops in reserve in Manchuria, ready to surge across the border once the UN was isolated, the Chinese seemed ready for the classic hammer-and-anvil operation that MacArthur had envisioned at Inchon—that is, the Chinese to the south preventing the UN from escaping, while the new armies from the north roared down to pound the UN troops.

The Chinese Trap Springs

The Chinese began their maneuvering for Unsan by setting dozens of forest fires in the mountains stretching south from the Yalu, then using the cover of vast clouds of smoke to avoid air reconnaissance while moving toward the battlefront.[7] On November 1 civilian and other observers reported thousands of soldiers moving in columns southwest of the town, with the stated mission of blocking the road beneath it. The Chinese advanced with tenacity. The afternoon of November 1, Major General Hobart Gay, commander of the 1st Cavalry Divison, sat in a command post with Brigadier General Charles D. Palmer, the division artillery commander, listening to radio chatter. They heard the pilot of an observation plane: "This is the strangest sight I have ever seen. There are two large columns of enemy infantry moving southeast over the trails. . . . Our shells are landing right in their columns and they keep coming."[8] By nightfall the Chinese had surrounded Unsan and the 8th Cavalry Regiment on three sides, south, north and west; the only ground not in Chinese possession was the ROK 15th Regiment positions to the east.

North of Unsan the Chinese moved in force in midafternoon, this time with a previously unseen weapon, 82 mm rockets fired simultaneously from four tubes mounted on a truck. The onslaught began with the eerie din of outsize brass bugles and shrill blasts of whistles, without discernible pattern to nervous GIs crouching in slit trenches and behind trees, but obviously signals for Chinese units. No longer could anyone in the Far East Command, general or private, deny the fact of massive Chinese intervention. The attack intensified as night fell, and by midnight the ROK 15th Regiment was overwhelmed; most of its men were killed or captured.

The next victim to the Chinese was the 3rd Battalion of the 8th Cavalry Regiment, trapped early on the morning of November 2, when the CCF cut withdrawal routes southeast of Unsan. The regiment's other battalions, the 1st and the 2nd, managed to break past roadblocks, albeit with heavy losses. The 3rd, however, was not so fortunate.

Realizing the road south was held by enemy forces, 3rd Battalion officers decided on an overland withdrawal and drew up vehicles bumper to bumper. Exhausted soldiers slept in truck cabs and beds and in foxholes, awaiting the order to withdraw. But a company of Chinese slipped through the security screen—the sentries thought they were ROKs—and suddenly the brassy sound of bugles cut through the still of the night. One soldier reported later: "Someone woke me and asked if I could hear a bunch of horses on the gallop. . . . Then bugles started playing taps, but far away. Someone blew a whistle, and our area was shot to hell in a matter of minutes."[9] Lieutenant W. C. Hill thought he was dreaming "when I heard a bugle sounding taps and the beat of horses' hooves in the distance. Then, as though they came out of a burst of smoke, shadowy figures started shooting and bayoneting everybody they could find."

Both sides reacted with confusion—a fact that saved the life of Captain Filmore McAbee. A bullet knocked off his helmet; seconds later another shattered his shoulder blade. With the enemy in pursuit, he ducked behind a jeep and emptied his carbine into a group of about thirty Chinese. Weakened from loss of blood, McAbee fell into a ditch. Three Chinese prodded him with bayonets. But they did not bother to disarm him; McAbee said later that they "jabbered to each other, seemingly confused." He quickly took advantage of the situation. He pointed down the road, with no purpose in mind other than to confuse the Chinese. They argued a bit more and then walked away. McAbee hurried toward the battalion command post, only to encounter more Chinese. They poked him with bayonets, then let him go, still carrying his carbine. McAbee finally reached the command post, wounded but alive.

The command post—a dugout in the side of a hill—became the final American refuge, with defenders beating back the Chinese with what Major Veale F. Moriarty, the battalion executive officer, called "cowboy and Indian" tactics—close-range pistol fire, fistfights, a strategically tossed grenade. Through strength of command Moriarty kept the battalion alive. During a brief dawn respite in the fighting he and others managed to bring more than 170 wounded troops back into the perimeter. There was no time to count the dead.

In view of the casualties and the Chinese strength, the only hope for survival of the 3rd Battalion was outside rescue. Such was not to be. The remnants of the 5th Cavalry Regiment made an attempt during daylight hours on November 2, but officers soon realized they could not break through the Chinese blockade. Lacking artillery, and with a thick haze of smoke covering the battle area, the two battalions attempting the rescue suffered some 350 casualties in a single savage afternoon of fighting.

Late in the day General Milburn, the corps commander, met with General Gay, the 1st Cavalry Division commander, in a quiet hollow a few thousand yards behind the battlefront. One of the cruelest demands of military command is that of sacrificing the few to save the many. Milburn talked with Gay and staff officers. He walked away from the group for a few moments of silent contemplation. Then he made the decision: Any attempt to rescue the 3rd Battalion would probably be futile and endanger the entire corps. This is the most heartrending decision of my entire career, Milburn told Gay and other officers; abandoning these men runs contrary to the traditions of the U.S. Army. I do not like the decision; I do not expect you to like the decision. But the decision is now made.[10] Such was the thrust of the message Milburn gave subordinates.

So orders were dispatched. Rescue attempts were abandoned; the surrounded 3rd Battalion was now on its own; if it were to survive, it must do so unassisted.

The message reached men of the battalion late in the afternoon, and officers and noncoms decided to wait until dawn to move.[11] Chinese artillery and mortar rounds fell with the dusk. Six times that night the Chinese charged, 400 or more men in each wave. The gravely wounded Captain McAbee, finally forced out of an overrun command post, looked with awe at the mounds of Chinese dead; more than 1,000 bodies lay around the defensive perimeter, he estimated.

The next day, November 4, barrages of phosphorus smoke alerted the battalion that a final-surge Chinese assault was coming. General Milburn's decision of the previous day was now personalized: To survive, men of the 3rd Battalion would have to leave some 200 wounded comrades behind for almost certain capture. "Shit, I don't like this," one man said to a friend, also a private. "I don't either," the friend replied. "Drink one for me, and screw one for me, if and when you get back to Tokyo." A valiant physician, Captain Clarence R. Anderson, stayed behind with the wounded and spent the rest of the war in POW camps. The battalion commander, Major Robert J. Ormond, died within hours of his wounds.

The men who escaped marched—crept, more accurately—all night in a cold rain to avoid the Chinese. They did not succeed. Several times they thought they had slipped through the Chinese lines, but the enemy kept reappearing. On November 5 they were again surrounded. But they refused to surrender. On the decision of the few surviving officers they split into small parties in the hope some might escape. Few did. Most of them were either killed or captured before sundown. The 3rd Battalion, 8th Cavalry Regiment, ceased to exist. The fighting around Unsan cost more than 600 officers and men.

Brink of Disaster

By November 2 General Walton Walker could do nothing but salvage remnants of a disaster. MacArthur's plans for the dash to the Yalu ruined by Chinese intervention, all Walker could do was hope to cling to a beachhead on the north bank of the Chongchon River, a toehold that he hoped would enable him eventually to resume the offensive. This task fell to the 27th British Commonwealth Brigade and the 19th Infantry Regiment of the 24th Division.

The CCF shrewdly pressed their continuing attack at the point where the ROK and Eighth Army lines met, near the town of Kunu-ri.* Their obvious aim was to break through the ROKs and flank EUSAK, forcing a further withdrawal. The Chinese attack pattern was repeated time and again: sudden appearances at night, from seemingly impassable mountain areas manned by neither the Americans nor the ROKs; fierce bravery in individual fire fights; an ability to emerge suddenly to the rear of enemy units.

An example: The night of November 5–6 CCF troops followed field telephone wires leading to positions of C Company of the 19th Infantry Regiment on a hill. Despite repeated warnings about the Chinese propensity for night fighting, many Americans were caught asleep in their sleeping bags and killed where they lay.

One American not caught by surprise was Corporal Mitchell Red Cloud, an American Indian from Friendship, Wisconsin.[12] He gave first alarm of the attack from a lookout post along the ridge, then was charged by a group of Chinese from only 100 feet away. Red Cloud returned fire with his BAR, but an enemy burst knocked him to the ground. He pulled himself to his feet, wrapped one arm around a tree, and delivered point-blank BAR fire until Chinese bullets killed him. Later comrades found a string of Chinese dead in front of his body. (Red Cloud's bravery brought him a posthumous Medal of Honor.) Another BAR man in the same company, Private First Class Joseph W. Balboni, suddenly noticed Chinese soldiers 75 feet in front of them. They charged. He met them with bursts of BAR fire and stood his ground until killed. A few days later a patrol found seventeen enemy dead in front of Balboni's body; the gallant GI received a posthumous Distinguished Service Cross.

The night of November 5–6 the Chinese directed major attacks at the American-British beachheads on the north bank of the Chongchon River. One especially beleaguered unit was C Battery of the 61st Field Artillery Battalion, attacked from the rear. The commanding officer, Captain Howard M. Moore, turned his 105 mm howitzers around and

*Ri is a Korean-language suffix meaning "village," used on first reference. Thus Kunu-ri or Koto-ri hereafter is referred to as Kunu or Koto.

directed point-blank fire against the Chinese—1,400 rounds in all, at ranges as close as fifty yards. The enemy intent was to push past the battery and destroy a bridge to the rear of its positions. It failed. By the time a British unit came to the battery's relief at dawn more than seventy dead Chinese lay around the gun positions. Elsewhere along the line on the same evening Australians used bayonets to hurl back another Chinese attack.

Portrait of the Enemy

As more prisoners fell into U.S. and ROK hands, interrogators began to piece together a clear picture of the stealth of the Chinese intervention. The troops crossed the Yalu into Korea beginning on October 13 or 14. Hiding in caves and in wooded areas by day, and marching only at night, they moved to positions on the southern slopes of the high mountain masses some fifty miles south of the Yalu—apparently the line the Chinese high command had decided the Americans and ROKs must not cross. There they had vantage points overlooking the approaches from which the Allies must come.

To their surprise, intelligence officers learned that no less than five full field armies of Chinese, each with three divisions, had slipped into Korea, nearly 100,000 men in all. Three of these armies came face-to-face with the Eighth Army and the ROK II Corps in the central mountains. Two others, or six divisions, remained in reserve in the hills to the west and did not participate in what came to be known as the First Phase Chinese Offensive. Contrary to assertions by Willoughby's analysts, the units were all-Chinese. Field interrogators found no instance in which North Koreans and Chinese were integrated into the same unit.

American field commanders reported the Chinese Army was far more sophisticated than the "Asiatic mob" so scorned by MacArthur. Lacking any weapons heavier than mortars, Chinese infantry attacked strong U.S. and ROK positions with excellent fire fight discipline, especially at night. Their patrols had marked success in seeking out U.S. positions. They planned attacks to strike from the rear, cutting escape and supply routes and then sending in frontal waves. The basic battle tactic was the *Haichi Shiki*, a V formation into which they allowed opposing troops to move. The Chinese then would close the side of the V while another force moved below the mouth to stop any attempts at escape and to block relief columns.

During their First Phase Offensive the Chinese showed surprising compassion in their treatment of prisoners, especially the wounded.

The North Koreans routinely shot wounded POWs in the head rather than try to care for them. The Chinese, conversely, in some instances put Americans on litters, carried them to the roadside, and then withdrew and held their fire so that UN medics could remove them. The Chinese had other than humanitarian motives: They would exhort the POW to "tell his comrades" of the humane treatment received from the Chinese and urge the Americans to "turn their guns against the officers." The Chinese troops apparently believed their own propaganda statements that American soldiers were oppressed victims of capitalism eager to flee their "imperialistic hell" for the freedom of Communist paradise.

According to "battle experience" booklets the Chinese distributed to their line troops after the first weeks of fighting,[13] the CCF officers had mixed feelings about the American GI. They admired American technology and the ability to coordinate mortars, tanks, and artillery fire as well as air strength, transportation, and the infantry rate of fire. But the Chinese Command thought little of the average American soldier as an individual fighter. A pamphlet, *Primary Conclusions of Battle Experiences at Unsan,* issued by the CCF Sixty-sixth Army, assessed the 8th Cavalry Regiment. American soldiers, when cut off from the rear,

> abandon all their heavy weapons, leaving them all over the place, and play opossum. . . . Their infantrymen are weak, afraid to die, and haven't the courage to attack or defend.
>
> They depend on their planes, tanks and artillery. At the same time, they are afraid of our fire power. They will cringe when, if on the advance, they hear firing. . . . They are afraid to advance farther. . . . They specialize in day fighting. . . . They are not familiar with night fighting or hand to hand combat. . . . If defeated, they have no orderly formation. Without the use of their mortars they become completely lost . . . they become dazed and completely demoralized. . . . At Unsan, they were surrounded for several days yet they did nothing. They are afraid when the rear is cut off. When transportation comes to a standstill, the infantry loses the will to fight.

In view of these weaknesses, the Chinese pamphlet suggested future tactics: Fight rapidly around the enemy and cut off his rear. Avoid highways and flat terrain when making attacks "to keep tanks and artillery from hindering the attack operations." Fight at night, and have a definite plan and liaison between platoons. "Small leading patrol groups attack and then sound the bugle. A large number will at that time follow in column."

* * *

Chinese "Volunteers"?

The Chinese publicly acknowledged their troops' presence in a radio broadcast on November 2, calling them a Volunteer Corps for the Protection of the Hydroelectric Zone who had entered Korea expressly to protect dams and power complexes along the Yalu. The use of the term "volunteers" perplexed Willoughby. He speculated that the Chinese, extremely subtle and obsessed with "saving face," were attempting to "have their cake and eat it too." By casting their troops as volunteers and insisting no organized units were in Korea, the Chinese did not risk the prestige of their army should it be defeated. But they could claim credit for helping North Korea in a time of need. Nonetheless, Willoughby concluded with a warning that caused chills in Washington:

> Although indications so far point to piecemeal commitment for ostensible limited purposes only, it is important not to lose sight of the maximum potential that is immediately available to the Chinese Communists.
>
> Should the high level decision for full intervention be made by the Chinese Communists, they could promptly commit twenty-nine of their forty-four divisions presently employed along the Yalu and support a major attack with up to 150 aircraft.*

These two messages, together with reports of EUSAK withdrawals before the Chinese, led the JCS on November 3 to ask MacArthur to appraise the situation. Despite the battlefield realities, the general would not entertain the prospect of a full Chinese intervention or that the situation was slipping out of hand. Replying on November 4, he called it impossible "to appraise the actualities of Chinese Communist intervention,"[14] even though his intelligence indicated several possibilities. The most ominous was that China intended to enter the war at full strength and openly. MacArthur did not expect this to occur; although he conceded full intervention was a "distinct possibility," it would represent a "momentous decision of the gravest international importance." He saw instead a combination of three other courses of action: covert intervention concealed for diplomatic purposes; the use of "volunteers" to keep a toehold in Korea; and, lastly, a miscalculation —i.e., that the Chinese came into the war with the expectation they would meet only ROK troops, who could be defeated without much difficulty.

In totality, the message had a reassuring ring. "I recommend against

*On paper, a Chinese field army consisted of three divisions of 10,000 men, or a total of 30,000 troops. In practice, however, Chinese units seldom fought at full strength. The range was from 7,000 to 8,500 soldiers per division, 2,200 per regiment, 700 per battalion, and 170 per rifle company. Thus in the cable above, Willoughby was indicating the Chinese could commit a force of about 232,000 men (twenty-nine divisions at 8,000 men each).

hasty conclusions which might be premature and believe that a final appraisement should await a more complete accumulation of military facts." In no way, either in tone or content, did the message imply that an emergency existed or that the situation was getting out of hand.

But all the while MacArthur's behavior belied the unconcerned tone of his message to the JCS. Lieutenant General George Stratemeyer had already planned increased bombing of North Korean arsenals and communications centers, using incendiary munitions for the first time. The order he prepared for his operational commander, Major General Emmett O'Donnell, Jr., was blunt: Burn the cities to the ground.

MacArthur wanted even more. When Stratemeyer took his plan to the Dai Ichi Building for approval, MacArthur outlined a far more drastic operation over a two-week span. "Combat crews," he ordered, "are to be flown to exhaustion if necessary."[15] He directed Stratemeyer to destroy the "Korean end" of all international bridges on the Manchurian border, which the air commander took to mean the first over-water span out from the Korean border. Next, the Far East Air Force was to begin bombing south of the Yalu and "destroy every means of communication and every installation, factory, city and village," excepting only Rashin and the Suiho Dam and other electric power plants. MacArthur did caution that "there must be no violation of the border."

One of the targets designated by MacArthur was Sinuiju, the North Korean city just across the Yalu from Antung, Manchuria. Sinuiju was an attractive target. Premier Kim Il Sung's fleeing government had taken refuge there, and its warehouses and dwellings sheltered key North Korean officials and troops. Two bridges, each about three-quarters of a mile long, connected the two cities; one was a combination rail and highway bridge, the other a double-track rail bridge.

MacArthur matter-of-factly told the army staff about the plan in a routine teleconference with the Pentagon. No one there saw any reason to question him. But Stratemeyer also chose to inform Washington of the operation, in an "information copy" of his orders to the air force. Someone there decided the information should go to higher channels, and within minutes Robert Lovett, the undersecretary of defense, was on the move.

When Lovett received the message,[16] the mission was scheduled to begin in three and one-half hours; thus the national security apparatus acted with dispatch. Lovett hurried to the office of Secretary Acheson, taking along Dean Rusk, the assistant secretary of state for Far Eastern affairs. Lovett did not like MacArthur's plans. Charts showed the Yalu very shallow near its mouth; hence destroying the bridges would not halt troop movements (although it would affect rail traffic). The danger of stray bombs hitting Antung and other points in Manchuria was "very great."

Rusk agreed, noting also the U.S. commitment not to take action involving attacks on the Manchurian side of the Yalu without consulting the British. The British Cabinet was meeting that very day to discuss the Chinese intervention, and "ill-considered action on our part might have grave consequences." The United States also intended to put the Chinese issue before the United Nations within a few days. Further, Rusk mentioned the possibility of Soviet involvement. The JCS were also dubious about the need for this particular bombing; General Collins, for one, thought MacArthur's abrupt turnaround displayed a "touch of panic."

After minimal discussion the decision was made that the attack should be postponed "until the reasons for it were more clearly known," Rusk wrote later. Lovett phoned Secretary Marshall, who agreed that "the action was unwise unless there was some mass movement across the river which threatened the security of our troops." A bureaucratic minuet ensued. Lovett called Thomas Finletter, the secretary of the air force, told him what had happened, and suggested the mission be held in abeyance until the President made a decision.

Acheson then telephoned the President in Kansas City—by happenstance, all this occurred on election day, and Truman made a point of casting his ballot, regardless of demands elsewhere—and they talked briefly. Truman would approve the bombing only to prevent an "immediate and serious threat" to American troops. Acheson told him MacArthur's report of the previous day contained no such statement, although he had mentioned reserves on the Chinese side of the Yalu. Truman first suggested that Acheson telephone MacArthur, then agreed that such communications on military subjects "should be through the military establishment."

An hour and twenty minutes before the ninety B-29 bombers were to take off on the mission, Lovett ordered MacArthur not to attack targets within five miles of the Manchurian border. He also asked for detailed information on the necessity for the bombing of Sinuiju and the Yalu River bridges. What puzzled the men advising Truman—Acheson, Marshall, and Bradley—was MacArthur's abrupt about-face. Only two days earlier MacArthur had warned Washington against precipitate action and recommended that everyone wait and see what the Chinese intended to do. By any measure, bombing Sinuiju was a marked escalation of the war.

The attitude of the British was especially on Truman's mind. Here the President was reacting to shadows rather than substance. Britain no longer ranked as a major world power. In the postwar years, the British Empire had contracted with the rapidity of a pinpricked balloon. Nonetheless, the Anglophile Acheson continued to treat Britain as a serious world power and also to give undeserved weight to the opinion of stumbling and hapless India, which received more attention than was merited from the State Department during the war.

MacArthur Angered

Cancellation of the Sinuiju mission infuriated MacArthur. He responded with an extraordinary message accusing Washington of endangering his command, implicitly appealing over the heads of the JCS to the President, and for the first time to the JCS revealing a dangerous battlefield situation:

> Men and matériel in large force are pouring across all bridges over the Yalu from Manchuria. This movement . . . threatens the ultimate destruction of the forces under my command. The actual movement . . . can be accomplished under cover of darkness and the distance between the river and our lines is so short that the forces can be deployed against our troops without being seriously subjected to air interdiction. The only way to stop this reinforcement . . . is the destruction of these bridges and the subjection of all installations in the north area supporting the enemy advance to . . . maximum . . . air destruction. Every hour that this is postponed will be paid for dearly in American and other United Nations blood. The main crossing at Sinuiju was to be hit within the next few hours and the mission is actually already being mounted. Under the gravest protest that I can make, I am suspending this strike and carrying out your instructions. What I have ordered is entirely within the scope of the rules of war and the resolutions and directions which I have received from the United Nations and constitutes no slightest act of belligerency against Chinese territory, in spite of the outrageous international lawlessness emanating therefrom. I cannot overemphasize the disastrous effect, both physical and psychological, that will result from the restrictions which you are imposing. I trust that the matter be immediately brought to the attention of the President as I believe your instructions may well result in a calamity of major proportion for which I cannot accept the responsibility without his personal and direct understanding of the situation. Time is so essential that I request immediate reconsideration of your decision pending which complete compliance will of course be given to your order.[17]

Surprised by MacArthur's sudden urgency and his vitriolic language —a lesser general would have courted cashiering for speaking so arrogantly—General Bradley telephoned the President and read the message to him. Truman, worried, spoke about the dangers inherent in bombing so close to Manchuria. He feared that an "overly eager pilot" might bring Soviet retaliation. Because MacArthur "felt so strongly that this was of unusual urgency," Truman told Bradley to authorize the Sinuiju mission.

Truman really had little choice since MacArthur's November 6 message left him open to blame should the American forces be overrun.[18] Truman correctly interpreted MacArthur's message as a for-the-record statement that could be resurrected to exonerate the general for any failure of the Korean mission and to put responsibility on Washington leaders who would not follow his advice.

Coming as closely as it did after MacArthur's use of non-ROK troops near the Yalu, the November 6 message put the JCS again on their guard. Thus the Joint Chiefs were stiffly correct in their reply, and they used language that reflected their skepticism.

They began with a subtle rebuke:[19] "The situation depicted in your message [of November 6] is considerably changed from that reported in last sentence your message [November 4] which was our last report from you." They agreed destroying the Yalu bridges would "contribute materially" to the security of the UN forces "unless" such action "resulted in increased Chinese . . . efforts and even Soviet contribution in response." Then they repeated what they had frequently told MacArthur: The administration wanted nothing done to "enlarge the area of conflict and the U.S. involvement to a most dangerous degree." The JCS authorized MacArthur to proceed with the bombing of Sinuiju and the Korean end of the Yalu bridges if he felt they were "essential to safety of your forces." They warned him to use "extreme care" to avoid hitting Manchuria.

The JCS signed off with a pointed suggestion that "we be kept informed of important changes in situation as they occur," reminding MacArthur that they had not received an estimate of the overall situation requested three days earlier.

Responding to the JCS on November 7, MacArthur offered further justification for the air offensive.[20] Intelligence had confirmed "beyond question" that organized Chinese units were in Korea. Although of unknown strength, they had seized the initiative opposite the Eighth Army and slowed the advance of X Corps in the east. If the enemy continued to increase his strength, MacArthur felt it might become necessary to give up hope of further advance, even to fall back. But he hoped to resume the attack in the west, possibly in ten days, if he could check the flow of reinforcements. "Only through such an offensive effort can any accurate measure be taken of enemy strength," MacArthur asserted.

To some Pentagon staff officers, the last sentence was incredible. One of them stated years later (after retiring with three-star rank): "The Chinese had already demonstrated in the EUSAK sector that they were strong enough to kick in MacArthur's teeth. They didn't ambush us—they met us head-on, stopped us, and then knocked us back. What MacArthur proposed was to stick his whole army in the goddamned dragon's mouth again when his own intelligence was telling him the Chinese were bringing in heavy reinforcements. MacArthur was awfully transparent: He was moving himself into a position where another collision with the Chinese was unavoidable. The prudent course would be to do your intelligence, then plan your operation. But then, MacArthur was never noted for prudence."

MacArthur concluded the November 7 message by implicitly calling President Truman and the JCS dolts. Bombing of the Yalu targets was the only way to halt a buildup threatening his command. It was routine interdiction of enemy communications "so plainly defensive that it is hard to conceive that it would cause an increase in the volume of local intervention or . . . provoke a general war." The inviolability of Manchuria and Siberia had been a "cardinal obligation of this headquarters" since the war began.

The passages evoked exasperation in Washington. MacArthur either was not hearing what he was being told or intended to continue chipping away at the JCS (and Truman) until he was granted the freewheeling authority he desired. The ever-diplomatic General Marshall, attempting to soothe MacArthur, replied with a long, conciliatory cable recognizing "your difficulty in fighting a desperate battle in a mountainous region under winter conditions . . . and necessarily limiting conditions."[21] He assured MacArthur he enjoyed the full support of the President and the State and Defense departments.

MacArthur's response, on November 8, was a lengthy tirade against the changing "character and culture" of the Chinese he claimed to know so well.[22] Once peaceful, the Chinese had become nationalistic and aggressive under Communist rule. MacArthur was convinced that the "Chinese Communist support of the North Koreans was the dominant one." Their moves in Korea, Tibet, and Indochina reflected "predominantly the same lust for the expansion of power which has animated every would-be conqueror since the beginning of time."

Although MacArthur did not say so outright, his message made plain that he considered his major enemy no longer North Korea but China. And his concern was not with stabilizing a local war but with halting Chinese "expansion" throughout Asia.

The Yalu Bombings

As these messages flurried across the Pacific, the issue that prompted them—bombing the Yalu bridges—finally got under way on November 8. Carrier and land-based planes launched the assault, which spread along the Yalu inland from both oceans. When carried out against supply dumps, railheads, roads, and bridges, the raids were extraordinarily effective. And also almost totally useless, in any practical sense: Chinese field armies did not travel by truck or rail; they walked, and they carried arms and supplies on their backs.

Bombing the Yalu bridges was a more complex matter. The ban on

flying over Chinese territory made bombing of the river spans dangerous, if not outright impossible. The normal bombing pattern would
have been for the B-29's to fly due north on a course parallel to the
bridges, drop their bombs, and make a sweeping U-turn to the south.
But to avoid penetrating Chinese airspace, the pilots were forced to fly
an awkward dogleg: to approach the bridges at a perpendicular angle,
always staying south of midstream of the meandering river. The Chinese packed the north banks with antiaircraft guns, and their fire drove
the B-29's to altitudes of more than 20,000 feet, where they were then
attacked by MIG-15 fighters.

The airmen worked a few days under the strictures, found them
unworkable, and then many decided to ignore them—in one of the
better-kept secrets of the war.[23] A flight commander, Noel Parrish, who
was to retire from the air force as a brigadier general, concluded that
the bridges could not be hit under the restrictions without heavy casualties. So he ordered his pilots to fly the due-north courses, release their
bombs as they reached the limit of North Korean territory, and then cut
back sharply to the south.

The pattern necessitated the B-29's flying over Chinese territory to
a depth of several miles. So, too, did fighter escorts, to keep away
Communist MIGs. The pilots kept the secret because to reveal it would
bring about, possibly, their own deaths, for exposing the violations could
put them under the command of an officer bent on following the letter
of the restrictions. Parrish did not apologize for breaking orders. The
Chinese, by his reasoning, would accuse U.S. aircraft of overflying Manchuria regardless; he preferred to save the lives of his air crews.

The Marines Are Apprehensive

Far to the east of the Eighth Army, meanwhile, the 1st Marine Division
had begun its mission in the X Corps area with a mixture of confidence
and apprehension. On October 30 General Edward Almond, MacArthur's chief deputy, flew into Wonsan for a briefing on what he expected
of the division. Almond talked with staccato sentences and ferocious
thrusts of his pointer stick. Gesturing at the map, he centered on the
area around the Chosin Reservoir, more than seventy miles from the
marines' position. Almond spoke as if outlining a leisurely Sunday stroll.
The marines were to move along the western shores of the reservoir,
then strike north for the Yalu. As support, the 7th Army Division was
to move east of the reservoir through the Sinhung Valley, then north
to the frontier town of Hyesanjin, opposite Manchuria.

"When we have cleared all this out," Almond concluded matter-of-factly, "the ROKs will take over, and we will pull our divisions out of Korea."[24]

Marine officers listened in skeptical silence. They had scouted the terrain ahead of them, by air and by foot, and they recognized its dangers. One of the first towns along the route was Sudong, where a ROK division had been mauled only a few days earlier by the Chinese. Although the CCF since had withdrawn from the area—or so intelligence said, anyway—the marines feared another surprise intervention. They did not shy from tough assignments. But the proposed operation did far more than take them from their traditional mission as an elite amphibious landing force. The marines were being converted into a roadbound infantry unit, operating at the army's direction.[25] Almond was proposing that a single marine division, approximately 8,000 men, string itself over a route sixty-four miles long, from the port city of Hungnam to the small town of Hagaru, on the southern tip of the Chosin Reservoir. The "road" was a narrow ribbon of dirt and gravel that rose from the coastal plain, in abrupt turns and switchbacks, into a tumbled region of mile-high peaks. The most rugged stretch was the thirty-five miles from Chinhung where the road left the coastal plain to Yudam. Funchilin Pass occupied eight of the ten miles immediately north of Chinhung—the roadway a twisting, one-way shelf, with a cliff on one side and a yawning chasm on the other, the ascent of the road steep enough to strain a jeep. Above Hagaru was another demanding obstacle, Toktong Pass, a 4,000-foot rise through a gloomy gorge onto a plateau leading toward Yudam.

Paralleling most of the route was a narrow-gauge railroad, much bombed during the first months of the war, yet still serviceable near the coast. Three power plants were strung along the Chongjin River south of the reservoir to provide electricity for chemical plants in the Hamhung area; other power lines spread to industrial centers elsewhere in North Korea and Manchuria.

The marines appraised the mission skeptically. To General Oliver Smith, the division commander, sending an infantry column scores of miles into enemy territory, with no flank protection, was military insanity. Almond was unsympathetic. For instance, Smith told Almond he wanted to build an airstrip at Hagaru, to bring in supplies and evacuate casualties, before moving north along the shores of the reservoir.

"What casualties?" Almond asked Smith.

The disgusted marine general recounted later, "That's the kind of thing you were up against. He wouldn't admit there even would be any casualties." (Smith ignored Almond and ordered the airstrip built; ultimately "we took 4,500 casualties out of that field.")

Colonel Alpha Bowser, the 1st Marine G-3, was also nervous when he looked at the maps and saw how far the marines and the 7th Army Division would be ahead of the right flank of the Eighth Army in the west.[26] He faulted "overoptimism" on the part of Almond and a willingness of MacArthur and his staff "to accept the fact that we could get away with this in that kind of weather." Bowser felt that Almond was "aggressive almost to a fault in my estimation. . . . Almond pictured this . . . as a sweeping victory that was in his grasp." Bowser thought the more prudent course was for the marines to prepare a winter defensive line and hold it until the weather broke.

A marine reconnaissance craft flew over the advance route in late October. The pilot, Major Henry J. Woessner, knew the ROKs had taken sixteen Chinese prisoners a few days earlier in the eastern part of North Korea. From the air he saw no sign of enemy troop movements anywhere around the Chosin Reservoir. But he noted—and reported—the formidable terrain through which the marines must march.

Under interrogation the sixteen Chinese prisoners had said that elements of four CCF divisions had crossed the Yalu in mid-October with the mission of protecting the Chosin Reservoir power complex; another reservoir, the Fusen, a bit farther north; and the flank of the CCF Army opposing the American Eighth Army to the west. X Corps intelligence dismissed the possibility the Chinese intended to fight around the reservoirs, the prisoners' contrary statements notwithstanding. The 1st Marine Division G-2 considered the sixteen prisoners an indication that "the CCF has decided to intervene in the Korean War" and with units rather than volunteer cadres. "However, until more definite information is obtained, it must be presumed that the CCF has not yet decided on full scale intervention."

But Colonel Homer L. Litzenberg, whose 7th Marine Regiment was to lead the march north, did not entirely accept these intelligence estimates. The evening before the regiment moved out, he called officers and NCOs to his command post, and told them they might soon be engaged in the opening battle of World War III.

"We can expect to meet Chinese Communist forces," he concluded, "and it is important that we win the first battle. The results of that action will reverberate around the world, and we want to make sure that the outcome has an adverse effect in Moscow as well as Peking."[27]

"Blitzin' Litzenberg" Arrives

Litzenberg's 7th Marine Regiment had arrived in Korea a full week behind the rest of the 1st Marine Division, coming ashore at Inchon on September 22. But it soon caught up with the other two regiments and moved so swiftly once it passed Seoul that officers, with joking admiration, called its commander Blitzin' Litzenberg.

Now, however, Litzenberg proceeded with caution. He knew Chinese were ahead of him near Sudong, the first objective on the road, but just how many he could only guess. So he moved his regiment—designated the 7th RCT (regimental combat team)—in gradual steps. The regiment's 1st Battalion, commanded by Lieutenant Colonel Raymond G. Davis, took the lead through the valley, with the 2nd Battalion trailing on the ridge lines, in what Litzenberg called a "walking perimeter." The 3rd Battalion brought up the rear. By Litzenberg's order, the column did not extend less than 4,000 or more than 6,000 yards in length—enough depth to give fighting room, but tight enough to ensure that the three battalions could support one another.

The march covered four miles toward Sudong the first day, October 31, with scattered opposition. The next day the RCT relieved ROK troops, and immediately the tempo of battle increased. Chinese opposition from the ridge lines bordering the road intensified. Marines staggered up the hills to blast them off (one company climbed 1,600 vertical feet from ground level over an average gradient of 25 percent). Planes flying low-level missions hit camouflaged CCF positions with 500-pound bombs, 20 mm shells, and rockets. By the night of November 2 the 7th Regiment was within a mile of Sudong, and men dug in for the night.

Shortly before midnight the Chinese jumped to the offensive. Bursting flares and bugle calls signaled an onslaught from each ridge line. When the Chinese met resistance, they fought savagely with machine guns and grenades; when they found gaps in the thin line, they poured into the valley. In the confusion of night Chinese seemed everywhere. Marines who had fought the Japanese in night attacks in the Second World War found familiar patterns in the Chinese tactics—calls in English for hospital corpsmen, accented cries of "Hey, Joe, where are you?" or "I got you, Chollie." The marines greeted the Chinese with quiet tenseness, firing only when the enemy exposed himself. A Russian T-34 tank broke through a roadblock and rumbled into the 1st Battalion's command post (CP), firing indiscriminately at mortar positions, vehicles, even individual riflemen. A 3.5 mm marine rocket stung the tank. Its turret swerved, and a single 85 mm shell—fired at virtual pistol range—wiped out the marine crew. The tank turned and rumbled away north.

At dawn the marines found they shared the valley floor with the Chinese. Enemy troops held the roadway between the 1st and 2nd Battalion CPs, and marine companies were scattered through the hills, many of them cut off from one another. Another Chinese regiment rushed to reinforce the attack.

Litzenberg did not panic. He ordered his surviving artillery and mortar sections to unleash a barrage at CCF positions. Meanwhile, UN aircraft lashed at Chinese targets on the hills with rockets and machine-gun fire, often hitting scant yards from marines. American riflemen rooted out individual Chinese from rocks and holes in the hills and in the valley. Litzenberg stressed a principle to his commanders: that to nullify Chinese night attacks, regardless of large-scale penetrations and infiltrations, defending units had to hold onto their positions until daylight. Then superior marine firepower ultimately would chop the Chinese masses into fragments.

That is exactly what happened all day long on November 3, with awesome Chinese carnage. One Chinese unit panicked under the pressure and tried to march out of the valley in daylight in column formation. Marine machine guns methodically blasted the column into ribbons. (Later the 1st Battalion was to count 662 Chinese corpses in its sector alone.)

The Chinese fought tenaciously. Two marine platoons of Easy Company hurled themselves against Chinese dug into positions on a high peak, only to be thrown back by what First Lieutenant Robert T. Bey called "the most concentrated grenade barrage this writer has had the dubious distinction to witness." An air strike finally hit the ridge; advancing marines found forty Chinese dead. Elsewhere a single Chinese sniper found the range on the 2nd Battalion aid station and shot down six marines in rapid succession—one of them Lieutenant E. W. Clark, a doctor wounded while treating a patient.

The fighting slackened at nightfall, and suddenly the marines realized the Chinese had vanished from the battlefield. Patrols encountered a few Chinese stragglers. Now the marines faced only a decimated North Korean force supported by four T-34 tanks. Advancing up the road to Chinhung, marines destroyed three of them with grenades and bazooka fire; a Corsair fighter plane demolished the fourth with a direct hit with a pair of five-inch rockets.

The advance continued the next day, November 4, with marines inching up a hairpin turn and a steep rise beyond Chinhung, exchanging artillery and machine-gun fire with scattered Chinese defenders. Several times the column stalled, only to be shaken free by intensive air support.

The Chinese had vanished—but why and for how long?

On the opposite side of Korea, in the Eighth Army sector, the night of November 5–6 also marked the high-water mark of the First Phase Chinese Offensive. Soon after dark UN units noted an eerie silence. The Chinese had broken contact, and now they withdrew in long columns marching northward.

The Eighth Army had been effectively halted along a line some sixty miles south of the Yalu. In the east, X Corps's advance had also been slowed, even though the Chinese commitment there was relatively light. ROK units remained in place along the east coast within striking distance of Manchuria.

Thus another element in a baffling puzzle. Why had the Chinese decided to break off the battle? Had their short-lived assault been a warning to the United States and the ROKs to come no closer to the Yalu? Were the Chinese signaling that should the UN offensive be resumed, the result would be total war?

The sudden break in the war gave both Washington officials and General MacArthur a chance to reconsider their war strategy and to decide what their future moves would be. And once again American attempts to fathom Chinese intentions proved staggeringly inaccurate, with a commensurately staggering loss of American and ROK lives.

CHAPTER THIRTEEN

The November Lull

When the Chinese vanished into the frozen North Korean hills, they left a mystery. Did the withdrawal reflect Mao Tse-tung's inherently cautious nature? Had the Chinese attempted to test the U.S. reaction to intervention or even to signal a willingness to negotiate? Or was the probe a reconnaissance, to be followed by a full-scale onslaught once the blooded armies had a chance to reinforce and resupply?

The American military, understandably, looked for military, rather than political, explanations. In hindsight, both factors seem to have been involved. And American analysis was gravely handicapped by shortcomings of both immediate and long-range intelligence about the Chinese Communist Forces.

The marines' first thought was that the Chinese armies had "fought themselves out." On the basis of prisoner interrogation reports and accounts from the Chinese Civil War, intelligence experts knew the Chinese foot soldier carried only three to five days' food—either rice or a Korean staple dish concocted from rice, dried peas, and millet seed ground together in a powder, which could be mixed with water and eaten cold in battlefield emergencies. Issues of ammunition were equally niggardly—essentially what a soldier could carry in his pockets or in a crude cloth roll pack. Resupply routes were practically nonexistent, although the Chinese did press into involuntary service Koreans with the traditional A-frame backpack.

During the First Phase Chinese Offensive marine reconnaissance saw many Chinese trucks on the northern fringes of the Chosin Reservoir. But these trucks were so precious and afforded such superb rocket targets for roaming Corsair fighter craft that the Chinese used them sparingly. Thus, in planning his tactics, the Chinese commander General Lin Piao was bound by a rigid stricture: His line divisions could fight three to five days before exhausting their food and ammunition. They then had to be replaced with fresh divisions.

Had U.S. intelligence paid more attention to the tactics of the Chinese Revolution, a more accurate explanation could have been deduced for the sudden enemy evaporation. In 1938, at the height of his battle with the Japanese, Mao Tse-tung wrote a lucid explanation of his guerrilla credo.[1] The book, *On Protracted War,* used words prophetic to the UN Command in Korea: "We have always advocated the policy of 'luring the enemy to penetrate deep' precisely because this is the most effective military policy for a weak army in a strategic defense against a strong army." He spoke of retreat as a tactic, through a rhetorical question and rhetorical answer: "Is it not self-contradictory to fight heroically first and abandon territory afterwards? One eats first and then relieves oneself; does one eat in vain?" And elsewhere Mao summarized his strategy in a slogan since immortalized in the annals of irregular warfare:

> Enemy advances, we retreat.
> Enemy halts, we harass.
> Enemy tires, we attack.
> Enemy retreats, we pursue.

But little of Mao's philosophy was known to the American military or intelligence community.[2] According to the political scientists Gene Z. Hanrahan and Edward L. Katzenbach, Jr., specialists in irregular warfare, translations of Mao's works had a "Communist-world-wide circulation." But they did not reach American military intelligence. Until Mao's works were published in London in 1954 and later that year by International Publishers in New York, they were "virtually unobtainable in the United States . . . including the Library of Congress . . . except for a stray pamphlet here or there," according to Hanrahan and Katzenbach. "They were not even in the [military] service libraries. . . ."

Lacking intelligence on how Mao fought previous wars, the military relied on uninformed guesses. The longer the Chinese delayed resuming the offensive, the more confident some officers became that they would not reappear. Buttressing this assumption was the onset of the bitter Korean winter. Days stretched into a week, then two weeks, then three weeks, and still no Chinese. During this period even Major General Oliver P. Smith lulled himself into the delusion the worst was over. "Even Genghis Khan," he remarked, "wouldn't have tried Korea in the winter."[3]

Whatever the reason—battlefield exigencies, diplomatic maneuvering, or simple indecision on the part of the Chinese leadership—the lull gave American strategists a chance to reevaluate war policies. MacArthur, for his part, made up his mind in a hurry. To this old soldier the

Chinese intervention was only a parting jab. He intended to resume his offensive—and so told the JCS—as soon as the Eighth Army could be regrouped and resupplied. MacArthur's intelligence section generated hundreds of pages of estimates during early November about Chinese intentions and capabilities; none, however, shook the general's core conviction that the best way to fight a war was to take the battle to the enemy.

Poor Presidential Advice

President Truman's advisers served him poorly during this period, by their own admission. Through vacillation, indecision, faulty judgment —and most of all, fear of offending MacArthur—the opportunity to keep the war on course was lost. Dean Acheson lamented in his memoirs: "The government missed its last chance to halt the march to disaster in Korea. All the President's advisors in this matter, civilian and military, knew that something was badly wrong, though what it was, how to find out, and what to do about it they muffed."[4]

The Pentagon's main offense was timidity, with the JCS cowering before MacArthur like schoolboys facing the town bully. When the JCS questioned the wisdom of the chasm between the Eighth Army and X Corps, now that the Chinese had moved, MacArthur imperiously slapped aside the query. "He always considered us a bunch of kids," admitted General Omar Bradley, the JCS chairman. "General MacArthur has always pretty much gone his own way."[5]

Officially MacArthur still operated under the JCS order of September 27—that should major Chinese forces intervene, he must take up defensive positions and ask further guidance from Washington. The Joint Chiefs, in asking MacArthur's comments on possible UN actions on November 8, reminded him the character of the war had changed and said it appeared necessary to reexamine his mission—"the destruction of the North Korean Armed Forces"—which had been contingent upon no Chinese intervention.[6] Although the JCS did not say so directly, the implication was that MacArthur should abandon his offense and defend what he held.

MacArthur Marches On

MacArthur, however, had no such intention. On the previous day, November 7, in pleading for lifting strictures on air operations, he had complained that the introduction of Chinese forces "in strength" into Korea "has completely changed the overall situation."[7] He now slid around this admission and took refuge in an October 9 JCS directive authorizing him, in the event of "open or covert employment anywhere in Korea of major Chinese Communist units," to continue operations so long as he had a *"reasonable chance of success* [emphasis added]."[8] In MacArthur's view, "it would be fatal to weaken the fundamental and basic policy of the UN to destroy all resisting armed forces in Korea to bring that country into a united and free nation." In this single passage, he managed to combine—and blur—the military mission assigned him by the JCS with the UN General Assembly recommendation on unification of October 7. He clearly did not intend to be bridled, the Chinese notwithstanding.

The general was confident his air power would stop Chinese reinforcements from crossing from Manchuria and would destroy Chinese troops already in Korea. After the air attacks he would complete destruction of the enemy with an offensive commencing on November 15 that would carry his banner to the Yalu. And once again MacArthur cast his plans in terms that suggested the JCS had no alternative but approval:

> Any program short of this would completely destroy the morale of my forces and its psychological consequence would be inestimable. It would condemn us to an indefinite retention of our military forces along difficult defense lines in North Korea and would unquestionably arouse such resentment among the South Koreans that their forces would collapse or might even turn against us.

Nor did MacArthur think much of a proposed British idea of a buffer zone along the Yalu. MacArthur compared this plan with the cession of the Sudeten region of Czechoslovakia to Germany in 1938. The proper UN action would be a resolution condemning China and threatening military sanctions if the Chinese did not withdraw. Yielding any part of Korea, even as a buffer zone, "would be the greatest defeat of the free world in recent times. Indeed, to yield to so immoral a proposition would bankrupt our leadership and influence in Asia and render untenable our position both politically and militarily." Halting his troops short of the Yalu "would follow clearly in the footsteps of the British who by the appeasement of recognition [of Communist China] lost the respect of all the rest of Asia without gaining that of the Chinese. . . ." MacArthur recommended "with all the earnestness that I possess that there be no weakening at this crucial moment and that we press on to complete victory. . . ."

MacArthur's cable arrived several hours before a JCS meeting on November 9, and it was effectively ignored. The JCS deliberations covered first Chinese intentions and then possible U.S. responses. The JCS saw three motives for the Chinese intervention:[9]

—The Chinese sought to protect hydroelectric power complexes along the Yalu and to establish a *cordon sanitaire* south of the river. If these were the motives, the Chinese might withdraw in return for a UN guarantee that neither Manchurian sovereignty nor the hydroelectric installations would be infringed. If such assurances were given, and the Chinese nonetheless remained in the war, "one possible explanation for China's behavior could be eliminated."

—Another possibility was an "undeclared war" to tie U.S. forces in Korea. The JCS did not wish the Korean War to sap U.S. strength and leave it unprepared for trouble elsewhere. Nonetheless, such a Chinese objective might leave an opening for a negotiated settlement.

—The third possible alternative was a Chinese attempt to drive the UN out of Korea. Such an effort could not succeed without Soviet air and naval power—an intervention which would signal the start of World War III and necessitate UN withdrawal from Korea.

So what should the United States do? The Joint Chiefs saw three alternatives: to force the war to a successful conclusion with a renewed offensive; to establish and hold a defensive line south of the Manchurian border; or to withdraw. The first option would require additional troops even if the Chinese did not materially increase the size of their commitment; the third was unacceptable and, if forced upon the United States, "could only be accepted as the prelude to global war."

The JCS clearly preferred the second alternative, the defensive line south of the Yalu. Such a course "might be a temporary expedient pending clarification of the military and political problems raised by Chinese intervention." The chiefs urged that "every effort should be expended as a matter of urgency to settle the problem of Chinese Communist intervention . . . by political means, preferably through the United Nations." The JCS called for public reassurances that the UN did not intend to take the war into China. They also suggested peace negotiations through nations recognizing Red China.

But having decided the best course was the defensive line south of the Yalu, the JCS made no effort to enforce it upon MacArthur. Had they done so, the pause in the war conceivably could have provided time for Acheson to seek a political settlement at the UN and elsewhere. MacArthur's mission, the JCS recommended, should not be changed, although it would remain under "constant review." Thus was MacArthur left free to take the offensive again.

The National Security Council was not ready to make any decisive moves when it met on November 9.[10] Acheson, presiding in the absence of Truman, suggested that the NSC "just discuss the situation" and have the staff make further studies and prepare a recommendation.

"We need to know more about where we are before we can decide where we are going," he said.

Acheson reviewed prospects of a political solution. He noted that the United States had carefully hedged its public statements about objectives. "In the UN we have never allowed any resolution to require expelling the Communists from all over Korea," the secretary said. "We also have not said that we would stay there until that objective has been achieved. Therefore, politically we are not committed to the conquest of all Korea *if something short of that can be worked out which is satisfactory* [emphasis added]." Here Acheson ignored previous UN resolutions on unification of Korea that MacArthur concurrently was citing as authority for his actions in the North. Yet neither he nor the JCS acted to reconcile the diverse policy goals being pursued in Washington and in Tokyo.

To General Walter Bedell Smith, the director of central intelligence, the unanswered question was the "extent to which the Chinese . . . were willing to act as the pawn . . . of the Soviets." Smith said the CIA estimated that the commitment of Chinese forces, with Soviet material assistance, indicated that the Soviets would risk general war in Korea. The Soviets presumably would like to have the United States in a general war with China, "which would mean that our European commitments would . . . go by the board.

"This raises the question as to what point the U.S. will be driven to . . . attack the problem at its heart, namely, Moscow, instead of handling it on the periphery. . . . [T]he Soviets take no risk, since they are perfectly willing to pull the rug out from under their satellite at any time and start talking peace," Smith continued. But "the Soviets could hardly contemplate giving up Korea and suffering a major defeat there."

Therefore, Smith concluded, "We are . . . facing the question of either going forward or back." The "political consequences of either standing pat or drawing back would be tremendous." He saw no "real reason to change the [CIA's] previous estimate that the Soviets are not prepared themselves to bring on a general war," even though they would like the United States to be at war in Asia. To Smith, "the danger was that the Soviets, as Oriental rug traders, would keep pushing us to the point where war is the only alternative." The Soviets could—and would—accept full-scale hostilities, such as those in Manchuria, without going to general war. "Democracies, however, are unable to accept such limited hostilities," he said. At some point the Chinese could be forced to react to attack on Manchuria by U.S. planes "since Chinese face would then be involved."

Speaking for the JCS, General Bradley reviewed the three possible Chinese intentions the military had discussed the previous day (the *cordon sanitaire* protecting the Yalu power complexes; a fixed line farther south; or driving the UN off the peninsula). Bradley thought the United States could hold its present positions, but "there would be an increasing question of how much pressure we could stand without attacking Manchurian bases." Holding the present line "would be a serious situation, since we would lose a lot of people if it continued indefinitely." Bradley noted that the Soviets recently had sent 200 to 250 planes into China. Since Russian-language conversations were no longer heard within the group, he assumed the planes "have been turned over to the Chinese and that the Russians have gone back home."

Although MacArthur thought that authority to bomb the Yalu bridges would enable him to push the Chinese out, Bradley felt this view "somewhat optimistic. But, after all," he continued, "MacArthur is the commander in the field. Until his directive is changed he is free to keep pushing forward. The JCS feel that the directive should not be changed now, but should be kept under constant review."

Secretary Marshall noted the U.S. military situation "is complicated by the wide dispersion on the east where we are vulnerable to an attack." (He referred to the X Corps area, where the 1st Marine Division was moving toward Manchuria.)

Bradley replied that MacArthur had split his forces to carry out his directive to occupy the country and to hold elections. (In actuality, Bradley's interpretation of MacArthur's orders was overly sweeping, although no one at the meeting questioned it.)

Responding to a question by Acheson, Bradley said MacArthur did not appear worried about his situation in the west. Acheson pressed further: Was any line better militarily than MacArthur's current position? Bradley replied that "militarily the farther back the line, the better off we would be." But "such a retrograde movement would probably lose political support and might lose the South Koreans' will to fight."

Acheson pressed the point. It was clear that "the Russian interest is their obsession with defense in depth." One way to relax the Soviet concerns would be a buffer zone in northeastern Korea under a UN commission, with a UN constabulary but no armed forces. For its part, Acheson continued, the State Department intended "to get after the Chinese Communists heavily in public in the UN, to make it clear that their units are not volunteers." In private ("and some in public") Acheson said, "We might explore such possibilities as a twenty-mile demilitarized area, ten miles on each side of the Yalu. Under such a plan, the Chinese Communists would be required to withdraw and we would hold elections and then get out." But Acheson pointed to a flaw in his own idea. If the Chinese accepted this plan, they would insist on withdrawing all foreign troops and establishing a government with equal representation from North and South Korea, "which would mean a Communist government."

After all this discussion the National Security Council decided to do nothing. MacArthur's directive would not be changed "at present." The general "is free to do what he militarily can do without bombing Manchuria." Concurrently political discussions would be undertaken when the Chinese Communists arrived at the UN. (Acheson admitted that the State Department has been trying "without success to figure some way to reach the authorities at Peking.")

The NSC minutes reflect no sense of urgency. In ordering further staff studies, the council set no deadlines, the only guidelines were that the staff should consult with the State Department, the JCS, and the CIA.

The NSC recommendations of November 9 make little, if any, sense, for they put the United States on contradictory political and military routes. Before the Chinese intervention, planners assumed the war could be ended without involving Peking. If the Chinese intervened, it was thought that the UN would stop military operations, retire to defensible positions, and await developments. But the first intervention, however brief, was enough to tell Washington that China could force the UN out of Korea. Nevertheless, the NSC intended to permit MacArthur to continue the same type of offense, now with the realization (admitted by Bradley) that bombing of Manchuria might be necessary for success. Yet when Acheson reported on the meeting to the President the next day, November 10, he spoke hollowly, even foolishly, of a parallel diplomatic effort to start negotiations. Acheson apologists —notably Richard Neustadt, an academic political scientist who served on the White House staff during the war—have argued that the secretary was reluctant to meddle in military strategy, especially since his conduct of Far East policy was already under attack.[11] "In immediate terms," Neustadt wrote later, "the risk was 'military'; if it justified reversing the commander in the field, then the Joint Chiefs must make the judgment and tell Truman." Such a statement is intellectual nonsense. Korean War strategy was a delicate balance of military and diplomatic initiatives, and Acheson had the right—even the obligation—to advise the President when a military matter made achievement of a diplomatic/political goal difficult or impossible. Acheson chose otherwise. Thus the combination of his reticence and MacArthur's brashness carried the United States farther toward disaster.

Truman, ironically, seemed to have had a better grasp of the problem than his advisers. Long after November 1950, adviser Neustadt asked whether he had become concerned about MacArthur's "end-the-war offensive." Although Neustadt conceded that Truman's answer was retrospective, he felt it reflected the essence of his viewpoint at the time:

What we should have done is stop at the neck of Korea right here [pointing to a globe]. . . . That's what the British wanted. . . . We knew the

Chinese had close to a million men on the border and all that.* . . . But [MacArthur] was commander in the field. You pick your man, you've got to back him up. That's the only way a military organization can work. I got the best advice I could and the man on the spot said this was the thing to do. . . . So I agreed. That was my decision—no matter what hindsight shows.

Thus MacArthur continued planning an offensive to win the war by year's end and under the same directives that had guided him during the early autumn.

MacArthur's Optimism Returns

Nor did MacArthur display any nervousness.[12] To the contrary, he was expansively optimistic in a November 14 conversation with William Sebald, his political adviser. His immediate objective, he said, was to destroy the Yalu bridges and thus isolate the area between Manchuria and the battle line. At the same time the Far East Air Force would destroy built-up areas to the enemy rear so the Communists could not "live off the country." MacArthur told Sebald that preparations for a drive to the Yalu were in progress and that it was essential to reach the river before it froze (which the CIA predicted would occur between November 24 and December 10). If his attack beat the freezing, the war would be over. Otherwise, he saw no alternative to bombing targets in Manchuria. Admittedly, if this were done, "the fat would be in the fire," for the Soviets almost certainly would intervene. He hoped such drastic action would not be necessary. If the UN succeeded in driving to the border, MacArthur felt the war would be over. The Chinese regime would have proved its desire to help a Communist neighbor and the ability to fight a modern war; they could then retire with "face" intact.

In a talk three days later, November 17, with Ambassador Muccio, MacArthur insisted that no more than 30,000 Chinese could have been infiltrated into North Korea.[13] Any larger number would have been detected by air. His "all out offensive" would clear the "whole area still in the hands of the North Koreans and Chinese Communists . . . within ten days." He would then escort all Chinese POWs to the frontier and release them and withdraw the Eighth Army to Japan, leaving the occupation to X Corps, assorted UN units, and the ROK Army.

The Chinese, in MacArthur's view, had delayed but not stopped his march toward occupation of all Korea.

*Actually the estimate was far lower.

Stalemate in the UN

Diplomatically the United States was stalemated in the UN during November. Action was along several lines. The main purpose of each move, however, was to attempt to assure the Chinese that the United States did not intend to infringe upon their territory.

On November 8 the Security Council voted to discuss a report from MacArthur on Chinese intervention and to invite a Chinese representative to attend. The United States agreed in the hope of starting a dialogue with China.

Two resolutions went before the Security Council. One, by the United States, called for removal of Chinese troops from Korea and assured that UN forces would remain there only long enough to establish a "unified and democratic government," under a special UN commission. The French countered with a resolution asking the UN Command, "with due consideration for the necessities of military safety," to take measures to prevent damage to the Yalu power installations. Much haggling ensued among the Pentagon, the State Department, and the French over acceptable language. State wanted the French language changed to read "without prejudice to military necessity," to allow MacArthur broader discretion.[14] The French agreed, provided the U.S. resolution included a statement affirming it was UN policy "to hold the Chinese frontier with Korea inviolate and fully to protect Chinese legitimate interests in the frontier zone." But the JCS called this addition "wholly unacceptable" since it would effectively "guarantee a sanctuary for attacking Chinese aircraft."

Nonetheless, the State Department overrode the JCS and decided to accept the French wording holding the Chinese border "inviolate." Such a resolution was introduced on November 10 by the United States and five other nations. But it swiftly fell victim to Soviet obstructionism. The USSR insisted that the subject should be discussed only in the presence of a Chinese representative.

On November 11 the Chinese curtly informed the UN they would not participate in any discussion of MacArthur's report or the resolution. Peking did agree to send a delegation of fourteen Chinese diplomats to Lake Success for consultations about Formosa. The original arrival date was set for November 14. But for unknown reasons, the Chinese chose to dawdle en route, in Moscow, Prague, and London, and did not arrive until November 24. Coupled with the breaking off of contact by Chinese troops in Korea, the Chinese refusal to debate convinced most Security Council members that no immediate action was necessary. The Security Council moved on to other matters. Warren Austin, the U.S. ambassador to the UN, told MacArthur by cable on November 15 that despite the lack of any formal vote,[15] the mere introduction of the resolution with U.S. sponsorship should reassure China the UN would not violate its borders.

Truman's inner circle shared Austin's confidence. Army Secretary Frank Pace, echoing feelings of the other civilian service secretaries, said, "You've got to remember that the Red Chinese had been threatening throughout the period.... Quite frankly, I guess it's a case of crying 'wolf' that often." Pace admitted that his thinking about Chinese intervention was influenced by what he heard from Tokyo. "Certainly General MacArthur had very clear ideas they would *not*, and I have to say that after Inchon I was very impressed with General MacArthur's capability to assess problems out there on the ground."

Allied governments did not share Washington's confidence. In mid-November numerous friendly diplomats passed warnings to Washington.[16] The Swedish ambassador in Peking reported large-scale Chinese Communist movements toward Korea. The Burmese embassy thought that the Chinese were ready to go to "any length" to aid North Korea and reported they were fostering "mass hysteria" on the basis of an alleged UN intention to invade Manchuria. The Netherlands on November 17 passed information to the State Department from its Peking ambassador that Chinese intervention in Korea was motivated by fears of aggression against Manchuria; if UN forces stopped fifty miles south of the Yalu, the Chinese would not move farther. The CIA, in appraising these reports, was skeptical. It thought that China's operations in Korea would "probably continue to be defensive in nature." The British military chiefs, in an advisory to Prime Minister Attlee's cabinet, said they saw no point in risking a major war for the minor triumph of conquering all of North Korea, which was "of no strategic importance for the democratic powers."

Nonetheless, Allied nervousness prompted further attempts by both President Truman and the State Department to allay Chinese fears of an invasion. At a citizens' conference on foreign affairs in Washington on November 15, Acheson sent an indirect message to Peking. It was essential to "clear away any possible misunderstanding that there may be in the minds of the Chinese." If they worried about their frontiers, then "everything in the world . . . is being done to make them understand that their proper interests will be taken care of." But if they were bent upon precipitating a "really grave crisis," then the United States would meet the crisis resolutely.

The next day, at a news conference, Truman cited the UN resolution on China as one of many actions attesting there was no intention to carry hostilities into China. Both the UN and the U.S. policy was "to localize the conflict and to withdraw its forces from Korea as soon as the situation permits." The United States, Truman said,

... will take every honorable step to prevent any extension of the hostilities in the Far East. If the Chinese Communist authorities or people believe otherwise, it can only be because they are being deceived by those whose advantage it is to prolong and extend hostilities in the Far East against the interest of all Far Eastern people.

Concurrent with the President's conciliatory gestures, the working-level staff at the Pentagon argued that nothing should be put in MacArthur's path as he marched toward the Yalu, especially not some proposals from "certain elements of the Department of State."[17] Particularly biting was a November 20 paper by Major General Charles Bolte, the Department of the Army's chief of operations (G-3), which ventured that British and French pressures "had great effect" on State for favoring a demilitarized zone along the Sino-Korean frontier. G-3, Bolte wrote, was "unalterably opposed" to a buffer. Making such an offer "could seriously restrain the U.S. (and UN) military position without any indication that any gain to the U.S. would be forthcoming from the Chinese Communists."

Bolte's paper argued the pros and cons of a renewed offensive, its dangers and its advantages, military and psychological. It stands as the only comprehensive rationale as to why the army—and then the Joint Chiefs—decided not to challenge its field commander.

The only reason an all-out offensive should not be undertaken, Bolte wrote, was that it would pose "too great a risk of global war." He thought the military situation a standoff; regardless of whether MacArthur attacked or stood still, the Soviets or Chinese would do what they had already decided.

Bolte did not worry about Chinese capabilities. "It is not envisaged that the Chinese Communists can succeed in driving presently committed UN forces from Korea, unless materially assisted by Soviet ground and air power." MacArthur's command "has sufficient forces to successfully hold any line in North Korea in the light of circumstances now prevailing." Bolte did not wish to interfere with plans and policies already in motion:

> A continuation of the offensive near the Sino-Korean border will no doubt increase rather than decrease the tenseness of the situation to some extent. Nevertheless, the decision to cross the 38th Parallel was based on the consideration that all of Korea should be cleared of Communist forces.
>
> Thereafter, any attack across the Korean border would be recognized internationally as a clear act of military aggression. The same principle applies to the present situation and it is believed, therefore, that we might have a better chance of localizing the conflict by driving all Communist forces from Korea. Moreover, there is great merit to the argument that a show of strength will discourage further aggression while weakness will encourage it.

Unless MacArthur stated he was unable to continue action, "to stop the offensive would be wholly unacceptable to the American public and not in consonance with the principles for which we have fought."

In a related paper, the army's plans division recommended even more drastic action than a ground offensive.[18] The Chinese should be given an ultimatum, either through the UN or by the United States unilaterally, to leave Korea; otherwise, the U.S. would launch air and naval strikes at military installations in Manchuria.

There was more: "The United States should take all necessary steps to assure the capability of prompt use of the atomic bomb against the Chinese Communists as, if and when directed by the President."

In coming months General MacArthur was to be criticized in Washington for his advocacy of harsh strikes against China. But the Pentagon staff was ahead of him in advocating use of nuclear weapons.

Ultimately the State Department forced a compromise, one far short of the threat of nuclear weapons but which nonetheless went beyond the British demand for a demilitarized zone. State's ascendancy in the bureaucratic struggle (a tribute to Acheson's persuasiveness) was reflected in the designation of Dean Rusk, an assistant secretary of state, to write a cable directing MacArthur to stop at a line not touching upon the Yalu, but *overlooking* it.*[19]

The Rusk directive opened with a blunt political warning:

> Other members of UN indicate growing concern over the possibilities of . . . a general conflict should a major clash develop with Chinese Communist forces as a result of your forces advancing squarely against the entire boundary between Korea and Manchuria-USSR. This might . . . result in loss of support within UN . . . [but] also involve increased risks of a military nature.

Rusk then mentioned the "sentiment" in the UN for a demilitarized zone along the frontier, to reduce Chinese fears of UN military action against Manchuria and the "corresponding sensitivity on the part of the USSR with respect to Vladivostok."

The consensus of the JCS, the secretaries of state and defense, and "other officials" was that MacArthur's mission should not be changed. But holding back from an assault to the frontier "might well provide an out for the Chinese Communists to withdraw into Manchuria without loss of face and might lessen the concern of the Russians as to the

---

*Circumstances suggest that although Rusk's intervention was polite, it was nonetheless invited by the JCS. He wrote what file papers state was a "revision" of a proposed JCS message to MacArthur. Rusk, in a covering note, recognized that State "does not have drafting responsibility with respect to this message" but thought that a "revised draft might provide the most convenient means of setting forth our views." Whereupon Rusk proceeded to write the entire message. He gave his home phone number (TE 8798) for use "if I can be of any assistance." The JCS radioed his message with only a few insignificant editing changes.

security of Vladivostok. This concern may be at the root of Russian pressure on the Chinese Communists to intervene in Korea." What Rusk appeared to be urging, through indirect but intelligible wording, was that MacArthur not drive all the way to the Yalu, but halt at defensible positions. The message stands as another splendid example of Washington's unwillingness to give MacArthur a plain-language order.

It also displayed Washington's unwillingness to engage in brinkmanship: to tell the Chinese and the Soviets that the UN intended to clear North Korea, per UN instructions, and to halt there and that any expansion of the war by the Chinese would be dealt with severely. The United States assuredly could not have "won" a land war in Asia with the Chinese. But its air power could have laid waste all major Chinese cities —a loss to which Chinese leaders would have had to answer. Throughout November U.S. actions were predicated on what the Chinese *might* do rather than what the United States *could* do.

The brief First Phase Chinese Offensive demonstrated to the Chinese they could punish UN forces with impunity, that officials in Washington would not order strikes against their rear bases. For the first time in U.S. military history, America was to fight a war in which the enemy homeland was tacitly declared off limits.

MacArthur, however, did not choose to obey the cautions of the JCS/Rusk cable. By the time it arrived in Korea he had launched a publicly proclaimed offensive to "end the war," regardless of what the Chinese did.

CHAPTER FOURTEEN

MacArthur Marches to Disaster

That MacArthur was ready to move was no secret; perhaps never in history has a general so throughly floodlit his plans for the enemy. "There are reports in the American press," a Washington dispatch stated in the *Times* of London on November 24, "that seven UN divisions—three of them American and four South Korean—as well as the British Commonwealth brigade, are ready for what is called the final push to clear the lower reaches of the Yalu River from the west coast to the point where South Korean troops have already reached it." The *Times*'s correspondent considered this advance publicity "certainly a curious way to fight a war." It was also costly of lives in the next days, for Communist diplomats in the West certainly told the Chinese what was to happen. Ironically, a ranking colonel in the Eighth Army—there is no reason to cite his name—had been broken from general rank before the Normandy invasion for blurting out a small part of the plan before unauthorized ears. He was permitted to remain in the army, with a notation on his file he should never again attain star rank. But his "leak" did not begin to approach in magnitude the flourish of trumpets with which MacArthur marched off to fight the Chinese.

On Thanksgiving Day, November 23, frontline troops enjoyed a more luxurious holiday meal than most other Americans: shrimp cocktail, stuffed olives, roast young tom turkey with cranberry sauce, sweet potatoes, fruit salad, fruit cake, mince pie, and coffee. At X Corps headquarters, Almond and other officers—including some unhappy marines such as General Oliver Smith[1]—attended a dinner featuring cocktails, tablecloths, napkins, chinaware, silverware, even place cards. To some officers the splendor seemed grotesquely misplaced for a war zone. But Almond enjoyed his comforts. There were jokes about troops being "fattened for the slaughter,"[2] but the overriding good news was that a unit of the 17th Regiment of General David Barr's 7th Army Division had reached the Yalu at the town of Hyesanjin. The 7th's advance from the sea had been swift and rather uneventful, with sub-zero temperatures, rather than Communist soldiers, the main obstacle. The regiment had one brushing contact with CCF forces, killing fifty men at the town of Paek-san. But the regiment stomped through snow and ice until November 21, when the 1st Battalion entered Hyesanjin and took ground overlooking the nearly frozen Yalu River. An exuberant General Almond flew up for the occasion and posed for pictures with well-bundled brass, Manchuria in the background. (Other officers were more apprehensive when they saw CCF sentries walking their rounds across the river.)

"Heartiest congratulations, Ned," MacArthur radioed Almond, "and tell Dave Barr that the Seventh Division hit the jackpot." Almond gave Barr and his men his own kudo: "The fact that only twenty days ago this division landed amphibiously over the beaches at Iwon and advanced 200 miles over tortuous mountain terrain and fought successfully against a determined foe in subzero weather will be recorded in history as an outstanding military achievement."

But in a private conversation at the X Corps Thanksgiving fete Barr confided to General Smith that the advance made him nervous.[3] According to what Barr said, "he had had to conduct the operation on a shoestring, never at any time having on hand more than one day's supplies. With almost impassable roads this was a risky procedure."

Because of Almond's continuing pressures, Barr was able to exercise none of the command caution that marked the 1st Marine Division's advance to his west. Barr's rapid advance, with short supplies and lack of flank security, across rugged terrain in miserable weather, was indeed a remarkable feat. But because of Almond, he later paid a cruel price. The 7th Division did not secure its flanks or prepare adequate supply lines; it sent a column sprinting through the mountains into the face of an unknown enemy, operating as if seizing an outpost on the Yalu would win the war. There was another significant difference between the advances of Barr and the 1st Marines: The army met only ragtag remnants of the North Korean Army, while the first days of the marine advance were against fresh Chinese troops. But Barr's rapid thrust gained him the congratulations of the victory-hungry MacArthur and Almond. It also doomed a large portion of his division to agonizing death by cold and Chinese bullets.

To MacArthur, however, reaching the Yalu was an event fraught with symbolism; his command had carried the war to the border with China with seeming impunity. Now he was ready to bring the conflict to a swift end. On November 24 he issued a communiqué to be read to all troops:

> The United Nations massive compression envelopment in North Korea against the new Red Armies operating there is now approaching its decisive effort. The isolating component of the pincer, our air forces of all types, have for the past three weeks, in a sustained attack of model coordination and effectiveness, successfully interdicted enemy lines of support from the north so that further reinforcement therefrom has been sharply curtailed and essential supplies markedly limited. The eastern sector of the pincer, with noteworthy and effective naval support, has now reached commanding enveloping position, cutting in two the northern reaches of the enemy's geographical potential. This morning the western sector of the pincer moves forward in general assault in an effort to complete the compression and close the vise. If successful, this should for all practical purposes end the war, restore peace and unity in Korea, enable the prompt withdrawal of United Nations military forces, and permit the complete assumption by the Korean people and nation of full sovereignty and international equality. It is that for which we fight.

Home by Christmas

The same day MacArthur flew to Eighth Army headquarters at Sinanju, on the Chongchon River, the *SCAP* landing on a bumpy airstrip. The day was bitterly cold (fifteen degrees) but clear, and the general pulled his parka over his head and squatted to give a playful pat to Ebbe, the pet dachshund mascot of General Frank Milburn's I Corps. After a briefing by General Walton Walker and other officers, he spent some five hours on a jeep tour of the front. During a talk with Major General John B. Coulter, commander of IX Corps, MacArthur remembered the Wake Island discussion in which he told General Omar Bradley he might be able to return some troops to America by Christmas. There are several versions—and interpretations—of what he said. According to a *Time* correspondent on the scene, MacArthur told Coulter and Major General John Church, commander of the 24th Division, "I have already promised wives and mothers that the boys of the 24th Division will be back by Christmas. Don't make me a liar. Get to the Yalu and I will relieve you."[4] Major General Courtney Whitney of MacArthur's staff, who was also present, wrote in his memoirs five years later that MacArthur said, "half in jest but with a certain firmness of meaning and purpose . . . 'If this operation is successful, I hope we can get the boys home by Christmas.' "[5] In his autobiography MacArthur said only that "in talking to a group of officers, I told them of General Bradley's desire and hope to have two divisions home by Christmas provided there was not intervention by Red China." MacArthur, unconvincingly, argued, "This remark was twisted by the press into a prediction of the success of our movement, and this false misinterpretation was later used as a powerful propaganda weapon with which to bludgeon me."[6] Indeed, MacArthur's adversaries used the "home by Christmas" statement against him, to his acute embarrassment. But the breast thumping of his own November 24 statement (not mentioned in his memoirs) makes absurd his claim that the press generated overconfidence in the offensive. A more credible explanation comes from a contemporary statement MacArthur gave to confidante Marguerite Higgins, a New York *Herald Tribune* correspondent to whom he had taken a liking. After the offensive collapsed, according to Ms. Higgins, MacArthur "privately admitted that he made a mistake in issuing such an optimistic communiqué."[7] MacArthur's after-the-fact excuse (an item of which the general kept an ample store) was that his references to withdrawing American troops "were intended as reassurances to the Chinese that we would get out of Korea the moment the Manchurian border was reached."

In his memoirs, published years later, MacArthur claimed he saw things on the front the day the offensive began that "worried me greatly." The ROK troops were not in good shape, and the entire line was "deplorably weak" in numbers. If the Chinese entered the war, MacArthur said he had decided he would abandon the offensive "at once" and stop any effort to drive north. If MacArthur in fact had made any such decision, it was conveyed neither to his field commanders nor to his staff, and Far East Command archives reveal no trace of any MacArthur directives calling for a withdrawal in the event the advance ran into Chinese.

But MacArthur did surprise everyone in midafternoon, when he reboarded the *SCAP*, by turning to pilot Tony Story and telling him, "Head for the west coast and fly up the Yalu."[8] Staff officers looked at one another in open astonishment. Even had the *SCAP* been armed and protected by a heavy fighter escort, the flight would have been dangerous. But the staff knew the futility of arguing with MacArthur when he had decided upon personal reconnaissance. He said he wanted to study the terrain and to look for signs of enemy activity. Don't worry about the lack of fighter cover, he said; the audacity of the flight was the best protection. Courtney Whitney for one wished he would don a parachute. MacArthur laughed. "You gentlemen wear them if you care to do so, but I'll stick with the plane." An accompanying newsman muttered to Colonel Sidney Huff, MacArthur's aide, "Sid, is this trip really necessary?"

At the mouth of the Yalu, Story turned east and flew over the river at an altitude of some 5,000 feet, high enough for the party to look deep into snow-covered Manchuria. Roads and trails were visible; none showed signs of extensive use. The snow, however, was deep enough to cover tracks of any recent traffic. The vista awed Whitney. "All that spread before our eyes was an endless expanse of utterly barren countryside, its jagged hills, yawning crevices, and all but the black waters of the Yalu locked in the silent death-grip of snow and ice." Whitney decided that MacArthur was right when he refused a parachute; in the event of emergency, it would be better to stay with the plane than to jump "into this merciless wasteland."

After MacArthur finished his tour, General Walton Walker stood on the airstrip, saluted farewell, and then watched the *SCAP* disappear over the horizon. "Bullshit," he murmured, to no one in particular, and got into his own jeep. Aide Mike Lynch remembered the remark vividly "because General Walker *never* used profanity no matter what the provocation."[9]

Walker sought out Major General John H. Church, commanding general of the 24th Division, and gave him a message for Colonel Richard W. Stephens, whose 21st Infantry Regiment would be in the vanguard of the attack: "You tell Stephens that the first time he smells Chinese food, pull back."[10]

A Nervous Willoughby

MacArthur's optimism, for once, was not shared by his intelligence chief, General Charles Willoughby.[11] Even as MacArthur planned his new offensive, Willoughby warned that even though the Chinese had broken contact, they "intend to go all out against UN forces in Korea." On November 10 an intelligence summary offered reasons why the "prediction of all-out action . . . is justified." The Chinese had initially delayed entry on the assumption that the North Koreans would win and therefore "were not prepared to intervene on short notice." Delaying their major effort until the war reached the frontier "greatly shortened their lines of communications," important because of UN control of air and sea. Willoughby also foresaw political advantages for the Chinese:

> In the frontier area, fullest advantage can be taken of the extent to which world opinion already is conditioned to acts of aggression and regards identification of a few regiments on the wrong side of a border as something less than overt action. . . .

It will be much easier to ship-up [*sic*] support of public opinion in China for major military operations if immediate threat to the Manchurian border can be claimed, which sources believe will be done despite the belief that CCF leaders are aware that the UN forces have no intention of crossing the Manchurian border.

Other daily intelligence reports on the same days told of Chinese buildups in Manchuria and North Korea. Between November 4 and November 11 estimated enemy strength in front of the Eighth Army increased from 40,100 to 98,400 men.[12] Daily POW interrogations revealed new Chinese units crossing the frontier. On November 15 Willoughby warned that "approximately 300,000 seasoned Chinese Communists troops" were massed north of the Yalu between Antung and Manpojin,[13] a distance of eighty miles. Intelligence reports from Canton, in southern China, stated that "large quantities of artillery, small arms, ammunition and other military stores" were being shipped north.

Willoughby became increasingly worried as he read these reports.[14] He wrote on November 7:

> The Chinese Communists have already displayed their ability to infiltrate troops into Korea with comparative ease. Utilizing back roads and the cover of darkness, it is entirely possible that the CCF could secretly move . . . this readily available force into position south of the Yalu in preparation for a counteroffensive. Logistic support . . . should be relatively simple . . . since supply lines would be extremely short.

The CCF "possesses a reinforcement capability of considerable potency—a capability which . . . could present a serious threat to UN forces. . . ."

Much later POW interrogation reports revealed reasons for G-2's difficulty in counting Chinese infiltrators.[15] The CCF capacity for forced march was phenomenal by any standard. In one documented instance, three divisions marched from Antung, in the northwestern corner of Manchuria on the Yalu, 286 miles to an assembly area in eastern North Korea in sixteen to nineteen days; one division averaged 18 miles daily for eighteen days, over rough mountain roads. The Chinese soldier's "day" began at dark, around seven in the evening, and lasted until three the next morning. By first light, at five-thirty, he was to have dug a shelter, camouflaged all equipment, and eaten. During daylight hours only scouting parties moved, to seek bivouac areas for the next day. If a Chinese soldier left cover by day, he was to freeze in his tracks and remain motionless if an aircraft appeared. Officers had summary authority to shoot violators.

Thus during October and November the CCF moved some 300,000 men into North Korea, men motionless and camouflaged, invisible to aerial photographs and observers.

In another ominous report G-2 warned on November 16 that the Chinese and North Koreans had "greatly increased" their defensive capabilities the first two weeks of November, making them "much less vulnerable" to air and amphibious assault. Guerrilla activity had also intensified, with "well-planned and well-executed" operations by groups of up to 1,000 men. "Since these groups operate against vulnerable sections of UN supply routes, they can neither be ignored, nor left to newly-organized police units. UN forces which could be valuable as mobile strategic reserves are thus tied down in rear areas." If the UN offensive were resumed, the army would "probably be forced to concentrate overwhelming strength for each offensive." Communist air support and near-zero temperatures from December through February would "further handicap UN offensive operations."

The Chinese exuded all the signs of an enemy ready for renewed combat—signals discerned by General Willoughby's intelligence section in Tokyo, but ignored by MacArthur.

Walker Is Cautious

In the Eighth Army area General Walton Walker was wary about sending his troops back into an arena where they had been routed, especially because of the uncertainty of what the Chinese intended.[16] So he delayed resuming the offensive, resisting confident hurry-it-up demands from Tokyo. Walker wanted to ensure that his men were amply supplied, and their flanks protected. The first advance order was issued on November 6, when EUSAK was still regrouping below the Chongchon. It set a date for November 15. But Colonel Albert K. Stebbins, Jr., the EUSAK G-4, or logistics officer, complained. The Eighth Army needed 4,000 tons of supplies daily for an offensive. No such quantities were arriving. The November 15 deadline arrived, passed, was reset for November 20, then reset for November 24. Walker devoted inordinate attention to tactical details. He wanted the attack to be closely coordinated, with all units under EUSAK control at all times. His orders, wrote army historian Roy Appleman, reflected "a considerable degree of caution and a certain respect for the enemy forces." Walker had confidence in the mission; he could reach the Yalu. Yet in private talks with correspondents at his headquarters, he was not nearly so confident. He told at least one reporter that his hesitation in advancing past the Chongchon River—and his silence despite barbed cables from MacArthur and Almond—were the result of his knowing he might have to prepare for retreat. Similar precautions might have saved the Eighth Army during the First Phase Chinese Offensive.

Walker delayed his march at considerable professional risk. Friends in MacArthur's headquarters whispered that he had almost lost his command because of the Eighth Army's retreat before the Chinese. MacArthur had disliked Walker since the early days of the war. Although no one put the proposition directly, Walker knew he must launch the offensive as MacArthur planned, and win it as MacArthur planned, or his army career was over.

The Pentagon watched MacArthur's end-the-war offensive with trepidation. Matthew Ridgway, seasoned on the European battlefields of the Second World War, looked at the disposition maps daily and worried about Walker's "dangerously exposed" right flank. Walker's only protection on the right was unreliable ROK troops. Ridgway also disagreed with the concept of MacArthur's march:

> Although MacArthur described this movement toward the Yalu as an "attack" it was really no more than an advance to contact. It is not possible to attack an enemy whose positions are not known, whose very existence has not been confirmed, and whose forces are completely out of contact with your own.
>
> While many a field commander was convinced in his heart that strong forces of Chinese were lying in wait somewhere, and while one or two harbored definite doubts of the wisdom of moving blindly forward with flanks ignored and without liaison with friendly forces on either side, no one flinched at the job and many reflected the glowing optimism of the Commander in Chief.

The Dismayed Marines

In the X Corps zone, in eastern Korea, the 1st Marine Division heard the call for the renewed offensive with dismay. General Oliver Smith felt that Almond's plans for the march north "were based on the assumption that we were pursing a defeated North Korean Army. The intervention of the Chinese Communist Army was discounted."[17] Smith thought the more logical line of advance would be up the northeast coast, where the marines could rely upon naval support and use amphibious envelopment tactics against enemy strongholds. But Almond insisted that the zone to the left was "the more critical area of advance and where the strongest enemy resistance was likely to be encountered." Almond wanted the 1st Marines to have the assignment as the "most battle-worthy division in the Corps."

In further talks with Almond on the first days of November Smith had learned that the corps was "expected to push rapidly forward to the Manchurian border before winter set in and that thus we would not become involved in a campaign under winter conditions." Smith disagreed, but since it was apparent that X Corps "was fixed in its decision," he prepared for a winter campaign. The order went out to logistics units: Start gathering all the cold-weather gear you can find.

Smith had been feuding with Almond since early November. As did other generals in the theater, Smith saw Almond as an alter ego of MacArthur's; arguing with the X Corps commander was tantamount to arguing with CINCFE himself. But the fact that he belonged to another service gave Smith additional courage. In view of MacArthur's strained relations with the Marine Corps during the Second World War, that a division commander had stood up to Dugout Doug—the marines' name for MacArthur—would not harm Smith's career. In his arguments Smith by his own admission frequently stepped beyond the line of prudence. Nonetheless, when the first Chinese encounters ended, he obeyed orders and told his troops to begin moving toward the Chosin Reservoir once again. The first days of the march Almond came up to offer the marines his congratulations on earlier success. When he heard of the heroism of Captain Thomas E. Cooney—a company commander who, despite two wounds, continued fighting for a key hill—he decided to award the man a Silver Star on the spot. The lack of a medal did not deter the ebullient Almond. He scrawled an inscription on a slip of paper, "Silver Star Medal for Gallantry in Action—Almond," and pinned it on Cooney's jacket.[18]

As MacArthur planned the new drive, a volunteer patrol left Chinhung at noon on November 8 to scout for Chinese. Leaving the main supply route (MSR, to the marines), they walked some twenty-five miles through rugged countryside along the road, reached the plateau just southwest of Koto-ri and the reservoir—and found no sign of the enemy. The patrol leader, Lieutenant William F. Goggin, radioed that the route was clear, and the 3rd Battalion moved on through the Funchilin Pass into Koto.

They did so in jolly good humor, encountering no opposition whatsoever—save for a small bear who wandered into a company perimeter the night of November 9–10. A marine private, frightened from his sleeping bag by the intruder, swore earnestly the next morning the animal wore a hammer and sickle emblem. The bear's nationality aside, a few marine shouts sent him scurrying.

But the marine euphoria proved short-lived. The evening of November 10 Lieutenant Colonel Ray Davis bedded down his battalion alongside a river in the Koto plateau; the weather was so warm he bathed comfortably in the stream.[19] Two evenings later the temperature was sixteen degrees below zero, with a fierce wind. "When we got up in the morning," Davis said, "none of the vehicles would start. Troops had their noses turn white, big spots on them, and their fingers were numb. It was just an absolutely unbelievable change in the temperature in twenty-four hours." Colonel Alpha Bowser watched marines come off the line "just like zombies, the cold was so severe. Cold-weather fighting is perhaps the most miserable type," he said. "There is nothing you can compare it with, wet, heat or anything. There is a sort of paralysis . . . at times that sets in in extreme cold."[20] When the savage weather struck, "our men were not conditioned for it," conceded Colonel Homer Litzenberg, commander of the 7th Marine Regiment. "The doctors reported numerous cases where the men came down to the sick bay suffering from what appeared to be shock. Some of them would come in crying; some of them were extremely nervous; and the doctors said it was simply the sudden shock of the terrific cold when they were not ready for it."[21]

But the marines made swift adjustments.[22] They learned to fire weapons periodically, day and night, to keep them from freezing. Platoons set up "warming tents" with diesel stoves vented through exhaust pipes; hot pots of coffee and caldrons of soup steamed on the stoves day and night, so that men could come in and revive themselves after patrols or hours on the line. When not on patrol, men crawled into sleeping bags for warmth—the rule being that at least one rifleman had to stay awake in each firing position or foxhole in case of attack. Many marines nonetheless developed the large blisters and discolored skin areas symptomatic of frostbite. When frostbite was diagnosed, the men were ordered evacuated. (Days later many men were found to have remained on the front despite blackened toes, which they concealed from medics. Their excuse was uniform: They had "not wanted to leave buddies.")

General Almond's orders to the 1st Marines went through several mutations during the first days of November. First, the marines' sole mission was to advance west of the Chosin and then drive due north to Manchuria. Then came a modification; the first phase of the advance went so smoothly that Almond now wanted the marines to send a salient out toward the Fusen Reservoir, some fifty miles to the northeast of the Chosin, to test enemy defenses there. The 7th Army Infantry Division, under Major General David Barr, meanwhile, followed the marines up the road to Hagaru, then ventured onto another road running up the rugged east side of the Chosin Reservoir.

A marine reconnaissance patrol soon found a fundamental flaw in Almond's plan: No road existed around the Fusen Reservoir. The only route was farther to the west, where Barr's 7th Division was already moving. Given these facts by Smith, Almond told the marines to abandon the advance on the Fusen Reservoir. But almost immediately Almond had another idea. The marines' rapid advance convinced him no serious Chinese opposition faced X Corps. He had seen the wild mountain regions for himself, on reconnaissance overflights, and the marines had told about the poor condition of the rutted paths that passed for secondary roads. Surely no sizable Chinese force could be operating in such a forsaken country. The *real* fighting, he felt, would be in the Eighth Army area to the west, where the 24th Army Division had been mauled by the First Phase Chinese Offensive.

Almond's solution, put into formal order by MacArthur on November 15, drastically changed the marine mission.[23] The order acknowledged that the UN Command force of some 100,000 men was opposed by an equal number of 100,000 "enemy" (Chinese or North Korean, the order did not suggest) but said they could be neutralized by superior American air power. Nonetheless, the CCF had an estimated 140,000 troops available north of the Yalu for reinforcements. So Almond (and MacArthur) wanted the 1st Marine Division to come to the aid of the Eighth Army advance by diverting part of its force westward, to Mupyong-ni, then drive due north to the Yalu. The 1st Marines, in effect, would constitute a blocking force against any Chinese attempts to come in on the east flank of the Eighth Army.

Smith rebelled.[24] "I went to Almond and said, 'After all, we can't make a main effort in two directions. We've got one main effort, which is going up this road by the Chosin Reservoir to the Yalu, and here you are telling us to be prepared for a major attack out to the northwest.'" Smith thought the diversion downright silly. He reminded Almond that the army's 3rd Infantry Division had recently landed in Korea and suggested that it be assigned to protect the Eighth Army's flank.

In actuality, Smith was ready to halt the marine advance at its present positions and dig in and wait out the winter. He wanted the 1st Marines to hold only enough territory to ensure the security of the Hamhung-Hungnam-Wonsan area—that is, a beachhead on the coast. One visit to his men near the reservoir convinced Smith they would be pressed to survive in the frigid climate, much less mount an offensive.

Disquieting intelligence also continued to reach the 1st Marines about Chinese intentions. Although only stray Chinese soldiers could be found on the actual battlefield, marine pilots flying sorties to the north reported a steady flow of trucks moving across the Yalu into Korea. Sinuiju, the city just south of the frontier, was raked constantly with rocket fire and blasted with bombs. But the bombardment—and endless flames from burning buildings in the city—did not abate activity. Successive adjectives from pilot reports told of the magnitude of southbound traffic from China: "heavy, very heavy, tremendous, and gigantic."

But how could pieces be fitted into the overall puzzle? On November 8 a patrol had ventured into the Sinhung Valley, perhaps ten miles east of Koto, and found a Chinese soldier sleeping in a house. The soldier related what marine G-2 considered an incredible story from someone of his low rank. He said China had decided to commit twenty-four divisions to Korea. After study, analysts decided the story was a plant:

that a foot soldier would not have been entrusted with such strategic information. Intelligence was wrong. Unlike modern armies, the Chinese troop indoctrination (as G-2 discovered later) included tolerably accurate information of what troops were being committed and what they were expected to accomplish.

General Smith, as uncertain as anyone about what the Chinese might attempt, made a crucial (and lifesaving) decision on November 15. He evaded Almond's orders, and deliberately.[25] "What I was trying to do," he admitted years later, "was to slow down the advance and stall until I could pull the First Marines behind us and get our outfit together." He told advancing units to "take it easy, that we'd fix an objective every day." X Corps wanted him to proceed to the Yalu. That he would do, but at his own pace. But there came a time when the momentum of his advance carried Smith beyond the point of prudence. "I told Litzenberg not to go too fast; he didn't want to go over the [Toktong] Pass and down to Yudam-ni because we had this tremendous open flank. But the pressure was being put on to get going. Finally I had to tell Litzenberg to go on over and occupy Yudam-ni."

Smith, however, took care to inform marine headquarters in Washington of the intolerable situation into which he was being thrust.[26] On November 15 he wrote a long letter to General C. B. Cates, the marine commandant, which indicated he did not trust what information might be reaching Washington via Tokyo. Smith outlined his tactical situation, described the terrain in which he was operating, and explained how he was being careful to keep his command drawn up tightly, despite conflicting demands from Almond.

> Although the Chinese have withdrawn to the north, I have not pressed Litzenberg to make any rapid advance. Our orders still require us to advance to the Manchurian border. However, we are the left flank division of the Corps and our left flank is wide open.
>
> There is no unit of the Eighth Army nearer than eighty miles to the southwest of Litzenberg. When it is convenient, the Corps can say there is nothing on our left flank.
>
> If this were true, then there should be nothing to prevent the Eighth Army from coming abreast of us. This they are not doing. I do not like the prospect of stringing out a Marine division along a single mountain road for 120 air miles from Hamhung to the border. (The road mileage is nearer 200.) I now have two RCTs [regimental combat teams] on this road and when Puller is relieved by the Third Infantry Division I will close him up behind.

"What concerns me considerably," Smith continued, "is my ability to supply two RCTs in the mountains in winter weather. Snow, followed by a thaw and a freeze, will put out my road." A railway ran part of the route but halted at the start of the mountains. Beyond, along the Chosin

Reservoir to the border, "there is nothing but mountain road." Airdrops in winter would neither supply two RCTs nor provide for their evacuation. Even visiting the units by helicopter was difficult because of the weather, their wide dispersal, and the altitudes at which they operated. Then Smith made a direct criticism of General Almond and his staff of a type seldom seen in a military communiqué:*

> As I indicated to you when you were here [Cates had been to Korea earlier on an inspection tour] I have little confidence in the tactical judgment of the Corps or in the realism of their planning. My confidence has not been restored.
>
> Planning is done on a 1:1,000,000 map. We execute on a 1:50,000 map. There is a continual splitting up of units and assignment of missions to small units which puts them out on a limb.
>
> This method of operating appears to be general in Korea. I am convinced that many of their setbacks here have been caused by this disregard for the integrity of units and of the time and space factor.
>
> Time and again I have tried to tell the Corps commander that in a Marine division he has a powerful instrument, but that it cannot help but lose its full effectiveness when dispersed. Probably I have had more luck than the other division commanders in impressing my point.
>
> Someone in high authority will have to make up his mind as to our goal. My mission is still to advance to the border. The Eighth Army, eighty miles to the southwest, will not attack until the 20th. Manifestly, we should not push on without regard to the Eighth Army. We would simply get further out on a limb. If the Eighth Army push does not go, then the decision will have to be made as to what to do next. I believe a winter campaign in the mountains of North Korea is too much to ask of the American soldier or Marine, and I doubt the feasability [sic] of supplying troops in this area during the winter or providing for the evacuation of sick or wounded.

Despite these misgivings, Smith said the marines were attempting to prepare for their assigned mission. The road linking Hamhung and Hagaru was being improved to handle tanks and heavy vehicles, and construction of the Hagaru airstrip was under way. Smith claimed not to be pessimistic (although the text of his letter belied his assertion). "Our people are doing a creditable job," he said, "their spirit is fine, and they will continue to do a fine job." But he repeated his concern about his "wide open left flank" and his misgivings about "the prospect of stringing out a marine division along a single mountain road for 120 air miles from Hamhung to the border."**

*The criticisms are not in the official marine history of the Korean War. Smith retained the letter in his personal papers.

**Commenting on Smith's concerns to marine historians after the war, General Almond said he was "very mindful of the skepticism of General Smith" and said he sympathized with his viewpoint. "However," he said, "in my mind, there was always the assistance to be gained by air supply either drop or landing them [sic], and the counterpart of that, the evacuation to be expected by plane from the air field that we were to build."

The same day he wrote the pessimistic letter to Cates, Smith was visited by Rear Admiral Albert K. Morehouse, chief of staff to Admiral Turner Joy, the FEC naval commander. "Since I felt I was talking 'in the family,' " Smith related later, "I told him frankly of my concern over the lack of realism in the plans of the Corps and the tendency of the Corps to ignore the enemy capabilities when a rapid advance was desired. I found in my deals with the Army, particularly with the X Corps, that the mood was either one of extreme optimism or of extreme pessimism. There did not seem to be any middle ground."[27]

The next day, November 16, Smith was in Hungnam when he encountered Major General Frank Lowe, who was in Korea as a sort of minister without portfolio of his old friend the President to report on the performance of reserve and National Guard units. Lowe happened to have with him map overlays showing the disposition of the Eighth Army, documents he had obtained during a casual visit to the 1st Cavalry Division a few days earlier. Smith eagerly examined the overlays, for they contained his first concrete information of the exact whereabouts of the other half of the UN Command fighting only a few score miles from his own lines. "Strange as it may seem," Smith marveled later, "this major general of the army reserve, who was the personal representative of President Truman in Korea, was the only means of physical liaison between the X Corps and the Eighth Army. All other communication between these commands was by dispatch traffic through General Headquarters."[28]

Another dubious marine was Colonel Lewis "Chesty" Puller, commanding officer of the 1st Regiment.[29] On November 10, the anniversary of the founding of the Marine Corps, Puller used a captured North Korean sword to slice a 100-pound cake (trimmed with radishes and jelly in the absence of candles). In accordance with marine regulations, he read a short tribute on the history of the corps, then thrust it into his pocket and gave an impromptu (and somewhat pessimistic) speech to assembled troops:

Now that's complied with, and I want to tell you something straight. Just do one thing for me—write your people back home and tell 'em there's one hell of a damned war on out here, and that the raggedy-tailed North Koreans have been shipping a lot of so-called good American troops, and may do it again. Tell 'em there's no secret weapon for our country but to get hard, to get in there and fight.

I want you to make 'em understand: Our country won't go on forever, if we stay as soft as we are now. There won't be an America—because some foreign soldiery will invade us and take our women and breed a hardier race.

Later, in the privacy of his quarters, Puller wrote his wife that "only a terrible defeat will change our present system, which is leading us to disaster."

Smith took what precautions he could; he delayed movements as long as he could, short of direct insubordination, and he ensured that his division kept secure flanks and ample supplies. In essence he commanded a cocoon of troops, drawn tightly together, their lifeline the MSR (main supply route) back down the mountains to the coast.

By November 24—the day the "final drive" offensive was to begin— all three regiments of the 1st Marine Division were operating east of the Chosin Reservoir, and RCT 7 had secured Yudam, about four miles to the west of the reservoir. Like it or not—and their officers did not—the marines were set to strike for the Yalu.

Eighth Army Moves

In the western portion of Korea MacArthur's plan called for the Eighth Army to attack on a broad front, starting from a line roughly paralleling the Chongchon River. From west to east, EUSAK consisted of the U.S. I Corps, composed of the U.S. 24th Division, the British 27th Brigade, and the ROK 1st Division; the U.S. IX Corps, including the U.S. 2nd and 25th Divisions, and the Turkish Brigade; and the ROK II Corps, made up of the ROK 6th, 7th, and 8th Divisions. The U.S. 1st Cavalry Division stood in reserve to the rear, near Sunchon.

The array made General Walker uneasy. The Korean peninsula widens drastically past the Chongchon River line, meaning his line of advance had to stretch as it moved north and draw even farther away from the X Corps positions to the east. A few days before the advance began, patrols of EUSAK and X Corps attempted to link up at the line separating the commands; because of the terrain and other problems, they did not locate each other. EUSAK's concerns and uncertainties were felt even by the press.

To writer James Michener, covering the war for the *Reader's Digest,* the "gravest of all memories" was an exchange at a press briefing as the offensive began.[30] After a staff presentation, George Herman, a young radio reporter for the Columbia Broadcasting System, asked, "General, you said your patrols had established contact with elements on the left flank 'believed to be friendly.' Were they friendly elements?"

"We think so," replied the general.

"Don't you know?" Herman persisted.

"We think they must have been friendly," the general said.

"Haven't you any liaison with the left flank?"

"No. We're operating separately. But we're sure the elements must have been friendly."

The UN Command learned otherwise a few days later.

The first two days of the Eighth Army advance troops met minimal resistance. In the far west the 24th Division raced ten miles toward its objective of Chongju; the 2nd Division, in the center-right of the line, reached Kujang-dong, some ten miles from its starting point of Kunu-ri. But on the right flank progress of the three ROK divisions was slow. By the second day the South Koreans had moved only a few hundred yards from Tokchon, their kickoff point. The ROK's inability to move alarmed Major General Laurence Keiser, commander of the U.S. 2nd Division, for he found himself outstretching the troops supposedly protecting his right flank. Air observers then brought word that the enemy was widening a highway leading toward Tokchon.

"Goddamn it!" Keiser exclaimed. "That's where they're going to hit. That will be the main effort—off our flank and against ROK II Corps."[31]

Keiser was right. That night the CCF hit the western end of the Eighth Army front with sledgehammer force, driving the ROK 1st Division back for some two miles. Chinese probes rippled along the EUSAK line, as if searching out vulnerable ROK units. (The American 24th Division, in the far west, was not touched the first days of the offensive.)

The Chinese found their opening on November 25. Their attack was merciless. With a brassy clang of cymbals, the wail of bugles, and the shrill blasts of whistles, the Chinese swarmed down upon and over the hapless South Koreans. The first units, per Chinese strategy, slipped through the ROK lines and set up barriers blocking retreat routes. Then came the main mass of CCF troops, running through the ROK lines by the hundreds. The ROK soldiers, many of them recruits snatched from the streets of Seoul and farmyards only a few days earlier, proved no match for the hardened Chinese. They broke and ran, tossing rifles and other equipment aside in a frantic attempt at survival. Within hours Walker's flank protection vanished; three ROK divisions simply dissolved in the face of the Chinese attack.

The ROK debacle meant the 2nd Army Division now stood naked, on its right flank, to the Chinese, an advantage the CCF swiftly exploited. General Walker, scanning his maps, saw the Chinese intention. Should they be able to sweep under his army and drive west to the Yellow Sea, scores of thousands of UN troops would be isolated.

The brunt of the Chinese attack next fell on the 2nd Division, in the line of advance just to the west of the ROKs—specifically, B Company of the 9th Infantry Regiment, which had had as its first mission the seizure of Hill 219, a prominent ridge on the east bank of the Chong-chon River.[32] As true of most EUSAK units, Baker Company was a mixture of greenhorns and veterans; one rifleman, Corporal Walter K. Crawford, of South Boston, Virginia, was only seventeen years old. About one-third of the 129 men and officers were black (including the executive officer, Lieutenant Ellison C. Wynn); a dozen or so were ROKs.

The men of Baker Company groused as they ate corned beef hash for breakfast and sipped coffee from canteen cups; each time the regiment fought, they said, Baker was in the vanguard. Now once again they had the dirty assignment. Not that they expected much of a fight. Most men, in fact, had even thrown away their steel helmets, calling them cumbersome and heavy; besides, newly issued pile stocking caps provided more protection against the cold. Nor did they bother to carry much ammunition—an average of one grenade per man and as little as sixteen rifle rounds each. Trenching tools? Lost on the road or discarded. Tinned rations? Too heavy. Travel with an empty pack, and rely upon Korean bearers to bring up food (and bedrolls) later in the day. Field telephone? The only one available did not work (although there was a tenuous connection to the rear via the telephone wire of the artillery forward observer). Thus the makeup of a typical company in EUSAK's end-the-war offensive.

Hill 219 proved to be a series of low knobs covered with loose rock and thickets of brush. Baker's lead platoon walked unchallenged to within twenty-five yards of the top, only to be halted abruptly by a shower of Chinese grenades. During a daylong fire fight Baker Company suffered many casualties—including Captain William C. Wallace, who had part of his ear blown off by a mortar—but could not dislodge the Chinese from well-constructed positions.

The regimental commander, Colonel Charles C. Sloane, Jr., viewed the hot battle briefly and then radioed 2nd Division headquarters: "I think this is different; it may be the real thing; we had better watch it." Division disagreed.

That night the Chinese struck in full force, overrunning and half destroying the 9th Regiment's 3rd Battalion, on the far left, and isolating the 2nd Battalion on the banks of the Chongchon. For Baker Company, however, the war evolved to the defense of two small knobs on the side of Hill 219: fourteen men on one of them, forty or so on the other, facing ten, twenty times as many Chinese.

Chinese crept to foxholes within twenty feet of the larger group, led by Lieutenant Theodore J. Weathered, and heaved grenades up onto the knoll. The space was so tight the GIs could not avoid the grenades; they could only kick them away or pick them up and try to toss them back before they exploded. Weathered was to estimate later that sixty grenades hit the knoll during two hours; forty were pitched out again. Time and again a shrill whistle blast could be heard through the din of battle, and the Chinese would jump from the foxholes and attempt to overrun the knolls. So the Americans learned to hoard their scarce grenades until they heard the signal. At the sound of the whistle they would hurl grenades down the slope. The Chinese repeated their mistake a dozen times, and dead bodies piled up high enough on the slope to provide an extra defense shield.

When the fighting slackened momentarily, Weathered called up to Lieutenant Wynn, commanding the beleaguered smaller group about 150 yards distant. "Fall back on us," he yelled, "it's better here."

Wynn agreed. "Get ready to run and I'll cover you," he told the other men.

But the strapping black officer had no weapon. Undeterred, he stooped and picked up an armload of rocks and canned C rations. He stood in clear silhouette on the brink of the knob and hurled rocks and cans at Chinese heads no more than twenty-five feet away. The audacity of his bravery so startled the Chinese that they momentarily stopped firing. A GI crawled out of the perimeter and stood alongside Wynn, swinging his empty rifle like a club, ready to knock down anyone who rushed the lieutenant.

Not until everyone else had escaped from the knob did Wynn retreat. As a last act of defiance before retreating, the enlisted man with him hurled his rifle down the hill at the Chinese.

When Wynn turned to leave, a Chinese grenade exploded in the air next to his head, blowing the side of his face away. He nonetheless remained on the hill until air strikes chased away the Chinese late in the afternoon, refusing bandages or morphine. "Give it to the men who are down," he said. Wynn finally fainted from loss of blood and was carried away; he spent 117 days in the hospital.*

Baker Company started the twenty-six hours of brutal fighting with 129 men; when it ended, there were only 34 men left, half a dozen of them "walking wounded."

George Company of the 9th Regiment, meanwhile, went unmolested the first night of the fighting, although units all around its positions on the Chongchon River were cut to pieces.[33] But at dawn on November 26 its turn came, and under circumstances that let George Company draw first blood. At daylight riflemen of the company were dug in along a high hill beside the river, shivering in the fifteen-degree cold and

*In my opinion, Lieutenant Wynn earned a Medal of Honor during the fight. But the paper work for such an award is voluminous, what with required eyewitness statements and recommendations from superior officers. Wynn's division was so battered during the next few days that not enough men survived to put him through for the medal. But he did win the Silver Star.

watching morning mists rise off the water. Master Sergeant William Long, yawning and stretching, saw a group of men moving along a creek below him, making no effort at concealment. Long watched them idly, thinking they must be Americans to be moving openly in such territory. But he kept watching them, and when they got to within 300 yards, he realized what he was seeing. "Chinks!" he yelled to his platoon. "They're Chinks."

The first burst of rifle and BAR fire knocked down about half to the ground; the survivors scrambled for cover in rice paddies and behind rocks in the creek bed. The company commander, Captain Frank E. Munoz, called up a tank. In five minutes George Company killed seventy men and captured twenty others.

That night, however, the Chinese fell upon George Company with a vengeance, driving both it and Fox Company from hills along the river. The Chinese attacked in unyielding waves, rifles and submachine guns blazing, hurling an apparently unlimited supply of hand grenades, overrunning American positions, and bayoneting men in their foxholes. In less than twenty minutes that evening, George Company lost more than seventy men killed.

The Chinese took as prisoners a private named Smalley and two ROKs attached to the division and marched them to a rear area. The interrogator, an officer who spoke perfect English, snapped his fingers, and the Koreans were marched away a few feet and shot down.

The officer turned back to Smalley. "We know all about you," he said, and proceeded to describe George Company and the names of its officers. "Now go back and tell your commander not to use fire bombs— napalm—against us. Your outfit is over there," he said, gesturing across the river. "Take off."

Expecting to be shot in the back, Smalley bolted for the river and managed to find remnants of his unit. He was one of many infantrymen captured and quickly released by the Chinese, apparently for propaganda purposes. But in Smalley's instance the tactic misfired. "Gimme a machine gun," he told Captain Munoz, his company commander. "I saw what they did to those ROKs."

Not every soldier was as determined a fighter as the spunky Smalley. During the retreat Munoz heard sobbing sounds coming from a shabby wooden shack along the river. Curious, he found a terrified American soldier crouched on the floor, tears rolling down his face.

"What're you doing in here?" Munoz asked.

"I don't know—I don't know," the soldier stammered between sobs.

"Come with me."

"Captain, I don't want to go out there—"

Munoz, impatient, grabbed the man by the arm and pulled him to his feet. "Get your ass on one of those tanks!" he ordered. The man obeyed.

Munoz gathered up other stragglers and wounded and made his way to the river. A group of Chinese rushed him. He drew his .45 pistol and shot down five of them. His party escaped to safety.*

Eighth Army in Disarray

November 26 was the day the Eighth Army began falling apart. No longer was the UN Command directing a coordinated offensive; now the war was a series of company-sized minibattles, with companies fighting alone and with no hope of reinforcement, flanked on every side by the onrushing Chinese, cut off from contact with superior headquarters. Nor could EUSAK stabilize the situation even long enough to bring its superior firepower into play. Author T. R. Fehrenbach, who commanded a unit in the 2nd Division (and also did a major study of the Korean War), noted, "Unable to maneuver where its wheels could not go, unable to see or communicate in these hills, the United States Army was being bitten to death rather than smashed down by numbers."

The magnitude of the 2nd Division's defeat came home to its officers in midafternoon of November 26. Colonel George Peploe, commander of the 38th Infantry Regiment, was holding the division's right flank in supposed coordination with the ROK divisions farther to the east. He looked from his command post to see an entire ROK regiment bolting through American lines. Their commander, his division shattered by the Chinese, had told his men to flee to the American zone to save their lives.

Peploe telephoned General Keiser, the 2nd Division commander. "I've got a whole ROK regiment coming into my area. What the hell shall I do with these people?"

Irritated at what must have sounded like a useless question, Keiser answered with a roar. "Take command of 'em and use 'em, dammit!"

Attempting to plug the sudden gap in the right of his front, General Walker rushed in the 5,000-man Turkish Brigade, which had been in the country only a few days. (The historian S. L. A. Marshall likened the maneuver to "applying an aspirin bottle cork to a bunghole in a beer barrel."[34]) The Turks had not been briefed; despite their obvious need for close coordination with the 2nd Division, no American advisers were attached to their unit; they were simply tossed into battle.

Within hours, however, came news of a stunning Turkish victory:[35] Meeting the "onrushing Chinese" for the first time, they had held their

---

*During the Chinese offensive Lou Cioffi of CBS received a cable from Fred Friendly, producer of the *Hear It Now* radio show. "Very much desire sound of Chinese bugles before attack." Cioffi wired back, "Request at once send one mile microphone cable."

ground and won a "bloody battle" at bayonet point and taken "hundreds of prisoners" as well. Second Division intelligence dispatched an interpreter, Lieutenant Sukio Oji, to interrogate the prisoners. He found them to be hapless ROKs who had blundered into the Turkish lines fleeing their own positions near Takchon. The dead "Chinese" were all South Koreans.

There was no mistaken identity the next day, November 27, when the Turks ran headlong into a vast Chinese force at the village of Wawon. Clear details of exactly what happened were never known. Regardless, the Turks fought, and most of them died. According to some reports, the officers threw their hats on the ground, marking a point beyond which they would not retreat, and "died upon their fur." Only a couple of Turkish companies survived the fight, and in much battered fashion.

MacArthur's offensive clearly had been halted. General Walker's goal was no longer that of reaching the Yalu. He must now try to save the Eighth Army from total destruction.

CHAPTER FIFTEEN

The Marines Escape a Trap

In the X Corps area, meanwhile, the 1st Marine Division in late November continued its cautious climb through snow and ice around the west shores of the Chosin Reservoir.[1] The Chinese Communist intervention notwithstanding, General Edward Almond still expected the marines to strike cross-country and link up with the Eighth Army to the west. As the march began, the troops were strung along more than forty miles of virtually impassable roads. At the head of the column, at Yudam, some five miles west of the middle portion of the reservoir, were two reinforced regiments—Colonel Homer Litzenberg's 7th and Colonel Ray Murray's 5th. Fourteen miles to the south (twenty by road) a reinforced battalion held Hagaru, at the southern tip of the reservoir. Most of the 1st Regiment, commanded by Colonel Chesty Puller, was yet another eleven miles south, at Koto. At Chinhung, ten miles south of Koto, a battalion commanded by Lieutenant Colonel Donald Schmuck defended the road where it began its sharp ascent into the mountains.

The marines did not find Yudam much of a prize when they moved into it late in the afternoon of November 26. Artillery shells had shattered most of the houses, and only a few miserably hungry and cold Korean civilians huddled in the ruins, unwilling or unable to flee to avoid the fighting. The first night the temperature dropped to seventeen degrees below zero, and marines made unfunny jokes about an "Ice Bowl." North winds screamed off the frozen reservoir and lashed at men huddled in tents and shallow holes on the valley floor and the adjacent hills.

Physically Yudam occupied the center of a broad valley surrounded by five large ridges, named in relation to their direction from the village: North, Northwest, Southwest, South, and Southeast. Each began at the rim of the village and extended several thousand yards in a snarl of peaks, spurs, and draws. A finger of the Chosin Reservoir poked toward Yudam between the North and Southeast ridges. The other four corridors leading from the village were highway routes.

The marine mission was to strike through the hills to the west for Mupyong, some fifty-five miles distant. As senior officer present, Litzenberg presided over a staff planning meeting that began at ten o'clock the night of November 27, in a windblown tent that offered little shelter to the officers huddled there. He began with disquieting news. The previous day three soldiers had been captured from the CCF 60th Division. Under interrogation, they said that the CCF 58th, 59th, and 60th divisions had reached the Yudam area on November 20. The prisoners, enlisted men, said the Chinese strategy was to wait until the two marine regiments had passed, then move south and southeast of Yudam and cut the main supply route (MSR). Both division and corps intelligence discounted the report because of its low-level source, although Chinese enlisted POWs in the past had proved markedly accurate in their information. G-2 felt that the CCF would continue to withdraw to the west and that the main battle would come in the hills outside Yudam. So division planning proceeded on this basis.

As subsequent captured documents proved, the enlisted men were correct. The CCF IX Field Army had secretly moved twelve divisions from Manchuria into the Chosin area. The commander, General Sung Shin-lun, had been commanding troops since his graduation from the Whampoa Military Academy at age seventeen and had headed a regiment during the Long March of 1934–35. His force was to carry out the eastern end of the overall CCF offensive. He was to move down the gap separating EUSAK and X Corps and then wheel east toward the coast, cutting off the 100,000-odd Americans and ROKs of X Corps. He would overwhelm the 7th Infantry Division force on the east side of the reservoir, then pick off the isolated 1st Marines. The Chinese apparently recognized the marines as their most potent foe. Before the battle the Chinese Command circulated thousands of copies of a pamphlet, *The Bloody Path*, by a Soviet Navy captain named G. Doidzhashvili, which painted a vile picture of the marines' past history and their presence in Korea:[2]

When in the summer of 1950 the American imperialist marauders . . . provoked the bloody holocaust in Korea, the Wall Street house-dog General MacArthur demanded that the American so-called "Marines" be immediately placed at his disposal. This professional murderer and inveterate war criminal intended to throw them into battle as quickly as possible for the purpose of inflicting, as it seemed to him then, a final blow on the Korean people.

In putting forward such a demand, MacArthur proceeded from the fact that U.S. "Marine" units have been trained more than any other type of American forces for the waging of the unprecedentedly brutal and inhuman, predatory war against the freedom-loving heroic Korean people.

It was precisely to U.S. Marines that the Ober-bandit MacArthur addressed the words: "A rich city lies ahead of you, it has much wine and tasty morsels. Take Seoul and all the girls will be yours, the property of the inhabitants belongs to the conquerors and you will be able to send parcels home."

The diatribe charged the marines with a "bloody trail of crimes against humanity" over a period of decades and called them a "pack of despoilers."

During this propagandistic buildup the Chinese were careful to stay out of sight. Aerial reconnaissance north of the reservoir showed no signs of any great troop masses, a tribute, once again, to the Chinese skill of camouflage and night movement. But Litzenberg knew the Chinese were in the area, and he took no chances.[3] He wanted strong patrols mounted on South and Southwest ridges and in the valley between them, for therein was the vital road link to Hagaru. If the MSR should be cut, both regiments would be endangered. The marines had managed to maneuver only one heavy tank, a Pershing, into Yudam, so heavy weaponry was limited.

Litzenberg's battle plan called for the 2nd Battalion of the 5th Marines, commanded by Lieutenant Colonel Harold S. Roise, to lead the attack west, the immediate objective being the peaks of Northwest and Southwest ridges and the westward road between them, a distance of about one and one-half miles. The 7th Marines would meanwhile provide perimeter defense for Yudam and be prepared to follow the 5th Marine attack. With this flank protection Litzenberg felt Roise could concentrate more strength for his drive through the low ground.

Litzenberg knew the plan contained a flaw, one beyond his control. The order sending the marines west in effect was an attempted envelopment and relied upon the assumption that the "holding force," the Eighth Army, would keep the enemy force from escaping. But when the attack began on the morning of November 27, EUSAK was already falling back; within twenty-four hours, it was in full retreat. Still, the marines had their orders from General Almond, and nothing could be done but to follow them.

The morning of November 27 frosted marines climbed from their sleeping bags and shelters and stamped their feet and clapped their mittened hands to restore circulation. They thawed field rations over oil fires—they knew by now that eating frozen food caused severe gastrointestinal distress—and warmed their weapons so that the actions would work (the hair dressing Wild Root cream oil, one ingenious trooper discovered, made a good improvised gun oil). Shortly after eight o'clock the companies began moving—one contingent to the west, down the crude road leading between Northwest and Southwest ridges and onto the slopes flanking it; the other, to the hills to the north and south of the hamlet for flank protection.

The northernmost company, How, of the 3rd Battalion, moved swiftly and by midmorning had seized its objective, Hill 1403, just behind the terminal height of Northwest Ridge, without opposition. To the south, George Company, commanded by Captain Thomas E. Cooney—Almond's "paper Silver Star" still in his pack—gained the peak of Southwest Ridge within minutes without opposition, then came under heavy small-arms fire from enemy troops on another high peak some 500 yards away, too distant to be a real threat, but nonetheless a nuisance.

The 5th Regiment's 2nd Battalion, assigned to drive down the floor of the valley between the two ridges, had considerably more trouble. Almost immediately after leaving the Yudam camp, the lead company —Fox, commanded by Captain Uel D. Peters—encountered heavy small-arms fire and then a series of sturdy but unmanned roadblocks. Covered by a mortar barrage, Fox Company veered off the road overland to hit at the north flank of the CCF positions, while Dog Company, of the 5th Battalion, continued along the road. Strong frontal fire finally brought both advances to a halt in midafternoon. Because of the swiftness with which night came, Lieutenant Colonel Roise ordered the troops to halt and dig in their defenses. The first day's march had covered a bare 1,500 yards of the 55 miles in the marines' attack mission.

Major John Hopkins, Roise's executive officer, produced a small flask of brandy in the battalion command post and carefully poured drinks into two canteen cups. "It's my birthday, Hal," he told Roise. "I bummed this from the doc."[4]

"To your health," Roise replied.

"To the longest fifty-five miles we'll ever travel—if we get there," Hopkins toasted.

To the south, Easy Company of the 2nd Battalion, commanded by Captain Samuel Jaskilka, set up positions on the south slopes of Southwest Ridge, his mission to protect the battalion rear. The terrain was awful—a narrow north-south corridor dotted with a few huts and some dwarfed trees and brush. A frozen stream ran up the middle of the draw. Jaskilka directed his troops in setting up his defensive perimeter. He was soon ready. He had a clear field of fire, and there was no cover for any Chinese who might appear.

Unbeknownst to both the marines and the CCF, the Chinese had already committed a tactical blunder that likely cost them the chance to wipe out the two regiments at Yudam. Had the CCF defenders fallen back along the road, say for two to three miles, the marines would have been drawn so far away from the Yudam base that their encirclement would have been hopeless. Instead, the Chinese had resisted the first day of the marine advance, and gains were modest—one of the few times, perhaps, in military history that "failure" to accomplish an objective actually proved to be a blessing.

When dusk came at around six o'clock, the mass of the marines had moved off the valley floor and into the hills: ten understrength rifle companies on the high grounds; two battalions of the 5th Regiment in the valley near the village; and two rifle companies, Charlie and Fox, of the 7th Regiment in isolated positions along the road to Hagaru. Fox was especially isolated: seven miles from Hagaru on one side, two mountainous miles from Charlie Company on the other. On North Ridge, two companies of the 7th Marines—Dog and Easy—sat on separate peaks with a gaping 500-yard saddle separating them. In marine parlance, their flanks were "hanging in the air," with no contact save an occasional patrol. The two companies' combined front stretched some two miles. Lesser gaps marred the line all the way around the perimeter.

One advantage the marines did possess was awesome supporting arms. Some four dozen howitzers—thirty 105 mm and eighteen 155 mm—were massed in the south end of the Yudam plain; there were 75 mm recoilless rifles and 4.2-inch mortars as well. But the ammunition dumps contained only about three days' supplies, and Litzenberg was not confident about bringing more trucks up the road. In any event, the marines were ready for the night.

When they tried to describe the cold later—be it to a war correspondent the next week, in a letter home the next month, in an interview three decades later—the marines, to a man, had to grope for words. "It was impossible," said one former sergeant, "to wear enough clothes to keep warm, much less comfortable. You were bundled so heavily, what with the gloves and the parka and the long john underwear and the hoods and what all, that you were bound to generate some body sweat. What happened, the minute you stopped moving around, it would turn to ice, right inside your damned clothes. Ever touch a piece of cold metal out of doors on a winter morning? Well, imagine trying to keep friendly with an M-one or a carbine. That steel was ice; put bare flesh on it, and you stuck, and the only way to get loose was to lose some skin. One time my *mouth* literally froze shut, my spittle mixed up with my whiskers."[5] The Marine Corps had spent millions of research dollars on a special cold-weather shoepac, but these boots offered no comfort when a man was immobilized for hours in twenty-below-zero weather. As marine historian Lynn Montross wrote, "Perspiration-soaked feet gradually became transformed into lumps of biting pain."

So, too, for weapons, especially the complex carbine and Browning automatic rifle (BAR). Men needed them to survive, yet in many the mechanisms froze so solidly they could not function. "I learned earlier in the campaign that in a real tight spot, you could break loose the action by pissing on it," said a young private, Brenton Case. "But, hell, how much water do you carry around with you? You do it once, you're done for the night, and even that freezes up again after a while."[6]

Thus the level to which the United States Marine Corps was forced for its own protection—freezing men crouched in holes on windswept Asian hills, their technology dependent upon the amount of urine in a private's bladder.

In the darkness, the Chinese moved. The assault battalions of the 79th and 89th CCF divisions drew the assignment to hit the two below-strength regiments in and around Yudam. Another division, the 59th, meanwhile had marched miles to the south, relying upon the gap between X Corps and EUSAK, and moved into position to strike at the MSR between South Ridge and the Toktong Pass, hoping to cut the road between Hagaru and Yudam. Three Chinese divisions against two American regiments, and the Chinese carried an advantage even greater than their three-plus to one numerical superiority: MacArthur's announcement a few days earlier told them exactly where the marines intended to go. Thus they could attack at times and places of their own choosing.

In the first hours of darkness small Chinese patrols made darting forays at the American lines, as if confirming weak points and looking for gaps. The occasional chatter of a Chinese voice, or of feet shuffling over the snow—the Chinese must have suffered; they wore flimsy canvas shoes with rubber soles—broke the silence.

A few minutes after ten o'clock the entire Yudam Valley errupted with fury. Bugles blared attack signals, mortar shells thumped into the American lines, Chinese soldiers suddenly stood up and hurled grenades at point-blank range, while others fired submachine guns.

Within minutes the war was a series of small unit actions, each with its own vignette of bravery and horror, war at its most primitive.

In the East Company area, Sam Jaskilka ordered his men to hold fire until the last possible minute: He had asked battalion for illumination mortar rounds, to light up the sector through which the Chinese were approaching. The light-providing rounds did not come; luckily, a machine-gun fire ignited a hut some 200 yards in front of Easy's positions. The valley was full of Chinese, who kept advancing through the flickering light, shooting-gallery targets for machine guns. (The next morning

Jaskilka counted more than 300 enemy bodies, some within 15 feet of his positions. He counted until he had walked out 100 yards. He dared not go farther, but he could see still more bodies farther away. "Easy Alley" someone called the defensive position he had chosen. Little else was "easy" at Yudam that night.

To Jaskilka's left, the Chinese found a gaping hole between Easy and Fox companies and poured through it en masse, driving toward Roise's command post and threatening to cut the road. A private first class, John Meade, took the initiative in forming a party to plug the hole.[7] He got half a dozen or so other men into positions where they could pour fire at the oncoming Chinese; when ammunition supplies were exhausted, he stumbled through snow to the company dump for more. Three times he made the trip carrying a load that would have staggered a man on a dry level field on a spring day. Meade would run down the line, dropping clips of ammunitions and grenades to other marines, then stand and fire himself. The fourth trip a bullet caught him in the leg, a wound so agonizing that buddies had to hold him to the ground while a corpsman treated him. The next day, when the attack had been broken, Meade was credited with having killed fifteen of the seventy-five Chinese piled outside the company's lines.

Across the valley to the north the Chinese assault struck first at How Company of the 3rd Battalion, deployed in an arc across the hills commanding the road leading out of the valley. How Company stood absolutely alone, something which the Chinese quickly discovered and exploited. Captain Leroy M. Cooke, the commanding officer, was killed in the first minutes of the attack; all save one of his officers were wounded. The company held, broke, held again. The Chinese called in reinforcements, who stumbled across the shell-torn corpses of earlier casualties to rush against How Company again and again. How fought back, but about four in the morning battalion officers decided continued resistance would be futile. How was ordered back into the main valley, leaving hundreds of dead Chinese in its wake. But the Chinese now held Hill 403, which gave them a commanding position at the north of the Yudam Valley. The marines appeared caught in a tightening vise.

And a bloody one. Easy Company of the 7th Marines (a different unit from Jaskilka's Easy Company, part of the 5th Marines) arrived late at the battle scene, its men gaunt and frostbitten, exhausted from the long trek up the mountain road. They had time for only a few hours' sleep on November 27 before taking up positions on the perimeter of Hill 1282, on North Ridge. The commander, Captain Walter Phillips, put two platoons on the summit and the third on a spur that dipped back toward Yudam. The marines put trip flares on the slopes below them and dug in.

The first Chinese attack was little more than a harassing action, with defenders easily beating back assault teams of submachine gunners and grenadiers. There was a period of silence, and Phillips remarked to another officer, "They thought they were coming after a single platoon, but they hit an entire company. They'll be back, and with more." He was right. Around midnight a weird cacophony of whistle shrills and bugle blasts cleaved the silence; under the din could be heard the crunch-crunch of thousands of feet crossing the snow. First Lieutenant John Yancey, a platoon leader, pleaded for illuminating mortars and artillery cover; none was available. Yancey, a gruffly profane man, already wore a Navy Cross won at Guadalcanal.[8] A reservist, he was plucked away from his liquor store in Little Rock, Arkansas, when the war began. The day he went ashore at Inchon—he heard days later— his wife had a baby. Like the other reservists in the 1st Marine Division (about half the total strength), he did not consider himself a professional military man. So Yancey and other marines waited and listened, and when the first shadows of an approaching Chinese could be seen in the darkness, they pulled the wires igniting the trip flares. Before them stretched oncoming rows of Chinese, at least four ranks before they vanished into the dim beyond the range of the flares. The Chinese sang unintelligibly, and they chanted, in English: "Son of a bitch, Marine, we kill! Son of a bitch, Marine, you die!" For two hours they charged, into the face of a cutting barrage of machine-gun fire and grenades. Some fell within ten feet of the marine lines. The marine casualties were heavy. Rifle slugs hit Captain Phillips in the shoulder and leg, but he refused evacuation. Grenade shrapnel slashed John Yancey's nose, and he gagged on blood, scarcely able to breathe. He, too, stayed in line.

About two in the morning the Chinese abandoned the attack, leaving behind what one marine called a "mat of human wreckage"—more than 200 dead, or almost every man in two companies. The marines had held Hill 1282.

But the Chinese came again, and in renewed force, two hours later, throwing squad after squad against two platoons of tired and desperate marines. Reinforcements hurried up from Yudam, climbing icy slopes in darkness and a minus-twenty-degree temperature. This time the Chinese swept through the American lines, and individual soldiers fought individual battles with rifle butts and bayonets. John Yancey, his nose wound still gushing blood, tried to form a defensive line around the company command post. A grenade exploded inches in front of his face, and a fragment ripped a horrible wound in the roof of his mouth. He continued fighting. So did Walter Phillips, already twice wounded. According to Andrew Geer, Phillips rushed toward the Chinese, flinging grenades on the dead run and shouting, "Hold on, men, this is Easy Company!" He snatched a rifle from the snow and thrust the bayonet into the ground. "We hold here." A few seconds later a burst of small-arms fire killed him.

Easy Company was now reduced to a handful of men. Lieutenant Raymond O. Ball, the executive officer, assumed command, although he was already immobilized by two wounds; moments later he was hit several more times, lapsed into unconsciousness, and died.

The redoubtable Yancey by now had only nine men left in his platoon, and he spurted blood with every breath. Coughing through the blood in his throat, trying to rally a counterattack, he blurted, "Gung ho, Marines, gung ho!"

One of the men who heard him was a rifleman named Stanley Robinson, who had been ordered to the aid station earlier that night with severely frostbitten feet. When Robinson heard his unit was endangered, he limped back to his position, his feet leaving splotches of blood in the snow. He heard Yancey's call, and he answered it. "Gung ho!" he roared, and the small band of men rushed up the hill toward the advancing Chinese, bayonets fixed and rifles blazing. A Chinese bullet hit Yancey in the face. This time he was blinded, and he sank to his knees. Incredibly he continued crawling toward the front, thrusting his rifle before him. But Easy Company could fight no longer. The Chinese swept over Hill 1282. They now had another open path to Yudam. The circle was drawing tighter around the two marine regiments.

To the east, on Hill 1240, was a repetition of Easy Company's valor-marked tragedy, this time with Dog Company of Captain Milton A. Hull the victim. Dog Company held, broke, counterattacked, broke again, and finally was smashed by overwhelming numbers of Chinese. When dawn came, Hull had been wounded several times, and he had only sixteen men left in fighting condition. The Chinese stood in front of him, on higher ground; on both his flanks; and on the slopes to his rear.

Dawn came on November 28 with an eerie silence. The Chinese still held the high ground they had seized during the night. However, to escape American air strikes, they went to cover, their camouflage making them invisible in the snow-covered hills and ravines.

General Oliver P. Smith had spent the night at Hagaru, hearing battle reports from Colonel Litzenberg over a squawky radio net.[9] Messages from western Korea told of the continued disaster befalling the Eighth Army. He reported the 1st Marine Division plight to Almond but by midmorning had heard nothing of substance in reply. To Smith's surprise, "No word was received from the X Corps as to any change in the plan"; that meant the 1st Marines should continue their drive west from Yudam. Smith realized the utter absurdity of any such attempted advance. "Under the circumstances, I considered it unwise to continue offensive operations. We were now engaged in a fight for our lives and it was necessary to assume the defensive at all points until the situation clarified." Acting on his own, Smith ordered the 5th and 7th regiments to consolidate their present positions—that is, to dig in at Yudam—and wait further instructions.

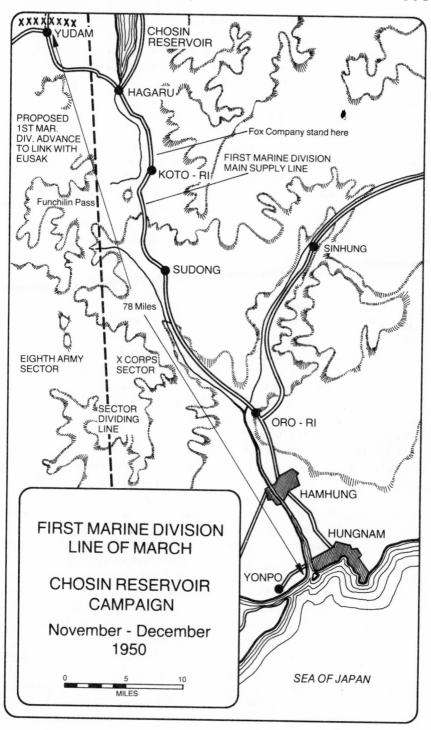

XXXXXXXX
YUDAM

CHOSIN
RESERVOIR

HAGARU

PROPOSED
1ST MAR.
DIV. ADVANCE
TO LINK WITH
EUSAK

Fox Company stand here

FIRST MARINE DIVISION
MAIN SUPPLY LINE

KOTO - RI

Funchilin Pass

SINHUNG

SUDONG

78 Miles

EIGHTH ARMY
SECTOR

X CORPS
SECTOR

SECTOR
DIVIDING
LINE

ORO - RI

HAMHUNG

HUNGNAM

FIRST MARINE DIVISION
LINE OF MARCH

CHOSIN RESERVOIR
CAMPAIGN

November - December
1950

YONPO

SEA OF JAPAN

0   5   10
MILES

"Damned Sorry for Those Chinamen"

News that the marines were in trouble flashed around the world.[10] At the marine training center at Camp Del Mar, California, an officer rushed into the office of Brigadier General Merrill Twining, the commander.

"General," he exclaimed, "a flash has come over the radio that the Chinese have the First Marine Division surrounded."

Twining casually looked up from his desk work. "All I can say, young man, is that I'm damned sorry for those Chinamen."

Late in the day on November 27 Smith finally did receive some orders from Almond's headquarters.[11] He was to bring one of his regiments back to Hagaru "to rescue the army outfit east of the reservoir." He could not believe what he heard. "My God," he exclaimed, "at that time we were being attacked by three CCF divisions ourselves. . . . It was manifest that we were up against a massive force. But we got no orders from the corps for two days to actually withdraw, so we couldn't do anything but defend, as I wouldn't withdraw without permission from higher authorities."

In Smith's view both Almond and MacArthur and their staffs were paralyzed. "Every four hours we sent in a report [to X Corps] of what was going on, but apparently they were stunned; they just couldn't make up their minds that the Chinese had attacked in force. . . . They just had to reorient their thinking."

Not until late on November 28 was Smith ordered to withdraw all his troops to Hagaru and "advance" to the coast. "That took them two days to figure out," he said disgustedly.

The order to draft plans for pulling the two regiments finally came to the field desk of Colonel Alpha Bowser, the division G-3, who in turn handed it to his executive officer,[12] Colonel Joseph L. Winecoff. "My God," Winecoff said, "I am going to have to go find a staff manual. It never even occurred to me that the Marine Corps would be involved in a retrograde or a withdrawal-movement."

Neither did General Smith. After finishing the plan, Bowser and Winecoff took it to Smith, whose CP was in an abandoned Korean hut. During the discussion someone used the word "retreat."

"Retreat" is not a term to be bandied about a marine command post, and Smith would hear no more of it. What was happening, he told his officers, was that "we are going to seize our own MSR. This is not really a retreat, because in every case we must attack."

The next day a British correspondent asked Smith for help on an article he was writing.[13] Should he call the marine movement a retreat or a withdrawal? "I pointed out to him that since we were completely surrounded, we could neither retreat nor withdraw but had to fight our way out." The press quote that eventually emerged—which Smith did not challenge—was: "Retreat, hell, we are simply attacking in another direction."

Ordeal on Fox Hill

Retreat or advance, one marine unit beyond the aid of General Smith or anyone else on the night of November 27–28—and for several tortured days and nights thereafter—was Fox Company of the 2nd Battalion of the 7th Regiment, augmented by heavy machine gun and 81 mm mortar sections to a strength of 240 men, about 50 more than the line marine company.[14] Commanded by Captain William E. Barber, Fox drew a perilous mission—to hold positions over the Toktong Pass, on the main supply route between Yudam and Hagaru, in an attempt to keep it open for the withdrawal that senior officers knew was now imperative. The Chinese had already cut the MSR in two places between the hamlets, but at points where Litzenberg felt they could be driven back. Holding Toktong Pass, however, was essential; if the Chinese gained this key high ground, two marine regiments would likely perish. Another unit, Charlie Company, of the same battalion, had already been driven from the Toktong area by overwhelming Chinese attacks; at one point enemy soldiers were placing grenades in socks and throwing them at the marines two at a time. The few survivors were withdrawn.

Fox Company did not have the option of withdrawal. Barber's orders were to hold the hill to the last man.

Fox Hill—as it came to be called in honor of the men defending it—was harsh terrain even by the demanding standards of eastern Korea. The hill ran steeply down toward the roadway, then ended abruptly in a 10-foot vertical cliff. A couple of flimsy huts stood between the cliff and the roadway. Small trees covered the lower slopes, changing to scattered brush nearer the top. From its highest point, Fox Hill fell away in a saddle some 900 yards long which one marine likened to a "swaybacked roof with steeply sloping sides"; the saddle eventually connected to a boulder-strewn ridge which lay outside Fox Company's perimeter. Barber did not like the looks of the saddle, for it formed a natural avenue of approach for the Chinese, who might sneak over from the unoccupied ridge. But with so much real estate to cover, and so few men, Barber had no choice but to close as tightly as he could.

Barber placed the 3rd Platoon, led by First Lieutenant Robert C. McCarthy, on the summit of the hill, facing north. The 1st Platoon, commanded by First Lieutenant John M. Dunne, tied in on the right flank; the 2nd, under Lieutenant Elmer G. Peterson, on the left. The headquarters section and a rocket squad were on the reverse slope. Barber placed his CP and the mortar sections at the base of the hill along the road. The layout resembled a reversed horseshoe, with Barber's contingent closing the gap at the bottom. Barber had further orders to send out security patrols during the daytime to check CCF attempts to breach the MSR.

As elsewhere in the 1st Marine Division, night brought cold even more numbing than that endured during the day. Officers were not completely satisfied with the position, but defending Fox Hill properly would have required an entire battalion. And the ground was so solid that marines could chop only meager holes for protection. As they settled in for the night, every man there expecting a Chinese attack before dawn, Lieutenant McCarthy remembered a fragment of a line from an old training lecture: "Moonlight favors the defenders."[15] Perhaps, he thought. But whatever advantage he obtained from the moon was offset by what sub-zero weather did to one's hearing: Either you kept your ears covered, or they froze. Deaf sentries, he thought. Half sentries . . . no ears. Only eyes. That sure as hell didn't favor the defender!

As the night wore on, men could hear the ferocious fire fights around Yudam, but nothing was seen or heard around Fox Company. Indeed, the night became so still that around midnight McCarthy roused out his squad leaders and admonished them to be more alert, their numbness notwithstanding.

At two-thirty o'clock the ridge at the end of the saddle literally came afire with a continuous blaze of muzzle flashes. The crash of gunfire, the peal of Chinese signal bugles, and shouted commands brought marines surging from their sleeping bags. "Here they come!" a young PFC yelled, unnecessarily.

Just as Barber feared, the first charge brought the Chinese surging across the long saddle, their white uniforms making them almost invisible against the snow. The Chinese intention in the first wave assault was to drive a wedge between the 2nd and 3rd platoons. But three marines took a stand at the juncture and refused to move. One of them, a giant twenty-one-year-old private named Hector A. Cafferatta, stood upright and took deliberate and deadly aim at the onrushing Chinese.[16] Another private, Kenneth Benson, crouched in a hole beneath Moose Cafferatta—a reservist now fighting a regular's war—trying to free the frozen bolt of his BAR. He could not believe what he heard. After each crack of Cafferatta's rifle he could hear the man grunt a number. "Nine . . . ten . . . eleven . . . twelve." Then Moose's rifle froze. With a roar of anger he ran a few steps forward and hurled his useless M-1 at the Chinese. He grabbed Benson by the shoulder. "Let's go, Bens, up there."

They stumbled into a shelter farther up the hill. Every man there was either dead or wounded. "Gimme a rifle," Cafferatta yelled. "Somebody gimme a rifle! Mine's busted!"

One of the wounded men shoved an M-1 toward Moose and said, "You shoot while I load." He began grabbing other rifles in the pit and jamming clips into their receivers. Cafferatta, at full and exposed height again, emptied rifle after rifle at the Chinese, pausing only to exchange an empty weapon for a loaded one.

The Chinese again resorted to hand grenades. According to marine historian Philip Pierce, some of the men in the shelter snatched up trenching tools and swung them like baseball bats, clubbing the grenades out of the way. But there were some missed swings. Two landed at Cafferatta's feet; twice he kicked them away. Another got past him and landed amid the wounded. Cafferatta dived wildly across the shelter, picked it up, lunged to his feet, and threw it away. It exploded before clearing his fingers, tearing shards of flesh from his hand; a severed finger dropped to the ground.*

The marines now fought with entrenching tools, with bayonets, with rifle butts, with their fists, a snarling primitivism which had men clawing at one another's throats and eyeballs in the snow, victory the only alternative to death.

The marines won. At the first hint of dawn in the sky a Chinese bugle wailed recall, and the attackers broke off contact and sped away into the hills. By six-thirty o'clock all was quiet on Fox Hill.

They gathered the marine bodies and laid them in two rows of ten corpses each. Corpsman Jim Morrissey was checking dog tags when he thought, that was like marines, lining up their dead in neat ranks. He paused a moment and let the haunting notes of taps pass through his mind.

But Fox Company's ordeal was just beginning.

CCF Attack Continues

All during the day on November 28 small-arms fire crackled around the Fox Company positions, but the Chinese attempted no new attacks. With fifty-four wounded, in addition to the twenty dead, and ammunition stocks running low, Captain William Barber repositioned his defenses and scavenged the battlefield for usable rifles and ammunition. Some Chinese were found to be carrying U.S. Thompson submachine

*For his bravery, Cafferatta received the Medal of Honor.

guns and Model 1903 Springfield rifles, apparently booty from the defeat of Chiang Kai-shek.

Radio messages during the day told Barber of the continuing turmoil at Yudam and the CCF attacks on Hagaru. Barber did not attempt to conceal Fox Company's plight from his junior officers. The 5th and 7th regiments were cut off; they had suffered heavy casualties; they had to fight their way down the road protected by Fox Company.[17]

"That's the only way out for their rolling stock," Barber said. "If we don't hold this hill, they haven't got a chance."

He looked at the tired, dirty faces of the men in his CP. A couple had flecks of ice on their faces and bloodstained bandages here and there. Barber sighed. "That's the story, gents. Let's get on with it."

Now was the time for improvisation. The marines resupplied themselves with whatever equipment they could find on the dead Chinese. (One blessing of the freezing temperature was that it preserved dead Chinese bodies, some 450 of which were counted in front of Fox Company that morning. The marines even dragged some of them up the hill and stacked them around their slit holes for shields.)

Private Ken Benson, still woozy from his close encounter with a Chinese grenade, worried most today about finding a new pair of gloves. He went down the hill to the hole where he and Moose Cafferatta had survived last night's action, and he cursed. Not only could he not find his clothes, but the Chinese had shot the sleeping bags full of holes and stabbed them repeatedly with bayonets, apparently on the assumption that marines were in them.

An idea. Take the dead men's sleeping bags, and stuff them with snow, and put them in a circle or a formation. The Chinese might think men are in them. When they come in for the kill . . .

Ken Benson spent the rest of the afternoon gathering sleeping bags, filling them with snow, and arranging his own private ambush.

That night Fox Company occupied the same general positions as the previous day, although in greatly reduced numbers. Nonetheless, Barber sensed a confidence in his men that they had endured the best— or the worst—that the Chinese had and that they could hold the hill again.

This time the rush of incoming mortar rounds signaled the renewed Chinese attack. The frozen earth shook at each impact, and the thump of high explosives and the whine of flying shrapnel tore the air.

Small squads of Chinese, eight or nine at a time, ran toward the line, yelling and firing, then withdrawing, obviously probing for gaps or weak points. This time the marines knew what to expect—the wave attacks, line after line of Chinese running into American rifle, mortar, and grenade fire in grisly precision, each successive group dodging around the torn corpses of the men who died earlier. The marines would blast one wave apart; seconds later in would come another. After two hours the 3rd Platoon could hold no longer. Pounding as relentlessly as a riptide, the Chinese tore through the line and pursued the 3rd Platoon down the slope. Barber and Lieutenant McCarthy ran to muster men to fill the breach. A rattle of machine-gun fire cut through the darkness, knocking both men down with broken legs.

Now that the Chinese had breached the American line, they seemed not to know what to do. Instead, some fifty of them walked aimlessly through the area behind the 2nd Platoon, as if waiting for a leader to emerge. They shouted; they talked; they blew bugles loudly. And they stood close together.

Lieutenant Elmer Peterson quickly appraised the situation and had his two machine guns turned around. In a few seconds of vicious fire the group of Chinese was slashed into a tangled mass of corpses. Not a single Chinese survived.

But the withdrawing Chinese in front of the perimeter did see a chance for one hit at the Americans—a semicircle of marine sleeping bags, as if the wounded had been given their own area from the battle. With savage cries the Chinese raced toward the dormant targets and began firing bullets into the bags and stabbing at them with bayonets.

Private Ken Benson sat a few yards away with his BAR, watching. He took careful aim and began firing. Six bangs, six Chinese bodies. He slung the BAR over his shoulder and walked back up the hill.

At morning light on November 29 the Chinese again broke contact and vanished into the hills. Barber's casualty count was much lower— five American dead and twenty-nine wounded. Still, Fox Company was down to less than half its effective strength, and Barber knew he would be on Fox Hill for several more days. But an airdrop in midmorning brought in ample supplies of ammunition and food, and for the third time Fox Company dug in for the night.

This time the Chinese kept their distance. They would occasionally blow bugles, as if signaling an attack; they would fire random rifle and mortar rounds. But the worst irritant was an amplified voice: "Fox Company, you are surrounded. I am a lieutenant from the Eleventh Marines. The Chinese will give you warm clothes and good treatment. Surrender now!"[18]

An angered Fox Company rifleman finally shouted, "Send up a flare, I want to talk to the son of a bitch." As the flare cut through the darkness, the rifleman emptied his M-1 in the general direction of the voice. It was heard no more.

Nonetheless, Fox Company remained sitting on a rather lonely hill, surrounded by thousands of Chinese, while the rest of the 1st Marine Division walked and rode to safety below them.

Ray Davis's Mission

But Fox Company was not forgotten. On November 30 Colonel Litzenberg looked around Yudam for the best man to lead a rescue mission. He was ready to begin moving the main contingent of marines down the road, a march the Chinese obviously expected. Still, sending a strong force through the hills would not only save Fox Company but also throw the Chinese off-balance. Litzenberg decided on one of the division's brightest, toughest young battalion commanders, Lieutenant Colonel Raymond G. Davis.[19] Litzenberg told Davis what he wanted: "It's obvious we can't bull our way down the road [to Fox Company]. I don't think the Chinese will expect us to move overland. [Fox Company] has to be relieved, and Toktong Pass held. Prepare to move out tomorrow morning."

Davis moved quickly. He segregated his sick and walking wounded and gave them responsibility for bringing out the battalion vehicles in the road column. Then he turned to his assault force. Each man would carry food for four meals, a canteen of water, and extra ammunition. What he chose to eat was his concern, for by now the men knew best what could be chewed in the cold. Most selected tins of bread and fruit, which when tucked into a fatigue jacket next to the stomach would not freeze. Davis doubled his mortar crews to share these heavy loads. Additionally each man in the column was to carry an extra 81 mm mortar shell. Fully loaded, every marine would be carrying about 120 pounds on his person—a packhorse load even on level ground in decent weather. Davis's men had lived in sub-zero temperatures for three weeks, seldom eating anything other than semifrozen rations. Each had angry gashes on his hands from digging foxholes in the frozen earth. Lean and lithe when they entered Korea because of marine physical conditioning, the men nonetheless had average weight losses of twenty pounds per man. When Ray Davis looked at his command, he saw faces gaunt with fatigue and hunger and occasionally tinged with the white of frostbite.

He lined them up, in battalion rank, and told them what they had to do—to walk across some bad hills, at night and supplied with only what they carried, and rescue Fox Company, and then hold the main supply route and save two regiments. There were grunts of assent, and the 1st Battalion moved from Yudam into the hills, their first objective a knob named Hill 1419 about 1,000 yards east of the road, held by a firmly entrenched CCF contingent that had resisted air, artillery, and frontal ground assaults for three days. All day the men slithered up the mountain, often crawling on hands and knees through the snow, always under heavy CCF fire. In a climactic heave a platoon headed by Lieutenant Leslie Williams fought hand to hand with the Chinese, breaking the back of the resistance.

By now it was seven at night, and pitch-dark. Davis looked at his thermometer and shuddered when he saw the temperature: minus twenty-four degrees. The day's exertion had left his men exhausted and wet with perspiration under their heavy clothing. Davis studied his map a few minutes, thinking, and he decided, if we stay here all night, as cold and as wet as we are, we won't be able to move tomorrow. This is going to be hell, but our best bet is to keep on pushing.

Davis ordered Baker Company, commanded by First Lieutenant Joseph R. Kurcaba, to take the point, with the battalion command group just to his rear for tight control. Davis squatted under his poncho, peered at a compass, plotted the direction; then the column was off through the night. As a secondary guide the lead man focused on a bright southern star. Ray Davis said years later:

> It was a numbing cold. There were some old pits where the Chinese had been, and to be sure we were going in the right direction, I would get down in them . . . and recheck my orientation with a compass.
> I remember twice crawling down, my poncho over my head, with a flashlight, getting my map oriented to check out the direction. I would fix my hand for a marker, turn the light out, and lift off the poncho and get out to check the direction, and I wouldn't remember what had happened down there under that poncho. I'd get up and just stand there in a daze. Two or three people standing around would have a few words to say, and by that time I had forgotten what it was I was trying to do.
> I'd have to go down and do this thing all over again. Everybody had to repeat back to you two or three times to be sure of what was supposed to happen. We were just absolutely numb in the cold.

As more and more marines passed over the trail, it became increasingly slick. "At this one place where we'd been sliding down, hanging onto rock," said Davis, "there were no roots left, and the incline was solid ice. It was like going down a sliding board. Just WHAM! and you'd hit the bottom."

The combined temperature and altitude made it impossible to melt snow for drinking water, even under a direct flame. So the men ate snow to get moisture. They carried dry socks and waist pads next to their bellies (the latter to guard against chafing from packstraps) and tried to remember to change them every few hours. Davis lived on dry crackers. "Everything else was frozen so hard that you couldn't get it thawed and eat it."

At one point that night, as the column crossed a series of ridges in deep snow, Davis tried to pass the word to the lead men to halt for a moment; he feared they were walking right into the enemy main force. "But it would never get passed by more than two or three men when one would say 'Shut up that noise,' and that was the end of it. So I had to beat my way all the way to the head of the column; when I got there,

I could hardly breathe, but I got them stopped, redirected in the way they were supposed to go."

At about two-thirty in the morning the column reached the top of the main ridge leading to Fox Company. The last yards "we had to climb on our hands and knees, holding onto roots and twigs to keep from sliding back down the icy trail."

Davis decided to pause here rather than attempt to make contact with Fox Company in the dark. Fox had no communications, and he did not want his relief column to be shot down in the night in the misapprehension they were Chinese.

But he also feared letting the marines fall asleep:

> The troops, when I got them off the top of the hill, they'd just fall out like flies. They couldn't stay on their feet, and I became alarmed about that to the degree that I got the companies each to organize three-man teams of noncommissioned officers to get the troops into position and go around and keep somebody on alert through the few hours we had before daylight.

Chinese snipers kept the battalion under sporadic long-range fire those hours. Davis survived one near miss; he had just crawled between two rocks and pulled the hood of the sleeping bag over his head when he felt a tug and then a sting on his head. An almost-spent round had gone through the cloth and "skinned my head."*

At daybreak the next morning—the sixth day that Fox Company had been on its battered hill—Davis's battalion marched across the saddle to the main positions. Barber saw them from afar and knew at a glance that the hooded figures were marines. Hundreds of feet below, on the MSR, he could see trucks winding south toward Hagaru.

Davis's men walked through remnants of the Chinese attackers as they neared Fox Hill. A hulking sergeant named Schaeffer called, "Come over here, Colonel, I want to show you something." Davis said, "He reached down and pulled this solid chunk up out of a hole, and it was a Chinese soldier. I said, 'Is he dead?' He said, 'No, his eyes are moving.' That's all he could move—his eyes." About half a dozen other quasi-alive Chinese were found outside the Fox Company perimeter; none survived.

Once on Fox Hill, Barber and Davis did a quick survey of casualties. Fox Company had twenty-two men so severely wounded they would have to be carried down the slope to waiting trucks. Two other men had to be restrained in improvised straitjackets after cracking mentally under the strain; both died before they could be evacuated.

Before leaving Fox Hill, Captain Barber toted up the cost of five days

---

*Thus by a fraction of an inch did Davis survive to earn a Medal of Honor and eventually ascend to the position of Commandant of the United States Marine Corps. Captain William Barber, Fox Company commander, also received the Medal of Honor.

and nights of battle—twenty-six men killed, eighty-nine wounded, including six of the seven officers, and three missing. Did Barber's surviving men wish to go down the hill to the main column?

No, Barber said, they would stay on Fox Hill with Davis's battalion, and help hold Toktong Pass until the last 1st Division truck had rolled through to safety.

As Lieutenant Colonel Ray Davis drove to the relief of Fox Company, the remainder of Litzenberg's command prepared to vacate Yudam and move south. After two rough days the fighting slackened. The Chinese, apparently, had maintained their schedule of fight-two-days, rest, fight-again, a formula necessitated by their poor supply system. No parachute drops of food and ammunition supported the CCF in the field; once a man consumed what he carried, either through his rifle or mouth, he had to drop out of line. "A wound to a Chinese was a death sentence," General Smith noted. "He was left to die of exposure. Marines could hear the cries of the Chinese wounded, cries which died away as they froze to death. On the other hand, in spite of the cold, marine wounded were cared for."[20] Had the Chinese possessed adequate logistical support and communications, Colonel Alpha Bowser, the division G-3, thought later, the marines would never have gotten out of the reservoir. "The First Marine Division was lucky," he said.[21]

One medical technique of which Smith spoke—medics melting frozen morphine Syrettes in their mouths—was put to use at the Yudam hospital run by regimental surgeon Chester M. Lessenden, a navy lieutenant commander. Lessenden worked under adverse conditions. Stray rifle fire had pinpricked his tent, and because of the overflow of wounded some men had to be left outside on straw pallets, covered with tarpaulins.

Once the Chosin ordeal had ended, Dr. Lessenden told Keyes Beech of the Chicago *Daily News* the problems he had encountered:

> Everything was frozen. Plasma froze and the bottles broke. We couldn't use plasma because it wouldn't go into solution and the tubes would clog up with particles. We couldn't change dressings because we had to work with gloves on to keep our hands from freezing.
>
> We couldn't cut a man's clothes off to get a wound because he would freeze to death. Actually, a man was often better off if we left him alone. Did you ever try to stuff a wounded man into a sleeping bag?[22]

Some of the wounded lay in the snow for seventy-two hours without moving and then were hauled out, strapped across truck radiators. "When we got to Hagaru," said Navy Captain Eugene R. Hering, 1st Marine Division surgeon, "the only way you could tell the dead from the living was whether their eyes moved. They were all frozen as stiff as boards."[23]

The order to leave Yudam was received on the afternoon of November 30, a day the Chinese began tightening the pressure on the perimeter. Units gradually fell back into the hamlet, maintaining positions only on essential high points. In overnight planning talks, the decision was that the operation should have two parts: one, a thrust to rescue Fox Company and hold Toktong Pass; two, to move the remainder of the regiment, and its equipment, down the MSR to Hagaru. General Smith had announced his determination not to abandon his equipment, in spite of strong opposition by General Almond. Smith said, "He wanted me to burn or destroy equipment and supplies, stating that I should be resupplied by airdrop as I withdrew. I told him my movements would be governed by my ability to evacuate the wounded, that I would have to fight my way back and I could not afford to discard equipment, and that, therefore, I intended to bring out the bulk of my equipment."[24] Almond did not argue.

Lieutenant Colonel Robert D. Taplett's battalion drew the mission of seizing and holding the commanding ground on both sides of the MSR leading south from Yudam while the main column got under way. Colonel Litzenberg shaped the column carefully. It would be led by the sole tank the marines had in Yudam, followed by an artillery battery that would pause after a few thousand yards and set up a base to provide covering fire for the rear guard. Artillery units in the perimeter would fire off most of their 155 mm ammunition before departing; the surplus artillerymen were converted into riflemen and formed into platoons. The wounded who were able to walk would do so, and carry rifles and fight. Only the most seriously wounded men were given space in the trucks which formed the center of the column. Litzenberg made a tough decision. The marines would suffer more casualties in the breakout, and he also had to pick up survivors for Fox Company. So the marines buried eighty-five of their dead at Yudam, unable to spare the limited space that would have been required to truck them out.*

Taplett's assault battalions moved out of Yudam and crunched down the snow-covered road to attack hills on either side of the MSR. Behind them, at a very cautious pace, came the trucks and the walking wounded. Recollected one survivor: "I'd walk three or four yards, then dive off the road behind a rock and shoot some Chinaman before he shot me. My knees were so tore up from jumping down on the rocks and ice that they hurt for months."[25] The cold was so intense that men's feet froze to the bottom of their boots and the skin peeled off when they took off their socks. Men who should have died from bleeding survived because the blood congealed and the flow stopped. "It was very strange to see blood freeze before it could coagulate," Lieutenant Commander Lessenden, the regimental surgeon, told Keyes Beech

---

*The remains were returned to the United States under the 1953 cease-fire terms.

later. "Coagulated blood is dark brown but this stuff was pinkish."

The march continued through the night, with the Chinese now counterattacking with determination—as if General Sung Shin-lun realized the quarry was escaping his net. More marine heroes emerged that night to frustrate the Chinese. Staff Sergeant William Windrich led a squad that ran along one sector of the front, trying to stop the Chinese from forcing a gap.[26] Within minutes, seven of twelve men were wounded, including Windrich, shot in the head. He kept fighting, then raced to his company CP for help in evacuating other men. Again rifle fire hit him, this time in the leg; again he refused to stop for treatment, telling the corpsman, "There isn't time. They're only small holes anyway." Windrich continued ranging along the column for an hour. Then he collapsed and died from loss of blood.

The next three days were a repetitive blur in which the marines and the Chinese contested hill after hill, ridge after ridge, with the bulk of the strong counterattacks coming at night. The first night the Chinese commander maintained tight control, with their troops using the inverted wedge formation to good advantage, squads striking simultaneously at the center and flanks of the American positions to probe within hand-grenade range. The marines would fight as long as they could, fall back, regroup, and fight again. Time and again single riflemen or machine gunners effectively sacrificed their lives by remaining in hopelessly overrun positions to cover the withdrawal of fellow marines. Private Barry Lester years later did not even know the name of the sergeant who saved his life; his decimated company had been merged with another, and although men shared slit trenches (and agony), introductions did not go beyond the Pat or Charlie stage.[27] Lester related:

"It was the first night, maybe the second, I don't know, the whole thing runs together. There were five of us spread along maybe twenty-five yards on the brow of a hill, on the flank. We shot back and forth with the Chinks three, four hours. They'd rush up, try to get in grenade range, then fall back, because we shot the shit out of them. I took a round in the calf of my leg, and it hurt, and I bled all over the place, but finally it stopped because it just froze up—or so the corpsman told me later, at any rate.

"Each time the Chinks rushed us they got closer and closer, and we were getting low on ammo, damned low, and we knew it was about time we went someplace else. Well, this sergeant, a guy I saw for the first time that afternoon, took a bad hit in his gut, and it must have nicked his spine, too, because he said he couldn't move his legs.

" 'Throw me your extra clips, all you've got, and get the hell back down to the MSR,' he yelled. 'I'll stay up here and cover you.' We did. I felt awful because I know there's no way he's coming off that knob. But I know there's no way we're going to carry him down alive either because when the Chinks know we are leaving, they're going to be right after our asses."

Lester and the other three marines emptied their pockets of clips, gave them to the sergeant, and slipped away into the darkness. They heard rifle fire from the knob for ten minutes more perhaps, then silence.

There were episodes of acute agony. A bridge collapsed under the weight of a truck, tossing some twenty wounded men through the ice covering a freezing stream. They had been riding on a bed of parachutes and explosive primer cord, and four of them became entangled beneath the truck. Despite the icy water, Lieutenant (jg) Morton I. Silver and an aide, Paul Swinn, plunged into the stream and cut the helpless men free. Another truck carrying wounded men was disabled shy of Hagaru when a bullet punctured its radiator. Silver assembled a detail of men which managed to push the truck to the top of a hill; they stood silently and watched it coast into Hagaru and safety. Lieutenant Colonel Joseph L. Stewart, the 5th Marine executive officer, told Beech, "It took a lot of Godlike characteristics to keep from letting men die."

At one point in the march Murray found Taplett in a temporary command post in a Korean hut. Wounded men huddled together for warmth in one room. Taplett, eyes glazed with fatigue, sat in another room before a smoldering fire, his boots off, picking ice from between his toes.

"How are you making out?" Murray asked him.[28]

"My feet are about to fall off," Taplett mumbled in response, "but we'll make it. Restore circulation and go forward." He pulled his boots back on and went outside to resume the march.

Air support complemented the on-the-ground bravery. Navy and marine pilots flew night missions, slamming napalm and bombs into the darkness, guided only by flares flickering across the frozen landscape. The pilots worked within 200 yards of marine positions, and even closer, and to avoid aiming errors, they scorched through the hills so low that some infantrymen swore their propellers chopped limbs off trees. The close-support planes took an awesome toll of Chinese; on one mission alone, to protect a marine battalion withdrawing at the tail end of the train, Corsairs hit a single ridge for twenty-five minutes with napalm and 500-pound bombs, leaving it "one of the most useless pieces of real estate in the world."

The Chinese began to fade under the pressure.[29] One rifle force made the mistake of breaking an attack at dawn and attempting to flee within range of marine machine guns. No one went out to count, but an officer with binoculars estimated 300 Chinese lay dead when the last volleys quieted. Farther down the MSR, Lieutenant Colonel Ray Davis came off Fox Hill to join the convoy, and by happenstance two of his companies surprised a large CCF force. The Chinese fled south on the road, not knowing that a marine force was coming up from Hagaru to meet the Yudam convoy. Colonel Litzenberg heard of this good fortune by radio. He turned to Lieutenant Colonel Ray Murray and said softly, "Ray, notify your Third Battalion commander that the Chinese are running southwest into his arms."

Bob Taplett, the 3rd Battalion commander, first tried artillery from Hagaru, but the range was too great for effectiveness. So he called for an air strike, even though the area was overcast. Again, luck for the marines. The overcast lifted just as the Corsairs arrived on target. The trapped Chinese, unable to get off the roadway, were hit by napalm and bombs from the air, mortars and heavy machine guns from both north and south. The CCF battalion—more than 700 men—was "completely eliminated," according to Taplett's battle report.

There was to be another fierce skirmish the next day when vehicles in the tag end of the column ran out of fuel. But the emotional high point of the Yudam breakout came at seven o'clock on the evening of December 3, when the first men of the column appeared on the outskirts of Hagaru. Someone called a halt, and the marines composed themselves with quiet, if pained, dignity and closed into a drill-field formation. Snow and ice encrusted their helmets, their parkas, their faces; some men walked on painfully frozen feet, wincing each time the hard purplish flesh touched the frozen ground; some stared blankly ahead, as if they did not know where they were, or why. But the marines marched into Hagaru with shoulders thrown back and their cadence even on the crust of the iced road.

Next came the walking wounded, blooded marine leaning against blooded marine, some with M-1's slung over their shoulders, others unable to do anything more but to cling to a supporting buddy. Captain Myron Wilcox had been shot through the jaw, and a huge mummy-fashion bandage encased his head; but he walked, and he walked proudly, determination keeping him and his comrades upright.

Next, the vehicles, many with unconscious wounded strapped across the hood on litters, some on the bare metal, 1,500 of them in all, perhaps a third of them frostbite cases.

"Many of them appeared dazed and uncomprehending at first," wrote the marine historian Lynn Montross. "Others wandered about aimlessly with blank faces. But there were few who had suffered any psychological disturbances that could not be cleared up with a good night's sleep and some hot food." The casualties were hastened to medical tents, and the other troops to mess tents for hot coffee.

That night Colonel Alpha Bowser sat in a hospital tent at Hagaru with General Smith and other officers. They suddenly heard voices singing Marine Corps songs.[30] "I looked at General Smith," Bowser said, "and I said, 'Our problems are over, we've got it made.' "

The marines took perverse pleasure the next day when suffering

Chinese began drifting in from the hills to surrender.[31] Some said they had eaten nothing in four days; many wore no shoes. Keyes Beech was riding in a jeep with a marine lieutenant when three Chinese crawled across the snow to the road, their bare feet frozen blobs of flesh. "That's the way I like to see them," the lieutenant said without pity. "I hope every one of the sons of bitches freezes to death."

During the march from Yudam, Hagaru somehow took on the illusion of a refuge, the point where the agony would end. Such was not to be; once the marines reached Hagaru, they had completed but the first leg of the trek out of the mountains. They must continue, first to Koto, then to the sea. But nothing in marine history could be worse than what they endured on the road from Yudam.

Respite from Battle

To the relief of the beleaguered marines, the Chinese did not attempt to attack their refuge of Hagaru, even after the Yudam column arrived. The marines saw several reasons. Hagaru defensive positions were fixed and clearly marked; hence CCF attacks would be vulnerable to American air support. The marines had no way to go but south. Wait until they withdrew onto the narrow road; some sixty-seven miles still separated them from the Sea of Japan, and the "war dogs of capitalism" could be destroyed at the CCF's leisure. The marines would use the lull to rest; the Chinese would use it to march their troops south and take up positions along the main supply route. The Battle of "Frozen Chosin" was by no means over.

Nonetheless, General Smith's division enjoyed the brief break from daily battle. The marines needed time to rest, to resupply, and to attend to some of the more grisly aftermaths of combat.

Smith made his first order of business the evacuation of casualties, via the airstrip he had insisted be built over General Almond's objections.[32] The first heavy flow of casualties, from the 2nd Army Division, began arriving on December 2. Smith's opinion of the United States Army sank even lower. Many unwounded soldiers, he said, would feign serious injury to get on an evacuation plane.[33] "They would go down to the strip and get a blanket and a stretcher and then groan a bit; the corpsmen would come along and put them on a plane." Captain Eugene R. Hering, the 1st Marine surgeon, alerted Smith to malingerers in the 2nd Division. The morning of December 2 he had 450 men in his hospital, and 914 were evacuated by air during the day. But at nightfall he still had 260 men in bed. Hering felt that "a significant number of men who were not casualties" succeeded in getting aboard planes. Screening tightened. These 2nd Division troops disgusted Smith. They had thrown away their weapons. Their conduct at Hagaru was disgraceful. "They didn't want to put up tents—they felt it was up to us to take care of them, feed them, and put up tents for them. We disabused them of that idea."

When the Yudam contingent staggered into Hagaru, Dr. Hering had a new guide for evacuees. According to Smith, "Some doctors were inclined to be sympathetic, others were hard-boiled. Dr. Hering finally set himself up as a final arbiter in doubtful cases. He used as his criterion the regimental surgeon of the Fifth Marines [Lieutenant Commander Chester M. Lessenden]. This doctor had frostbitten feet but could still hobble. If men were in no worse shape than [Lessenden] they were not evacuated."[34] By December 5, 4,312 casualties had been flown from Hagaru.

Smith gave priority to flying out bodies, which upset X Corps. Major General Clark L. Ruffner called Colonel Gregon A. Williams, Smith's chief of staff, to demand that the dead be left at Hagaru, and the space be given the wounded. Smith cut him short. The marines "have a particular reverence for their comrades killed in battle," even to the point of risking their lives to bring in bodies. He would not leave them "in a desolate village in northeastern Korea which we were about to evacuate. We just slipped the bodies in, and it was very simple—they were frozen stiff, there was no putrefaction or anything like that. We sent them all out, 138 in all."

Another irritant was kibitzing from MacArthur's headquarters. When frostbite victims appeared in Japan hospitals, the Far East Command blamed the cases on a "lack of leadership."

"That made me mad as a hatter," Smith exclaimed.[35] He sent an angry letter to General Clifton Cates, the marine commandant:

> Here I have just given a Silver Star to a sergeant who pulled off his mitten in order to heave a grenade, and he got frostbitten fingers. Are you going to court-martial that man for not taking proper precautions against frostbite? Are you going to court-martial his battalion commander, his regimental commander, his division commander?

The issue died of absurdity.

Hagaru, however, was a temporary respite. Air Force C-119 transport planes parachuted in vast quantities of supplies—372 tons of ammunition, artillery shells, gasoline and diesel fuel, and rations, which Smith called "the margin necessary" to sustain division operations.

Smith recognized the five quiet days as a false peace. Intelligence reports told of massive CCF buildups along the MSR to Koto—seven divisions confirmed, two probable, meaning a nine to one Chinese advantage. The march plan was much the same as had brought the marines from Yudam: advance elements to seize the high ground along the road; next a mixed column of walking wounded, riflemen, and more than 1,200 vehicles; then the rear guard. Overhead would be the greatest concentration of tactical aircraft of the entire war, a flotilla of more than 100 fighter craft from land and carrier bases.

Marguerite Higgins of the New York *Herald Tribune* hitched a ride into Hagaru on December 5.[36] She listened to Lieutenant Colonel Ray Murray brief officers exhausted from the trek from Yudam. "They had the dazed air of men who have accepted death and then found themselves alive after all. They talked in unfinished phrases. They would start to say something and then stop, as if the meaning was [*sic*] beyond any words at their command."

Higgins felt she detected a harsh tone in Murray's voice: "This is no retreat. This is an assault in another direction. There are more Chinese blocking our path to the sea than there are ahead of us. But we're going to get out of here.

"Any officer who doesn't think so will kindly go lame and be evacuated. I don't expect any takers." There were none.

The night of December 5 artillery at Hagaru fired saturation barrages at both sides of the roadway south, a thunder of 155 mm shells that smashed into the massed Chinese. (The barrages also disposed of surplus 155 mm ammunition the marines could not carry with them.)

At daybreak on December 6 the column moved south through a clinging silver fog. The artillery battalion was to proceed about five miles—slightly more than half the distance to Koto—and set up fire bases to protect the line of march. General Smith stayed in Hagaru until midafternoon, when he was confident the march was satisfactorily under way. Then he boarded a helicopter and flew south to a new command post in Koto. The flight took eleven minutes. The rest of the division would not have such an easy trip.

The march got off to an auspicious start. Some 1,500 yards south of Hagaru marines found a group of Chinese sleeping in a small village and killed two dozen of them. Then opposition stiffened, with Chinese mortar fire several times halting the column. Chinese roadblocks were frequent, often utilizing wrecked American vehicles. Lead tanks shoved them aside.

The few prisoners taken showed that the Chinese were in far worse physical shape than the marines. Frozen, starved, demoralized by superior American firepower, many threw down their arms at the first opportunity. Litzenberg ordered all huts along the route burned.[37] "We'll leave no warming pens for the enemy behind us."

The marines fought through the night, Litzenberg deciding the dangers of fighting at dark—the Chinese-preferred time—were outweighed by the risks of the enemy's being able to maneuver into the position for attack. Again there was an abundance of heroism. A tank stalled under heavy machine-gun fire, blocking the following company. The terrain and the angle of fire favored the Chinese. Sergeant Leland Ehrlich assembled his squad and yelled, "I'm going to get them." He raced across the road and up the steep slope, stumbling and sliding over the ice. The surprised Chinese turned the machine gun on him. They killed him, but before they could reposition their fire, marine bullets cut down the crew. Two trucks carrying wounded were hit by Chinese fire and burst into flame. Fully visible to the Chinese because of the glare, Master Sergeant William J. McClung ran to the truck and pulled off several men. An enemy bullet killed him. But the road reopened.

At five-thirty on the morning of December 7 the lead company made contact with units from Colonel Chesty Puller's Koto base. They had taken twenty-two hours to travel the nine miles. Ninety minutes later the first men staggered into Koto—only to be told to return to the MSR and keep it open for the remainder of the troops. An artillery battery had no sooner set up positions than an observer spotted 800 Chinese massing for attack. The cannon roared at ranges of from 100 to 500 yards, killing all but several dozen of the enemy.

Meanwhile, the rearguard units at Hagaru staggered under ferocious Chinese attacks. The first morning of the withdrawal, marines had managed to seize a key hill which the Chinese had held to good advantage since early November 29. The marines needed the promontory to cover the withdrawal, so they went out and took it—Chinese opposition collapsing after only a few hours' resistance. To reach the crest, the marines hauled up machine guns, mortars, even men, by ropes secured to the icy crest with pitons. But this was only the first round of a twenty-two-hour battle, for the Chinese returned, in force. Corsair fighters won the round for the marines in midafternoon, when they caught a huge Chinese force trying to force their way across a saddle leading to the hill. CCF soldiers surrendered en masse, more than 200 of them to a single American platoon. (The marines kept the prisoners only a few hours, then disarmed them and turned them loose with a day or so of rations to fend for themselves.)

But all the Chinese did not quit. During the early morning hours of December 7 they launched an attack that Yudam survivors called the "most spectacular, if not the most fiercely contested, battle" of the entire Chosin Reservoir campaign. In the words of marine historian Lynn Montross:

Never before had they [the marines] seen the Chinese come on in such numbers or return to the attack with such persistence. The darkness was crisscrossed with a fiery pattern of tracer bullets at one moment, and next the uncanny radiance of an illumination shell would reveal Chinese columns shuffling in at a trot, only to go down in heaps as they deployed. Marine tanks, artillery, mortars, rockets and machine guns reaped a deadly harvest, and still the enemy kept on coming with a dogged fatalism which commanded the respect of the Marines. Looking like round little gnomes in their padded cotton uniforms, groups of Chinese contrived at times to approach within grenade-throwing distance before being cut down.[38]

The CCF dead before the 2nd Battalion positions on the hill were estimated at 800.

The tail end of the convoy caught the last-gasp resistance of the Chinese, and at close hand. Erstwhile clerks of the Division Headquarters Company secured light machine guns on the top of truck loads; bandsmen became machine gunners to keep the enemy away until burning trucks could be pushed off the road. But the Chinese kept coming. At daybreak First Lieutenant Charles H. Sullivan—six feet four inches, 240 pounds—fired his last carbine rounds at advancing Chinese. He rose to his full height and with a roar hurled the weapon like a javelin.[39] The bayonet drove into the chest of a Chinese soldier fifteen feet away. The other Chinese broke and ran. Sullivan pulled the bayonet from the corpse, wiped off the blood, found more ammunition, and continued fighting.

At nightfall on December 7 the tail end of the column had cleared Hagaru, and demolition teams left behind them a caldron of flame, smoke, and explosions—remnants of ammunition and fuel supplies that could not be carried out. The marine engineers smashed crates of rations and surplus clothing with a bulldozer, then soaked them with fuel oil.

Nonetheless, the prospect of finding food tempted Chinese soldiers to run through the flames to pick through debris. The marines paused to fire parting artillery rounds at them.

A pathetic flotsam of war trailed the marines—civilian refugees, thousands of them, women and children and old men, carrying whatever belongings they still owned. Hagaru no longer existed, nor for that matter did any of the other villages caught up in the Chosin Reservoir campaign. The engineers warned the civilians repeatedly that bridges and the roadway were packed with explosives and that anyone walking over them could be blown skyward. The warnings did not deter the North Koreans; they raced across bridges seconds before engineers blew them up. They had lived five years under Kim Il Sung. They apparently did not think the Chinese Communists would improve their lives.

The Koto phase of the evacuation finally ended thirty-eight hours after it had begun, with 10,000 troops and more than 1,000 vehicles safe. The marines lost 103 men dead, 506 wounded, and seven missing, a total of 616. Their survival, in the end, was due to General Oliver P. Smith's refusal to be cowed by Generals MacArthur and Almond—a stubbornness that saved the lives of 10,000 marines.

Bridging a Gap

Psychologically the worst of the Chosin Reservoir withdrawal was that it came in stages: The marines crawled from Yudam to Hagaru, rested only briefly, and then were away for the march to Koto. Now they must find energy for the last miles to the sea, and safety, another forty-three miles to Hungnam.

The marines had reached the limits of physical endurance. Most of the unwounded suffered severe diarrhea and helplessly soiled themselves as they strained through mountain passes and hills. No one dared pause during the Hagaru–Koto march to light a fire to warm rations, so the marines ate half-frozen food or went hungry. No one had enjoyed more than a brief warming-tent respite from sub-zero temperatures for more than a week. Those who walked did so in slow motion; some wounded had not moved from their litters for three days.

And at Koto the cruel Korean winter greeted the exhausted marines with a final insult: a snowstorm that piled half a foot more of dry snow on the ground, creeping into the crevices of parkas and sleeping bags, making walking numb agony.

General Smith's first concern, again, was evacuating the wounded. This time, however, he did not have the luxury of Hagaru airstrip, only a smaller field unable to handle the R-4D transport planes (the marine-navy version of the workhorse C-47, or DC-3). So marine aviators used obsolete torpedo bombers, TBMs, which could land on the tight space and carry out six to nine wounded per flight. None of the three pilots —Lieutenant Truman Clark, John Murphy, and Alfred F. "Little Mac" McCaleb—had ever flown TBMs before. No matter. Aided by a landing control officer using flags, they flew repeatedly into Koto on December 9 and carried out more than eighty wounded men. Marine Private Leland Gordon was lying on a litter alongside the landing strip during the evacuation. He had been hit in the upper right leg, and the morphine dulled but did not eliminate the hurt. "I remember hearing a plane and looking up through this goddamned snow. I could barely see beyond my nose. All of a sudden there was yelling, and it was on the ground, and people had my litter up and I was aboard and away."[40]

Smith's plan duplicated the Yudam and Hagaru evacuations: Battalions would seize the high ground on either side of the MSR while the main column moved down the road, supported by leapfrogging artillery units. Colonel Lewis Puller, who had sat out the Chosin campaign thus far in fretful frustration, would hold Koto until the column cleared the hamlet, then do rearguard duty. Lieutenant Colonel Donald Schmuck's 1st Battalion of the 7th Regiment, in a maneuver intended to throw the Chinese off guard and slow their progress toward Koto, would feint northward along the MSR and set up blocking positions.

However, intelligence reports brought news that could reduce the entire marine effort thus far to futility and leave the entire division stranded at Koto.[41] The Chinese had blown a bridge that cut a critical gap in the roadway to safety—and at a place that left no room for a bypass. Spanning a twenty-nine-foot chasm became the most delicate part of the entire seventy-eight-mile march.

General Smith frowned when he heard the report, for he knew the bridge well; he had passed over it on November 16, while driving up the road from Chinhung, and thought at the time its destruction could cause his troops much trouble. The bridge was three and one-half miles south of Koto.

"At this point," Smith said, "water coming from the Chosin Reservoir by tunnel emerged from the side of the mountain and was discharged into four penstocks [large concrete pipes] which descended steeply down the mountainside to the turbine of the power plant in the valley below. Where the penstocks crossed the road there was a concrete substation, without a floor, on the uphill side of the road covering the penstocks. On the downhill side of the substation was a one-way concrete bridge. The drop down the mountain side here was sheer. There was no possibility of a bypass. The integrity of this bridge was vital to us, for without it we would have been unable to get out our vehicles, tanks, and guns."

The CCF recognized the bridge as an excellent bottleneck and had blown it twice, on December 1 and December 4. The first time marine engineers replaced it with a wooden structure; the next time, with a steel treadway span. (Treadways are two long strips of steel placed far enough apart to accommodate the treads of tracked vehicles.) Now they had blown it for a third time.

Lieutenant Colonel John Partridge, an engineer officer, decided the best solution was to air-drop treadway sections into Koto, then truck them to the gap. But the sections weighed 2,500 pounds, a heavy load for a parachute. He asked the air force to test-drop one at a base in South Korea. The air force did. The section crumpled. Another engineer officer, Captain Hersel Blasingame, jury-rigged a double parachute; this time the test drop was successful. Partridge told Smith his plan the night of December 5–6, and the general cross-examined him at length, only to find that Partridge had foreseen all possible contingencies and backups. "I could see that Partridge was becoming annoyed," Smith said. "He finally informed me in no uncertain terms that he had gotten us across the Han River, that he had provided roads for us, that he had provided airstrips for us, and that he would get us a bridge. I told him to go ahead with his plans."

Early the next morning Partridge flew over the gap site to see the exact dimensions of the problem. The cold was so severe he could not even make notes. But he estimated the total gap was about sixteen feet.

By happenstance, an engineer in Colonel Chesty Puller's regiment, Lieutenant Charles C. Ward, had been a member of a treadway bridge company in Italy in the Second World War and had attended the Army Engineer School course on treadways. Four trucks in Ward's section could handle the treadways; thus the operation was off to a good start. The drop was arranged for nine o'clock the morning of December 7, and Koto marines were warned to keep out of the way lest a bridge section fall on their heads.

Although only four treadway sections were required, the air force dropped eight, one of which fell outside American lines. Additionally, the air force parachuted a number of plywood center sections to fit over the treadways, to accommodate smaller vehicles with a narrower wheel base than tanks and self-propelled artillery. The treadways would carry a load of fifty tons; the plywood, twenty tons. With both the metal spans and the plywood in use, the bridge would ensure the unbroken passage of tanks and vehicles.

The engineers spent the next day and a half getting the treadway sections to the gap, handicapped by increased heavy snow, continuous fire fights along the route, and other mishaps. When they reached the bridge, they found to their astonishment the CCF had blown out another ten-foot section, plus the abutment on the south side of the road. The total gap thus increased to twenty-nine feet; the treadway sections on hand would span only twenty-four. The engineers did not pause. Someone spotted a pile of old railroad crossties just below the bridge site. Sixty Chinese POWs were put to work hauling the ties up to the roadbed and filling sandbags. By midafternoon on December 9 the work was done. Partridge apologized to Smith. He had promised the bridge itself could be erected in one and a half hours; it actually took three.

The bridge opened for traffic, and vehicles began rumbling across at two miles per hour. Colonel Partridge watched the scene with a quiet sense of accomplishment and also a recognition of unexpected beauty: "The sensation throughout that night was extremely eerie. There seemed to be a glow over everything. There was no illumination and yet you seemed to see quite well. There was artillery fire and the sound of many artillery pieces being discharged. There was the crushing of many feet and many vehicles on the crisp snow. There were . . . North Korean refugees on one side of our column and marines walking on the other side. . . . Every once in a while there would be a baby's wail. There were cattle on the road. Everything added to the general sensation of relief. . . ."

South of the bridge, by a mile or so, was the last major obstacle, the Funchilin Pass, dominated by Hill 1081. For this battle the marines relied upon a relatively fresh unit, the 1st Battalion of the 1st Regiment, commanded by Lieutenant Colonel Donald Schmuck, which, despite aggressive patrolling to the south of the MSR, had not engaged in major action. So the "First of the First" was rested and scrappy when they moved north through darkness and a swirling snowstorm at two o'clock on the morning of December 8.

This time the marines seized the advantage of darkness from the Chinese, marching in near-zero visibility, their snow-covered parkas giving protective coloration. Not a single Chinese was encountered, yet it took the marines six hours to walk six miles on the slippery road. At Hill 1081, under snow cover, they surprised hundreds of Chinese in a bunker area and killed or routed every one of them. The Chinese had so little warning they left kettles of rice cooking. (They also left millions of body lice; the marines decided to forgo the comforts of the bunkers that evening.)

For the troops driving south, progress was tedious but steady, with marines fighting scores of squad-, platoon-, and company-sized actions, weather a larger obstacle than the Chinese. The most poignant scene was the MSR roadway just above a roadblock intended to keep the Chinese from pursuing the marines south.[42] Unavoidably the block also served as a dam to block the flow of hundreds of homeless refugees, who huddled together in the driving snowstorm. The marines were not callous; they had no choice, for both the North Koreans and the Chinese had disguised themselves as civilians in past engagements. One marine recalls a "low-pitched wail of misery" from the huddled civilians. The night of December 8, with the temperature well below zero, medics crept past the roadblock to assist two women in childbirth.

Mercifully the snow ended on December 9, and the savage small-unit fire fights resumed. The strain of two weeks' fighting without relief began to take its toll of the Chinese. Two companies passing along the bridge site checked out a group of foxholes some yards off the roadway and found fifty Chinese. "They were so badly frozen," said Major W. D. Sawyer, "that our men simply lifted them from the holes and sat them on the road." They eventually were put into a POW column.[43]

Shortly before three o'clock the morning of December 10 the first marines began trickling into Chinhung. But the Chinese had some last-gasp strength. Later that afternoon Korean civilians warned that the previous night large numbers of Chinese had infiltrated the village of Sudong, just south of Chinhung on the MSR. Troops of the army's 3rd Infantry Division had responsibility for this area; they sent out patrols but found no enemy. But around midnight, when the marine column passed through Sudong, Chinese swarmed from behind houses in the villages with grenades and burp guns, killing several truck drivers and setting their vehicles ablaze. For a few minutes confusion reigned, with the Americans unable to find the enemy in the flickering light of the fires. Then an army lieutenant colonel, John U. D. Page, and a marine private, Marvin L. Wasson, took on the Chinese challenge, routing some twenty Chinese blocking the head of the column. Page was shot dead, Wasson received two grenade wounds. After first aid Wasson, a jeep driver, fired three white phosphorus shells from a 75 mm recoilless rifle into a house the Chinese were using for shelter. The Chinese bolted into the open and were cut down by machine-gun fire. Wasson was not finished. He then volunteered to shove burning trucks of exploding ammunition off the road. Wasson carried a new name away from the battle, "The Spirit of '76," a title bestowed by an army officer.

The last Chinese blow hit the rear of the column, forty tanks guarded by a much depleted platoon of twenty-eight men commanded by Lieutenant Ernest C. Hargett. Thousands of Korean civilians trailed in the rear, intermingled with CCF soldiers. Because of the ice and the narrowness of the road, the tanks proceeded a few inches at a time, with dismounted crewmen trying to keep them steered onto solid ground.

Shortly after midnight a mishap. The brakes froze on the ninth tank from the rear of the column, halting the tail of the column. Thirty-one tanks continued, leaving the others stranded about 2,000 yards south of the treadway bridge. As crewmen tried to make repairs, five Chinese came up from the refugees, in single file. The lead man said, in English, they wished to surrender.

Hargett, suspicious, stepped forward to talk, guarded by Corporal George A. J. Amyotte, who carried a BAR. The lead Chinese jumped to one side, and the men behind him raised hidden burp guns. Hargett pulled the trigger of his carbine; it had frozen. So he sprang forward and swung the weapon like a club, smashing the head of one of the enemy soldiers. Amyotte fired four swift rounds from his BAR; the remaining four Chinese fell dead.

The ruse was the prelude for a sudden Chinese attack from the high ground to the side as well as from the rear. A grenade blast wounded Hargett. He kept on his feet but decided the time had come to abandon the tanks and strike for safety. As Hargett and the remaining twenty-four men started fighting their way to safety, crewmen finally freed the frozen brakes on the stalled tank; it and two others rumbled on down the road. One crewman, Corporal C. P. Lett, had never driven a tank before. But he shouted, "I'm going to get this tank out of here even if I get killed doing it!" He guided around the obstacles and on down the ice-covered road.

During the last minutes of the encounter an explosion blew a young private, Robert D. DeMott, over the side of the road and down into the ravine. Other men thought he had been killed and did not try to retrieve his body. Some minutes later he regained consciousness and struggled to the road to find it clogged with refugees. He moved swiftly through them into Chinghung—the last marine to escape the Chosin Reservoir. Now the marines had only a brief march over flat country to reach the safety of Hungnam-Wonsan. The worst ordeal in marine history had ended.

The last miles the marines found energy for song, a biting parody of "Bless 'Em All," an old marching ditty of the British Indian Army:

> Bless 'em all, bless 'em all,
> The Commies, the U.S. and all:
> Those slant-eyed Chink soldiers
> Struck Hagaru-ru
> And now know the meaning of U.S.M.C.
> But we're saying goodbye to them all,
> We're Harry's police force on call.
> So put back your pack on,
> The next step is Saigon,
> Cheer up, me lads, bless 'em all![44]

An Enclave at Last

Until December 9 General Smith intended to take up defensive positions on the coast, around the port of Hungnam, and hold an enclave. But MacArthur realized the danger of such a deployment. True, the Chinese Communists had broken off major actions, following the attack-lull-attack cycle dictated by their resupply problems. MacArthur had been burned twice. He knew the Chinese would be back, and he did not want to risk attempting to stand off several field armies from a tight coastal perimeter subject to air attacks. So MacArthur passed new orders: As soon as X Corps reached Hungnam, its troops should board transports and sail south to Pusan. In the west Walton Walker's Eighth Army should retreat to successive defensive lines to the south and attempt to hold a perimeter in the Seoul-Inchon area. If the CCF chose to bypass EUSAK and strike for the south, MacArthur was hopeful he would be able to maul their extended supply lines. In the same order MacArthur finally agreed to end the split command that had plagued X Corps and the Eighth Army since the Inchon landing. Once the corps withdrew to Pusan, it would pass under command of General Walker as part of EUSAK.

What the marines planned at Hungnam was an "amphibious landing in reverse," with some 100,000 men—marines, U.S. soldiers, and ROKs —to be withdrawn from a gradually tightening perimeter protected by air strikes and naval barrages.

The chief worry was that the Chinese would maneuver artillery batteries into range of the port and lob shells into the vast supply dumps.

Such did not happen; there were a few desultory mortar barrages, but the Chinese behaved as if they had lost their capacity to fight.

Recognizing the futility of trying to empty the quarter-mile-long warehouses laden with foods, soap, lard, coffee, and fruit juices, supply officers threw them open to anyone around. *Time* correspondent Dwight Martin walked through the supply depot:

> G.I. and Korean stevedores ate steadily all day long, casually hacked open six-pound tins of pork luncheon meat to make one sandwich, gallon tins of fruit juice for one swallow. Outside one warehouse, a black-bearded U.S. sergeant dug his plastic C-ration spoon into a ten-pound tin of corned beef with the delicate disdain of an overweight debutante at a *smorgasbord*.[45]

Lines of Korean women walked through endless stacks of flour and rice and carried away 50- and 100-pound bags strapped to their backs or balanced on their heads. At the dock area was a line of spanking-new Japanese-made railroad freight cars, their crisp white sides bearing the insignia of the U.S. Army Transportation Corps. An officer looked at the rail cars and other heavy equipment and said, "God, we just got most of this stuff in here. If the gooks keep on coming, we're going to have to turn right the hell around and blow it all up again. God help the taxpayers."

Loading of the troop transport ships progressed smoothly for the 400-mile voyage to Pusan, with all the marines loaded by December 14, and the surviving army troops guarding the perimeter the last few days. Next, Smith gave permission for as many Korean civilians as possible to be snatched off the beachhead—elderly men and women carrying their possessions on their backs, mothers with babies strapped into white cotton-cloth slings, curious youngsters, some without parents, eager for the "big boat ride" to the south. In the rush some 4,000 people managed to rush aboard a single LST, sinking it firmly into the mud. ROK soldiers fired burp guns into the air, and everyone got off while the skipper managed to maneuver his craft into open water. Then the Koreans reboarded. Another ship, a large commercial vessel, carried away 12,000 civilians. (Some of the Koreans seemed as frightened of their own government as of the Communists; in the Seoul area, South Korean Army firing squads killed some 700 people suspected of collaborating with the North Koreans. Western clergymen protested many of the executions were without sanction of trial; the military commander replied firing squads were "more convenient" than hanging, and he did not intend to stop.)

Now began systematic destruction of the supplies that could not be taken to Pusan.[46] The army's 175th Engineer Combat Battalion jammed a 2,100-foot railroad bridge with steam engines and boxcars, aided by

Korean railroadmen. "When the Koreans learned that the rolling stock was to be destroyed," said Lieutenant Carroll W. Gruth, "they became reluctant and had to be prodded to do the job. By contrast, the engineers found the job enjoyable, release for their pent-up emotions." A span was blown, and cars and engines were pushed through the gap into the ravine. The engineers filled some of the cars with drums of gasoline for maximum destruction. Then wooden cribbings of the bridge were set afire, and the entire structure was left to collapse. "The heat was so intense that a locomotive became cherry-red and its whistle started blowing," Gruth said.

By Christmas Eve the entire perimeter was cleared. The U.S. military intended to leave nothing behind for the enemy. Two cruisers, seven destroyers, and three rocket-firing vessels stood in line a few hundred yards offshore and unleashed a hellish barrage at the abandoned town —nearly 34,000 shells and 12,800 rockets, a heavier rain of fire, indeed, than that preceding the Inchon invasion. The parting roar was the detonation of 400 tons of frozen dynamite and five hundred 1,000-pound bombs. "The entire Hungnam waterfront seemed to be blown sky-high in one volcanic eruption of flame, smoke, and rubble which left a huge black mushroom cloud hovering over the ruins," said a marine witness.

On Christmas Day General Smith ruefully remembered MacArthur's boast of a month ago about American troops being "home by Christmas." To the contrary, the 1st Marine Division was bound for Pusan to regroup and to prepare to commence the war all over again. The congratulatory messages the generals exchanged about the skillful escape from the CCF did not conceal the core fact of what had happened: The Chinese had thrown X Corps out of the battle.

But the Chinese did so at frightful cost. Between October 26 and December 15 the 1st Marine Division had 4,418 battle casualties—604 killed in action, 114 dead of wounds, 192 missing in action, 3,508 wounded in action. There were another 7,313 nonbattle casualties, mostly minor frostbite or indigestion cases quickly returned to duty. In addition, 8 marine pilots were killed, 4 missing, another 3 wounded.

By their own admission in documents captured later in the war, the Chinese opposing the marines suffered 37,500 casualties—15,000 killed and 7,500 wounded by marine ground forces, plus 10,000 killed and 5,000 wounded by air operations.[47] In postbattle analyses of their performance, Chinese commanders were candid. The CCF 26th Army complained that because of transportation problems:

> The troops were hungry. They ate cold food. They were unable to maintain the physical strength for combat, the wounded . . . could not be evacuated . . . the fire power of our entire army was basically inadequate. When we used our guns there were no shells and sometimes the shells were duds. . . .

The CCF Twentieth Army lamented that although "we succeeded in the separation and encirclement of the enemy . . . we failed to annihilate the enemy one by one. . . ." This analysis blamed tactical rigidity of senior commanders for not exploiting advantages—that small units were not permitted to strike swiftly, even when they wanted to, and thus marines could break off contact and escape. (The marines agreed; during the Hagaru attack the Chinese hit the strongest points of the American line on successive nights, thus permitting a battalion to hold off a much superior force.) The CCF Twenty-seventh Army complained especially about the severe weather and the lack of warm clothing and shelter:

> The troops did not have enough food, they did not have enough houses to live in, they could not stand the bitter cold, which was the reason for the excessive non-combat reduction in personnel (more than 10,000 persons), the weapons were not used effectively.
>
> When the fighters bivouacked in snow-covered ground during combat, their feet, socks, and hands were frozen together in one ice ball; they could not unscrew the caps on the hand grenades; the fuses would not ignite; the hands were not supple; the mortar tubes shrank on account of the cold; seventy per cent of the shells failed to detonate; skin from the hands were stuck on the shells and the mortar tubes.

The Chinese indeed ran X Corps out of "Frozen Chosin" but at a price that effectively took its Ninth Army Group out of the war for crucial weeks. Now Smith had the chance to rebuild and refit X Corps in the relative comfort of the old Pusan Perimeter.

CHAPTER SIXTEEN

Washington Reacts to Disaster

Shortly after midnight on November 28 Washington began to realize the magnitude of the disaster MacArthur had brought to the American military. A cable from the Far East Command told of the collapse of the ROK II Corps and the pending retreat of the Eighth Army back across the Chongchon River. This cable arrived at the Pentagon message center a few minutes before 1:00 A.M. Four hours later MacArthur admitted his offensive had failed, in a message that characteristically absolved himself of blame for the misadventure:

> The developments resulting from our assault movements have now assumed a clear definition. All hope of localization of the Korean conflict to enemy forces composed of North Korean troops with alien token elements can now be completely abandoned. The Chinese military forces are committed in North Korea in great and ever increasing strength. No pretext of minor support under the guise of volunteerism or other subterfuge now has the slightest validity. We face an entirely new war. . . .[1]

MacArthur continued that the "pattern of Chinese strategy" now had become clear. The initial intervention in late October had been to check the UN advance. This accomplished, the Chinese broke contact to build overwhelming strength for an offensive, probably to be launched in the spring. (The timetable MacArthur offered on behalf of the Chinese did not make much sense. Why would Chinese commanders leave more than 200,000 troops in the open, exposed to months of bitter Korean winter, if their use in battle were not planned for four months? Billeting them in Manchuria seems more logical.) In MacArthur's view, the ultimate Chinese objective was the "complete destruction of all United Nations forces in Korea."

Then MacArthur complained that his command had been given a mission beyond its capability, a carping refrain that was to become infuriatingly familiar to the JCS the next months. He wrote:

> At the present moment the freezing of the Yalu River increasingly opens up avenues of reinforcement and supply which it is impossible for our air potential to interdict. It is quite evident that our present strength of force is not sufficient to meet this undeclared war by the Chinese with the inherent advantages which accrue thereby to them. The resulting situation presents an entire new picture which broadens the potentialities to world embracing considerations beyond the sphere of decision by the Theater Commander. This command has done everything humanly possible within its capabilities but is now faced with conditions beyond its control and its strength.

MacArthur said he intended "to pass from the offensive to the defensive with such local adjustments as may be required by a constantly fluid situation." He completely ignored what he had said only three days earlier, when he launched the "end the war" offensive. He had been warned, by his field commanders and by the JCS, as well as his own intelligence officers, of the risks he incurred.

General Omar Bradley telephoned Truman at 6:15 A.M. to break the bad news.[2] Bradley and the other chiefs had discussed the situation the previous day, and while it was "serious," they doubted that it was "as much a catastrophe as our newspapers were leading us to believe." Bradley told Truman that the Chinese had "come in with both feet."[3]

The President immediately called the National Security Council into session.[4] Bradley's main concern was the danger that the Communists might decide to use their full air potential. U.S. intelligence estimated that Manchurian airfields stored at least 300 bombers. If these bombers entered the war, they could hamper U.S. supply lines (of the 3,000 tons of materials used daily by EUSAK, 1,000 tons came by air) or destroy American planes standing wing tip to wing tip at Korean air bases. Bradley called the fields "very vulnerable"; one raid already had damaged six U.S. planes.

Was there any possible defense against raids? Truman asked. Only by bombing Manchuria or by withdrawing planes to Japan, General Hoyt Vandenberg, the air chief, replied.

Defense Secretary Marshall warned about involvement in a general war with Communist China, either unilaterally or as a UN member. "To do this would be to fall into a carefully laid Russian trap," he said. The United States should neither go into Chinese territory nor use Chinese Nationalist troops.

Bradley disagreed with MacArthur's complaint that he did not have enough men to perform his mission. "MacArthur has enough there," he said; in any event, "there are no more ground troops which we could now send." (Army Secretary Frank Pace noted that only one division, the 82nd Airborne, remained in the United States and that National Guard units would not be ready until March 15. Even "filter replacements" would not be available until January 1.)

Marshall expressed concern about the exposed X Corps troops in northeastern Korea. Marshall "assumes that he [MacArthur] will withdraw his advanced forces." The problem should "be considered here in Washington" because it related to the question of direct war with China; nonetheless, "it would not be helpful to interfere with MacArthur's operations on the spot."

Vice President Alben Barkley, an acutely political man, brought up what he recognized to be a dangerous public relations problem for the administration: MacArthur's widely quoted "home by Christmas" remark. Barkley "wanted to know whether [MacArthur] did make the statement and, if so, did he know what was pending, and if he did know, why did he make it."

Truman replied that MacArthur "did make the statement and the Vice President would have to draw his own conclusions as to why." Bradley suggested that MacArthur "might have had in mind making the statement for the effect it would have on the Chinese in order to make it clear to them that we would get out after the attack."

The President wanted nothing said that would cause MacArthur "to lose face before the enemy." Marshall agreed; the administration should "regard the statement as an embarrassment which we must get around in some manner."

The talk then turned to what should—or could—be done about what Barkley called the "very gloomy" situation. Marshall had no answer. "We want to avoid getting sewed up in Korea," he said. But the question was: "How could we get out with honor?"

Acheson felt the country was "much closer to the danger of general war." He still saw the Soviet Union as the ultimate villain and manipulator in the war. Nonetheless, "we would not, at this time, say the USSR is responsible because we could not do anything about following such a charge . . . due to [sic] the attitude of our allies." But the United States should pursue its condemnation of China as an aggressor in the United Nations. The secretary of state would advise MacArthur there was no need for him to occupy northeastern Korea, "We can't defeat the Chinese in Korea; they can put in more than we can," Acheson said. Acheson would give "very, very careful thought" to air strikes against Manchuria. "If this is essential to save our troops, it must be done." But if the United States did enter Manchuria, "it would be very hard to stop and very easy to extend the conflict." If America were successful in

Manchuria, the "Russians would probably enter to aid their Chinese ally without considering it war with us. We would get more deeply involved. One imperative step is to find a line we can hold, and hold it. This would help meet the views of our allies and show them we are not aggressive and we await the next Chinese move."

Marshall wrapped up the meeting with the comment that the MacArthur offensive was necessary to find out what the Chinese Communists were up to. "Now we know," he said.

Truman did take one precautionary step. After the meeting ended, he telephoned Marshall and directed that all messages from the JCS to MacArthur must "be processed through the Secretary of Defense to the President personally."

The JCS Question MacArthur

MacArthur's first public reaction to the debacle was an incredible claim that the Chinese, not his command, had been caught by surprise. A press communiqué from his headquarters on November 29 essentially condensed his message to the JCS which depicted the crisis as an "entirely new war." But he also entered a claim that the JCS considered an outrageous howler: The UN offensive had "forced upon the enemy a premature engagement" and disrupted plans for a "later surprise assault upon our lines in overwhelming force."

But all the Joint Chiefs did was to watch and worry and let MacArthur continue unimpeded by the advice of outsiders. Admiral Sherman worried about the situation in the northeastern section, where naval vessels supporting X Corps were dangerously close to Vladivostok. Sherman wanted MacArthur to be ordered to withdraw the corps to a consolidated defense line. But the other chiefs remained reluctant to give MacArthur direct orders, contenting themselves with queries which they hoped would draw his attention to the danger.[5] "What are your plans regarding the coordination of the Eighth Army and X Corps," they asked on November 29, "and the positioning of X Corps, the units of which appear to us to be exposed?" The JCS did grant MacArthur permission to shift from the offensive to the defensive, as he had requested in his first alarm message. "Strategic and tactical considerations are now paramount," the chiefs said. The JCS suggested—but did not order—that MacArthur consider closing the gap between the two commands and form a continuous defensive line across the peninsula.

The same day the JCS again refused MacArthur's revival of the twice-rejected request that he be permitted to use Chinese Nationalist troops in Korea. MacArthur noted Chiang Kai-shek's offer had been refused earlier because of fears that a Communist invasion of Formosa was imminent and that their use in Korea might give China a pretext to enter that war. Since these considerations no longer applied and no other manpower was readily available, MacArthur wanted to negotiate directly with Chiang for use of his troops.

In a draft reply the JCS said use of Nationalist troops would probably bring Formosa into war with China. Secretaries Marshall and Acheson edited the message to stress the political and diplomatic considerations. Truman personally approved the final draft:

> Your proposal . . . is being considered. It involves world-wide consequences. We shall have to consider the possibility that it would disrupt the united positions of the nations associated with us in the United Nations and leave us isolated. It may be wholly unacceptable to the [British] commonwealth countries to have their forces employed with Nationalist Chinese. It might extend hostilities to Formosa and other areas. Incidentally, our position of leadership is being most seriously compromised in the United Nations. The utmost care will be necessary to avoid the disruption of the essential allied lineup in that organization.[6]

MacArthur now behaved in a fashion at once contradictory and puzzling—actions bespeaking a man who was both confused and frightened, one who did not wish the reality of his situation to detract from the illusion of his intentions. The first step in this odd sequence was the summoning of his two field commanders, Generals Walker and Almond, to Tokyo on November 28 for a "council of war" ("at a time they could ill afford to be away," General Collins commented caustically[7]). No record exists of their conversation; the decision, however, was that the Eighth Army must withdraw as far as necessary to avoid being flanked by the Chinese.[8] X Corps, meanwhile, would abandon MacArthur's march-to-the-Yalu orders and withdraw into the Hamhung-Hungnam area (the course of action which the marines' General Smith had urged, and MacArthur had rejected, only two weeks earlier). There was brief discussion of a suggestion—ridiculous in the recitation—that the 3rd Army Division drive westward from the Wonsan area on the east coast to strike at the Chinese operating against EUSAK's right flank, about halfway across the Korean peninsula. This idea came from General Edwin K. Wright, the X Corps chief of staff, in response to a MacArthur question about what the corps could do to relieve pressures on the Eighth Army. To Almond's credit, he intervened and with a few deft flickers of his pointer at the map showed the group that the proposed route lay across the Taebaek mountain range. Regardless of what the map showed, no roads existed in the area. Try it, he said, and the entire 3rd Division would be lost. Incredibly Almond then agreed to support the idea, provided General Walker would undertake to supply the division once it crossed to the west side of the Taebaek Mountains. Walker was able to do no such thing, and he wisely remained silent. MacArthur said he would decide later. (A few hours later he briefly ordered, then canceled, the proposed drive.)

MacArthur announced these decisions—tantamount to a forced retreat of his entire command—in a November 29 cable that nonetheless downplayed the JCS fears about his troops and defended his positioning of them.[9] Rather than being threatened with decimation, MacArthur claimed, X Corps actually was challenging the main supply lines of the Chinese arrayed against the Eighth Army and was also tying down six to eight Chinese divisions that otherwise might be free to move against EUSAK's flank. How X Corps could fulfill such a mission once it was withdrawn into the coastal region was something MacArthur did not explain. What he was ordering his troops to do, and what he was telling the JCS they *were* doing, did not match. General Smith, for his part, had been around MacArthur long enough to seize the opening he had wanted for weeks. Once X Corps was authorized to pull back from its abortive offense, he told the 1st Marine Division to start thinking of ways to preserve itself.

MacArthur, however, did not heed the JCS suggestion that his command be formed into a single line. Doing so would be "impracticable" because of the distances involved, the numerical weaknesses of his troops, and the logistical problems caused by the mountainous spur through the middle of Korea.

The JCS did not find MacArthur's words reassuring.[10] General Bradley, reading his photostated copy of the message, scrawled doubting comment after doubting comment in the margin, especially the claim about X Corps's "threatening" enemy supply lines. He put a huge question mark alongside MacArthur's reasons for not joining the corps with EUSAK. Army historian Robert J. Watson interviewed Bradley two decades later and found the general still remembering this message —of the scores received from MacArthur—as "insulting." Bradley told Watson, "with some emotion," that MacArthur "treated us as if we were children." What remains inexplicable is why the JCS tolerated such behavior.

Less than two hours after receipt of this message the Joint Chiefs heard from MacArthur again, this time in a message tinged with panic.[11] Despite all efforts at air interdiction, the Chinese continued to strengthen their troops. Intelligence reports said enemy troops were reaching the front in two night marches, making possible a "continuous and rapid buildup." He saw further Eighth Army withdrawals as inevitable. "Everything leads to the conclusion," he said, that the CCF intended "the complete destruction" of the UN Command.

This somber news brought the JCS into their fourth session in as many days, from 3:10 to 4:55 P.M. on November 29.[12] Again, however, the

Joint Chiefs were reluctant to give MacArthur direct orders. They did state in slightly stronger words their fear that a "progressively widening gap" might develop between the Eighth Army and X Corps. The JCS felt it important that X Corps units be "extricated from their exposed position as soon as practicable" and that the two commands "be sufficiently coordinated to prevent large enemy forces from passing between them or outflanking either of them." The JCS cast these concerns into the form not of a directive but of a "hope" that MacArthur would consider them in planning his next moves.

When the message went to Marshall for review, he added an instruction to MacArthur that "the entire region northeast of the waist of Korea [the X Corps area] should be ignored except for strategic and tactical considerations relating to the security of your command."

The next spring, at hearings following MacArthur's dismissal, Bradley was asked why the JCS had taken no direct action to close the gap. Bradley replied:

> Well, . . . we were a little bit worried, looking at the map from here. . . . We did not send him any message as to our worries about the disposition because you cannot fight a battle or conduct a battle from 7,000 miles away, which we were. You must let your field commander fight that battle.[13]

General Collins thought that Bradley "might have added that just as the JCS could not conduct the battle from 7,000 miles away, neither could General MacArthur from a distance of 700 miles."[14]

A Beleaguered Truman

For Harry S. Truman, the bad news from the battlefield presaged the worst month of his presidency. As December 1950 began, he headed a beleaguered government that was simultaneously losing a foreign war and alienating traditional allies such as the British. Now domestic opposition also crushed down upon him, a turn signaled by Republican successes in the November 1950 congressional elections. The Democratic majority in the Senate was cleaved from twelve to two; in the House, from seventeen to twelve. The defeated senators included three of Truman's strongest voices on Capitol Hill: Scott Lucas of Illinois, the majority leader; Millard Tydings of Maryland, chairman of the Armed Services Committee; and Francis J. Myers of Pennsylvania, the majority whip. Conversely the Republicans added such strongly pro-Nationalist China figures as Richard Nixon of California, Everett Dirksen of Illinois, and John Butler of Maryland as well as retained administration foes Robert Taft of Ohio, Bourke Hickenlooper of Iowa, Eugene Milliken of Colorado, Homer Capehart of Indiana, and Alexander Wiley of Vermont. Furthermore, the victorious Republicans during their campaign had castigated Truman for the "loss" of China and other gains of communism, even attributing Western setbacks to a "conspiracy" within the administration itself. They wanted a more vigorous anti-Mao policy, less deference to Western allies such as Britain, and less economic aid, plus a "housecleaning" of the State Department, from Acheson on down. Richard Stebbins, of the Council on Foreign Relations, noted that administration foreign policies had never been immune from criticism, although it was questionable whether the critics were an important segment of American opinion.[15] But "after November 7 there could no longer be any doubt that large numbers of Americans were out of sympathy with the Administration's methods and dubious about its objectives." Arthur Krock wrote in *The New York Times* the day after the votes were counted that the State Department was the "loser" in the election.

Robert Taft saw the election results as a clear road map to the presidency in 1952. His overwhelming win in Ohio made him the front-runner for the GOP nomination, and he did not intend to run the "me-too" internationalism campaign which he felt had defeated Thomas E. Dewey in 1948.[16] Taft's friendly biographer, William S. White, capsuled the Ohioan's thinking. Winning the White House required a "smashing, rock-breaking sort of campaign full of nothing but attack, to put him, or any other really solid Republican, over anywhere." And Taft was ready to abandon the foreign policy bipartisanship that had marked American politics in the postwar period. He concluded that the Democratic majority in Congress would prevail on domestic issues but that the Republicans possessed a cornucopia of issues on security issues: the secret deals with the Soviets at Teheran, Yalta, and Potsdam; the loss of the atomic monopoly; Alger Hiss and other cases of alleged espionage; the Communist triumph in China. And now Truman had bungled the Korean War.

The eye of Taft's attacks became Acheson, who, in the words of political scientist John W. Spanier, was the "symbol of America's global involvement and the target upon whom most of the accompanying fears and disappointments focused."[17] That the Republicans—Senator Joseph McCarthy in particular—succeeded in picturing Dean Acheson as "soft on communism" remains a ridiculous irony of American politics. The view certainly was not shared by the Kremlin. Acheson was instrumental in shaping the Truman Doctrine, which put the United States behind Greece and Turkey when the British suddenly abandoned their historic responsibilities there, thereby preventing a Soviet sweep into the Middle East, South Asia, and North Africa. Acheson helped devise the Marshall Plan, which put economic props under Western Europe, and the North Atlantic Treaty Organization, which brought West Germany into the U.S.-European military bloc. And the Sunday of the North Korean invasion Dean Acheson was the first Truman adviser—ahead even of the Joint Chiefs of Staff—to recommend that the challenge be met militarily.

But Acheson did not command great personal popularity in Washington. He served a constituency of one—Harry Truman—and even friendly Democratic senators felt uncomfortable around him. The November 1950 election results made congressmen realize that close identification with Acheson was politically dangerous.

Taft began his campaign against administration foreign policy on November 13 with a demand that the United States "re-examine" the scope, methods, and character of its military and economic aid to Europe. (The acerbic Acheson, in reply, likened Taft to a "farmer [who] goes out every morning and pulls up all his crops to see how they have done during the night.") Several days later Taft challenged Truman's stated intention to send four divisions to bolster European defenses and to appoint General Dwight D. Eisenhower as NATO commander. With his close ally Senator Kenneth Wherry, Taft introduced a sense-of-the-Senate resolution asking that no troops be sent to Europe pending formulation of a NATO policy "by the Congress."

The ensuing debate, which stretched into the spring of 1951, put the Truman administration at a distinct disadvantage. It also raised some questions which Truman aides found difficult to answer publicly. Sending a trip-wire force to Europe, one incapable of standing down the Red Army, was tantamount to inviting commitment to a losing land war. Putting troops on frontiers of Soviet satellites was provocative, and useless, anyway, because they would be vulnerable to atomic attack. Besides, why bother protecting Europe when you are unwilling to make a maximum effort in the Far East on behalf of Nationalist China and South Korea? Taft and his proponents would use air and naval power; to them, Europe was expendable. "In my opinion," Taft said at one point in the debate, "we are completely able to defend the *United States itself* [emphasis added]."

Politically the foreign policy debate limited Truman's freedom of movement in Asia. Given the GOP denunciations of his administration for having "lost" China, under no circumstances could he make a peace which seated Peking in the UN or withdrew the American shield that protected Chiang Kai-shek. Douglas MacArthur, from Tokyo, saw what was happening, and many of his provocative statements of December 1950 obviously were issued in the expectation that he could rely upon the Taft Republicans for protection.

But when Taft spoke on Asia, he suffered from glaring inconsistencies. In June 1950 he thought North Korea's aggression was inspired by

President Truman in an informal chat with his key advisers on the Korean War: from left, special assistant Averell Harriman, Secretary of Defense George C. Marshall, Truman, Secretary of State Dean Acheson, Treasury Secretary John Snyder, Army Secretary Frank Pace, and General Omar Bradley, chairman of the Joint Chiefs of Staff. (*National Park Services/Abbie Rowe, Courtesy Harry S. Truman Library*)

Despite mutual antipathy, President Truman and General Douglas MacArthur manage broad smiles for one another at the Wake Island conference, October 1951. (*Department of State, Courtesy Harry S. Truman Library*)

Above: A grief-stricken American infantryman, whose buddy has been killed in action in the Pusan Perimeter defense, August 1950, is comforted by another soldier while a corpsman in the background fills out a casualty tag. (*U.S. Army photograph*)

At right: Korea's foreboding terrain — soaring mountains, meandering valleys — posed special problems for an American army accustomed to operating on roadways. A signalman leans precariously over a cliff while repairing communications lines near Chechon. (*U.S. Army photograph*)

Infantrymen of the 25th Division shield themselves behind rocks from exploding mortar shells during action in central Korea. (*U.S. Army photograph*)

U.S. Marines advance to a new position after knocking out an enemy bunker. (*Defense Department photograph [Marine Corps]*)

Infantrymen direct 75 mm recoilless rifle fire against enemy positions during defense of the Pusan Perimeter. (*U.S. Army photograph*)

The port of Inchon blazes after a pre-invasion bombardment by naval guns and bombing raids by U.S. planes. (*Defense Department photograph [Marine Corps]*)

Scaling ladders at the ready, U.S. Marines ride landing craft toward the Inchon seawall. (*Defense Department photograph [Marine Corps]*)

Landing craft beached in the Inchon mudflats off-load supplies the day after the invasion. (*National Archives*)

President Syngman Rhee of the Republic of Korea, center, chats with visiting Secretary of the Army Frank Pace, right; Ambassador John Muccio is at left. (*Department of Defense, Courtesy Harry S. Truman Library*)

General Douglas MacArthur congratulates General Oliver P. Smith, commanding general of the First Marine Division, for the successful Inchon invasion. Surface amity between the two generals concealed deep differences on war strategy. (*U.S. Army photograph*)

Communist prisoners are herded through the streets of Seoul by marines following recapture of the South Korean capital. (*Defense Department photograph [Marine Corps]*)

Marines trudge down an isolated mountain road in sub-zero temperatures to escape a Chinese Communist trap in the area around Chosin Reservoir in December 1950. General Oliver Smith insisted on evacuating equipment, thereby preserving the First Marine Division's fighting capability. (*U.S. Marine Corps photograph*)

Marines fought off an assault by three Chinese divisions during an epic five-day march down mountain trails to the sea. Heavy snowfalls added to the marines' misery. They prevailed, however, and brought out the wounded and their equipment. (*Defense Department photographs [Marine Corps]*)

Blazing napalm removes a Chinese Communist roadblock that had stalled the marine march down the mountains from Chosin Reservoir. (*Defense Department photograph [Marine Corps]*)

Lieutenant General Matthew B. Ridgway, grenades clipped to his chest, visits a battlefield with General MacArthur in April 1951, a few days before succeeding him as U.S. commander in Korea. (*U.S. Army photograph*)

Their cold-weather gear reminiscent of that worn by the Chinese enemy, soldiers of the 25th Infantry Division watch phosphorus shells hit Communist-held areas in February 1951. (*U.S. Army photograph*)

Marines work their way through a battered Korean village during the renewed UN offensive of spring 1951. (*U.S. Marine Corps photograph*)

Mass assaults by the Chinese resulted in tremendous casualties during the spring 1951 offensive. Marine machine guns and rifles cut down more than 400 of the enemy during a single ten-hour engagement on the central front. This scene was repeated dozens of times all along the front. (*U.S. Marine Corps photograph*)

Marines also suffered during the offensive: *Above,* a wounded marine sips hot coffee and *at right,* awaiting evacuation to a rear area hospital, three other men help one another down from a steep ridge where they were wounded. Rapid helicopter evacuations and the presence of field hospitals close to the lines enhanced the chances of survival for wounded men. (*Defense Department photograph [Marine Corps]*)

A South Korean guerrilla receives preliminary parachute training at the CIA island base in Pusan harbor. Guerrillas were later parachuted into North Korea and Communist China for sabotage and intelligence missions. (*Hans Tofte Collection*)

Hans Tofte, left, directed the Central Intelligence Agency's covert operations against the Communists during the Korean War; with him are Colonel "Dutch" Kraemer, a marine officer detailed to the CIA, and a South Korean guerrilla leader. In the background is a C-46 from the private air force amassed by the CIA during the war; "Civil Air Transport" was ostensibly a civilian company based in Nationalist China. (*Hans Tofte Collection*)

A South Korean military policeman displays a sampling of weapons seized in the prisoner-of-war compound on notorious Koje-do Island. Communists made knives and spearheads from the steel supports in their shoes, while sharp daggers were made from oil-drum metal. Rifles were fashioned from discarded wood, the hand grenades from C-ration cans. (*U.S. Army photograph*)

the Soviets and feared it might "lead to a war with Soviet Russia. It is entirely possible that Soviet Russia might move . . . to help the North Koreans and that the present limited . . . conflict might cover the entire civilized world." But then he began listening to MacArthur. When China entered the war, he could not see "that any bombing of China without invasion can be regarded by Russia as an aggressive move against Russia itself, or reason for war." He supported MacArthur's calls for bombing Manchuria, for a naval blockade of China, and for use of Nationalist troops either to invade or to threaten invasion "to keep South China in an uproar." He did not worry that a "tougher" U.S. policy in Asia would turn the Korean War into a nuclear holocaust. Oddly, however, he did not wish a "tougher" policy in Europe because it *would* provoke the Soviet Union. Thus he voted against ratification of the NATO treaty and the sending of U.S. troops to Europe.

Taft also did an unembarrassed about-face over the correctness of Truman's response in Korea. In June opposing Communist aggression was consistent with America's national interests. But once the Chinese entered, the United States had been "suckered" into war by the UN, a "weak reed." Truman had "rashly sent to Korea any American soldier who was available." Taft could not decide what he wished: At various times he advocated withdrawal of American troops to Japan, Okinawa, and Formosa; a few days later he would back MacArthur's demands for more aggressive moves against China.

To the lay citizen not seeped daily in diplomatic and political nuance, Taft's criticisms were a confusing and demoralizing refrain. Americans knew from their daily newspapers that things were going poorly in Korea and that the American army might have to withdraw. Truman's vacillation was as confusing as that of Taft; he would not acknowledge the fact that the country was at war, nor would he order the mobilization necessary to put the United States on a war footing. He wished to fight a war without disturbing America's daily life. Business, labor, consumers, farmers—all wished to enjoy the continued pleasures of the postwar economy. But public discontent with the war grew weekly. In the end Harry Truman was to satisfy virtually no one.

An episode on December 13 signaled the Republican determination to drive Truman from office.[18] The President had called leaders of both parties to the White House to discuss proclaiming a national emergency, increasing production of military equipment, and imposing certain economic controls.* Acheson thought that Senators Taft, Wherry, and Alexander Smith were "unusually quiet and noncommittal" during the meeting. Later, as secretaries tidied the room, one found a memorandum on stationery of the Republican Policy Committee. The paper

---

*Tax increases and price controls enabled Truman to keep a tight rein on the economy during the war. Inflation was 6.6 percent the first year of the war and only 1.6 percent in 1953.[19]

bore no signature, but it was where Wherry had been sitting. The memo advised against any Republican participation in the national emergency proclamation, "in order to preserve the party's position in case of possible impeachment proceedings." After some discussion someone on the White House staff telephoned Wherry to report that a "sealed envelope" had been found after the meeting and to ask whether he had lost anything.

"So that's where I left it!" Wherry exclaimed. The envelope was returned—sealed, but its contents known to Truman.

MacArthur Passes the Blame

His army in retreat, MacArthur struggled to preserve his image as an infallible battle commander. The record suggests he knew he had talked himself into grave trouble; if his army were to be "home by Christmas," it would be in defeat, not in victory. So MacArthur energetically rewrote the history of the previous week, surely one of the swiftest attempts at revisionism ever attempted. MacArthur sensed Americans and Europeans alike would search for a scapegoat; hence the importance of recasting the purpose of his offensive and explaining that it had failed because of political strictures imposed by Washington, not strategic blunders in the field. The barrage of interviews and special "statements" from MacArthur's headquarters was dizzying: on November 28 a special communiqué to Ray Henle of the obscure *Three Star Extra* radio news program; on November 30 a reply to a query from Arthur Krock, chief Washington correspondent of *The New York Times,* the most esteemed daily journalist in the country; on December 1 an interview with *U.S. News & World Report;* and a lengthy cable to Hugh Baillie, president of the United Press. Other interviews and messages were given or cabled to Ward Price of the London *Daily Mail* (to reach foreign audiences) and to Barry Faris, managing editor of International News Service. MacArthur stressed three themes in these statements:

—First, he repeated the claim originally made in his November 28 cable to the JCS that his offensive prematurely forced the Chinese hand, ruining plans for a surprise offensive that would have destroyed his command and conquered Korea "in one invincible movement."

—Secondly, he denied that his thrust deep into North Korea had provoked the Chinese intervention. Every move he made had been in accord with UN resolutions. He hit at "misleading anonymous gossip" that he had been directed to stop at the 38th parallel, Pyongyang, or "any other line short of the international boundary." (Technically MacArthur was accurate; however, he glossed over directives that only

ROK troops, not Americans, operate in territories immediately adjacent to Manchuria.) The "decision by the Chinese Communist leaders to wage war against the United Nations could only have been a basic one, long premeditated and carried into execution as a direct result of the defeat of their satellite North Korean armies. . . ."

—Thirdly, and most vociferously, MacArthur objected to press descriptions of his "planned withdrawal" from North Korea as a "retreat." (MacArthur certainly succeeded in concealing his intention from his field commanders.) He blamed "ignorant" correspondents who could not distinguish between a skilled withdrawal and an army "running in full flight." MacArthur did credit the Chinese with some "tactical successes" but said these were possible only because of overwhelming numerical superiority and at "staggering personnel cost." He was especially angry about "irresponsible comments" in the European press and criticized the "somewhat selfish though shortsighted viewpoint" of Europeans who considered the defense of their own continent more important than Asia.

—Finally, MacArthur implicitly criticized his superiors in Washington for forbidding him to strike at Communist forces across the Yalu.

He told *U.S. News & World Report:*

Q. Are the limitations which prevent unlimited pursuit of Chinese . . . forces and unlimited attack on their bases regarded by you as a handicap to effective military operations?
A. An enormous handicap, without precedent in military history.
Q. What accounts for the fact that an enemy without air power can make effective progress against forces possessing considerable air power?
A. The limitations aforementioned, plus the type of maneuver which renders air support of ground operations extremely difficult and the curtailment of the strategic potentiality of the air because of the sanctuary of neutrality immediately behind the battle area.
Q. Is there a significant lesson in this for U.S. planning?
A. Yes.

The next two questions dealt with use of the atomic bomb, and MacArthur's replies were chillingly evasive.

Q. Can anything be said as to the effectiveness or ineffectiveness of the [atomic] bomb in the type of operations in which you are now engaged?
A. My comment at this time would be inappropriate.*
Q. In the type of warfare now going on in Korea, are there large enough concentrations of enemy troops to make the bomb effective?
A. My comment at this time would be inappropriate.

*The questions have the quality of batting-practice pitches served for a purpose. MacArthur could have ruled out this question, and the following one, and refused any answer whatsoever.

MacArthur painted a dark picture of his travail: "Never before has the patience of man been more sorely tried nor high standards of human behavior been more patiently tried and firmly upheld than during the course of the Korean campaigns."

Truman was infuriated by these statements, and especially by the *U.S. News & World Report* article, for the magazine was his dedicated enemy. So far as the President was concerned, MacArthur had committed the sin of consorting with political enemies. Truman later told intimates he had been intending "to fire MacArthur" for some months. But with the UN Command in trouble Truman felt compelled to defend the general against critics, especially Europeans. He told a press conference on November 30, "They are always for a man when he is winning but when he is in a little trouble they all jump on him with what ought to be done which they didn't tell him before." MacArthur "has done a good job and he is continuing to do a good job." But Truman that evening scorned MacArthur in the privacy of a diary entry:

> This has been a hectic month. General Mac as usual, has been shooting off his mouth. He made a pre-election statement that cost us votes and he made a post-election statement that has him in hot water in Europe and at home. I must defend him and save his face even if he has tried on various and numerous occasions to cut mine off. But I must stand by my swordmates, and wouldn't Mac "love" that statement from a man he considers "inferior."

MacArthur's press statements disgusted Robert Lovett, the undersecretary of defense, who told Dean Acheson that MacArthur was "scared" and was issuing "posterity papers."[20] Lovett disputed MacArthur's claim that no authoritative source had advised him that it would be unwise to push forward to the border. He called the statement "false and mendacious." He also found it "one of the most extraordinary things he has ever seen . . . that the General should have sat down at a time like this" to write messages to the press.

As MacArthur's critical statements continued, Truman finally moved to silence him. On December 6 he issued two orders, directed at all executive officials—but clearly targeted for MacArthur. The first directed that no speech, press release, "or other public statement concerning foreign policy" be issued without clearance of the State Department. The purpose was to ensure that information made public "is accurate and fully in accord with the policies of the United States government." The second directive was more explicit. It stated that officials overseas, including military commanders and diplomatic representatives, should "exercise extreme caution in public statements, to clear all but routine statements with their departments, and to refrain from direct communication on military or foreign policy with newspapers, magazines or other publicity media in the United States." The order slowed the commentary from MacArthur's headquarters, but only for the moment. Quieting MacArthur did not equate with silencing him.

Loose Nuclear Talk

Despite his efforts to hush MacArthur, the President himself touched the sorest nerve among European allies—and many Americans as well —with careless talk about using nuclear weapons in Korea. Since the war began, the Pentagon had done continuing studies of circumstances under which atomic weapons might be used. On November 20, a week before the MacArthur offensive, General Lawton Collins told colleagues it was "conceivable that the JCS will be required to present their views concerning the use of the atomic bomb in Korea on short notice. It is also conceivable that, in the event of an all-out effort by the Chinese Communists, the use of atomic bombs against troop and material concentrations might be the decisive factor in enabling the UN forces to hold a defensive position or to effect [an] early drive to the Manchurian border."[21] He advised a contingency study on the use of nuclear weapons.

Nothing apparently was done on his suggestion for another week, when the Chinese entered the war in force. On November 28 Rear Admiral W. G. Lalor, the JCS secretary, sent a "priority" requirement to the Joint Strategic Survey Committee.[22] Should the Soviets intervene, Lalor desired recommendations on "the possible use of the atomic bomb as a factor to discourage such continued intervention and/or to assist in the evacuation of UN forces from Korea." He asked comments on the possible number of bombs, target areas, and considerations as to "use, timing, transportation etc." He also asked for comments on the "use of conventional and atomic bombs against China, with or without previous ultimatum."

Even the *possible* use of atomic weapons was a closely held secret in the JCS bureaucracy. Lalor's memo bore an admonition: "The only copy of this memorandum is in the possession of the Secretary, Joint Chiefs of Staff. The JCS direct that knowledge of the subject matter herein be very closely guarded."

The JCS staff study was still in progress on November 30, when President Truman was drawn into a discussion of nuclear weaponry at a press conference. The President used language that was both loose and legally inaccurate.

Q. (by Anthony Leviero, *The New York Times*): Mr. President, will attacks in Manchuria depend on action in the United Nations?

The PRESIDENT. Yes, entirely.

Q. (Leviero): In other words, if the UN should authorize General MacArthur to go further than he has, he will?

The PRESIDENT. We will take whatever steps are necessary to meet the military situation, just as we always have.

Q. (Jack Dougherty, New York *Daily News*): Will that include the atomic bomb?

The PRESIDENT. That includes every weapon that we have.

Q. (Paul R. Leach, Chicago *Daily News*): Mr. President, you said, "every weapon that we have." Does that mean that there is active consideration of the use of the atomic bomb?

The PRESIDENT. There has always been active consideration of its use. I don't want to see it used. It is a terrible weapon and it should not be used on innocent men, women and children who have nothing whatever to do with this military aggression—that happens when it's used.

Merriman Smith, the veteran correspondent for the United Press, apparently thought the President had put the case stronger than intended. He gave Truman a chance to back away.

Q. Mr. President, I wonder if we could retrace that reference to the atomic bomb. Did we understand you clearly that the use of the atomic bomb is under active consideration?

The PRESIDENT. Always has been, Smitty. It's one of our weapons.

Q. (Robert Dixon, International News Service): Does that mean, Mr. President, use against military objectives or civilian—

The PRESIDENT (interposing). *It is a matter that the military people will have to decide. I am not a [the] military authority that passes on these things* [emphasis added].

Reporters returned to the subject a few questions later.

Q. (Frank Bourgholtzer, NBC News): Mr. President, you said this depends on the United Nations action. Does that mean that we would not use the atomic bomb except on a United Nations authorization?

The PRESIDENT. No, it does not mean that at all. The action against Communist China depends on the action of the United Nations. *The military commander in the field will have charge of the use of the weapons, as he always has* [emphasis added].

President Truman was flatly wrong, as the pained White House press office said a few hours later in a "clarifying statement." Under the Atomic Energy Act, only the President can authorize use of the atomic bomb. But before this statement was issued, both the Associated Press and United Press had flashed Truman's misstatement around the world, causing "much excitement at home and abroad," as Edward T. Folliard wrote in the Washington *Post.* British officials said they were "shocked and astounded" by the statement, which they took to mean that the unpredictable MacArthur had been given a free hand to use the atomic bomb against the Chinese.

Although Truman was never noted for precision of language, his misstatement of presidential authority on such a sensitive issue was so glaring that it is suspicious. In his own memoirs (at times poor history), Truman says the press misunderstood him, although he does not bother to quote his own assertion that use of nuclear weapons "is a matter that the military people will have to decide." There is a smidgen of evidence that Truman did not misspeak: that he intended to warn the Chinese, and the Soviets, that escalated violence in Korea risked all-out war.[23]

The circumstances: The afternoon of November 30, a few hours after Truman's press conference, Baron Silvercruys, the Belgian ambassador in Washington, met with Dean Rusk, the assistant secretary of state. Silvercruys noted that the Belgian foreign minister, Paul Van Zeeland, in his capacity as president of the Council of Ministers, spoke frequently with other Western European leaders. Accordingly he could "convey any opinions we might have" to those men. Rusk responded that while the United States was prepared to "do everything possible to avoid a general breakout of the war, we were not going to withdraw from Korea."

In Rusk's account, Baron Silvercruys then referred to Truman's statement about the atomic bomb "and asked if I meant that we were going to use it." Rusk replied, "I could not say whether or not we were going to use the atomic bomb." Silvercruys said he "presumed" the President meant he would be guided by recommendations of military field commanders since the President alone could authorize the use of the atom bomb.

Rusk said nothing further about nuclear weapons during the conversation. But as he walked Silvercruys to the elevator, the Belgian said that if the United States did intend to bring the atomic bomb into the war, "he could not see any particular value to using it against Chinese cities. Why not go a little further and destroy the Soviet facilities for manufacturing atom bombs?" Silvercruys noted these facilities "were not located at too great an air distance from the scene of our present operations."

Rusk did not respond. But the thrust of his statement meant that a friendly ambassador was handed an ambiguity for his foreign minister to spread in European capitals. If Truman were indeed attempting a nuclear bluff, his message would reach the Chinese and Soviets in short order.

Whatever Truman's motive, his comments started a furor in the British Parliament which the U.S. embassy called "the most serious, anxious and responsible debate on foreign affairs conducted by the

House of Commons since the Labor Party came to power in 1945."[24] Some 100 Labor MPs signed a letter to Prime Minister Clement Attlee protesting any use of the bomb. The discontent in Parliament was general, including even the staunch American friends Sir Winston Churchill and Anthony Eden, both out-of-power Conservatives. Another Conservative leader, Richard A. Butler, said that "British people as a whole wished to be assured before their fate was decided [by an extension of the war to China] that they were helping to decide their own fate."

During the debate Attlee's aides frantically telephoned the U.S. embassy. The prime minister said he would like to wind down the debate by announcing he intended to meet Truman to discuss "problems of mutual concern."[25] The President quickly agreed, momentarily relieving the tension in Parliament, which adjourned with a chorus of cheers.

UN Allies Revolt

Concurrently the administration heard rumblings from the United Nations, where Ambassador Warren Austin reported a swelling "lack of confidence" in MacArthur because of feelings that he was not "sufficiently responsive to direction."[26] On November 29, even before Truman provoked the uproar over atomic weaponry, Sir Gladwyn Jebb, the British UN ambassador, and Jean Chauvel of France bearded Ernest A. Gross of the State Department in a long gripe session about U.S. policy. They stressed European fears about being "on the front lines and wide open to all-out Soviet military attack." They did not want to let the "Asiatic octopus squeeze out all our common strength." Jebb was blunt: Should six Labor members abstain on a confidence vote on Korea, Attlee's government would fall. Thus Attlee had little room for maneuver.

Truman's nuclear remarks brought the Western ambassadors trotting back to UN Ambassador Austin late in the afternoon of November 30 in deep alarm.[27] Chauvel said the Dutch representative had asked him "with tears in his eyes" whether he saw any chance of avoiding war. Jebb said other Western Europeans shared with the British "the tremendous apprehension" that the United States was committing them to war in Asia "at an impossible time and under the most difficult possible strategic conditions." The Europeans did not want to condemn China as an aggressor because this was tantamount to attempting "reconquest and liberation of areas" already seized by Peking.

The unified front of the United Nations was eroding rapidly.

Washington Considers Withdrawal

Overnight cables reaching Washington November 30–December 1 told
of a rapidly deteriorating battlefield situation. At eight-thirty that morning (a Friday) one of the more somber assemblages of the war gathered
in the JCS conference room.[28] For the first time since the early days of
the war serious discussion was heard on whether the United States
should admit defeat and retire from Korea altogether.

One key factor was what Dean Acheson called the "virtual state of
panic which seemed to exist among our friends" in the UN. Many were
complaining, he said, that U.S. leadership had failed and that the "present difficulties are the fault of General MacArthur's action." Acheson
thought it essential that unity be restored for the sake of European
security.

Acheson proposed finding a line that could be defended militarily and
then using it as the basis for opening political negotiations on ending
the war. He saw dangers: The Chinese might refuse to accept a static
line. And even if the United States vacated Korea and the Chinese
withdrew into Manchuria, the ROKs would still have to cope with the
North Koreans. "The question was where that would leave us," Acheson
said.

"In any event," he continued, "we must do something in Korea, and
we must do something to counter the rapid resurgence of neutralism
in Germany." Acheson wanted to speak to the General Assembly the
following week but not until the United States had an agreed plan of
action.

But Acheson wanted guidance from the military. If holding a line was
impossible militarily, "we are confronted with a new set of problems
and must proceed on different assumptions."

General Bradley could offer only pessimistic conjecture. Unless X
Corps could regroup, "it is hard to stabilize a line. One cannot tell now.
If our losses are heavy in the east, we may not have enough troops to
hold a line." Bradley mentioned intelligence reports of very heavy
traffic coming in from Manchuria. "We may have to fall much further
back," he said. He repeated what the JCS, with Truman's approval, had
told MacArthur the previous evening: that from the standpoint of the
UN mission, it was unnecessary to hold the territory north of the waist
and that except for considerations involving the security of his command, "he could ignore the area."

But what would be the most advantageous thing to do? asked Acheson.

Again, neither Bradley nor General Lawton Collins could give an
answer (one result being that General Marshall told Collins to leave for
Japan and Korea that very day to seek some answers).

Admiral Forrest Sherman said that "from a strategic point of view" the United States should get out of Korea and retire to the Japanese islands. However, he said, abandoning Korea "would be dangerous to Japan due to airfields in Korea." Thus the United States should hold Korea at the waist as a long-term strategic plan.

Sherman was amazed that the Chinese had let the UN maintain sole control of the air. He took sharp, if unstated, issue with MacArthur's demand that he be permitted to bomb Manchurian airfields. "We should not interfere with this situation until our position is straightened out," he said. At present the "advantage of keeping our air on our side of the frontier outweighs the disadvantages." If Russian air came in, "we might not be able to hold." But even if the situation stabilized, should the United States send other fleet elements and troops to Korea at the expense of Atlantic defenses?

Bradley did not want to decide in advance what to do if the Chinese sent in planes. Hitting back "might draw in the Soviet air. If this is true, we may have to defer striking."

General Collins strongly supported Bradley. "If we hit back," he said, "it is a strong provocation of the Chinese and might possibly bring in Soviet air and even submarines. The only chance then left to save us is the use or the threat of the use of the A-bomb. We should therefore hold back from bombing in China even if this means that our ground forces must take some punishment from the air." To Collins, "Korea was not worth a nickel while the Russians hold Vladivostok and positions on the other flank."

General Walter Bedell Smith, director of central intelligence, reported that a new CIA estimate "makes a much better case than . . . previously thought for Russian plans for war soon." The Soviets' first purpose was to defeat European rearmament. "They probably do not plan on war now but are willing to have it if they can bog us down in Asia," Smith said. The CIA chief's advice was direct: "We should get out of Korea now, although we do not solve the problem by getting out. The Russians are sure we don't intend to get into war in Asia, and so feel that they can push us as far as they want. . . . They could bleed us to death in Asia while defeating the rearmament effort in Europe."

Robert Lovett, the deputy defense secretary, tried to bring a consensus: that although Korea was not a decisive area, losing it might jeopardize Japan. Thus "it was best to hold in Korea for political moves. We should regroup our troops and stall for time. The outcome might be a mutual withdrawal from Korea."

There was more talk about what should happen in the event of massive Chinese air attacks, with both Bradley and Smith agreeing that if "real Russian support of the Chinese developed, we would have to evacuate and probably would be engaged in war." That meant, interjected Collins, either the "threat or the use of the A-bomb."

Acheson finally put the question directly: What did the military people think of accepting a cease-fire and going back to the 38th parallel? He asked whether, from a military point of view, that would be "the best choice and whether they [the brass] would consider we were lucky to get such an arrangement."

Generals Bradley and Collins and Admiral Sherman concurred, although both Marshall and Collins said "we should not agree on it yet."

As the discussion ended, General Marshall said, somewhat wanly, that "the acceptance of the cease-fire would represent a great weakness on our part." No one cared to pursue the thought. What had happened, in the space of an hour's time in the sanctity of a Pentagon conference room, was a U.S. decision to abandon any thought of victory in Korea, to make the best deal possible on the basis of a yet undefined truce line, and get out of the war.

The United States was not to win in Korea.

Questions from Congress

By happenstance the day of the crucial Pentagon meeting (December 1) also happened to be the day when President Truman asked Congress for a $17 billion supplemental appropriation to support the war—four times the Pentagon's pre-Korea annual budget. To muster support, he invited congressional leaders to the White House for a briefing on the war and the overall world situation.[29]

The congressmen were not pleased with what they heard. Was it not true, asked Representative John McCormack (Democrat of Massachusetts) that "it was a well known fact that the Chinese Communists had been present in Manchuria in large numbers?"

"Yes," replied General Bradley.

"Isn't there a command intelligence at MacArthur's headquarters?" McCormack asked sarcastically.

General Walter Bedell Smith of the CIA talked about ominous signs from the Soviets. "In the past ten days, events in the Soviet areas of Europe had been very quiet and this in itself was a disquieting fact," Smith said. The Russians had just finished "very large scale maneuvers" involving some 500,000 men and concentrating on airborne operations and river crossings. Between 60 and 70 percent of the Soviet armed strength was estimated to be west of the Ural Mountains, arrayed against Western Europe.

Senator Kenneth Wherry wanted to know how Smith got his figures. Smith said the military figures came from "military attachés, from defectors, from deserters, and from 'other means.'" Wherry asked if CIA used "all sources."

"We have no morals," Smith responded. (Laughter greeted this statement.)

Smith next talked about guerrilla forces operating in China. Their equipment, he said, "was very poor," but "efforts were under way to improve it."

Senator Wherry asked what kind of help was being given the guerrillas. Smith would not answer in detail, but he did say that "assistance was being given in the form of money, advice and 'objectives.'"*

Truman then moved to the point of the meeting. The $17 billion supplemental request he would send Congress had been "raised significantly" because of the Chinese attack. He asked that Congress act swiftly. The crisis had accelerated military procurement by about eighteen months. "We are trying to get by mid-'52 what we wanted for mid-'53," the President said.

As the meeting ended, Truman urged the congressmen to remember they had heard "extremely secret" information. "Don't tell anybody— not even your wives. What you heard here today is something I don't even hear unless I push these people into telling me."

Senator Richard B. Russell (Democrat of Georgia) was sorry he had heard all he had heard. He didn't think he talked in his sleep, and he hoped he wouldn't tonight.

A U.S. Suit for Peace?

Whether viewed from Washington, Tokyo, or the myriad battlefields in Korea, Saturday, December 2 ranked as one of the gloomier days of the war. At an early-morning meeting in the State Department, Dean Acheson told subordinates to begin thinking about how to approach the Soviets or Chinese, or both, about a cease-fire. There was continued talk about a UN resolution, but Acheson made plain that the overriding factor was the "extremely pessimistic" view the Pentagon had of the battlefield situation.

The CIA, in a report circulated in midmorning, concluded that "it is highly improbable that the Chinese Communist regime would have accepted this risk without explicit assurances of effective Soviet support."[30] The agency predicted that the Soviets would "come openly to the military support of Communist China, under terms of the Sino-Soviet Treaty, in the event of major U.S. . . . operations against Chinese territory." The Soviet Union "is prepared to accept, and may be seeking to precipitate, a general war between the United States and China,

*See Chapter Seventeen below.

despite the inherent risk of global war." But whether the Soviets were ready for global war themselves was a question the CIA said it could not answer.

Staff discussions continued at the State and Defense departments and the CIA throughout the day; by nightfall Acheson and General Marshall were ready to report to Truman at the White House.

Bradley said it bluntly.[31] In forty-eight to seventy-two hours the military situation would reach a "crash state." Logistically X Corps could be evacuated within five days, but he wondered about "the manner of the evacuation unless the cease-fire were secured." The 7th Army Division "might be saved," and the 3rd Division, near the ports, "could get out." But "we could not take our troops out and leave the ROK Capital and other divisions behind."

Marshall said that even a "Dunkirk type" of evacuation might be imperiled if the Chinese launched air attacks. The dilemma, Marshall said, was "between saving our troops and our national honor."

Truman asked about MacArthur's repeated requests for operations across the border. Acheson said any such decision should be based "solely on whether it would hurt or help our troops." He felt "we need a very good military judgment on whether knocking out the Chinese airfields would bring in the Russians." The decision should be made not by MacArthur but by Secretary Marshall on the advice of General Collins, then en route to Tokyo and Korea.

Then Acheson attempted a move to supplant MacArthur as the U.S. commander in the Far East. He did so by indirection. Acheson suggested that Collins "should stay in Tokyo" for the duration of the crisis. As the secretary of state well knew, the presence of the army chief of staff would put MacArthur in a subordinate role. ("I had lost all faith in MacArthur's judgment," Acheson wrote in his memoirs.) But not a single member of the Joint Chiefs spoke in support of Acheson, and his idea died without a seconding voice.

So the discussion returned to possible UN Security Council action, which Truman considered nothing more than a "good stall for time." A larger question was the price the Chinese would ask "as payment for a settlement." Acheson thought "the least they could ask was that we go south of the 38th Parallel." Marshall did not think they would "ask for this little." Acheson saw escalating demands: the United States' leaving Korea; a Chinese seat in the United Nations; abandonment of Formosa; even bringing the Chinese into the Japanese peace negotiations, with the ultimate goal of squeezing the United States out of Japan.

No one wanted to take responsibility for asking the Chinese for a cease-fire. Marshall noted the crisis might peak before the scheduled meeting between the President and Prime Minister Attlee three days away. The British should be consulted before any "definitive action was taken." Marshall saw a way for the United States to save some semblance of pride. "It would be better to have Mr. Attlee suggest a settlement rather than having [*sic*] us bear the burden of making the suggestion."

The talk turned to domestic considerations. Acheson wanted to have the armed forces "built up as quickly as possible," to have the President declare a national emergency, and to establish controls on prices, wages, and production. Truman agreed. Then he told Acheson, Marshall, and Bradley to meet with the Joint Chiefs the following morning and report to him immediately thereafter.

For the Truman administration, the Korean War was now a salvage operation.

China at the UN

The Chinese Communist emissaries, meanwhile, had arrived at the Lake Success headquarters of the United Nations, but Western attempts to deal with them were futile.[32] In an information cable to American diplomatic missions, Acheson said their attitude was "completely intransigent and non-conciliatory." Even attempts for talks by delegations friendly to Peking "have been repulsed," and the Chinese "are being isolated from contact with all delegations except that of Soviet." State wanted pressure brought upon friendly governments to support a General Assembly resolution condemning China, along the lines of the Security Council resolution vetoed by the Soviets.

Circumstances suggest the Chinese delegates could not move without specific instructions from Peking. The Indian delegate B. N. Rau finally met the Chinese general Wu Hsiu-chuan late the evening of December 1 (a "hardheaded soldier," Rau called him[33]). Also present was a lower-ranked "adviser" named Ch'iao Kuan-hua, who bore a number of titles in the Chinese Foreign Ministry, including that of director of the International News Bureau. Rau thought that Ch'iao was the "brains" of the group. Yes, the Chinese might have dinner with the Indians, but not for forty-eight hours. (The U.S. delegation's Ernest Gross thought that Rau was "following [a] weak appeasing line.")

That night Gross encountered Rau at a dinner party. Rau pulled him aside with the message that the Chinese were now ready to talk, at 10:30 A.M. the next day. "Because of Rau's tendency to leap out of the water at flies, I undertook to sound some warnings," Gross advised the State Department. He thought some of Rau's enthusiasm the result of "political immaturity." But he wanted to avoid "entrapment" that might create "false hopes among UN members." Thus Gross lectured Rau. The Soviets often diverted free world attempts at negotiations by the "propaganda trick of pretending to want 'discussions.'" He warned Rau against "falling into this familiar trap." Although the United States was "not eager to talk" with General Wu, "if Wu had anything on his mind, we were prepared to listen."

Behind the polite diplomatic language was a message: The United States, although cautiously skeptical, was ready for any signal the Chinese cared to offer on ending the war.

A Grim Washington

James Reston of *The New York Times* perceptively summarized the mood of Washington on Sunday, December 3:

> Every official movement in the capital today, every official report from Tokyo, and every private estimate of the situation by well-informed men reflected a sense of emergency and even of alarm about the state of the United Nations army in Korea. Not even on the fateful night twenty-three weeks ago when the Korean War started was the atmosphere more grim.

For the Pentagon, the news began on a somber note with a Tokyo dispatch shortly after midnight.[34] The UN Command had lost more than 11,000 men dead, wounded, missing, or captured on November 30 and December 1. The 2nd Infantry Division had lost more than 6,380 men, nearly half its strength. The Turkish Brigade was believed to have lost 1,000 men of 5,000. Between them, the Eighth Army and X Corps could put no more than 110,000 men in the field, whereas intelligence estimated the Chinese forces at 256,000, the North Koreans at 10,000.

No sooner had this pessimistic information been digested than MacArthur added his gloomy voice.[35] X Corps was being withdrawn into the Hamhung area "as rapidly as possible." The Eighth Army situation was becoming "increasingly critical," with General Walker now talking about holding a line not at Pyongyang but around Seoul. MacArthur saw no benefit (nor "practicability") in uniting the two forces. Both were "completely outnumbered," and joining them would hamper flows of supplies through separate logistical lines.

He also saw no advantage in forming a line across the waist of Korea. The road distance would be about 150 miles, meaning each of the seven U.S. divisions would have to hold a front of 20 or more miles "against greatly superior numbers of an enemy whose greatest strength is a potential for night infiltration through rugged terrain." MacArthur felt that such a line, with no depth behind it, "would have little strength and as a defensive concept would invite penetration with resultant envelopment and piecemeal destruction." The concept might have worked against the weaker North Koreans, "but against the full forces of the Chinese army [it] is impossible."

Next, MacArthur complained that Washington did not yet comprehend "the basic changes which have been wrought by the undisguised entrance of the Chinese Army into the combat." Twenty-six Chinese divisions were in battle, with a "minimum" of 200,000 troops in the rear moving toward the front. The terrain diminished the worth of American air support; with the enemy concentrated inland, naval gunfire was not effective. The Defense Department had repeatedly told MacArthur no more troops were available. But MacArthur again asked for "ground reinforcements of the greatest magnitude." Otherwise, his command would be forced into successive withdrawals "with diminished powers of resistance after each move," until pushed into "beachhead bastion positions."

MacArthur praised his command's morale and efficiency, even though "it has been in almost unending combat for five months" (a misstatement: The war had been in progress for five months, but the bulk of the American divisions did not enter Korea until mid-September, two and one-half months later). ROK combat effectiveness was "negligible." The other foreign contingents were too small to be influential. What MacArthur wanted was a greatly enhanced army and greatly changed rules under which he could fight:

> The general evaluation of the situation here must be viewed on the basis of an entirely new war against an entirely new power of great military strength and under entirely new conditions.
>
> The directives under which I am operating based upon the North Korean forces as an enemy are completely outmoded by events. The fact must be clearly understood that our relatively small force now faces the full offensive power of the Chinese Communist nation augmented by extensive supply of Soviet material.
>
> The strategic concept suitable for operations against the North Korean army which was so successful is not susceptible to continued application against such power.
>
> This calls for political decisions and strategic plans in implementation thereof, adequate fully to meet the realities involved. In this, time is of the essence as every hour sees the enemy power increase and ours decline.

Gloom at the Pentagon

Ranking State and Defense officials had read the MacArthur communiqué when they gathered at the Pentagon[36] at nine-thirty on Sunday morning "amid deepening gloom," in Acheson's words.[37] MacArthur's complaints brought solace to no one. General Matthew Ridgway, heartsick at the battering of the U.S. Army, gave the briefing on military developments. He was not optimistic. He was not sure whether X Corps would be able to disengage and reach the port of Hungnam or whether the Eighth Army could arrive in Seoul before the Chinese. If the troops reached the beachheads of Inchon, Hamhung, and Pusan, they could hold until a decision was reached on evacuation.

Acheson snapped the meeting to the key question: "Has the military situation reached a point at which it is necessary for us to get a cease-fire?"

Bradley responded that a cease-fire would be "fine" if the price were not too high: "Do we get out of Korea and do they?" The military situation would improve if American troops could get into the beach-heads. The United States was fast losing the initiative. If a cease-fire could not be obtained within forty-eight hours through the UN, "must we conclude that we must take action ourselves?" One course suggested by Bradley was "saying to the Chinese Communists that since they refuse a cease-fire we consider we are at war." He foresaw blockading of the coast, bombing, and "a good many other things to bother them, though we would probably not use the A-bomb."

Acheson was not so ready for a cease-fire as was Bradley. If such a U.S. offer were made, and rejected, it would nonetheless start a UN debate. The United States must consider the security of its troops and its position in the Far East "and the whole world." The secretary of state wanted no precipitate retreat: "There is danger of our becoming the greatest appeasers of all time if we abandon the Koreans and they are slaughtered; if there is a Dunkirk and we are forced out it is a disaster but not a disgraceful one." If the Chinese and Soviets were to ask terms, "it would seem all right to withdraw to the 38th Parallel" (although he quickly added this seemed "too easy" and doubted the enemy would agree).

As a diplomat Acheson did not want to be drawn into negotiations over Formosa, for the United States had no international support on this issue. Other countries, he said, "agree that Formosa is not ours and have no sympathy with our position." But he could find "moral force" support for a cease-fire at the 38th parallel. The United States "must anticipate" that someone—here he mentioned Clement Attlee—would propose a cease-fire, and State's role then would be to persuade other governments to "hold on to what is decent and right."

General Bradley repeated that a cease-fire would be militarily useful, "if the cost is not too great." But "time has now run out on that proposition and we must consider it."

Acheson wanted to "consider carefully" any direct moves against the Chinese. If a cease-fire were rejected, "and we have to fight our way out, all military steps against the Chinese should relate to the evacuation of our troops." He did not wish "mere retaliation," for "if we get into general war with China, and there are grave chances of general war with the Soviet Union soon, then we would fight without allies on our side."

Admiral Sherman wished no compromise. The United States had lost men; "one can say we have lost a campaign, but we are not defeated." He would not ask for a cease-fire. "The only sound basis for dealing with the Chinese Communists would say that unless you stop you are at war with the United States." If the Chinese chose war, "we get our troops out as best we can and fight the war. If we don't take this course, others will begin to push us around. If any one can kill that many Americans and not be at war, we are defeated."

Bradley did not think the Chinese would settle for a cease-fire. He saw a "race to get into the beachhead." The question was not only how long the military could hold the beachheads but also "how long the American public will stand this without saying we are at war with China."

"The great problem is that we are fighting the wrong nation," Acheson said. "We are fighting the second team, whereas the real enemy is the Soviet Union."

Bradley would not put men into China. But he "wondered whether we could come home and just forget the matter."

Acheson "certainly" would not. He asked the Joint Chiefs what the effect of war with China would be on the U.S. ability to fight the Soviet Union, "which would like to see us tangle with the Chinese." If U.S. resources were devoted to a war with China, "we cannot build up strength in Europe."

Another point, Acheson continued, was the effect war with China would have on America's allies. He "thought many of them would quit us and deal with the Soviet Union." The French, Acheson said, "are so weak and shellshocked they are anxious for a deal which would give them an illusion of safety."

The talk next turned to security measures that might be imposed if the United States decided to evacuate. Was censorship desirable? Acheson asked.

Admiral Sherman said it "was most desirable but it was difficult. Perhaps the best way was to get the reporters out of the place."

Acheson recalled General William T. Sherman's policy during the Civil War: "Tell the correspondents all his plans and then lock them up in jail."

Acheson finally asked the key question: Did anyone present doubt that it would be desirable to have a cease-fire on the 38th parallel if some other country suggested it?

No answer was heard—nor any dissent either, according to Philip Jessup's notes of the meeting. However, Bradley did express concern about the "reaction in Congress and among the military forces." How much could be abandoned, he asked, without further action against Communist China? He doubted whether the Chinese would accept the 38th parallel "if we crossed it first."

Bradley saw two questions: politically, whether the United States should ask for a cease-fire; militarily, "when we draw back to the beachheads, do we begin to evacuate our troops or do we fight to a Dunkirk?" Personnel, but not the equipment, could be evacuated swiftly from Inchon. "We can get out more if we begin at once. The same is true of Pusan but there was a question about Hamhung. An immediate decision must be made on whether we begin to withdraw."

Was the equipment vital? Acheson asked. "We have nothing else," Bradley replied, "but you cannot call it vital."

"Should we evacuate the ROK forces?" Acheson asked.

"We could not leave them if they wanted to come out," said H. Freeman Matthews of the State Department.

Marshall returned to the point of "starting from a complete admission of defeat," which he did not like because of the "psychological elements." Politically Marshall "thought it would be useful if someone would put up the proposal of a cease-fire on the 38th Parallel before we get there. Once we are in the beachheads the Chinese Communists can overrun South Korea."

Should the ROK Army be evacuated to Japan? Jessup asked. Rusk thought not. "The Communists were very active among the Koreans now in Japan and it might be risky to bring in the Korean Army." Another home would have to be found for the ROKs.*

Bradley thought the other conferees were not taking seriously enough a view of the American rout and its consequences elsewhere. "If the Chinese attack on us in Korea is not war," he said, "would it be war if they overran our zone in Berlin?" Bradley recalled that "we used to say that an attack on a platoon of United States troops meant war." He did not wish the American army next to be "overrun by East Germans in Berlin." Bradley doubted that the United States could accept a forced withdrawal "without striking back" at the Chinese. He did not

*During the next few months a JCS planning committee cast about for a place that might receive hundreds of thousands of Korean refugees. Japan was dismissed because of "racial antagonisms," and the American-controlled islands of Saipan and Tinian because of sensitive security installations there. The committee finally decided upon the islands of Savaii and Upolu, in the Western Samoa group, administered by New Zealand under a UN mandate. These islands had a population of only 68 persons per square mile, contrasted with 358 per square mile in the American Samoan group; some 328,000 South Koreans could be relocated there. "Advantages are: the Koreans should be able to sustain life with a minimum of outside aid; the location would not interfere in military operations during a global war.... Disadvantages are: the distance of approximately 4,000 miles from Japan;... living facilities are currently not available in the area." The talk about establishing a "new Korea" was kept hush-hush because "the political and psychological effects world-wide would be ... unfavorable."

want war with China. "The effect of pulling out or being kicked out without war with Communist China would, however, be very bad." But he "would not propose any retaliation until after we had completed the evacuation."

Acheson wanted to handle any cease-fire as legalistically as possible. He sketched the diplomatic dilemma. American public opinion would not tolerate the administration's proposing a "cease-fire on any basis." The United States "can't have a cease-fire and still go on fighting the Chinese unless they violated the cease-fire and renew their attack because in that case we alone would be starting a war in violation of the UN order." If the United States must continue the war, "we must not take the course of ending the hostilities; we must be forced out of Korea and therefore we must resist a suggestion of a cease-fire. In that case, we would have to try to get condemnation of the Chinese and have them branded as an aggressor."

Acheson brought the meeting to a conclusion. The President would want to talk with Prime Minister Attlee before making any decisions, especially one that might involve all-out war with China. So what should MacArthur be directed to do? Admiral Sherman urged that he be ordered to get his troops into the beachheads at once. (MacArthur, it will be recalled, had mentioned withdrawal into beachheads as one of the few strategic options open to him in an earlier cable.)

During the meeting Bradley had been jotting notes. Now he read the draft of an order telling MacArthur "to hold the beachheads as long as required pending settlement of the general situation."

Marshall objected. He questioned whether it was necessary to go into so much detail on the situation and future developments. He thought it would be sufficient merely to approve regrouping in the three bases held by U.S. forces (Inchon, Wonsan, and Hamhung-Hungnam).

No vote was taken, not even an informal show of hands. But the consensus was clear: MacArthur's army should retire to seaports and prepare for an evacuation, the first time in history that the American military withdrew from a war without victory.

To Matthew Ridgway, the meeting was a traumatic experience.[38] As a soldier he recognized much of the problem lay with MacArthur, the general's sleight of hand with orders and his petulance. Ridgway sat in amazement as his superiors talked about every other subject save MacArthur. Although Acheson and Marshall were there, as representatives of the President, "no one [was] apparently willing to issue a flat order to the Far East Commander to correct a state of affairs that was going rapidly from bad to disastrous." Although both "responsibility and authority" were in the room, no one would speak.

Finally, Ridgway's conscience overcame his discretion. "With deep feeling" he said that the group had "already spent too damn much time on debate and that immediate action was needed." Such was owed to the soldiers in the field; ultimately the men in the JCS room must answer for their lives. Twenty men were present, the top officers of the American military. Ridgway's statement was answered with complete silence (although a navy colleague did scribble a note, "Proud to know you").

The meeting broke up. Utterly frustrated, Ridgway went over to General Hoyt Vandenberg, who had been a cadet at West Point when Ridgway taught there. Ridgway saw no need for doubletalk. He reported:

> "Why," I asked him, "don't the Joint Chiefs send orders to MacArthur and *tell* him what to do?"
>
> Van shook his head.
>
> "What good would that do? He wouldn't obey the orders. What can we do?"
>
> At this I exploded. "You can relieve any commander who won't obey orders, can't you?" I exclaimed.
>
> The look on Van's face was one I shall never forget. His lips parted and he looked at me with an expression both puzzled and amazed. He walked away then without a word and I never afterward had occasion to discuss this with him.

Immediately after the Pentagon meeting, Acheson, Marshall, and Bradley reported to Truman.[39] By Acheson's account there were two possibilities: to continue hostilities with the Chinese or to stop the fighting "before the disintegration moved too far in order to save our forces." He clearly rejected the first alternative, for he never mentioned it again; to him, the problem was the mechanics of withdrawal.

Acheson saw three distinct areas to be considered during the evacuation: the east coast, Inchon, and Pusan. The east coast withdrawal, he said, "is solely concerned with saving troops," for there was "nothing to be gained politically by making a stand there." (Acheson's advice here was consonant with that of the JCS, which wished MacArthur to withdraw X Corps from its disastrously exposed positions at the Chosin Reservoir.) Acheson gave lip service to protocol. He told Truman he "didn't wish this to appear as advice because it was a strictly military matter. However, if the military did need some kind of political action, such as a cease-fire, in order to carry out the evacuation on the East Coast, then the military should let us know." The decision on Inchon could wait a few days, but Acheson suggested that if Eighth Army troops must be withdrawn from this port to avoid encirclement, they should be relanded and refitted in Japan, not farther south in Korea. Acheson said it would be "dreadful" to abandon the ROK soldiers so far from their homes. They should be picked up "some way or other and relanded in South Korea to filter back to their home towns." The main thing was not to abandon them.

Acheson next raised the question of the price America "would have to pay for the events in Korea." If the United States proposed a cease-fire and it were accepted, "we would need to understand that we can't do things like bombing Manchuria and will be required to observe it ourselves." On the other hand, "if we think the probabilities were that it will not be accepted, then that would be another thing." (Implicit in Acheson's statement was the possibility that in this case the United States would be free to bomb Manchuria.)

The consensus was that Truman would wait until talking with Clement Attlee before making any decision. Acheson "was inclined to think we shouldn't go ahead alone, and it was left that way."

In conclusion, Bradley had Truman approve a message ordering MacArthur to concentrate his troops, which was dispatched later that afternoon.[40] The order read: "We consider that the preservation of your forces is now the primary consideration. Consolidation of forces into beachheads is concurred in."

When Acheson finally went to bed that Sunday night, he mused that he would not be surprised if he were awakened by an announcement of global war.

The Joint Chiefs shared Acheson's fear. On December 6—the same day the Chinese occupied Pyongyang and continued their hot pursuit of the battered Eighth Army—the JCS sent a somber warning to all American commanders worldwide: "The JCS consider that the current situation in Korea has greatly increased the possibility of general war. Commanders addressed [should] take such action as is feasible to increase readiness without creating atmosphere of fear."[41]

The Pentagon meeting also left Dean Rusk dejected. Back at the State Department, he expressed concern about the morale of the Joint Chiefs, who "all appear to be extremely dejected." He did not think the military was "in the frame of mind for the best possible effort which we could make" in Korea.

Perhaps the problem was MacArthur's field performance. Rusk suggested a devious means of sidelining the general. General Lawton Collins would leave the JCS to assume command of troops in Korea, with MacArthur relegated to "spending full time on the Japanese peace treaty." Such a sham assignment would be a public repudiation of MacArthur, one he would not be apt to suffer silently. Talking of relieving a field commander was none of the State Department's business, and Rusk apparently realized it, for the memorandum of the meeting glides swiftly past his suggestion with no further discussion indicated.

George Kennan did not like the idea of getting into negotiations. A request for a cease-fire would appear to the Soviets "as a suit for peace." The Soviets would "want to extract every possible advantage and to damage wherever possible the prestige of the United States . . . their reply would inevitably be an arrogant one." If there was validity to the theory that negotiations should be from conditions of strength, "this was clearly a very bad time for an approach to the Russians."

But what was needed immediately was a "real estimate from the military on its capacity to resist." Rusk said, "We must make the best stand possible if we are unable to get a cease-fire at the 38th Parallel." If a cease-fire could not be achieved, the United States must hold as long as possible and force the Chinese to pay the highest price possible for expelling UN forces; simply to "bow out" would have disastrous effects on the U.S. world position.

Acheson reported these conclusions later that morning by phone to General Marshall, who gave qualified agreement: First it would be necessary to see whether X Corps could be evacuated; and secondly, the U.S. "must not dig ourselves into a hole without an exit." Acheson agreed.

But at the same time the State Department's diplomats were urging that the UN force stand and fight, the Pentagon's top civilians took the opposite tack. The three service secretaries gave Marshall advice directly opposite to that of Acheson. UN forces, if pursued south of the 38th parallel, should be withdrawn. But the United States should refuse to recognize defeat and should thereafter blockade China and prepare to bomb China's lines of communications, while being careful to avoid commitment of ground forces on the China mainland. "The broad lines of our policy," they wrote, "should not be to accept the present military defeat as any more than the loss of a battle or campaign." But the recommended reprisals, they stressed, should be taken only with UN approval. Marshall knew the latter proviso made the secretaries' proposal meaningless. The U.S. problem was persuading the UN majority not to expand the war, but to remain in it in any force whatsoever.

Daily the American press ran front-page "situation maps" showing the Chinese encircling X Corps and driving a pincer around EUSAK. "America's worst military licking since Pearl Harbor," said *Newsweek*. "Perhaps it might become the worst military disaster in American history. Barring a military or diplomatic miracle, the approximately two-thirds of the U.S. Army that had been thrown into Korea might have to be evacuated in a new Dunkirk to save them from being lost in a new Bataan." "It was defeat—the worst defeat the U.S. had ever suffered," lamented *Time* the same week. And *Time* implicitly called upon the Truman administration for tougher action (but with no specific suggestions on exactly what should be done):

> If this defeat were allowed to stand, it would mean the loss of Asia to Communism. If it were allowed to stand, no Asian could evermore put any stock in the promise that had given him hope against Communism—the promise that the U.S. and its allies would come to his help. And no European would be able to believe, with any firmness, that the U.S. was the

bulwark against Communism that it professed to be before the disaster in Korea.

The American public received the grave battlefield news with a matter-of-fact shock that oddly did not affect the day-to-day lives of most citizens. People continued to flock to big-weekend college football games and to jam department stores for their Christmas shopping. A survey by *Time* correspondents found the most frequently heard comment was: "It looks bad." One wounded veteran of the Second World War said, "I quit turning on my radio—I don't want to hear the bad news." MacArthur's home-by-Christmas comment (which *Time* loyally but inaccurately said had been "misconstrued" by the press) left citizens snippish, for the sudden adverse turn of the war caught them by surprise. An Iowa filling-station attendant criticized the administration for not being more forceful: "They piddled around and piddled around. I wonder what the hell they are thinking about?"

Although the administration had been careful not to blame the Soviets for fomenting the war, many Americans nonetheless were ready to strike at the Russians, the real villain. "Hit the main Bolsheviks," said Detroit salesman Zacharias Cosmas. "The tail won't bite you if you hit the head." A New Orleans policeman, Ernest F. Curtis, said, "We should declare war on Russia officially and then drop all the A-bombs we can on her."

But the general public attitude, *Time* found, was confusion and "half-believing matter-of-factness," the attitude a person might have upon being told he suffered from terminal cancer.

The British Pay a Visit

Dean Acheson detested Prime Minister Clement Attlee, and on the eve of his arrival in Washington he recalled with relish Winston Churchill's description of him as a "sheep in sheep's clothing."[42] The meetings, which lasted four days beginning on December 4, thus unsurprisingly were marked by sour exchanges between the two supposed allies.

Attlee said at the outset the UN had no choice but to negotiate its way out of Korea, even at the price of abandoning Formosa and giving Peking the Chinese seat in the UN.[43] The matter was "serious and very distasteful" and would cause the UN to "lose face . . . especially in the Far East." This did not bother Attlee. "The British [have] had to face some hard situations in [our] history. . . . We must not get so involved in the East as to lay ourselves open to attack in the West." In his memoirs Acheson quoted Attlee as continuing that there was nothing more important than retaining the good opinion of Asia (this statement is not in the formal conference notes). "I remarked acidly that the security of the United States was more important," Acheson recounted.

Truman stated the U.S. position. A cease-fire would be acceptable, but only on terms that did not mean abandonment of South Korea or Formosa or seating China in the UN. If China refused a cease-fire and continued fighting, the United States would commence a variety of military, political, and economic harassments, including inciting anti-Communist guerrillas in China. Attlee remained noncommittal, and the meeting ended on an uncomfortable note; clearly the United States and Great Britain were in dangerously sharp disagreement.

That evening Acheson sought out Sir Oliver Franks, the British ambassador, at a reception and gave him a blunt warning.[44] The U.S. must have a single foreign policy for both parts of the world, East and West. "If we surrender in the Far East, especially if this results from the action of our allies, American opinion will be against help in the West to those who had brought about the collapse," Acheson said. If the United States voluntarily left Korea, "the Filipinos and Japanese would run for cover."

Acheson suggested a way out of the impasse: A simple cease-fire resolution would be put before the General Assembly, which the U.S. could get passed easily. "It is probable the Chinese would not accept the cease-fire and that others would then urge us to pay a price. We would ignore such arguments." If the United States were then forced to "take a Dunkirk," it would at least "prove that we are not ready to surrender but are standing up to attack. It would be much easier to hold opinion on that course than by desertion and surrender." Under no circumstances would Acheson "reward" the Chinese for their Korean intervention.

Acheson's plain talk bore fruit.[45] The next morning, December 5, Franks told him the British would support the cease-fire resolution. Acheson thanked him but brushed aside a suggestion that the Chinese be asked to join in the UN debate.

When Truman and Attlee met again that day, the President emphasized that the United States would not quit Korea voluntarily, even if the UN Command were subjected to bombing.[46] Truman "did not like to go into a situation such as this and then to admit that we were licked." He would rather "fight it to a finish." The President pointedly told Attlee that "we do not desert our friends when the going is rough."

Later in the talks Attlee raised what he called a "difficult and . . . delicate question," that of MacArthur's conduct of the war. The prime minister said there was a "general feeling in Europe that . . . MacArthur was running the show and also a feeling that other participating countries had little say in what was done."

General Bradley and Secretary Marshall sprang to MacArthur's defense. MacArthur was operating under a UN mandate, and the British were consulted regularly on military issues. Bradley bridled at a suggestion that a committee formulate war policy. If the British or any other country did not like what was happening, "they should say so and they would be given assistance in withdrawing."

The remainder of the talks were marked by sharp arguments over the proper approach to take to bring China back to friendship with the West—the British pleading for a sympathetic tack, the Americans taking the position (stated by the State Department's George Kennan) that "We owe China nothing but a lesson." Truman hoped eventually to "bring them to realize that their friends are not in Siberia but in London and in Washington."

Attlee "didn't think we could make them realize that by continuing military action against them." Truman "quite agreed, but we couldn't leave the Koreans to be murdered." The President offered an analogy: "If they licked us in Korea that was one thing, but after Dunkirk the British didn't surrender but went right on. . . . Perhaps we in the United States [have] inherited from the United Kingdom the spirit of not liking to pick a fight but of standing up to it when it comes to us."

The primary reason for Attlee's visit, his concern over use of nuclear weapons, was overshadowed by the nasty exchanges about overall war policy.[47] Truman and Attlee finally talked over the subject privately the last hours of the conference, without any aides present. Truman told Attlee the United States and the United Kingdom had "always been partners in this matter and that he would not consider the use of the bomb without consulting with the UK." Whereupon the prime minister injudiciously asked that the agreement be put into writing.[48]

"No," Truman snapped. "It will not be in writing. If a man's word isn't any good it isn't made any better by writing it down."

When Truman and Attlee announced their decision on U.S.-U.K. consultation before use of the bomb, Acheson and Robert Lovett of the Defense Department exchanged agonized glances. American law forbade the President to make any such promise, and besides, Truman had repeatedly promised he alone would decide when use of the bomb was necessary. "We are teetering on the edge of great trouble and you must carry the ball," Lovett whispered to Acheson.

Acheson spoke quietly with the President. Sharing responsibility for the bomb would uncork a "most vicious offensive" in Congress against both the administration and Great Britain. A better course, Acheson said, was a promise to keep in touch with Attlee in any situation that might lead toward world war.

Attlee went away assured that Truman had no plans for use of nuclear weapons in Korea. What he did not know was that during the very course of the talks Truman had authorized unassembled nuclear bomb components to be flown to the Far East and stowed aboard a U.S.

carrier. Truman indeed did not want to use the bombs—but he was ready and willing to order them dropped if necessary to prevent an American military disaster.

A Six-Month War?

The underlying uncertainty in all these talks was lack of specific knowledge on the breadth of Chinese intentions. The first offensive, in retrospective, was clearly intended to warn the UN away. The second offensive, which had staggered MacArthur's force, was still of unknown purpose. A highly sensitive CIA report sent to the White House on December 7 did offer some guidance. The context of the message (heavily censored when declassified through FOIA) indicates it came from a trusted foreign source. According to the report:

> . . . [T]he Chinese Communists felt that use of the atom bomb in Korea as tactical support of UN troops would not precipitate war, but use of strategic atom bombing inside of Manchuria was another matter, and in that case, the decision on war would be left to Soviet Russia.
>
> However, the source reports that Communist officials are "absolutely confident" UN will not use the atom bomb and, when pushed back to the 38th parallel, will either withdraw from Korea or reach an agreement with the Chinese.

According to the CIA source, the Soviets "have apparently convinced the Chinese Communists that the U.S. is incapable of war for the next six months and that settlement of the Korean difficulty must occur within that period." The Chinese were said to be worried about "having their best trained and equipped armies in Manchuria and North China and agreed only to enter the Korean War after the Soviets promised 300,000 Soviet troops plus naval and air support in case of war with the U.S."

The CIA report came to Washington within seventy-two hours of the time Truman flatly told Prime Minister Attlee that the United States did not intend to use nuclear weapons in Korea. Among the people in the British Embassy privy to the Truman-Attlee talks were the Soviet spies Philby and Burgess. Reports on the talks went directly to the Foreign Office's American desk, headed by yet another Soviet agent, Maclean.

A deep distrust of the accuracy of MacArthur's battlefield reports permeated the conversations in Washington at every level. MacArthur's swings were mercurial and daily. He would warn of the disaster befalling his command and the reinforcements and expanded bombing authority he needed to control the situation. Then he would carp about correspondents' reports that his army was "in retreat" rather than making a skilled withdrawal. One result, as noted earlier, was the decision on December 1 to dispatch General Collins to the Far East. Field commanders under MacArthur had no direct communication with the Defense Department; messages were cleared through Tokyo, and if MacArthur or subordinates did not like them, they were rewritten or discarded. But even MacArthur would not dare try to prevent the army chief of staff from visiting the field generals.

General Bradley laid out a wide panoply of options for Collins to discuss with MacArthur, including possible air and naval attacks north of the Yalu.[49] The first draft directive asked Collins to determine the advantages and disadvantages of arranging a cease-fire; however, Bradley had second thoughts about taking such a defeatist option to a battle commander and deleted it.* In essence, he asked Collins to find out the actual situation in the Far East.

Collins flew to Tokyo on December 4 and spent about four hours talking with MacArthur. He heard nothing beyond what MacArthur had been saying in cables daily the past week:[51] that the United Nations should meet the Chinese challenge with its "full power" and that "directives and strategic plans" should be changed accordingly—that is, MacArthur be given free rein to take the war to China. MacArthur claimed to face an army of more than 500,000 Chinese and 100,000 North Koreans, a horde able to envelop any static defensive position and force the Eighth Army back to the Seoul-Inchon area. His command could hold beachheads only if the Chinese did not launch a full-scale attack.

Were any reinforcements available or likely? he asked Collins, a question to which he had repeatedly been given the answer. No, replied Collins.

So far as MacArthur was concerned, therefore, the only solution was to arrange an armistice "on [the best] terms available" and as soon as possible. Although MacArthur never brought himself to say so directly —his ego would not admit defeat, only blame external sources for causing it—his message was clear: The army he commanded could not stand in Korea and hold a line. Unless Washington gave what he wanted, he was ready to retire from the battle.

Collins offered the hope that the enemy would give the UN Command a breathing spell. He said it was the "probable intention" of the JCS to order EUSAK back to Japan and then to reinforce it.

He cabled the JCS a brief summary of MacArthur's view[52] and then flew to Korea to talk first hand with the commanders on the scene. He

---

*But two days later Bradley, after reconsideration, told Collins to ask MacArthur's views on a cease-fire anyway.[50]

had every reason to expect to find a thoroughly whipped army, one which would soon be forced off the peninsula in disgrace, unable to stand down the enemy, for such was the thrust of the messages MacArthur had been sending to Washington the past days.

Collins worked long hours.[53] Only three hours or so after ending his meeting with MacArthur, he was in Seoul to talk with Walker. Walker did have problems, and he admitted them. The 2nd Division had been "badly hurt"—i.e., almost destroyed—as had the Turkish Brigade. But now that Walker had had a few days to regroup his troops and assess the damage, the picture was by no means one of unrelieved gloom. The 1st Cavalry and the 24th and 25th Infantry divisions were in good shape. The ROK 5th Division was in fair condition, although other ROK units would have to be taken out of line for refitting. Walker did not think he could hold Pyongyang; he worried about the Chinese sweeping through the gap between his Eighth Army and X Corps. If EUSAK tried to hold around the Seoul-Inchon area, it well might be encircled. He did not want a forced withdrawal through Inchon, for he feared it would be costly in men and equipment. "On the other hand," Collins stated, "he could withdraw on Pusan without further serious losses and, if reinforced with the X Corps, could hold the old Pusan Perimeter indefinitely."

So much for half of MacArthur's force in the field. Walker was ready to stand and die again, if necessary, just as he had done the previous summer. Collins concluded, after spending the next day in the field, that "although the situation in the Eighth Army was sticky, there was no panic." Leaving the Seoul airport on December 6, Collins was asked by reporters whether the United States would use atomic weapons against the Chinese. "Certainly not from what I saw yesterday," he replied. Would EUSAK be encircled by the Chinese driving down its right flank, the "X Corps gap"? Collins replied, "I think the Eighth Army can take care of itself."

Collins flew next to Hungnam to meet with General Almond, the X Corps commander. Again the picture was mixed. The 7th Army Division had been hurt, as had the 3rd. But the 1st Marine Division, the linchpin of the UN operations in eastern Korea, was in the process of withdrawing from the Chosin Reservoir relatively intact. "General Almond is convinced, and I concur," Collins told the JCS, "that he can hold the Hungnam bridgehead for a considerable period without serious losses and that he can successfully withdraw by sea and air from the bridgehead, if necessary, without excessive loss of men or equipment."

Thus did a second field commander directly dispute MacArthur's estimate of the battlefield situation. MacArthur obviously did not recognize the capabilities of his own troops. He was so caught up in political machinations—his demands to take the war to China, to use Chinese Nationalist troops, to blame the British and other Europeans for his troubles—that he overlooked the first function of a commander: to perform his assigned mission as best he could within his ability to do so, without carping at the source of the order.

Collins lacked MacArthur's longevity of rank and prominence. Yet his inspection trip to the front—MacArthur had not been there since he launched his end-the-war offensive on November 27—convinced him that the general either did not know what was happening in his theater or looked toward an expanded war as part of a grand scheme or as a means of saving his command from annihilation.

In a sense, Collins's inspection visit was a watershed for MacArthur. The Joint Chiefs for months had questioned MacArthur's political meddling, his petulant public statements, his strategic maneuvers. Now Collins was prepared to add another indictment: that MacArthur had failed tactically and did not know his own battlefield situation.

Collins met again in Tokyo on December 7 with MacArthur and his top staff.[54] As a framework for discussion, Collins offered three sets of conditions, the first two assuming continuation of a total attack by the Chinese, the third a Chinese agreement not to go south of the 38th parallel.

Under Condition One, the assumption was that there would be no UN air action against China; no naval blockade; no reinforcement by Nationalist Chinese troops; no increase in UN ground forces except possibly four National Guard divisions commencing in April 1951; and no use of the atomic bomb.

MacArthur "felt strongly" that if all or a major part of these limitations were imposed on him, with a continuing strong Chinese attack, "this would represent essentially a surrender." An armistice would be a political matter, "helpful but not essential from a military standpoint." American forces would have to be withdrawn from Korea, "but we should not be precipitate in seeking an armistice." MacArthur did agree with his field commanders—on the basis of Collins's report—that EUSAK and X Corps could be withdrawn safely, with or without an armistice.

Condition Two envisioned tougher actions: a naval blockade; air reconnaissance and bombing of the Chinese mainland; "maximum employment" of Nationalist Chinese troops; and "possible use of the atomic bomb." Under these conditions, MacArthur said, "we should continue to hold the best possible positions in Korea." He would move X Corps by water to Pusan and then overland to join up with the Eighth Army. These combined forces, under Eighth Army command, would then hold a "position across the peninsula as far to the north as possible." MacArthur wanted 50,000 to 60,000 Chinese Nationalist troops "as rapidly as possible" from Formosa. MacArthur also looked to mainland China action. "Other Chinese Nationalist forces should be introduced into South China, possibly through Hong Kong," he told Collins. (This proposal was diplomatically and politically absurd; MacArthur knew that the British, who controlled Hong Kong, were looking for a way out of the war and that under no circumstances would they permit their crown colony to be used as an entry point for Nationalist guerrillas.)

Condition Three was contingent upon a Chinese Communist agreement not to advance south of the 38th parallel. In this event, the UN should accept an armistice, but with strictures: a prohibition against North Korean or Chinese troops moving south of the 38th parallel; the withdrawal of all North Korean guerrillas to above the parallel; and supervision of the armistice by a UN commission. MacArthur said this "would probably be the best arrangement that could be obtained" unless the UN agreed to the Condition Two operations.

Collins agreed that if the UN did not support fully its troops in the face of continued all-out Chinese attack, MacArthur "should be directed to take the necessary steps to safeguard his command and prepare plans for evacuation from Korea." However, he disagreed with MacArthur on a key point (although he did not argue it). Even with the limitations placed on the UN Command, he did not feel the Chinese could force it out of Korea. "I based this judgment primarily on the views expressed by the field commanders, Walker and Almond," Collins said. Arriving back in Washington on December 8, Collins told reporters that the UN forces "would be able to take care of themselves without further serious losses."

The army chief went immediately to the White House to join the talks among Truman, Attlee, and their advisers.[55] He brought the first mildly good news the conferees had heard: that "although the military situation remained serious, it was no longer critical."

As it happened, the final communiqué had already been drafted, so Collins's findings had no direct influence on the outcome of the talks themselves. But at least the British visitors could return home with the knowledge that the Korean situation was no longer desperate. Nonetheless, more cliff-hanging weeks faced the UN effort in the war.

Futility at the UN

Events in mid-December demonstrated the futility of seeking peace through the United Nations, despite U.S. efforts. Ambassador Warren Austin found that most nations shared the British view that China should be "bought off" with concessions. UN members were willing to oppose aggression by a minor country such as North Korea; confronting Communist China was another matter entirely. Austin was pessimistic about the UN's helping to reach a settlement on terms acceptable to

Washington. In the words of Richard Stebbins, writing contemporane-
ously for the Council on Foreign Relations:

> Most of the non-Communist world seemed less troubled by Peking's
> bullying of the United Nations and generally lawless behavior than by the
> chance that the quarrel between the United States and Communist China
> would precipitate general war. . . . A good many delegations now seemed
> to consider restraint of Communist China less important than restraint of
> the United States.[56]

On December 5—soon after both the British and the Americans
agreed to seek a cease-fire under UN auspices—thirteen Asian and Arab
states proposed to ask the North Koreans and Chinese not to cross the
38th parallel, in the hope that the old border could become a truce line.
Both Truman and Attlee quickly assented. The Indian delegate, Sir
Benegal N. Rau, then put the question to Peking and Pyongyang; several days lapsed, and he received no reply. India next sought—and
obtained—assurances from Washington that if the Chinese stopped at
the parallel, UN forces would not renew their invasion of North Korea.
But the Communist bloc remained silent.

On December 11 the Arab-Asian bloc introduced two resolutions in
the General Assembly. One would establish a three-man commission to
seek a cease-fire; the other would call for a conference on Far Eastern
affairs. The approach was tailored to satisfy the U.S. insistence on an
unconditional cease-fire and also the Chinese demand for consideration
of broader Asian problems.

The question went before the National Security Council on December 11.[57] The Pentagon distrusted the idea, on several grounds. The
military feared a continued buildup of enemy forces at the front without their being subjected to UN air attack; should the Communists
decide to break the cease-fire, they could have massive amounts of men
and supplies at the 38th parallel. The military also wished to hold
certain strongpoints north of the parallel. Speaking both for the Pentagon and the State Department, Dean Rusk told the council that specific
conditions should be discussed before the United States agreed to a
cease-fire. General Marshall wanted a supervisory UN commission; otherwise, "we would not have any protection against major violations,"
and he "had had plenty of experience with such violations" during his
year in China.

Truman said he had made clear to Prime Minister Attlee that "we
would not surrender to these murderous Chinese Communists. We will
have to be pushed out, and that will take them a long time." Under any
truce, "there must be free access to all of Korea, since we can't sit still
and let the enemy build up."

Secretary Marshall said the United States was in a dilemma. A cease-fire could stop American air and naval activity and permit a Chinese buildup. "If we objected, they would say that we had not lived up to the cease-fire. On the other hand, if we oppose a cease-fire, our friends would think that we were objecting to a peaceful solution." Marshall urged finding "some position that appears reasonable, even if the other side refuses to accept it."

Vice President Barkley thought that any conditions attaching to a cease-fire should appear in a UN resolution and not be "behind-the-scenes understandings of any sort." He felt it important that the United States not be cast in the position of opposing a cease-fire and that it was "very important that the other side bear the onus" for any rejection.

The final recommendation, approved by the President, was a qualified acceptance of a cease-fire "which does not place UN forces at a military disadvantage and which does not involve political concessions."

Soon after the NSC adjourned, the Joint Chiefs queried MacArthur about the "acceptable" military conditions for a cease-fire. MacArthur replied that he wanted five safeguards:[58] (1) All ground forces must remain in their positions or be withdrawn to the rear; (2) no resupplies other than those needed for the health and comfort of troops; (3) no aircraft flights by either belligerent across the front lines; (4) no movements of refugees across the line in either direction; and (5) supervision by nations not involved in the fighting, with "unlimited freedom of movement."

The Joint Chiefs expanded these conditions in a memo sent to General Marshall on December 12.[59] The cease-fire should be limited to Korea and remain in force until the "Korean question" was permanently settled. A demilitarized zone some twenty miles deep should be established, with its southern boundary roughly following the 38th parallel. Guerrillas on either side of the parallel should receive safe passage to their main force, and POWs should be exchanged on a one-for-one basis.

At the United Nations, meanwhile, the General Assembly's Political and Security Committee (the First Committee, in UN jargon) had spent several desultory days discussing the "Chinese presence" in Korea and had sought Peking's views on a cease-fire.[60] On December 13 the First Committee approved establishment of a three-member committee (headed by the General Assembly president, Nasrollah Entezam of Iran) to determine possible cease-fire terms. (India's Rau and Lester B. Pearson of Canada were selected as the other commission members.) The next day the General Assembly approved the cease-fire resolution by a wide margin and with U.S. support.

But the Chinese were not about to talk of peace under any terms other than total U.S. capitulation. General Wu, the Chinese representative, refused even to meet with the cease-fire committee; he left Lake

Success for home. Peking announced on December 21 a flat rejection of the Arab-Asian proposal, saying all UN actions taken without Chinese participation were illegal. Then, two days later, Foreign Minister Chou En-lai, in a broadcast over Peking Radio, assailed any UN action. The 38th parallel, as a demarcation line, had been "obliterated forever" by the "invasion" of North Korea. China would not consider a cease-fire without an accompanying "favorable disposition" of Far Eastern political issues: withdrawal of "foreign" troops from Korea; settlement of Korean affairs by "the Korean people themselves"; withdrawal of "American aggressive forces" from Formosa; and seating of Peking in the UN. This harsh rebuff ended the UN peace effort. On January 2 the First Committee told the General Assembly that "no recommendation in regard to a cease-fire can usefully be made . . . at this time."

If the United States wanted a halt to the fighting, it must look elsewhere than the UN. The only alternative to the unilateral withdrawal now was to stand and fight and to convince the Chinese to negotiate.

The Battle Command Changes

On December 22 General Walton Walker hurried into the Eighth Army's general officers' mess, a comfortable dining area serving fresh foods flown in daily by courier plane from Japan. The mess offered a brief refuge from war, but few officers tarried there. Brigadier General Francis W. Farrell, the commander of the Korean Military Advisory Group, remembered, "I was there that day with some of my Koreans, and I was wolfing down my food and ready to be on my way."[61]

Walker was not known to outsiders as an introspective man; hence Farrell was surprised when the general suddenly began talking about his Second World War idol, General George S. Patton. "I find it ironic," Walker said, "that a man who lived as Patton did would die in a traffic accident." Farrell heard the remark and thought nothing of it. Then Walker finished his food, summoned his jeep driver, and set out to present unit citations to the 20th Division and the British Commonwealth's 27th Brigade and a Silver Star to his son, Captain Sam Walker, a 20th Division company commander.

Walker was an impetuous passenger-seat driver; if something slowed his jeep's progress, he was apt to snap, "Move on around it." Today a long column of South Korean Army trucks occupied his lane. His driver swung over and to the left to "double-column it," in army parlance. But one of the South Korean trucks pulled out of line and directly in front of Walker's jeep. The driver skidded; the vehicle swerved off the road and into the ditch.

Walker was pulled from the jeep with massive head injuries. (He disliked wearing his heavy steel helmet when not in active combat zones; it was found in his lap.) Sped to a field hospital, Walker was pronounced dead on arrival.

General Farrell heard of the accident later in the day and remembered Walker's remark about Patton. "That gave me a chill for a long time," he said.

General MacArthur gave Walker in death the praise he had denied him in life. He told correspondents in Tokyo that he had "recently recommended a promotion for Walker to the four-star rank of a full general." If MacArthur, in fact, had done so, he had neglected to say anything about the matter to anyone in the Defense Department. The truth was that MacArthur and other brass, including General Collins, had been looking for an opportunity to fire Walker for four months. But the spunky general died with both his rank and his Eighth Army intact, even if battered.

CHAPTER SEVENTEEN

Ridgway Takes Command

The evening of December 22 General Matthew Ridgway was dining with Old Army friends at Fort Myer.[1] Midway through an after-dinner cocktail came a telephone call from General Lawton Collins that "turned my evening upside down."

Ridgway returned to the drawing room, finished his drink, nodded to his wife, and they left without a word being said about why he had been called to the phone. He remained silent even when they reached their home. "She could get some sleep even if I couldn't." Over coffee the next morning he broke the news: General Walton Walker had been killed in an accident. Ridgway was to "report without delay" as his successor. Mrs. Ridgway did not blink. "Like the courageous thorough-bred she is, she accepted it with the characteristic fortitude of an Army wife."

What Ridgway did not know was that Collins and MacArthur had picked him as Walker's successor months earlier, when they decided a new general should be put at the head of American forces. (In his memoirs Collins says Ridgway was selected in advance because of Walker's constant exposure to danger in the field and the possibility he might be killed in action. Collins tactfully did not reveal he had recommended that Walker be fired.)

After hurried briefings at the Pentagon, Ridgway learned he was to leave for Asia that very evening. He had hoped to spend Christmas at home, but there could be no two-day delay. He did not have the heart to break the news to his wife. He asked General Wade H. Haislip to make the call for him. General Collins asked if Ridgway wanted any staff to accompany him. "No," he replied, "I'll go this one alone. It's Christmas, and even a bachelor will have made plans."

Matthew Ridgway was fifty-five years old that December, an austerely handsome man who literally had spent his entire life in the United States Army. He was born in Fort Monroe, Virginia, son of a Regular Army artillery colonel. At West Point (class of 1917) he managed the football team and played on the hockey squad. The West Point yearbook commented, "Beyond doubt, the busiest man in the place." One of his classmates was General J. Lawton Collins, the man who sent him to Korea; another was General Mark Clark, who was to succeed him there.

Ridgway missed fighting during the First World War and spent the between-war years in the ho hum assignments of a peacetime army. He did time in China, Nicaragua, and the Philippines. Besides patience, he also learned Spanish, which made him a favorite at Latin American embassies during Washington assignments. In 1942 he was tapped as commander of the 82nd Division, and at an opportune time: Pentagon strategists had decided to convert two divisions to airborne, and the 82nd was one of those chosen. Airborne divisions were to become the army's elite, and Ridgway was with them from the start. He led the 82nd Division into battle in Normandy on D-Day, then commanded a corps. Ridgway was not universally loved. He could decorate a division commander for bravery, then lead him aside and dress him down for not advancing rapidly enough. "A kick-ass man," a subordinate said of him. "You could save the whole damned division, and be thanked—but make sure you had your brass polished."

After the war the Pentagon made Ridgway a military diplomat, with assignments on the United Nations Military Staff Committee and then chairman of the Inter-American Defense Board (the latter the coordinating group for hemispheric defense) and later commander of the Caribbean area. Brought back to the Pentagon in 1949 as deputy chief of staff of the army, Ridgway was soon recognized by the army network as a future chief of staff.

Besides iron will and ability, Ridgway carried another attribute to Korea. He had run the West Point sports program during the 1920's, when MacArthur was commandant there, and he could view the general with both respect and reservations. He knew well the MacArthur failings: "his proclivity to a bit of bombast and boasting"[2] and his penchant for "taking credit for [things] that actually hadn't happened." Ridgway noted MacArthur's love of the limelight

that continually prompted him to pose before the public as the actual commander on the spot at every landing and at the launching of every major attack in which his ground troops took part; his tendency to cultivate the isolation that genius seems to require, until it became a sort of insulation ... that deprived him of the critical comment and objective appraisals a commander needs from his principal subordinates; the headstrong quality . . . that sometimes led him to persist in a course in defiance of all seeming logic; a faith in his own judgment that created an aura of infallibility and that finally led him close to insubordination.

At a December 26 meeting in Tokyo, MacArthur indicated that Ridgway was to have more tactical leeway in the field than had been granted General Walker.[3] The best MacArthur hoped for was "tactical success —inflicting a broadening defeat making possible the retention . . . of South Korea." Military success of any kind "would strengthen our diplomacy." At the end MacArthur said simply, "Matt, Eighth Army is yours."

A Decision to Hold in Korea

Coincident with the change of command in the Eighth Army, the Joint Chiefs of Staff and the State Department wound up their long attempt to synthesize military and political goals.[4] The clear victor was Dean Acheson, who was in the ironic position throughout December of trying to convince the JCS that the military could hold in Korea while his diplomats pursued peace via negotiation. Dozens of Pentagon briefing papers churned out during December made clear the military's belief that Korea was "the wrong war in the wrong place at the wrong time," as General Bradley put it. As is true of many compromises, the result satisfied no one, neither in Washington nor in Tokyo.

The December meetings began to climax on the evening of December 26, when Truman summoned Secretaries Acheson and Marshall and General Bradley to Blair House to discuss, in Truman's words, "whether we could hold our position there [in Korea], what we should do if we could not."[5] Acheson said agreement seemed clear on what he called the "big objective," to take a stand against aggression on a collective security basis and retain that position as long as we could. "Reverses did not warrant withdrawal. We were not hopelessly outnumbered in Korea and . . . the Chinese Communists had the burden of being on the offensive. . . . We should test out the Communists and see whether they had the vast power that they were supposed to have. . . ." Nonetheless, Acheson said, eventual disengagement was essential because "we had never intended to keep a large force there." But any withdrawal should be done without loss of forces because "they represented so large a part of our strength."

Acheson asked Marshall about the directives which had been given MacArthur. He "did not understand" why he had taken the 3rd Army

Division out of Japan and put it back in Korea when the defense of Japan was of primary concern. Marshall replied there had been so many directives issued that he feared "there was some confusion about them." He thought they should be "reconsidered and rewritten as necessary." Agreement was general that MacArthur must not risk the destruction of his forces since nothing remained to protect Japan. The generals agreed to rewrite MacArthur's directives.

Acheson briefed subordinates on the Blair House meeting the next morning, and the consensus was that State should draft options for the President to consider since (as Acheson said) "we assume the Pentagon is doing these things." Rusk saw only three ways to end the fighting: win a military victory and stabilize the situation, which "was not within our capabilities"; make it "in the interest of the Chinese Communists to accept some stabilization by making it so costly for them that they could not afford not to accept"; or "get out in defeat voluntarily or under pressure and then continue our harassing tactics." Rusk preferred the second option.

But would this bring in Russian air power? None of the State officials felt so; the opportune time for air strikes—during the evacuation from the North—had passed. If the Soviets had wanted a general war, then had been the time to start one, for destroying the American armies would have left Japan defenseless.

Rusk wanted State to move fast with its recommendations lest it be preempted by either the Pentagon or MacArthur. Ambassador Jessup said he "would think that [Marshall] would want the decisions made here rather than in the field by General MacArthur."

But the military was not waiting.[6] On December 26 the JCS approved a memorandum to Marshall reflecting the mood of their December 22 meeting. Since the United States could not reinforce MacArthur, the Chinese appeared strong enough to expel his army. If UN troops were to be driven out of Korea, the United States should select the time and place for evacuation, instead of being driven out "under conditions approximating a military rout." The JCS memo ignored the State Department's view that political considerations required prolonged resistance. The chiefs argued that the "decision to evacuate should not be based on political grounds; rather, it should be based on our best military judgment as to whether and how long it is possible to maintain combat forces in Korea." They felt that the last opportunity for orderly withdrawal would occur when UN troops reached the Kum River, just north of Taejon. If it became necessary to retreat to this line, and the Chinese began massing forces for a new attack, MacArthur should be ordered to begin withdrawing to Japan. The JCS sent along a draft directive incorporating their recommendations.

At Marshall's insistence the draft was discussed on December 28 with Acheson and Rusk, who demanded a revision to emphasize the political advantage of resisting in Korea as long as possible and inflicting maximum damage on the Chinese. The final version, approved by President Truman, contained many of the ambiguities that had marred earlier attempts to give MacArthur direction, although its authorization of withdrawal was so specific that Defense Undersecretary Robert Lovett called it a "jig is up" message. The JCS sent the directive to MacArthur on December 29.

It appears from all estimates available that the Chinese Communists possess the capability of forcing UN forces out of Korea if they choose to exercise it. The execution of this capability might be prevented by making the effort so costly . . . that they would abandon it, or by committing substantial additional U.S. forces . . . thus seriously jeopardizing other commitments including the safety of Japan. It is not practicable to obtain significant additional forces for Korea from other members of the United Nations. We believe that Korea is not the place to fight a major war. Further, we believe that we should not commit our remaining available ground forces to action against Chinese Communist forces in Korea in face of the increased threat of general war. However, a successful resistance to Chinese-North Korean aggression at some position in Korea and a deflation of the military and political prestige of the Chinese Communists would be of great importance to our national interests, if this could be accomplished without incurring serious losses.

Your basic directive to furnish such assistance to the Republic of Korea as may be necessary to repel the armed attack and to restore international peace and security in that area requires modification in the light of the present situation.

You are now directed to defend in successive positions, as generally outlined in your [message of 7 December], inflicting such damage to hostile forces in Korea as is possible, subject to the primary consideration of the safety of your troops. Every effort should be continued to mobilize the maximum Korean contribution to sustained resistance, including both conventional and unconventional means.

Since developments may force our withdrawal from Korea, it is important, particularly in view of the continued threat to Japan, to determine, in advance, our last reasonable opportunity for an orderly evacuation. It seems to us that if you are forced back to positions in the vicinity of the Kum River and a line generally eastward therefrom, and if thereafter the Chinese Communists mass large forces against your positions with an evident capability of forcing us out of Korea, it then would be necessary, under these conditions, to direct you to commence a withdrawal to Japan.

Your views are requested as to the above-outlined conditions which should determine a decision to initiate evacuation, particularly in light of your continuing primary mission of defense of Japan for which only troops of the Eighth Army are available.[7]

When MacArthur read this message, longtime aide Courtney Whitney said later, "I cannot recall when I have seen heartache etched so

vividly on his countenance."[8] To MacArthur, the message indicated a
"loss of the 'will to win' in Korea."[9] Truman's determination to free and
unite that land "had now deteriorated almost into defeatism. Washington planning was not directed toward methods of counterattack, but
rather toward the best way to run; no solution was advanced as to the
problem, even with Nationalist Chinese troops,* but rather towards
unrealistically expecting the impossible from men who had gone in to
fight one war, had won it, and were now trying to fight a much bigger
one." MacArthur claimed that "the thought of defeat in Korea had
never been entertained by me." (To the contrary, several times in
preceding weeks he had cabled Washington that in fact, he was defeated and had no alternative but to withdraw.) Without the "artificial
restrictions" imposed by diplomats, MacArthur claimed he could not
only save Korea but "also inflict such a destructive blow upon Red
China's capacity to wage aggressive war that it would remove her as a
further threat to peace in Asia for generations to come."

So MacArthur argued back, in what Whitney called "his most important single comment on the Korean war."[11] He began with an insinuation that Washington could not possibly have made a final decision since
the message went so contrary to his own thinking.[12] "A comprehensive
estimate of relative capabilities in the Korean campaign," he cabled,
"appears to be dependent upon political-military policies yet to be
formulated." The "entire military resource of the Chinese nation" had
been committed against the UN Command. Because of the concentration of China's forces in Korea and Manchuria, other sections of the
country were vulnerable. MacArthur with water-drip persistence
urged on the JCS four actions previously rejected but which he said the
administration should undertake should it care "to recognize the state
of war which has been forced upon us by the Chinese authorities: (1)
to blockade China's coast; (2) to destroy China's industrial war-making
capacity, through air and naval bombardment; (3) to reinforce the UN
Command with Nationalist Chinese; and (4) to allow the Nationalists to
undertake diversionary action against the mainland."

MacArthur argued that these actions "could severely cripple and
largely neutralize China's capability to wage aggressive war and thus
save Asia from the engulfment otherwise facing it." Pressure on UN
troops in Korea would be relieved, and a decision could then be made
whether to carry on the fight there or to deploy forces to the offshore

---

*A CIA "National Intelligence Estimate" on December 27 said Chinese Nationalist
troops "would not be a major factor"[10] affecting the ability of UN forces to hold a
defensive line, and their presence would upset allies and "whatever chance might remain" for a political settlement. The CIA said the USSR "would probably welcome a
unilateral U.S. decision to use Chinese Nationalist troops . . . as (a) further embroiling the
U.S. in hostilities with Communist China without engaging the USSR; (b) dividing the U.S.
from its allies; and (c) providing plausibility for international Communist propaganda
concerning alleged U.S. military aggressions and support of reactionary regimes."

islands, meanwhile continuing navy and air action against China.

The general did recognize that the same actions had been rejected earlier as likely to provoke general war. But now China was fully committed, and "nothing we can do would further aggravate the situation" insofar as that country was concerned. The Soviet reaction was "a matter of speculation." MacArthur acknowledged that the Soviets were showing increasing attention to Japan; thus he wanted four more divisions there.

He then challenged directly the fundamental priority of the Truman administration's foreign policy, reopening arguments he had repeatedly lost in the past:

> I understand thoroughly the demand for European security and fully concur in doing everything possible in that sector, but not to the point of accepting defeat everywhere else—an acceptance which I am sure could not fail to insure later defeat in Europe itself. The preparations for the defense of Europe, however, by the most optimistic estimate are aimed at a condition of readiness two years hence. The use of forces in the present emergency in the Far East would not in any way prejudice this basic concept. To the contrary it would insure thoroughly seasoned forces for later commitment in Europe synchronously with Europe's own development of military resources.

In conclusion, MacArthur agreed that given the continuing restrictions on his operations, the JCS tactical estimate was sound. Evacuation should be accomplished only through a "successively contracting defense line south to the Pusan beachhead." No "anticipatory decision" needed to be made until the "beachhead line" was reached. Queried on which "beachhead line" he had in mind, MacArthur jibed back that unless there were "some possibility of policy change or other external eventuality favorable to the strengthening of our effort in Korea," withdrawal could commence "at any time." But "if a reasonable possibility does exist for favorable developments"—that is, a policy change in Washington—he would delay evacuation until his troops were driven into the old Naktong River line above Pusan.[13]

Regardless of the cable traffic between Washington and Tokyo, and whether MacArthur won or lost his pleas for more troops and wider authority, survival of the UN Command became the responsibility of General Matthew Ridgway and the 100,000-odd American troops in the field and their ROK and UN allies. If they could hold a line, stop the Chinese, and hurt them enough, perhaps the Truman-Acheson-JCS strategy would contain the war. If not, the UN was to be driven from Korea. So in the last days of December Ridgway set about doing his job as a soldier, forgetting the politico-military squabbles raging between MacArthur and superiors 7,000 miles away.

Ridgway in the Field

As if to welcome the new commander to war,[14] shrill Chinese attack whistles and the thud of mortar barrages hit the Eighth Army front early on the morning of New Year's Eve, only a few hours after General Ridgway had arrived in Korea. The attacks, along a multimile front in the western portion of Korea, again centered on the ROKs, who scattered during the first hours of fighting.

Ridgway gave rapid orders: Retreat if you have to, but make the Chinese pay for every yard they advance. Soon he realized that EUSAK could not hold. He ordered a fallback, even though retreat meant the loss of Seoul once again. By January 4 EUSAK had been forced some thirty-five miles to the south, to a line running along the Kum River. The Chinese then ran out of supplies and halted their advance.

Tactically Ridgway did not consider the retreat too great a loss. One advantage gained was that the Eighth Army now had a line across the waist of Korea—from Pyongtaek east through Wonju to the east coast at Samchok. The refurbished X Corps was sending men north from the Pusan Perimeter. Ridgway now had a line on which he could stand and fight. And although no one knew it at the time, the Eighth Army had retreated, on an army basis, for the last time. Kinks would be taken out of the front in the months ahead, and individual units would retreat from time to time, only for short distances, but never again would EUSAK be forced back.

A few weeks earlier, while Ridgway was still in Washington, the Joint Chiefs had called the Kum River line a "last ditch position" and said if the UN were forced that far south, withdrawal from Korea should be considered. Ridgway, however, gave no thought to withdrawal. He had told Washington he would need time to rebuild the Eighth Army, now that his command was anchored on a line from which he could maneuver.

His first days on the line he decided upon the concept by which he would fight the war. "Real estate" was irrelevant; Ridgway would not advance simply to occupy a few square miles of ground which the Chinese might seize from him a few days later. What he wanted from his command, stated in most graphic form, was dead Chinese.

A few days into command Ridgway realized how deeply the Eighth Army had been hurt, physically and psychologically, by its ordeal of the past weeks. He wrote General Collins in a personal letter:

> There was a definite air of nervousness, of gloomy foreboding, of uncertainty, a spirit of apprehension as to what the future held. . . . It was clear

to me that our troops had lost confidence. I could read it in their eyes, in
their walk. I could read it in the faces of their leaders, from sergeants right
on up to the top. They were unresponsive, reluctant to talk. I had to drag
information out of them. There was a complete lack of that alertness, that
aggressiveness, that you find in troops whose spirit is high.[15]

Ridgway, in truest Old Army fashion, started turning his command
around by kicking individual asses. He personally stopped a retreating
convoy of six ROK trucks, asked where the men were going, and ordered them back toward the front, a directive enforced by the carbine
of a military policeman Ridgway brought to the scene. Beginning on
December 27, he spent three days in the field, talking with everyone
from privates to generals. He would assemble troops by the scores, by
the hundreds, and tell them nothing was wrong with the Eighth Army
that confidence would not cure. He later said:

> I told them their soldier forebears would turn over in their graves if they
> heard some of the stories I had heard about the behavior of some of our
> troop leaders in combat. . . . In time of battle, I wanted division command-
> ers to be up with their forward battalions and I wanted corps commanders
> up with the regiment that was in the hottest action. If they had paper work
> to do, they could do it at night. By day their place was up there where the
> shooting was going on.[16]

He wanted "maximum punishment, maximum delay" of any Communist advances. In a briefing of 1st Marine Division officers he demanded their troops "bleed Red China white." At a staff conference on
January 5 he issued a general directive "to seek every opportunity to
punish the enemy . . . to seek occasions where the enemy may be drawn
into a trap where strong forces on his flanks may counterattack and cut
him up." Ridgway gave his commanders a standing order: "Stimulate
offensive spirit among all troops." He ordered staff officers to get into
the field every few days. "No amount of imagination can replace the
actual witnessing of an operation." Troops were not to be given sacrifice missions. "All troops are to be informed that we will not abandon
them or cut off units," he said. "They are to be fought for unless it is
clear that relief will result in the loss of equal or greater number of
troops."

Reviving an essentially defeated army was not an easy task. As a
former airborne commander Ridgway was used to officers and soldiers
with aggressive spirits. Many of his frustrations he vented through letters to General Collins. On January 8 he complained of a "lack of
aggressiveness among some corps and division commanders."[17] During
his first battlefield tour he found American units facing a numerically
strong enemy dug into fortified positions. The American officers, Ridgway recounted, felt that "any major offensive action on our part would

fail and probably with heavy losses." He agreed, but he did order that the American units should take advantage of air superiority and "our enormous armored superiority" for daytime attacks. Ridgway's letter to Collins continued:

> During daylight of the first day following the hostile attack, my instructions were not complied with.
>
> That night I repeated them in person and during the next daylight period both Corps, at my insistence, made an effort, but in my opinion, an inadequate one.
>
> Again and again I personally instructed both Corps commanders to so conduct their withdrawal as to leave strong forces so positioned as to permit powerful counterattacks with armored and infantry teams during each daylight period, withdrawing those forces about dark as necessary.
>
> These orders, too, failed of execution.

Ridgway had no time to run a training school for officers. If those in line could not produce, he wanted them out of Korea. He set up a screening board to weed out the incompetent and the weak (and complained that more names were not being submitted for review). He called upon his Old Army network for friends he could put into command jobs and trust. Colonel Dan Gilmer, for example, was teaching at the Army War College at Fort Leavenworth, Kansas, when Ridgway asked him to take a regiment. (The JCS let Ridgway choose his officers outside Pentagon channels.) Ridgway warned Gilmer that Korea could be a problem. "I am ever conscious," he wrote, "of the similarity to an animal trainer in a cage full of lions and tigers. So long as the trainer is alert in every fiber of his mental and physical being, he has the advantage, but time is his inexorable enemy. One major slip, one bit of carelessness, one dropped guard, and he may be in trouble."[18] Gilmer came to Korea.

Ridgway insisted that staff officers and commanders "go out, get off their hunkers, and visit the troops in the field . . . not just be operating from a nice comfortable desk in the rear headquarters." As he put it:

> I didn't want any staff officer to get a message which required action and have him sit around, smoke a cigarette and think it over and maybe go take a walk. I wanted him to reach for the telephone or reach for his hat and get going on the action that was called for.[19]

Ridgway was also dissatisfied with field reports from commanders which would "give you the circumstances . . . of why a unit withdrew. Well, you get the impression that they withdrew under pressure. Well, they hadn't done any such thing; they were changing their lines to get better terrain or something like that." To Lieutenant General John B. Coulter, deputy commander of EUSAK, he complained:

We still have far to go to attain the standards of toughness of body and soul of American troops, who as you so well remember, in each of several Civil War battles, with fewer men engaged than we now have in line, suffered in a few hours double the number of casualties that this command has had in six months of fighting.

Ridgway told Collins he intended to be "ruthless with our general officers if they fail to measure up." Soon he was relieving generals of their commands—for a career military man, tantamount to professional execution. The officer corps is a pyramidal system. Men enter through graduation either from West Point or an officer candidate school. Success is measured by promotion. "Star grade"—the rank of general—was the pinnacle. Now Ridgway had to do unpleasant chores. Some of the Eighth Army and X Corps generals had not performed, so they must be sacked.

The first to go was Major General Robert B. McClure, who had commanded the ill-starred 2nd Infantry Division for only a bit more than a month.[20] McClure inherited the shattered command shortly after the First Phase Chinese Offensive, during which, from November 27 through December 2, it suffered some 3,000 casualties, including most platoon, company, and battalion leaders. McClure picked up the division on December 6 and spent a month trying to rebuild it, a process still underway when the Chinese launched their New Year's Eve offensive.

At the time the 2nd Division was responsible for holding Wonju, a key center in central Korea below the Han. In this engagement McClure fell into Almond's fatal displeasure. During the fighting McClure realized the Chinese were threatening to sever his main supply route (MSR), which ran through a deep defile to the south of the city. Rather than risk having his men cut off and decimated, as had happened during earlier Chinese drives, McClure decided to fall back through the defile and cover Wonju with artillery fire. But to withdraw, he needed the permission of General Almond, his corps commander. Colonel Paul Freeman, a regimental commander, later a four-star general, related:

> McClure was unable to reach General Almond. He finally made this decision on his own. In a blinding snowstorm we were ordered to pull out of Wonju to . . . a position north of this defile, probably some twelve miles, and to establish minefields, booby traps, and so on.
>
> That night we received orders that we were to retake Wonju, that the evacuation of Wonju had not been agreed to by the corps commander. . . . By this time the snow was very deep. All of our mines and booby traps had been covered so that they couldn't be removed.

One battalion set out on the mission, ran into heavy fire, and received McClure's permission to withdraw. Freeman stated that supporting artillery was "far to the rear with the commander" and "we didn't have the teamwork that we would normally have had." The next day Freeman dispatched two of his battalions to retake Wonju; during the fight, as a snowstorm raged, a furious Almond arrived on the scene. As Freeman understated, "there was some dissension as to whether his instructions and orders had been carried out." Among other things, a battalion commander was found not to have a map or sketch of the relative positions of his companies. No battalion staff was in the forward command post. "Very little" artillery was brought on target, and there was no coordination between the attacking rifles companies and artillery support. McClure's days as a EUSAK general were numbered.

With Ridgway's approval, Almond set out making a formal case for removal.[21] On January 9, a week after this ill-fated battle, Almond visited the 2nd Division area again. What he wanted was undisputable evidence that McClure was not doing his job. Almond did not have to look hard. He found artillery pieces strewn around the rear area with no protection against infiltrators. The division artillery officer was not at the front, and half his thirty-six cannon were not in use. "At the time of my visit to the forward area," Almond reported, "a battery fired two rounds short and into the center of the right assault battalion—a most discouraging occurrence for troops engaged in combat operations." He wrote Ridgway that these conditions "indicate not only a failure to operate in the full spirit of delay and destruction of enemy forces, but also careless control of divisional operations."

Almond visited the 2nd Division area again four days later. This time he found men without gloves, sleeping bags, parkas, or overcoats. Foxholes and fields of fire were poorly sited. The division had not destroyed a nearby village with artillery, despite a direct order to do so (Almond's report suggests, but does not state, that North Korean or Chinese troops used the village as a refuge). From an observation post Almond called in artillery fire on a target. Twelve minutes lapsed before the first shell arrived. "Much too slow," he said. Almond checked elsewhere. Soldiers had never fired their crew-served bazookas. One 57 mm crew "could not hit within 300 yards of the target 700 yards away."

Ridgway fired General McClure the next day, with an oblique comment that sounded more like a warning against the man than a recommendation: "I believe that General McClure's long record of superior accomplishment will justify the assumption that he does have high potential in some other assignment."

Ridgway did not need inspection reports before dismissing four other generals (David G. Barr of the 7th Division, John H. Church of the 24th Division, Hobart R. Gay of the 1st Cavalry Division, and William B. Kean of the 25th Division) whose replacements had been decided upon before he left Washington. Ridgway tactfully told a conference of his senior aides on January 8, "We must get some of the seasoned fellows back. We will pull some of the men who have been in combat a long time and send in some of the younger general officers."[22] The Pentagon, while supportive, advised Ridgway to tread carefully to avoid any congressional inquiry into what General Wade Haislip, the army vice chief of staff, called the "wholesale relief of senior commanders."[23] Haislip told Ridgway to depict the replacements as routine replacements, with press statements coming from the Department of the Army in Washington, rather than from the field. "Achievements and awards while in Korea should be stressed," Haislip counseled. The public relations ploy worked. *Time,* for instance, managed to make the sackings sound like promotions, saying that the replaced generals "are back in the U.S. for jobs of first importance."[24] By late February Ridgway had assembled a new cadre of division commanders, all major generals in the age range of forty-nine to fifty-one years: Charles D. Palmer, 1st Cavalry; Blackshear M. Bryan, Jr., 24th; Claude B. Ferenbaugh, 7th; and Joseph S. Bradley, 25th.

In letters to Collins, Ridgway spoke tartly of the battlefield stamina of American troops compared to that of the Communists. He acknowledged that

> unless you have seen this terrain, not only from the air but from a jeep, it will be hard to visualize the difficulty of operations. Yet the other fellow manages and he seems never to lack ammunition, the heaviest load in his logistics stream, though, of course, he uses impressed human carriers and every local form of transportation—oxen, camels, ponies and two-wheel carts.

He wanted a "toughening of the soul as well as of the body" in training. He visited POW camps at Pusan and found the North Korean and Chinese prisoners "in appearance but a shade above the human beast. It is by the use of such human canaille that the Soviets are destroying our men while conserving their own."

Ridgway intended to deal roughly with an enemy that hid behind civilians. At a command conference on January 8 the question arose of what to do with enemy soldiers posing as civilians. "We cannot execute them, but they can be shot before they become prisoners," the minutes state.[25] One general had another suggestion. "We just turn them over to the ROKs and they take care of them." Ridgway asked MacArthur for permission to use poison gas "as a last resort to cover the withdrawal and evacuation from a final beachhead where pressure might be so great as to justify resorting to extreme measures."[26] Using gas "would afford an invaluable tactical advantage." MacArthur refused. "I do not believe there is any chance of using chemicals on the enemy in case evacuation is ordered. As you know, U.S. inhibitions on such use are complete and drastic and even if our own government should change this attitude, it is more impossible that . . . the United Nations" would approve.

Troops and officers alike soon knew Ridgway as a stickler for detail. He would stop a marine radioman so laden with communications gear that he could not stoop to tend flapping laces of a combat boot and tie the man's shoe himself. He emphasized terrain studies. "We must know roads, good and bad; we must know where armor can operate, where it cannot." When Ridgway ordered a unit to attack a certain sector, "I knew if it involved infantrymen crawling up 2,000-foot ridges with their weapons, ammunition and food on their backs or whether they could move heavy equipment in, could ford the streams, or could find roads where wheeled vehicles could advance."[27] He and his pilot, Captain Mike Lynch, ranged over the entire front, their L-17 liaison plane touching down on roads atop dikes in rice paddies or darting into small towns to land on level streets. "General Ridgway was like a cat on a hot tin roof where combat was concerned," Lynch related. "He wanted to be in on it."[28]

Lynch was a pilot with the derring-do to take Ridgway where the general wanted to go. He had learned early to spend his spare time scouting for odd landing places that could be used in emergencies. One such spot he found was in a town near the Han River. A fairly broad road ran through the town and dead-ended at a T intersection. "I got into the town the first time by flying under a wire, then up and over a bridge and down again," Lynch said. "Four months later, when I was flying for Ridgway, he had an operation where the 187th Regimental Combat Team was to jump north of the town. The 1st Cavalry, however, got out of the blocks in a hurry as its part of the operation and seemed to be able to beat the 187th to the objective. General Ridgway wanted to know where we should cancel the 187th's jump because if the enemy had moved out of town, it would be a waste." But was the enemy in the town?

"Let's go down and look," Ridgway told Lynch.

Another Ridgway aide on a larger command plane protested over the radio net, "There's no place to land down there."

"I did it before," Lynch told Ridgway. "I can get in, but it's going to be a hairy son of a gun."

"Go," Ridgway said.

Lynch landed without incident. He handed Ridgway a carbine, and they walked through the town, checking bridges for explosives and booby traps. "Then the lead units of the 1st Cavalry came rolling into town, led by Charlie Dog Palmer [an inevitable army nickname for someone with the initials C. D.]. So the first thing General Palmer saw was the Eighth Army commander and a bunch of little Korean kids waving American flags."

The criticisms of American generals and enlisted men Ridgway was careful to keep private. In press briefings he emphasized that he faced a job of rebuilding the Eighth Army. His personality and candor gave Ridgway remarkably good press relations. To Walker, reporters had been a nuisance. He felt the press had not given him enough credit: that his defense of the Pusan Perimeter had been completely overshadowed by MacArthur's splashy Inchon landing. When Walker did not snarl at reporters, he ignored them. Ridgway, however, recognized that the public image of the war inescapably was shaped by what battlefield reporters wrote, and he courted them. He persuaded James Quirk, formerly one of General George Patton's public information officers, next an executive of the Philadelphia *Inquirer,* to return to active duty to handle his press relations. Quirk had a sense for the small comforts and services that helped the working press. He posted a large-scale map at the press billet in EUSAK Headquarters with a tactical overlay that was frequently updated. He installed a phone bank at the billet so reporters could call in dispatches from the field. He built a soundproof booth for radio broadcasters. Stories about Ridgway reflected press fondness for him. To the American public he became the "can-do general" who was ferocious toward the enemy, firm but understanding of his men. Some reporters chuckled about the two live grenades Ridgway wore clipped to his field jacket. Captain Mike Lynch, however, insisted these criticisms were unfair. "General Ridgway was regularly in shooting situations. We had mortar shells drop all around us on several takeoffs. After a 187th RCT jump, we took prisoners within several yards of the plane."

But Ridgway could be harsh about what he considered inaccurate or uninformed reporting. On January 8 he refused to permit Marguerite Higgins of the New York *Herald Tribune* to file a dispatch saying "American officials" and "high army sources" felt that the Korean situation was "hopeless."[29] In a note to MacArthur, Ridgway explained: "Since she has been here Miss Higgins has not interviewed anyone authorized to speak for this headquarters. It is not known what government officials she has talked to." Her opinions "did not reflect the views of this headquarters." Ridgway alerted General Doyle Hickey, MacArthur's chief of staff, that Higgins was "mildly indignant" and might be heard from again.

Ridgway dealt with MacArthur respectfully and circumspectly, his inner doubts about his commander notwithstanding. He frequently interjected praiseful paragraphs about MacArthur into routine messages to Tokyo, and he was careful to avoid critical remarks that might get back to the general. He was always mindful of the famed MacArthur ego and of the consequences of offending it. On February 16 Earl D. Johnson, an assistant secretary of the army, sent Ridgway a Drew Pearson column stating that "Ridgway has profited from the mistakes of General MacArthur in turning a tragic defeat into Korean victory."

Johnson wrote: "Without passing on the pros and cons of this argument, you recognize even more clearly than I do the need for not allowing such talk to produce an unfavorable emotional reaction on the part of General MacArthur. You can count on me to take whatever action possible to offset this unfortunate approach."[30] Ridgway understood. He replied that the subject "is a most delicate one, in which I must proceed very carefully, for in spite of the singleness of purpose on my part . . . it would be so easy . . . inadvertently or thoughtlessly to find some completely innocent act or utterance misconstrued."[31]

MacArthur made Ridgway's task easier by keeping away from Korea the first weeks of the change of command. Ridgway played by the book. He sent MacArthur cables almost daily telling of his work to restore the Eighth Army to fighting trim and of his intention to launch limited counteroffensives once he felt his force was ready. He and MacArthur shared commiserations about the indefinite JCS mandate under which the command operated. But Ridgway took pains to explain to commanders why they could not have the reinforcements they wanted and why they could not take the war to China. He talked frankly. "To support the army in Korea," he said, "our mobilization base has been destroyed and our supply warehouses and shelves are bare. The United States is not capable of any major effort anywhere in the world except Korea."[32] But he sought to instill in the officers the "fullest confidence that we can stay indefinitely while delay merges into defense, and then offense."

One result of the candid briefings was a dampening of rumors of a general withdrawal from Korea, in acknowledgment of imminent defeat. Ridgway knew that men would fight once they knew they were in Korea to stay and that the boats were not coming in the near future. By late January, after a month's vigorous work and a wholesale purge of unwanted officers, Ridgway looked toward the offensive.

MacArthur's Recommendations Rejected

General Ridgway's success in stopping the New Year's Eve Chinese offensive stiffened the JCS resolve to reject MacArthur's December Hobson's choice of either a wider war or withdrawal from Korea.[33] MacArthur's last flurry of cables in December had asked that the JCS "reconsider" their veto of moves against China, upon pain of mandatory retreat. The JCS did not change their mind. After a polite two-week lapse of time, on January 9 the JCS cabled MacArthur that while the retaliatory measures he recommended would be "given careful consideration," he should accept several conclusions. "There is little possibility of policy change or other external eventuality justifying strengthening of our effort in Korea," they said. Blockading China must await either stabilization of the American position in Korea or withdrawal; even then, a blockade would require negotiations with the British because of "the extent of British trade with China through Hong Kong" as well as UN concurrence. Naval and air attacks on China "probably can be authorized only if the Chinese Communists attack United States forces outside of Korea." The JCS rejected (for the fourth time) use of Nationalist Chinese in Korea. Then they restated MacArthur's directive: to defend in successive positions, "inflicting maximum damage" to the enemy "subject to primary consideration of the safety of your troops and your basic mission of protecting Japan. Should it become evident in your judgment that evacuation is essential to avoid severe losses of men and material you will at that time withdraw from Korea to Japan."

MacArthur read the message with anger; aide Courtney Whitney said he considered it a "booby trap" that demanded contradictory alternatives: to hold in Korea if possible; otherwise, to withdraw.[34] He responded by asking the JCS for "clarification," a code word that meant he intended to reargue the issue.[35] (MacArthur had tried the same ploy in December.) It was "self-evident," MacArthur cabled, that the UN Command was not strong enough both to hold in Korea and to protect Japan. Strategic dispositions "must be based upon overriding political policy establishing the relativity of American interests in the Far East." A beachhead line could be held for some time, but not without losses. "Whether such losses were regarded as 'severe' . . . would to a certain extent depend upon the connotation one gives the term." (The JCS had not offered their own definition of "severe.")

The UN Command had accomplished its original mission by driving the North Korean Army out of South Korea. It had never been intended to "engage the armies of the Chinese nation." The UN troops

are tired from a long and difficult campaign, embittered by the shameful propaganda which has falsely condemned their courage and fighting qualities in misunderstood retrograde maneuver, and their morale will become a serious threat to their battle efficiency unless the political basis upon which they are asked to trade life for time is clearly delineated, fully understood, and so impelling that the hazards of battle are cheerfully accepted.

In conclusion, MacArthur threw down the gauntlet to Washington: It must decide, and immediately, whether to remain in Korea. The decision, he cabled, was

of highest national and international importance, far above the competence of a Theater Commander guided largely by incidents affecting the tactical situation developing upon a very limited field of action. Nor is it a decision which should be left to the initiative of enemy action which in effect would be the determining criteria [*sic*] under a reasonable interpretation of your message. My query therefore amounts to this: Is it the present objective of United States political policy to maintain a military position in Korea—indefinitely, for a limited time—or to minimize losses by evacuation as soon as it can be accomplished?

As I have before pointed out, under the extraordinary limitations and conditions imposed upon the command in Korea its military position is untenable, but it can hold for any length of *time up to its complete destruction if overriding political considerations so dictate* [emphasis added].

When General Marshall brought MacArthur's message to the White House, President Truman was "deeply disturbed."[36] MacArthur was, in effect, charging that the "course of action decided upon by the National Security Council and by the Joint Chiefs of Staff and approved by me was not feasible." Dean Acheson was more biting. "Here was a posterity paper if there ever was one," he asserted, "with the purpose not only of clearing MacArthur of blame if things went wrong but also of putting the maximum pressure on Washington to reverse itself and adopt his proposals for widening the war. . . ."[37] For Acheson, "nothing further was needed to convince me that the General was incurably recalcitrant and basically disloyal to the purposes of his Commander in Chief." Secretary Marshall, after reading the paragraph on troop morale, said to Dean Rusk, "When a general complains of the morale of his troops, the time has come to look into his own."

MacArthur's glum estimate of the military situation puzzled the Joint Chiefs, who had felt that Ridgway's performance the first week of January had shown that the Eighth Army could hold its own. Admiral Sherman said he and colleagues felt "some disappointment" at being asked to "clarify" instructions that had seemed perfectly clear. General Marshall told a Senate committee a few months later that "we were at our lowest point" about the time this message came in.[38] But General Collins sympathized with MacArthur's dilemma and also expressed some pique at the State Department.[39] During periodic meetings after the Chinese intervention "the Chiefs constantly tried to pin down . . . just what our remaining political objectives were in Korea." The diplomats "would always counter with the query, 'What are your military capabilities?' " To Collins the "discussion would almost invariably come down to the age-old question of the chicken and the egg." The State Department, in Collins's view, wanted to attain the maximum military results. "But the military would have to assume all the responsibility if things went wrong."

Despite his irritation, Truman did agree that sending the message was "the proper procedure for [MacArthur] to voice his doubts and to ask for reconsideration."

On January 10, a Sunday, Dean Acheson called an informal meeting of key State and Pentagon figures at his home.[40] Acheson was irritated and said so. The previous month he and others had spent days reaching agreement that the military should give diplomacy time to work. Now MacArthur raised the same issues again. Acheson was at the end of his patience. He wanted suggestions on how MacArthur could be persuaded, once and for all, that the United States was pursuing a specific course and that his incessant carping was unwelcome.

But Acheson realized he was talking as a diplomat, not as a soldier, and with a keen sense of protocol he tried to persuade the military that he was not encroaching on its territory. He talked at length about the *political* importance of continued military resistance. Acheson agreed that military considerations should determine how long UN forces continued fighting and that no requirements should be put on EUSAK that would impair its later usefulness in Japan. But he said it would be "valuable to gain time." A new cease-fire effort was under way in the UN. If UN troops could hold until it was completed, there would be a good chance that if it failed, the UN could be persuaded to condemn China as an aggressor.

After more discussions and reviews of drafts, at the White House and elsewhere, President Truman decided to use three separate channels to bring MacArthur into obedience.[41] First, he approved a JCS message repeating (for the third time) MacArthur's operating directive. On the basis of "all the factors known to us, including particularly those presented by you in your present message," it appeared to the chiefs "infeasible under existing conditions" to hold a position in Korea for a protracted period. But it would be in the interest of the United States and the UN to gain further time for diplomatic efforts. Thus the JCS stressed the importance of inflicting "maximum practicable punishment" on the enemy and of not evacuating Korea "unless actually forced by military considerations."

Secondly, Truman approved sending Generals Collins and Vandenberg to Korea both to obtain firsthand information on the current battle situation ("stripped of MacArthur's colorful rhetoric," Acheson said) and to counsel MacArthur on the reasoning behind Washington's decisions. By talking to the general directly, without the formalese of cable traffic, Truman hoped he could make his case.

As the two generals traveled to Tokyo, Truman drafted a personal letter to MacArthur. The President clung to the thought that if the general understood the rationale behind American foreign policy, he would cease his criticisms. Truman had heard the rumors that MacArthur's palace guard screened his cables and that many important papers never reached his desk. So on January 13 Truman sent MacArthur a lengthy "personal message" to bring him "up to date on our foreign policy."

The message summarized what had been stated at NSC and other meetings the past several months: that a "successful resistance in Korea" would demonstrate that neither the United States nor the UN would accept aggression; that it would "deflate the dangerously exaggerated political and military prestige of Communist China"; that it would buy time for a buildup of world resistance to Communist expansionism. Truman asked MacArthur's "judgment as to the maximum effort which could reasonably be expected" from his command.

An overriding aim, Truman continued, was to "consolidate . . . the nations whom [sic] we would desperately need to count on as allies in the event the Soviet Union moves against us." Pending the buildup of military strength, "we must act with great prudence in so far as extending the area of hostilities is concerned." Truman could understand MacArthur's impatience. Nonetheless, "steps which might in themselves be fully justified and which might lend some assistance to the campaign in Korea would not be beneficial if they thereby involved Japan or Western Europe in large-scale hostilities."

Truman recognized that continued resistance with available forces might be impossible and that American strategic planning depended on preserving enough military strength to defend Japan. If the UN Command were driven from Korea, it might be advisable for MacArthur to continue resistance from Cheju-do or other islands. But it must be made clear to the world that any expulsion from Korea was the result of "military necessity" and that "we shall not accept the result politically or militarily until the aggression has been rectified."

The last statement made it plain that Truman intended to retaliate against the Chinese should MacArthur be forced from Korea—a point which the general never seemed willing to accept or trust.

By happenstance, MacArthur received the Truman letter shortly before Collins and Vandenberg arrived in Tokyo.[42] At the outset of their talks he complained no one had ever made clear to him just how long and under what conditions the Eighth Army was to hold in Korea or who was responsible for the security of Japan. He then read the President's message and said it removed part of the uncertainty. "That, gentleman," MacArthur said, "finally settles the question of whether or not we evacuate Korea. There will be no evacuation." To Truman, he replied simply, "We shall do our best."

But MacArthur balked at assuming responsibility for both Korea and Japan. The Eighth Army had its hands full fighting the war. Collins referred him to the JCS directive of January 12, which stressed the importance of remaining in Korea while leaving it to MacArthur to determine whether the UN Command could do so without being destroyed. Collins pointed out that the President had indicated the great importance he attached to a prolonged defense in Korea in order to allow time for political action in the UN. As for Japan, even if reinforcements were approved at once, they could not arrive for six weeks, meaning MacArthur would still be responsible for protecting Japan.

MacArthur found no comfort in this statement. He replied "with some emotion" (General Collins's phrase) that he should not be held responsible for the defense of Japan while the Eighth Army was in Korea. He repeated his request that the four National Guard divisions be sent to Japan at once. Collins and Vandenberg replied they had not been mobilized for that purpose.

Next, Collins and Vandenberg turned to a long options paper that had been evolving through the JCS bureaucracy since November. The final version—approved by the JCS and read but *not* approved by Secretary Marshall or anyone else—was a list of "proposed actions" to be taken against China in the event the UN was forced to evacuate Korea. In the words of General Marshall the proposals "were put forward as tentative courses of action to be pursued if and when this possibility came closer to reality."[43] When the January 12 list was originally put together, evacuation was a keen possibility. But by the time the list reached MacArthur, as Marshall noted, "the situation . . . began to show signs of improvement." Marshall emphatically stated, "None of these proposed courses of action were vetoed or disapproved by me or by any higher authority. Action with respect to most of them was considered inadvisable in view of the radical change in the situation which originally had given rise to them."

Of the sixteen points listed in the proposals, eleven related directly to Korea. But of the four specific requests made by MacArthur on November 30—in the cable that so irritated the JCS—only one was adopted without qualification, that pertaining to removal of restrictions on Nationalist forces. Two others, naval blockade and bombardment of the mainland, appeared as carefully hedged contingent possibilities. The fourth MacArthur request, the use of Nationalist troops in Korea, was not even discussed; the JCS were not about to plow this familiar ground once again. The major points listed were:

—Continue and intensify the existing economic blockade of China.
—"Prepare now to impose a naval blockade of China and place it into effect as soon as our position in Korea is stabilized, or when we have evacuated Korea, and depending upon circumstances then obtaining."
—Remove restrictions on air reconnaissance of China coastal areas and of Manchuria.
—Remove restrictions on operations of Chinese Nationalists and give logistical support to operations against the Chinese Communists, including "all practicable covert aid" to Nationalist guerrilla forces in China.
—Initiate damaging naval and air attacks on objectives in Communist China at such time as the Chinese attacked UN forces outside Korea.

The exact manner in which Collins and Vandenberg presented the January 12 "options list" to MacArthur is not on record, for no notes were kept of their meeting. In Senate hearings later in 1951 both generals insisted MacArthur was told the January 12 list had not been adopted as planned actions, but only as options to be considered should the Chinese eject his command from Korea. Obviously there was a communications failure. To MacArthur, the list became identified as policy parameters within which he could operate (and comment). Either Collins and Vandenberg did not adequately explain the difference between "proposed actions" and "intended actions," or MacArthur did not understand them. Within months the January 12 list was to become the subject of acute political dispute, with MacArthur citing the points as evidence that he did not violate policy in discussing them publicly and the administration and the JCS using them to argue the opposite side of the case.

Truman had tried through three channels to inform MacArthur of why he was proceeding as he did in Korea. Now only events could tell whether MacArthur had heard, understood, or intended to heed what he had been told.

Eighth Army Moves Again

By late January General Matthew Ridgway was ready to take the Eighth Army on the march again.[44] X Corps units, now under the unified EUSAK command, moved up from the Pusan area into line, again on the east side of the country. Several strategic considerations guided Ridgway's decision to take the offensive. The winter was rapidly winding down. Soon torrential spring rains would sweep Korea, washing out bridges, culverts, and roadways, flooding lowlands and rice paddies. Bad weather meant no American air support. Also, Ridgway was curious about the whereabouts and intentions of the CCF. Intelligence reports estimated that an army of 174,000 Chinese lay in front of his positions. Few, however, were visible to aerial reconnaissance. Ridgway finally flew twenty miles behind the enemy lines in a slow AT-6 advance trainer with General Earle E. Partridge, the Fifth Air Force commander, at the controls to look for signs of the Chinese. The craft flew at treetop level, often dipping below surrounding ridges. "Hardly a moving creature did we spot," Ridgway wrote, "not a campfire smoke, no wheel tracks, not even trampled snow to indicate the presence of a large number of troops." So the Eighth Army would have to go in on the ground to see what was happening.

This time, the Eighth Army moved prudently, rather than in replica of what Ridgway called "the reckless and uncoordinated plunge toward the Yalu" MacArthur had conducted in November. A single commander, Ridgway, controlled all units, which in turn were tied together at their mutual flanks. When the offensive began, on January 25, Ridgway was proud that the Eighth Army "soon proved itself to be what I knew already it could become: as fine a fighting field army as our country had yet produced."

Ridgway made no grandiose promises of success; he was conducting a probe, and his advance would depend on the enemy strength he encountered. He did not care about real estate; he wanted Chinese bodies. In the west he set as the tentative advance line the banks of the Han River; in the east, an area marred by rugged mountains, he would stay farther south of the river. He saw no military value in moving beyond the Han "unless Communist China should elect to withdraw north of the 38th Parallel." For this initial offensive Ridgway was dubious about attempting to go as far as the 38th parallel, which he called "an indefensible line with forces now available." Retaking Seoul "would involve placing an unfordable river through or in rear of our defensible position." Unless a "sudden opportunity arose for the trapping and destruction of a major portion" of the CCF, he would consider "an effort at its recapture unsound," although he did have plans for a future later recapture of the city.

MacArthur generally agreed with Ridgway's plan, although he would push beyond the Han until he met the limit of CCF resistance. "As far as Seoul is concerned," MacArthur cabled, "the re-occupation of Kimpo Airfield and . . . Inchon . . . would unquestionably be of marked value. . . . The occupation of Seoul itself would . . . present certain diplomatic and psychological advantages which would be valuable, but its military usefulness is practically negligible."[45] Ridgway, however, stuck with his more conservative plan.

The broad-front attack—IX Corps in the west, X Corps in the east—moved about two miles daily the first week, despite sudden warm rains that turned the frozen ground to eight to twenty inches of slimy brown mud. With his west flank anchored on the Han, Ridgway concentrated on straightening a southward bulge in the center of the line, in central Korea, with the 1st Marines in the forefront. The CCF lost up to 2,100 casualties a day the first week.

Then the Chinese stiffened. Again the break of a ROK regiment led to a slaughter. An American artillery battery, supported by an infantry guard, was moving up a narrow highway three miles northwest of Hoengsong, apparently without any flank guards. The units were to support the ROK 8th Division, a few miles to the north. They bedded down for the night. The CCF counterattacked, the ROKs broke and ran, and suddenly the Chinese swarmed over the artillerymen. Of more than 500 men, only 2 survived. One, a corporal, related: "The Chinks hit us about 2 A.M. There was shooting all over the place. They sent me and fourteen other riflemen out to secure the guns. We helped get them into convoy, but only three of us came back."[46]

The next day the artillery convoy managed to move southward to escape the Chinese momentarily. But that night they encountered another ambush. The other survivor, a private, related:

> The Chinks hit the driver in the front machine, and that stopped the column. Everybody got rattled. As soon as somebody fell, the Chinks would grab his weapon. Somebody hollered "There's one!" and I fired. But it was only a tree. Somebody hollered "Let's get out of here." I turned around and the world seemed to explode at my feet. Blood gushed everywhere. I knew I had had it then and there. . . .

The Hoengsong ambush was the most concentrated loss of American lives in the entire war, some 530 men—a tragedy that began with the break of a ROK unit and was compounded by poor tactical maneuvering of the U.S. unit.

Another tough battle was fought by the 2nd Division's 23rd Regimental Combat Team (RCT), commanded by Colonel Paul Freeman and aided by a French battalion led by a redoubtable lieutenant colonel named Ralph Monclar, as gallant a soldier as ever fought in any war.[47] Monclar's dress uniform bore every military medal France offered; he had been wounded seventeen times and walked with a severe limp. When the war began, he was a lieutenant general, an inspector general of the Foreign Legion. But he wanted the honor of leading the French contingent to Korea, so he voluntarily took a reduction to lieutenant colonel. Monclar's battalion was with Freeman's RCT assault on an area beyond the Han River known as the Twin Tunnels, named for two parallel railroad tunnels that went through a mountain there. On February 3 the combined forces moved into a road junction village named Chipyong, already much battered by air and artillery bombardments. Small units went forth for reconnaissance and ran into a strong Chinese counterattack. At one point Freeman decided that prudence dictated withdrawal. Both Almond and the division commander agreed and asked for Ridgway's approval. The printable portion of Ridgway's reply was: "No!"

Freeman did not flinch. He called his battalion commanders, told them to strengthen the perimeter, and said, "We're going to stand and fight."

The CCF attack came at two in the morning in division force with a cacophony of bugle and whistle calls and chanting of political slogans. The French responded by cranking up a hand-powered siren which sent its own eerie wail howling over the battlefield. The fighting raged through the rest of the night and into the day, with Freeman desperately trying to focus artillery fire on an enemy intermingled with his own troops. To the presumed astonishment of the Chinese, the Frenchmen—most of them former Legionnaires, like their officers—removed their helmets and tied red scarves around their heads. They yelled an honored Legion battle cry, "Camerone!" the name of the Mexican village where 65 Legionnaires stood and died under an assault by 2,000 Mexican soldiers in 1863. Then they went after the Chinese with slashing bayonets and smashing rifle butts. When a group of American artillerymen (impressed into duty as riflemen) broke and fled, Captain Thomas Heath stood and pounded at them with his fists, shouting, "Goddamn it, get back up on that hill! You'll die down here anyway— you might as well go up on the hill and die there!" Twice he forced them back to the battle; twice they broke again. The Chinese kept coming. Another captain, William Klutz, grunted over a field phone, "Let's kill as many of these sons of bitches as we can before they get us." But counterattacks failed, victim of overwhelming Chinese manpower, and Freeman at last was forced to call upon a final reserve of one ranger company to plug a widening gap in his line.

Screaming and yelling as they attacked, the rangers halted the Chinese. In the wild melee the Chinese and the rangers scrambled over the crest of the hill—lunging at one another with bayonets, dodging tossed grenades, occasionally finding the opening to fire a rifle shot. Beaten down by the three to one Chinese manpower advantage, the surviving Americans began fighting their way off the hill. If they lost, the Chinese had a gap in the American line which could be quickly exploited.

A single man took up the slack. Captain Robert Elledge, an artillery liaison officer, had been wounded earlier in the fight but decided to return on his own. At roadside he found an abandoned four-barrel .50 caliber machine gun mounted on a half-track. He yelled to a nearby tank crew, and between them they managed to swing the gun around until its muzzle faced the enemy. Elledge fired the motor. It started. He leveled the gun and fired behind the retreating Americans, cutting down the pursuing Chinese. A Chinese bazooka crew crept close and tried to knock out the gun. Elledge silenced them with a burst. He held the position until daybreak.

Now came three American tanks, guns blazing, followed by an overflight of fighter planes with napalm and phosphorus bombs, leaving the hill covered with hellish flames. Colonel Freeman, close by at the rear, rushed up hastily assembled reserves to plug the gap.

The Chinese held the hill all day long despite the counterfire. Their resistance ended at sundown, and they slipped away to the rear.

Ridgway came up the next day, and he and Freeman walked over the battlefield. Freeman was no combat virgin. He had gone through the 2nd Division debacles in North Korea in November and December, and he had survived the best that the Chinese had to offer. Of this day, however, he said, "That was probably the most desperate fight that I participated in during my entire time in Korea, and we were very lucky that we weren't overrun because we were truly making our last stand."

Counting enemy casualties is usually a matter of estimate rather than exactitude, especially when deaths are caused by napalm and high-explosive artillery shells. But at the Twin Tunnels, U.S. soldiers counted some 4,000 confirmed Chinese dead.

The significance was not lost on Ridgway. Individual groups of UN soldiers had broken under superior fire and resisted orders to return to combat. But the regiment's officers, to a man, had stood their ground, even when they expected to die. Enough enlisted men—the vast majority—also remained firm. For the first time in the war an all-out Chinese offensive had been broken.

Furthermore, the Chinese broke off major contact all along the line of advance. Ridgway realized that the way was now clear for him to force a crossing of the Han River east of Seoul, cutting enemy supply lines and trapping CCF forces massed in the west. The Eighth Army's performance had not been perfect—but it had bested the Chinese in head-to-head fighting, and Ridgway felt proud of what he had done in six weeks in command.

MacArthur Claims Some Credit

The first weeks of the Ridgway command, General MacArthur stayed away from Korea, and with good reason. To the public, Korea was a lost war, and MacArthur wanted no further identification with a losing cause. With most of the war news bad, MacArthur even ordered that press communiqués be released by EUSAK headquarters in Korea, rather than from the Dai Ichi Building. Ridgway did not mind MacArthur's absence, for he could conduct his daily business without the dominating presence of a senior general.

But the success of Ridgway's late January offensive rekindled MacArthur's interest. He could not resist the reflected glory of a victory, especially when he might be able to claim credit for what someone else had done.

The rank vanity of his superior commander came sharply home to Ridgway in an incident in February. On February 18 Ridgway drafted a plan for what he called Operation Killer, intended to exploit the gains of the earlier drive. The Eighth Army was to attack across the Han River with two divisions. Four CCF field armies were reported to be in the area in and south of Pyongyang. Operation Killer was a probe with the purpose of "inflicting maximum losses" on the enemy, with a minimum to the UN.[48]

Early on the morning of February 19 Ridgway outlined the plan to key EUSAK generals. There was discussion about details, but by breakfast time the plan was firm. To Ridgway, Operation Killer was the "final implementation of the plan I had nourished from the time of my taking command of the Eighth Army—and had done so it may be said in the face of a retreat-psychology that seemed to have seized every commander from the Chief [MacArthur] on down."

The same day Ridgway brought in correspondents assigned to Eighth Army headquarters for an off-the-record briefing. He wanted to put his campaign into context. The Eighth Army had stopped the Chinese counterattack, he said. "We have resumed the initiative, and in two or three days we shall attack." The background statement told the newsmen that they should prepare to be in the field; it was not intended for publication that would alert the enemy of what was to happen.

To the dismay of the Eighth Army censors (and the press) MacArthur flew into Korea on February 20, the eve of the offensive, and told the same reporters, on the record, "I have just ordered a resumption of the offensive."

The statement staggered Ridgway.[49] Not only did it tell the Chinese that the Eighth Army would be moving the next day, but it also implied that MacArthur had personally conceived the operation. "The implication was clear," in Ridgway's opinion. "He had just flown in from Tokyo, had surveyed the situation, discussed it with his subordinates, and had then ordered the Eighth Army to attack." No such thing had happened. Neither MacArthur nor his Tokyo staff had anything to do with the operation. Ridgway now knew the outer bounds of MacArthur's ego.

The episode gave army censors a fit. By coincidence, the previous day Major General Henry I. Hodes, the EUSAK deputy chief of staff, had lectured chief censor Lieutenant Colonel Melvin B. Voorhees and his three top assistants. His theme was what to do when a general officer violated security regulations in press statements. The guiding rule for censors, Hodes said, was: "No matter who is quoted, your job is to safeguard the security and welfare of the army."

Thus, when the press dispatches on MacArthur's news conference landed on the censors' desks, the officers faced a true dilemma. In the words of Voorhees, a former newspaper executive, "Here was a news story which should be suppressed for security reasons, even though it emanated from a general officer. Yet it came from the one officer who possessed the undoubted authority to make any statement regarding military operations he chose."

Voorhees signed and passed the dispatches for publication.[50] He felt that MacArthur's press officer, Major General Courtney Whitney, had timed the release for maximum publicity, the eve of the Washington

Birthday holiday in the United States. "All good press agents know that the way to get a page-one 'break' in daily newspapers is to hit the slack pre-holiday hours when every newsroom is seeking material with which to fill space," Voorhees commented.

Ridgway learned a hard lesson from the "Commander in Chief's efforts to keep his public image always glowing." MacArthur's press statements endangered the lives of the men fighting for him. Invariably, when a major offensive was to be launched, MacArthur visited the attack units and figuratively fired the starting gun, a practice good perhaps for troop morale, but also invaluable to enemy intelligence. But pep talks to the troops are best done discretely, not with the amplification of a Tokyo public relations staff. In a carefully worded cable to Tokyo, Ridgway asked MacArthur to forgo visits to the front on the eve of other operations, for security reasons. He did not want to withdraw the welcome mat; he did not want to intrude on MacArthur's prerogatives as commander. Yet the fact was that his very presence was a distinct signal to the enemy. MacArthur agreed. He would remain away from operations until they were well under way.

Keeping MacArthur away from the front before offensives was one thing; silencing him, another. And to Ridgway's rage, some of the things he said hurt Eighth Army morale. At Suwon on March 7, for instance, he said that only a stalemate could result in the war unless he were permitted to attack the Reds in their Manchurian sanctuary. Eighth Army troops called this his "die for a tie" speech, and in the words of Colonel Voorhees, "its effect on their attitude toward the future was not inspirational."[51] Ridgway had to devote considerable energy the next few weeks convincing the troops they were not fighting in vain.

To close observers MacArthur was an exhausted man that spring, a general who had lost his aura of glamour and omnipotence. William Sebald, the political adviser in Tokyo, who had worked closely with MacArthur for years, found him "tired and depressed." Lieutenant Colonel Adam A. Komosa, an adviser to the ROK 9th Division, recalled a MacArthur inspection tour to one of his units, which was just above the 38th parallel, the northernmost position along the UN line. "MacArthur was slumped in the front seat of his jeep as though he were completely exhausted," Komosa related. "He did not manifest his usual confidence and flamboyance. That famous scrambled-egg hat didn't look very dashing on that day either. He was a beaten man."[52]

But MacArthur's flow of public statements was undiminished. As the spring wore on, and Ridgway's success continued, MacArthur's statements were at once defensive and belligerent. For one thing, he decided to issue yet another justification for and explanation of the disastrous "home by Christmas" campaign.

No longer was the November drive a reconnaissance, MacArthur's initial post failure claim. Now he portrayed it as a skillful strategic maneuver.[53] "Our field strategy, initiated upon Communist China's entry into the war, involving a rapid withdrawal to lengthen the enemy's supply lines with resultant pyramiding of his logistical difficulties and an almost astronomical increase in the destructiveness of our air power, had worked well." The sentence is complex, and it deserves a rereading. Washington received the bald claim with incredulity.[54] The State Department's Herbert Feis said that if stretching out Chinese supply lines were MacArthur's objective, "obviously it would have worked better if we'd gone all the way to the Philippines." Dean Acheson was astounded at MacArthur's recasting of the record. "It is hard to conceive a more mischievous or stupid statement for anybody to make than this one. . . ." He called the statement "the most obvious and childish attempt to . . . pretend that we really foxed the Chinese by this headlong retreat down the peninsula . . . most absurd!"

Another sentence in the statement ran directly contrary to the policy being shaped by Acheson and Marshall in Washington and by General Ridgway on the battlefield. "The concept advanced by *some* [emphasis added; MacArthur preferred to criticize insinuated rather than named adversaries] that we should establish a line across Korea and enter into positional warfare is wholly unrealistic and illusory." Acheson commented, "Well, this is exactly the attitude which all our allies had; it was one which was being discussed in the government at the time he had his statement; and it was the one that was later adopted by the government of the United States. . . ."

MacArthur Builds a Record

What the JCS wanted—and the State Department and other administration elements accepted—was a cease-fire with restoration of the prewar status quo—that is, with Korea divided near the 38th parallel.[55] Such a decision was reached on February 6, with the chiefs rejecting four other listed alternatives: reinforcing the UN to unify Korea by force; deliberate withdrawal; military stalemate without any agreement; or an attempt to "settle the Korean question" by defeat of the Peking regime. "Congress wants us out of Korea," General Collins said, "and if we are going to stay any length of time we ought to be deciding as to the reason for our staying and getting the word to the people."

The JCS once again discussed the January 12 list, although they took no action other than deciding to keep the options under consideration. No one favored taking the war back to North Korea in force, although Ridgway was authorized to seize specific tactical objectives across the 38th parallel to protect his defense line.

The decisions of late January and early February marked a significant convergence of the views of the JCS and State Department. They wanted to end the war with diplomacy, not expanded fighting. The urgency of December and early January had been dispelled by the steady battlefield gains of the Eighth Army.

MacArthur, however, had his own plans. In a series of messages in February he asked again for permission to bomb Manchuria. "It can be accepted as a basic fact," he wrote, "that unless the authority is given to strike enemy bases in Manchuria, our *ground forces* as presently constituted *cannot with safety attempt major operations in North Korea* [emphasis added; major ground operations in North Korea, as MacArthur should have known, were the last thing the JCS wished at this stage]."[56]

What MacArthur began to formulate, in planning only partially shared with Washington, was a long-range scheme for destroying the Chinese forces in Korea. His target would be Chinese supply lines. First, he would regain the Seoul line as a base of future operations. "I would then clear the enemy rear all across the top of North Korea by massive air attacks."

If the JCS denied him permission for the bombing, MacArthur had an even more bizarre idea, one the international (and domestic) repercussions of which he did not address. "If I were still not permitted to attack the massed enemy reinforcements across the Yalu, or to destroy its bridges, I would sever Korea from Manchuria by laying a field of radioactive wastes—the byproducts of atomic manufacture—across all the major lines of enemy supply."[57] The destruction of North Korea had left it barren of supplies, and food or munitions used by the Chinese had to come across the Yalu. At any given time the CCF had only about ten days' supply of food and ammunition. Once these supplies were exhausted, MacArthur would use American reinforcements and Chinese Nationalists to "make simultaneous amphibious and airborne landings at the upper end of both coasts of North Korea, and close a gigantic trap. The Chinese would soon starve or surrender. Without food and ammunition, they would become helpless. It would be something like Inchon, but on a much larger scale."

MacArthur's maneuver ignored several relevant facts. The JCS had told him, repeatedly, that he would not be given either reinforcements or use of Nationalists and that American policy did not foresee taking the war to the north again. Nuclear experts consulted by the JCS said the "nuclear waste band" would contaminate underground water and rivers for decades. The JCS ignored MacArthur. They wanted no "super-Inchon" or "dirty belt."

Even as Ridgway advanced, killing thousands of Chinese weekly as he contested the CCF for each bloodstained acre, MacArthur complained he needed more freedom of maneuver. "Our field strategy," he said in late February, "a war of maneuver with the object of inflicting as heavy a punishment upon the enemy as possible . . . has worked well. But we must not fall into the error of evaluating such . . . successes as decisively leading to the enemy's defeat."

MacArthur pushed. On February 15 he again asked the JCS for permission to bomb the North Korean port of Rashin, off limits since September.[58] Vast unidentifiable supplies went through the port and its rail marshaling yards, reconnaissance planes spotting 332 railroad cars on a single day. MacArthur called Rashin "the last major profitable strategic target in North Korea." Destroying it by visual bombing "will be a major loss to the enemy . . . conversely, its immunity from attack remains a major threat to our forces." Although some subordinate staff officers favored the bombing, Marshall and his deputy, Robert Lovett, objected. Besides risking a Soviet reprisal, an attack would have little military effect because the rail connections did not run to the south and because the North Koreans could simply move their supply operations across the border to Vladivostok. The JCS consequently did not even put the matter before the President, although they did acknowledge to MacArthur the negative decision was political rather than military: "Decision has been reached on higher governmental levels that restrictions on Rashin must remain in effect for the present."[59]

A few days later MacArthur revived another long-rejected issue—bombing the Yalu hydroelectric plants.[60] The JCS had first raised this possibility in December. MacArthur, after reconnaissance, reported the installations were "mainly inactive," and bombing them would serve no military purpose. On February 26, however, he forwarded an "urgent" request for permission to bomb the plants. The JCS said no, citing MacArthur's December statement about the inactivity of the plants.[61]

Why did MacArthur make requests that the JCS almost certainly would deny? Exploring the intricacies of MacArthur's motivation was a puzzling pastime even for his intimates. In Washington the JCS and other officials could only speculate. One State Department official thought he knew the answer. MacArthur was methodically constructing a record for use in his defense should the war suddenly turn sour again. By documenting a series of proposals and their rejection, he was putting himself into a position to blame "Washington" for any future battlefield failures.

Ridgway Fixes a Line

By late February General Ridgway's renewed offensives had straightened the UN line across the waist of Korea. For the first time since the

Chinese had appeared in the war UN forces stood along a relatively stable line, with (in the words of army historian James F. Schnabel) "no gaping holes, no soft spots, and no enemy salients threatening to tear it in two."[62] In the east, ROK units had gone several miles past the 38th parallel and dug into deep defensive positions which could be protected by both naval gunfire and carrier-borne aircraft. For the third time American and ROK forces had recaptured Seoul from the Communists (although the capital was so battered by now, and bereft of population, that its possession was mainly symbolic). Despite his occasional carping, MacArthur rather cheerfully cabled Washington on March 1 that he was "entirely satisfied with the situation at the front, where the enemy has suffered a tactical reverse of measurable proportions. His losses have been among the bloodiest of modern times."[63] Pleased by the northward progress of his forces in the field, MacArthur noted, "The enemy is finding it an entirely different problem fighting 350 miles from his base than when he had this 'sanctuary' in his immediate rear, with our air and naval forces practically zeroed out."

This cable was the last optimistic statement MacArthur was to send the JCS. It was so optimistic, in fact, so free of MacArthur's usual backbiting, that Admiral Sherman wondered what mischief MacArthur might be plotting.

New Diplomatic Initiatives

Just as Matthew Ridgway rebuilt the Eighth Army, Dean Acheson rebuilt the American diplomatic initiative in the war.[64] Acheson did not succeed in starting negotiations, but he did maneuver the Chinese into a position where none but avowed Soviet bloc nations could support them in the United Nations.

To Acheson's tactical delight, the New Year's Eve Chinese offensive came while the UN was still trying to digest the Chinese rejection, in late December, of overtures by its cease-fire commission. To him, the rejection and the new offensive were evidence of China's intention to make good its "oft-repeated threat" to drive UN forces from Korea. It would be "incomprehensible" for the UN to ignore this intention and thus to signal that " 'big' aggressions can succeed with impunity." The administration began drafting a resolution condemning China as an aggressor and soliciting support from other nations.

To Acheson's chagrin, the cease-fire commission refused to accept the Chinese rejection as final and on January 11, with only a few hours' notice to the United States, submitted a new formula designed to meet some of the demands set forth by Peking. The plan had five parts: (1)

an immediate cease-fire; (2) a political meeting for restoring peace; (3) withdrawal by stages of foreign troops, with "appropriate arrangements" for the Korean people regarding their government; (4) arrangements for unification and administration of Korea; and (5) a conference, after the cease-fire, of the United Kingdom, United States, Soviet Union, and Communist China, "to settle Far Eastern problems," including the status of Formosa and China's representation in the United Nations.

The first four of these measures were innocent enough. The fifth, however, which implied American willingness to surrender Formosa and admit Communist China to the UN, gave the administration what Acheson called a "murderous" choice. Supporting the plan meant the "fury of Congress and the press"; rejecting it could cost the United States its majority support in the UN. But to Acheson, any plan involving concessions to the Chinese was repugnant to elementary concepts of justice and legality, in view of the Korean aggression. Still, as foreign policy historian Richard Stebbins wrote, the proposal "still retained considerable appeal in circles which felt that Peking had been unfairly treated in the past and must be conciliated at almost any cost in order to avoid a possible general war."[65] British Prime Minister Clement Attlee fell in with the commission's proposal, proclaiming somewhat loftily: "We should, in the name of a common humanity, make a supreme effort to see clearly into each other's hearts and minds."

With Attlee declared in advance as favoring the seating of Peking in the UN, the United States would be outnumbered three to one in the posthostilities conference. So Acheson ran the problem through his lawyer's mind, weighing what the Chinese and Soviets would conceivably do. He concluded that the Chinese would want even more from a UN settlement, that they would reject the proposals. He talked with Truman, who agreed the United States should accept the plan and bide its time. So when the plan was formally introduced, Ambassador Warren Austin said the United States would vote in its favor.

"Shocking appeasement," shouted Senator Robert A. Taft; even loyal Democrat Tom Connally, chairman of the Senate Foreign Relations Committee, complained sharply to the State Department. Just wait, counseled Acheson (who nonetheless worried when the "political roof fell in" in Congress). The UN approved the plan by overwhelming vote and transmitted it to Peking.

Just as Acheson expected, the Chinese reply totally vindicated his strategy. A cease-fire without political negotiations was wholly unacceptable. The Chinese strongly repeated their earlier demands—prior Chinese admission to the UN and U.S. withdrawal from Formosa—as the price for any negotiations whatsoever.

His trap successfully sprung, Acheson called the Chinese reply further evidence of a "contemptuous disregard of a world-wide demand for peace."[66] The UN had explored every possibility for finding a peaceful settlement in Korea. "Now," he said, "we must face squarely and soberly the fact that the Chinese Communists have no intention of ceasing their defiance of the United Nations."

Despite British and Indian opposition, the General Assembly on February 1 declared Communist China an aggressor by a vote of 44 to 7, with 9 abstentions. (Burma, India, and five Soviet bloc members opposed the resolution; Sweden, Yugoslavia, and seven Asian and Arab states abstained.) The resolution called on Peking to "cause its forces and nationals . . . to cease hostilities . . . and to withdraw from Korea." It reaffirmed UN determination "to continue its action in Korea to meet the aggression" and called upon members "to continue to lend every assistance" to the action in Korea. Finally, it created two special bodies: a committee to consider, as a matter of urgency, "additional measures to be employed to meet this aggression" and a three-man group to be available "to bring about a cessation of hostilities," in effect a cease-fire commission.

Acheson's adroit manipulation of the United Nations produced a diplomatic coup of the first order. A group of neutrals had proposed a peace plan which the Chinese—not the Americans—rejected. Now the Chinese flew the outlaw banner; Peking, not Washington, opposed peace.

For the Chinese, opposing the cease-fire caused a ghastly human disaster. By overreaching themselves, apparently in the belief that a UN majority would support their demands, the Chinese rejected an opportunity to end the war on far better terms than they were to accept two and one-half years later.

The 38th Parallel Issue Again

Ridgway's offensive revived a problem which the JCS and State Department had debated since December with no resolution: Should the UN forces reach the 38th parallel again, what should they do? Technically MacArthur still operated under the directive the United Nations had issued when it entered the war: to repel the aggression and to restore peace and security in the area. As noted earlier, the UN directive also incorporated the long-standing goal of bringing about the "establishment of a unified, independent and democratic Korea." These directives remained in effect even after MacArthur was given the tactical mission, after the Second Phase Chinese Offensive, of maintaining forces in Korea as long as possible without endangering either his command or the defense of Japan.

By the same token, MacArthur still possessed the authority to cross the 38th parallel under orders given him by Washington on September 27 and confirmed on October 7 by the UN General Assembly. But because of the changed political situation, Acheson felt that any decision to move above the parallel required discussions with allied governments.

Thus commenced a peculiar minuet in which neither the State Department nor the JCS were willing to propose a definite course. "Indeed," Acheson remarked, "so insistent was each [department] upon having guidance from the other that it gave rise to some sharp expressions suggesting avoidance of responsibilities."[67] To Acheson, reentry into North Korea would "create a severe crisis within the free world and could lead to the withdrawal of certain allies [notably the British] from the war."[68] Acheson conceded that all of South Korea must be recaptured to deny the enemy his main objective. Nor would Acheson forbid minor ground actions across the parallel to interrupt enemy offensive preparations. Stopping the war at the frontier would make negotiations easier. Acheson could not foresee the North Koreans' entering into a truce which gave the UN (and the ROKs) even a slight toehold in their territory. If the objective was to inflict "maximum punishment" on the enemy, this could best be done by stabilizing a front along the 38th parallel, rather than stretching supply lines by going farther north. Air and naval actions in the North would continue. In any event, Dean Rusk of the State Department told the JCS ("in confidence") the main reason for a policy statement was Averell Harriman's feeling that it was necessary to "firm up" Truman's thinking on the 38th parallel.

The JCS protested.[69] So long as UN political objectives remained unchanged, its military forces should not be barred, for political reasons, from crossing the parallel. The prohibition would let the Chinese mass for battle with impunity. The no-cross rule would be one-way, for the Chinese would go as they wished. The JCS said it would be difficult for MacArthur to keep up offensive operations, or even maintain a strong defense, without freedom of maneuver.

Yet the Joint Chiefs thought it premature to recommend what MacArthur should do when he reached the parallel. Until then the JCS considered any decision "militarily unsound." Discussions with allies would leak to the enemy, the JCS feared (and with reason; in addition to Soviet agents Philby, Burgess, and Maclean, the British Labor government was laden with people unfriendly to the UN cause). What the JCS wanted was for the State Department to specify a course to reach U.S. political objectives.

The strength of the JCS objections convinced Acheson that the State recommendation opposing crossing the parallel should not be sent to Truman. Marshall agreed. He also wanted to keep the discussion from other governments as long as possible.

MacArthur, with secondhand knowledge of the intense intra-administration debate, tried to force a decision in roundabout fashion. On March 2 he sent the JCS a semimonthly report for the UN on his operations during the last two weeks of February, a routine paper that usually talked about the military situation. MacArthur included a sentence that the State Department recognized as a political bombshell:

> While President Truman has indicated that the crossing of the parallel is a military matter to be resolved in accordance with my best judgment as a theater commander, I want to make it quite clear that if and when the issue actually arises, I shall not arbitrarily exercise that authority if cogent political reasons against crossing are then advanced and there is any reasonable possibility that a limitation is to be placed thereon.[70]

State officials immediately saw the loopholes in a statement that at first glance might appear as a disclaimer of any intention to cross the parallel. They saw no profit in unnecessarily highlighting the issue for UN allies and asked that MacArthur delete the sentence. He did.

But battlefield events within a few days brought the parallel issue to public attention. On March 7 General Ridgway launched Operation Ripper, intended to drive a broad wedge into the center of the enemy line and separate the Chinese in the west from the North Koreans in the east. The major target, Chunchon, was less than ten crow-flight miles from the 38th parallel. With Chunchon in hand, the Eighth Army stood only two days' march from the frontier.

On March 15 a reporter asked Truman whether UN forces would go beyond the parallel. "That is a tactical matter for the field commander," he replied. "A commander in chief seven thousand miles away does not interfere with field operations. We are working to free the Republic of Korea. . . . That doesn't have anything to do with the 38th Parallel."

Although Truman's statement was vague, it dealt with a subject on which MacArthur had been forbidden to comment only a few days earlier. The general grumbled to Tokyo intimates about a "one-sided gag; they can say what they want in Washington, but this old soldier cannot obtain approval on any statement more significant than a morning report" (the company-level form reporting how many men are present for duty on a given day).

The same day of Truman's press statement, by coincidence, the State Department finally agreed on a draft statement on war aims in Korea. Although two months' discussions and some minor revisions lay ahead before final approval, the State paper did constitute an agreement between the JCS and State on some "fairly simple and sensible conclusions," as Acheson called them.

The paper effectively gave up the idea of unifying Korea by force. UN forces should continue to inflict maximum losses on the enemy and should regain control over territory south of the 38th parallel. UN ground forces should be permitted to conduct "aggressive defensive operations" approximately ten to twenty miles north of the parallel "as may be required by the tactical situation."[71] When the 38th parallel was reached in force, the United States should seek a cease-fire along the lines communicated to the UN Cease-fire Committee in December 1950. Should the enemy refuse the terms, UN forces

> should continue to inflict maximum attrition. They could undertake raids north of the border to keep the enemy off balance and to disrupt offensive preparations, but there should be no general advance, nor any attempt to hold territory in North Korea. The United States should continue to deflate Communist China's prestige by inflicting heavy losses on its troops in Korea, and should continue economic and diplomatic actions against its government. But no military actions directly against mainland China were contemplated.

The draft superseded the options list the JCS had drafted on January 12. The paper was significant to MacArthur for two reasons: It defined the parameters of where he could operate beyond the 38th parallel, and it rejected his prospective operations against mainland China. To be sure, the draft did not represent a final decision by the National Security Council or by the President. But it did inform MacArthur, and in explicit terms, of the JCS-State consensus of how the war should be waged. And the JCS were MacArthur's superiors.

MacArthur, however, was not to be dissuaded from speaking his mind. The December 6 presidential directive requiring clearance in Washington of statements by administration and other officials quieted the general for months. (One administration official suggested that Truman's order had less to do with MacArthur's unaccustomed silence "than the fact that he [MacArthur] had just gotten his ass kicked off and really had nothing to say, even on his own behalf.") But now MacArthur was ready to commence once again his propaganda campaign against the administration he served, and in such a bizarre fashion that within weeks serious discussion was held within the Pentagon and White House as to whether America's supreme commander in the Far East was a rational man.

The CIA Comes of Age[72]

In early 1951 a Chinese Communist inspection officer reported to Peking that its troops in Korea were sick, starved, and frozen, surviving the sub-zero winter on a few unthawed scraps of potatoes daily. "When the fighters bivouac in snow-covered ground their feet, socks and hands freeze together in one ice-ball; they cannot unscrew the caps on their hand grenades; the fuses will not ignite . . . skin from their hands sticks on shells and mortar tubes. . . ." With no shelter the Chinese lived in disease-producing misery, and scores of thousands of men lay immobilized by pneumonia and intestinal diseases.

Although the Chinese had slackened the tempo of battle after their December victory, General Matthew Ridgway knew the lull would be short-lived. After the two previous offensives the Chinese had been forced to pause a few weeks to regroup and to replenish their supplies, which were brought in over the ice-coated mountains of North Korea by human bearers. All Ridgway could do was try to bring his own men back into fighting form—two army divisions had been virtually destroyed in December—and hope that he would be able to beat back an enemy with a numerical advantage of four or five to one.

Although Ridgway didn't know it, his command was about to receive vital help from an unlikely congeries of sources: a Danish-American spymaster, the Nationalist Chinese Coast Guard, and an anonymous U.S. espionage agent in the Indian government.

In mid-January Central Intelligence Agency station chiefs throughout the Orient received an urgent message from headquarters in Washington. The message relayed "hard" intelligence received from an agency plant in the Indian government of Prime Minister Jawaharlal Nehru, which, despite professed neutrality in the Korean War, gave frequent propagandistic and diplomatic support to the Communist Chinese. Now Nehru's support was to become material as well. According to the agent, the Chinese had chartered a Norwegian freighter and dispatched it to Bombay, India, to take on a cargo of medical supplies provided by the Indian government. The shipping manifest was impressive: It included three full field hospitals, plus assorted drugs ("enough to give at least three shots of penicillin to every enemy soldier north of the 38th parallel," according to one American intelligence agent), surgeons, physicians, nurses, and other medical personnel and gear.

Washington's message to the field agents was blunt: The ship and its cargo must be stopped from reaching the enemy "at any cost." The message did not dwell on humanitarian aspects of the shipment. Should the medical supplies reach Chinese armies in the field, they would put them into shape for a renewed offensive that could cost thousands of American and ROK lives.

But intercepting the ship was a matter of considerable diplomatic sensitivity. Although Norway was a member of the United Nations, it nonetheless had permitted its vast shipping interests to continue trading with the enemy, despite diplomatic protests from the United States and other UN members with troops in the field. The U.S. had shied away from declaring a blockade of China because of fears of offending the British, who also had continued trading with China as a means of protecting their crown colony of Hong Kong.

Thus the dilemma: How could the United States halt the shipment without provoking a diplomatic furor that could shatter an already fragile diplomatic alliance? The message from CIA headquarters did not address this issue; it simply instructed field agents to do the task, and do it quietly, and the expense be damned. But the message did carry an implicit but unstated warning: Do not embarrass the United States government.

Thus began Operation TP-Stole,* an act of unabashed (and successful) piracy of the ship of another nation on the high seas without even a bow in the direction of international law. The CIA had joined the Korean War, and with boots and fists flying.

The directive ultimately reached Atsugi, Japan, and the desk of Hans V. Tofte, a handsome Danish-American with thinning blond hair and a touch of his native Scandinavia in his voice. Virtually unknown outside the insular intelligence community, Tofte nonetheless carried a reputation among peers as one of the more remarkable operatives of the twentieth century. And what had happened in his life *before* he read the cable about the Norwegian vessel tells much about why he was superbly suited for the mission.

Tofte's experience in Asia began in the early 1930's, when at age nineteen the East Asiatic Company, a Danish shipping firm, sent him, the son of a Danish sea captain, to Peking to learn Chinese as the first part of a planned career abroad. The firm was an equivalent of the East India Company that the British long used as their colonial agent in India, and it had offices up and down the coast of China. "When you went overseas for the company," Tofte related, "you did so with the understanding you would be there twenty-five years or so, with marriage not permitted the first ten years." After two years of Chinese-language studies in Peking, Tofte lived in Kirin, Manchuria, for eight years, traveling there and in the northern part of Korea on behalf of his company. He developed strong ties with the White Russian aristocracy, refugees from the Communist Revolution, living in the area, and he came to know the twists and turns in virtually every railroad and highway. (Later, as a CIA officer, Tofte would bemusedly plot Chinese troop movements over the rail lines he had traveled as a young man and give his guerrilla teams precise locations—bridges and other bottlenecks— where traffic would be particularly vulnerable to a saboteur's bomb.)

When the Second World War broke out, Tofte returned to Denmark

---

*For administrative purposes, the CIA assigns a digraph designation to related operations in a given area. Korea War operations bore the prefix "TP."

and joined the underground. But he recognized reality: The Nazis were not to be defeated from within an occupied country. Using bogus papers, he managed to escape to Spain (flying nervously on a German plane) and thence to the United States. In New York he sought out William Stephenson (later famed as "The Man Called Intrepid"), who ran British intelligence operations in America. Tofte offered his services, and Stephenson dispatched him to Singapore, where he organized native crews to run supplies over the Burma Road to the Chinese fighting the Japanese in the interior. He organized guerrilla bands of tribesmen and fought valiant but ultimately futile delaying actions against the Japanese. When Singapore fell, Tofte returned to the United States and surrendered his rank of brevet major in the Indian Army to enlist in the American army as a private.

Because of his background, Tofte was detailed to the Office of Strategic Services, the wartime intelligence and espionage organization from which the CIA eventually evolved. Now commenced the most dazzling of Tofte's Second World War exploits.

Working with Major General William "Wild Bill" Donovan, the OSS chief, Tofte was instrumental in devising a scheme to compel the Germans to divert strategic troops from the campaign in Italy to Yugoslavia. The British had been parachuting arms, ammunition, and other supplies into the mountain strongholds of Yugoslav patriots who were conducting a pinprick war against the Germans. The impetuous Tofte thought this effort too slow and too limited. Drawing upon his maritime background, he organized a flotilla of old and otherwise worthless coastal vessels, manned them with refugee Yugoslavs, and set up a seaborne supply service across the Adriatic from the Italian port of Bari to the island of Vis off the Yugoslav coast.

By October 1943 Tofte's strange little navy contained forty-four vessels—old schooners, trawlers, and rusty tramp steamers—that darted across the sea at night, each ship carrying as much matériel as the British airdrops had supplied in a month. Josip Broz Tito, later president of Yugoslavia, gratefully received the arms, and his partisan bands tied down scores of thousands of German troops. The United States awarded Tofte the Legion of Merit.

When the war ended, Tofte had invitations to remain in American intelligence. Although the OSS was disbanded within months after the fighting stopped, intelligence professionals knew a replacement agency would eventually emerge. Tofte declined, for he did not wish to spend his life in a quasi-military organization. He returned to Copenhagen as manager of an American overseas airline, maintained contact with the chief of the Danish intelligence service, and occasionally carried covert documents to the U.S. In the late 1940's he married an American woman and moved to Mason City, Iowa, to run her family's printing business.

By now the Central Intelligence Agency was in existence—a minute organization, distrusted by the military and the State Department bureaucracy, but with considerable internal ambitions. Tofte visited Washington during Christmas 1949 and heard fervent recruitment pleas from two old war friends, Desmond FitzGerald, the CIA's deputy director for plans (i.e., head of covert operations), and Major General Richard Stilwell, head of Far East operations. During a lunch at the Sulgrave Club, Tofte politely but firmly refused to join the CIA. He was leading a comfortable middle-American life in Iowa—the Rotary Club, the Episcopal Church, a Boy Scout commissioner—and he wanted no part of a peacetime bureaucracy. He did agree to talk with Frank Wisner, another wartime colleague now in CIA clandestine services. The setting befitted the CIA's orphan status, a cluster of ramshackle wooden "temporary" buildings near the Reflecting Pool.

"We sure need you," Wisner said.

Tofte again declined. "But if there is another war, you can count on me," he said.

In June 1950 Tofte went to Fort Riley, Kansas, for two weeks' active duty training as a lieutenant colonel in the army reserve. He heard about the war on Sunday morning and thought, War has come, and Jesus, I am caught in Fort Riley in uniform! The expected call from Wisner came early the next morning. "Is this enough of an emergency for you?" Wisner asked dryly. It was, Tofte said. "Can you get in here now?"

By Tuesday Tofte was at agency headquarters in Washington. He recognized that because of his background in the Orient and his linguistic ability (by now he spoke six languages), he was a natural for assignment to Korea. Stilwell and Wisner arranged for briefings, but they could give Tofte few orders. "There was no book to go by," he said. "This was the first time that CIA was to function in a hot war."

As general guidance Tofte was told to look to the CIA functions mandated by Section Five of NSC 10/2, the National Security Council directive which outlined the spy agency's mission: covert political action, covert psychological warfare, covert paramilitary operations, covert sabotage, and economic warfare; evasion and escape plans for pilots downed behind enemy lines; and a "stay-behind" organization of operatives in the event the Communists overran either Japan or Korea.

"Basically I was told to choose a site and build an operations base outside Tokyo, big enough to handle one thousand people, with our own communications. Whatever else happened, I was on my own."

Tofte telephoned his wife in Mason City and asked her to meet him when his Tokyo-bound flight stopped briefly in Minneapolis. She brought him two suitcases of clothes. "I never went home."

Tofte did insist upon one thing before accepting the Korean assignment. He had secondhand knowledge of the way things were run in MacArthur's headquarters and of the martinet qualities of Major General Charles Willoughby, the theater G-2, with whom he must work intimately. So he refused to maintain his reserve rank of lieutenant colonel. He would go to Tokyo only with an agency rank equivalent to major general, the same as Willoughby's. The CIA agreed.

Tofte's precaution proved wise, for the CIA had a bare toehold in MacArthur's theater. Only in May had General Stilwell succeeded in obtaining MacArthur's permission for the agency to operate in his portion of Asia. MacArthur's antipathy to clandestine intelligence independent of his command dated to the Second World War, when he absolutely refused to admit OSS agents to the Pacific theater. A military traditionalist, he disdained the free-lance qualities of agents working independent of his headquarters, and only immense pressures from Washington forced his reluctant agreement with Stilwell a few weeks before the war began.*

When Tofte arrived in Tokyo, he found that the CIA presence there consisted of "six poor lost souls" working from a hotel room. This unit, under Georges Aurell, maintained uneasy liaison with what Tofte called "the tight little island" of MacArthur's staff. A more substantial operation was at Yokosuka Naval Base near the port of Yokohama, where William Duggan conducted intelligence operations under auspices of a CIA branch with the meaningless title Office of Special Operations, or OSO. Tofte set about organizing his own unit for covert activity, the Office of Policy Coordination, or OPC.

First, however, he had to bring the recalcitrant Willoughby into line. Their first clash came when Tofte, a man un-shy about asserting his importance, insisted on being billeted in a suite at the Imperial Hotel, best in downtown Tokyo. Impossible, huffed Willoughby, the Imperial is exclusively for generals, admirals, and other "top military men of special importance." Tofte asserted his "rank" of major general and received the suite. He also demanded that the military supply him a two-star flag for his automobile. When it was not forthcoming, he had one made for himself.

"I decided that the only way to deal effectively with Willoughby was to kick him in the pants every chance I got, to let him know I was tough as he was, or tougher," Tofte related. So when Willoughby made what came to be his "monthly threat" to throw Tofte and the CIA out of Japan, Tofte would tell him, "Shut up, you work for me, I'm an American citizen and a taxpayer, and you can't order me around."

*Willoughby took the CIA's insistence on running its own intelligence networks in Asia as a personal affront. People active in CIA intelligence gathering at the time say he was mistaken. The CIA's position was that it needed sources independent of the military and State Department to ensure that ingrained biases did not affect the national intelligence estimates given the President.

But Willoughby and Tofte did share a common ability for languages, a fact that gradually moderated "but did not entirely end" the hostility between them. "I would call him one day and speak in Russian, the next day in Chinese. It got to be sort of a sport, and he would laugh about it. But I made one thing plain to him. 'I will not speak with you in your goddamned German,' " Tofte said, recalling his days with the Danish underground.

Tofte benefitted from having an experienced bureaucrat as his Tokyo deputy—Colwell Beers, who had previously served the government with the U.S. Forest Service and the Hoover Commission (a postwar agency on efficiency in government). "Beers was a hell of a good bureaucrat," Tofte said. "He kept me out of jail because he knew his way around government and how to handle the paper work and details. We became a formidable team."

Tofte and Beers spent the first week driving around the environs of Tokyo, looking for a site for the new CIA base. "It wasn't all work. We took along picnic lunches and swam off the Imperial Beach." In fact, they were eating lunch as they walked around Atsugi Air Force Base, forty-seven miles south of Tokyo, with a splendid view of Mount Fuji, when they came across an isolated area of some fifty acres. "I had a beer in one hand and chicken sandwich in the other, and I pronounced, 'This is where the base will be.' " Still eating and drinking, Tofte and Beers paced off where various buildings would be located. Engineers and a construction battalion were at work within the week.

Next Tofte needed people. He sought them in the military, the only pool of available manpower. Recognizing upper-echelon hostility to the CIA, he concentrated on second- and third-level staff officers. "One of my responsibilities was to establish an evasion-and-escape [E&E] operation across Korea to rescue downed fliers. For obvious reasons, this had great appeal to the air force and the navy, for they wished security for their fliers. Thus I was able to persuade these services, and the army as well, to assign men to me."

Tofte assembled two officers each from the air force, the army, and the navy and locked them into his Tokyo conference room with orders to draw up an E&E plan. "If a pilot was hit up around the Yalu River, in MIG Alley, and he had twenty minutes' flying time before going down, it made a colossal difference if he knew where he had to head for." Tofte laid down these specifications for the E&E plan:

—Two islands off the east and west coasts of Korea above the 38th parallel as the main E&E destinations for downed airmen, manned by CIA agents and communications personnel.
—A "belt" across the peninsula to be saturated with trained guerrillas

as guides, working from fixed inland positions that would be given pilots as part of their combat briefings.

—Covert agents and E&E observation points to be established along the east and west coasts just below MIG Alley at twenty-mile intervals, equipped with communications gear.

—Two CIA-controlled indigenous "fishing fleets" to patrol the coasts to look for downed fliers, using actual black-market operations as cover.

—Briefings of fliers on E&E techniques by CIA agents before their missions, and debriefings of rescued airmen once the system went into operation.

—A supply of $700,000 worth of one-ounce gold bars bearing the chop of the old Bank of China, so that each pilot could carry three or four bars in his uniform to pay native Koreans for help. Tofte knew the gold was obtainable in Formosa.

After some revisions and discussion, the air force and army accepted Tofte's plan. The only demurrer came from Willoughby, who said that because of currency restrictions, the Formosan gold could not be brought into Japan. Tofte did not bother to argue. That night he flew to Formosa, made a private deal with the exile Bank of China, and returned to Japan with the $700,000 of gold. Within a month parts of the E&E plan were working.

The next step was to create guerrilla bands, both for E&E duties and for sabotage and paramilitary operations. CIA interrogation teams screened Koreans in refugee and POW camps near Pusan, paying particular attention to North Korean refugees and their motivation for leaving their country. Those found to be interested in liberating the North from the Communists were offered guerrilla assignments. Tofte recognized that the motivation might be something other than ideology. "The refugees were down-in-the-mouth, bored with nothing to do. Joining the guerrillas would give them a chance to get out, to eat three meals a day, to have something to do. They would be buddies with a purpose, rather than shuffle around the camp." Through the screening CIA found enough trained radio and telegraph operators—chiefly from the South Korean Telegraph Company—to form communications sections for the guerrillas.

For a training base, Tofte took over Yong-do, a small island in the Bay of Pusan at Korea's southern tip. There a CIA detachment headed by Lieutenant Colonel "Dutch" Kraemer, a marine officer, trained some 1,200 Korean guerrillas for action in the North. Potential leaders were screened and transferred for extensive training to another base in Japan, Chigasaki, some ten miles from Atsugi, on the beach of Sagami Bay.

The training continued through the fall of 1950 and the early months of 1951, with agents periodically being pulled out and dispatched to

E&E duty in the North. The format was the same basic guerrilla course Tofte had taught other Asians in the early months of the Second World War: weaponry, use of small boats for covert landings, sabotage techniques, covert communications, espionage, and the other tradecraft skills long used by behind-the-lines agents.

CIA borrowed underwater demolition experts from the navy for training and for launching actual missions. Small landing craft would stand offshore below the horizon while the infiltration and sabotage teams inflated their rubber boats and rowed to the beach. "I wanted it known [to the Koreans] that the Americans took the guerrillas in by hand. This gave the Koreans respect for us, and the military services also."

Tofte's empire expanded by leaps and bounds. Several years earlier the CIA had taken control of General Claire Chennault's old "Flying Tiger" air force from the Second World War—American mercenaries and regulars who fought for Chiang Kai-shek against the Communists —and transferred it to Formosa, where it was renamed Civil Air Transport, or CAT. Now forty of the aircraft, bearing Nationalist Chinese markings along with the CAT emblem, were transferred to Japan and Korea for Tofte's use. The pilots and ground crews were on the CIA's payroll. Tofte took a comfortably outfitted C-47—number XT-854—for his personal plane, for flights around the string of six CIA training stations in Japan and others in Korea. He also took over a small house on Yong-do Island overlooking Pusan Harbor, highest point in the area, which he used for a retreat and for planning conferences. "This was one of the best views in Asia, and getting down there away from all the clamor in Tokyo enabled us to work better and faster."

Tofte's mandate gave him responsibility for covert action in a wide swath of Asia outside Korea: eastern Siberia as far inland as Lake Baikal; all of Mongolia and North China, including Manchuria; and the Kurile Islands and the Ryukyus, the latter under Soviet control. One particularly delicate target was the major Soviet naval base at Vladivostok, Siberia. The Soviets used many Koreans and Chinese for casual labor at the base; thus insertion of CIA operatives was relatively easy. At any given time after late 1950 CIA had at least half a dozen agents working there, watching Soviet naval movements and keeping alert for any sign of possible Russian intervention in the war.

The base was so closely guarded, however, that Tofte's agents dared not use radios for communication. "We relied on 'carrier pigeons'— other Korean agents who would take messages back and forth. Damnably dangerous work, but necessary."

By air and sea, agent teams penetrated Manchuria and eastern Siberia; other specially trained units based at the Atsugi CIA facility went into the Shantung Peninsula and the Tientsin area of North China. For political reasons there were strictures on the use of the CAT planes for insertion of agents on missions into China and the Soviet Union. "We couldn't have planes with Chinese Nationalist markings flying over these countries, so we relied upon the Far East Air Force," Tofte said. General Earle E. Partridge, the FEAF commander, thankful for the CIA's help in rescuing his downed airmen, readily agreed to furnish planes and pilots for these dangerous behind-the-lines missions. MacArthur, however, early on decided that Tofte's operation was becoming too big, independent—and dangerous. On October 25, 1950, MacArthur cabled the Joint Chiefs of Staff that Tofte's Office of Policy Coordination, "which [was] operating under special agreements, had been intermittently violating these agreements." He reported that a recent incident, an airdrop of an agent into Soviet territory from a FEAF plane, had taken on "serious proportions." Accordingly he advised the JCS that he intended to suspend the project. He had already "directed the agencies of his command that they would not participate in similar projects without his specific authority."

The JCS replied two days later that "no responsible official in Washington questioned [MacArthur's] command authority over the operations of the CIA in his theater or in areas projected therefrom." Nonetheless, the JCS "hoped he would afford such support to authorized intelligence and covert operations of CIA as would be consistent with CINCFE responsibilities."*

As the weeks passed, Tofte's force at the Atsugi base alone rose to more than 1,000 people living in a secure compound within the airfield. The CAT aircraft gave CIA a mobility independent of the military. "We never asked for military orders in Japan or Korea," Tofte said, "but wrote our own to look like the official papers without which nobody could move. We ignored the embargo on bringing indigenous personnel in and out of Japan and moved hundreds of guerrillas and agents in and out of our own training and staging camps both in the war zone and throughout occupied Japan."

These sub-rosa activities did not entirely escape Willoughby's attention. CIA personnel found themselves under surveillance by Japanese policemen working for army counterintelligence; Tofte was so angered he gave fleetingly serious consideration to "drowning" one particularly obnoxious officer working for Willoughby. In moments of frustration Tofte would say that MacArthur had three enemies: the Russians, the Chinese, and the North Koreans. "I had four," he said. "Those three, plus MacArthur."

Occasionally Washington-dispatched oddballs did come through

---

*Although Tofte spoke freely of Korean operations in many interviews, because of security strictures he would give scant details of CIA activities in China and the USSR. Despite the passage of three decades the CIA refused my Freedom of Information Act requests for access to the voluminous reports Tofte filed during his tenure in Korea. "At the end," he told me, "the monthly reports were the size of a Manhattan phone book."

Tofte's domain. One man, a Cherokee Indian code-named Buffalo, had been asked in Washington, "How would you like to kill [North Korean Premier] Kim Il Sung?" "I'll start today," he supposedly replied, and left for the Far East. Buffalo was so suspicious of the world that he would not go near a conventional CIA office, even a deeply covert one; he insisted on meeting Tofte and other officers "at sunset near the wall of the Imperial Palace." Buffalo had been offered what Tofte called a "grand prize of a considerable amount of money" if his assassination mission succeeded. It obviously did not, and exactly what Buffalo did after leaving Tokyo was never known to the CIA.

In the area of psychological war Tofte managed not only to tarnish the Soviet Union's reputation in Japan but also to earn a $104,000 profit for CIA in the process. Soviet policy at the time was to encourage leftist groups in Japan to resist MacArthur's democratization process and to make the Japanese citizenry wary of too close an alignment with the United States. The implication was that bystander Japan could be destroyed in a U.S.-USSR war.

Tofte's chance for propagandistic mischief arose in late 1950, when the Soviets began freeing hundreds of Japanese soldiers who had been "lost" in Siberia since the Second World War ended. "There were many lovey-dovey stories in the leftist press in Japan about how nice the Russians were to free these men," Tofte said. He sensed other motives. The American military presence in Japan, save for staff people, consisted of a military police battalion. Tofte feared that the released POWs, and the surge of pro-Soviet sentiment, might give the Russians a propaganda advantage. He and deputy Colwell Beers talked about a countermove but could not find any suitable ideas.

Willoughby inadvertently gave them an opening. Someone on his staff obtained a diary kept by a Japanese colonel who had spent the postwar years in a Siberian labor camp, a grim experience. "Willoughby didn't know what to do with the diary, so he sent it over to CIA as a sort of joke," Tofte said. Tofte skimmed a translation and announced to Beers, "We're going into the movie business. We are going to make a movie about how it is to be a prisoner of war in Russia."

At Tofte's urging MacArthur lifted a ban that had prevented the Japanese film industry from reopening after the war. A request went to CIA headquarters for a film director and writer. Working chiefly with Japanese film technicians—but under CIA direction—crews built a replica of a Russian prison camp in the snowy vastness of Hokkaido, Japan's northernmost island. Tofte ordered, among other items, four rail cars of tomato catsup. Why? Beers asked. "Because this is going to be the bloodiest movie ever," Tofte replied.

That it was. "I knew we were on the right track when Communists tried to sabotage the set. The movie was a dreadful exposure of the Soviets. The Japanese film industry loved it because it put actors and technicians back to work after a long layoff. Audiences loved it because it was a damned good film. We opened at twenty Japanese theaters simultaneously, and it ran for weeks, a smash hit at the box office. Eventually it played at more than seven hundred theaters. It created tremendous indignation and anti-Soviet feeling. And when we added up the figures, CIA took out a profit of a hundred four thousand dollars, which was turned over to the U.S. government."

A more conventional covert warfare operation was carried out at the behest of the National Security Agency, created concurrently with the CIA as the nation's code-breaking and communications-intercept organization. NSA technicians had trouble intercepting North Korean and Chinese messages in the early months of the war. The Chinese used an underwater telephonic cable across the Yellow Sea for most of their message traffic between troop commands in Manchuria and their general headquarters in Peking, a line on which the NSA could not eavesdrop because of its location far behind enemy lines. So the NSA came to the CIA with a request: Was there any way the CIA could disable the cable, thereby forcing the Chinese to use radio broadcasts susceptible to monitoring?

Tofte received the query in his morning cable traffic ("It was always fun opening the mail, for one received the oddest things") and began thinking about the problem. By happy circumstance, he happened to know a bit about the cable in question, for in prewar days he had owned a vacation house on the Manchurian coast. "The cable went into the water about six hundred yards from my garden fence. Further, it was owned by a Danish company, the Great Northern Telegraph Company." Through discreet inquiries Tofte managed to plot the cable's course across the Yellow Sea and the depth at which it could be found. His source even volunteered that cable breaks were particularly annoying when the two severed ends drifted away from each other.

Several days later a flotilla of "Korean fishing boats" converged in the Yellow Sea. The cable was tugged to the surface by grappling hooks and cut. Separate vessels snatched up the loose ends and sailed away in opposite directions. Soon NSA monitors were overhearing and deciphering radio traffic between Chinese forces in North Korea and Manchuria and the defense ministry in Peking.

(Radio-intercept capabilities—and results—remain one of the more closely guarded secrets of the U.S. government; thus an accurate evaluation of Tofte's cable caper is impossible for an outsider. But one early intercept that came to Tofte's attention gave him immense personal pleasure. "The High Command in Peking warned the field commands that fifty thousand guerrillas were loose between the lines. Actually we had about twelve hundred men in the field, no more.")

But in terms of overall importance to the Korean War effort, no other CIA operation approached the one directed against the Norwegian ship carrying a load of medical personnel and supplies to the Chinese Communists.

No one in Tokyo—including Hans Tofte—was very optimistic about TP-Stole. The ship flew the flag of a neutral nation, and for obvious diplomatic reasons the United States did not dare challenge it openly on the high seas. Tofte talked with the navy, which politely said it could do nothing, not even with unmarked covert ships. Nor did the air force care to risk a covert bombing, for the source of the raid would be transparent to the international community. But Tofte did persuade the two services to keep the vessel under surveillance as it steamed north. A U.S. destroyer hovered just over the horizon, tracking the freighter and radioing frequent location reports to Tofte in Japan.

Tofte knew Washington was serious when CIA headquarters authorized him to spend $1 million on TP-Stole without any further authorization. To Tofte, the lifting of normally tight CIA fiscal restrictions meant stopping the ship was "definitely an act-first-and-talk-later proposition."

CIA station chiefs from throughout East Asia gathered with Tofte in Tokyo to plot means of stopping the ship. At one point it appeared the vessel might put into Hong Kong for supplies. Al Cox, the station chief for the port, drew explosives and other special equipment from CIA-Atsugi and hastened back to Hong Kong, "to plan a sabotage operation under the noses of the British authorities if necessary," in Tofte's words. But the ship did not pause. It continued north.

Tofte knew time was running short. All he could wheedle from the Far East Air Force was a promise to bomb the ship—the Norwegian flag notwithstanding—if it put into a North Korean port. Such was unlikely, however, for the UN controlled the seas off Korea. If the ship docked at a more logical destination in Manchuria or South China, the FEAF's hands were tied.

Scanning a map, Tofte saw only one possible intercept point. He boarded one of his CAT planes and flew to Formosa for a conference with Generalissimo Chiang Kai-shek, whom he had met during his Burma Road guerrilla days early in the Second World War. Al Cox, the Hong Kong station chief, joined him. Luckily Chiang remembered Tofte, and he did not blink when the Danish-American spymaster asked his help in an audacious plot. He called in a Nationalist Chinese Coast Guard commander, one Wong, and said, "Give Mr. Tofte what he wants."

Soon a flotilla of Nationalist gunboats—Al Cox and other CIA agents aboard—moved out to sea and, guided by U.S. Navy communications, intercepted the freighter just north of Formosa. The Americans remained belowdecks during what Tofte termed a "fairly discreet piracy under CIA supervision." Chinese boarding parties took command of the freighter, held the Norwegian crewmen incommunicado, and systematically transferred its cargo to their own ships. Tofte let the Chinese have the medical supplies as a prize of war; the nurses, doctors, and other medical personnel were never heard of again, and he does not speculate as to their fate. Now empty, the freighter and its crew were permitted to resume their voyage, knowing only they had been looted by Asian pirates on the high seas. TP-Stole was a success.

To Tofte, the "operation justified the entire CIA budget for the next three to five years. By delaying the enemy's spring offensive for three months, it saved probably seventy-five thousand American lives, for when the Chinese came, General Matthew Ridgway had had time to organize his artillery positions. The Chinese were mowed down by the thousands when they launched their attack."

Tofte returned the $1 million. "I didn't need a penny of it; Chiang Kai-shek did everything." Years later he happened to be dining at the India Club, a private luncheon establishment for shipping executives in Manhattan. Two maritime lawyers were discussing a claim involving a mysterious episode in the Far East. As they talked, Tofte realized the ship involved was the one he had pirated in 1951. He suppressed a smile and remained silent.

The exploits of Hans Tofte in Asia, and of other agents elsewhere in the world, brought a new respect for the CIA to Washington. Thus the Korean War marked the agency's growth into one of the more powerful units of American government. Raw figures suggest the magnitude of the CIA's surge in three years.[73] In 1949 the agency's Office of Policy Coordination (OPC), the cover name for covert activities, had total personnel of 302, a budget of $4.7 million, and seven foreign stations. By 1952 OPC had grown to a strength of 2,812 direct employees plus an additional 3,142 "overseas contract personnel"—a catchall category that included both deep cover agents and flunkies—a budget of $82 million, and forty-seven stations.

Another factor contributing to the CIA's growth was the domineering presence of General Walter Bedell Smith, a man willing to wield authority. The stunning success of the Chinese intervention gave Smith the opportunity to bring even MacArthur into grudging acceptance of the CIA's role in the national security establishment. With President Truman's blessing, Smith visited MacArthur in January 1951. What transpired between them remains a secret. But MacArthur thereafter did not interfere with CIA activities in his theater.

CHAPTER EIGHTEEN

MacArthur Is Sacked

The accepted Truman historiography, one fostered by the late President himself, pictures Douglas MacArthur as a recalcitrant general who finally stepped over the bounds of acceptable behavior in a series of public statements in March and April 1951 that challenged administration policy. General Charles Willoughby, MacArthur's intelligence chief, for one, could not accept this reason. In bitter memoirs Willoughby charged that "it must seem that all of the Administration's 'reasons' masked something deeper."[1]

What Willoughby insinuated was that MacArthur had fallen victim to sinister forces in the State Department and in the British Foreign Ministry, even to covert Communist agents influencing Truman and American policy. But he unwittingly touched a deep Truman administration secret. Douglas MacArthur was fired not for his public statements but for foreign machinations that President Truman could not tolerate.

The true story of the MacArthur dismissal was known to only a few people in Washington. The "public" story, in Truman's estimate, justified his dismissal regardless. And from the distance of three decades it is still impossible to determine who in the administration knew why Harry Truman was firing MacArthur and who knew only the public reasons.

The circumstances that ensured MacArthur's downfall began with the creation, in 1947, of the National Security Agency (NSA), an ultrasecret department the existence of which was seldom publicly mentioned during the Korean War.[2] The NSA was responsible for safeguarding the sanctity of U.S. government communications through the development of elaborate encrypting machines and other devices and for monitoring the messages of other nations, both friend and foe. (The NSA had other secret duties as well. Its closely guarded installations, for instance, housed high-level Soviet bloc defectors during their debriefings.)

Eavesdropping on friendly nations is a dirty business, regardless of national security justifications; as recently as the 1920's Secretary of State Henry L. Stimson stormed that "gentlemen do not read one another's mail," an attitude long outdated in foreign ministries and intelligence agencies around the world. Nations avoid embarrassing one another by the expedient of not talking about communications intercepts.

In the spring of 1951 the main NSA monitoring station in Japan was at Atsugi Air Force Base just outside Tokyo. The main mission was monitoring Chinese communications. But NSA technicians routinely eavesdropped on messages which resident foreign diplomats dispatched to their capitals. Much of this snooping was prompted by nothing other than bureaucratic curiosity: Were the diplomats saying the same thing to their ministries as they were to American officials in Tokyo?

Technicians doing the actual intercepts and decoding of such messages do not deign to analyze what they "hear." Transcripts are passed up the bureaucratic line, first to the NSA's Washington headquarters, which during the Korean War occupied ramshackle buildings at Arlington Hall, an army post in the near-Virginia suburbs of Washington, and then to designated officials of the intelligence community, the State Department, and the Pentagon. Intercepts are tightly held information even in agencies which use the intelligence they contain. At times the intercept material is disguised as coming from another source entirely to shield its actual origin.

Two of the Tokyo embassies monitored in 1951 were those of Spain and Portugal, countries run by right-wing dictators and countries for which Douglas MacArthur long had an affinity. In mid-March 1951 President Truman was handed a sheaf of intercepted messages from Spanish and Portuguese diplomats in Tokyo in which they told superiors of conversations with General MacArthur. The gist of the talks was that the general was confident that he could transform the Korean War into a major conflict in which he could dispose of the "Chinese Communist question" once and for all. MacArthur did not want Portugal or Spain to be alarmed if this happened. The Soviet Union would either keep out of the war or face destruction itself.

The intercepts were seen by Truman and three, perhaps four, of his closest advisers. The thrust of the messages, if not the actual transcripts, was made known to the Policy Planning Staff of the State Department, where director Paul Nitze and associate Charles Burton Marshall were still trying to shape a policy to end the war.

When Truman read the messages, his jaw tautened, his open palm slapped the top of his desk. This is outright *treachery,* he said, in the flat tones that meant he was controlling his rage. Truman no longer had any choice. MacArthur must be stripped of his command. Despite his assurances to Washington that he would obey policy, he had told foreign governments he intended to do no such thing, that he would continue pecking at "political restrictions" until he forced the United States into what he considered a necessary wider war.

But the source of the information meant that neither Truman nor anyone else in the administration could use it publicly. The United States, in 1951, was not about to admit that it snooped on friendly countries. The case for firing MacArthur would have to be built elsewhere, on his public utterances, of which there were many.

The stricture handicapped Truman. Had he been able to reveal the Portuguese and Spanish conversations, MacArthur would have been destroyed overnight. Americans might accept MacArthur's public criticisms of U.S. policy as an extended form of free speech. But conniving to reverse policy was another matter entirely.

Thus was Truman locked into an ironic situation. At the very time MacArthur complained that Washington forced him to fight a "limited war" in Korea, he benefited from the fact that the White House had no choice but to wage a "limited war" against him as well when Truman finally decided to move.

MacArthur Speaks Out

Unfortunately for MacArthur his own public statements gave Truman ample grounds for dismissal even without use of the communications intercept material. If it is assumed he recognized Washington's sensitivity to his criticism (as he should have, after Truman's December 6 gag order), MacArthur's statements beginning in early March 1951 were professionally suicidal, as if he were probing the limits to which he could go. Jealousy seems another motive. MacArthur had complained in December he could not possibly hold in Korea without reinforcements. Ridgway, once in command, did not receive additional troops, and he advanced with a success that stood in stark, layman-visible contrast with MacArthur's self-inflicted disaster of November-December.

So MacArthur began sniping at Ridgway and his "accordion war." He told General Courtney Whitney that "Red Chinese aggression in Asia could not be stopped by killing Chinese in Korea, no matter how many, so long as her power to make war remained inviolate."[3] He did not seem able to understand that Ridgway's strategy was to establish and hold a defensible line as a first step toward negotiating an end to the war. He repeatedly demanded that decisions on what should be done next be made at the "highest international levels"—ignoring Washington's repeated statements that policy had been decided.

On March 15—the same day that Truman was deliberately vague in press statements about penetration of the 38th parallel—MacArthur took his criticisms out of the privacy of his inner circle. In a statement to Hugh Baillie, president of the United Press, he criticized stopping the Eighth Army's advance to the 38th parallel as short of "accomplishment of our mission in the unification of Korea." Acheson commented, "He had been told over and over again that this was not his mission."[4]

Nine days later MacArthur performed what Acheson termed "a major act of sabotage of a government operation." The Eighth Army's successful advances, and its drive to the proximity of the 38th parallel, convinced the administration the time was auspicious for a new try at peace. The prewar status quo had been virtually restored, and EUSAK nearly matched the strength of the Chinese and North Koreans. Now the UN could bargain from a position of equality. Truman felt that "it would now be in their interest at least as much as ours to halt the fighting."[5]

But what sort of deal should be offered the Chinese? The discussion was on two levels: a public statement that the President could issue and a secret consensus on what the United States would accept in negotiations or even be willing to discuss. Politically the administration hoped that its peace initiative would gain support from allies and neutrals. Militarily the Joint Chiefs of Staff felt that the Eighth Army's improved posture since December enabled the United States to insist on a harder bargain. But Robert Lovett, acting defense secretary during a brief illness of George Marshall, did not entirely agree. Forwarding the JCS "harder bargain" memorandum to Acheson, Lovett expressed "general agreement" but added that it would be "fitting" to include the questions of Formosa and of China's admission to the United Nations in considering settlement terms.[6] (The United States, it should be remembered, initially refused to discuss these points in December, when the Chinese insisted they be part of any negotiating agenda. But the next month, during the UN peace initiative, Acheson did not object to their inclusion on an agenda, although he made it plain that the United States would not agree to either point. Whereupon the Chinese refused the UN bid for peace talks. The Chinese behavior convinced Acheson that Peking was not ready to negotiate.)

Acheson, Marshall, and the JCS met on March 19 to review the draft of the proposed public statement. They decided to inform MacArthur of the pending presidential announcement and to solicit his recommendations. Truman, from his Little White House vacation retreat in Key West, Florida, approved, and the JCS on March 20 sent a message to MacArthur:

State Department planning a Presidential announcement shortly that, with clearing of bulk of South Korea of aggressors, United Nations now preparing to discuss conditions of settlement in Korea. United Nations feeling exists that further diplomatic efforts toward settlement should be made before any advance with major forces north of 38th Parallel. Time will be required to determine diplomatic reactions and permit new negotiations that may develop. Recognizing that parallel has no military significance, State has asked JCS what authority you should have to permit sufficient freedom of action for next few weeks to provide security for United Nations forces and maintain contact with enemy. Your recommendation desired.[7]

MacArthur's reply, on March 21, effectively ignored the JCS request for comment.[8] He complained again about restrictions on his command, which "renders it completely impracticable to clear North Korea or to make any appreciable effort to that end." His existing orders covered the situation quite well, he said.

The next several days State and Defense officials refined the proposed presidential announcement and reviewed it with Washington ambassadors of nations with troops in Korea.[9] The statement offered no concessions. It ignored the conditions Communist China had cited earlier as criteria for talks. But it did offer open-ended diplomatic language: "The Unified Command is prepared to enter into arrangements which would conclude the fighting and ensure against its resumption . . . including the withdrawal of foreign troops from Korea." It also offered, indirectly, discussions of the issues raised by Peking: "A prompt settlement of the Korean problem would greatly reduce international tension in the Far East and would open the way for the consideration of other problems in that area by the processes of peaceful settlement envisaged in the [UN] Charter. . . ." Diplomatically the language was the perfect opening gambit for negotiations. It conceded no points in advance, but it did hold out the possibility of concessions during actual talks.

Truman commented, "The thought behind this was that a suggestion of our willingness to settle, without any threats or recriminations, might get a favorable reply."[10]

Three days later, as the State Department discussed the draft proclamation with other governments, MacArthur cut the ground from beneath the President by issuing his own call upon the enemy to talk peace.[11] "Had he deliberately sought to do so," a JCS study concluded, "the UN commander could hardly have found a more effective way to arouse the President's wrath."

Although MacArthur later innocently dismissed the statement as a "routine communiqué," it was no such thing. He knew enough about Chinese pride to realize that his "peace overture" was an incitement to continue the war, not to end it. MacArthur's statement was released to the press, without any prior review by, or notification to, the Joint Chiefs of Staff.

MacArthur called China a vastly overrated military power. "Even under conditions which now restrict the activity of the United Nations forces and the corresponding military advantages which accrue to Red China," he continued, "it has been shown its complete inability to accomplish by force of arms its conquest of Korea." (MacArthur had told the JCS otherwise, repeatedly, over the past several months.) He offered the Chinese an ultimatum, not negotiations:

> The enemy . . . must be now painfully aware that a decision of the UN to depart from its tolerant effort to contain the war to . . . Korea through expansion of our military operations to his coastal areas and interior bases would doom Red China to the risk of imminent military collapse. . . .
>
> Within my area of authority as military commander, however, it should be needless to say I stand ready at any time to confer in the field with the commander in chief of the enemy forces in an earnest effort to find any military means whereby the realization of the political objectives of the United Nations in Korea, to which no nation may justly take exception, might be accomplished without further bloodshed.

MacArthur, expectedly, later denied any improper conduct. Questioned at Senate hearings after his dismissal, he said, "The notice I put out was merely that which every field commander at any time can put out: that he would confer with the opposing commander-in-chief in an endeavor to bring hostilities to an end." But did he not know of the State Department initiative then being circulated to UN allies? "Yes, I received such a message. It had nothing to do with my statement whatever, though. . . . There is nothing unusual or unorthodox or improper that I can possibly read into the statement that I made on March 24."

In this testimony MacArthur did not skirt the truth—he outright lied. Later that year, speaking to a friendly convention of the American Legion, MacArthur boasted that he had uncovered one of the most "disgraceful plots" in American history.[12] He viewed the Acheson peace move as a sellout, a political move that would end the war without victory, with disastrous consequences to the United States and South Korea. To aide Courtney Whitney, the Lovett memo offering to discuss the status of Formosa and the Chinese UN seat was evidence of a "sinister element at work . . . a plot . . . that had . . . reached the top echelons of the Administration."[13] Oddly, however, the record shows that MacArthur was not even told of this shift until March 30, or six days after his statement undercut the peace initiative. Other MacArthur loyalists had their own after-the-fact explanations. General Willoughby offered the dubious thesis that MacArthur was actually supplementing the Washington overture with a "smart stroke of psychological warfare" intended to "back up the peace campaign that was being waged in the United Nations."[14] Taking yet another tack in his memoirs, MacArthur tried to justify the statement as a "military" action because he issued it in his "authority as a military commander" speaking in the "local voice of a theater commander."

Whatever his reasons, MacArthur had thrown down the gauntlet one time too many. His statement, in Secretary Marshall's words,

> created a very serious situation with our allies, along the line of their uncertainty as to just how we were proceeding: the President bringing something to their attention, and gauging their action to find agreement with him, and before that can be accomplished, the leader in the field comes forward with a proposition that terminates the endeavor of the Chief Executive to handle the matter. It created, I think specifically, a loss of confidence in the leadership of the government.[15]

To Truman, the issue of who ran U.S. foreign policy was more important than the diplomatic furor caused by MacArthur's "pronunciamento," (the word used by the Norwegian ambassador when he inquired at State exactly what the Americans were doing). "What was much more important was that once again General MacArthur had openly defied the policy of his Commander in Chief, the President of the United States."[16]

The Spanish and Portuguese cables had made MacArthur's dismissal inevitable. Now Harry Truman had a case he could use publicly.

Washington Is Angered

Robert Lovett, the undersecretary of defense, heard of MacArthur's peace-talk statement late in the evening of March 23, Washington time and immediately went to Dean Acheson's home with Dean Rusk, Lucius Battle, and Alexis Johnson, of the State Department, for a conversation that lasted until one the following morning. Acheson said of the session with Lovett: "Bob, under pressure, is usually inclined to make wisecracks and to be quite entertaining about a thing. . . . This evening, he had no humor. He was just as mad as he possibly could be, and his prescription was that General MacArthur had to be removed, and removed at once."[17] Acheson thought Lovett's mood was "of immediate annoyance and anger" and did not reflect Pentagon institutional thinking. "I was quite convinced that a good deal of steam would go out of the boiler by the next morning."

Inwardly, Acheson seethed, for he felt the peace initiative might have provoked a meaningful Chinese response. Still angry years later, he said, "MacArthur shot his face off and made a proclamation of his own . . . [a statement containing] everything that you can say to make any sort of a reception of a negotiated proposal impossible." The UN allies thought the situation "an unbelievable performance. They didn't know who was running the government of the United States. I don't think anyone suspected that this was a deliberate double-cross, but they [sic] would have been very justified in doing it."

MacArthur was not to be silenced. During a battlefield visit, while his "peace" message was still circulating in a stunned Washington, he told a press conference that the 38th parallel was of no consequence; that the air force crossed it at will; that ground forces had done so in the past and would do so again; that the issue "had been discussed thoroughly in the past and resolved." Acheson called this statement a "bombshell."

But what should the administration do in response? Truman first acted as if he could not believe what had happened. To a Cabinet meeting, he complained that he "had a sad experience with MacArthur, who beat the gun on a statement" he was to make. Truman said it was a "disloyal act to the commander in chief."[18]

On March 24, a day after MacArthur's "peace" statement, Truman met with Acheson, Lovett, and Rusk. All agreed that the December 6 order on clearing foreign policy statements had been clear and explicit and that MacArthur had violated it. The unspoken implication was that MacArthur had exposed himself to court-martial, which the general would probably have welcomed, given his confidence in his position and the opportunity for a public forum. One Truman intimate stated a court-martial was not discussed as a serious possibility. "MacArthur had enough things going for him without making him a martyr as well," this person said. But Truman did decide upon a legalistic maneuver on March 24 that was a clear signal to MacArthur that the President thought he had disobeyed instructions. On Acheson's recommendation, Truman ordered the JCS to send the general a two-part message, reminding him of the December 6 directive and directing that if the Communist military leaders requested an "armistice in the field, you immediately report that fact to the JCS for instructions."[19] (In Senate hearings later that spring MacArthur was to claim, implausibly, that he did not regard this message as a "rebuke" and never connected it with his March 24 statement inviting negotiations.)

The next several days, Truman's reminder notwithstanding, MacArthur continued to poke at administration policy. In an interview with Lieutenant General H. G. Martin, military correspondent for the London *Daily Telegraph*, MacArthur asserted his troops "were circumscribed by a web of artificial conditions." For the first time in his military career he "found himself in a war without a definite objective." On the 38th parallel issue, the politician had encroached upon the domain of the soldier. "The situation would be ludicrous if men's lives were not involved." MacArthur implied that the 6,000 to 7,000 monthly casualties in his command were being killed or wounded in vain. "These and still heavier losses would be accepted readily *if only they were being incurred for a definite purpose* [emphasis added]." In another interview—one given earlier, but published the weekend when MacArthur's future was debated in the administration—the general responded to a query by the *Freeman* magazine. The editor cited a news report that the ROK government was releasing draftees for lack of equipment and asked MacArthur why the United States did not supply them. MacArthur replied that the question "involves basic political decisions beyond my authority." He lied. MacArthur had recommended on January 6 that the United States not supply weapons to the "Korean Youth Corps."

Republican senators picked up MacArthur's themes. Homer Ferguson of Michigan proposed that a congressional committee go to Tokyo and ask MacArthur how the war should be conducted. James H. Duff of Pennsylvania said "someone in authority" should decide policy and "the rest ought to abide by it."

To Truman, MacArthur's performance "had the earmarks of a man who performs for the galleries."[20] His historical mind likened his dealings with MacArthur to those President Lincoln had had with General George McClellan during the Civil War. McClellan had his set ideas on how the war should be run, and if Lincoln gave him an order he did not like, he ignored it. Like Lincoln, Truman gave MacArthur "much wearisome thought," then relieved him.

The public catalyst was a letter MacArthur had written on March 20, three days before he torpedoed the peace talks. On February 12 Representative Joseph Martin, Republican House leader, said in a floor speech he thought it "sheer folly" that Chinese Nationalist troops had not been used in Korea. He sent MacArthur the text and invited comment. On April 5 Martin read MacArthur's reply in a floor speech:

I am most grateful for your note of the eighth forwarding me a copy of your address of February 12. The latter I have read with much interest and find that with the passage of years you have certainly lost none of your old time punch.

My views and recommendations with respect to the situation created by Red China's entry into war against us in Korea have been submitted to Washington in most complete detail. Generally their views are well known and generally understood, as they follow the conventional pattern of meeting force with maximum counterforce as we have never failed to do in the past. Your view with respect to the utilization of the Chinese forces on Formosa is in conflict with neither logic nor this tradition.

It seems strangely difficult for some to realize that here in Asia is where the Communist conspirators have elected to make their play for global conquest, and that we have joined the issue thus raised on the battlefield; that here we fight Europe's war with arms while the diplomats there still fight it with words; that if we lose this war to Communism in Asia the fall of Europe is inevitable, win it and Europe most probably would avoid war and yet preserve freedom. As you point out, we must win. There is no substitute for victory.

Truman first heard of the MacArthur letter when news wires carried accounts of Martin's floor speech. He read the text with fury. The second paragraph, on use of Nationalist Chinese, "was in itself enough of a challenge to existing national policy" to warrant MacArthur's firing. MacArthur had been fully informed why the administration would not use the Nationalists, and only eight months earlier he had endorsed the decision. When he changed his position later and asked they be used, he was informed that administration policy had been set. "So, by praising Mr. Martin's logic and traditional attitude," Truman felt, "he was in effect saying that my policy was without logic and violated tradition."[21]

The President called the last paragraph "the real clincher." It showed that MacArthur either did not understand or did not choose to accept America's determination to have a presence in both Asia and Europe. In his memoirs Truman sarcastically wrote, "I do not know through what channels of information the General learned that the Communists had chosen to concentrate their efforts on Asia—and more specifically on his command." Truman was astounded that MacArthur paid no heed to the effort and sacrifice that had been required to "stem the Communist tide in Iran—in Greece—at Berlin. Perhaps he did not know how strenuously the Kremlin wished to block the emergence of a united front in Western Europe." Truman did not like MacArthur's "belittling comment about our diplomatic efforts" and his grandiose statement that "there is no substitute for victory."

Truman's personal hatred of MacArthur—it can be called by no other words—spilled over into his diary that evening. After noting that "MacArthur has made himself a center of controversy, publicly and privately," he summarized the general's private life: "He has always been a controversial figure. He has had two wives—one a socialite he married at forty-two, the other a Tennessee girl he married in his middle fifties after No. 1 had divorced him." Truman was about to give MacArthur a grand dose of controversy.

The next morning—Friday, April 6—Truman called Acheson, Marshall, Bradley, and Harriman to his office and asked point-blank what should be done about MacArthur. General Bradley was "terribly upset," in Truman's words. "He and Averell Harriman said I ought to fire MacArthur forthwith." Harriman, in fact, thought Truman should have sacked MacArthur two years earlier, when in the spring of 1949 he would not come home for consultations because of a claimed press of business in Tokyo. Harriman recollected Truman's having had to send Army Secretary Kenneth Royall to Tokyo to dissuade MacArthur from supporting an economic bill in the Japanese Diet that was directly contrary to occupation policy.

As for Acheson:

> [My] own view was very clear as to what should be done from the very first minute. It was perfectly clear to me that an issue had been created which could only be resolved by the relief of General MacArthur. But it was equally clear to me that whatever the President did he would have to do with the unanimous support of all his military and civilian advisers. If he acted without [their] support . . . greater trouble was likely to occur than if he didn't act at all. But . . . it should be with a completely unified front, with no cracks in it whatever.[22]

Marshall advised caution. He wanted to think about the matter further. He warned Truman that a firing might make it difficult to get the military appropriations bill through Congress.

To Bradley, the main concern was military discipline. He saw MacArthur's actions as a "clear case of insubordination." The general deserved to be relieved of command. But he thought it prudent to consult the JCS before making a recommendation. MacArthur commanded enormous respect in the professional officer corps. But the Regular Army had even more respect for command authority, and a JCS endorsement of any decision to relieve MacArthur would dampen reaction by the general's uniformed supporters.

Acheson, ever the lawyer, summarized the discussion. He, too, thought it essential that Truman have the unanimous support of the JCS. He did not want a dismissal to appear an impetuous action by a piqued President. He told Truman, "If you relieve MacArthur, you will have the biggest fight of your administration."

Truman told the advisers to "meet and talk it over and to come back with a report." To Truman, the Martin letter was not the major issue. MacArthur's scuttling of the peace initiative was "inexcusable."

That Friday afternoon Marshall, Bradley, and Harriman met in Acheson's office. Marshall was nervous. He was known in the military as a man not enamored with MacArthur; he would not lead the move against him. He suggested calling MacArthur home for consultation and delaying any final action until then. Acheson strongly opposed the idea. "To me this seemed a road to disaster," he said. The Republican right wing's use of Senator Joseph McCarthy as a battering ram against the administration and the clumsy preliminary moves toward impeachment (exposed by Senator Wherry's misplaced memorandum) convinced Acheson that "their attachment to constitutional procedures was a veneer at best." MacArthur's histrionic skills made Acheson wary. "To get him back in Washington in the full panoply of his commands and with his future the issue of the day would not only gravely impair the President's freedom of decision but might well imperil his own future." Truman especially wanted Marshall on his side. So before Marshall left, the President suggested that he read the cable traffic between MacArthur and Washington since the war began.

In his diary that evening Truman again commented on the general: "MacArthur shoots another political bomb through Joe Martin. . . . This looks like the last straw. Rank insubordination." Truman capsulized the VFW speech furor of the previous summer and his trip to Wake Island "to see him and reach an understanding face to face." He continued: "I've come to the conclusion that our Big General in the Far East must be recalled. I don't express any opinion [at that afternoon's meeting] or make known my decision."

Over the weekend the vise tightened around MacArthur. In a meeting on Saturday Marshall told the President he had read the cable traffic and concluded that "MacArthur should have been fired two years ago." Truman called Representative Sam Rayburn of Texas, the speaker of the House, and Chief Justice Fred Vinson to the White House. Both were trusted political and personal friends from Truman's congressional years. "We talked for a long time. The Chief Justice advised caution," Truman said. "He said the authority of the President of the United States was at stake. . . . they said I would have to weigh the situation very carefully and come to my own conclusion. Rayburn was worried about the political aspect."

After they left, Truman "got out the books" on American history. He read again of Lincoln's problems with General McClellan. One story that particularly tickled him was how Lincoln dealt with McClellan when he commented on political affairs. The story goes that Lincoln was asked what he would reply to the general. "Nothing—but it made me think of the man whose horse kicked up and stuck his foot through the stirrup. He said to the horse, 'If you are going to get on, I will get off.'"

The seminal meeting was held on Sunday afternoon across the Potomac from the White House, in the Pentagon office of General Omar Bradley, Chairman of the Joint Chiefs of Staff. MacArthur in effect was tried by a jury of his professional peers.

Ironically the Joint Chiefs discussed MacArthur's future as UN commander at the very time they had decided to expand significantly his authority, subject to presidential approval.[23] The JCS spent April 4—the day before Martin revealed MacArthur's letter—discussing "as a matter of urgency" approaches to allies to determine their "willingness to support possible action against mainland China." Admiral Sherman, the navy chief, toughened the draft to state that "preparations should be made" for attacks against the mainland, rather than that such actions should be kept "under continuing review." Translated from Pentagon bureaucratic language, Sherman's change (accepted by the other chiefs) meant that air and naval forces should start mustering men and equipment to strike at specific targets.

Next, on April 5, the JCS responded to intelligence warnings of possible Soviet intervention by approving a draft order authorizing MacArthur to attack air bases in Manchuria and nearby China in the event of a major air attack on UN forces. Over the next several days the JCS obtained approval of the draft from the secretaries of state and defense and Truman. Under normal procedures the next step would be to send the draft directive to MacArthur for use in contingency planning. But the general's troubles with Truman interrupted the process. The JCS decided to withhold the order and even the knowledge of its existence from MacArthur.

In explaining the decision in a JCS memo, Bradley wrote the most damning words possible against MacArthur. The order was not sent to MacArthur, he said, because the JCS feared he might "make a premature decision in carrying it out."[24]

General Bradley had cold feet about firing MacArthur. Before the Sunday meeting he suggested that Marshall write a personal letter to MacArthur pointing out the problems his public statements were causing the President. He and Marshall went so far as to write a draft.

The Joint Chiefs gathered at two o'clock on Sunday afternoon around a conference table in Bradley's office—Collins of the army, Sherman of the navy, Vandenberg of the air force. For the first time they learned the depth of what Bradley called the "MacArthur problem." Bradley said that the President was considering relieving MacArthur and that Secretary Marshall wanted the chiefs' "strictly military views." Although Truman did not know it, the JCS welcomed the chance to deal with MacArthur. Colonel Chester Clifton, Bradley's aide, said the JCS "had become disenchanted with MacArthur a long way back—as far back as February or January in any event—and on military rather than on political grounds."[25] JCS complaints involved MacArthur's conduct of operations (splitting his forces and launching the November offensive with inadequate intelligence); the feeling he had lost confidence in himself and was forfeiting the confidence of his troops; the "petulance and ill-tempered complaints" in his cables to Washington; and evidence he was jealous of Ridgway's success in stabilizing the front. Today the talk centered on MacArthur's attacks on administration policy, not on his battlefield conduct.

The talk lasted about two hours. No formal record was kept of the meeting (this account is based on Collins's memoirs and a memorandum by Sherman), but the early consensus was that MacArthur must go. One face-saving gesture was discussed, that of permitting him to remain as supreme commander in Japan, a post the chiefs knew was dear to MacArthur. But the problems of Japan and Korea were so interwoven that the theater could not be run by two commanders. In the end the chiefs decided that MacArthur should be relieved and that Matthew Ridgway was the best choice as his successor.

At four o'clock the chiefs—a "sad and sober group," Collins described them—moved down the corridor to Marshall's office. The setting was one of the most impressive in Washington. Marshall sat behind a massive oak desk that General John Pershing had deposited at the War Department many decades ago. The windows looked out across a verdant strip of the Virginia shores of the Potomac, then to the White House, the Capitol, and the Washington Monument. The view encompassed the institutions to which a professional soldier must answer: the President, the Congress, and the military traditions of George Washington.

Marshall had suffered through the spring from influenza; he wheezed today. He sensed the verdict that was to be delivered. He could not welcome it, in one sense, for it inevitably would be construed as a slap at the profession to which he had devoted his life. Nor did any of the Joint Chiefs enjoy the business at hand. Each man was an officer who sensed the shame of the words "relieved of command." General Collins put it well: "It was not easy to be a party to the dismissal of a distinguished soldier."

Marshall asked each chief directly what should be done about MacArthur. Each prefaced his statement by saying he was speaking from a "military point of view only"; no one wanted politics to taint the proceedings. Sherman maintained that if the United States were to be successful in limiting the Korean conflict and in avoiding World War III, "we must have a commander in whom we can confide and on whom we can rely." Collins believed the President "was entitled to have a commander in the field whose views were more in consonance with the basic policies of his government and who was more responsive to the will of the President as Commander in Chief." Vandenberg did not disagree.

No formal vote was taken. The JCS did not recommend that MacArthur be relieved. They simply gave their views to Marshall for transmittal to the White House. They went against MacArthur on two grounds: the need for the President (and for themselves) to be able to rely completely on subordinate commanders, and the principle of civilian control of military power. Bradley summarized the JCS thinking a few weeks later in Senate testimony. Since MacArthur was not in "entire sympathy" with administration policies in the Far East, "it was difficult to have him do certain planning. . . ." Bradley continued:

For military success we have always held that, whenever the superior authority loses full confidence in a subordinate, whether or not such loss of confidence is justified by the facts, the subordinate must be changed. . . .

In this instance, there is little evidence that MacArthur ever failed to carry out a direct order of the Joint Chiefs, or acted in opposition to an order. However, it can be shown that at times, when MacArthur did not receive the orders he desired, or disagreed with the basic policy being followed, he would take his case to the public. This sometimes would reveal what the JCS were planning not to do, and it would cause considerable embarrassment and lack of confidence in MacArthur's attitude on further operations when they did not coordinate with his ideas. All of this tended to create doubt, confusion, and uncertainty in the minds of the public of military leadership at a time when confidence in that military leadership was very essential.

All members of the JCS have expressed from time to time their firm belief that the military must always be controlled by civil authorities. They were all concerned in this case that if MacArthur was not relieved, a large segment of our people would charge that civil authorities no longer controlled the military.

The professional military had returned the equivalent of a guilty verdict, with a sentence that was tantamount to capital punishment: General Douglas MacArthur should be stripped of his command and brought home.

The President Decides

The Oval Office is where a President of the United States does his tough work. The outsize room juts off the west rear of the White House, with ceiling-to-floor doors opening onto the Rose Garden. The President's desk is at the back of the U-shaped room. The office did not awe Truman. Early in his tenure he put a placard on his desk: "The Buck Stops Here."

"The Buck" at nine o'clock on Monday morning was MacArthur. Bradley led off by reporting that the JCS were unanimous that MacArthur should be relieved. (Bradley never stated his own view, which no one asked. In Senate hearings later that spring he said he had "indicated agreement only by not expressing disagreement.") There was no hesitation elsewhere. Marshall wanted MacArthur out. Acheson and Harriman were "very emphatic" that he be relieved. Not until each adviser had spoken did Truman reveal he had already made up his mind. Soon after reading MacArthur's March 24 statement, he had decided the general must be relieved.

The discussion then turned to the most efficacious means of telling MacArthur he had been fired. Acheson thought it was "unwise to send this through military channels because this would be a grave humiliation and embarrassment to General MacArthur, to have almost everybody in his headquarters know he was relieved before he knew. . . ."

By coincidence, Army Secretary Frank Pace was on an inspection tour of the Far East and was in Korea that very day. Truman directed that the relief notice be sent to Pace, who would hand-deliver it to MacArthur at his home in the U.S. embassy in Tokyo at ten o'clock in the morning of April 12 (ten in the evening of April 11, Washington time). Two sets of messages were involved. One would be the formal military change of command orders to MacArthur, Ridgway, and General James Van Fleet, who would succeed Ridgway as the Eighth Army commanding general. Joseph Short, the White House press secretary, would prepare the public explanatory statement to be released as soon as MacArthur was notified he was relieved.

At about three in the afternoon of Tuesday, April 10, Truman received and signed the relief orders. He gave them to Acheson for transmittal to Ambassador John Muccio in Pusan, with instructions to deliver them to Secretary Pace, who was at the front with Ridgway. Everyone involved was sworn to secrecy. For obvious political and public relations reasons, if a popular field commander must be fired, the ceremony must be proper.

Through no assignable fault, the administration's plan fell apart. The State Department used commercial cable facilities for messages to Pusan; somehow they broke down, and the first cable to Secretary Pace never arrived. Then a tipster in Tokyo told the Chicago *Tribune* that MacArthur was about to be sacked, and Washington correspondent Walter Trohan got on the story.[26] "A few probes in sensitive areas lay bare the White House intent," Trohan wrote. He told *Tribune* Pentagon correspondent Lloyd Norman to check sources there. "I undertook to beard Joseph Short," Trohan wrote. "It wasn't much of a bearding because Short, who was a nice fellow personally and completely devoted to Truman, confirmed the story by his evident panic." Truman aide George M. Elsey, Jr., conceded: "there was a degree of panic" in the White House that night, "some concern that MacArthur might get wind of . . . [his firing] and might make some grandstand gesture of his own. There were rumors flying around that he was going on a worldwide broadcast network and there was some suspicion that he was going to resign with a grandstand announcement. In effect the White House was . . . I'm sorry to say it, was *panicked* by fear that MacArthur might get the jump."*[27]

*Elsey came to the White House in 1942 as a naval intelligence officer assigned to the Map Room, the military situation center. He remained as a civilian aide to Truman, and one of his many duties, beginning in 1951, was keeping a file on MacArthur "because these

Not wishing the first news of the MacArthur firing to come through an unfriendly newspaper, the White House decided to make a public announcement at one o'clock the morning of April 11. (Ironically the *Tribune*'s tipster lost confidence in his exclusive and told the paper to drop the story. Thus the *Tribune* "scoop" was not printed until after the White House announcement.)

Joseph Short passed out the papers. First was Truman's formal announcement that "with deep regret" he had concluded that MacArthur was unable to give his "whole-hearted support" to American and UN policies. Recognizing his constitutional responsibilities and the additional responsibilities imposed by the UN, Truman was relieving MacArthur and designating Matthew Ridgway as successor. The President continued:

> Full and vigorous debate on matters of national policy is a vital element in the constitutional system of our free democracy. It is fundamental, however, that military governors must be governed by the policies and directives issued to them in the manner provided by our laws and Constitution. In time of crisis, the consideration is particularly compelling.

Truman acknowledged that MacArthur's "place in history as one of our greatest commanders is fully established." The nation owed him a debt of gratitude. "For that reason I repeat my regret at the necessity for the action I feel compelled to take in his case."

Thus was MacArthur's relief announced in the dead of night—albeit no fault of the White House—and in a hurried fashion that made the act appear a shameful deal, rather than the decision of a President who had decided to stand firm against a military titan whose prestige, if not his rank, predated Truman's by a full two decades.

Pace Receives Orders

In view of the undelivered cable and the Chicago *Tribune* leak, Army Secretary Frank Pace's role in the MacArthur firing became a comic-opera sidelight.[28] Pace had misgivings about even meeting MacArthur; although now he was MacArthur's nominal superior, "I had to remember that when he was chief of staff of the United States Army, I was at the Hill School in Pottstown, Pennsylvania [a prep school]." Unaware

situations were so tense, and so fraught with potential trouble." Elsey clipped and annotated newspaper and magazine articles and even talked with correspondents "when directed and when approved." Thus the Truman White House went into combat with MacArthur with loaded dossiers.

of the furor over MacArthur in Washington, Pace was puzzled when during his first day in Tokyo he received a cable from Defense Secretary Marshall: "This is explicit. Repeat, this is explicit. You will proceed to Korea and remain there until you hear from me. MARSHALL."

"It didn't say a day, a week, a month, a year," Pace recollected. So he said farewell to host Douglas MacArthur and flew to Korea. There Matthew Ridgway took him on a tour of the battlefield and field hospitals and on a flight over enemy lines. The second evening Pace was napping in a command post, hail drumming on the roof, when he received a phone call from General Leven C. Allen, the Eighth Army chief of staff. Allen read a cable from Marshall: "Disregard my cable number 8743. You will advise General Matthew Ridgway that he is now the supreme commander of the Pacific, vice General MacArthur relieved. You will proceed to Tokyo where you will assist General Ridgway in assuming . . . his command. MARSHALL."

Stunned, Pace replied, "You'd better read that once more, Lev. I don't want to relieve General MacArthur on one reading." Allen read the cable again.

Recognizing that he had been thrust into a sensitive situation, Pace quietly asked Ridgway to step outside the command post for a private talk. Hail was still falling. Pace took a few steps outside and looked at the grenades festooning Ridgway's chest. "Matt," he exclaimed, "take off those damned grenades. If one of these hailstones hits that grenade, there'll be no secretary of the army and no commander in Korea."

For privacy, they walked a few dozen yards to a Korean graveyard. Pace told Ridgway what he had heard from General Allen.

"I can't believe it, Mr. Secretary," Ridgway said.

"I can't either, so I'll repeat it," Pace replied. "You're now the supreme commander. Now let's go get that cable that I'm to disregard."

Pace finally received a copy of the first cable some hours later. It read, "You will proceed to Tokyo where you will advise General Douglas MacArthur that he is relieved of his command."

Privately Pace was relieved that he did not bear the onus of personally firing MacArthur. Back in Washington, he told friends that firing MacArthur would have been "no problem." He continued: "I'd commandeer the first plane and fly to Tokyo. Being there after hours, I would have gone directly to General MacArthur's headquarters. I would ring the bell, shove the order under the door, and run like hell!"

* * *

MacArthur Is Notified

MacArthur, however, was to learn of the shattering of his career in perhaps the worst possible fashion.[29] He was not totally unaware of Washington's displeasure and of the possibility that he might be in trouble. His political officer, William Sebald, noted that Tokyo was "flooded with press reports indicating an 'open break' between MacArthur and the administration." These rumors apparently led to the Chicago *Tribune*'s abortive scoop.

Yet the rumors did not penetrate MacArthur's quarters. He had worked at his Dai Ichi Building office in the morning, reading routine cables from the front. A few days earlier the first breath of an early spring had touched Tokyo, bringing out sprouts on the chrysanthemum bushes and signaling an end to winter's harshness.[30] April 11, however, began with thick, misty clouds and a drizzle of rain, a threat to the annual afternoon garden party of Prime Minister Shigeru Yoshida. Keira Huff, wife of Colonel Sid Huff, MacArthur's pilot, fretted. "Oh, dear!" she exclaimed. "Why does it always have to rain on the day of the prime minister's garden party?"

Huff paid little attention. He had received a call from a press association reporter. "Be sure to listen to the three o'clock news broadcast," the reporter said. "We think President Truman is going to say something about MacArthur's resignation."

Surprised, Huff tried to call MacArthur, who he knew was entertaining Senator Warren Magnuson of Washington and William Sterns, an executive of Northwest Airlines. MacArthur would not leave his guests to take the call, so Huff left a message asking Mrs. MacArthur to phone him as soon as possible.

Huff then turned on the radio. The first part of the news broadcast contained nothing unusual. Then at the very end the announcer said, "Stand by for an important announcement." A few moments later Huff heard a brief flash from Washington: MacArthur had been relieved of all command.

Before Huff could digest the news, the phone rang. Mrs. MacArthur was on the line. "Did you call, Sid?" she asked.

"Yes. It's important. I just heard a flash over the radio from Washington saying that the General has been relieved of all his commands."

"Wait a moment," Mrs. MacArthur said. "Repeat that, Sid. The General is here." Huff repeated the message, slowly this time, so she could have the exact words to convey to MacArthur.

There was a pause. "All right, Sid," Mrs. MacArthur said. "Thanks for calling."

A few minutes later a Signal Corps messenger brought to Huff an "important message" for MacArthur in a small brown envelope. Huff drove his car to the embassy compound, parked, and walked through perhaps a dozen reporters waiting at the gate. "What's the news?" one shouted. "Has he got the word yet?"

Huff held up the envelope. "This is probably it," he said. He went through the wide reception hall, under the bright flags signifying the general's past commands, and up the stairway to the door of MacArthur's bedroom. There Mrs. MacArthur met him.

"Here it is," he said, handing over the envelope. "Anything I can do?"

No, there was not. Jean MacArthur, her face taut, tears flowing down her cheeks, handed Douglas MacArthur the brown envelope. He opened it and skimmed the papers inside. Then he hugged her and said, "Jeannie, we're going home at last."

A Sick President?

When General Ridgway arrived in Tokyo on April 12 to assume command, MacArthur invited him over for a private talk.[31] Ridgway listened in silent astonishment to MacArthur's bizarre rationale for his firing.

MacArthur claimed to have been told by an "eminent medical man," who in turn received his information from Truman's personal physician, General Wallace Graham, that "the President was suffering from malignant hypertension."* MacArthur continued that "this affliction was characterized by bewilderment and confusion of mind," that because of it, Truman had written "both the letter to the music critic and the one about the marines." MacArthur claimed the physician had told him the President "wouldn't live six months."

Regardless of what MacArthur might have been told, the statements about Truman's health were not true. The President did suffer from high blood pressure. But no one who worked with him during his White House years ever noted any signs of mental instability. The irony is that both the President and MacArthur entertained doubts about the other's mental stability. In Truman's instance, however, he had been willing to give MacArthur a clean bill of health after General Frank Lowe's discreet observation trip to his headquarters in September 1950.

Continuing their conversation, MacArthur told Ridgway that he had already received a variety of offers to speak and write about his dispute

---

*"Malignant hypertension" is a medical term meaning a person has a blood pressure so dangerously high that he must be hospitalized; there is often concurrent damage to the kidneys and eyes. My internist of fifteen years, asked directly if a man could function as president of the United States with such a condition, answered, "emphatically not!" That Truman suffered from high blood pressure was a known fact; no evidence suggests that the severity was anything approaching the degree described by MacArthur, whose information was admittedly second-hand.

with the President—one for $150,000; another for $300,000 for fifty speeches to "raise hell"; yet another for $1 million ("which again he did not enlarge upon," Ridgway noted). MacArthur expressed "amazement" that he had been fired. Nonetheless, he was not overly displeased because he "had always had a hankering" to retire to New York.

MacArthur's statements about Truman's health disturbed Ridgway, but not in the way the general intended. When Ridgway left MacArthur's study after the hour talk, it was not the President who he felt was of confused mind. It was Douglas MacArthur.

CHAPTER NINETEEN

The General's Return

General Douglas MacArthur left the Orient at dawn on April 16 not as a disgraced soldier but as a departing hero. The morning was damp and gray, but the five-star flag on the fender of MacArthur's Chrysler limousine snapped briskly during the drive to Atsugi Airport, past crowds which journalists estimated at 200,000, standing silently to pay farewell to the man who had ruled their nation as surrogate emperor for five years. The strains of the last days marked MacArthur; his face was drawn and gray, and his battered cap with the gold lace looked to one man like a tacky relic, rather than a symbol of past greatness. Artillery pieces boomed a nineteen-gun salute as MacArthur stood at attention on the tarmac alongside General Ridgway. Then he shook hands with his successor and climbed the steps to the *Bataan*. The military band struck up "Auld Lang Syne," and the *Bataan* disappeared into the low-hanging overcast. For the first time in almost fourteen years Douglas MacArthur was not the dominant American military personage in Asia.

For MacArthur the next days were a montage of admiring crowds, laudatory speeches, and public adulation, the outpourings of a citizenry eager to pay homage to a personage of mythical stature. For the moment America seemed to overlook the reason MacArthur was home again; his heroism and leadership dated to the First World War, and he was to receive, six years late, the adulation the nation had given fellow generals of the Second World War. He arrived at Hickam Air Force Base in Hawaii after midnight; nonetheless, thousands of persons were there to cheer him, and many more lined a forty-mile parade route the next day. Then on to San Francisco, where ecstatic citizens broke through police lines at the airport—again after midnight—and jostled with one another to get close to the general. It took police half an hour to get MacArthur to his car and another two hours to crawl fourteen miles through yelling crowds to the St. Francis Hotel. People stood in the square around the hotel for hours, shouting into the night.

MacArthur's demeanor throughout was regal: the returning conqueror home to receive just tribute. He did not deign to mention President Truman or make other than oblique references to the reason he was in the United States, rather than Asia. He did allude briefly to the episode in a talk at the San Francisco Civic Center that also signaled he himself might have aspirations on the presidency:

> I have just been asked if I intended to enter politics. My reply was, "No." I have no political aspirations whatever. I do not intend to run for any political office. I hope that my name will never be used in a political way. The only politics I have is contained in a simple phrase known to all of you —"God Bless America!"

The first fits of public indignation against Truman seemed genuine. The Los Angeles City Council adjourned in "sorrowful contemplation of the political assassination" of MacArthur. People in San Gabriel, California, burned the President in effigy. OUST PRESIDENT TRUMAN bumper stickers appeared by the thousands, overnight. The legislatures of Illinois, Michigan, California, and Florida passed resolutions condemning the President and supporting MacArthur ("irresponsible and capricious action," said the Illinois solons). Truman threw out the first ball at the Washington Senators' opening game without incident, but when his departure was announced in the eighth inning, the crowd booed him. A Houston clergyman became so agitated in dictating a telegram to Western Union ("Your removal of General MacArthur is a great victory for Joseph Stalin . . .") that he was stricken in mid-sentence and fell dead. Western Union objected when a woman in Charlestown, Maryland, wanted to call Truman a "moron" in a telegram. After riffling through *Roget's Thesaurus,* they settled upon the word "witling." A Denver man started a "Punch Harry in the Nose" club. Several veterans mailed their Second World War medals to Washington. The *Congressional Record* simmered with angry telegrams that legislators inserted on behalf of constituents (many of whom apparently found no Western Union objections to strong language): "Impeach the imbecile. Impeach the Judas in the White House who sold us down the river to the left wingers and the UN. Impeach the B [sic] who calls himself President. Impeach the little ward politician stupidity from Kansas City. Impeach the red herring from the presidential Chair. . . ." On the telegrams rolled by the thousands.

The right-wing press barons—Hearst, Colonel Robert McCormick of Chicago, the Luce publications, and Scripps-Howard—raged. Hearst's New York *Journal-American* suggested that Truman had been crazed with drugs when he fired the general. "Maybe the State Department gave him some kind of mental or neural anodyne." Nick Kenny, poet-columnist for the New York *Daily News*, depicted in stilted verse the general's reactions as arrows bounced off his breastplate and knives sank into his unprotected back. "Great soldier, statesman, diplomat/ Keep high your shining sword!/ 'Tis your name that they applaud!" Harry H. Schlacht, resident poet on the *Journal-American*, outdid Kenny with a rousing verse entitled "We Thank Thee, Heavenly Father, for General MacArthur." McCormick wanted Truman "impeached for usurping the power of Congress when he ordered American troops to the Korean front without a declaration of war." He cabled Walter Trohan, his Washington correspondent and political operative, "Impeach Truman."[1] Trohan knew what the cable meant; he was to persuade friendly congressmen to start impeachment proceedings against the President, a cause the GOP leadership said it would not pursue. Trohan sidestepped the order.

Reaction abroad was somewhat different. In the British House of Commons, cheers rang out when Foreign Secretary Herbert Morrison announced the news. The London *New Chronicle* editorialized, "Mr. Truman has taken the bull by the horns and pushed him out of the China shop." In a bit of journalistic hyperbole, the *Frankfurter Allgemeine Zeitung* said, "The whole world stopped breathing for a moment over his fall." The Communist world, predictably, exuded jubilation. "Victory for the Chinese and Korean people in the fight to resist American aggression," said Peking Radio. Budapest newspapers lauded the dismissal of a "bloody-handed hangman, murderous, carnivorous fascist." But in Moscow the *Literary Gazette* warned, "Having removed the general who failed, Wall Street does not intend to renounce his risky policy."

MacArthur approached Washington amid a rising fire storm of criticism of Truman and Acheson, the latter widely identified by the antiadministration press as the lurking villain who had cut down the hero. From the first hours after the firing Truman's Republican opponents had behaved with fury. House Minority Leader Joseph Martin, at stage center because of his role in the letter incident, caught the first afternoon's headlines with a terse comment about the "possibility of impeachment." Senator Joseph McCarthy was even more blunt. The recall was a "Communist victory won with the aid of bourbon and Benedictine. . . . The son of a bitch should be impeached." Senator Robert Taft thought it would "be hard to deliberately invent a more disastrous series of policy moves than this Administration has adopted during the past thirteen months. . . . The State Department is a branch of Downing Street. . . ." Senator William Jenner of Indiana roared, "I charge that this country today is in the hands of a secret inner coterie which is directed by agents of the

Soviet Union. Our only choice is to impeach President Truman."

Martin wanted a confrontation. He telephoned MacArthur's office in Tokyo to invite him to address a joint session of Congress. MacArthur tentatively agreed. But hearing MacArthur from the prestigious podium of Congress itself was a prospect that made Democrats shudder. They hemmed and hawed at Martin's proposal most of the afternoon. Then Martin issued an ultimatum: Unless the invitation came that very day, MacArthur would proceed to New York and address the nation by radio. Were the Democrats too cowardly to listen to MacArthur in person in Washington? Martin asked sarcastically. Representative Adolph Sabath, a rousingly partisan Chicago Democrat, said he would hold hearings in the Rules Committee, which he chaired, on a resolution inviting MacArthur to address Congress "to explain . . . his . . . failure to comply with the orders of his superiors and . . . disregarding the instructions of the President, the Commander in Chief." The Democratic leadership managed to curb Sabath but did insist that the speech be to a joint *meeting* of Congress, not a joint *session,* a parliamentary distinction of interest only to purists. The Democrats wanted the event to be not an affair of state but a voluntary gathering which members could choose to attend if they saw fit.

The speech issue resolved, the next dispute was the format of the hearings at which both Republicans and Democrats wanted to elicit testimony from MacArthur. The general was willing to air his side of the controversy publicly. So, too, were the Republicans, who wished the entire nation to hear the proceedings via live radio and television. This the Democrats would not accept, for reasons involving both public relations and national security. Senator Richard Russell, the chairman of the Senate Armed Services Committee, was unconcerned with the quality of live entertainment MacArthur might provide. The hearings necessarily would deal with military secrets, and Russell was not a man to share security information with the Communists. "We are entering doors that have been barred," he said, "we are unlocking secrets that have been protected in steel safes." With their majority the Democrats prevailed, even though *Time* blamed partisan politics for the decision "to keep General MacArthur's thundering rhetoric out of earshot of the microphone and his dramatic profile off the screens of twelve million television sets." But the national security issue prevailed. The Senate's penchant for institutional procedures knocked down a GOP demand that the inquiry be done through a special committee. No, replied Russell, the job could be done adequately by the combined Senate committees on armed services, which he chaired, and on foreign relations, headed by Tom Connally of Texas.*

---

*To ensure against any criticism that the Democratic majorities on the combined committee meant MacArthur would face a biased forum, Russell retained as his chief adviser retired General Verne Mudge, who had commanded the 1st Cavalry Division

The public uproar of support for MacArthur meant few prominent Democrats dared defend the President the first few days. One Senator who did was Robert Kerr of Oklahoma. After listening to harsh Republican oratory, he threw down the gauntlet:

> The Republicans are making a lot of noise on this floor today, but they are dodging the real issue. If they . . . believe that the future security of this nation depends on following the MacArthur policy, let them put up or shut up. Let them submit a resolution, expressing it as the sense of the Senate, that we should either declare war against Red China, or do that which would amount to open warfare against her. . . . If they do not, their support of MacArthur is a mockery.

The Republicans did not fall into Kerr's trap. The White House watched MacArthur's march to the eastern seaboard and the congressional appearance with a mixture of apprehension and amusement. The night after the firing Truman delivered a national radio broadcast to explain the reasons for his action. For the first time he revealed publicly his intention, negated by MacArthur, to seek a settlement of the war through direct negotiations with the Chinese. He stressed the necessity of keeping Korea from becoming a general war. Cooperation of America's allies was essential. "The free nations have united their strength in an effort to prevent a third world war," the President said. "That war can come if the Communist leaders want it to come. But this nation and its allies will not be responsible for its coming."* Truman was confident that history, and MacArthur's own utterances, would soon redound to the administration's advantage. The morning after the firing he harked back to the disobedient General George McClellan, fired by President Lincoln during the Civil War. Truman said of MacArthur: "He's going to be regarded as a worse double-crosser than McClellan. He did just what McClellan did—got in touch with minority leaders in the Senate. He worked with the minority to undercut the Administration when there was a war on."[4] (Truman perhaps noted another possible parallel between MacArthur and McClellan: The Civil War general ran for the presidency after being fired. He lost.)

Despite his personal dislike of MacArthur, Truman ordered that he be received in Washington with correct military honors. Thus, when MacArthur arrived at Washington, on April 14, after midnight, Defense

---

under MacArthur during the Second World War.[2] Mudge did the bulk of the liaison with the Pentagon.

*Marshall, in a strong memo to Paul Nitze, opposed a presidential address, saying, "The ground for the relief is one of military authority and discipline. . . . The President does not have to give an accounting. . . . The American public understands the basis of the action. It needs no further enlightenment. . . . To labor in a public speech the issues between the President and MacArthur would bring the issues to the level of public controversy. . . ."[3]

Secretary Marshall and the Joint Chiefs greeted him, as did Truman's military aide, Major General Harry Vaughan. In all, half a million cheered MacArthur during his twenty hours in Washington, half of them in one enormous throng on the Washington Monument grounds. By Truman's order, government workers and schoolchildren received half a day off to greet MacArthur, which boosted the crowd considerably. The emotional—and theatrical—highlight was his address to the joint meeting of Congress.

Congress assembled in the House chambers at noon, and a few minutes later Mrs. MacArthur took an honored visitor's seat in the gallery; the assemblage rose and applauded in greeting. Then in filed a column of uniformed officers who had served with MacArthur—Willoughby and Whitney prominent among them—along with MacArthur's young son, blinking at the unaccustomed pomp; they took the chairs normally reserved for the President's Cabinet at a joint session. (No Truman Cabinet member honored MacArthur with his presence.) The bright television lights came on, and the chamber buzzed with anticipation. MacArthur let them wait for about ten minutes, the suspense building all the while. Finally, at 12:31 P.M., he appeared at the door with an escort of representatives and senators. The crowd in the public galleries stood as one and cheered and applauded; so, too, did most of the congressmen, although some Democratic members remained conspicuously seated. The doorkeeper's voice rang through the chamber: "Mr. Speaker, General of the Army Douglas MacArthur."

MacArthur stepped forward into a thunder of applause, trim and formal in an Eisenhower jacket barren of his many medals and ribbons, back rigid and face impassive, his every nuance captured by television cameras (still a rarity in the Capitol) and beamed to an East Coast audience of scores of thousands of viewers. He strode to the podium, stood silently until the applause stilled, then spoke in a deep and resonant voice.

In his first sentences MacArthur referred to Truman (though never by name) as someone who was to be more pitied than despised; never once did he concede that the President might have been right in their dispute. "I address you," he said, "with neither rancor nor bitterness in the fading twilight of life, with but one purpose in mind: to serve my country." Applause and cheering greeted the sentence; he was to be interrupted fifty times in the next half hour.

Then MacArthur proceeded to argue the case that the Joint Chiefs and other administration figures had heard repeatedly in his cables—and rejected—for the past six months or more. He slapped at critics who said he ignored Europe or wanted to restore a rejected past upon Asian peoples. The issues are global, he said, and so interlocked that to consider the problems of one sector oblivious to those of another is to court disaster for the while. While Asia is commonly referred to as the gateway to Europe, it is no less true that Europe is the gateway to Asia. . . . There are those who claim our strength is inadequate to protect on both fronts. . . . I can think of no greater expression of defeatism.

(MacArthur knew better; he had been told repeatedly U.S. troop strength and the JCS estimate that the United States would not be ready even to think of a two-continent war for two more years.)

To MacArthur, Asians had "found their opportunity in the war just past to throw off the shackles of colonialism and now see the dawn of new opportunity." He had great praise for Japan, for the Philippines, for the Nationalist Chinese government, which from Formosa "has had the opportunity to refute by action much of the malicious gossip which so undermined the strength of its leadership." (Here MacArthur spoke in political code words intelligible to the Republican right wing. The "malicious gossip" was the State Department's China White Paper of July 1949, compiled under the direction of Acheson, which blamed Nationalist corruption for its defeat by the Communists.)

Since the Korean War began, MacArthur continued, the U.S. strategic frontier had shifted to embrace the entire Pacific, down the island chain from the Aleutians to the Marianas.

> Any major breach of that line . . . would render vulnerable to determined attack every other major segment. . . . This is a military estimate as to which I have yet to find a military leader who will take exception. For that reason I have strongly recommended in the past . . . that under no circumstances must Formosa fall under Communist control.

Next, MacArthur got around to the Korean War. Although he was not consulted before Truman decided to intervene, "that decision, from a military standpoint, proved a sound one." The UN forces hurled back the North Koreans and had victory in their grasp when China intervened, creating a "new war and an entirely new situation . . . which called for new decisions in the diplomatic sphere." Such decisions, MacArthur said bitterly, "have not been forthcoming." He flung down his own challenge and program:

> While no man in his right mind would advocate sending our ground forces into continental China . . . I felt that military necessity in the conduct of the war made necessary (1) intensification of our economic blockade against China; (2) imposition of a naval blockade against the China coast; (3) removal of restrictions on air reconnaissance of China's coastal area and of Manchuria; and (4) removal of restrictions on the [Chinese Nationalists]

on Formosa, with logistical support to contribute to their effective operations against the Chinese mainland.

For entertaining these views, all professionally designed to support our forces committed to Korea and to bring hostilities to an end with the least possible delay and at a saving of countless American and allied lives, I have been severely criticized in lay circles, principally abroad, despite my understanding that from a military standpoint, the above views have been fully shared in the past by practically every military leader concerned with the Korean campaign, *including our own Chiefs of Staff* [emphasis added].

The concluding six words of the sentence were either a deliberate falsehood or a clumsy and inaccurate recasting of the record. The four points cited by MacArthur indeed had been "recommended" by the JCS, in their January 12 list, but only as options that might be pursued if the Chinese launched all-out air attacks. By inaccurately claiming the endorsement of the JCS, MacArthur cast Truman and Acheson as civilians who overrode the professional military. In the weeks to come the JCS were to throw MacArthur's claims back into his face.

Republicans in the audience came to their feet with cheers as MacArthur issued his indictment. He showed no sign of emotion whatsoever, standing with hands firmly gripping either side of the lectern, pausing only to take an occasional sip of water. He continued citing his woes:

> I called for reinforcements, but was informed that the reinforcements were not available. I made clear that if [the command were] not permitted to destroy the enemy-built-up bases north of the Yalu, if not permitted to utilize the friendly Chinese force of some 600,000 men in Formosa, if not permitted to blockade the China coast to prevent the Chinese Reds from getting succor from without, and if there were to be no hope of major reinforcements, the position of the command from the military standpoint forbade victory.

Replying to critics who said he wished to start a world war, MacArthur said strongly, "I know war as few other men now living know it, and nothing to me is more revolting. . . . But once war is forced upon us, there is no other alternative than to apply every available means to bring it to a swift end. War's very object is victory."

MacArthur built slowly toward his climax. He would not attempt to placate Communist China, saying that like blackmail, appeasement "lays the basis for new and successively greater demands until, as in blackmail, violence becomes the only other alternative."

Next, MacArthur was the accessible general who went into the foxholes to talk with the troops. "Why, my soldiers asked me, surrender military advantages to an enemy in the field?" (No contemporary account of MacArthur's visits to Korea mentions any pauses to chat with troops. That a foot soldier would deign to raise strategic questions with such a regal commander as MacArthur belies credulity. His statement was theatrical hokum.)

Now MacArthur was ready to say farewell. He leaned forward over the podium, and his voice dropped several registers, although he could still be clearly heard in the hushed chamber.

> When I joined the army, even before the turn of the century, it was the fulfillment of all of my boyish hopes and dreams. . . . The hopes and dreams have long since vanished, but I still remember the refrain of one of the most popular barracks ballads of that day which proclaimed most proudly that old soldiers never die; they just fade away.
> And now like the old soldier of that ballad, I now close my military career and just fade away, an old soldier who tried to do his duty as God gave him the light to see that duty. Goodbye.

Anyone familiar with the nuances of American foreign policy, and the weaknesses of the American military, could easily pick any number of factual and logical holes in MacArthur's speech. But as *oratory*—words intended to seize the emotions and the hearts of his listeners—his performance ranked as one of the more powerful political experiences of the mid-twentieth century. Many congressmen wept openly as he finished; so, too, did men and woman around the country who heard and saw the speech on radio and television. For the moment, MacArthur occupied the high ground.

Through his press spokesman Truman made a great official show of ignoring MacArthur during his day in Washington, even to the point of letting it be known that he did not watch the congressional address on television. Truman did, of course, for he was curious as to how MacArthur would be received. "Nothing but a bunch of bull shit," he exclaimed, "some of those damned fool Congressmen . . . crying like a bunch of women."[5] Truman "knew that once all the hullabaloo died down, people would see what he was." Dean Acheson felt like a father with a beautiful daughter who lived on the outskirts of an army post, with constant fears about her chastity.[6] When she finally came home and announced her pregnancy, he threw up his hands and exclaimed, "Thank God that's over."

Adulation for the General

By the indices of public acclaim, MacArthur moved through the next days with the grandeur of a Robert E. Lee or a Black Jack Pershing. For a nation tired of a can't-win war and confused about what Harry Truman was trying to accomplish halfway around the world, MacArthur's speech offered what seemed at first blush to be a splendid alternative, a call for restoration of American grandeur and might, even be it at national risk. Americans cheered MacArthur for many reasons—to give him the homage he had earned in the Second World War and never returned to claim; to support the Fourth of July patriotism that had somehow slipped away after the defeat of the Axis powers in 1945. MacArthur stood also in vivid contrast with Truman: a soldier of heroic proportion versus a man still considered an accidental President by many Americans.

So recording companies rushed out phonograph records of the MacArthur speech, and knickknack vendors offered replicas of the famed corncob pipe with outsize stem and little drinking mugs graced with the MacArthur countenance. People tore his pictures from magazines and newspapers and put them on the wall, as they had done for Franklin Roosevelt years before, in another era when America had reached out for a hero.

The most resounding display came in New York City, which "roared and shrilled itself into near-exhaustion," as *The New York Times* put it. The parade route stretched nineteen and one-half miles through Manhattan, from the Battery to midtown and back again, and an estimated 7.5 million people (twice the crowd that had greeted General Eisenhower in 1945) leaned from windows and roofs, climbed traffic standards, and jumped up and down at curbside for a glimpse of the general. In the Wall Street district the blizzard of ticker tape, wadded newspapers, and torn telephone books—the traditional salute to heroes—was so thick that television technicians complained their cameras had trouble penetrating it. MacArthur sat in the back of an open limousine and enjoyed every moment of it, pausing at City Hall for greetings from Mayor Vincent Impellitteri and at St. Patrick's Cathedral, from Francis Cardinal Spellman, most prominent Catholic prelate in America, who walked down the stairs, resplendent in red robes, to reach into MacArthur's car to shake hands.

Overhead, skywriting planes hired by the city spelled out WELCOME HOME and WELL DONE in heavenly letters two miles long. People in the sidewalk crowds brandished homemade placards and banners with such slogans as GOD SAVE US FROM ACHESON and MACARTHUR SHALL NEVER FADE OUT.

After the New York homage MacArthur retreated into Suite 37-A of the Waldorf-Astoria Hotel to prepare for the Senate hearings. (The management gave him the $133-a-day suite for $450 monthly, and here he was to live until he died in 1964. "Here's where we lighted, and here's where we stay," he told Jean.) This appearance, he knew, would be far tougher than his ceremonial appearance in Congress. He faced a hostile Democratic majority. If MacArthur indeed had a case against

Truman's conduct in Korea, he must make it in a setting where for the first time in his career he would be questioned by men unawed by his rank.

For MacArthur, the Waldorf suite became a "Little Dai Ichi," a replica of his Tokyo headquarters, where he continued to draw a full general's salary of $19,541, with a government-owned Constellation aircraft at his disposal, as well as Whitney and other staff. The well-wishers, chiefly prominent Republicans, arrived to pay tribute. MacArthur's Waldorf neighbor, former President Herbert Hoover, came away from his session muttering about "the reincarnation of St. Paul in the *persona* of a great General of the Army who had come out of the East." The nonstate visitors included New York Giants manager Leo Durocher, who brought little Arthur some autographed baseballs.

But MacArthur's main business was assembling the case he intended to make to the Senate. The circumstantial evidence is that as far back as January he realized he might one day have to defend himself publicly against Truman. That month he called an old army aide, a sergeant, out of retirement and had him scour Far East Command files for documents on his differences with the JCS. Working with eight assistants, the sergeant over the next four months accumulated twenty-one military footlockers of documents. These were flown back to the United States on the same plane that carried MacArthur; another seven packing cases, closely guarded, followed by ship.

By late April, the visitors reported, MacArthur had hit upon his strategy for the hearings. He would not make any formal statement. He would appear empty-handed and offer to answer questions. MacArthur was too shrewd to make a frontal attack on the President or on the Joint Chiefs. He would strike for the administration's weak point, Dean Acheson. MacArthur told any number of Republican senators—including some who would sit on the committee—that he would make Acheson his "major target."

Two questions remained uncertain the last days of April. Now that the Republicans were MacArthur's *de facto* sponsor, how far would they go in supporting his advocated positions? And once the tumult and shouting died away—Americans are always good at instant causes—how broad was public acceptance, or understanding, of what the general said? Denser Republicans apparently did not listen carefully to MacArthur's speech; one, Senator William Jenner, exclaimed excitedly his joy that MacArthur opposed military aid to Europe. MacArthur, of course, did no such thing. Senator Robert A. Taft, who did understand MacArthur's two-continent strategy, proclaimed, "I have long approved of General MacArthur's program." Taft, in fact, had fought to weaken the draft, to restrict the dispatch of troops to Europe, and to scrap the North

Atlantic Treaty Organization because it might incite the Russians to war. A few days after MacArthur's speech Taft also repeated one of his old themes: that "we must not overcommit this country. . . . There is a definite limit to what we can do." MacArthur, however, had said firmly, "There are those who claim our strength is inadequate to protect on both fronts. . . . I can think of no greater expression of defeatism." The discrepancy caused Taft no public embarrassment; he continued to laud the general. There were other GOP inconsistencies as well. Republicans had noisily berated Truman for dispatching troops to Korea in the first place; MacArthur's complaint was that Truman had not sent enough men. And while Senator Edward Martin of Pennsylvania decried "the hasty midnight decision which ordered our troops . . . into Korea," MacArthur said the decision, "from a military standpoint, proved a sound one."

But having adopted MacArthur, the Republicans for the moment were stuck with him. He possessed definite utility value. He could be used to harass the administration, to help the Republicans build their case that Truman was a bumbling President ill-served by the likes of an Acheson. But any Republican who made a sober analysis of what MacArthur advocated, and how sharply his proposals differed from the midwestern isolationists then in the mainstream of their party, would find ample grounds for reconsideration.

Public opinion was yet another matter. A Gallup Poll soon after MacArthur's speech found 54 percent of the public favoring his proposals to blockade the China coast, to bomb Red Chinese bases in Manchuria, and to help the Nationalists invade the mainland, while 34 percent opposed. Only 30 percent wanted total war with China, but a slim majority (46 to 38 percent) thought that Chiang Kai-shek's army could whip the Communists on the mainland if supported logistically by the United States. And by a six to one majority Americans felt the United States should defend Formosa from Communist attack. In the shorthand of polls, the first rounds clearly belonged to MacArthur.

Yet his support had soft spots.[7] Upon close reading the speech contained disturbing nuances. For instance, MacArthur had said that if the United States followed his proposals, the Soviets "will not necessarily" enter the war. Did the United States really want to risk all-out war with Russia to settle the Korean conflict? News accounts the first days told of "floods of telegrams and letters jamming the White House mail room," most of them angry denunciations of the President. Indeed, the written public response was brisk and initially opposed to the firing by a two to one margin (8,677 versus 4,322 the week ending April 13). But two weeks later the mail had almost balanced (10,448 favorable, 10,617 opposed). Through May 7 the White House received 84,097 communiqués, 37,708 supporting the President, 46,389 opposing him, or roughly 45 percent pro, 55 percent con. But since people are more inclined to write letters when angered than when pleased, the White House considered the mail response a standoff, even a slight edge.

Further, the White House and objective press observers agreed that hostile publishers stirred much of the pro-MacArthur sentiment to discredit Truman, whom they had not forgiven for winning the 1948 election despite their strong contrary advice to the electorate. From Korea, writer James Michener called press coverage of the dismissal one of the "muddiest days of American newspaper history," and he blamed it on publisher antipathy toward Truman.[8] "One radio man," Michener said, "had to interview seventeen soldiers before he got one who would allow his voice to break and ask pathetically why they were doing this to the General. What the other sixteen said would have made better—but unwanted—stories." Commanders in the field in Korea did not view the firing as a national disaster. Murray Schumach of *The New York Times* wrote from Eighth Army headquarters, "The widespread feeling among officers of field rank is that the relationship between General Headquarters in Tokyo and the Eighth Army in Korea will become more pleasant. . . ."

The White House rejoiced when such opinion leaders as the New York *Herald Tribune* (a Republican newspaper) supported Truman's right to command the support (or at least the silence) of his generals. Such was the proposition on which Truman intended to base his case. But the White House also recognized that the Senate hearings during the coming weeks would be essentially a political fight, with MacArthur using the forum to attack administration policy in all Asia, not just Korea, and the Republicans exploiting every opportunity to embarrass the President. So the administration moved to defend itself, through classic tactics that two generations later would be known as hard-ball politics.

The White House Strikes Back

The White House's first public relations strike against MacArthur involved secret transcripts of the Wake Island Conference, at which the general stated flatly the Communist Chinese would not intervene in the war. As noted earlier, the transcripts were chiefly the work of Vernice Anderson, a State Department secretary traveling with the Truman party; notes by General Bradley and others augmented her account, and copies of the compilation were sent to MacArthur's headquarters in December 1950. The existence of the notes was no secret. On November 13, 1950, columnist Stewart Alsop wrote in the New York *Herald Tribune* that MacArthur had assured the President at Wake that the danger of Chinese intervention had passed. When the obscure conservative publication the *Freeman* wired MacArthur asking him to confirm or deny the truth of this report, it received this reply: "The statement [from Alsop] quoted in your message . . . is entirely without foundation in fact. MACARTHUR, Tokyo, Japan." MacArthur's denial of a comment he definitely had made angered the administration, for it displayed a willingness to lie when it served his cause—and when he thought he could get away with it. But the White House bided its time, waiting for the apt moment to knock the props from under the general with his own words. Columnist Drew Pearson published minor excerpts from the actual notes on January 23, including MacArthur's boast that his army could "take care" of the Chinese if they crossed the Yalu.

Soon after MacArthur's firing, Anthony Leviero, White House correspondent for *The New York Times,* began putting together a definitive account of the Wake Conference. One of the people Leviero contacted was George M. Elsey, the White House aide who had been assembling material for a counterattack on MacArthur.[9] Leviero said he wanted to sort out the conflicting versions of what MacArthur and Truman had said to each other. Elsey told him nothing during their first conversation but did mention the interview the next morning to Truman at a staff meeting. He also told Truman Leviero was "exceedingly eager to consult . . . whatever written memorandum or record there was" of the Wake Conference.

"The President thought this over briefly," Elsey said, "and asked if I had a copy in my files. I said I did, and the President said, 'Okay, go ahead and tell Tony he can have it.' " Elsey passed the transcript to Leviero the same day. *The Times* published the story on April 21,* and the MacArthur camp exploded with rage. The White House, declared General Courtney Whitney, was out to "smear" MacArthur through selective leaks of classified information; he also criticized "surreptitious notetaking" and questioned the accuracy of the composite transcript. Columnist George Sokolsky saw the episode as evidence of a degradation of public morals under Truman's reign. Republicans on the joint Senate committee demanded access to all Joint Chiefs of Staff documents on MacArthur. The White House would not get away with making only part of the record available.

In moving to counter MacArthur, the White House sought to amass a broad array of citizens' groups behind the administration, using trusted officials in the bureaucracy to enlist support.[10] Kenneth W. Hechler of the White House staff, the coordinator, ticked off a long list of things-to-do and things-in-progress in a White House memo. Both the State Department and the Defense Department were preparing hostile questions for friendly senators to ask MacArthur. White House aide

---

*Leviero won a Pulitzer Prize.

Theodore Tannenbaum was attempting to stir up a congressional investigation of the China Lobby, the loose coalition of conservative businessmen, congressmen, and religious leaders vociferously supporting the general. "You will no doubt want to talk with the responsible people in Congress about how to get this thing started," Hechler advised White House lobbyist John A. Carroll.

The Democratic National Committee, through publicity man Charles Van Devander, assembled dossiers on such senators as Taft, Wherry, and McCarthy to stress their "inconsistency" in urging military force in Asia and opposing strengthening European defenses. The DNC distributed scores of thousands of copies of a Truman speech outlining administration policy.

Hechler noted "some miscellaneous work on MacArthur materials which may be useful if the debate ever reaches the 'dirty tricks' stage." For example, Hechler wrote:

> Van Devander, in cooperation with Representative Pat Sutton [a Tennessee Democrat] is having the Signal Corps dig out the photographs of the wading ashore at Leyte. These photographs, when placed together, show ... [this] was done in the face of a barrage of newsreel cameras, while on the edge of the photograph are a number of engineers and other service troops standing dry on a solidly constructed pier. I have my doubts about the usefulness of such materials, but have no objection to assembling them.

Searches were also being made in the Roosevelt Library at Hyde Park, New York, for Second World War material derogatory to MacArthur. Another White House aide, Phileo Nash, was given permission to work with "non-governmental organizations which can participate" in the effort to counter MacArthur.*

In public Truman referred to MacArthur with scorn and ridicule. In a press conference on April 26—in remarks deliberately designed to anger the haughty general—Truman reminded reporters that technically MacArthur was still under his orders. Five-star generals do not retire; they serve for life and thus remain subordinate to the President. Yes, Truman said, he did "hold the strings" over both MacArthur and General Whitney ("MacArthur's press secretary," he called him), but he did not intend to pull them. The President indicated that the more

---

*The administration public relations effort continued after the Senate hearings concluded.[11] Edward Barrett, a State Department publicist, told the White House his section "would like to collaborate with a private publisher in New York in bringing out an inexpensive paper-backed book within the very near future, containing the meat of the MacArthur hearings." Truman approved. The result was a book, *The General and the President*, by Arthur M. Schlesinger, Jr., and Richard Rovere. Correspondence in the Truman Library indicates the sole White House role was in providing presidential speech texts to the writers; there is no hint that the White House attempted to influence the content of the book. But the administration initiative did contribute to its side of the story being told by a Pulitzer Prize-winning historian and distinguished political journalist.

MacArthur and Whitney talked from their retreat in the Waldorf-Astoria Hotel, the more they hurt their own cause. Truman laughed out loud when a reporter noted Whitney's statement that MacArthur did not have the "faintest idea" why he was fired. "Everybody else knows why," Truman said, joining in the general laughter.

The Generals Prepare

At the Pentagon, however, the mood was far from jovial as the Joint Chiefs prepared for the hearings.[12] The first step was a preparation of a lengthy memorandum summarizing every message exchanged between MacArthur and the JCS from June 25, 1950, the day the war began, and April 11, the day he was fired. Colonel E. F. Cress, who directed the staff work, warned the chiefs that they should expect "personal attacks on the integrity of the JCS as a body and as individuals." Cress saw three lines of inquiry: strategy in the Pacific and elsewhere; the relief of MacArthur; and the "timing and manner of his dismissal." Cress feared that if any JCS member used prepared statements or documents in his testimony, it would trigger a spate of calls for the official records, "thus jeopardizing military security and adversely affecting current and projected operations" as well as relations with other nations. (Cress appeared especially fearful that derogatory remarks about the ROK Army would get into the record.) Thus Cress suggested that each chief "go into seclusion, as General MacArthur has done, and so prepare himself that he can testify without notes at the hearings." The JCS agreed. Members of the Senate committees would receive the JCS summation of the Washington–Tokyo cable file for background information, but the military high command would go to the hearings armed with no documentary material. Marshall urged the chiefs to "apply their energies to trying to find out how much could be given to the committee rather than what we were not going to give. . . ." But he had qualms about discussing plans and strategy for a war still in progress. "If I may say so," Marshall said, "I have felt through a good deal of this as though I were sort of acting as an intelligence agent for the Soviet Government and the Chinese Communist government, but they don't provide one for me."

CHAPTER TWENTY

"Opening Closets
of Secrets"

The morning of Thursday, May 3, MacArthur walked down the marble corridors of the Senate Office Building toward Room 318—informally, the Senate Caucus Room, the main arena for first-class Senate hearings —in matter-of-fact fashion, acknowledging the crush of reporters and photographers with a gesture that was half wave, half salute.[1] His dress was also understated: a battle jacket bearing no emblems, rather than his five stars of rank; dark slacks; khaki shirt and tie. He carried no briefcase. His aides stayed a few unobtrusive steps to the rear. MacArthur was entering combat alone and with empty hands.

Virtually every member of the United States Senate, a good proportion of their aides, and more than enough press awaited him in the caucus room. MacArthur nodded to Chairman Russell, took a seat in a straight-backed chair at the witness table, and fumbled around in an inside coat pocket until he found an old briar pipe. He placed it before him on the table—he did not light it until half an hour into the hearings, and then only after asking permission to smoke—and settled back in obvious anticipation. He was no longer the field commander chafing under restrictions that forbade him to strike out at the "damned fools in Washington," the words he had used so frequently to Willoughby and Whitney. He now sat in the witness chair at the express invitation of the United States Senate, and he intended to make the most of the forum.

That the public and press were excluded from the hearing room irritated MacArthur, for he wanted the widest possible audience—to document that he had not been a disloyal soldier, the slur of the detested Harry Truman and the liberal press, and to force the administration, through the sheer power of his testimony, to acknowledge that he was right and change its policy in Korea. MacArthur *believed* he was in the right on both points. Not a phrase in his voluminous public statements and private papers shows the slightest hint of a doubt of his own certitude.

Although he was not to be heard publicly, a compromise between the Democrats and Republicans ensured that his words would be released promptly and with minimum censorship. Under the agreement the stenotype record would be rushed to an anteroom every five minutes or so and be transcribed onto a mimeograph stencil. The testimony would be reviewed by Vice Admiral Arthur C. Davis of the Pentagon and Adrian Fisher of the State Department. If any sentences violated security, Davis sliced them out with a razor blade. Then the stencil was run through a mimeograph machine, with reporters grabbing sheets as they emerged. Chairman Russell told MacArthur that if he felt that any of the deleted material was "essential to the presentation of your views," it would be restored, and corrected pages released.*

Richard Russell, in his opening statement, was all things: the senator facing "momentous questions . . . vital to the security of our country and the maintenance of our institutions of free government"; the respecter of MacArthur's past achievements as "one of the great captains of history"; the nonpartisan who wanted "the whole truth, without the color of prejudice or partisanship, and with no thought as to personalities."

The gentlemanly aura lasted only a few moments. Senator Wayne Morse interrupted MacArthur as he commenced his testimony. "Mr. Chairman," Morse asked, "are you going to swear the witness?"

MacArthur looked at Morse in unpleasant fashion, as if to say, "Is not my uniform affirmation enough of my honor?" Russell explained to the general that the committee had decided to put all witnesses under oath because of the uncertainty of the course of hearings. So MacArthur swore to tell the truth, the whole truth, and nothing but the truth, so help him God.

The general began with the disarming statement that he did not appear "as a voluntary witness at all, but in response to the request of the committee." He had no prepared statement because "my comments were made fully when I was so signally honored by the Congress in inviting me to appear before them." This statement took about a minute.

MacArthur's virtuosity; his conviction; his smattering of knowledge on such diverse subjects as the Magna Carta, nineteenth-century corn laws in Great Britain, and the daily calories consumed by Japanese

---

*The reporters paid 12 1/2 cents per page.[2] The investment eventually became considerable, for 8,000 pages went through Davis's hands. For a while there was an active resale market at 3 cents a page.

farmers; his ability to speak in concise and grammatical sentences for fifteen, twenty, thirty minutes at a time dazzled many of the senators —for the first day. When given unimpeded rein, MacArthur could use a single question as the mere starting point for a lecture on military strategy, Oriental psychology, and the futilities of limited war. His stamina, for a man of seventy-one years, was awesome. No, he did not care to break for lunch; he would be content to munch a sandwich at the witness table and continue testifying.

The first hours of his testimony MacArthur disposed of the senators' easy questions with the aplomb of a .400 hitter in batting practice. He dismissed any thought of a Soviet capability to seize Japan by air and sea assault. The Soviets were deluded by their own propaganda statements that the United States planned to attack them. Although Soviet air might be strong initially, weak logistics would prevent a sustained air war. Then MacArthur began to gripe.

He had constantly asked for more troops than had been supplied. Naval and air forces operated at a fraction of their efficiency because of policy strictures. The "great strategic concept" of stopping supplies from reaching the front, of hitting enemy troops in their mustering areas, the concepts developed "over the years and centuries . . . are not permitted over there." Turn loose the air force, MacArthur said, and "I do not believe it would take a very great additional component of ground troops to wind this thing up." Otherwise, "you would not be able to supply enough ground troops in Korea to be able to safely clear North Korea."

Russell then led MacArthur into a discussion of specific recommendations he had made to the Joint Chiefs and their response. After the Chinese entered the war, MacArthur recommended that "the wraps be taken off the forces in Formosa." There were other communications with the JCS about the blockade and bombing of Communist China. MacArthur next talked about the January 12 options list drafted by the Joint Chiefs. This list was crucial to MacArthur's case. He had constantly maintained that he and the JCS were in accord on broader military action; the January 12 list was the trump card he had displayed in his congressional speech as evidence that his end-the-war strategy was not the harebrained scheme of a single general, but the considered judgment of the military hierarchy.

MacArthur was wrong—dreadfully wrong, documentably wrong. Yet he stated his positions with such unflinching certitude, even in the face of contrary written evidence, that one must speculate as to motive. The simple answer is that MacArthur truly misunderstood the nature of the JCS options list, that he mistook worst-possible-scenario possibilities for definite decisions. The devious answer, one not entirely out of step with MacArthur's behavior the first months of 1951, was that the general was confident he could sweep the JCS along with him, that the Pentagon generals shared his disgust with Truman and would support him publicly.

"The position of the Joint Chiefs of Staff and my own so far as I know were practically identical," MacArthur said.

On January 12 the Joint Chiefs of Staff presented a study to the Secretary of Defense embodying these conditions:

That we were to continue and intensify now an economic blockade of trade with China;

That we were to prepare now to impose a naval blockade of China and place it into effect as soon as our position in Korea is stabilized or when we have evacuated Korea, and depending upon circumstances then obtaining;

Remove now the restrictions on air reconnaissance of China coastal areas and of Manchuria;

Remove now the restrictions on operations of the Chinese Nationalist forces and give such logistical support to those forces as will contribute to effective operations against the Chinese.

According to MacArthur:

Those views which were put forth on January by the JCS were unquestionably the result largely of the conferences which were going on constantly between my headquarters and Washington. I was in full agreement with them and am now.

As far as I know, the JCS have never changed these recommendations. If they have, I have never been informed of it.

MacArthur interjected here a statement that his relations with the JCS "have been admirable. All members are personal friends of mine. I hold them individually and collectively in the greatest esteem. If there has been any friction between us, I am not aware of it."

Either the general was unbelievably obtuse—the military grapevine is a two-way circuit for messages, and the JCS had distrusted him in earnest beginning in January—or through flattery and a peace offering he was inviting the JCS to join the winning side of a campaign to change administration policy. He would not blame the chiefs for the nonexecution of the supposed "recommendations." Instead, he pointed a furtive finger at his old adversary General George Marshall. The JCS, he said, had sent the "recommendations" to the secretary of defense and supplied his headquarters with an information copy. "A decision putting this into effect never arrived," MacArthur continued. He could only "assume" that a veto was exercised either by Secretary Marshall or by President Truman.

In actuality, of course, no "decision" was ever made because the options presumed an all-out Chinese attempt to drive the UN Command from Korea, with both air and ground attacks. No such offensive ever materialized. General Matthew Ridgway stabilized the front, rendering moot the options list.

Nonetheless, MacArthur's testimony provided headlines for the first day of the hearings. Secretary Marshall had "vetoed" JCS recommendations for stronger action against the Chinese. The testimony—and the headlines—were false.

MacArthur did not encourage follow-up questions, nor did Russell have the background (or the inclination) to ask them. A few moments later MacArthur interrupted a harmless inquiry about the U.S.-UN Command relationship to suggest to Russell, "If you can get three or four days off, go over to Korea. You will learn more in forty-eight hours in that atmosphere than you will learn in forty-eight weeks at this distance. They would give you the heartiest of welcome, and you would have an indelible impression. You have been *playing with soldiers* long enough to be something of a soldier yourself [emphasis added]."

Russell did not rise to the bait. "I do not want to go to Korea right now, General, because I am trying to be objective in this matter, and I know that any man who gets over there with troops and under fire would immediately to [*sic*] go shouting for airplanes, more troops, blockade the coast, bomb the Chinese. Because when a man is under fire in the Pacific area, that is the most important thing in the world."

On another ticklish subject, his flat statement at the Wake Conference that the Chinese would not enter the war, MacArthur sought to shift the error onto other persons. Yes, he did have "knowledge" that the Chinese had massed along the Yalu. But "my own reconnaissance, you understand, was limited entirely to Korea." Besides, the Chinese themselves "were putting out, almost daily, statements that they were not intervening, that these were volunteers only." Sources other than Peking that misled MacArthur, by his account, included Secretary Acheson, who had said in September there was "little chance, and no logic," in Chinese intervention, and the CIA, which in November saw "little chance of any major intervention." Here MacArthur was correct.

MacArthur had an ample store of blame to spread around on the subject. "Now, you understand," he lectured the senators, "the intelligence that a nation is going to launch a war is not . . . intelligence that is available to a commander, limited to a small area of combat. That intelligence should have been given to me."

MacArthur approached the next subject, the ill-conceived division of the Eighth Army and X Corps, in much the same vein. No, he told Russell, the disposition was not based on the assumption the Chinese would not intervene. He disposed his forces "upon the basis of the enemy that existed, and the orders that I had to defeat them." He had the North Korean Army beaten and would have finished it in short order had not the Chinese entered the war. "As a matter of fact," he said, "the disposition of those troops, in my opinion, could not have been improved upon, had I known the Chinese were going to attack."

To MacArthur, restrictions on American air power allowed the Chinese success. "Thousands and hundreds of thousands of troops were permitted to concentrate on the Yalu," he said, "only two nights' march down to the front lines." The great mass of them "moved down after we had started our reconnaissance in force, north." (The "reconnaissance in force," of course, was MacArthur's home-by-Christmas campaign that ended so disastrously.)

This statement puzzled Russell, who knew a bit about international law. "It does not seem to me that we would have bombed them *before* they came in," he said. "That is the thing I do not understand about it."

MacArthur did not understand. "What is that, Senator?"

"You said if you had been permitted to bomb them before they crossed the Yalu; but the Chinese army—"

"If I had been permitted to bomb them before they crossed the Yalu, Senator, they would never have crossed," MacArthur replied. Bombing would have severed the Chinese's logistical base and prevented them from advancing in force against the Eighth Army.

Russell did not like what he heard. "I see," he said. "Of course I can see the handicap you were under in not bombing them before they crossed; but it would have been a rather dangerous thing to bomb them *before* they crossed."

The senator offered MacArthur an opportunity to back away from his advocacy of preemptive bombing. "Of course, you would not have advised that they be bombed until they had disclosed their hand, that they were coming into the war and thereby precipitate a contest between Red China and ourselves, would you, General?"

Indeed, he would. The "extraordinary groupment" of troops along the Yalu originally had been massed opposite Formosa. "When they were withdrawn [and sent north] . . . I would have warned China that, if she intervened, we would have regarded it as war and we would have bombed her and taken every possible step to prevent it. That is what I would have done, and it seems to me that this is what common sense would have dictated should have been done."

Again MacArthur was glaringly inconsistent. In October, in response to a direct question from President Truman, he said the Chinese would not intervene. MacArthur said nothing at Wake about obtaining permission to bomb any "extraordinary groupment" of Chinese. Now, six months later, he offered hindsight solutions to a problem he had not even recognized when it appeared and implied that some unknown force in Washington had denied him prerogatives he had not requested.

MacArthur next went into a lengthy defense of his home-by-Christmas offensive, which he again sought to explain as a probe of Chinese strength.

When we moved forward we struck him in tremendous force—or he struck us, and we withdrew. The concept that our forces withdrew in disorder or were badly defeated is one of the most violent prevarications of truth that ever was made. Those forces withdrew in magnificent order and shape. *It was a planned withdrawal from the beginning. . . .*

The whole reversal of the movement was a strategic one. . . . If I had known the Chinese troops were there I wouldn't have done any differently.

In another statement that caught the afternoon headlines, MacArthur avowed that Chiang Kai-shek's Nationalist troops were "excellent . . . exactly the same as these Red troops I am fighting." The first days of the war MacArthur would have left the Nationalists to defend Formosa. But later they could have been used to "great advantage" in Korea. "It would have been a 100-percent different picture if they had not been held in leash."*

Save for his unstated but implied disagreement with MacArthur on bombing China before it sent troops into Korea, Senator Russell treated the general gently. The courtly Georgian was not a fire-and-brimstone legislator. His questioning, in essence, elicited from MacArthur the broad and unqualified statements that are a cross-examiner's delight. To Russell, the more MacArthur orated, the better; the hostile questioners need only bide their time.

The senior Republican present, Styles Bridges of New Hampshire, certainly caused MacArthur no problems. MacArthur did not question the right of the President to dismiss him. "The authority of the President to assign officers or to reassign them is complete and absolute. He does not have to give any reasons or anything else. That is inherent in our system." Therefore Bridges assured himself that MacArthur had never disobeyed any military orders. "No more subordinate soldier has ever worn the American uniform," the general said of himself. Bridges helped MacArthur impeach the accuracy of the Wake Conference notes. "There would have to have been a lot of eavesdropping to get any report by anyone who wasn't in that room," the general said.

Russell had heard enough. Come, now, General, did you not receive and read the Wake transcript? MacArthur stuttered a bit here. "I didn't —if I remember correctly—I filed the copies; I didn't even check them."

"I beg pardon?" Russell inquired.

MacArthur repeated: "I did not read the copies—the copy that was sent me. I merely put it in the file. I have no idea of whether it was authentic . . . or not. By that time, Senator, that incident was about as

*Thus did MacArthur put a phrase into the American political language. For the next three presidential elections the populace heard talk of "unleashing" Chiang Kai-shek.

dead as the dodo bird. They had no bearing on what was taking place in Korea then."

Russell pressed on. He had personally sent MacArthur a copy of the notes once they reached the committee. Could he not state whether they were accurate?

MacArthur sidestepped the question. "I got the copy just as I was stepping into the plane, so have not had a chance to read it," he said. "I had no stenographic notes myself. . . ." But he did concede that "in general" the notes were accurate.

Under questioning by Senator Alexander Wiley, a Wisconsin Republican, MacArthur moved into more substantive criticisms of U.S. policy. He was a loyal soldier

> operating in what I called a vacuum. I could hardly have been said to be in opposition to policies which I was not aware of even [sic]. I don't know what the policy is now. You have various potentials:
>
> First is that you can go on and complete this war in the normal way and bring about just and honorable peace at the soonest time with the least possible loss of life by utilizing all of your potential.
>
> The second is that you bring this thing to an end . . . by yielding to the enemy's terms. . . .
>
> The third is that you go on indecisively, fighting with no mission for the troops except to resist and fight in this accordion fashion—up and down—which means that your accumulative losses are going to be staggering. It isn't just dust that is settling in Korea, Senator; it is American blood.

To General Marshall, MacArthur's "American blood" statement was the most heinous thing the general could have said. "A soldier can be very easily made to feel sorry for himself, particularly when he is in most disagreeable, unattractive, and dangerous localities, and particularly when he has been called upon to make a tremendous effort over a long period of time. . . ." Marshall felt that MacArthur's statement cut into the morale of Matthew Ridgway's army.

But none of MacArthur's inquisitors showed any concern for the individual soldier fighting the war. To Senator Wiley, a more pertinent —and exculpatory—question was whether MacArthur had helped formulate China policy in the late 1940's. No, he replied; except for one invitation to appear before a congressional committee in 1946 (which he could not accept because of duties in Japan), no "Washington authorities" ever asked his views. Wiley clearly thought this omission a grave error:

> Do you know of any man in America that has had the vast experience that you have had in the Orient, getting acquainted with various nations in the Orient? Do you know of any other man that has lived there so long,

or known the various factors and various backgrounds of the people, and their philosophy, as yourself?

MacArthur was self-effacing. "That is a very flattering estimate you make, Senator. I think that I have probably lived in the Far East as long as anybody that I know of, in an official position in the United States. Whether I have profited by it, by the wisdom that you imply, is something else again."

What advice would he have offered about postwar China? He would have given "such assistance to the conservative government of China as to have checked the growing tide of communism." A compromise between the Communists and Chiang Kai-shek had "just about as much chance . . . as that oil and water will mix."

During a short noontime break (sandwiches were brought to the hearing room) MacArthur casually mentioned his hope the afternoon session would be short, for he had an engagement elsewhere that evening. That the general intended to spend only a single day with the committee surprised members.

According to one staff member, "The Senators thought he was behaving damnably highhandedly. You don't cover an entire war in a one-day session."[3]

When the committee reconvened, Senator Morse objected to MacArthur's leaving after a single day of testimony. No senators had had time to study the Pentagon's paraphrased cables; Morse's own cross-examination would take no less than three hours. "Unless we go into this thoroughly," Morse said, "it is not going to be fair to the General, nor to the American people or any other party concerned."

Chairman Russell agreed, although with apologies to MacArthur. "As much as we dislike to inconvenience you in any way, I know that you will give this committee time to really develop this matter." Southern iron was audible under the soft words, and MacArthur did not argue.

For the first part of the afternoon MacArthur had an easy time, with Republican questions giving him repeated chances to flail the administration. By trying to contain the Korean conflict without general war, the administration was introducing "a new concept into military operations—the concept of appeasement, the concept that when you use force, you can limit that force. . . . To me, that would mean that you would have a continued and indefinite extension of bloodshed, which would have . . . a limitless end." If UN allies would not support the United States in Korea, he would continue the war "alone, if necessary. If the other nations of the world haven't got enough sense to see where appeasement leads after the appeasement which led to the Second World War in Europe, if they can't see exactly the road that they are following in Asia . . . then we had better protect ourselves and go it alone."

MacArthur then returned to the theme that the war squandered lives. Casualties already approached 65,000 men, and the conflict had lasted "almost as long as General Eisenhower's decisive campaign which brought the European War to an end." If the administration continued its "indecisive" course, "you are going to have thousands and thousands and thousands of American lives that will fall. . . . Then the great question is—Where does the responsibility of that blood rest?

"This I am quite sure—It is not going to rest on *my* shoulders."

An armed conflict, MacArthur continued, must be ended in the quickest possible way through military victory. ". . . if you do not do that, if you hit soft, if you practice appeasement in the use of force, you are doomed to disaster."

If the administration pursued the January 12 five points, Senator Leverett Saltonstall asked, would the war spread to Manchuria and China? MacArthur conceded it might. "I don't think that if you apply the measures that I advocate . . . that you will necessarily confine the area of the conflict to Korea, but I believe it will give you an opportunity to hit the enemy where he is assembling to hit you." MacArthur said repeatedly, however, he did not advocate using American ground troops in China.

The questioning toughened as the afternoon wore on and junior Democratic senators had their turn with the general (each member had ten minutes the first round, the order based on seniority). By this time Pentagon staff officers were feeding questions to friendly members, pointing to areas where MacArthur had misstated the record or was otherwise vulnerable. Senator Lyndon B. Johnson, a freshman Texan, for instance, through persistent questioning pinned down MacArthur on his assertion that the JCS supported the January 12 options. Johnson obviously knew MacArthur was wrong, that the JCS had listed the options for use in the event America was chased from Korea. Shrewdly Johnson let MacArthur ramble on, knowing this particular trap, now set, could be sprung at the Democrats' will.*

Senator Morse (who said he prepared "as a lawyer . . . looking for theories") pinned the general into a firm position on another issue: whether his March 24 statement demanding that the Chinese surrender or be destroyed undercut the Truman message of a few days earlier about the new administration peace initiative. Truman's move "had nothing to do with my statement whatsoever," MacArthur insisted. The President was "constantly" trying peace feelers, he continued. MacArthur "would be surprised" if the JCS or anyone else testified that his

---

*Johnson also made MacArthur squirm by asking if his proposals would require a rise in the then ceiling of 3,462,000 men in the armed forces and universal military training. MacArthur pleaded ignorance on both subjects. "I have never given [universal military training] the slightest thought," he said. MacArthur, in fact, had given both subjects sufficient thought to know his Republican friends opposed them.

notice to the Chinese leadership had anything to do with his firing.

The questions by Johnson and Morse, although needling, stopped far short of a frontal attack on MacArthur. But Senator Brien McMahon of Connecticut did not even bother with the ritualistic bow in honor to MacArthur's military reputation taken by the earlier interrogators. McMahon at the time chaired the Joint Atomic Energy Committee, and he knew as much as anyone in Washington the ghastly aspects of nuclear war and of America's then inability to fight simultaneously in Asia and Europe. The cloakroom mutterings that "nuking the Chinks" would end the Korean War "sent McMahon into nightmares," according to Pat M. Holt, a young Foreign Relations Committee staff aide. McMahon, with his insider's knowledge of nuclear capabilities, recognized that the true adversary was the Soviet Union. The Chinese had no nuclear weapons; to McMahon, the Korean War was a "sideshow, a diversion from the main event." And he felt that MacArthur's proposals moved America toward the main event.

McMahon had done his homework; he had listened to MacArthur; he benefited from the pitfalls dug by Lyndon Johnson and other senators. He began by saying he did not apologize for the time he intended to take "because we are here discussing the survival of our Nation, which means the future of civilization itself." He turned to MacArthur. "General, we are faced, are we not, with global problems in the ambitions of Communist Russia?"

"Unquestionably," MacArthur said.

"You have given that problem a great deal of thought, I assume?" McMahon continued. MacArthur apparently sensed he was being led down a path of indefinite course, for he did not answer immediately. "Don't you hear me, General?" McMahon coached.

MACARTHUR. Yes. Yes, I have, sir.

McMAHON. And, therefore—

MACARTHUR. With particular attention, of course, to my own theater.

McMAHON. Pardon me?

MACARTHUR. With particular attention, of course, to my own theater. My responsibilities are in my own theater.

McMAHON. That is correct. As you have said on three or four occasions today, you [were] a theater commander. I believe you said to Senator Johnson that as a theater commander you had made no determination in your own mind on either universal military service or . . . the amount of troops . . . that we should have for global defense.

MACARTHUR. That is correct. That problem did not fall within my responsibilities or authorities.

McMAHON. I take it, therefore, General, that you have not clearly formulated in your own mind . . . how we are going to put on a global defense if Russia decides to make global war upon us.

MACARTHUR. I have my own views, Senator, but they are not authoritative views, and I would not care to discuss them. Because I understand I am here to discuss my own theater. There are other authorities that have all those responsibilities and authority. They are not mine, and I therefore would not superficially inject [*sic*] myself into those discussions.

McMahon had led MacArthur into an admission that a theater commander did not have the broad knowledge (much less the authority) to coordinate global military strategy. He was, in effect, a spear carrier with responsibility for only a part of the world; like it or not, people in Washington had a broader mandate than did Douglas MacArthur. McMahon now hit the general head-on.

McMAHON. I take it, General, that you believe that what we do in following your recommendations will not necessarily bring the Soviets into the war. Is that correct?*

MACARTHUR. That is my belief.

McMAHON. Suppose, General, you are wrong about that. You could be wrong about it, couldn't you?

MACARTHUR. Most assuredly.

McMAHON. You did not believe at one time that . . . Red China would come into the conflict in Korea.

MACARTHUR. I doubted it.

McMAHON. They did. You now doubt that the Soviets—

Here MacArthur felt a challenge to his infallibility. He interrupted McMahon. "In that," he said, "I was . . . supported by practically everybody. The American government through its Central Intelligence Agency, who [*sic*] were the best-informed authorities, presented that fact."

McMAHON. In other words, everybody that had to do with it turned out to be wrong.

MACARTHUR. Practically, although, Senator, I think everybody realized that that risk was involved. When we first entered Korea that was inherent to it and it was a calculated risk that was taken.

McMAHON. And now, of course, we can't all agree that there is a possibility that the Soviets will come in if we adopt the recommendations that you recommend that we carry out.

MACARTHUR. There is that possibility, but there is the certainty . . . that if you don't carry out those recommendations, you are going to lose Americans by the thousands every month. . . .

I believe that what you argue are possibilities. . . . Everyone will admit that, but what I am arguing about is a certainty.

There is no question about the war being in Korea. There is a great question whether the war would extend some place else. You have got a war on your hands, and you just can't say, "Let the war go on indefinitely

*MacArthur had so testified earlier.

while I prepare for some other war," unless you pay for it by the thousands and thousands and thousands of American boys.

Now that is the responsibility of those who make this decision, and it is a responsibility, as far as I am concerned, I repeat I wouldn't want on my shoulders.

Your policy, as you enunciated it here, Senator, means—

MCMAHON. I haven't enunciated it yet. I am simply asking for information as to your views. You see, General, what I want to find out from you is this—that if you happen to be wrong this time and we go into all-out war, I want to find out how you propose . . . to defend the American nation against this war.

MACARTHUR. That doesn't happen to be my responsibility, Senator. My responsibilities were in the Pacific, and the Joint Chiefs of Staff and the various agencies of this government are working day and night for an over-all solution to the global problem.

Now I am familiar with their studies. I haven't gone into it. I have been desperately occupied over on the other side of the world. . . .

McMahon did not relent. MacArthur had no more information on American nuclear capability "than the average officer would have." MacArthur had asked about "the potentialities and possibilities of the use of the atomic bomb in my own theater." But he said he had never recommended its use. MacArthur did not mention the "band of radioactive waste" he had advocated planting along the Yalu in January. Although the general was not privy to intelligence about Soviet nuclear capability, he did not consider enemy nuclear weapons a threat in Korea. "I don't believe for a minute . . . that the enemy has the potential or the inclination to use his limited atomic weapons in . . . Korea or China."

McMahon next had MacArthur admit that he knew of the civil defense program "only in a general way."

MCMAHON. Have you thought about the possibility of the Russians launching a surreptitious attack on the United States and its vital production centers, through atomic sabotage?

MACARTHUR. In a general way only. Once again, that isn't my theater of responsibility, Senator.

MCMAHON. I understand that, General. I am just trying to introduce a few of the considerations that the JCS and their Commander in Chief . . . must have in mind in determining what kind of action should be taken in any specific theater.

McMahon bore on. He reminded MacArthur of an administration statement a few days earlier (by Mobilization Director Stuart Symington) that the United States would not be strong enough to repel a Soviet attack until 1953. MacArthur interrupted. "And in two years," he asked, "what will be your casualty rate of American boys in Korea?"

McMahon replied, "And, General, I ask you what our casualty rate will be in Washington, D.C., if they put on . . . an atomic attack . . . to say nothing of the American boys who are going to die in the air and sea in this logistical support of the troops into China." McMahon wanted to "stop, look and listen and see where we are before we plunge into a course that may take us over the precipice before we are ready."

"The only thing I am trying to do, Senator," MacArthur said, "is to settle the thing in Korea. . . . I believe it can be brought to a decisive end without the calamity of a third world war." The war would continue far longer, with greater risks, "if we practice appeasement. . . . That is all I am saying. I am saying it with the acute consciousness of the dreadful slaughter that is going on in Korea today. . . ." MacArthur totaled up the casualties thus far: 65,000 Americans and more than 140,000 ROKs, plus uncountable civilian deaths. The North Koreans and Chinese had an estimated 750,000 casualties, plus 140,000 more in "our prison bull pens," meaning more than a million people killed, wounded or captured in fewer than eleven months. MacArthur said:

> I have never seen such devastation. I have seen, I guess, as much blood and disaster as any living man, and it just curdled my stomach, the last time I was there. After I looked at that wreckage and those thousands of women and children and everything, I vomited.
> Now, are you going to let that go on, by any sophistry of reasoning, or possibilities? . . . What are you going to do? Once more I repeat the question. What is the policy in Korea?
> If you go on indefinitely, you are perpetuating a slaughter such as I have never heard of in the history of mankind. . . .
> Your entire drift has been not to do anything, just keep on fighting, losing and bleeding there; and I think we should make some extraordinary effort to bring it to an end.

MacArthur continued to insist that the American military had the capacity to defend in Europe and Asia simultaneously. "If you say that we haven't, you admit defeat. If the enemy has that capacity and is divided on all these fronts, we should be able to meet it." Again he put himself into a trap, and McMahon closed it skillfully. Did MacArthur think "that we are ready to withstand the Russian attack in Western Europe today"? MacArthur replied:

> Senator, I have asked you several times not to involve me in anything except my own area. My concepts on global defense are not what I am here to testify on. I don't pretend to be the authority now on those things.
> When I was the Chief of Staff twenty years ago, that was my problem, and I would have answered it. The Chiefs of Staff or others here are the ones to answer that query, not me.

Through these statements MacArthur unwittingly admitted what the President, Acheson, and the JCS had maintained all along: that he was a tiresome meddler in affairs on which he was ignorant and that he was blind to needs other than those of his own Far East Command.

McMahon next chipped at MacArthur as a China expert. First, he elicited MacArthur's comment he considered himself "pretty well informed" both two or three years earlier and at present. Then McMahon read a letter the general had written to the House Foreign Affairs Committee on March 3, 1948, responding to a request for his views on Asian affairs. MacArthur replied that China, as a military theater assigned to the U.S. Navy, was "controlled outside the scope of my existing authority." He had no representatives there, and "apart from general background knowledge, such detailed information as has been made available to me has been derived largely by indirection." MacArthur was not familiar with government studies, nor had he been able to visit China for "many years" (not since 1937, according to his later testimony). With this background, he wrote, "you will readily perceive that I am not in a position to render authoritative advice with reference to the myriad of details on which a definitive policy for this particular area must necessarily rest."

All MacArthur could do was nod and acknowledge he had written the letter. Further exchanges with McMahon as the first day's testimony closed did not help his cause. Did he believe in the concept of collective security? McMahon asked.

"What do you mean by 'collective security'?" MacArthur asked.

McMahon tried again. "Do you believe in the concept of collective security upon which our foreign policy is based?"

"What do you mean by 'collective security'?" MacArthur repeated.

"I mean the attempt to weld together a military alliance to keep the peace such as we have attempted to do in the North Atlantic Pact," McMahon said.

"I have only a superficial knowledge of the North Atlantic Pact, Senator," MacArthur replied. (The pact was one of the major military-political events of the late 1940's and had been discussed *ad infinitum* in both the popular and the professional press.) "I am not prepared to discuss it in any way, shape or manner."

"Neither its provisions nor its implementation?" McMahon asked.

"I have only the ordinary knowledge that any officer would have on it," MacArthur responded. "You have experts on that." He noted the Senate had heard recently from General Eisenhower and others.

Through his own testimony MacArthur labeled himself a commander with parochial interests and knowledge. No longer could he posture as the master world strategist whose view from the Dai Ichi sanctuary was superior to that of diplomats and other professional militarists.

When the first day's session ended, at 6:10 P.M., the general pushed past waiting newsmen without comment and flew back to New York.

One day's exposure to probing senators unimpressed by the MacArthur legend did not whet the general's appetite for continued interrogation. He returned the next morning, as agreed, but aide Courtney Whitney approached Chairman Russell before the session began to request a favor. In the interest of MacArthur's finishing his testimony that day, rather than have to return, could not the luncheon recess be waived? Coffee and sandwiches could be brought into the hearing room, as had been done the previous day, but Whitney suggested that the questioning proceed over lunch. Russell agreed not to recess; however, he told Whitney the questioning would continue for as many days as the senators felt necessary.

On the second day under questioning by Senator Estes Kefauver of Tennessee, MacArthur modified his absolute opposition to sending American ground troops into China. He saw no objection to U.S. advisers, say, 500 of them, accompanying Chiang Kai-shek's army if he moved against the mainland. He did not see the use of a "few hundred technicians . . . [as] a matter of any serious import."

MacArthur did not accept the assumption, by the British, the Indians, and others, that U.S. support of Chiang Kai-shek would lessen U.S. prestige in Asia. "To the average Asiatic, Chiang stands out as the great symbol against communism. . . . Those that are inclined towards Communism oppose him, completely and absolutely. . . ." Supporting Chiang did not imply approval "of everything he says and does. But it does mean that he assists us in our resistance to this world menace; and that any choice between him and communism would naturally resolve in his favor."

But Senator Henry Cabot Lodge wondered at the consequences if Chiang were to land on the mainland and be wiped out. Would not Formosa then fall? MacArthur called the question hypothetical and thus unanswerable. But not under "any circumstances whatever" would he permit Formosa to fall to the Communists.

MacArthur by late afternoon had convinced Chairman Russell of the validity of his cause. As far back as August Russell had entertained "the terrible dread . . . of hordes of Chinese intervening" in the war. In retrospect, he would have withdrawn from Korea and then laid siege to China by land and air until they stopped the "predatory attacks upon Korea." He did not like the "accordionlike movements up and down Korea by land forces." Hitting the Chinese "will certainly stop the slaughter of our men on the ground." So why not withdraw and punish the Chinese from a distance?

Russell's advocacy of action against China disturbed the administration. As chairman of the Armed Services Committee Russell wielded unique powers over military spending, and his control of the purse strings in turn gave him substantial influence over military policy. As the administration had made clear, the United States did not want total war with China. Yet MacArthur was about to finish his testimony with the dominant figure on the committee—and a Democrat at that—in agreement with his chief demand for a change in war policy.

Senator Wayne Morse saved the day for the administration. Russell was excusing MacArthur from further testimony—this at the tag end of a second long day of questioning—when Morse insisted that he continue on the stand until all members had questioned him to their satisfaction. After brief but spirited debate Morse prevailed. MacArthur would have to make one final run through the gauntlet.

MacArthur's third and last day of testimony opened with profuse apologies from Chairman Russell that he had been subjected to a "marathon session." Then the junior Democrats took over; they had digested MacArthur's testimony and the JCS cable traffic, and their note pads were crammed with questions furnished by Pentagon staff officers.

Senator Lyndon Johnson led off. Try as he might, he could not persuade MacArthur to make any substantive comment on the need for more American men to be put under arms or on the merits of universal military training. Again, MacArthur recognized the ambivalence of his Republican sponsors, and he refused to take sides in the intraparty debate regardless of his resultant inconsistency. MacArthur would talk at length about his problems in bringing divisions to fighting strength and in integrating ill-trained ROKs into his divisions. But he pleaded ignorance on the overall manpower problem.

Johnson suddenly moved to the most significant question directed to MacArthur during the three days: "I want to ask you this question, General. Assume we embrace your program and suppose that the Chinese were chased back across the Yalu, and suppose they refuse to sign a treaty and to enter into an agreement on what their future actions will be, what course would you recommend at that stage?"

MacArthur tried to evade an answer, calling the question hypothetical. "I can't quite see the possibility of the enemy being driven back across the Yalu and still being in a posture of offensive action."

Johnson was not to be denied. He mentioned the "accordion thing that you are talking about" when the sides alternately advance and retreat. "Now suppose we inaugurate this program that you have advocated and suppose it has the elements of success that you envisage. They go back across there, they still retain large mass formations there, what course are we going to have to take?"

"I don't think they could," MacArthur insisted.

"Are we going to have to keep a large number of men there to protect our position?" Johnson insisted.

"I can't visualize an enemy who has been cleared of Korea staying in a state of belligerency," MacArthur said. If the Chinese became convinced they could not hold south of the Yalu, "I believe that a rational treaty could be drawn up with him at that time." But Johnson had made his point: Going to war with China would involve more than tossing a few bombs across the frontier. Under further questioning MacArthur would not even estimate whether his plan would require 100,000 or 500,000 more men for Asia. "I believe that the major thing to do is to take off the inhibitions and let us use the maximum of force we have."

"Well, General," Johnson said, "we have to estimate the number of men required if we embrace these programs, and we not only have to estimate them, we have to be able to supply them. And when you present a positive program, such as you have presented, it is going to be our responsibility to be sure that we have the units and the forces required to carry it out."

In a long discussion with Senator Morse, the general discounted fears the Soviets might enter the war. Their support "has paled out" as events progressed; he had read intelligence reports of supplies furnished the Chinese, and "it seemed to me that was pretty weak support if China was becoming hard pressed."

When the war began, MacArthur said, there was much anxiety about Soviet intervention in direct combat roles. But the Soviets showed surprising restraint even when an American plane accidentally bombed a Russian airfield. Although the United States apologized for the error and offered compensation, the Soviets never sent a bill. American reconnaissance flights near Siberia did not cause "the slightest increase" in the number of Soviet troops there. Despite Soviet noise at the UN, "out on the battlefront it has been quite the contrary," MacArthur said.*

In a prescient statement—one with more foresight than that then possessed by the State Department—MacArthur saw Soviet fears "of this new Frankenstein that is being gradually congealed and coalesced in China." He doubted that the Soviets wanted the Chinese to become powerful enough to challenge the USSR; to the contrary, Moscow wished to keep China under control.

MacArthur's testimony finally ended at 7:10 P.M. on May 7. MacArthur had been in the witness chair for almost twenty-three hours, and

---

*Publicly the Soviets had made only one public admission its personnel were in North Korea.[4] A Radio Pyongyang broadcast on March 20 noted the arrival of an "anti-epidemic medical unit" from Russia, assistance certainly needed according to U.S. intelligence reports. But the broadcast specified that the unit was to assist "at various places *behind the battleline* [emphasis added]." The Soviets obviously wanted to signal the United States they were not actively entering the war.

his testimony filled 787 typed pages. He left with fulsome praise by the committee members ringing in his ears.

Douglas MacArthur had put his views on conduct of the Korean War, and his policy differences with the Truman administration, squarely on record. The point he sought to make above all, as a matter of personal honor, was that he had not been disobedient to President Truman. He stated late the last day:

> I resent, with every fiber in my body, any inference that can be drawn that I have been, in any degree, insubordinate or disrespectful of the President of the United States, or the policies of this country, or even of the policies and directives of the United Nations.

Now the stage was turned over to others, to the military and diplomatic architects of administration policy.

The Administration's Turn

The Joint Chiefs of Staff and their subordinate officers spent the weekend in a sentence-by-sentence analysis of MacArthur's testimony. The major point they challenged—and unanimously—was MacArthur's repeated assertion that they had "approved" the four actions proposed on January 12—that is, the intensification of the economic blockade of China, a naval blockade, removal on restrictions on air reconnaissance of Manchuria and the Chinese coast, and removal of restrictions on the operations of Chinese Nationalist troops. MacArthur had been emphatic that he felt the steps to be established policy; could he possibly have been misled by General J. Lawton Collins when he outlined the options to the general in Tokyo in mid-January? No, Collins replied; to the contrary. He had read the JCS paper directly to MacArthur to avoid any possibility of misinterpretation by any staff member. If MacArthur did not recognize the memo as "options," the fault was his, not Washington's. Thus the JCS had no choice: They must perform the distasteful task of showing a national hero to be wrong.

Secretary George C. Marshall, leading off for the military on Monday, May 7, began by saying it was a "distressing necessity" that he had to testify "in effect in almost direct opposition to a great many of the views and actions of General MacArthur." He called the general a "brother Army officer, a man for whom I have tremendous respect." Then he rebutted MacArthur for hour after hour.

First was MacArthur's assertion that Marshall had overruled the JCS in their opposition to turning Formosa over to Communist China and to seating Communist China in the United Nations. MacArthur made these comments when reviewing the peace announcement that President Truman had intended to make in late March. What the administration, in fact, had proposed, Marshall testified, was that the United States would not "oppose discussion of these questions." The long-standing policy of the United States, he continued, was to "deny Formosa to Communist China and to oppose the seating of the Communist Chinese in the UN." There had been "no deviation from that policy whatsoever" and no wavering in American determination to keep them out of the armistice terms. Putting the issues on the agenda for discussion was a pragmatic decision, since other parties were certain to raise them anyway. But discussion did not equate with approval.

On the January 12 options, Marshall gave a lengthy explanation of the grave military situation as 1951 opened and the fact that the United States was "faced with the very real possibility of having to evacuate our forces from Korea." The JCS courses cited by MacArthur were put forward as tentative, to be considered for implementation "if and when this possibility came closer to reality." At about the same time the JCS memorandum went to the National Security Council for review, the military situation improved dramatically, with Ridgway regaining the initiative. Thus it became unnecessary to put any of the options into effect. "None of these proposed courses of action was vetoed or disapproved by me or by any higher authority," Marshall said firmly. "The ultimate decision with respect to them was simply rendered unnecessary at that time—or unwise, to put it better—in the view of the Chiefs of Staff."

On following days the other chiefs echoed what Marshall said about the January 12 paper. The most detailed account came from General Omar Bradley, the JCS Chairman, who said the chiefs as far back as late November had directed a staff committee to study actions that might be taken in the event the United States and China became involved in total war. The resulting committee report carried a preamble setting forth this qualifying contingency. Somehow the qualifying language was omitted from the final JCS memorandum, leaving only a statement that the listed courses of action had been *"tentatively agreed* [emphasis added]." But to Bradley—and his colleagues, they said later—it was perfectly clear that the memorandum was merely a "study," not a directive or set of instructions to MacArthur. Nothing in the memorandum said the decisions were final.

Marshall stood in essential disagreement with almost every point MacArthur made about the conduct of the war. He did not share MacArthur's confidence that his proposed moves against the Chinese would not lead to a broader war:

> He [MacArthur] would have us accept the risk involving not only an extension of the war with Red China, but in an all-out war with the Soviet

Union. He would have had us do this even at the expense of losing our allies and wrecking the coalition of free peoples throughout the world. He would have us do this even though the effect of such action might expose Western Europe to attack by the millions of Soviet troops poised in Middle and Eastern Europe.

The fundamental divergence, Marshall continued, was between a theater commander with a limited mission and that of the President, the secretary of defense, and the JCS, who "must weigh our interests and objectives in one part of the globe with those in other areas . . . so as to attain the best over-all balance."

Marshall found it understandable that a theater commander would "become so wholly wrapped up in his own aims" that the directives he received from higher authority "are not those that he would have written for himself." Military history was replete with such instances. But what was new in MacArthur's case was the "wholly unprecedented situation of a theater commander's publicly expressing his displeasure at and his disagreement with the foreign and military policy of the United States." Marshall then cited the core reason why Truman fired MacArthur:

> It became apparent that General MacArthur had grown so far out of sympathy with the established policies of the United States that there was grave doubt as to whether he could any longer be permitted to exercise the authority in making decisions that normal command functions would assign to a theater commander. In this situation, there was no other re-course but to relieve him.

Each of the other chiefs, in turn, confirmed their support of the decision to relieve MacArthur, strictly on military grounds. None would accuse him of military insubordination; each maintained, in essence, that the accumulative effect of his statements, culminating in the sur-render ultimatum to the Chinese on March 24 and the Martin letter left the President no choice. And although there was much criticism of some of MacArthur's tactical moves, notably the split between the Eighth Army and X Corps, the chiefs seemed reluctant to question the judgment of a field commander (although both Collins and Bradley firmly said they would have deployed differently). But Collins's opinion of MacArthur's overall conduct of the war was implicitly stated during an exchange with Senator Alexander Wiley. "From a purely military standpoint," Wiley asked, "would you be willing to state that General MacArthur's conduct of the Korean War was compatible with the out-standing record he . . . compiled in the conduct of the war in the Pacific from 1941 to 1945?"

"That is a difficult question to answer, Senator," Collins replied.

"Do you want to answer it?"

"If you insist, I will answer it. I prefer not to," Collins said. Wiley did not insist.

Marshall spent most of his testimony reviewing in detail the administration's decision to limit the Korean War to gain time for mobilization of enough military strength to counter any Soviet moves, a process that would last until 1953. In the process, Marshall disputed several assertions MacArthur had made as a matter of undisputed fact.

Perhaps foremost among the questionable MacArthur claims was that of the combat ability of the Chinese Nationalists. MacArthur spoke of an army of half a million men, fully capable of operations against the Chinese mainland, given the logistical support of the United States. Any reservations he had about the fighting prowess of the Nationalists he couched in words so general as to be meaningless. Marshall, however, put the Nationalists into more accurate perspective.

MacArthur had testified that when he went to Formosa in August 1950, he thought the Nationalist Army "excellent." They lacked trucks, artillery, and other "modern refinements." But they "are capable of being made into a very excellent force. . . . [T]he force represents a potential of a half million first-class fighting men."

MacArthur's comments were based on spot observations during a one-day visit, largely ceremonial. In testimony censored from the 1951 hearing transcript Marshall summarized the findings of a thirty-seven-officer survey team that MacArthur sent to Formosa later in August 1950. The mission reported that the Nationalists' "condition of training and equipment, as to ground troops, and as to air troops, and as to naval troops, was so low that they could not be depended upon to defend the island" of Formosa. Thus MacArthur's cited army of "a half million men" could not be relied upon even to defend their home base, much less fight in a foreign country.

At another point MacArthur had minimized Nationalist equipment shortages. No matter. From the 500,000 men, enough arms and other gear could be found to send 35,000 to 40,000 troops to Korea. Marshall thought otherwise. "Under recent conditions in Formosa," he said, "such a small force would represent the core of Formosa's defense. It would seem questionable to strip Formosa of such a force *even if it were in existence* [emphasis added]." Nor did the JCS see any reason to squander precious American equipment on the Nationalists. An internal JCS memo in November 1950 noted that the "record of the Chinese Nationalist troops for losing the equipment furnished them [during the war with the Communists] increases the reluctance of the Joint Chiefs to equip them and employ them in battle." Marshall did not trust the morale of the Nationalists to hold if they went into battle with the Communists, to whom they had lost ingloriously only a few years earlier.

General Bradley went even further. The Nationalists' morale was so poor they might defect to the Communists at the first opportunity. If a Communist force managed to land on Formosa, Bradley testified, they might rely upon defections to take the island. General Collins felt the same way. "We were highly skeptical that we would get anything more out of these [Nationalist] Chinese than we were getting out of the South Koreans, because these were the same people that were run off China in the first place."

Nor did the JCS support MacArthur's contention that the Nationalists could run any meaningful operations against the mainland. Marshall did not feel that the Nationalists "have . . . the ability to sustain an operation without getting so involved that we would have to be drawn into their support." Neither the JCS nor the CIA saw any possibility of Chiang Kai-shek's finding meaningful popular support should he attempt to return to the mainland. Given his limited strength, Chiang could not possibly succeed without the support of the Chinese populace. Bradley did not think this would happen.

> The trouble of it is Chiang is not accepted by a large part of the Chinese. . . . Chiang has had a big chance to win in China and he did not do it. From a military point of view in my opinion I don't think he would have too much success in leading the Chinese now.
>
> It's true that some of them [the mainland Chinese] are getting tired of the Communists and might be more loyal to him now than they were before, but in my opinion he is not in position to rally the Chinese people against the Communists even if we could get him ashore.

But the Joint Chiefs recognized the political appeal of "unleashing Chiang Kai-shek," as MacArthur had put it. In deference to the China Lobby they did not rule out eventual Nationalist operations against the mainland. Bradley saw no capability "right now" for any such move. "Their leadership is poor; their equipment is poor; and their training is poor. When that has been improved to a point where it means something, then I think this thing should be reconsidered and that action taken up again." Secretary Acheson, testifying a few days later, would not even think of mainland operations. The "first task" of the Nationalists was defending Formosa. "I don't think you can talk much about anything else they could do. It wouldn't make any sense at present time."

All this testimony was stricken from the record released to the public and the press. The Joint Chiefs faced a Hobson's choice in censoring the statements about Chiang's weaknesses. Letting MacArthur's inaccurate testimony go unchallenged cast the JCS as the men who would not use a supposedly fighting-fit ally in Korea. But publicizing the true condition of Chiang's army, especially the probability his troops would defect the first chance they received, would give the Communist Chinese intelligence of inestimable value. So the JCS, through the censor, kept this testimony secret.

The JCS decision reverberated in American public life for the remainder of the 1950's and well into the 1960's. Republican politicians spoke windily about "unleashing" Chiang Kai-shek, as if only a restraining rope kept the Nationalist general from scattering the Communists with a few yelps and snarls. The issue was false. The American leash did not inhibit Chiang; it saved him. Had he been set loose, the Communists would have finished the Chinese Civil War in short order.

Marshall was unsympathetic toward MacArthur's war strategy, with its "terrible possible consequences." MacArthur, because of his "preoccupation with Korea," did not realize the problems Washington was having with allies and the "extraordinary difficulty" of maintaining a majority in the UN. Marshall preferred the Ridgway approach of inflicting "the greatest number of casualties we could in order to break down not only the morale but the trained fabric of the Chinese armies."

In a sense, Marshall said, Korea was comparable to the Berlin blockade crisis of 1948–49, when the Soviets blocked Western access by ground to a city isolated in the Soviet zone of Germany. Marshall was secretary of state at the time. There were times when the struggle over Berlin "also looked like a stalemate, but we kept our head and in the end won a noble victory," Marshall said. "There were those who wanted to end this situation by smashing through the Russian blockade, even though this might have precipitated a war. . . . We refused to take a risk as long as there were other means of accomplishing our ends." Similarly, the struggle in Greece to defeat Communist insurgents took eighteen months, and policy critics said that "this was a hopeless adventure and . . . we were . . . wasting our economic and military assistance to that country."

Marshall could not condone MacArthur's conduct. When a military commander writes a letter to a member of Congress, he

> has to use considerable discretion. I have had to write a good many thousand . . . but I don't think I would ever be involved myself in a criticism of the Commander in Chief to any Congressman of either party concerned. . . . You preach loyalty all the time. You are dealing with an organization where a man receives an order from even a captain which leads to his death or his wound, and he has to obey that order. . . . [T]hat has to be instinctive. Now, if the example at the top is contrary to that, then you have got a very serious situation.
>
> I thought it would have been immensely profitable if General MacArthur, on his own motion, had responded to invitations to come over and talk to the President about a great many of these things, and come in touch with reactions which didn't reach him, except in a rather vague way, in Japan.

On MacArthur's specific plans, Marshall was unsympathetic. China's vastness made it immune to air attack. "When you bombard a coastal city, or an interior city, I don't think you accomplish a great deal." The Japanese, despite having troops "all through China," were not able to take the country. Marshall would prefer to kill Chinese in Korea. The first North Korean force had been demolished by MacArthur; the first Chinese army put into Korea was "pretty largely torn to pieces, almost decimated"; now the new Chinese troops "have been really so torn to pieces that they are not capable of effective action and will not be for some time to come." No army could continue to sustain the losses being suffered by the Chinese.

Even as he testified, Marshall sensed (and so indicated to the senators) that during the next few weeks American policy would succeed to the point where the administration would no longer have to address the question of expanding the war to end it. That the Chinese were continuing their spring offensive encouraged, rather than discouraged, Marshall. Ridgway's Operation Killer (see above) had taken an awesome toll of Chinese during April and early May. In Marshall's words:

> The best possibility that we see at the present time is . . . a continuation of the attack by the Communists, with the hope that we get fair weather, and inflict such tremendous losses on them in proportion to what has occurred in the past two weeks that we have broken the power of their trained armies.*

(In his testimony two weeks later General Bradley agreed. "I believe the general feeling is that we would be in a much better position to propose political terms after we have stopped this spring offensive than we would have been had we tried to get a negotiation and an armistice before we had shown them that they could not chase us out of Korea.")

On MacArthur's insistence on speaking his mind, even when he ran counter to administration policy, Marshall recalled his frequent "difficult scenes" with President Roosevelt over Second World War policy and instances in which he was "frequently embarrassed" before congressional committees. Yet "I honestly thought it was ruinous for me to come out in opposition to my Commander in Chief." He argued with Roosevelt in private; once decisions were made, he stuck with them. MacArthur should have done the same or resigned. Marshall cited another example of command loyalty: General John J. Pershing led an expedition into Mexico in 1916 after the renegade revolutionary Fran-

---

*During the week of May 17–23 alone, General Collins testified a few days later, the Communists had almost 90,000 casualties, bringing their total to an estimated 1,025,000 killed, wounded, and captured.

cisco "Pancho" Villa. President Wilson, wanting to confine the action directly to Villa, rather than risk general war with Mexico, ordered Pershing not to commandeer Mexican national railway trains, even though there was no other transport. Later Pershing was ordered to withdraw when he was on the verge of capturing Villa. Pershing, although frustrated, did not say a word to his own staff, much less the public, about the reason.

Marshall disputed MacArthur's claim that bombing restrictions gave the Communists an unfair advantage. In testimony censored at the time, Marshall said that "the loss of advantage of our troops on the ground [by not bombing Manchuria] was actually more than equalled by the advantages which we were deriving from not exposing our vulnerability to air attacks." UN targets in Korea were concentrated; the Chinese were scattered and fluid. The JCS were concerned about "extremely vulnerable" Pusan, Korea's only deepwater port and the major choke point for UN supplies. "Because the docks are close together, and the ships are close together," Marshall testified, "the depots can be only scattered to a certain extent."

Marshall and the chiefs alike stressed that the Communists were also fighting a limited war. Rebutting a statement by Senator Walter George of Georgia that the Chinese were waging "all-out war," Bradley replied that "they have not used air against our front line troops, our ports, . . . our bases in Japan or against our naval forces." On the whole, Bradley thought, "we are fighting under rather favorable rules for ourselves." General Hoyt Vandenberg, the air chief, agreed that "this sanctuary business, as it is called, is operating on both sides."

In censored testimony, Vandenberg also offered practical reasons for not bombing beyond the Yalu. Communist air bases above the border employed radar-controlled antiaircraft batteries, "and we found out from operating along the Yalu, they are very accurate." Nor did the United States have the air strength to mount sustained air attacks:

> The air force of the United States . . . is really a shoestring air force and these groups that we have over there now doing this tactical job are really about a fourth of our total effort that we could muster today, and four times that amount of groups in that area over that vast expanse of China would be a drop in the bucket.

The JCS did not reject MacArthur's pleas for authority to bomb military installations in Manchuria out of hand, Marshall said. The main deterrent was the fear of retaliatory Chinese air strikes. General Collins, the army chief, elaborated a few days later. As Collins noted, MacArthur's first request for bombing authority came when X Corps was being supplied through Hungnam. Had bombing been permitted north of the Yalu, we were dreadfully afraid that might be the thing that would release the Russian planes . . . and possibly submarine attack during the perilous evacuation from Hungnam. Troops evacuating from a port of that character, in commercial ships, are terribly subject to air and underwater attack; and in my judgment, it would be a much too risky procedure.

Similarly the JCS withheld permission for maximum bombing of North Korean targets for postwar political strategy. According to General Collins, the United States looked toward a united Korea once the war ended, something the North Koreans might not accept "if we were to just bomb their cities."

Neither Marshall nor the military chiefs shared MacArthur's view that the ROKs were "very fine troops." In heavily censored testimony, Marshall, Bradley, and Collins offered scathing appraisals of the ROKs. During the most recent Chinese attack, Marshall said, one ROK division, the 6th, did a "complete foldup, practically with no resistance whatever." The ROKs fell back eighteen to twenty miles under the first assaults, with "no fighting, really, whatsoever . . . so that the troops on either side were put in a very dreadful dilemma." Questioned by Senator Johnson, Bradley estimated that the ROKs had lost enough equipment to outfit ten divisions in the eleven months of the year. "Everytime they are hit by the Chinamen," Collins said, "they just plain run."

One cross Marshall bore stoically was tedious questioning about American policy in China during the years he was President Truman's special representative there and secretary of state. Another was an exhausting repetition of questions by his adversaries; time and again he went through the events of the days preceding MacArthur's dismissal and his explanation of why the United States did not accept Chiang's troops for use in Korea.

Only once did Marshall display personal animosity toward MacArthur. A few minutes before he left the witness chair on his seventh day of testimony, Senator John Sparkman of Alabama read a United Press story giving MacArthur's views on a message President Truman had sent him on January 13. This communiqué recognized that MacArthur might find it necessary to evacuate Korea but urged that he hold as long as possible for diplomatic reasons. General Courtney Whitney, speaking for MacArthur (according to the UP account), said that Truman intended to pull out of Korea and to "make Eighth Army the scapegoat" for the defeat. Would Marshall care to comment? Sparkman asked.

Truman's message spoke for itself, Marshall said; not in "the most remote manner" did the President intend to make the Eighth Army a scapegoat. Marshall blushed, and his voice became rigid. "That would almost be treasonable."

Sparkman agreed and then began reading the article again. Marshall interrupted him. "I didn't select this aide [Whitney], you know." When

Sparkman continued, Marshall cut him off abruptly, coldly. "I don't care to discuss it, Senator."

Marshall never raised his voice. But no one who heard him doubted that he held General MacArthur and his entourage in utter contempt.

The separate chiefs who followed General Marshall the next weeks added little new to the swelling volumes of testimony; to a man, however, they opposed MacArthur's proposals. General Bradley summarized the prime strategic consideration motivating JCS planning: "Red China is not the powerful nation seeking to dominate the world. Frankly, in the opinion of the JCS, this strategy would involve us in the wrong war, at the wrong place, at the wrong time and with the wrong enemy." Taking on China would only guarantee a "larger deadlock at greater expense" without any assurance of victory in Korea. Following MacArthur's proposals would present a "real danger" of bringing the Soviets into the war.

Led by Senator Alexander Wiley, the Republicans did inject one new issue into the proceedings: that since the President permitted Bradley to testify, he should relate his conversations with Truman about MacArthur's dismissal. The GOP senators suspected a sinister force was behind the firing—the detested Acheson, perhaps even the British. Bradley refused, saying he considered himself a confidential adviser, and Chairman Russell upheld his right not to repeat presidential conversations. (The committee, in turn, upheld Russell's ruling by an 18–8 vote.*)

With administration figures relating closely parallel stories and not yielding under cross-examination, even when questioned half a dozen times on the same point, the Republicans grasped at secondary issues. Senator William Knowland of California professed great indignation that Vernice Anderson had taken notes at Wake Island unbeknownst to General MacArthur (or so the general claimed). "Suppose it had been an assassin behind that partition?" Knowland asked. Bradley corrected him: Ms. Anderson was not "behind a partition"; she was in another room, a trusted public employee with a top secret clearance. Senator Charles W. Tobey, New Hampshire Republican, wanted to end the hearings during Bradley's testimony. "I am impressed with the futility of much that is going on here and very definitely so." Tobey thought the hearings a waste of time:

> Here are a lot of . . . well-intentioned men, with absolutely no military training or gumption . . . coming in here to pose questions to men whose life-long service has been in the military establishments. . . . We have got the whole country by the ears putting out bulletins. Mr. Stalin subscribes

*Senator J. William Fulbright of Arkansas was the only Democrat to vote to compel Bradley to reveal the presidential conversations. More than a decade later, during the Vietnam War, he consistently took the same position in contesting aides of President Johnson who claimed "executive privilege" on White House discussions of the war.

to it day by day. . . . And so what are we doing? We are asking questions many of them being very, very piddling. . . .

When the hearings ended, MacArthur would still be out of a job, the JCS would still run the military, troops would still fight in Korea. Tobey wished to "ring the curtain down."

Although the Republicans poked at Bradley for two more days, Tobey's point was heeded. The evidence was that MacArthur had stepped out of line—in both the surrender ultimatum and the Martin letter—and that Truman had acted within his authority in firing him. At the start of the May 24 session the GOP moved to stop the hearings. Senator Bourke Hickenlooper proposed that the three service chiefs not be called personally but that they read the previous testimony and stipulate whether they agreed with it. Hickenlooper claimed further military testimony would be repetitious; he wanted to move on to Dean Acheson, a more vulnerable target. But Senator Russell demurred. The Republicans had been loud in demanding the hearing and generous in condemning the administration. The Republicans had used the word "whitewash." Russell gave no quarter; the committee would sit until every relevant witness had been heard.

The Democratic majority had another reason for dragging on the hearings. One means of smothering public indignation is to so overwhelm the citizenry with a subject that they tire of it. For three weeks the "MacArthur hearings" dominated the news, to the point where the American public was ready to turn to summer vacation and baseball.

Acheson on the Stand

When Secretary Dean Acheson appeared as a witness, the Republicans saw an opportunity to have profitable sport with the administration on the fall of Nationalist China. An unshaken GOP tenet was that Truman bungling, at best, or manipulation of the State Department by Communist agents, at worst, had caused Chiang Kai-shek's loss to the Communists. Thus Acheson was to spend the longest time before the committee of any witness—from 10:06 on Friday morning, June 1, through Saturday afternoon, June 9, at 5:05 P.M. The first two days Acheson endured rambling, disjointed questioning that veered from demands he recite again and again the sequence of events leading to MacArthur's firing to his explanation of various State Department memorandums.

But Acheson managed to make the points he wished: Following MacArthur's plans risked bogging America in a strategically useless war.

In all probability the Soviets would have intervened to help the Chinese, under their mutual assistance treaty, or lost face as leader of the Communist world.

But Acheson's most important statement was directed beyond the senators to the Communist Chinese and the North Koreans. In the past several weeks the administration had lost confidence in the UN as a bargaining forum to end the war. Acheson and others considered it too unreliable and unpredictable a body to coordinate peace talks. The strongly divergent views of UN members meant a risk of the United States' being elbowed into unsatisfactory peace terms. The United States decided to devise its own approaches, with the aim of stopping the fighting, even if under less than perfect terms.

Acheson used the Senate hearings as a megaphone to offer the Communists sharply scaled-down American war aims. No longer did the United States insist on fulfilling the long-standing UN mandate to unite Korea. Although unification remained a long-range goal, the U.S. was willing to settle the war under other terms. If the Communists would give the United States assurances that hostilities would not be resumed against South Korea, it would accept a cease-fire around the 38th parallel and agree to remove all foreign troops—i.e., the UN—from the war, provided foreign troops—i.e., the Chinese—left North Korea as well. In effect, Acheson was telling the Communists they could stop the fighting if they so desired.

Although he did not explicitly admit that the United States had reduced its war aims, he offered an elaborate and detailed explanation of why Washington was now willing to end the war on terms that represented the situation existing when it began.

Driving the Chinese back to the 38th parallel would contain "Communist imperialism" and deny the aggressors their victory. True, the war might not end. But continuing it on a smaller front would be easier —and less costly in lives—than the expanded war MacArthur sought. Even if the war was extended, there was no guarantee of "victory," but there were considerable risks to the alliance through which the United States hoped to halt communist aggression worldwide. Asking the allies to join in such a perilous venture as war in China put unfair burdens on them. Acheson explained:

> We cannot expect that our collective security system will long survive if we take steps which unnecessarily and dangerously expose the people who are in the system with us. . . .
> The power of our coalition to deter an attack depends in part upon the will and mutual confidence of our partners. If we, by the measures proposed, were to weaken that effort, particularly in the North Atlantic area, we would be jeopardizing the security of an area which is vital to our own national security.

Acheson would not accept MacArthur's contention that the war could not be won if confined to Korea. In his view the word "won" was irrelevant. "It doesn't make any difference exactly where the fighting may end. The point is, is a settlement going to be made or is it not going to be made where the Chinese will not have the will and the desire to come back in and fight again?"

Continued punishment would eventually lead the Chinese to stop fighting, Acheson said. He did not wish a war of extermination with the Chinese. He wanted a balance to be struck that would ensure peace in Korea.

But Acheson's critics did not seem interested in his exposition of Korean policy; time and again they returned to "the State Department's loss of China" and implicitly demanded that he grovel in apology. Acheson defended the administration as best he could, but he feared that "a hash would be made of this complex matter if it was covered only by hit-or-miss questions and answers." So late in his second day, Acheson offered a counterproposal: Give him a day of preparation, and he would attempt a comprehensive statement on U.S. policy toward China since 1945. The committee agreed, and Acheson gathered a thick sheaf of State Department documents and retreated to his farm in rural Maryland for the weekend. "Aided by coffee and a farmhouse policed into silence by his wife, with a security guard at the gate," he culled through the papers for weary hours, making a pile of notes.

On Monday morning Acheson delivered an extraordinary three-hour exposition. Speaking with notes, he told of the disintegration of China's ancient society under the impact of a modernizing society and of the unsuccessful attempts of the United States to mediate the competing forces of nationalism and communism. He flatly rejected any American fault for the collapse of the Chiang government. American aid, he said, could not ensure the survival of any government, could only supplement its own efforts. Nor could the United States make decisions on behalf of another government, even one it was attempting to salvage.

Acheson pictured a China in chaos in 1945, a "territory" that had not been a nation for decades, with the Communists and Soviets controlling the northern provinces and Manchuria, the Japanese controlling the major cities and rail and road system, and the Nationalists clinging to the southern quadrant of the country. The realistic conclusion by American study missions was that the Nationalists would have to fight for years to dislodge the Communists and that chances of victory were slim. General George C. Marshall, in China as a presidential emissary, tried unsuccessfully to negotiate a cease-fire and to persuade the Nationalists to institute social and political reforms to gain broader mass support. Both efforts failed. Congress eventually voted the Nationalists $400 million in economic and military aid (versus $570 million asked by the administration) but refused to send military advisers into combat areas. (Although Acheson tactfully did not say so, the lesser aid package was voted by the Republican-controlled Congress elected in 1946.) Even with that help, the Nationalists began collapsing militarily in late 1948, going from a three to one numerical superiority to a one to one and one-half disadvantage. A U.S. Army intelligence estimate in January 1949 said the Nationalist military position "has declined beyond possible recoupment." General David Barr, head of the U.S. military mission, said the Nationalists had the "world's worst leadership." Eighty percent of the American military equipment had been lost. The United States decided not to take over the war, and Chiang collapsed.

That, in much summarized form, was the story Acheson told the committee—nothing new, to be sure, for the China collapse had been reviewed in detail before various congressional groups previously. The statement did not completely satisfy Acheson's adversaries; one of them, Senator Owen D. Brewster of Maine, accused the secretary of taking "unfair advantage" of the senators through greater knowledge of the subject matter.

The remainder of Acheson's testimony was a resounding defense of administration conduct of the war and total rejection of MacArthur's plans to take the conflict to China. He would not challenge MacArthur's motives: If the general thought bombing Manchuria would end the war sooner, he meant it. But "it was our fear he would not bring it to an end."

Acheson also was questioned intensely about the reasons the United States had withdrawn its troops from South Korea in the late spring of 1950. The United States, he said, had recognized the situation was dangerous but "trusted in the fact that the invasion would not take place until the South Koreans were able to handle themselves better." (Acheson did not reveal that the State Department had, in fact, urged that troops remain in Korea longer and that they were withdrawn at Pentagon insistence.)

Strategically Acheson felt the Chinese had blundered by entering the war, for it cost them almost certain conquest of Formosa, which now was beyond their grasp indefinitely. No longer did the world community consider Formosa leftover business from the Chinese Civil War. Much of the world now viewed China as an "international outlaw." Nor would China have any voice in the Japanese peace treaty, as it might have anticipated had it kept out of Korea. And China had forfeited any immediate hope for a UN seat.

Conversely the United States made several major gains. Foremost was the demonstration that it would live up to its commitments to other nations. The expanded war gave impetus to a rearmament effort the American people and Congress otherwise would not have supported. "I think it brought home to people very strongly the extent of the danger to which the whole world was subjected, and which the whole world faced," Acheson said.

The questioning rambled on interminably, with Acheson quizzed about such infuriating irrelevant subjects (for a hearing concerned with the military situation in the Far East) as lending money to Mexico to develop its oil resources; the connection between Acheson's former law firm and Iran; the fact that Assistant Secretary of State George McGhee had wed the daughter of the international oil geologist Everett de Golyer; soybean speculation by renegade refugees of the Chinese Nationalist regime; the admission of German scientists to the United States; and why the War Department sent one general rather than another to China to a study mission in 1945. Even Acheson's supposed friends turned into bores who cluttered the record with tediously repeated questions; Wayne Morse, the most frequent culprit, simply ignored what had already been asked and conducted his interrogation as if he were the only senator present.

When Acheson finally finished, a State Department friend asked what he intended to do that weekend. "I have a plan that will test my capacity for the consumption of alcohol," the secretary replied, "and if another war erupts before I finish, it must be waged without my services."

The Hearings Wind Down

For all practical purposes, Acheson's testimony ended the substantive portion of the hearings, although they dragged on for several more weeks with peripheral witnesses who had little to add, either affirmative or negative, to what had already been said.

On the last day of his Senate testimony, Secretary George Marshall had stated that the decision to relieve MacArthur was made with the awareness that it would be controversial. But Marshall added, "It was also felt that after the height of the emotional wave passed, there would be some sober thinking." Marshall's attitude irked Senator Bourke Hickenlooper. "That might be interpreted as an assumption by the Administration that the American people would lull themselves into a situation of indifference after a period of time," he said. "I think sober thinking and lull are not comparative terms," Marshall replied.

Marshall's judgment proved correct. Even as the hearings continued, MacArthur traveled the country in quest of new adulation. But he found attention diminishing. People would turn out to see him for curiosity value, but not to listen to his speeches. In Chicago a noontime motorcade attracted an estimated 3 million people. But that evening, when he spoke at Soldier Field, only 50,000 were there, half the stadium's capacity. And MacArthur became increasingly demagogic. In a speech to the Texas legislature he charged that the foreign policy formulated by "civilians" in the American government (MacArthur made the word sound dirty, even sinister) was "largely influenced, if not indeed in some instances dictated, from abroad and dominated by fear of what others may think or others may do." As he continued across the country, he sounded not so much like a returned statesman as he did a conventional conservative Republican campaigning for election. In Seattle he charged that "our political stature has been sadly impaired by a succession of diplomatic blunders and reckless spendthrift aims at home. . . . There is a growing anxiety in the American home as disclosures reveal graft and corruption over a broad front in our public service." He decried "political ineptitude and economic incompetence." MacArthur also found himself adopted—once his government logistical support ended—by people from the far right of American politics. Texas oilmen H. L. Hunt and Clint Murchison put a plane at his disposal. And gradually the American public tired of hearing MacArthur espouse political ideas that they had rejected in 1948, when they elected Harry S. Truman President.

To much of the press—especially the Luce magazines *Time* and *Life* —MacArthur's travels were an event of the emotional magnitude of Caesar's returning to Rome after his successful campaigns. Less excitable observers told a different story.[5] Lawyer Maury Maverick, a distinguished political leader in San Antonio, Texas, sent President Truman a long memorandum describing MacArthur's reception in his city. WELCOME MACARTHUR flags were first offered by hawkers for $1. The price dropped to 15 cents when no one wanted them. The police had anticipated a crowd of 500,000; only 80,000 or so appeared, most of whom seemed to be people en route to lunch. The centerpiece of MacArthur's visit was a speech at the Alamo. "When he began talking," Maverick said, "people craned their necks and then departed, giggling or chewing gum . . . nobody listened to the rumbling oratory." The main confusion was created by army troops who blocked intersections so that MacArthur's caravan could pass unimpeded. Another Texas lawyer-politician, Harry L. Seay of Dallas, also monitored MacArthur's travels in the state. In Houston MacArthur drew 20,000 to Rice Institute Stadium, which seated 80,000, far less a crowd than Truman had attracted there in a 1948 campaign appearance. At the Cotton Bowl, in Dallas, 25,000 were in the 75,000-capacity stadium, and many left before he finished speaking. "His trip to Texas was a FLOP," Seay wrote the President, "and many of his friends admit it."

Although MacArthur perhaps did not recognize it at the time, there was a core reason for his swift passage. The Republicans who brought him to Washington and gave him a forum before the Congress and the Senate hearing did so with a mixture of concern over war policy and a desire to torment the administration. MacArthur mistook the affectionate attention as an invitation to mount a political crusade and drive Truman from the White House. The Republican plans for dealing with Truman, however, in June 1951 did not extend much further than titular leader Senator Robert A. Taft. MacArthur, to the Republicans, had a place and a purpose. Once he had testified, and castigated the administration, and received the cheers of the nation, there was no further use for him. MacArthur basked in the limelight from mid-April through mid-June. Afterward he was a lonely old man in a Manhattan hotel suite, as far removed from any role in the Korean War as a raw recruit in a New Jersey army training camp.

The next spring MacArthur attended a Phillies-Giants baseball game in the Polo Grounds. Near the end he crossed center field with Jean and Arthur and headed for an exit as the band played "Old Soldiers Never Die." The crowd applauded respectfully; then a brass-voiced shout came from the bleachers: "Hey, Mac! How's Harry Truman?" The bleachers exploded with guffaws—the only recorded instance in which anyone ever laughed at Douglas MacArthur to his face.

CHAPTER TWENTY-ONE

The Secret Road to Peace Talks

When Communist Chinese representatives arrived at the United Nations in December 1950, the UN Command was at its lowest ebb, with evacuation possible at any hour. China held victory in its grasp; the panicked General MacArthur saw his only options as either expanding or abandoning the war.

Thus the State Department was astounded to receive a feeler from the Chinese delegation that seemed to point toward a willingness to open peace talks.[1] The contact was indirect. A Chinese delegate was a member of the Young China Party, one of several splinter organizations in the delegation not formally affiliated with the Chinese Communist Party. Soon after arrival at Lake Success, this person contacted a Chinese student attending American University in Washington, who in turn passed a message to an acquaintance at the State Department: The Chinese were willing to exchange "information" on a nonofficial basis.

The State Department reacted warily. With China on the verge of battlefield victory, what could it gain by back-channel talks with Washington? Charles Burton Marshall, of the State Department's Policy Planning Staff, was designated to pursue the lead. "I saw this as a typical diplomatic cutout where you can disavow anything that is said," Marshall said. "It is hard to authenticate whether the other side is trying to inform you or mislead you." Marshall soon was convinced that the "opening" was authentic but with an ulterior purpose: The Chinese aim was to block the UN resolution condemning Peking as the aggressor in the Korean War. The State Department decided that the aggressor resolution was more important than any wink-and-nudge signal and persuaded the General Assembly to condemn China.

Undaunted, the "contact" sent word to Marshall that he would "try to remain in touch." The State Department responded with a challenge. As Marshall put it, if he indeed had the unofficial blessing of his government, "they [the Communist Chinese] should spring a certain American held in jail in Shanghai on espionage charges." What Washington did not know was that the accused spy had already been shot. Thus the tenuous opening petered out.

As the "accordion war" dragged through the spring and early summer of 1951, with Matthew Ridgway's Eighth Army slowly winning back the battlefield advantage, the United States probed constantly for openings for armistice talks. One handicap was that the administration did not recognize the legitimacy of the Peking regime.[2] As Assistant Secretary Dean Rusk stated in May 1951, "We do not recognize the authorities of Peking for what they pretend to be. It is not the government of China. It does not pass the first test. It is not Chinese." And as Acheson stated at the MacArthur hearings, "the perplexing question" was with whom a peace could be negotiated. Although the Chinese bore the brunt of the fighting, the North Koreans and Soviets would want a voice in any settlement (although Acheson still considered the North Koreans and the Chinese "Moscow-trained Communists" who would do "what Moscow wants them to do"). But Acheson gave the Chinese a broad hint that the United States could be flexible, remarking that "we would have to deal with the Chinese Communist authorities." Even though he considered Peking a "sort of rump government," Acheson saw no alternative: "[Y]ou would deal with them as the authority which is fighting your troops, and if they desire to stop fighting your troops, I don't think there is any problem about dealing with them."*

According to Acheson, the United States "cast about like a pack of hounds searching for a scent."[4] Kremlinologist Charles Bohlen spent frustrating days trying to start a dialogue with a Soviet diplomat in Paris. Ernest Gross and Thomas Cory of the UN delegation thought they had picked up a signal from the Soviets at Lake Success. Before they could pursue the hint, *The New York Times* printed a story about a rumored peace contact, and the Soviets vanished. Still later in the spring a Western European "with some credentials of reliability" suggested the Chinese would listen to a proposal for negotiations.

---

*Another lamentable handicap was the State Department's purge of Chinese specialists because of attacks by Senator Joseph McCarthy. "We had trained a generation of dedicated Foreign Service officers to speak and understand Chinese, to cultivate the leaders of Chinese Communism, to understand what they planned," wrote journalist Theodore White,[3] who spent the Second World War in China. But when the United States needed these experts, they had been exiled to such posts as Kenya, Bonn, and Iceland. The best of them, John Stewart Service, had been dismissed from government and worked for a plumbing manufacturer in New York City for $9,000 a year.

After long discussions in the State Department, Acheson directed Charles Burton Marshall to pursue the lead, but in deepest secrecy.[5] "McCarthyism was then active," Marshall recollected, "and the MacArthur uproar was at the forefront of attention. Because of these touchy circumstances, utmost secrecy was applied. Five or six persons—no more—in the executive branch were informed. Only oral instructions were given."

The plan was for Marshall to travel incognito to Hong Kong and "hunt up four possible go-betweens" suggested by the CIA. Marshall carried a message intended to convince the Chinese that Washington and Peking should patch up their differences, that the Soviet Union was the "real strategic enemy" of both powers. Marshall was to remind the Communists of the U.S. attempt to keep open its embassy after the war, of its initial refusal to guarantee the Nationalists' Formosan sanctuary, and of its lack of direct involvement in the Civil War. Marshall was to recognize the new government's "psychic need for an external enemy," a role that fell to the United States. The "embittering effects" of the Korean War were bound to be felt a long time by both parties; nonetheless, "China must not become involved in the Soviet Union's side in a war against the U.S." Once hostilities wound down, Marshall foresaw an arm's length relationship during which "a substitute external enemy for Peking would probably materialize in the Soviet Union." This would provide a "logical occasion for moving towards overtly improved relations between the U.S. and China."

Unfortunately for Marshall, once he reached Hong Kong, he could not deliver his message. Two of the four contacts suggested by the CIA were of dubious reliability, contactable only through third-party cut-outs. (The use of a third party enabled Marshall to convey his message without any face-to-face contact, thereby affording the United States "deniability" in the event the Chinese decided to claim that their enemy was suing for peace.) Marshall thought them "too chancy" to entrust with a message. But eventually he did leave some information with the editor of a non-Communist newspaper and with a person who was a distant relative of Mao Tse-tung's wife. Still, these conduits had all the guaranteed efficacy of putting a note into a bottle and tossing it off the San Francisco docks. Later there was vague circumstantial evidence that Marshall's signal had reached the Chinese leadership. However, no overt response developed. So Washington knew it must look elsewhere for an opening to peace.

*   *   *

The Kennan Approach

In mid-May 1951 Freeman Matthews of the State Department had an idea.[6] George Kennan, formerly of the State Department's Policy Planning Staff and the foremost Russian expert in American government, had taken a leave of absence to the Institute for Advanced Study at Princeton to write a book on U.S.-USSR relations. Thus Kennan for the moment was not an official member of the American diplomatic community. He was a man the Soviets trusted; they respected him as a scholar and diplomat who spoke with objective candor, not propagandistic cant. With Acheson's approval, Matthews suggested that Kennan approach Yakov Malik, the Soviet UN ambassador, with a message roughly as follows: The United States and the USSR seemed on a collision course over Korea, something the Americans felt neither power wanted. Both countries seemed to be drawn further along by the Chinese. Would it not make better sense for all concerned if an armistice and cease-fire were sought in Korea, perhaps along the line of the present troop dispositions? Kennan was to ask how Moscow viewed the situation. As Acheson summarized the instructions, "If hostilities were to end, it was a good time to set about ending them."

Kennan wrote a longhand note to Malik, asking for a meeting without stating the purpose. Within hours Malik telephoned and asked Kennan to his summer house on Long Island for lunch. The meeting, on May 31, went smoothly—after an initial embarrassment when Malik dumped a tray of fruit and wine in his own lap. In a sense it was the day for which Kennan had trained since he became a diplomat in 1925. He spoke to the ambassador in fluent Russian; he approached the subject in roundabout fashion, knowing that Malik could make no commitment at an exploratory meeting on such a sensitive issue. Malik asked a few questions after hearing Kennan, then suggested they "meet again when he had had the opportunity to consider Kennan's points"—meaning he must consult Moscow.

That the Soviets were as eager as the Americans for peace was revealed by a prompt reply. Less than a week later, on ·June 5, Malik called Kennan to his office and told him the Soviet government wanted a peaceful solution in Korea. But because the Soviets had no direct involvement in the war—a hairsplitting technicality, but one which Kennan did not challenge—any approaches should be made to the Chinese and the North Koreans. "No doubt existed in any of our minds that the message was authentic," Acheson wrote in his memoirs. "It had, however, a sibylline quality which left us wondering what portended and what we should do next."

The first few days of June the State Department concealed the Malik approach from allied ambassadors for two reasons: to avoid raising false hopes and to avert public leaks that might abort the initiative. On June 5, for instance, Assistant Secretary Dean Rusk cautioned the ambassadors from putting any credence into "peace feeler" stories in the press.[7] On June 8 another assistant secretary, John Hickerson, solicited allied views on peace talks without mentioning the overture to Malik. The immediate question was whether President Truman should make any statement about peace terms and, if so, whether he should do so in the name of the sixteen nations fighting in Korea or unilaterally. The United States, Hickerson said, was wary about binding itself in advance; thus the thought was that specifications for a cease-fire "should be couched in general terms." Details should await a display by the enemy that he was ready to start talking. Hickerson did say that "if the enemy were willing to stop fighting and to accept a settlement in the general area of the 38th Parallel there would be a basis for discussion." But since the Chinese continued fighting, he saw no immediate hope for a cease-fire. Hickerson said further that "we had no draft of a statement, were willing to discuss all courses of possible action, and had no firm position in the matter except that the enemy must be convinced, and willing, to stop fighting before an honorable negotiated settlement could take place."

For American purposes, the important point was that the allied ambassadors had given Washington free rein to pursue an armistice. The ambassadors wanted to be told what was happening. But the mechanics would be entrusted to the State Department.

Now all Washington could do was await a further Soviet reply. The Soviets must talk with leaders in Peking and Pyongyang, so the silence did not alarm the State Department. Indeed, the answer arrived sooner than expected and through an unusual forum. The UN, since its inception, had sponsored a weekly public affairs radio broadcast open to any member nation. The Soviets had ignored it. Now Malik demanded time on the June 23 program. In his talk—delivered in what grammarians could call first-nation-personal—he said the "Soviet people" believed the war could be settled. Continuing, Malik said, "The Soviet people believe that, as a first step, discussions should be started among the belligerents for a cease-fire and an armistice providing for mutual withdrawal from the 38th Parallel." Can such a step be taken? Malik asked. "I think it can"—he answered his own question—"provided there is a sincere desire to put an end to the bloody fighting in Korea." (To American analysts, the word "bloody" indicated battlefield casualties were hurting the Chinese.)

Malik's response caught the State Department by total surprise.[8] When the United States learned Malik had asked for time on the UN radio, it expected to hear only propagandistic bombast. But to analysts the follow-up of the broadcast was significant. Soviet press and radio gave it what Dean Rusk called "good play," and two days later newspapers in Peking announced, in effect, that Chinese authorities approved Malik's proposal. But the Chinese thereafter were ambiguous. If Americans wanted peace, Peking Radio said, they could accept the Chinese terms. Malik's speech was also littered with ambiguities of the sort that enchant diplomats. When he mentioned the "Soviet people," did he in fact mean the "Soviet government"? He talked of "belligerents," yet denied any Soviet involvement, and the Chinese insisted on being called volunteers. According to Dean Rusk, "The degree of coordination and understanding between the Chinese Communists and the Soviet Union was another and very important unanswered question." Efforts to gain clarification from Malik were impossible because the ambassador was "indisposed," a diplomatic means of avoiding unwanted conversations. Rusk indicated some suspicions that the entire exercise might be propaganda: "[T]he men in the Kremlin are master propagandists, propaganda being a major instrument of their foreign policy."

The Soviet position came out in bits and pieces.[9] Alan Kirk, the U.S. ambassador in Moscow, after several requests obtained an audience with Andrei Gromyko, the deputy foreign minister. Gromyko felt that military representatives of the belligerents in Korea should conclude a military armistice limited to military matters. No political or territorial issues should be raised. Gromyko insisted he knew nothing of China's attitude on cease-fire talks.

The State Department interpreted the Soviet answer as a signal that the Chinese would welcome an approach.[10] The department moved to rally support of its allies. First, responding to an American request, the UN legal adviser Abraham H. Feller held that the United States had the right to conclude a cease-fire or armistice without UN authorization so long as the negotiations were limited to military matters and results were reported to the Security Council. Ambassadors of countries with troops in Korea unanimously favored negotiations.

But a snag developed at the Pentagon.[11] On June 28 Rusk outlined to a JCS-State meeting a recommendation that Ridgway broadcast an invitation to enemy commanders to a conference. General Vandenberg, the air chief, did not like the idea because it put the UN Command in the position of suing for peace. Vandenberg hotly questioned stopping the fighting when the enemy was being "hurt badly." But Bradley saw problems in public support of the war if the UN ignored this opportunity for peace. Collins and Sherman agreed, and Vandenberg did not press his argument. The JCS directed a staff group to work with State on drafting a broadcast for Ridgway.

Ridgway's statement, broadcast at eight o'clock in the morning of June 29, Tokyo time, was carefully honed:

As Commander in Chief of the United Nations Command I have been instructed to communicate to you the following:

I am informed that you may wish a meeting to discuss an armistice providing for the cessation of hostilities and all acts of armed force in Korea, with adequate guarantees for the maintenance of such armistice.

Upon the receipt of word from you that such a meeting is desired I shall be prepared to name my representative. I would also at that time suggest a date at which he could meet with your representative. I propose that such a meeting could take place aboard a Danish hospital ship in Wonsan harbor.

Dean Rusk explained the wording of the statement to allied ambassadors a few hours before Ridgway spoke.[12] The main purpose was to discover whether Communist commanders were interested in meeting in the field to discuss a cease-fire. "We felt that it was important to continue with the idea that the other side had taken the initiative in this matter," Rusk said, "but not say that they were suing for peace, thereby raising prestige obstacles. But we did desire to put the responsibility on the Communists, to get the idea across that they had brought the topic up."

Casting Ridgway as the UN commander was a means of avoiding use of the word "government," which Rusk said was "to accommodate the other side." There were other nuances intelligible only in the diplomatic world. "We did not pretend that Ridgway himself had been approached, but rather that he had been informed that an approach had been made. We did not suggest a date, but in order to move the whole matter ahead a step we had proposed a place, aboard a Danish hospital ship in the harbor of Wonsan, which, we felt, would be convenient to both sides." Although the ship was in Korea to serve the UN Command, the Danish government "would be happy" to make the vessel available, under its own flag, for the talks.

Would the allies be consulted as the talks progressed? asked Australian diplomat David Williamson McNichol. Rusk answered ambiguously. He would discuss developments "which could be reasonably discussed," but other things "might better be kept quiet." He did not think anyone would "like to see the peace we all hope for ruined by premature public debate."

To Rusk, starting talks was paramount. "Our choice . . . is clearly an acceptable cease-fire or an expansion of the conflict." No one disagreed.

The Communists replied to Ridgway's broadcast in relatively short order. On July 2 Peking Radio acknowledged Ridgway's message and continued:

. . . we are authorized to tell you that we agreed to suspend military activities and to hold peace negotiations, and that our delegates will meet with yours.

We suggest, in regard to the place for holding talks, that such talks be held at Kaesong, on the 38th Parallel.

If you agree to this, our delegates will be prepared to meet your delegates between July 10 and 15, 1951.

The message was signed by Kim Il Sung, as "commander in chief of the Korean People's Army," and General Peng Teh-huai, "commander in chief of the Chinese People's Volunteers."

Washington read the response with caution.[13] Dean Rusk found it peculiar that Kim Il Sung, the North Korean president, had joined a statement saying "we are authorized" to begin negotiations since he ostensibly was head of his government. There was hesitation about Kaesong as a meeting place, for military reasons.[14] Kaesong, in western Korea, lies a few miles south of the 38th parallel. In July 1951 it was under Communist control, with the nearest Eighth Army units ten miles away. The Joint Intelligence Committee of the JCS, although judging Kaesong an "acceptable" site, warned that it offered "definite political and psychological advantages to the enemy." The committee overlooked a more salient fact. Kaesong in past centuries had been the Korean capital, and holding talks there could be interpreted as evidence that the Communists held the upper hand in the war.

Several parts of the message, especially the cease-fire proposal, disturbed Ridgway.[15] He did not intend to surrender the five months he had spent rebuilding the Eighth Army and regaining the battlefield advantage. He cabled the JCS he considered a cease-fire "wholly unacceptable" and said he would reject it "unless otherwise instructed." Ridgway cited intelligence reports of a Chinese buildup leading to another offensive. If he must negotiate, Ridgway wanted the date advanced.

The JCS—their every step coordinated with the White House and the State Department—forbade Ridgway to urge an earlier meeting. Negotiations were in hand; they must not be permitted to escape. The JCS gave Ridgway specific language to use to reply to the Communist broadcast which made plain that the start of the talks did not mean an end to the fighting. Ridgway's dictated response said that "agreement on armistice terms has to precede cessation of hostilities." After some other public exchanges, both sides agreed to a meeting of liaison officers in Kaesong on July 8.

Another prenegotiation item was extricating the United States from an unwitting, yet potentially grave mistake of Dean Acheson. During the MacArthur hearings Acheson had talked imprecisely of a cease-fire along the 38th parallel—a line recognizing the then-military realities. But in the ensuing months the Eighth Army had extended its lines in a pie-shaped wedge beginning roughly north of Seoul on an easterly slant to about thirty-five miles north of the 38th parallel. The Imjin

River basin area, a maze of small streams and marshy lands west of Seoul and south of the 38th parallel, was bypassed by the advance since it was of no military value. Giving this worthless territory to the Communists was also of bargaining value. The JCS and the UN Command intended to negotiate an armistice which would leave American and ROK troops some miles north of the 38th parallel. The de facto abandonment of the Imjin River lands could be passed off as a "trade" of lands—the UN surrendering land south of the parallel in exchange for more valuable land north of the parallel. The center of the UN line was anchored by the so-called Iron Triangle, a series of high points between the towns of Pyonggang (not to be confused with Pyongyang, the North Korean capital, some miles to the northwest), Chorwon, and Kumhwa. When first sketched on a map as an objective for Ridgway's advance, the front was dubbed the Kansas Line, and it was here that the UN Command was to hold positions—with some minor fluctuations—for the two years remaining in the war.

To Ridgway, the deployment of his major forces during the cease-fire was a paramount concern.[16] He saw no military significance in the 38th parallel. In the first discussions of acceptable cease-fire terms the JCS and Ridgway envisioned a demilitarized zone twenty miles deep, centered on troop positions at the time of agreement. Thus Ridgway's forces would have to pull back some ten miles. Ridgway at one point considered a drive even farther north, to gain twenty miles beyond the Kansas Line. But after inspecting the terrain, he told the JCS that the drive, while "tactically and logistically feasible at present, would entail unacceptable casualties."*[17]

U.S. Peace Terms

In June the JCS had sent Ridgway extraordinarily detailed instructions, developed by Pentagon and State officials, on the conduct of the

*Lieutenant General James Van Fleet, who had succeeded Ridgway as EUSAK commander after MacArthur's firing, was to complain bitterly later that in June 1951 he had the Communists "on the run" and "I was crying to turn me loose."[18] Van Fleet said he wanted to pursue the Communists all the way to the Yalu. Ridgway agreed a further advance was possible, but it was not worth either the cost in casualties and the surrender of the strategic advantage then held by EUSAK. "Seizure of the line north to the Yalu . . . would have been merely the seizure of more real estate," Ridgway stated. "It would have greatly shortened the enemy supply lines and greatly lengthened our own. It would have widened our front from 110 miles to 420, and beyond that front would lie Manchuria and the whole mainland of Asia, in which all the wealth and manpower of this country could have been lost and dissipated."[19] Several of Van Fleet's cables to Ridgway in June 1951 show him endorsing the no-advance strategy he later criticized. Collins, for one, thought Van Fleet's belated complaints "political."

negotiations.[20] With only minor changes these instructions became the blueprint that Ridgway and his successors followed for the next two years. The top secret message began by listing "general policy."

> Our principal military interest in this armistice lies in a cessation of hostilities in Korea, an assurance against the resumption of fighting, and the protection of the security of United Nations forces. . . .
> We lack assurances either that the Soviet Union and Communist China are serious about concluding reasonable and acceptable armistice arrangements or that they are prepared to agree to an acceptable permanent settlement of the Korean problem. In considering such an armistice, therefore, it is of the utmost importance to reach agreements which would be acceptable to us over an extended period of time. . . .
> Discussions between you and the commander of opposing forces should be severely restricted to military questions; you should specifically not enter into discussion of a final settlement in Korea or consideration of issues unrelated to Korea, such as Formosa and the Chinese seat in the United Nations; such questions must be dealt with at government level.

The JCS wanted Ridgway to be tough, to advance initial bargaining positions beyond the irreducible conditions which the United States would accept. But he must not allow the talks to break down, except in case of enemy failure to accept his minimum position. He must avoid the appearance of "overreaching" in a way that would cause international opinion to question the good faith of the UN Command. U.S. prestige must not be engaged in any position to the extent that retreat to the minimum position would be impossible. The Joint Chiefs recognized that negotiating with the Communists would be difficult but assured Ridgway that this fact was "fully appreciated here."

Next, the JCS laid out the "minimum" U.S. position. The armistice would be confined to military matters in Korea and continue in effect until superseded by other arrangements. The respective commanders would order a cessation of hostilities. A demilitarized area would be established across Korea. Ground forces would either remain in position or, if in advance of the demilitarized zone, move to the rear. A "military armistice commission" with members chosen equally by either side would "have free and unlimited access to the whole of Korea" to oversee the truce. No air, ground, or naval reinforcements could be introduced, although the exchange of units or individual personnel on a man-for-man basis would be permitted. And there should be no increase in the levels of war equipment in Korea at the time the armistice became effective.

Mindful of Communist disdain for formal agreements elsewhere in the world, the JCS put great emphasis on the military armistice commission. Its freedom of operation was deemed "essential." It must be led by "competent assistants," designated by each commander, and have

"numbers sufficient to enable it to carry out its duties and functions."
The UN would not consider any armistice arrangements to be effective
until the commission was functioning.

On another "essential" point, the establishment of a demilitarized
zone, the JCS ordered Ridgway to do tough bargaining. The chiefs
desired a twenty-mile-wide zone "based generally upon the positions
of the opposing forces at the time the armistice arrangements are
agreed upon." (Here the UN hoped to skip around Dean Acheson's
careless language about a cease-fire line at the 38th parallel.) The JCS
told Ridgway:

> If it becomes necessary for purposes of bargaining for you to agree to
> some withdrawal of UN forces, you may do so to the extent that your
> present strong military position and your ability to carry out your military
> mission are not placed in jeopardy. . . .
>
> For purposes of negotiation, your initial demand might be that the
> Communist forces must withdraw twenty miles or more along the entire
> front.
>
> If the Communist commander refers to statements attributed to United
> States government officials that the United States is prepared to accept a
> settlement on or around the 38th Parallel, you should take the position that
> such statements are not applicable to an armistice in the field but are
> properly the subject for governmental negotiation as to a political settle-
> ment.
>
> Further, you should state that in any event the military arrangements
> you propose involve certain areas under Communist military control south
> of the 38th Parallel [the Imjin River floodplains northwest of Seoul, as
> noted above] and certain areas under UN control north thereof. The net
> result, while military in character, does not prejudice political and territo-
> rial questions which would be for further considerations by appropriate
> authorities.

Another point for negotiation, seemingly innocuous at the time, involved prisoners of war, who would be "exchanged on a one-for-one
basis as expeditiously as possible." Until the POW exchange was completed, Red Cross representatives would be permitted "to visit all POW
camps to render such assistance as they can." Dean Rusk told allied
ambassadors on July 3 the man-for-man POW swap was necessary
"since a wholesale repatriation of prisoners . . . would virtually restore
intact to North Korea forces equivalent to the number it possessed at
the time of the aggression and thus entirely change the military situation." The situation was "difficult" because the UN held some 150,000
Communist POWs, and the Communists "less than 10,000 UN personnel."

The JCS directive held the seeds of future settlement. But it also
contained bargaining points over which the Communist and the UN

were to haggle seemingly endlessly the next two years—first, on the location of the cease-fire line and, secondly, on the disposition of prisoners. But in late June and early July 1951 neither point seemed significant. The important fact was that a negotiated end to the war now seemed in sight.

To the Truce Table

In selecting the head of the UN negotiating team, General Matthew Ridgway wanted a senior officer with the self-control to endure expected hours of Communist abuse without losing his temper and ending the talks with a harsh reply. UN strategy would be orchestrated in Washington, and the format of each day's UN presentation detailed in cables. Ridgway expected the Communists to try to talk the UN into submission, to win their case through ennui. Ridgway wanted an adversary, as he told one associate, "who can sit for six hours and neither blink nor think of taking a break for a pee."

So Ridgway decided upon Admiral C. Turner Joy, a much-decorated veteran of the Second World War now in charge of naval forces in the Far East. Joy spent his nonwar career in explosives development. His war experience led him to conclude that the best way to beat an enemy was to destroy him. As did other American commanders, he personally hated the Communists and their ideology, and he was uncomfortable with the political strictures of the Korean War, but he did his job well and without public complaint.

Ridgway rounded out the UN negotiating team with Second World War combat veterans. Major General Henry I. Hodes, the deputy chief of staff of the Eighth Army, had led an infantry regiment in Europe. Major General Laurence C. Craigie, vice commander of the Far East Air Force, had commanded a fighter wing in North Africa. The best known to the public, perhaps, was bluff Rear Admiral Arleigh A. Burke, the deputy chief of staff of the Far East Naval Forces, famed as "31-Knot" Burke because of his daring handling of destroyers in the Pacific campaign. The ROKs chose Major General Paik Sun Yup, a corps commander who had impressed the Americans as "perhaps the most able officer in the ROK Army."

Asian experts gave Ridgway's team painstaking psychological advice on dealing with the Chinese and Koreans. Care must be taken not to cause them to lose face unnecessarily. Orientals desired a "golden bridge" of withdrawal they could use to back away from an uncomfortable position without appearing to abandon it.[21] The necessity of English, Korean, and Chinese translations meant semantical and linguistical problems. Ridgway cautioned about "basic and sustained misunderstandings arising from inaccuracies in translation."

Ridgway held high hopes for the negotiations. If the team could cap the Communist military defeat with skillful handling of the armistice, "history may record that Communist military aggression reached its high water mark in Korea, and that thereafter Communism itself began its recession in Asia."

Preliminary Skirmishes

The UN liaison party, headed by Air Force Colonel Andrew J. Kinney, flew by helicopter into Kaesong on July 8, and Communist propaganda gamesmanship began immediately.[22] The town, a small, dusty cluster of buildings on the lee side of low mountains, had served as a rest station for travelers on the main road from Seoul to the north. Although Kaesong was supposedly neutral for the meeting, Communist soldiers brandishing machine guns surrounded the unarmed Americans and menacingly waved the weapons for Communist reporters and photographers. To the Communists, the UN was suing for peace, and the Communists intended to make the most they could of this "fact."

Kinney thought fleetingly of ending the mission and returning to Seoul for further instructions but decided to proceed. He unwittingly won the next round. The Communists led his party to a teahouse which was to be the meeting place, an ornate one-story building with a curving tile roof and sculptured bonsai trees in the front courtyard. The Communists had hauled in wooden conference tables, and armed soldiers stood around on the outside, as if guarding the place. The building's once-graceful lines were marred by bullet and shell marks, and several outbuildings had been destroyed. But it was the most pleasant structure Kaesong offered. Before the Communists could direct them, the Americans marched into the teahouse and took the row of seats facing the south. There was an awkward silence, and the Communists gestured, no, no, you must sit in the other row of chairs, the ones facing north. "We are comfortable here," Kinney said, and refused to move. Later he learned that according to Oriental tradition in peace negotiations, the conquering nation faces the south and the defeated party the north.

The first exchanges contained no hint of cordiality from either side. Kinney presented the list of UN delegates and asked the same of the Communists. Whereupon the Communists recessed for three hours, apparently to review the UN list and select equal-ranking officers.

During the recess Kinney refused Communist offers of food, liquor, and cigarettes, not wishing to accept even minor gifts under the scrutiny of Red cameras and reporters. The UN party ate the lunch it had brought.

After the break the Communists announced their delegation would be headed by Colonel General Nam Il of the Korean People's Army. They proposed that the first meeting be on July 10, two days later, also in Kaesong, and promised to clear the road from Panmunjom, a frontline village six miles to the east. UN vehicles would be marked with white flags, and the Communists would ensure the safety of UN personnel en route to and in the conference area. All members of the UN group save the delegates would wear arm brassards for identification.

When Kinney left Kaesong, he felt uneasy that negotiations were to be conducted in Communist-controlled territory. The experiences that day convinced him the Communists intended to exact maximum propaganda. Kinney told Ridgway and Joy of his concerns. But the die was cast; the UN would proceed, even though Kinney's warnings alerted the delegation on what they should expect.

Thus neither Admiral Joy nor anyone else was surprised on the morning of July 10 when Communist "escort" vehicles met his convoy at Panmunjom. Three vehicles filled with Communist officers in full dress uniforms swung into the front of his convoy and preceded it into Kaesong. Communist photographers thronged by the roadside, and escort officers waved victory salutes. This time the Communists resolved the seating issue by barring the UN delegates from entering the teahouse by the north doors.[23] When Joy and the others stepped inside, the Communists already occupied the psychologically advantageous seats. The Communists also took not-so-subtle revenge on Admiral Joy for the earlier slight. When he sat at the table, he sank almost from sight. The Communists had given him a chair much shorter than normal. Across the table General Nam Il towered a full foot over the admiral. "Chain-smoking Nam Il puffed his cigarette in obvious satisfaction as he glowered down on me, an apparently torpedoed animal," Joy wrote later. Before Joy obtained a larger chair, "Communist photographers had exposed reels of film." Joy felt that in isolation such tactics were childish. "It should be borne in mind, however, that a great multitude of these maneuvers can add up to a propaganda total of effective magnitude."

There was worse. Heavily armed Communist guards stalked the grounds around the teahouse, following closely any UN person who stepped outside. During a recess a guard pointed a burp gun at Joy and "growled menacingly." One proudly explained to Colonel Kinney that his medal was for "killing forty Americans."

Joy knew he faced negotiators with political as well as military expertise. American intelligence had screened the list of Communist negotiators and told Joy quite a bit about them. Nam Il, the supposed leader, was Korean by birth only. Son of a family that had fled to Siberia to escape the Japanese, he was a Soviet citizen who had spent most of his life in the USSR. As a Soviet captain he fought the Germans at Stalingrad, and later, as chief of staff of a division, he helped take Warsaw. After returning to North Korea, Nam Il became minister of education and converted the ministry into a key propaganda agency of the government. In 1950 he helped the Defense Ministry plan the attack on the South. (In August 1953, reverting to his political role, Nam Il became foreign minister.) Nam Il astounded Russian and Eastern European advisers to the North Korean Army with his tremendous capacity for alcohol.[24] Pawel Monat, a Polish colonel who served in Korea (and later defected to the West), once sent Nam Il three dozen "giant" bottles of vodka as a gift; the general consumed them within a month and inquired about getting more.

Nam Il was ridden with considerable nervous energy. Seldom would he display emotion; occasionally his face flushed with anger, but his expression most often was feigned astonishment. Joy soon recognized that Nam Il, despite his title, was subordinate to the Chinese general Hsieh Fang. Of murky background, Hsieh was believed to have studied at military academies in Japan and Moscow and to have played a major role in the kidnapping of Chiang Kai-shek by the Chinese Communists in 1936. Subsequent developments in Hsieh's career suggest Soviet trust in his reliability. From 1940 to 1945 Hsieh served the Japanese government in occupied China. Immediately after peace he became chief of propaganda for the northeastern Chinese provinces. Such progression is unusual in the Soviet intelligence services; a man who has served "the other side," even though under direct orders, is usually considered contaminated once the assignment ends and is either liquidated or assigned a meaningless job. But in 1951 Hsieh was put into a position of the utmost importance to Soviet foreign policy.

A spare and angular man with close-cropped hair, Hsieh impressed —even unnerved—Joy, who remembered the Shakespearean lines "Yond Cassius has a lean and hungry look . . . such men are dangerous." He spoke without reference to his colleagues. If he had business to state, he did so without burdening the record with propagandistic statements. Joy decided Hsieh made the decisions for the Red delegation.

The other member of the delegation who spoke was Lee Sang Jo, a North Korean general who had fought in China against the Nationalists and returned to Pyongyang with the first group of Soviet-oriented officers in 1945. Chunky and often physically filthy, Lee had one impressive characteristic: He would permit flies to crawl over his face without brushing them away.[25] "Apparently he thought this showed iron self-control," Joy said. "For my part, I concluded he was simply accustomed to having flies on his person."

Joy's immediate concern was to put the UN bargaining position on the record, if only to satisfy political exigencies.[26] He knew well the admonition from the JCS that the talks were to be broken off only under duress. The Communist arrogance infuriated him. He wished to gather his fellow officers and march out of the teahouse. But he had no choice. So he carried out his instructions, beginning with a long statement of the UN position.

Joy said, bluntly, that the UN delegates intended to discuss military matters pertaining to Korea, and nothing else, either political or economic. So far as the UN was concerned, the fighting would continue until agreement was reached on an armistice, and the armistice commission at work. He then presented a nine-point agenda drawn up by the UN delegates:

1. Adoption of the agenda;
2. Location of and authority for International Committee of the Red Cross to visit POW camps;
3. Limitation of discussion to purely military matters related to Korea only;
4. Cessation of hostilities and acts of armed forces in Korea under conditions that would assure against resumption of hostilities and acts of armed force in Korea;
5. Agreement on a demilitarized zone across Korea;
6. Composition, authority and functions of a military armistice commission;
7. Agreement on principle of inspection within Korea by military inspection teams;
8. Composition and functions of these teams; and
9. Arrangements pertaining to prisoners of war.

General Nam Il countered with a proposed return to the June 1950 status quo, with both sides withdrawing to the 38th parallel and all "foreign" troops leaving Korea. He wanted an immediate cease-fire and the establishment of a twenty-kilometer demilitarized zone along the 38th parallel. Once this was done, POWs would be exchanged, and peace would be at hand.

To Joy, the Communist proposals were overly simplistic. He wished a formal agenda, in which disputed points were laid out, one by one, for discussion and resolution. Removing "foreign" troops from Korea was a political matter, for the United States would not abrogate its right to keep armed forces in a friendly nation by invitation. Accepting the Communist terms would re-create the situation that had prevailed when the North Koreans invaded a year ago and would tilt the military balance to the Chinese; their "terms" offered no verification that Peking's "volunteers" would be withdrawn.

The next session, on July 11, was equally unproductive. This time the main argument was over Red Cross visits to POW camps. Nam Il quickly termed the subject "political" and chastised the UN for raising it. (Even the official U.S. Army history of the talks agreed with Nam Il: "As long as the UN delegation insisted on excluding non-military matters, the Communists had a point."[27])

Joy also managed to mishandle instructions from Ridgway, who told him to "make an issue" of freedom of movement in the conference area, teeming gun-waving Communist guards, and access for Western press correspondents.[28] Otherwise, the UN would not negotiate further. Unfortunately for Joy, he read the statement, then added that he desired an "answer . . . the first thing in the morning." Such was not what Ridgway had in mind, as he promptly told Joy in a scorching cable. Ridgway's "single idea" was that Joy read the statement and hand it to the Communist side. He wanted Communist action, not comment. The statement was a declaration of intent, "explicit and unambiguous." Communist propagandists were exploiting the talks; the Western press was rawhiding Ridgway because of its exclusion from Kaesong. That evening Ridgway dressed down Joy severely and warned him that he would do as told or else. Then, characteristically, Ridgway told Joy he started with a clean slate; as he wrote in his diary that evening, the incident was now "water over the dam." But he did "point out that I might in the future desire to follow the same tactics, and therefore I thought it important that there be a complete understanding between us."

Joy recouped the next day.[29] When Nam Il remained adamant about admitting the Western press, Joy forcefully told him that the UN delegation would return with the reporters or not at all. The stand put the burden squarely on the Communists: They must accept either the newsmen or a delay in the negotiations. But the Communists pressed the UN to the limit. When the newsmen appeared at Panmunjom as part of the UN convoy, the Communists refused the vehicles passage. True to his threat, Joy ordered the convoy turned around. Two days of talks between the liaison staffs followed, and the Communists capitulated. Western newsmen would be admitted, and armed soldiers would be kept away from a five-mile circle around Kaesong and the road connecting the truce site and Panmunjom.

Nonetheless, the overall Communist attitude raised doubts in Washington as to whether they wished serious talks. Briefing allied ambassadors on July 12, Dean Rusk said that it had become "evident that the other side was going to make propaganda capital out of certain . . . matters of form we had been prepared to overlook." By "negotiating by propaganda broadcast," the Communists had "nailed themselves publicly to a fixed position from which they can hardly retreat." Rusk thought this showed "they entered the talks in anything but a negotiating frame of mind." American intelligence showed a "continued and substantial buildup of enemy troops at the front."

To Joy's chagrin, resolving press access to Kaesong did not mean progress on other issues.[30] It soon became apparent that the Communists sought an agenda composed of "conclusions favorable to their basic objectives," whereas the Americans saw the agenda as a list of topics to be discussed. As an analogy, Joy said Americans meeting to arrange a baseball game might adopt an agenda as follows: (1) place the game is to be played; (2) time the game is to start; and (3) selection of umpires. The Communist agenda would be: (1) agreement that the game is to be played in Shanghai; (2) at night; and (3) with Chinese officials as umpires.

The agenda haggling lasted for ten sessions, which flowed "with all the speed of a stiff concrete mix," Joy said. Each statement made by Nam Il had to be translated into English and Chinese; each Joy statement, into Chinese and Korean. But the Communists gradually yielded. On July 16 they agreed to eliminate specific mention of the 38th parallel from the agenda and suggested the more general phrase "establishment of a military demarcation line between both sides to establish a demilitarized zone as a basic condition for a cease-fire." Joy reported an improvement in tone, and he felt the Communist side had been instructed to narrow the gap on the agenda. Interpreting developments for allied ambassadors on July 16, Dean Rusk said the Communists saw the Kaesong talks as a permanent peace settlement, especially on withdrawal of foreign troops. Rusk considered this issue "not a suitable topic for military armistice discussions." He rejected the Communist insinuation that the Koreans settle their problems themselves. This would guarantee a prompt resumption of the war once UN troops left.

As July progressed, the Communists modified their stand on troop withdrawal. "Foreign troops" were "those troops sent to Korea under the instructions of their government." Such could not be accepted by the UN, for the Chinese still insisted their troops in Korea were volunteers. So the Chinese changed the definition: Foreign troops were soldiers "not Korean and not in the Korean army." Dean Rusk remained suspicious, for the change "left the way open for the Chinese to sidestep into the North Korean Army." Rusk called the issue "troublesome," but he told allied ambassadors on July 18 the United States would work toward compromise language.

On July 19 Nam Il challenged the bargaining faith of the UN. "War is not travel and troops are not tourists," he said. "Should the cease-fire be ordered and armistice achieved, [and] the foreign armed forces still stay where they are, it is clear that the intention . . . is not . . . to let them enjoy the scenic beauties of Korea. . . ." The UN delegation felt the statement was intended to create political pressure to force the UN to accept the Communist agenda item.

General Ridgway had complained in early July of press talk about "Let's get the boys back home" and "the war-weary troops."[31] Ridgway intended to stamp out such talk in his command. "If this be 'thought control,' then I am for it, heart and soul," he told the JCS. "To condone it would be a cowardly surrender of everything for which we have fought and plan to fight." But Ridgway could not dampen press speculation that an armistice was at hand. The State Department asked allied ambassadors for forbearance; the United States did not want to be pressured into yielding on substantive issues, as the Communists clearly were pressing it to do.[32] The Australian ambassador, Percy C. Spencer, apparently expressing the sentiment of the other envoys, strongly agreed. If the United States decided to break off negotiations on the troop withdrawal issue, "the public must be prepared" for such a contingency. However, the United States did not intend to get into a propaganda war with the Communists; any public statements would come from Ridgway, not officials in Washington and elsewhere. (The State Department did notice that Soviet propaganda media simply repeated North Korean statements on the armistice talks without adding any commentary that would commit the Soviet government to any given position.)

The first weeks of the talks the Chinese brought reinforcements and supplies into North Korea at an accelerated pace.[33] Intelligence estimates in mid-July put Communist strength at seventy-one divisions and three brigades, composed of almost 500,000 men (61,000 North Koreans at the front, 159,000 at the rear; 65,000 Chinese at the front, 200,000 at the rear, plus 7,000 guerrillas). Supplies arrived at the rate of about 600 tons daily in excess of daily requirements; on the basis of past battle experience, the Communists amassed enough munitions to support a sustained attack by forty-five divisions for nine to eleven days, or a seventy-one-division attack for four to seven days. The longer the talks dragged, therefore, the stronger the military suspicion that the Chinese were using the battle lull to prepare for strong offensives before the summer ended.

Ridgway proposed using superior American air strength to give the Chinese an incentive to end their "obstructive and stubborn" tactics.[34] On July 21 he told the JCS he intended an "all out air strike on Pyongyang," employing 270 bombers and fighter planes. Leaflet drops in advance of the raids would guarantee against "unnecessary killing of non-combatants." The raids would strike a "devastating blow . . . [at] the . . . buildup of supplies and personnel in . . . this . . . key area." But the JCS thought the raids "questionable at this time."[35] Truman agreed. The raids were canceled. Ridgway now knew that he could not back firmness at the bargaining table with firmness on the battlefield.

But on the key bargaining issue of troop withdrawal, Ridgway would not budge.[36] On July 20 he told the JCS he intended to instruct Admiral Joy to inform the Communists that unless they dropped the troop withdrawal demand, the UN would recess the talks until something "new and constructive" was heard. Ridgway set a deadline for the Communists of seven o'clock on the morning of July 21. He told the JCS he was confident the enemy would not "break off" talks over the issue.

The JCS decided to clear Ridgway's proposal with the State Department.[37] Because of Tokyo-Washington time differences, State heard the proposal only two hours before Ridgway's deadline. Dean Rusk vehemently objected. The proposed action might cause a break in negotiations and challenge the Communists' prestige so directly they would find it difficult to concede. Further, the action could create the public appearance of a major concession by the Communists. The JCS told Ridgway to withhold his ultimatum pending further instructions.

In a lengthy cable sent on July 21, incorporating both State and Defense department views and approved by President Truman, Ridgway was assured of complete backing on his position on troop withdrawal but was also warned that it could be a "breaking point" because of the strong stands taken by both sides.[38] "It is important that, if and when breakdown of negotiations occurs, the onus for failure shall rest clearly and wholly upon the Communists," the JCS said. The message also outlined new bargaining strategy that would permit the enemy to air his views on troop withdrawal unilaterally without any stated UN agreement to accept them.

The Communists agreed to drop their insistence on troop withdrawal from the agenda in return for assurance that the subject would be discussed at governmental level after the armistice. At a session on July 26 the parties agreed. Thus the fifth agenda item became wondrously broadly worded "recommendations to the governments of the countries concerned on both sides." Agreeing on the agenda had consumed ten full meetings of the delegations, plus innumerable staff sessions. Now the question in Washington and other UN capitals became: Would the Communists offer a counterconfrontation in an attempt to regain the upper hand in the talks?

Drawing a Demarcation Line

With the troop withdrawal issue tacitly put aside, the UN negotiators hoped to speed the pace of the talks. They were sorely disappointed. Immediately the Communists renewed their demand that the 38th parallel be the demarcation line when the truce was signed. To call the Communists obstinate is to understate; regardless of the UN pleas, the Communists pointed to the parallel, said that was the only line they would consider, and refused to discuss the issue further. The parallel "was consistent with historical fact and basic to the armistice talks." The war had begun with one belligerent violating the line (the ROKs, by

Communist account). The war therefore could not be stopped with one belligerent in violation of the line. Finally, since no stable battle line existed, the 38th parallel stood as the best demarcation point since each belligerent had forces on both sides of the line.

The UN delegation rebutted with arguments that the Communists seemingly could not hear. Would the Communists have accepted the 38th parallel as a demarcation line in July and August 1950, when the UN Command struggled to hold the Pusan Perimeter? Would the UN have accepted the 38th parallel in November 1950, when its forces were on the brink of the Yalu? In terms of military reality, Joy argued, there were three zones in the war: the air zone, which the UN controlled up to the Yalu; the sea zone, also under unchallenged UN control; and, finally, the ground zone, which the UN controlled beyond the 38th parallel. Withdrawal of American air and naval forces would be the equivalent of the withdrawal of North Korean and Chinese troops far to the north of their present positions. So the UN delegation pressed its demand for a demilitarized zone twenty miles in depth, its southern border following roughly the present battle line. In return, the UN would halt air activity from the northern border of the line to the Yalu, and naval actions from the southern border of the line north to the Tumen River on the east coast and the Yalu on the west. The United States, Dean Rusk told allied ambassadors on July 27, intended to stand firm on these terms. He heard no dissent.

The Communists responded with the harshest language of the talks. "Seeing that you make such a completely absurd and arrogant statement," Nam Il demanded of Joy on July 28, "for what actually have you come here? Have you come here to negotiate for peace or just to look for an excuse for continuing the war?" Joy bit his tongue and replied to Nam's "inappropriate, irrelevant and discourteous question" only because an answer had been specifically requested. The very presence of the UN delegation at Kaesong evidenced its intent to seek an honorable and equitable basis for an end of hostilities. Joy would not tolerate further billingsgate from the Communists. If Nam Il persisted in his "rudeness, discourtesy and immature remarks," the UN would conclude that the Communists were not bargaining seriously and that the "prospect for peace in Korea would be greatly dimmed." (Here Joy relied upon the U.S. intelligence estimate that the Communists wished the talks to continue and that they would eventually yield if pressed.)

Whereupon Nam Il changed his tone to "patient reasonableness," dropping the strident language, although still maintaining his previous bargaining position. (The suspicious Joy decided that Nam was either probing for a compromise offer by the UN or awaiting further instructions from Peking. By now the admiral had detected a pattern in the Communist arguments. After a one- or two-day break Nam Il would speak firmly on the issue at hand. But if the UN offered any new ideas, he would filibuster away the rest of the day, obviously powerless to bargain without specific authorization from superiors.)

So there the talks lodged, neither side willing to talk about an alternative demilitarized line (although the UN delegates, in contingency planning, were prepared to discuss kinks and curls in any final line, subject to the battlefield situation at the time of signing). In fact, at one point on August 1, Admiral Joy "expressed a willingness to discuss any line related to the present military situation other than the 38th Parallel."

"I have made my stand already," Nam Il replied. The Communists' willingness to surrender territory south of the parallel "with military value" was evidence of good faith. (Actually, all the Communists held below the parallel were the useless river estuary lands west of Seoul.) The UN's proposed line was "favorable for defensive purposes only to the UN forces and [was] therefore not equal for both sides."

Would the Communists make any other suggestions for a line? Joy asked. No, Nam Il replied, his stand was "unshakable."

But Joy kept at his task, hopeful that logic would eventually find a crevice in Nam Il's position. The UN held twice as much territory north of the parallel as the Communists did south of it. But the UN was not interested in real estate; its concern was military security during the armistice. The 38th parallel was unrealistic because it was "not recognizable from the ground," the cause of many prewar border incidents.

The first two days of August Peking Radio began broadcasts which U.S. intelligence interpreted as signs the Communists were preparing world public opinion for a break in the talks. One broadcast stated that "American and Rhee troops violated the Kaesong neutral zone on fourteen occasions." There were also accusations that the UN delegates were "using threatening attitudes towards the North Korean delegates such as is used toward a defeated country."*

Joy felt his deepest frustration on August 11, after listening to Nam Il present what he called a "well worn argument" for the 38th parallel. Nam ended by stating, "At present we have nothing more to say."

"Neither do we," Joy responded. The two sides sat in absolute silence for two hours and eleven minutes. Joy broke it. "Would you like to say something?"

"At present I have nothing to say," Nam Il replied. As the meeting broke up, he stated he intended to continue discussing the 38th parallel the next day.

Reporting the episode to Washington, Ridgway saw "no evidence of change or likely change in position of enemy."[39]

---

*Having read the previously top secret policy directives from the JCS to the UN negotiators, as well as Ridgway's private cable file, I find this claim ludicrous. Truman and everyone else in official Washington wanted out of Korea. Ridgway kept a tight rein on Kaesong; in view of his penchant for obedience, I think it unlikely that any underling would have done anything to give the Communists a pretext for breaking the talks.

[The UN delegation] strongly believes that now is the time to intensify efforts to influence world opinion by pointing out the arbitrary, intransigent and unreasoning attitude of Communist delegation and their obvious desire to deadlock negotiations if UN does not meet their original demand. ... The record to date is devoid of evidence of Communist good faith and is recently replete with evidence of intention to force us either to yield on issue of 38th parallel, or to break off the conference.

Once again Ridgway was ready to risk a break in the talks to force the Communists from their intransigence. He intended to instruct his delegation to meet the Reds once more—on August 11—and tell them the UN "flatly, formally and finally" refused to consider the 38th parallel as the demarcation line. It would discuss a line based upon the present military situation or put the truce line issue aside for the moment. If no satisfactory response was heard in seventy-two hours, the UN "will consider the conference terminated by the deliberate act of the Communists." Ridgway asked JCS approval "or other instructions" by FLASH message.*

The Joint Chiefs quickly curbed Ridgway.[40] "Your instructions require that you not break off meetings without previous instructions from Washington," General Bradley cabled on August 10. "You should continue meetings until further guidance received." The JCS, although sympathetic to Ridgway's frustrations, worried that he would put himself into a position in which the Communists would call his bluff and break the talks. A long cable dispatched on August 11, approved by the President, reiterated Washington's desire to keep the talks going.

In view of possibility of communications delays and of necessity for highest level consideration, you should not set in motion any action contrary to above directives without prior JCS authorization. Termination of discussions is of such governmental importance as not to be left to exigencies of clearances or communications by some deadline hour.

If the talks did fail, the JCS wished the Communists to be clearly responsible. Any issue causing failure must be one that would bring world condemnation to the Reds. "It will not be enough for us to say that Communists are at fault because they do not agree with us," the JCS said. "It must be abundantly clear that we have used persistence and patience to obtain agreement on terms which will appeal to world opinion as reasonable and just." The chiefs noted the Communists had some justification for their hard-line stance: Both Secretary Acheson and Secretary-General Lie, in statements in the spring, had misled the Communists into expecting the UN to accept the 38th parallel as the

---

*FLASH meant that a reply was expected within the hour, with a yes or no answer, and explanations to follow.

demarcation line. The Communists would need time to adjust. In the meanwhile, Ridgway should be patient and firm.*

The Communists concurrently began applying pressures of their own by accusing UN forces of violating the neutral area around Panmunjom. In mid-July they had charged that UN soldiers had fired toward Panmunjom, and a few days later that UN planes strafed one of their trucks near Kaesong. Then, during the lunch recess on August 6, a company of armed Chinese soldiers marched through the truce area, within 100 yards of the house assigned the UN delegation.[41] Joy protested heatedly to Nam Il that no troops other than military police were to be permitted within half a mile of the area. Ridgway thought the episode serious enough to warrant a telecon with Washington. He wished an explanation and an apology, the alternative being an end to the talks. The language of diplomacy, Ridgway said, was "inappropriate and ineffective" in the talks. "To sit down with these men and deal with them as representatives of an enlightened and civilized people is to deride one's own dignity and to invite the disaster their treachery will inevitably bring upon us." He intended to tell his delegates to stand up to the Communists, "to employ such language and methods as these treacherous savages cannot fail to understand, and understanding, respect." He cited numerous examples of insulting language in the transcripts and repeated his belief that the Communists considered an armistice a shortcut to the attainment of their objectives at minimum cost.

Truman, however, was not prepared to rupture the talks.[42] He clung to a belief that the Chinese were "sick of the whole thing and wished they had never gotten into Korea." Ridgway was ordered to remove the threat; he should demand an explanation and agree to resume talks when one was given and the enemy agreed to follow the rules.[43] The Communists offered a low-keyed explanation of their "mistake," calling it "minor." The reply did not satisfy Ridgway, who again asked Washington to refuse to continue negotiations until he received firm assurances against future violations.[44] That failing, he wanted a new site where the UN itself could "guarantee against violations." But Washington again took the cautious tack. "To impose new conditions now would be difficult to justify in many important quarters," the JCS cabled Ridgway.[45] He should send his negotiators back to Panmunjom but warn the enemy against any further violations.

Having pushed Washington and found no resistance, the Communists continued their charges of "violations," making new charges almost

---

*In his memoirs Acheson conceded the Communists were genuinely surprised that the UN would not settle at the 38th parallel. He explained away his critical diplomatic blunder by saying that the Communists "would never imagine that what appeared to be trickery was wholly inadvertent on our part. It was exactly the sort of maneuver in which they would have delighted."

daily.[46] The most elaborate came around midnight on August 22, when Colonel Chang, a Chinese liaison officer, radioed Colonel A. J. Kinney of the UN delegation to claim a bombing and strafing of the Kaesong conference site by American planes. With Joy's approval, Kinney took a party to the scene in a drenching rainstorm. When he arrived at about 1:45 A.M., he found Chang and a group of Communist reporters and photographers, all in a "mood of high excitement."

According to Chang, "everyone" at Kaesong had heard a plane approach, then a bomb explode. He insisted on showing suspect "physical evidence": a rumpled piece of metal which Kinney said resembled an aircraft oil tank and a small depression in the ground perhaps thirty inches wide and ten inches deep. There was no evidence of burning, and Kinney suspected the hole could have been made by a partially buried grenade. The Chinese also talked vaguely of rocket fire, although they could produce no evidence. Kinney also noted the "napalm tank" was flush-riveted, whereas ones used by the Far East Air Force were of rougher construction since they were used only once. He soon had had enough of the Chinese show.

"I'm getting very impatient with this nonsense," Kinney said. Whereupon a Chinese soldier stepped forward to claim he had seen an American plane "with its lights on" during the raid—an absurdity, to Kinney, because no pilot goes into combat with his plane illuminated. As Kinney turned to walk away, Chang thrust his hand into his tunic pocket and pulled out a sheaf of prepared notes. Armistice talks were being suspended indefinitely, he declared.

The propagandistic nature of the predawn confrontation and the clumsily fabricated "evidence" convinced Ridgway the Communists had contrived the episode as a pretext for ending the talks. He speculated about the reason. Ridgway felt the Communists wished to stall progress on an armistice until talks opened later that year on the Japanese peace treaty in the hope that Peking could somehow wheedle something out of the settlement—a truce in Korea, perhaps, in exchange for a role in postwar Japan. But the episode seemed clearly tailored to put blame for the break on the UN.

Matthew Ridgway did not care. His Eighth Army continued to make good progress in the field, even though it did not attempt any significant advances.[47] The most important gain during the summer was a sharp increase in the effectiveness of the ROK Army. A training program produced officers and noncoms whose ranks depended upon military skills, not the whim of a political or local warlord. UN artillery gradually built up to the point that Chinese mass assaults became mass suicides. Now seasoned in battle, American and ROK troops no longer panicked at the sound of Chinese attack bugles and whistles. They burrowed deeper into reinforced bunkers and called in hails of artillery shells. And as winter approached the bleak Asian countryside, improved logistical support meant that the UN Command would be better outfitted to endure the cold.

Nonetheless, disturbing omens were seen on the battlefield. The last weeks of August and the first few days of September the Communists markedly increased their troop strength by 61,000 men to a total of around 700,000. Further, many of the new arrivals were what U.S. intelligence called "Soviet and/or other Caucasian troops."[48] The Soviets had assignments only a scant step removed from combat roles: antiaircraft and coastal defense specialists, security forces, counterespionage agents, military advisers, and signal and radar personnel. The other Caucasians, although of undetermined national origin, served with artillery, medical, and service units. Because of spotty intelligence coverage, neither the CIA nor the Far East Command would rule out flatly the possibility that the Soviets were on the fighting front. Another disturbing factor was that enemy air activity seemed moving steadily southward, an indication of mounting Communist air strength. As U.S. diplomats told allied ambassadors at a Washington briefing on October 2, the Communists had effective air control over northwestern Korea. Nonetheless, unless peace was reached, Assistant Secretary Dean Rusk noted a feeling in the UN Command "that this coming winter will be a serious one for the enemy."

Diplomatically the United States and its allies let the Chinese know in a hurry they could expect no role in the Japanese conference. Branded an aggressor by the UN, China would not be welcome at any peace table until it ended the Korean War. Militarily the Chinese leadership apparently realized within a very few weeks that its forces were ill-prepared to spend another winter on the Korean battlefield. They soon looked for a pretext to mask a resumption of the talks they had so peremptorily abandoned.

Ironically they found an opening via an admitted accidental strafing of Kaesong by an American fighter plane. No casualties resulted, and the UN immediately apologized for the incident, attributing it to pilot error. This was on September 10.

Ridgway, meanwhile, had been sparring with Washington over his demand that the UN refuse to return to Kaesong under any circumstances. To return to the old site under the old rules would simply invite more of the same troubles. He wanted the authority to demand that the Communists accept another site; otherwise, no further talks should be held. Once again Ridgway found Washington nervous about appearing responsible for ending the talks. In a series of cable exchanges during the first days of September the administration reluctantly authorized Ridgway to propose a new site which afforded expectations of reasonable security. But the JCS still avoided giving him blanket permission to refuse to return to Kaesong.

The September 10 accidental bombing came in the midst of these maneuvers, and the JCS immediately saw the opportunity to put the talks together again.[49] They told Ridgway that a UN apology—no one disputed that the American plane had been out of bounds—would give the Chinese a chance to save face. If the Chinese did not give a satisfactory answer within a week, the JCS would reconsider Ridgway's desire to end Kaesong's neutrality.

After several exchanges of messages and meetings of liaison officers,[50] Ridgway decided the Communists did not intend to return to Kaesong in good faith. He used the issue of resumption of the talks to precipitate a confrontation with his superiors in Washington. First, Ridgway made clear, in cables to the JCS, that he was determined not to hold further talks at Kaesong unless directly ordered to do so. And even if the talks resumed, there or elsewhere, he wanted to make no further concessions. Ridgway felt strongly, and so told the Pentagon in a telecon on September 26, that the Communists "urgently needed an armistice" because of their unfavorable military situation and the onset of winter.

The JCS disagreed, primarily because of earlier Ridgway reports of continued Communist military strength. Other Ridgway cables had indicated the truce talks benefited the Communists because of the neutrality of the Kaesong area and the psychological letdown among UN troops when the talks began. Clearly nervous at the domestic and international political consequences of the talks failing, Truman dispatched JCS Chairman Bradley and Charles Bohlen of the State Department to the Far East the last days of September for a firsthand look at the situation. The trip proved pivotal in swinging the administration behind Ridgway.[51] Bohlen admitted later he had left Washington convinced that an acceptable armistice was a matter of "real urgency." But after visiting troops in the field and conferring with commanders, both he and Bradley decided that the UN military superiority was so great it would be to the U.S. advantage to draw out the talks for strategic reasons. Bohlen also supported Ridgway on the site question, saying that there "could be no question" of forcing him to resume talks at Kaesong "under present conditions."

That Ridgway resolved his differences without resorting to public protests pleased the JCS. General J. Lawton Collins, the army chief, remarked to a subordinate, "Had MacArthur still been out there, he would have taken his case to the papers and we would have been accused of all sorts of nefarious things. Ridgway was different. He was a soldier who made his case, then accepted the decision of his superiors and followed orders and kept his mouth shut."

As it turned out, the Communists were ready to compromise on the site. On October 4 Ridgway asked the Communists to suggest a new meeting site midway between the front lines. Three days later the Communists proposed Panmunjom, the small village six miles east of Kaesong. Liaison officers agreed on a circular conference site 1,000 yards in radius from which all armed personnel save military police would be excluded. The same rule applied to circles three miles in radius centered on the UN delegation headquarters at Munsan and the Communist headquarters at Kaesong. Access would be via the Munsan–Panmunjom–Kaesong road, with a neutral strip 200 meters wide on either side. With the site set, the belligerents could talk about the issues again.

The Communists Compromise

Now commenced some of the more sophisticated bargaining of the peace talks, with the Communists at once moving away from previous positions and simultaneously grasping for new advantage.[52] But the most significant first step of the renewed talks was a Communist abandonment of insistence on the 38th parallel as a truce line. The UN opened on October 25 by repeating its proposal for a demilitarized line based upon the line of contact. The Communists the next day turned down the UN proposal but for the first time countered with a suggested line of its own that was not strikingly out of line with what the UN had indicated it would accept. The Communist plan called for the UN to surrender a good deal of favorable terrain in exchange for worthless ground on the Ongjin and Yonan peninsulas. But Ridgway and Joy saw the proposal as an opportunity to move the talks off dead center.

The next several days the main issue was control of Kaesong, an ancient capital of great symbolic significance. As Ridgway cabled the JCS, "its possession by the UN or its demilitarization would be viewed in Asia as damaging to Communist prestige and enhancing our own. . . ."[53] Because Kaesong lay on the main invasion route to Seoul, a score of miles to the south, Ridgway wanted it either under UN control or in a neutral zone.[54] He had been on the verge of seizing Kaesong in midsummer 1951—indeed, he had several battalions within its bounds —but held off a final offensive because he assumed that as an armistice site it should be neutral. Now Ridgway was not about to let Kaesong slip away by default.

So strongly did he feel on Kaesong that once again the JCS had to caution him against binding himself into an uncompromisable bargaining position. As Ridgway told General Bradley on his fall visit, he intended to give the Communists a proposed demarcation line as a "final offer." Somehow Ridgway got the notion the JCS supported him. He said in a cable on October 28, "I plan little change in our proposed zone except to reflect further Eighth Army advances." The chiefs promptly warned him (in a cable approved by President Truman) that no one had approved the current UN offer as "final" and stressed he should be willing to make minor adjustments if necessary to reach agreement with the Communists. The JCS did recognize the difficulty of a field commander's surrendering "hard-earned ground," although they also noted rising public sentiment against breaking the talks over Kaesong.[55] *The New York Times,* for instance, had asked rhetorically on November 11 why the delegates were "backing and filling over a seeming trifle" when agreement had been reached on the "big issues." *The Times* did not understand Ridgway's insistence on a defensible peace line; hence the editorial was misleading. But it was an example of the public eagerness to compromise and end the war. To the public, the Communists had agreed to end the war generally along the battleline, as the UN had sought all along; now American negotiators should finish the details and sign a treaty.

An even more pressing factor, given the timidity of Western European nations, was the ambivalence of the Soviet Union. On the one hand, the Soviets were shaken by a congressional appropriation in October of $7 billion for foreign technical and military aid to friendly nations, mostly to strengthen NATO members. A few days later NATO voted to admit Greece and Turkey as members, a major broadening of the area of NATO responsibility and strength. The Soviets were not silent. In October they exploded their second and third atomic bombs and announced plans for an ambitious nuclear program. Prime Minister Joseph Stalin publicly pledged friendship to Communist China and published a message of thanks for Soviet aid from Kim Il Sung, the North Korean president. And Alan Kirk, retiring as U.S. ambassador to Moscow, received a gloomy reception on his final call to Soviet Foreign Minister Andrei Vishinsky. In response to a direct question, Vishinsky said the Soviets would not pressure Communist negotiators in Korea to modify their bargaining position.

What the Soviets intended clearly was a challenge of allied resolve. Congress might vote money, but would the NATO members spend it? The Soviets took the offensive at a United Nations General Assembly meeting that opened in Paris on November 6. (The UN floated annual meetings among major member states during its formative years, although it maintained a permanent base in New York.) Foreign Minister Vishinsky carried a shopping bag of billingsgate intended to unnerve nations living in proximity to the Soviet Union. He wanted NATO dismantled. He wanted a UN ban on nuclear weapons (an act that would have stripped Western Europe of its only meaningful protection from Soviet attack). He wanted a world "peace meeting" to include Communist China (ignoring the fact that China was technically at war with the UN). Finally, he demanded a Korean truce along the 38th parallel and withdrawal of all foreign and "volunteer" troops within three months.

The propagandistic nature of Vishinsky's bombast aside, it posed acute political problems for the United States. American relations with the United Kingdom had improved measurably since the election of a Conservative government and Winston Churchill's selection as prime minister. Nonetheless, Acheson was not confident he could hold European support for the Korean War. Although eleven of the fourteen NATO members had troops fighting there, the Europeans worried more about their own frontiers than they did a distant Asian battlefield.

Acheson, however, did succeed in obtaining a major promise from the new British government. At a meeting at the American Embassy in Paris in early November, Acheson told Anthony Eden, now the British foreign minister, that he "very frankly" expected the Chinese not to accept any verification that they were obeying armistice terms.[56] In the event of violations, Acheson wanted to put the Chinese on notice in "no uncertain terms" that "no holds would be barred" in the American response. He spoke of bombing Chinese military bases ("not necessarily limited to airbases across the Yalu") and blockading the mainland. Eden reported these contemplated "drastic actions" the same evening to Prime Minister Churchill. The British went part of the way with Acheson. They would support the bombings, asking only that they be consulted in advance. But perhaps mindful of Hong Kong's tenuous existence as a coastal enclave, Churchill would not pledge support of the naval blockade. Nonetheless, the British support on the bombing issue encouraged Acheson to proceed with an armistice on less than promising terms.

So the United States—which is to say, Acheson—backed away from what Ridgway had been told, in effect, was a carved-in-stone UN position that a cease-fire must be simultaneous with setting of a demarcation line. On November 6, the opening day of the General Assembly meeting, Ridgway was ordered to accept "in principle" a demarcation line along the battle line and then propose to discuss other issues.[57] If the enemy flatly rejected this proposal, Ridgway was to yield even further—to agree to return to negotiations at Kaesong, as the Communists still demanded, if they would accept a demarcation line at the battlefront. But the JCS attached a key caveat. By freezing the land forces in place, the UN would be abandoning its valuable air and sea superiority. Hence acceptance of a cease-fire along the battlefront must be contingent upon a time limit for completion of all agenda items. If the deadline were not met, the demarcation line would be subject to revision.

Recognizing they now had a propaganda advantage, the Communists moved swiftly to maneuver the UN into a politically untenable position. On November 7 they proposed that the fighting stop immediately, all troops withdraw two kilometers, and inspection teams go into the field that very day to check the line of contact on maps. Despite its surface attractiveness, the proposal had major pitfalls. Each side could veto any adjustments in the line proposed by the other. There was no practical machinery for resolving disputes over such revisions. What the Communists were seeking, Ridgway told the JCS, was a *de facto* cease fire."[58] He intended to stand inflexibly on the principle established by the UN at the start of the talks: that the line of contact as of the effective date of the armistice must be the line of demarcation. Otherwise, the Communists could take advantage of a break in the fighting to fortify positions in front of the Eighth Army and bring in men and supplies for a renewed offensive, immune from any attack by the U.S. air arm. If the Communists indeed wished peace, Ridgway argued, force them to accept an entire package, not just points of immediate military value. Not having mutual inspection teams would leave the UN vulnerable to sudden surprise attacks.*

American diplomats found allied ambassadors shaky on Kaesong.[60] J. H. van Roijen of the Netherlands felt that the UN was "placing undue emphasis upon the retention of Kaesong and that continued fighting . . . was in fact unnecessary." The British and South Africans also had reservations, saying in effect that any demarcation meant a decrease in the fighting. But John Hickerson of the State Department defended Ridgway's view. Decreased fighting levels, although attractive at first blush, also decreased pressures on the Communists to negotiate. If the Communists showed a disposition to settle all issues soon after accepting a truce line, the situation would be different. But they displayed no such intention. Hickerson said it would be "almost impossible to maintain troop morale" if the actual line were fixed immediately and that regardless of future advances by the UN, the gains would have to be surrendered when the war finally ended. About ten enemy divisions "had been used up" since the start of talks in June, and the enemy must be kept off-balance if the talks were to succeed.

But the allied unease gave the Truman administration a clear choice: It could either support Ridgway, its commander in the field, or yield to the fretful European ambassadors. Ridgway lost. The administration cut the ground from beneath him, not for the first or the last time.[61] "We feel here," the chiefs cabled Ridgway on November 9, "that early agreement on principles governing selection of line of demarcation satisfying our major requirements has considerable importance." They also worried that the Communists, having made what could be considered a major concession, might revert to their old demand for the 38th parallel as a demarcation line if rebuffed.

Ridgway resisted.[62] In a cable to the JCS reporting on a November 10 armistice meeting, he said the Communists were so certain of pre-

---

*Privately Assistant Secretary Dean Rusk told allied ambassadors the United States did not expect the Communists to accept unlimited inspection; hence the United States would settle for "selective types of inspection at key points which would give the opposing commanders adequate insurance against any surprise onslaught."[59] He asked this bargaining flexibility be kept secret.

vailing that they used "brutally rude" language toward UN representatives. One Communist officer called Major General Henry I. Hodes a "turtle egg," one of the more insulting epithets in the Chinese language. Another Chinese officer slurringly referred to Admiral Joy as the "senior delegate . . . whose name I have forgotten." Ridgway pleaded for leeway; why force him to make concessions to an adversary who openly insulted his officers? He wanted "more steel and less silk" in the American position. The JCS had misgivings, but no true choice, given Acheson's dominant role in the debate. On November 13 the JCS directed Ridgway to accept the present line of contact as a demarcation line, with an understanding it must be renegotiated if other issues were not resolved within one month.[63] The agreement did not mean a ceasefire; ground action would continue. The message bore the approval of President Truman.

The stunning reversal of negotiating strategy angered Ridgway, and his response was forceful and biting.[64] "Premature acceptance" of the present line, regardless of any adjustments later, "must inevitably delay the possibility of obtaining an acceptance and honorable armistice." After reviewing the history of the abandoned position, Ridgway concluded with language MacArthurian in tone:

> I feel there is substantial probability that announcement to the Communists of the course you have directed will increase Communist intransigence and weaken our future positions on every substantive point. Having grown up with this developing situation, I have a strong inner conviction, admittedly based on the Korean as contrasted with the world situation, that more steel and less silk, more forthright American insistence on the unchallengeable logic of our position, will yield the objectives for which we honorably contend.
>
> Conversely, I feel that the course you are directing will lead step by step to sacrifice of our basic principles and repudiation of the cause for which so many gallant men have laid down their lives. We stand at a crucial point. We have much to gain by standing firm. We have everything to lose through concession. With all my conscience I urge we stand firm.

Ridgway's plea went unheeded. Once again the Truman administration bowed to international pressure and gave threatened happenings elsewhere precedence over the immediacy of the Korean War. In a directive approved by the President—but, peculiarly, not so stated in the text—the JCS on November 14 ordered Ridgway to accept the Communist proposals.[65] The deadline for agreement on other truce issues would be a month.

The Washington decision stung Ridgway. He felt himself in the position of a poker player who must constantly ask someone else for permission to play his hand. Admiral Joy was the man who dealt with the Communists face to face and knew the nuances of their bargaining positions. Ridgway could not lay down a "final position" on the table and stand behind it. Joy felt the cut keenly. As he wrote in his armistice memoirs, the "delegation, and indeed, General Ridgway, never knew when a new directive would emanate from Washington to alter our basic objective of obtaining an honorable and stable armistice agreement." Joy wrote:

> In such circumstances it is most difficult to develop sound plans, to present one's case convincingly, to give an appearance of unmistakable firmness and finality.
>
> It seemed to us that the United States Government did not know exactly what its political objectives in Korea were or should be. As a result, the United Nation delegation was constantly looking over its shoulder, fearing a new directive from afar which would require action inconsistent with that currently being taken.[66]

Years later General J. Lawton Collins, the army chief of staff, acknowledged that Ridgway had ample grounds to complain.[67] Instructions the JCS sent Ridgway were often "vacillating" and showed a "lack of firmness" that justifiably distressed Ridgway and the UN delegation. "I must admit," Collins wrote, "that . . . the JCS occasionally had the same feeling in our consultations with the State Department and civilian leaders more directly responsible politically to the American people. Yet we had to admit that we could not guarantee the success of military courses that General Ridgway, or we ourselves, supported."[*]

Loyal soldier Ridgway carried out his orders, albeit with reluctance. On November 17 his negotiators told the Communists the UN would accept the current line of contact as a demarcation line, provided other issues were resolved within the month. Sensing they held the upper hand, the Communists demurred. They insisted that the line not be revised, even after expiration of the one-month limit, until all other agenda items had been settled. Given its instructions, the UN delegation had no recourse but to begin tracing the line of contact on battlefield maps.

Ridgway was to be disappointed on other issues as well. All fall he had tried to persuade the JCS to establish a firm position on what sort of postarmistice inspection he should require of the Communists. Time and again Ridgway warned the chiefs the Chinese would use the lull to reinforce their troops. He wanted three verifications: joint observer teams at ports of entry and communications centers throughout Korea, with freedom of movement over lines of communication; joint aerial observation and photoreconnaissance over all Korea; and joint observa-

*Ridgway, as noted, desired a much-escalated bombing program, extending to nuclear warheads if their use could be proved feasible.

tion of the demilitarized zone (DMZ). As a final position he would waive aerial observation. On November 13 he asked for a swift decision. He had learned through experience, he noted in a cable to the JCS, that unless UN negotiators could be confident as to "firm national policy," they would be at a disadvantage. The Communists would become aggressive at the first sign of UN vacillation. Ridgway pleaded for a decision, one way or another. If Washington would not support his position, "it is requested that I be informed earliest as to the position in this regard which will be accepted as a final concession. . . ."

The JCS disappointed Ridgway, informing him on November 16 that although both ground and aerial observation was desirable, neither was worth breaking negotiations. Ridgway protested that the UN delegation had been ordered to accept a position "more advantageous" to the Communists than the Communists' own proposal. Ridgway was also disturbed at language in a JCS message stating that it was not in the "military interests" of the United States to be "tied up in Korea indefinitely." Any withdrawal from Korea within eighteen months of an armistice, he said, would result in "incalculable damage" to the American position in the Far East and would be tantamount to a betrayal of the Korean people.

The JCS, in a series of conciliatory messages, sought to assure Ridgway there was no intention of an "immediate withdrawal," although military and diplomatic realities might cause a "phased withdrawal" of U.S. troops. But the JCS promised no precipitate abandonment of the ROKs. The Joint Chiefs again stressed their central point: They did not want the talks broken over the inspection issue.

As Ridgway anticipated, heated arguments arose with the Communists over control of particular sectors when negotiators tried to draw a demarcation line on the map.[68] In one instance, both sides claimed control of a hill in central Korea. General Henry Hodes, confident that UN troops held the questioned hill, arranged for a telephone connection between the American commander there and the UN "verification team." Yes, the American replied, his troops held the hill. A UN interpreter overheard a *sotto voce* comment from the Chinese negotiator to a staff officer: "Never mind, it will be ours tonight." A warning was passed to the UN unit to expect an attack; nonetheless, the Chinese seized the hill.

By November 27 the line of demarcation had been established. The agreement stated that both sides accepted the principle that the line of contact would become the military demarcation line and that following completion of the armistice agreement, both sides would withdraw two kilometers to create a demilitarized zone. If the armistice were signed within thirty days, the line of contact already determined by UN and Communist staff officers would become the demarcation line, regardless of changes dictated by the battle situation during the period. Ridgway made it clear his troops would continue fighting during the thirty days.

Conceivably the war now could end within thirty days—a fact quickly circulated among American soldiers, Ridgway's desires notwithstanding. The fault apparently lay with the imprecise language of General James Van Fleet, the Eighth Army commander.[69] In a directive to his corps commanders Van Fleet stated that although his troops should be aware that hostilities would continue, the Eighth Army should "clearly demonstrate a willingness to reach an agreement." The order filtered to company level, someone spoke to newsmen, and the Associated Press dispatched an article stating: "UN troops on the Western front were ordered to stop all offensive fire against the Communists today and shoot only in self defense." The story went on to say that the order "came about twenty-four hours after the UN and Communist negotiators agreed on a provisional cease-fire line."

The story was not true, and it gave exactly the impression that Ridgway had feared—that is, that the agreement on a demarcation line meant the end of the fighting. Cables flew between Washington, Tokyo, and Rome (where General Bradley, the JCS chairman, was on a tour) and the vacationing Truman at Key West. The JCS, admitting to "confusion and excitement here," asked Ridgway whether he or Van Fleet "might have engendered these reports." Both denied any responsibility. (The Eighth Army later traced apparent responsibility to a company commander who had unwittingly told an AP reporter of his new orders.)

The press story, and the troop reaction to it, vividly supported the very arguments Ridgway had made against the administration's bargaining strategy—arguments Truman had rejected upon advice of Dean Acheson and other counselors. Thus Truman reacted with embarrassed fury, attacking the press rather than the untenable situation created by his administration's fuzzy and confused bargaining techniques. "I hope everyone understands now that there has been no cease-fire in Korea and that there can be none until an armistice has been signed," Truman said. "Any premature slackening of our effort would cost more U.S. casualties in the long run than need be lost."

So now the administration and the UN Command could only wait to see if the concession brought results.

Proposals, Counter Proposals, and Stalemate

For most of December the UN Command and the Communists did give-and-take bargaining that gave occasional hints of success but ended with both sides cemented to unshakable positions.[1] The UN's goal was to prevent the Communists from rebuilding their army and renewing the assault on the South, hence an insistence on inspection and a ban on increases of military forces and equipment in either half of the country. The Communists first rejected these demands out of hand, then on December 3 made an unexpected move toward compromise: Both sides would refrain from introducing troops or weapons "under any pretext," and observation commissions from "neutral" nations would screen the ports of entry. But even this "compromise" contained a serious germ of trouble. Under questioning, the Communist delegates said their prohibition on introduction of troops would forbid rotation or exchange of units or weapons. The UN position was that replacements must be permitted on a one-for-one basis; otherwise, normal rotation of American troops would not be possible, and the UN Command would swiftly diminish in strength. UN policy provided one year of duty in Korea for each man, or the replacement of about 35,000 men monthly. This meant a force of 420,000 men could be completely rotated in a year. Yet the Communists initially proposed a rotation rate of only 5,000 per month, meaning a duty tour of seven years for American soldiers in Korea and about fifteen years for the Chinese (whose army numbered about 1 million men). Although Admiral C. Turner Joy denounced this scheme as "obvious nonsense," the Communists were to cling to it for months.[2]

Another portion of the new Communist proposal included what had been a secondary issue: the rebuilding, by both sides, of such facilities as airfields and railroads. Admiral Joy felt the rebuilding would permit an increase in Communist combat effectiveness; hence he opposed it as contrary to what the UN sought in an armistice. The Communists did not have a single operative airfield in all North Korea. MIG aircraft operating along the Yalu flew from Manchurian bases immune from attack. With North Korean bases rebuilt, the Communists would be able to strike deep into South Korea. "We of the UN delegation could see no reason why the Communists should be allowed to develop an impor-tant military capability during the . . . truce," Joy stated. But the JCS overrode Joy and sent Truman a draft message accepting the Commu-nist proposal. Truman, vacationing in Key West, Florida, was in no mood to be so conciliatory; he would deny the Communists permission to rebuild North Korea even if it meant leaving South Korea in ruins indefinitely. In a cable flashing with presidential temper, Truman stated that "we have expended lives, tons of bombs and a large amount of equipment to bring these people to terms."[3] The Communists con-tinued to operate effectively even without airfields, and Truman de-manded that the JCS explain why these facilities should be rebuilt.

The Joint Chiefs, replying on December 8, cited the "strong feeling" that the military armistice "may be the only agreement we will have for a long time."[4] The economy of both Koreas depended upon rebuild-ing the facilities. "[W]e feel it would be impracticable to keep all of Korea in a state of devastation," the JCS told Truman. Furthermore, the Communists felt so strongly on the issue they would break the talks if denied it.

The chiefs convinced Truman.[5] On December 10 he approved a new JCS directive to Ridgway containing four major points: continued insis-tence on troop rotation; rehabilitation of airfields; withdrawal from offshore islands north of the demarcation line; and acceptance of neu-tral observer teams (rather than teams from the belligerents).

Now the Communists became intransigent again. Rebuilding the air-ports was not a negotiable issue. The "neutral" observer teams should not be answerable to any superior commission and they could not con-duct aerial observation. To Ridgway, it quickly became apparent that the Communists were again maneuvering for an armistice without any inspection organization; the "two sides were drifting farther apart." He warned the JCS against any extension of the thirty-day period specified in the demarcation line agreement (due to expire on December 27). On December 18 he stated that any extension would have a "harmful effect on the mental attitude" of his men and possibly on American public opinion.[6] He urged that Washington set "final positions" and break off the talks if the enemy proved obdurate. "Every time that the UNC [United Nations Command] delegation abandons a position which it has strongly held," he said, "its future position and bargaining strength are proportionately reduced."

To Ridgway the key question on which the fate of the armistice depended was whether the enemy would accept a prohibition on increasing his military capabilities during an armistice. "If the enemy will not accept, or will long delay, an armistice which contains a prohibition against airfields," he stated, "the question arises why the enemy is so seriously concerned about airfields." The only way to determine the answer was to press the Communists to the "point of ultimate decision and choice—an armistice, or airfields."

Responding, the JCS said they wished to avoid setting "final" conditions because of such uncontrollable variants as allied support and public opinion.[7] They believed the public supported an armistice and grew impatient only when the UNC appeared to be quibbling over minor details. Again they flatly told Ridgway the United States did not want to be put into a position where the talks were broken by American initiative.

The thirty-day limit expired on December 27 with no armistice in sight. The first few days of January 1952 the UNC offered several minor concessions, including surrender of its demand for aerial observation. But enemy negotiators rejected each probe, and attempts to find a common ground on the staff level were to no avail. On January 1 Admiral Joy summed up the situation. The Communists, he said, would "grow old sitting at the table" if they expected the UNC to yield any further.[8]

Some American-British Saber Rattling

Although Ridgway had not been told the details, Washington's seeming "weakness" in not sticking to a firm negotiating position stemmed from a conviction that no inspection process would ensure against renewed Communist attacks. As noted earlier, Secretary Dean Acheson and Prime Minister Winston Churchill had agreed in Paris in November in a joint Anglo-American declaration that any postarmistice expansion of the war would result in direct UN attacks on mainland China. The issue was discussed later in November in meetings in Rome between Acheson, Bradley, and Robert Lovett—who had replaced the ailing General

George Marshall* as secretary of defense in September—and the British Chiefs of Staff.[9] Acheson felt it might be impossible to reach an armistice agreement that would provide for a truly adequate inspection system. Lovett added that no inspection limited to Korea would ensure against a renewal of war since the major Communist bases were north of the Yalu. What Acheson asked of the British was a joint declaration threatening reprisals if the Chinese broke the armistice. The British seemed more sympathetic to bombing Manchuria than to a naval blockade. On December 19 the JCS asked Ridgway's views on a warning to the Chinese that "renewed aggression in Korea would result in a new war which would bring upon China the full retribution which the U.S. and her allies deem militarily desirable."[10]

Ridgway did not think his command could carry out much of a "full retribution."[11] The Chinese surely intended to reinforce their air strength once a truce was signed, and he had been told the UN could expect no significant reinforcements. Ridgway asked the JCS if the State Department understood the implications of such a warning. "In my opinion the retributive potentiality of UN military power against Red China would be non-effective unless the full results of precipitating World War Three were to be accepted, and the use of atomic weapons authorized," he cabled on January 7.

Once again Ridgway was ignored.[12] On January 10 the JCS sent him, for comment, an even weaker version of the U.S.-UK "declaration" drafted by the State Department. Consequences of breaching an armistice, the draft said, "would be so grave that, in all probability, it would not be possible to confine hostilities within frontiers in Korea." Ridgway now more than ever felt this approach was senseless. With its "presently available resources this command would be incapable of posing a threat to Communist China sufficient . . . to deter it from renewed aggression." The only sensible approach, he said, was to tidy up the entire armistice into a single package, with no issues left for settlement later.

In the end both sides tacitly agreed to leave the issue of airfield rebuilding alone for the moment and move to other business. And within several days in early January 1952 the UN Command and the Communists were at loggerheads on the issue that was to dominate the peace talks for eighteen more months: prisoners of war.

---

*Marshall suffered a recurring kidney problem for which he had undergone surgery in 1948; when he became secretary of defense in September 1950, he told President Truman he did not wish to serve more than one year.

The POW Issue

The disposition of prisoners of war—an item the enemy showed little inclination to discuss during 1951—was a problem which pitted the conflicting demands of international law against humanitarianism. As such, it appeared almost tailor-made for an adversary bent upon dragging out negotiations through ceaseless raising of new, tangential issues.

The problem, in a perhaps too concise nutshell, was which prisoners should be released after an armistice, and to whom and under what circumstances. On the surface, international law was very specific: Article 118 of the Geneva Convention of 1949 (which the United States signed immediately but did not ratify until mid-1951) stated flatly: "Prisoners of war shall be repatriated without delay after the cessation of hostilities." This clause was aimed directly at preventing a recurrence of the Communists' keeping scores of thousands of prisoners in slave labor camps long after the Second World War ended. Its drafters did not foresee a situation wherein large numbers of prisoners might not want to be repatriated. Soon after the Korean War began, the three major belligerents—the United States and the two Korean governments—announced they would adhere to the Geneva Convention. In actuality both Korean regimes frequently violated rules on treatment of prisoners the first months of the war. The ROKs routinely shot North Korean prisoners rather than go to the trouble of caring for them; so, too, did the North Koreans, who bound and shot groups of American GIs. The North Koreans also ignored the Geneva stipulation that prisoner lists be exchanged, reporting the names of only 110 UN troops when their compounds actually held more than 65,000 men.

But these legalities aside, a large number of the "Communist" prisoners held by the UN Command were ex-ROK and ex-Nationalist Chinese soldiers who had been forced to serve in the North Korean Army. Furthermore, scores of thousands of Chinese Communist soldiers told allied interrogators they wished to go to Formosa rather than return to China. Forcibly repatriating these soldiers meant their possible enslavement, even death. A corollary problem was the thousands of South Korean civilians taken prisoner by the North Korean Army the first weeks of the war and pressed into service as laborers. As civilians these people were not POWs in a legal sense, yet their captivity could not be ignored.

Such, in essence, was the broad outline of the complex situation facing the UN Command when the Communists, beginning in November 1951, first showed signs of interest in talking about the POW question.

The JCS and the UN Command, earlier in 1951, had discussed a congeries of approaches to the issue.[13] One idea that was attractive from the outset was a legalism that would give prisoners a choice of where they would be repatriated. The idea came from Brigadier General Robert A. McClure, the army chief of psychological warfare. In a memorandum to General J. Lawton Collins on July 5, McClure proposed that Chinese POWs who were former Nationalists and who feared punishment by the Communists for surrendering be sent to Formosa. Since Formosa was still legally a part of China (a position argued strongly by the Communist government), the stratagem would enable the United States to comply with the Geneva Convention, technically at least. It would also permit it to avoid forcibly sending prisoners to a country where they did not wish to live. McClure even suggested that some Chinese POWs would prefer to be put ashore on the mainland clandestinely to make their way to home villages or guerrilla-held territory.

Ridgway, however, felt this to be an "unrealistic approach."[14] He favored a one-for-one exchange of prisoners, which would mean an early recovery of UN prisoners in Communist hands. This plan gave the UN a great numerical advantage since it held far more prisoners than did the Communists. Ridgway would screen, then release to the ROK government, about 40,000 South Koreans being held by the UNC, chiefly men who had been impressed into the North Korean Army. Any prisoners still held after the one-for-one exchange would choose where they wished to go. But once a formal peace was signed, Ridgway saw no alternative to returning all Communist prisoners. To do otherwise, however humanitarian the motive, would establish a precedent dangerously contrary to the Geneva Convention and could conceivably prevent the return of U.S. POWs after future wars.

The debate continued in Washington for most of the fall, with frequent shifts of position by the parties involved (the Joint Chiefs of Staff, Lovett, and Acheson).[15] The JCS initially saw the possibility of an immense propaganda coup should the UN offer sanctuary to Communist soldiers who chose not to return to either China or North Korea. But they also conceded that making the prisoners part of an "ideological struggle" could cause the enemy to break off talks and refuse to return UN prisoners. Dean Acheson took the legalistic view, calling for "strict observance of the provisions of the Geneva Convention." Lovett wanted an all-for-all exchange to avoid "bargaining with the welfare of our own prisoners."

President Truman entered the discussion on October 29.[16] He was becoming increasingly testy about the lack of progress in the peace talks, and he saw the POW issue as one on which the UN negotiators should take a firm stand, the obligations of international law notwithstanding. An all-for-all swap would be inequitable in view of the vast disparity in the numbers of prisoners held by the two sides. Prisoners who had "willingly surrendered" to the UN would be "immediately done away with" if returned to the Communists. Regardless of the complications, Truman would not accept an all-for-all exchange unless the UN received "some major concessions which would be obtained in no other way." His position was transmitted to General Ridgway in late November as the official U.S. bargaining position.

U.S. interrogators immediately interviewed POWs who had resided south of the 38th parallel before the outbreak of war and within days designated some 37,000 of them as civilian internees and placed them in separate compounds.[17] At the conference table the UN offered to have all POWs screened by "joint teams" of belligerents prior to release. Those not wishing to be exchanged would remain under control of their captors. But Ridgway remained dubious of any exchange other than an all-for-all.[18] He felt it "highly improbable" that the enemy would agree to an "individual preference" exchange that likely would result in a large-scale defection of Communist POWs. He saw as a "final position . . . an all-for-all exchange to include the forced exchange of those POWs not desiring to return to Communist controls."

The Communists swiftly bore out Ridgway's prediction. On December 9 their negotiators insisted that both sides release all POWs immediately upon signing of the armistice. Pressed for a list of UN prisoners, the Communists on December 18 reported holding 4,417 UN POWs (of whom 3,198 were American) and 7,142 ROKs, a total of 11,559.[19] UN negotiators thought these figures incredible; the first months of the war the Communist radio had reported some 65,000 captives. U.S. intelligence estimated that the list contained only about one-half the U.S. prisoners actually held. Nonetheless, the JCS told Ridgway that the press was not to be given any information on the list "so as to avoid creating an emotional atmosphere here [in the United States] or a situation from which neither side can withdraw."[20]

The UN list, conversely, contained 132,474 names—95,531 North Koreans, 20,700 Chinese, and 16,243 former ROKs who had been captured and pressed into the enemy army. (Another 37,000-odd former ROKs, as noted, had already been screened and reclassified.)

Pressed to explain the discrepancy between their earlier claimed number of captives and the formal list, the Communists offered a variety of reasons.[21] Many POWs had died from sickness or bombings of prisoner camps. Others had been released at the front and chose to go home rather than resume fighting. The UN put little credence in these claims, calling the Communist list "fraudulent and dishonest," and bridled at the prospect of releasing 130,000 enemy POWs in exchange for fewer than 12,000 UN soldiers. The Communists replied by demanding the release of the 37,000 "reclassified" ROKs who had been put into their army. The POW release should not be a "trade of slaves," the Communist negotiators argued. The UN was trying to turn over part of the prisoners to a "certain friend" in the Republic of Korea and part of them to "another friend" in Formosa.

Reporting on the talks to allied ambassadors on January 8, U. Alexis Johnson of the State Department glumly noted that Communist negotiators were using "wild . . . accusations, vituperation and . . . emotionally lurid language." In his view the Communists were not interested in peace through negotiations. The Communists, he felt, wished to pursue peace through a special meeting of the UN Security Council, something the United States wished to avoid lest the Soviets try to repeal the resolution of July 1950 under which the war was being waged. Even though such a move would be legally dubious, the Soviet Union could be expected to reap maximum propaganda from it.

For General Ridgway, January 1952 was one of the more frustrating months of the war. The Communists obviously did not wish to bargain on repatriation; they wanted each of their soldiers back, regardless of national origin, and would discuss no alternatives. President Syngman Rhee, asserting himself more forcefully now that peace appeared a possibility—Rhee essentially had had no policy role in the war since mid-1950—told Ambassador John Muccio he did not object to absorbing North Korean POWs who did not wish to return home. But he hoped the bulk of the Chinese would be sent back to China because he did not want them sitting in the ROK indefinitely, "just eating rice." Nor was Generalissimo Chiang Kai-shek enthusiastic about receiving Chinese POWs in Formosa, even though he approved giving them a choice on not returning to Communist control. Chiang apparently did not wish to risk having thousands of soldiers of unproved loyalty introduced into his armed forces.

Even more distressing to Ridgway were signs of further compromise in the United States' "firm" position against forced repatriation. On January 15 the JCS told him the United States' "final" position, approved by President Truman, was that the UN would agree to an all-for-all exchange except that "no forcible return of POWs would be required."[22] But before putting this position on the bargaining table, UN negotiators should make certain that all other possibilities had been exhausted. The JCS warned that "in face of pressures which could develop" if loss of some 3,000 UN prisoners were balanced "against the welfare of an indefinite number of Communist prisoners in our hands," further changes in bargaining strategy might be necessary. Ridgway could read between the lines: The Truman administration—that is, the President and Dean Acheson—were so anxious to be out of the war that continued Communist intransigence would cause step-by-step abandonment of America's negotiating goals. Ridgway literally begged for less publicity about the negotiations. Each time the Communists read in the press about discussions "at high policy levels in Washington," they invariably waited for further concessions. Ridgway wanted to stop the "authoritative speculation" stemming from Washington.

But to Harry Truman, the major obstacle to peace lay not in Panmunjom, but in Moscow. Writing in his diary on January 27, 1952, the President mused about giving the USSR an "ultimatum with a ten day expiration limit." Unless the Soviets nudged the Chinese toward settlement, the United States would bomb Manchurian military bases, blockade China, and enter into "all out war" with the USSR if necessary.* Truman also discussed with aides the possible use of nuclear weapons should the Chinese violate any armistice agreement.

Circumstantial evidence strongly supported Truman's belief that the Soviets prevented progress in the talks. In early February 1952 the negotiators discussed the composition of the proposed "neutral" organization that would ensure against armistice violations. The UN Command, through the State Department, suggested Norway, Sweden, and Switzerland, each of which agreed to serve. The Communists, after proposing that the body be named the Neutral Nations Supervisory Committee, nominated the Soviet Union and two of its satellites, Poland and Czechoslovakia. The Communist delegation blandly added, "If the Soviet Union could not be nominated as a neutral nation, there would be no neutral nation at all existing in the world." The exasperated Admiral Turner Joy exclaimed:

> The guns, the aircraft, the tanks, the marine mines, the ammunition, the fuel, the trucks, and the military advice that had been used by Communist forces in the Korean War came from the Soviet Union. When my senior liaison officer first established contact with the Communists at Kaesong, he was held at the point of Russian machine guns, conveyed to the meeting place in a Russian jeep, even offered a bottle of vodka.[23]

But to Joy's astonishment, the UN delegation was directed to oppose the USSR as a commission member not on the ground that it supported North Korea in the war, but because the countries shared a common border. The JCS told Ridgway it was "inadvisable" to state the UN did not consider the USSR a neutral because proof of Soviet participation in the war "would be difficult to substantiate." Ridgway complained in response that Washington's unwillingness to disclose the real reason for excluding the USSR left the enemy free to make propaganda statements lauding the Soviets which he could not refute. To Joy's chagrin, again and again the Communists taunted his delegation: "Why do you give no logical reason for opposing the great, peace-loving USSR as a member of the Neutral Nations? You give no reason because you have none. You are unable to deny that the USSR is a true neutral in the Korean conflict." Even after years of reflection, Joy was "unable to perceive any sound reason for such timidity. . . ." To him the Communist insistence on the Soviet inclusion as a "neutral" was a "red-herring technique" intended to divert attention from other issues and to force

*Truman's complete diary entry is quoted in the Introduction; see page xxv.

UN concessions. Joy and other officers also did not wish to permit Soviet observers to glean technological secrets from U.S. equipment as they inspected material coming into South Korea. "It was utterly fantastic that any nation would expose its most critical military secrets to the eyes of its enemies," Joy said. Yet the Communists insisted on doing just that for months more of fruitless bargaining.

Exploitation of the POWs

The POW issue came to an ugly head beginning in late February 1952 with the Communists realizing that the United States would not force the repatriation of any prisoners. Truman announced the decision publicly; he explained in his memoirs, "Just as I had always insisted that we could not abandon the South Koreans who had stood by us and freedom, so I now refused to agree to any solution that provided for the return against their will of prisoners of war to Communist domination." The Joint Chiefs, transmitting the decision to Ridgway on February 27, called it the "final U.S. governmental position," one that would be maintained "without use of any subterfuge."[24] Ridgway was directed to screen the prisoners and remove from POW status those who he believed would be fearful for their lives if returned to Communist control and would violently resist repatriation. Persons thus reclassified would be held separate from other prisoners and their names removed from the POW lists given the Communists. The Communists would then be told that the UN was ready for an all-for-all exchange on the basis of the revised lists and that the UN considered this course of action had been forced by the Communist failure to accept voluntary repatriation on a fair basis. The Communists now made a decision of their own: They would seek to gain through contrived chaos what they could not gain through negotiation.

To set the scene, a brief overview of the POW situation is in order. One major problem stemmed from the fact that the UN had captured extraordinary numbers of prisoners in a short time. In August 1950 the UN held fewer than 1,000 POWs. But by November, with the Inchon invasion and the rapid drive into North Korea, the total rose to more than 130,000. Caring for them posed mammoth logistical and administrative problems; although the prisoners originally were cooperative, no doubt relieved to be out of the war, housing them in the Inchon and Pusan areas created security problems. In January 1951, when the Chinese intervention drove the UN Command far to the south of Seoul, General Douglas MacArthur asked the JCS for authority to move the POWs (by now numbering some 137,000) out of Korea for security reasons, even to the United States. "POWs have been docile, coopera-tive and ready to work at all assigned tasks," he said.[25] Since they were not accustomed to the same standard of living as Americans, they could be maintained in modest facilities and fed less than "Occidentals." The JCS refused this request, for unstated reasons, but did urge MacArthur to shift the POWs out of the combat zone, perhaps even to the Ryukyu island group south of Okinawa.

As it turned out, MacArthur was so occupied elsewhere he did noth-ing else about the POWs before his dismissal in April 1951. His successor, General Ridgway, decided to shift the POWs to the uninviting but available island of Koje-do, a few miles south of the mainland. About 150 square miles in area, Koje-do was a barren jumble of rocky hills, with little flat land suitable for POW camps; it also teemed with about 200,000 natives and civilian war refugees. Ridgway, however, saw it as a "choice between evils," for no other site existed to house the prisoners.

Koje-do was tailor-made for trouble.[26] American military police con-structed four vast barbed-wire enclosures, each in turn split into eight compounds, into which were crammed some 130,000 Korean and 20,000 Chinese prisoners. The compounds, intended to hold 700 to 1,200 men each, were soon overloaded to as much as five times capacity. Even the space between compounds was eventually used for POWs. The ROK Army recognized Koje-do as a convenient dumping ground for in-competent soldiers; these poor-caliber guards aggravated the tense situ-ation.

To the Chinese and North Korean leaderships, the POW compounds were an extension of the battlefield. As military intelligence discovered, via interrogation of prisoners and captured documents, the Commu-nists organized a special unit to take the lead in making POWs con-tinued combatants. The unit, attached to headquarters of the North Korean People's Army, had two missions: to train agents who would permit themselves to be captured so they could take on specific leader-ship missions in the camps and to furnish intelligence to the Communist negotiators at Panmunjom. These agents were instructed specifically to spread propaganda among POWs to the effect that the war would end with Korea united under Communist rule and that UN withdrawal was imminent. The prisoners were promised "high respect and considera-tion" when they returned home, an inducement for voluntary repatria-tion.

If persuasion failed, the cadre enforced discipline with beatings, kan-garoo courts, even "executions" of dissidents. By early 1952 the Com-munists had a *de facto* shadow government in Koje-do, poised to move on command.

The signal came in February 1952, when UN guards began a screen-ing of POWs to determine which wished to be repatriated. As Ridgway had anticipated, the vast majority did not want to return to either China or North Korea. Then the screening teams reached Compound 62, which housed some 5,600 inmates, and which was under firm control of the special cadre. When U.S. guards moved into the compound on the morning of February 18, they were attacked by some 1,000 to 1,500 Koreans wielding crude but deadly weapons—steel-tipped poles, knives, flails, clubs, even a hand-fashioned firearm or two. The UN troops opened fire, killing 55 POWs outright (another 22 died later) and wounding another 140. The UN lost 1 man dead and 38 wounded.

Five days later, on February 23, the Communists put the incident into the forum of world propaganda, protesting the "sanguinary incident of barbarously massacring large numbers of our personnel." The UN understandably rejected the charge, but the Communists continued complaining of the "massacre." General James Van Fleet, the Eighth Army commander, replaced the camp commandant with Brigadier General Francis T. Dodd; nonetheless, riots and incidents continued, with prisoners signing petitions with their own blood and tattooing anti-American slogans on their bodies. These episodes lent a modicum of surface credence to Communist claims that UN brute force was preventing captives from choosing to return home.

An unexpected development in mid-April, meanwhile, signaled a possible break in the negotiating stalemate. Asked to estimate how many prisoners might be returned after screening, UN negotiators told the Communists they anticipated about 116,000. This figure apparently was more than the Communists had anticipated, and the enemy suggested that screening be resumed to prepare a "final list" of prisoners to be returned. Further discussions would follow.

To the Communists' dismay (and the surprise of the UN as well, by all evidence), of 106,376 POWs and civilian internees questioned, only 31,231 wished to return.[27] Another 44,000 at Koje-do either refused screening or could not be interviewed because of the terrorism gripping the camp. Thus the UN informed the enemy that only about 70,000 prisoners would be returning.

The announcement stunned the Communist negotiators, who had to fight to maintain their composure. The next day, April 20, the Communists called the 70,000 figure "completely impossible" and suspended the talks.

The Truman administration decided to make one more compromise effort. For weeks intensive debate had raged between General Ridgway and officials of the State and Defense departments about the format of a "final offer" he would make directly to General Nam Il, the head of the Communist negotiating team. A concurrent public broadcast by President Truman would attempt to portray to world opinion that the UN was offering concessions and that peace was at hand if the Communists really wanted it. The break in the talks after the POW dispute prompted President Truman to proceed with the "final offer" on a modified basis. (The "offer" went through too many gradations to warrant its being detailed here.)

On April 28 Admiral Joy challenged the enemy to "join us in seeking a compromise solution which both sides may accept." The United States offered a concession: It would place "no restriction . . . on the rehabilitation and reconstruction of airfields." In exchange it demanded that the Communists accede to the U.S. positions on the composition of the neutral commission to oversee the peace (that is, that the USSR not be a member) and the exchange of prisoners. "As you know," Joy stated, "our position regarding prisoners of war is the exchange of 12,100 prisoners . . . of our side for approximately 70,000 of your side."

To the astonishment of Joy, the U.S. proposal "created as much stir as a pebble dropped into the ocean."[28] The Communists recessed briefly; then General Nam Il stated that "our side fails to see how your proposal . . . can really be of help to an overall settlement of all the remaining issues." Joy replied that the offer was "final and irrevocable," whereupon Nam proposed an indefinite recess.

The break did not alarm Joy, for he realized that Nam Il could make no policy decisions without consulting superiors in Peking and Pyongyang. When the Communists returned to the table on May 2, Nam Il assailed the UN proposal at length, then ended with what he called an important concession: The Communists would abandon their hitherto rigid insistence on the USSR's being a member of the "neutral" commission. But he had a condition of his own, what he called a "reasonable compromise" on the POW issue. It was no such thing. Nam Il demanded the return of 132,000 prisoners, insisting that no Chinese soldiers be left under control of the UN. His "concession" was that the Communists would forget about the 44,000 former ROK soldiers who had been pressed into the enemy army. Joy replied that the UN offer was an "integrated whole" and that individual elements were not subject to bargaining. So he formally rejected the Communist proposal.

The significance of the Communist move was that the enemy was now ready to rest the entire armistice on a single issue, that of forced repatriation of prisoners. Rather than bear the onus of stopping the talks, Joy did agree to return within several days to discuss the Communist proposal further after consultation with Washington. But President Truman did not intend to make any additional concessions. In a lengthy public statement he said that the UN had made earnest efforts toward peace and that the offer given the Communists was fair. On the prisoners, Truman was emphatic: "We will not buy an armistice by turning over human beings for slaughter or slavery."

Now the Communists had drawn a line, and they intended to stand upon it and rely on world opinion to force further UN concessions. Their major weapon was the cadre underground in the Koje-do prison camp, which had almost instantaneous communication with the Communist high command in Pyongyang. The cadres' proclivity for mischief was no secret to the American military. In late April, for instance, intelligence agents received word of a Communist plan to try to seize the Koje-do commandant, General Dodd, and hold him hostage to force further UN concessions. The birth of this scheme coincided with the Communist rejection of the UN proposal on the prisoner swap. Now there was to unfold one of the more incredible episodes of the war.

Despite the intelligence warning that the POWs intended to capture him, General Dodd walked into the Communists' hands.[29] On May 7 he agreed to meet leaders of Compound 76, known to be under militant control. Dodd and an aide, Lieutenant Colonel Wilbur Raven, stood outside an open gate, listening to well-worn complaints about food, clothing, and medical attention. They ignored or did not notice about twenty POWs walking back toward the compound after emptying buckets of latrine sewage, a so-called honey bucket detail. The group suddenly rushed Dodd and Raven, seized the general, and carried him into the compound. Raven managed to grab onto a gatepost and hold on until help arrived, saving himself from capture. But the Communist POWs now held a prize prisoner of their own.

By coincidence, the episode occurred the very day that Lieutenant General Mark W. Clark arrived in Japan to replace General Ridgway as UN commander in chief.* Thus responsibility for U.S. actions the next several days was divided between Ridgway (the supreme commander until he actually left the Far East); Clark, who was dubious about chances for immediate settlement, but who had no say over Ridgway's actions; and General James Van Fleet, the Eighth Army commander, and Dodd's immediate superior. Each general had his own views on how to handle the crisis; the mechanics eventually left each sour toward the other.

Clark's reflexive reaction was to "let them keep that dumb son of a bitch Dodd, and then go in and level the place." Clark said in his memoirs, "You don't negotiate with prisoners of war, particularly fanatical Communist POWs who consider themselves combatants despite capture." Ridgway felt the same way. As a soldier Dodd had accepted the risk of violent death when he entered his profession. "In wartime," Ridgway said, "a general's life is no more precious than the life of a common soldier. . . . If, in order to save an officer's life, we abandoned the cause for which enlisted men had died, we would be guilty of betraying the men whose lives had been placed in our care."

Van Fleet, however, had other ideas. He flew immediately to Koje-do and heard the prisoners' initial demands (relayed by Dodd). They wanted recognition of a "POW association" as a spokesman for the prisoners and telephone and jeep communication between the several

---

*For a discussion of the change of command, see Chapter Twenty-three.

compounds. Ridgway, upon his arrival at Koje-do, promptly reversed Van Fleet. He directed that a battalion of tanks be hastened to the island. "If the Reds resisted or delayed in carrying out our demands, I was determined to shoot and to shoot with maximum effect."

Van Fleet tarried in carrying out Ridgway's order, partially because of a delay in the arrival of the tanks, partially because of what Ridgway said were "other reasons not clear to me." (This account, based upon memoirs of the principals, should be read with the realization that the three generals did not agree on what should be done at Koje-do.) Dodd sent out a message (to Brigadier General Charles F. Colson, his successor) which listed a long set of charges that UN guards had killed and injured prisoners. The statement—written by the Communists—also contained alleged Dodd admissions that camp authorities were "guilty" of these offenses.

Colson had ordered his troops and tanks to be ready to move into the compound at ten o'clock on the morning of May 10. But the Communists interrupted these moves by sending out a list of demanded confessions to myriad crimes. In immediate and crude translation, the key demands were:

> Immediate ceasing the barbarous behavior, insults, torture, forcible protest with blood writing, threatening, confinement, mass murdering, gun and machine-gun shooting, using poison gas, germ weapons, experiment object of A-bomb, by your command.
> Immediate stopping the so-called illegal and unreasonable repatriation of North Korean People's Army and Chinese People's Voluntary Army.
> Immediate ceasing the forcible [screening] which thousands of POWs of NKPA and CPVA be armed and falled in slavery [sic].

To Ridgway, the demands asked the UN Command to "plead guilty to every wild and utterly baseless charge the Red radio had ever laid against us"; the repatriation policy "would have been shot right from under" the UN negotiators at Panmunjom. Ridgway, unfortunately, was not at the scene; Colson let the ten o'clock deadline slip away into the evening and then signed a reply that was tantamount to an admission of the Communist charges:

> . . . I do admit that there have been instances of bloodshed where many POWs have been killed and wounded by UN forces. I can assure in the future that POWs can expect humane treatment in this camp according to the principles of international law. I will do all in my power to eliminate further violence and bloodshed. If such incidents happen in the future, I will be responsible.

The Communists haggled for even further admissions the next twenty-four hours, then freed Dodd on the evening of May 11. He had been held slightly more than four days. The next day General Clark denounced the "confession" as "unadulterated blackmail" and said that any concessions made by Colson and Dodd "should be interpreted accordingly.* Dodd, in his own statement to the press, said that the "demands made by the POWs are inconsequential and the concessions granted by the camp authorities were of minor importance." Van Fleet said much the same thing.

Clark thought otherwise, and emphatically. Phrases such as "I can assure in the future that POWs can expect humane treatment" implied past mistreatments. A promise against "no more forcible screening" admitted to something that had not happened. Even though the press had been kept away from Koje-do during the incident, the Communists quickly publicized the UN "admissions," and their negotiators used them to taunt UN delegates at Panmunjom.

Although an Eighth Army board cleared Dodd and Colson of any misconduct, Clark convened another investigative panel that recommended reducing both generals to the rank of colonel. The Department of the Army approved the action, effectively ending the careers of both Dodd and Colson.

The UN Command next moved to break Communist control of the camps, by smashing their so-called leadership and dispersing POWs to smaller, more secure compounds. The new Koje-do commander, Brigadier General Haydon L. Boatner, with more than ten years' Asian service, knew he must impose discipline firmly but gradually, relying upon written orders (certified with an official seal, or chop) rather than verbal commands.[30] As a first test he ordered Chinese POWs to remove a Communist flag and statue of Stalin from their compound and gave them a specific deadline of noon the following day. When the Chinese did not comply, infantrymen and two tanks entered the compound sharply at noon, tore down both statue and flag, and withdrew within five minutes, a decisive act intended to show the Chinese Boatner meant business.

When the new commander was ready to move the Communists to new compounds, again he gave written orders with a specific date. The Chinese sent word they would not move voluntarily. Boatner did not discuss the issue; "POWs don't negotiate," he announced. He sent paratroopers and half a dozen tanks into the compound and methodically smashed the resistance, his troops using concussion grenades and tear gas. The battle raged for two and one-half hours, with the POWs hurling Molotov cocktails, spears (killing one American), and rocks; thirty-one prisoners died. Once the tumult died, the Communist "spokesman" was

---

*Ridgway left his command the afternoon after Dodd's release. Clark begged him to release a final statement on Koje-do before he departed. Ridgway smiled and said nothing as he walked toward the plane ramp with his wife. "As he waved goodbye," Clark said later, "I visualized him throwing me a blazing forward pass."

dragged from the compound by the seat of his pants, and the prisoners marched to their new quarters. UN troops found staggering weapons arsenals: 3,000 spears, 1,000 Molotov cocktails (bottles filled with gasoline and armed with cloth wicks), 4,500 knives, and uncountable clubs, hatchets, barbed-wire flails, and hammers. They also unearthed the bodies of sixteen murdered prisoners.

A few days later Boatner—under firm security—talked to several "representatives" of the POWs to inform them of the camp rules he intended to enforce. A young POW who previously had claimed to be a "leader" started "shouting violently at me. I told him quietly and politely to shut up [Boatner spoke fluent Chinese]. He did not, so I ordered guards to take him to solitary confinement where he stayed for the remainder of his captivity."

The Koje-do revolt was over.

The Germ Warfare Campaign[31]

The *de facto* defection of half their captured soldiers posed a propaganda problem of mammoth proportion for the Chinese and North Koreans. For months their broadcasts had denounced the tyrannical regimes of Chiang Kai-shek and Syngman Rhee; now the "volunteers" who had marched away to fight these dictators were deciding to stay and live under their rule. The raw figures on the number of Chinese and North Koreans who said they would "violently" refuse repatriation were a matter of record. As a propaganda rebuttal the Communists offered "germ warfare"—infectious diseases supposedly spread by the United States via a weird assortment of carriers such as potato bugs, lice, rats, and fleas. The Communists created the germ warfare issue from whole cloth, promoted it through their front groups, and persuaded uncountable millions of people throughout the world that the United States practiced bacteriological genocide in Asia.

Measured objectively, the campaign should have collapsed by weight of its inherent absurdity. Pictures from North Korean and Chinese news agencies showed citizens in "germ-hunting parties" picking up black specks from the snow with chopsticks, supposedly "germ-laden flies" dropped from American aircraft. (When the non-Communist press queried how flies survived the fierce Korean winters long enough to circulate any germs, the Communists quickly explained the Americans had developed a cold-resistant mutant.)

Germ warfare was a propaganda theme that had obsessed the Soviet Union for years. It proved a useful tool during Stalin's bloody purge trials of 1938–39, which featured "confessions" of discredited officials that they spread anthrax among cattle. The same charges surfaced frequently during the Second World War (against the Germans) and in postwar Japan (when the Soviets sought to disrupt a final peace treaty with the Japanese). Other cold war variations included allegations that the United States experimented with plague among Canadian Eskimos, financed a West German germ warfare research institute, and intended to use biological warfare rather than nuclear weapons because of the "clearly capitalistic reason that it destroys people without damage to property."

In the late spring and early summer of 1950, just prior to the start of war in Korea, the campaign became even more esoteric. Now the Americans were accused of dropping potato bugs on East German and Czechoslovakian farmland. High concentrations of such insects were said to be found along flight paths of American aircraft, and the Communist media ran photographs of "potato bug containers" said to be attached to parachutes and balloons. A CIA agricultural analyst noted the charges coincided with crop failures in the complaining countries. "It is clear," one officer wrote, "that the Soviet bloc used these charges to divert attention from their own inability to cope with a natural disaster, to stamp the U.S. with the label of aggressor, and to heighten tension in the orbit states."

Thus U.S. intelligence was not surprised when germ and chemical warfare charges surfaced in Korea in the spring of 1951, when the Communists were suffering major reverses. The first accusations involved supposed shipments of mustard gas to Korea, a report spread by the Catholic Committee for World Peace and Against Communist Aggression—a Soviet front, despite the misleading name. Various front groups such as the Hungarian Red Cross asked the UN to move against the "American imperialists to prevent the atrocity of using poison gas . . . in their war of aggression in Korea." Then Communist media would transform undocumented charges into issues being given serious consideration by the UN. The reality was that U.S. intelligence regularly during 1951 received reports of widespread epidemics of smallpox, typhus, and amebic dysentery in North Korea. The same diseases were also encountered in the South.

The campaign widened in 1952 to include "confessions" by American airmen that they had participated in germ warfare bombings. This was not accidental, for the Soviet representatives in North Korea "reprimanded the North Koreans and Chinese Communists for failing to produce a better propaganda case on bacteriological warfare," according to an American intelligence report.

By happenstance, the Chinese had two American airmen as prisoners, Lieutenants Kenneth L. Enoch and John Quinn, captured when their B-26 was shot down on January 13, 1952. After five weeks' intensive interrogation Enoch and Quinn broke and gave the Communists what they wanted. In written and filmed statements the airmen said the United States had begun planning bacteriological warfare in August 1951, with first actual operations mounted on January 3, 1952. Communist media used the statements as the centerpiece for a massive worldwide propaganda campaign, commencing with articles published in *Pravda* on successive days after May 6. Tape recordings of the "confessions" were widely circulated. The two lieutenants were subjected to a mass interview with Chinese and Korean "newsmen and scientists" that stretched over ten days, highlights of which were made into a "documentary" movie. (One participant was the renegade Australian journalist Wilfred Burchett, then a correspondent for the French Communist paper *Ce Soir,* who two decades later was a frequent and detested visitor to American POWs in Vietnam.)*

Their campaign now supported by live witnesses, the Communists now sought to make germ warfare a major issue.

Bak Hon Yong, the North Korean minister for public affairs, charged that the Americans had dropped flies, fleas, ticks, mosquitoes, and spiders to spread contagious diseases. A few days later Chou En-lai, the Chinese foreign minister, followed with a statement about how sixty-eight formations of American aircraft had made no less than 448 sorties over areas of northeastern China, scattering germ-bearing insects. (Statistical exactitude is a device propagandists use to give credence to otherwise unprovable allegations.) Communist journalists toured North Korean villages, gleaning eyewitness accounts from peasants of the ravages of germ warfare. The Communists mounted a vigorous national inoculation campaign. No one escaped—not even Major General William Dean, a captive since July 1950.[33] The shot "made my arm swell more and created a harder lump than any of the hundreds of shots I've received in our own army," Dean wrote later. The "monster shots" gave "all of North Korea . . . fever and sore arms." All in all, the Communists succeeded in stirring up such a hate-American campaign that (according to Dean) "a downed airman had virtually no chance of getting away from his wrecked plane or parachute." Chinese and Korean officers who wanted the fliers for intelligence purposes had to race farmers and villagers; the latter usually won. The Communists had succeeded all too well in convincing villagers that the timeless diseases that had ravaged Korea could now be blamed on American imperialists.

Internationally the Communists set up "germ warfare" displays in Peking, featuring the written and sound-recorded film confessions of Lieutenants Enoch and Quinn, scores of insects gathered in the Korean

*James Angus MacDonald, who fought in the war as a British officer and later did the definitive study of the conduct of U.S. marines in captivity,[32] notes that previous to these confessions the Communists gave the same relative treatment to aviation and ground personnel. "After January 1952, aviators were singled out for a special brand of treatment designed to wring bacteriological warfare confessions from them," MacDonald wrote.

countryside, and statements of villagers. A blizzard of petitions from "international bodies" orchestrated by the Communists fell upon the world's foreign ministries and the United Nations.

Realizing the value of "confessions," the Communists put intense pressure on captured fliers to give statements. Enoch and Quinn helped indoctrinate new captives with a crude theatrical performance at POW camps depicting how they received orders for germ warfare missions. One marine flier, Judson C. Richardson, was told bluntly he would never leave Korea when he denied that the United States waged bacteriological warfare. He refused to cooperate and survived.

Another uncooperative pilot was a marine, Master Sergeant John T. Cain, a prematurely gray man who had deep empathy for the Korean people and who grieved over the destruction the war had brought to their land.[34] He befriended nine small children who lived near his base and paid for their education. On July 18, 1952, he was flying a light observation plane over enemy lines when he was shot down and taken captive. Because of his gray hair and lack of insignia, the Chinese decided Cain must be a senior officer, at least a colonel, and brushed aside protestations he was a sergeant. The initial interrogation produced nothing, so Cain was taken to an isolated part of the infamous Pichongni prison camp for intensive interrogation. Eventually the Chinese stuck him in a hole five feet square and six feet deep. In October the water in the hole was two inches deep, and it froze around Cain's feet. He did not break. He was pulled out and made to stand at attention for five to eight hours without interruption.

By mid-November the Chinese realized Cain was an unusual man. They told him they were tired of playing with him. They marched him to a hillside, blindfolded him, and stood him in front of a squad of riflemen. Rifle bolts clicked. Are you ready to talk? the commander asked, in authentic B movie dialogue. No, replied Cain. The Chinese returned him to solitary confinement and then to his original POW camp. He had called their bluff and survived.*

Another marine who did not fare nearly so well was Colonel Frank H. Schwable, chief of staff of the 1st Marine Air Wing, shot down on a reconnaissance flight on July 8, 1952. Schwable carried copious identification, and the Communists had no trouble in concluding they had captured a blue-ribbon prisoner. (For inexplicable reasons, the Department of Defense, four days after Schwable's capture, issued a press release giving considerable data on his career. Save for General Dean, Schwable was the highest-ranking American officer captured during the war.)

Perhaps because of their inability to break other marines in captivity, the Chinese gave Schwable special treatment. They thrust him into a

_____

*After his release the Marine Corps gave Cain a letter of commendation with ribbon.

filthy hole alongside a Korean house, on a near-starvation diet, and denied him latrine privileges and medical attention. Schwable was pulled from his hole daily for badgering interrogation. When the cold weather came, the Chinese gave him no blanket.

Schwable realized from the outset that the Chinese wanted to use him for propaganda purposes. In December he began to break, but with a rationalization. The Communists had specimens of his signature; whenever they wished to affix it to a germ warfare document, they could do so. Schwable suffered from constant diarrhea. The Chinese made him squat in unnatural positions. He later confessed that he was confused, that he was convinced that he had no alternative:

> In making my most difficult decision to seek the only way out, my primary consideration was that I would be of greater value to my country in exposing this hideous means of slanderous propaganda than I would be by sacrificing my life through non-submission or remaining a prisoner of the Chinese Communists for life, a matter over which they left me no doubt.

On January 21, 1953, Colonel Schwable signed a confession affirming his knowledge of germ warfare activities conducted by the 1st Marine Aircraft Wing. He named fellow officers (not in captivity) as being involved. He gave considerable information about the composition and personnel of marine units and of aircraft technology. As was the case with Enoch and Quinn, he was forced to record the "confession." In the words of James A. MacDonald, "It was a much more sophisticated version than the efforts of earlier captives and one of the most damaging to emerge from North Korea."*

Other pilot confessions followed; the earlier statements seemed to put an imprimatur of approval on anyone who wished to follow.

Joseph Manto, an army captain, and a marine lieutenant named Turner, decided to put the "bug hunts" into perspective. First, they acquired a dead mouse, no challenge in the vermin-ridden POW camp. Turner then made a minute parachute and lettered "U.S. Air Force" on the canopy. Manto tied the dead mouse to the parachute and tossed it onto a bush where the Chinese would be sure to discover it. Sure enough, a Chinese sentry saw the mouse. He backed away, in a frenzy, pointed his rifle at the tiny, dangling corpse, and shouted frantically for help. Other Chinese scurried to his rescue. After consultation one care-

---

*After the war a Marine Court of Inquiry reviewed Schwable's conduct and concluded he had resisted Communist pressure and torture "to the limit of his ability before giving in." The court also considered Schwable's record: Naval Academy graduate, twenty years of military service, including World War Two night fighter duty. It ruled he should not be subjected to disciplinary action. But it also said his future usefulness as a marine officer was "seriously impaired" by his conduct as a war prisoner. The ruling effectively ended Schwable's career.

fully lifted the mouse off the branch with a pair of tweezers and dropped it into a glass bottle and immediately popped in the cap. The mouse went into a local exhibit as further evidence of imperialistic American bacteriological warfare.

Manto, Turner, and other prisoners took care the next few days not to laugh out loud around guards.

The "mouse caper" was a rare instance of POW camp levity. To prisoners frustrated at the lack of progress at Panmunjom, the most interesting news of 1952 was a change of both political and military leadership. Unbeknownst to the POWs (or anyone else, for that matter) the war was soon to enter its climactic months.

CHAPTER TWENTY-THREE

A Change of Political Command

President Harry Truman had carried a secret around with him since April 16, 1950, a full two months before the Korean War began.[1] He did not intend to run for reelection. When his term ended, he would have been in public office thirty years. He believed in the two-term rule. "In my opinion eight years as President is enough and sometimes too much for any man to serve in that capacity," Truman wrote in his private diary. "There is a lure in power. It can get into a man's blood just as gambling and lust for money have been known to do."

But shrewd politician that he was, Truman chose to say nothing publicly until the time of his own choosing. He did speak privately with Chief Justice Fred M. Vinson, whom he considered "the most logical and qualified candidate." But Vinson begged off for reasons of health. Truman gradually shared his secret with other Democratic leaders, and by January 1952 he had decided upon Adlai E. Stevenson, the governor of Illinois, as the "best all-around candidate." Stevenson met twice with Truman but would say neither yes nor no, to the President's irritation. Stevenson was still vacillating on March 29, when Truman made a surprise statement at the annual Jefferson-Jackson Day Dinner in the National Guard Armory in Washington that he would not run again.

Although Truman asserted boldly in his memoirs he could have won reelection, circumstances suggest otherwise. The public was disgusted with a firecracker string of scandals that shook his administration beginning in 1950: corruption in the federal tax service; "five percenters" who pushed government contracts to friends in return for such payoffs as mink coats; funneling of Reconstruction Finance Corporation loans to such speculative ventures as gambling casinos in Miami and Las Vegas, with payments to such high Democratic officials as William M. Boyle, Jr., the party's vice-chairman, easing the paper work. Although no one ever accused Truman of taking a dime, the aura of hustlerism permeated the White House (the President's military aide, Major General Harry Vaughan, for instance, matter-of-factly told an audience how easily he had sold his $55 watch for $500 on the German black market). Cumulatively the Truman scandals were Washington's sorriest hour since the Teapot Dome affair of the Harding years. Truman paid a high price in public support. In late 1950, when the Korean War went well, Truman enjoyed a "favorable" rating in the Gallup Poll of 46 percent, highest of his time in office. But during the last two years of his term, approval never rose above 32 percent, and at times it dipped as low as 23 percent. With the support of less than one citizen of four, Truman clearly faced an uphill fight had he chosen to run again.

The task would have been all the more formidable in 1952 because the Republicans nominated a midcentury hero, Dwight David Eisenhower, a man of indefinite politics but a deserved public reputation for strength and decency. Politicians of both parties had tempted him with the presidential nomination since his triumph in the European campaign, and Truman had said in more than one forum that he had offered to step aside for the general in 1948. Ike—everyone called him that— spent the postwar years as army chief of staff, as president of Columbia University, and as the first commander of the North Atlantic Treaty Organization. In late 1951 Eisenhower began dropping hints to Republicans visiting his Paris office that he was available. Korea was a definite factor, he told Herbert Brownell, long an associate of former Governor Thomas Dewey of New York (and later Ike's attorney general). Eisenhower saw very deep dissatisfaction throughout the country over Truman's handling of the war. Eisenhower had the idea he could win the GOP nomination simply by issuing a statement. Brownell felt otherwise: Winning the nomination over Senator Robert A. Taft of Ohio would be considerably more difficult than winning the election, he counseled the general. The last three elections Taft's isolationist midwesterners had seen their party nominate an "eastern internationalist" (Wendell Willkie in 1940; Dewey in 1944 and 1948); now the Taftites wanted their turn. So they fought it out in the primaries, with Taft bounding to an early lead. In early April Eisenhower told the President that his "surprising development as a political figure" was interfering with his military duties, and he asked to be replaced as NATO commander. As his successor, Truman chose General Matthew Ridgway, a tribute to the latter's success in Korea. The reshuffling took General Mark

W. Clark, hero of the Italy campaign of the Second World War, to Korea to replace Ridgway.*

Opening his campaign on June 2 in his hometown of Abilene, Kansas, Ike called for a "decent armistice" in Korea but did not specifically criticize administration policy there. The most pressing issue in the campaign, he avowed, was "liberty versus socialism." He asked for the abolition of "useless" federal agencies and the "rooting out" of "subversive elements." In a major speech some two weeks later, billed as an "Answer to Abilene," Taft criticized Eisenhower for refusing to condemn the Truman administration's war policies. Although Taft offered no new policies to pursue in Korea, one promise stood in sharp contrast with Eisenhower: He would bring General Douglas MacArthur back into government, although in an unspecified capacity. Eisenhower knew better. He said only he would "listen to anything MacArthur had to say." (The previous spring, shortly after MacArthur's firing, Eisenhower wrote an old friend that "I've kept my mouth closed in every language of which I have ever heard."[2])

No such silence came from MacArthur. He credited himself (unduly) with frightening Truman out of the election; now he set his sights on stopping Eisenhower on behalf of Taft—perhaps even himself. The GOP chose him as keynote speaker for its convention in Chicago in early July. MacArthur made plain in his private talks his willingness to heed destiny should it summon him. "His role as keynoter is just a starter," observed *U.S. News & World Report*. "He is ready to lay aside his uniform, retire from the army, do anything necessary to . . . defeat his five-star colleague." All spring MacArthur had evoked cheers with his attacks on Truman's conduct of the war. Now he wished a chance to vindicate his reputation.

MacArthur's opposition to his fellow general was both philosophical and personal. He considered Eisenhower the embodiment of the "George Marshall wing" of the United States Army, oriented toward Europe rather than Asia. Eisenhower was a staff man, not a fighter; patriotic though he was, he lacked MacArthur's messianic opposition to communism. As army chief of staff MacArthur had made Eisenhower his protégé and taken him to Manila as a key aide after his first retirement. They disagreed politically then (Eisenhower even having the audacity to wager considerable cash that Roosevelt would win reelection in 1936); MacArthur saw no changes in the younger man save for the worst. So the MacArthur campaign groups mushroomed: Americans for MacArthur in California; Demand MacArthur in Texas; Fighters for MacArthur in Pennsylvania.

A few weeks before the convention MacArthur and Taft had breakfast in the general's retreat in the Waldorf.[3] According to General

*Clark's last assignment had been chief of army field forces, responsible for training.

Courtney Whitney, MacArthur promised Taft his support, both for the nomination and in the campaign (making no mention of his own lingering ambitions for the prize). Taft, in return, promised to appoint MacArthur head of the armed services if he became President. This was the MacArthur camp's version. By Taft's account, he intended to ask the convention to nominate MacArthur as his running mate and then announce he would make the general a "deputy commander in chief" with shared responsibility for "the formulation of all foreign policy bearing upon the national security."

As it happened, all these schemes came to naught, for by the time the convention opened Eisenhower had won procedural test votes on enough contested delegates to put him within reach of the nomination. Thus MacArthur's only chance to thrust himself back into national prominence was his keynote address: If he could excite the delegates sufficiently, perhaps he could yet swing the convention to Taft (or to himself). The omens were poor. The Ike forces easily won platform planks affirming U.S. commitments to Europe, and the bandwagon seemed unstoppable. MacArthur certainly was no barrier. Even to friendly observers the speech was one of the poorest of his career. His voice frequently broke, and he bobbed up and down as if trying to give emphasis to key sentences. "He said nothing but sheer baloney," wrote C. L. Sulzberger of *The New York Times.* "One could feel the electricity gradually running out of the room. I think he cooked his own goose and didn't do much to help Taft."[4]

MacArthur flew back to New York on the *Bataan* that night with lingering hopes the convention might still summon him to duty. The call did not come. Ike won on the first ballot, with 595 votes to Taft's 500 (MacArthur received 10 diehard votes; other candidates had 100 or so among them). But although Taft did not win the nomination, his followers infused the convention with the main theme that was to mark the campaign: rousing anticommunism and attacks at the "slimy traitors" active even now "in the Red Dean's State Department." The words were those of Senator Joseph McCarthy of Wisconsin, and as the band played "The Marine Hymn," delegates carrying fish-shaped placards labeled "Acheson," "Hiss," and "Red Herring" paraded in front of the platform. McCarthy spoke with a roar: "We can't fight Communists in the Acheson-Lattimore* fashion of hitting them with a perfumed silk handkerchief at the front door, while they batter our friends with brass knuckles at the back door!" He called on "millions of *loyal* Democrats" to realize their party had "deserted" them. Turning to Korea, McCarthy pledged that if the Republicans won, "we won't be in any war which we are afraid to win." The real issue of the election

*Owen Lattimore, an academic analyst of Chinese affairs, was then under attack by McCarthy.

was whether the United States should "continue to squander her blood, waste her resources, and sacrifice her position of world leadership—just that and nothing more." Continuing the same theme, young Senator Richard M. Nixon of California, tapped by Ike as his running mate, shouted that "the American people have had enough of the whining, whimpering, groveling attitude of our diplomatic representatives, who speak of America's fears, rather than of America's strengths and of America's courage."

The formal platform, brimming with talk about "traitors in high places" and "arrogant bureaucrats," took the Democrats to task for a long string of diplomatic failures ranging from Yalta to China. The language on Korea, however, was relatively mild, centering chiefly on Truman's decision not to obtain a formal declaration of war: "We charge that they have plunged us into war in Korea without the consent of our citizens through their authorized representatives in the Congress, and have carried on that war without will to victory."

The foreign policy plank was the work of John Foster Dulles, who in the past six months had maneuvered to make himself Ike's chief foreign policy adviser. Although he continued to serve the State Department as a special adviser through early January, Dulles had become increasingly critical of the Truman-Acheson doctrine of containment. Dulles realized that two decades of continuous power, with all their accretions of grievances, meant an imminent end to Democratic rule. At the core of the problem was the Korean War. In the view of Townsend Hoopes, a young Defense Department official, "Because its conduct ran so hard against the grain of war-making in the simpler American past, it was producing strains, anxieties, and problems of credibility that became fertile breeding grounds for the new unilateralism and a vicious demagoguery."[5] Dulles hoped to be a part of the new guard occupying Washington.

Rather reflexively Dulles cast his lot with Eisenhower. He thought Taft narrowly isolationist and conservative, with unflinching hostility toward Europe's myriad problems. Through his New York law firm (Sullivan & Cromwell) Dulles had long associated with continental businessmen and officials, and he thought it dangerously shortsighted for America to turn its back on such an important bloc of nations. Although Eisenhower's views on world affairs were largely unknown (as, indeed, were his views on almost any subject at hand), Dulles thought he would be amenable to a "basically generous and pragmatic internationalism." So Dulles set about attracting the general's attention, first with memos sent to Eisenhower through Dewey and Lucius Clay, a retired general, now an investment banker and a key backer, then with a visit to Paris. His views came together in an essay published in *Life* magazine on May 19, seven weeks before the convention, entitled "A Policy of Boldness." The article is significant because among other things, it signaled the approach Eisenhower and Dulles would use a year later to end the Korean fighting.

Although Dulles saw strong points in such Truman actions as the Marshall Plan, formation of NATO, and intervention in Korea (the latter he called "courageous, righteous, and in the national interest"), on the whole he thought American policy a series of reactive, negative, emergency measures that did not strike at the root of the problem of Soviet expansionism. "We are not working, sacrificing and spending in order to be able to live *without* this peril—but to be able to live *with* it, presumably forever. . . . Ours are treadmill policies which, at best, might keep us in the same place until we drop exhausted."

So what should be done? Dulles proposed a concept that came to be known as massive retaliation. As he put the case: "There is one solution and only one: that is for the free world to develop the will and organize the means to retaliate instantly against open aggression by Red armies, so that, if it occurred anywhere, we could and *would strike back where it hurts, by means of our choosing* [emphasis added]." Dulles argued for the existence of a "moral or natural law," to which men and nations must conform or ultimately face ruin, and he saw America as the chosen agent of God's vengeance. "This law has been trampled by the Soviet rulers, and for that violation they can and should be made to pay." The free world had the "means" for retaliation—(the code word meaning nuclear weaponry); now it must "develop the will" to use such power "instantly."

Emmet John Hughes, a *Life* editor who helped Dulles write the article, kept pressing Dulles to define his policy intentions more specifically. "What are you proposing that U.S. policy should *do?*" Dulles preferred to remain vague: He had laid down the broad objectives; now let the Soviets wonder how he intended to carry them out if Ike became President.

Eisenhower, in private, fretted about Dulles's views on massive retaliation; he also told C. L. Sulzberger of *The New York Times* he thought the attacks in the platform on Truman "were a bit savage." But he made a pragmatic decision. He did not offer serious objection to the platform language because he needed the Taft wing of the party to win. And as far as specifics were concerned, Ike would work these out at his leisure over the next few months.

The Democrats: "Madly for Adlai"

Although one of the more reluctant candidates in history, Adlai Stevenson finally bestirred himself enough in July to win the Democratic nomination, which proved something of a hollow prize. As has so often been true in the twentieth century, the Democrats so battered themselves in convention that the party could not unite itself by November. The fights this time were over party loyalty, civil rights, and the degree of fealty that must be sworn to the accomplishments of Harry S. Truman. To win, Stevenson had to beat back such popular party figures as the South's beloved Richard Russell; Averell Harriman, the patrician former New York governor, much favored by eastern liberals; Estes Kefauver of Tennessee, who had struck a popular public chord the past two years with televised hearings on the underworld; and Stuart Symington of Missouri. Although a two-term governor of a large state, Stevenson was by no means a national figure. His dumpy, balding personal appearance, while exciting the mother instinct in some women, struck other people as hopelessly nondescript. Stevenson's admirers—and they could be fervent—sought in the governor a reincarnation of Franklin D. Roosevelt; that, sadly, he was not. Stevenson could be sincerely eloquent, and he is one of the few politicians I have encountered whose speeches still "read well" three decades in the tomb. His early hesitancy notwithstanding, Stevenson promised the convention to work hard to win, albeit on a high moral road. "Better we lose the election," he said in his acceptance speech, "than mislead the people; and better we lose than misgovern the people."

A few days later Stevenson deliberately disassociated himself from Truman. His campaign headquarters, he said, would be in the Illinois capital of Springfield. He fired the Democratic national chairman, Frank McKinney, and replaced him with his own man, Stephen A. Mitchell, a Chicago lawyer. He also told a reporter one of his major goals would be to "clean up the mess in Washington," a line that could have been lifted from the GOP platform. "By this inadvertence," Truman fumed, "Stevenson provided the Republican opposition with the audacity to go ahead with the two phony issues of the Eisenhower campaign—corruption and Korea."[6]

But Stevenson could not shake off his party's recent past, and he found himself contesting separate Republican campaigns. One was epitomized by Senator Karl Mundt's formula: $K_1 C_3$ (Korea, Crime, Communism, and Corruption). The other was Eisenhower, who heard the chant "We Like Ike!" wherever he went. Marquis Childs of the St. Louis *Post-Dispatch* wrote: "Millions were happy to take him on faith, on his face, on his smile, on the image of American manhood, on the happy virtue of his family life." Eisenhower happily stayed on the high perch while Joe McCarthy and Richard Nixon exploited the "treason in high places" theme (the latter saying a Stevenson victory would mean "more Alger Hisses, more atomic spies, more crises . . .").

Still, the Eisenhower campaign seemed to lack the vital spark that would ensure victory. Stevenson's soaring eloquence impressed television audiences, and although Eisenhower commanded the editorial support of much of the nation's press, America's intellectuals backed the man columnist Stewart Alsop called an "egghead." Eisenhower kept Korea out of the formal campaign these first weeks, apparently by design. As a professional soldier he disdained saying anything that might harm his old comrades now in charge of the war. On June 5 he supported continuing the limited war while seeking a "decent" armistice. On August 21, pressed to explain how his policies as President would differ from those pursued by Truman and Acheson, he chose to attack the Taft-MacArthur approach, saying they risked involving the United States in a war with China that would be "far more difficult to stop than the one we are in now."

Then Eisenhower stepped across the line into rank (and highly inaccurate) partisanship on Korea.[7] In a speech on the origins of the war, Eisenhower said:

> The terrible record of these years reaches its dramatic climax in a series of unforgettable scenes on Capitol Hill in June of 1949. By then the decision to complete withdrawal of American forces from Korea—despite menacing signs from the North—has been drawn up by the Department of State.

Eisenhower's statement was instantly and embarrassingly refutable. The initial recommendation for withdrawing U.S. troops from South Korea came in May 1947 from Secretary of War Robert Patterson, a Republican. On September 26, 1947, the Joint Chiefs of Staff said the United States had "little strategic interest" in maintaining troops and bases in Korea. American manpower could be put to better use elsewhere. Among the JCS members signing this memorandum was General Dwight D. Eisenhower, then army chief of staff. Further, as documented earlier (see Chapter One), the State Department, not the American military, argued for a slower pace of American withdrawal in 1949–50; the Defense Department prevailed. This statement, and others in the same speech, angered Truman, who thought Eisenhower's misuse of the record "politically and morally intolerable." The President could understand his extreme isolationist foes using Korea politically, "but I will never understand how a responsible military man, fully familiar with the extreme delicacy of our negotiations to end hostilities, could use the tragedy for political advantage."

Eisenhower's staff, to the contrary, worried whether the general was making maximum use of Korea. He was a professional soldier; surely the public expected more from him than banalities. When would Eisenhower say specifically what he intended to do to end the war and to get American troops home from the Asian quagmire?

The idea came from Emmet John Hughes, the *Life* editor recently signed on as an Eisenhower speech writer, during a dinner at his Greenwich Village apartment with Herbert Brownell, Ike's campaign manager.[8] "He [Hughes] had the idea that there should be a promise . . . by General Eisenhower . . . to go to Korea and take a personal look at the situation there, with a view to stopping the war," Brownell recollected. By Hughes's recollection, the origin of the speech "rose from the need to say something affirmative on the sharpest issue of the day—*without* engaging in frivolous assurances and *without* binding a future administration to policies or actions fashioned in mid-campaign by any distorting temperatures of domestic politics."[9] Korea was the "most distracting and the most dramatic" issue of the day, and it was military. "The candidate, who happened to be the nation's most renowned military figure, pledged himself to look at the area personally." Hughes felt the statement was "natural and appropriate, almost to the point of being banal."

As Brownell and Hughes talked, they decided on the short phrase "I will go to Korea." After several speech drafts the idea was handed to Eisenhower, who was not so sure about it. On his campaign train one evening, rocking across upper New York State, Eisenhower read the draft to several persons to mixed reaction. Ike finally told Brownell to decide. Make the speech, Brownell counseled.

Eisenhower did, in a talk at the Masonic Temple in Detroit on October 24. Speaking to what passed for a national TV audience in 1952, Eisenhower wound up a talk by saying his administration would give first priority to ending the Korean War: "That job requires a personal trip to Korea. I shall make that trip. Only in that way could I learn best how to serve the American people in the cause of peace. I shall go to Korea."

The statement enraged Truman, who asserted Eisenhower "must have known that he was weakening our hand in negotiations" and misleading the American people into thinking peace would follow swiftly on the heels of his election.[10] Stevenson, characteristically, tried to laugh off an obvious coup by his opponent. "If elected," Stevenson said the next day, "I shall go to the White House."

The Democratic audience chuckled and clapped, but political writer Jack Bell of the Associated Press wrote, "For all practical purposes, the contest ended that night."

And it did. For the first time since 1932 America voted for a Republican President, giving Eisenhower a victory of landslide proportion, 33,936,234 votes to 27,314,992. Now Eisenhower had his opportunity to seek peace in Korea.

* * *

Sputtering Peace Talks

A silent but very interested observer of the American elections was President Syngman Rhee. And regardless of what the Americans voted, he did not intend to discuss a peace on any terms approaching those considered attainable by the UN. Rhee had taken the United States— and the UN—at their word when they came into the Korean War; now he intended to hold them to it. The week the peace talks started, in June 1951, Rhee had laid down his demands in a letter to the State Department:

1. Complete withdrawal of Chinese forces from Korea.
2. Disarmament of North Korea.
3. UN commitment to prevent any third-party support of the North Koreans.
4. South Korean participation in any UN consideration of "any aspect of the Korean problem."
5. Preservation of the sovereignty and territorial integrity of Korea.

In sum, Rhee wanted UN adherence to its resolutions calling for a free and united Korea, devoid of any foreign troops. The elderly president had seen much of his nation destroyed in quest of these goals; he did not intend to compromise for anything less, regardless of how badly the United States wished to leave the war. His obvious fear was that the Americans would settle the war at the 38th parallel (as indeed Washington was ready to do, give or take a few tucks in the battle line).

Rhee's attacks, which continued throughout late 1951 and early 1952, caused no especial concern to Ambassador John Muccio or other U.S. officials in Korea. But Muccio did note that Rhee "becomes increasingly exacerbated at each indication [that] armistice may eventuate."[11] When Francis Cardinal Spellman of New York, the most prominent U.S. Catholic dignitary, visited Seoul, Rhee enjoined him in front of Muccio and General Van Fleet to "ask every Catholic in the United States to pray that there will be no cease-fire." To Muccio's distress, the antiarmistice sentiments spread to moderate members of Rhee's government, with one minister charging the UN of "yielding to arrogance and insults of the traitorous Communists."

Reading these and scores of similar cables sent from Seoul to the State Department the first months of 1952 leads me to a harsh conclusion unrefuted by any document, written or commented upon, at any level of the U.S. government—to wit, the Truman administration's expectation was that Rhee, for some undefined reason, would accept *any* negotiated settlement the UN might achieve. Here Muccio and other diplomats fell into an almost fatal delusion. President Truman indeed wished a settlement before his term of office ended, for the Korean War was a seminal event of his administration, one he did not wish to hand to Eisenhower. But instead of looking for ways to accommodate Rhee, Muccio—on Acheson's orders—in effect told the South Korean he *must* cooperate. Whereupon Rhee "became hot under the collar" (Muccio's words) and insisted that his government would never accept a cease-fire and that Truman should be told he was "mistaken" in negotiating with the Communists.[12] Ridgway, who monitored Muccio's reports, warned that Rhee's attitude might "gravely endanger" any settlement.[13] He detected a Rhee threat to withdraw ROK forces from the UN Command, and he had no assurance that he could control ROK forces should an armistice be signed.

But no one in Washington—that is, the President, the State Department, or the Joint Chiefs—wished to bargain with Rhee or even to offer him further explanations. A February 27, 1952, cable to Ridgway suggested that he present any armistice as a *"fait accompli"* and then take the "strongest measures to insure ROK compliance."[14] Truman followed this message with a personal warning to Rhee that was tantamount to a blackmail demand: Rhee must follow American guidance or else forfeit any postwar support.[15] Although couched in convolutedly diplomatic language, the note was nothing less than an "or else" ultimatum to an ally:

> The degree of assistance which your government and the people of Korea will continue to receive in repelling the aggression, in seeking a just political settlement, and in repairing the ravages of that aggression will inevitably be influenced by the sense of responsibility demonstrated by your government, its ability to maintain the unity of the Korean people, and its devotion to democratic ideals.

Rhee, however, would not be cowed. He dropped hints about withdrawing the ROK Army from UN control; he intimated to Ambassador Muccio he was "quite pleased by evidence that he was keeping other countries guessing" about his actions.[16] One of his official spokesmen even announced the ROK would veto any armistice signed under "dishonorable circumstances" and that the South Korean negotiator did not actually represent his country since the UN had appointed him. And in a public statement on April 24 Rhee disdained talk of a cease-fire. "I am still opposed to any cease-fire which leaves our country divided," he said. "No matter what arguments others may make, we are determined to unify our fatherland with our own hands."

He, however, had problems even retaining control of South Korea.[17] Many Koreans resented Rhee's autocratic methods, and these hostilities came to a head in the National Assembly in the summer of 1952. Under the Korean constitution, legislators elected the president, and indications that summer were that Rhee would not be returned to office. With his characteristic disdain of opponents, Rhee demanded that the Assembly change the constitution to provide for a popular general election, confident of his ability to sway public opinion. When the Assembly refused, Rhee declared martial law in the Pusan area—where the legislature was sitting—and arrested more than a score of its members on obviously false charges of treason and complicity with the Communists. He cited "military necessity" as his reason and claimed the support of General Van Fleet, whose command had been plagued with guerrillas in the area. (Van Fleet denied any such backing.) Heated exchanges between Rhee, President Truman, and the State Department ensued, and Rhee escalated the crisis by threatening to withdraw ROK troops from combat zones to "insure order" in Pusan. UN protests about the martial law did not move Rhee.

General Mark Clark, torn between prosecuting a war and placating Rhee, warned superiors on May 31 that it might be necessary "to tolerate actions by Rhee which are abhorrent and endure embarrassing political incidents precipitated by him." But when Rhee's machinations threatened Clark's military situation, he was prepared to take either of two actions: continue to urge Rhee to moderate his crackdown in the "forlorn hope" he would listen to reason or "take over and establish some form of interim government"—in other words, topple Rhee with a coup and install more amenable leaders.

But Clark was pessimistic about moving against Rhee. He had already alerted one army regimental combat team for movement from Japan to Korea, and he had spoken with the ROK Army chief of staff about ensuring the support of the ROK Army should Rhee attempt to use it against his internal enemies. Any ROK Army units taken out of their combat missions would lose UN logistical support, Clark said, and the Eighth Army would block their movement toward Pusan. Clark, however, cautioned Washington against "hasty action . . . [or] idle threats." He did not have the troops to withstand a major Communist offensive, retain control of rebellious POWs on Koje-do Island, and "handle major civil disturbances in our rear at the same time." He recommended that the UN swallow its pride until Rhee, through "illegal and diabolical actions," created a militarily intolerable situation. At that point, Clark said, he would muster all his forces, establish martial law or military government if necessary, and take "any steps" directed by the U.S. government to correct the situation.

On June 2, Generals Clark and Van Fleet confronted Rhee in person, pointing out the dangers that the enemy might take advantage of the confusion by launching a major attack.[18] Rhee was not moved. He could control any situation, he would not interfere with the war, but he would "comply with the will of the people." He was so emotional that the American generals wondered whether he had lost his reason. At one point Rhee even accused the United States of building up the Japanese Army to "take over in Korea" after U.S. troops were withdrawn. Clark was willing to give more time, although as he told the JCS:

> . . . until such time as we are forced to take drastic military action, pressure should be exerted on Rhee through diplomatic channels. I am also convinced that I cannot take any partial action such as offering protection to national assemblymen without causing an upheaval which might require us to assume complete control, which we can ill afford to do.

Ambassador Muccio, perhaps Rhee's best—and most patient—friend in the American community, could make no headway with the president. Rhee would not deal with the Assembly because "Communists controlled it," and his orchestrated mass demonstrations took on ugly anti-American tones. On June 14 Muccio threw up his hands and told the State Department the time had come for a direct threat of UN intervention. He would use as an agent the ROK Army, acting on orders from the UN transmitted through the Eighth Army.

President Truman agreed with Muccio.[19] On June 25 the State Department prepared a directive—approved by the Joint Chiefs and cleared by the President—for Muccio and General Clark. They were to confer "earliest" to prepare plans for military and political action if intervention became necessary to prevent interference with UN military operations. Preferably Truman would order intervention, but in an emergency Clark was authorized to act on his own initiative. The scenario was outlined along these lines:

If Rhee took any action that threatened the war effort, or imposed any further strictures on the National Assembly, Clark and Muccio, on behalf of both the United States and the UN, would demand that he desist. If Rhee refused, Clark would order the ROK chief of staff* to assume control of the South Korean Army and take control of the Pusan area. The authority and functions of the ROK government would be preserved insofar as possible, and constitutional government would remain intact.

Given this broad authority, Clark prepared a contingency plan for a coup. Rhee would be invited to Seoul on a pretext. Once he left, UN troops would move into Pusan in force, seize Rhee's key supporters and vital installations such as government and communications offices, and take control of the existing martial-law government through the ROK chief of staff. Rhee would be directed to proclaim the end of martial law and permit freedom of action by the National Assembly. If he refused, he would be held incommunicado in protective custody, and the prime minister would issue the desired proclamation.

*Other Washington–Seoul cables suggest the chief of staff would side with the United States in any showdown with Rhee.

To Clark's relief, the coup was not consummated.[20] On July 3 the National Assembly reversed itself and voted to amend the constitution to permit the president to be elected by popular vote. Imprisoned members were released, and Rhee lifted martial law on July 28. On August 5 Rhee was reelected by landslide vote. Thus the immediate crisis eased. But the Truman administration had made a basic policy decision that would provide guidance for the future: It would not hesitate to remove President Rhee from office by force if necessary to attain U.S. goals in the war.

A Stagnant Battle: "Trench Warfare"

All through the myriad sideline happenings—the American elections, the stalemated negotiations, the diplomatic problems with President Rhee—the war itself had essentially ground to a halt. The opposing armies faced each other like two wary and weary giants, contenting themselves with probes and patrols, all the while consolidating their defensive positions. The UN front, with scores of thousands of reinforced bunkers dug into the Korean hills, connected by a series of communications trenches, resembled a front line from the First World War. Neither the UN nor the Communists showed any willingness to go beyond the demarcation line that had been agreed upon in November 1951. To General James Van Fleet, even minor attacks "will not, in my opinion, justify the costs."[21]

General Matthew Ridgway, politically sensitive to the Truman administration's intention to get out of the war, detailed his reasoning in a long cable to the Joint Chiefs on March 1, 1952, that in effect capsulized the UN military conduct the remainder of the war. Ridgway's key conclusions were as follows:

> A major ground offensive in Korea, having as its objective large scale destruction of hostile personnel and matériel, would require acceptance of a serious risk of successful enemy counter-offensive which could inflict heavy matériel and personnel losses on our own forces.
>
> Even if our operations were successful and hostile counter-offensives, if launched, were defeated, the operations would still exact heavy U.S. battle casualties.
>
> Employing all . . . forces available for this effort, the operation, even though successful, could do no more than deal a hard blow to Communist forces. . . . It could not inflict a decisive military defeat.
>
> Without substantial organizational reinforcement, a major ground offensive would offer too marginal a chance of success to justify its undertaking.[22]

The Joint Chiefs accepted Ridgway's assessment. A reinforcing factor was the sharp increase in enemy strength. An intelligence estimate circulated in the Pentagon in April noted that from July 1951 to April 1952, the Communists had increased their manpower from about 500,000 to more than 860,000.[23] There were also significant improvements in armor, artillery, and unit firepower. The long lull enabled the enemy to improve supply routes (despite constant UN air and naval attacks) to their best condition since the war began. The G-2 estimate also noted that other Communist forces in the Far East included 3.6 million Chinese regulars and some thirty-three Soviet divisions, or another 330,000 men. The UN Command totaled about 547,100 troops—259,000 Americans, 250,000 ROKs, and 37,700 from other UN nations.

Given the strictures on ground operations, the UN Command pounded the Communists incessantly by air, with particular attention paid to the vast hydroelectric plants along the Yalu. In one three-day period in June 1952, navy and air force planes flew more than 1,400 sorties against the power plants, badly damaging Suiho, the largest, and putting ten others out of commission. The resultant power blackout in North Korea lasted for two weeks. Britain's Labor Party protested strongly the "escalation" of the war, and there were murmurs of dissent from the French. But General Clark was not moved: The plants helped the enemy; thus they were fair game for attacks.

Clark also found ways to harass the enemy psychologically.[24] Since MacArthur's success at Inchon the Communists displayed acute fear of further amphibious assaults, concentrating coastal artillery and troops at such likely invasion points as Wonsan, on the east coast. In October 1952 Clark decided to move the 1st Cavalry Division from Japan to Korea, and he saw the operation as an opportunity to alarm the enemy. "The more he worried, the more troop strength and effort would have to be diverted to building defenses behind the lines," Clark reasoned.

So the cavalry units went through intensive amphibious training, climaxed with a full-scale landing rehearsal. They then boarded attack transports, battle-loaded and ready to fight; low-echelon officers thought the troops were en route to a combat landing. Meanwhile, air and navy forces struck at the "target" beaches around Wonsan in raids that paralleled what the American military had done preceding amphibious landings since the Second World War. When the armada neared Wonsan, some of the troops left the transports and climbed into assault boats which circled in regular preattack formations.

"Our intelligence reported that the enemy was in a tailspin on the beach near Wonsan," Clark recollected. Communist reinforcements were hastened to the area. After several hours the American troops reboarded the main transports and sailed south to Pusan, their true destination.

But Clark made no progress when he reopened a long-decided old debate: the use of Chinese Nationalist troops in Korea.[25] Clark had been in command barely two weeks when—on May 27, 1952—he told the JCS he was worried about having enough manpower to perform his dual missions of defending Japan and pushing the war in Korea. Bringing in two divisions of Nationalists would be of value psychologically and militarily, he argued. General Walter Bedell Smith, the director of central intelligence, supported Clark, saying that the Nationalist troops on Formosa were a "wasting asset" unless used.[26] Moving two divisions to Korea would not materially weaken island defenses, he said. Truman, however, would go only so far as to authorize "additional study." The State Department flatly opposed any such use of the Nationalists, citing certain adverse world reaction.

The Joint Chiefs discussed the issue through the fall of 1952, finally deciding on November 21 that Clark should receive the requested two divisions. By this time, however, Eisenhower was President-elect, and the lame-duck Truman administration did not wish to undertake such a drastic revision of policy. The question was left for Eisenhower to decide. Eisenhower never gave the issue serious consideration: He had his own plans for peace in Korea, and they did not include the Nationalist Chinese.

Truman's Last Chance

Throughout the summer of 1952 the UN and the Communists exchanged subtle variations of proposals on disposition of the prisoners of war, with no progress. Both the Soviets and the Chinese presented ideas that at first blush seemed promising, then trailed away. Other ideas were floated by such diverse personages as Vincent W. Hallinan, presidential candidate of the far-left-wing Progressive Party (that a cease-fire be declared, with the POW question to be discussed later) and President Miguel Alemán of Mexico (that POWs declining repatriation be given immigration status by UN nations).

The Joint Chiefs, as well as the UN negotiating team, ticked off the obvious defects of both these schemes. The Communists desperately wanted a cease-fire so they would be spared further UN air attacks. Ending the fighting without resolving the POW issue would leave the UN powerless to obtain the terms it wanted. Through a series of recounts and reclassifications of POWs, the Communists now demanded the return of around 83,000 men; the UN found only around 70,000 willing to accept repatriation. (These figures varied from month to month as the result of deaths, escapes, and new captures.)

In September pressures mounted on President Truman to break the stalemate at Panmunjom. Although positions varied from day to day, the State Department, under Secretary Acheson, seemed willing to accept a form of President Alemán's plan—to move for an immediate cease-fire and to give nonrepatriates asylum in other UN countries. This scheme gave an obvious political advantage to Adlai Stevenson, the Democratic presidential candidate, for "stopping the fighting" would undercut a dominant issue being pressed by Eisenhower. But the Defense Department—led by Secretary Robert Lovett—argued against any makeshift settlement; to do so would display fatal weakness and undermine military pressures being applied to the enemy.[27] Concessions, Lovett said, would "be unlikely to move the Communists, who were influenced only by force." The Joint Chiefs agreed, stating (in the words of General Hoyt Vandenberg of the air force) that an armistice would create pell-mell pressures to "bring the boys home," as happened at the end of the Second World War.

The onus for decision clearly rested on President Truman. State and Defense disagreed. The President frequently pointed out to visitors a sign on his desk, "The Buck Stops Here." This day the buck stopped squarely on Truman's desk, and his decision helped doom Stevenson's campaign. Agreeing with Secretary Lovett, Truman saw "no real prospect of getting an armistice" except by continuing military pressure. He wanted "additional military effort" to force the enemy to accept the "reasonable proposals" the UN had offered. Truman directed that the talks be postponed indefinitely, rather than give the Communists the impression they could expect concessions by convening at a specific future date.

At another meeting two days later, on September 24, Acheson warned that moving for an indefinite recess could cause diplomatic problems at the UN. Acheson displayed signs of personal nervousness. His persuasive abilities had brought the United States into the war; when things went wrong, the same persuasive abilities had caused the United States to fight a limited war. Now Acheson seemed determined to end the war before he left office. He saw any number of political problems should the United States not obtain a cease-fire. The UN General Assembly could establish a commission to conduct the war, which would "make it impossible for us to fight a war there effectively."[28] Looking over his shoulder at his hard-line Republican antagonists, Acheson said an indefinite recess in the peace talks would be evidence that the administration was at a loss on what to do in Korea. The "impatient element" which had been advocating that the UN "shoot the works" in Korea might have a resurgence. Acheson clearly wanted out of the war.

Truman strongly disagreed. The United States faced the question of whether "we should do anything in the world to get out of Korea."[29] Here he was demonstrably tougher than Acheson. Truman was not willing to seek an armistice "just for the sake of an armistice," especially if China would be left in a position to renew the fighting. He had worked for "seven years to avoid a Third World War." Accepting the sort of armistice proposed by the "State Department" (he kindly did not use Acheson's name) would revert the country to the same position as that in September 1945, when "we tore up a great fighting machine" which should have been kept intact. Accepting a false armistice would mean the United States lost the gains it had made in Korea since June 1950. Truman then asked for comments.

Pentagon spokesmen endorsed Truman's hard-line approach. William C. Foster, speaking for the Defense Department, would increase military pressures, including use of Chinese Nationalist troops (Truman demurred), more intensive bombing, and expansion of the ROK Army. General Walter Bedell Smith, the director of central intelligence, felt there could be no real armistice in Korea as long as China "had the potentiality for further devilment." Every means of putting pressure on the Chinese should be exploited. The Chinese Nationalists, Smith said, were a "pistol at the head" of the Chinese Communists.

Truman listened to the debate, then came down hard on the side of the military. The UN negotiators would present a proposal against forcible repatriation, based upon the POW screening lists already compiled. The chief negotiator, Major General William K. Harrison, Jr.,* would lay the proposal on the table and give the enemy ten days for reply. If the Communists rejected it, the United States would declare an indefinite recess and "be prepared to do such other things as may be necessary." Truman flatly refused to defer the POW issue for later political discussions. In a personal message to General Clark the next day, September 26, Truman repeated the instructions and added that they should be "presented with the utmost firmness and without subsequent debate."[30] Military pressure during the ten-day waiting period "should not be lessened."

On October 8 the Communists' chief negotiator, General Nam Il, rejected the UN proposal as "unacceptable." Whereupon General Harrison declared a recess until "you are ready to accept one of our proposals or to make a constructive proposal of your own, in writing, which could lead to an honorable armistice." Dean Acheson, announcing the recess in Washington, was firm on the principle of voluntary repatriation. "We shall not trade in the lives of men," Acheson said. "We shall not forcibly deliver human beings into Communist hands."

The recess stung the Communists, for now they had lost the propa-

*Harrison had replaced Admiral C. Turner Joy on May 22. At his last negotiating session Joy told the Communists, "There is nothing left to negotiate. I now turn over the unenviable job of further dealing with you to . . . General Harrison. . . . May God be with him."

ganda forum of Panmunjom. But a note on October 16 from Kim Il Sung, the North Korean premier, and Peng Teh-huai, head of the Chinese "volunteers," pointed up the futility of continued talks. The note demanded an immediate resumption of the talks and an armistice on the basis of "total repatriation of all prisoners." Thus the talks ended, with diplomacy at a dead end.

CHAPTER TWENTY-FOUR

Eisenhower: Peace at Last

In the predawn hours of November 29, 1952, the time when New York is at its quietest, sleepy men dressed for winter travel appeared quietly, singly and in small groups, at designated locations around Manhattan, to be met by limousines that rolled silently out of the dark.[1] Charles E. Wilson, who was to be secretary of defense in the new administration, waited alone and without luggage at the southeast corner of Fifth Avenue and Fifty-eighth Street. Thirty blocks farther north, Herbert Brownell, Jr., the attorney general-designate, stepped out of his town house. The largest group, journalists and photographers sworn to secrecy, herded by press secretary James Hagerty, walked out of cavernous Penn Station up a ramp normally used by mail trucks. And finally, at 4:30 A.M., a Secret Service agent slipped from Ike's home at 60 Morningside Drive and lured the uniformed patrolman on duty down to the corner for a conference on an imaginary subject. Once the officer's back was turned, Eisenhower hurried out the door to a waiting car. The President-elect was off to Korea to fulfill his campaign pledge, under security so tight not even uniformed New York officers were to know about his movements.

Because of the security problems inherent in a national leader's visiting a war zone, the Secret Service hit upon a scheme to conceal Eisenhower's presence in Korea until he had come and gone, what George Humphrey of the Treasury Department called "the most hush-hush, cloak and dagger . . . you ever heard in your life." As Ike flew toward Korea, a steady flow of prominent visitors came to Morningside Heights and emerged to give the press the implication they had conducted business with the President-elect in person. In fact, by midday Saturday, Ike's Constellation was far over the Pacific.

Ike flew away in a swirl of minicontroversy from critics—including some in his own party—who insisted the effort was not worth the risk. But Eisenhower emphatically said he intended to carry out his pledge. He had no "patent medicine" to solve the war, but he wanted information; to break faith with the American public so early would brand him as just another politician. (The security proved justifiable: An hour after Eisenhower completed his mission and left for home—on December 5 —eleven Communist fighter planes attacked the Seoul airport.)

By any measure, however, the trip was little more than what an angered President Truman had charged during the campaign: a political stunt of value chiefly for public relations purposes. Ike began by irritating President Rhee, who had the idea he could use the visitor's prestige to spur his own lagging popularity and to rekindle enthusiasm for the war among the weary Korean people.[2] Rhee's idea was for Ike to spend a full week in Korea, speaking to the National Assembly and presiding over a mammoth military review. Ike's entourage of advisers permitted no such use of the general. Eisenhower intended to spend only seventy-two hours in South Korea, most of that with his military leaders, chiefly General Mark Clark, the UN commander, and General James Van Fleet, commander of the Eighth Army. Eisenhower swept through Korea in a frenzied manner that reminded Merriman Smith of the United Press of the just-completed campaign. He reviewed troops near the front, crunching over the ice-crusted battlefield; he talked to the wounded in an American mobile army surgical hospital (MASH); at times the thud of artillery shells could be heard in the distance. During these three days he found only a total of one hour to spend with the unhappy Rhee, in two meetings.

Nor did Rhee find solace in Eisenhower's general comments at a press conference the day the trip ended. Hagerty wished to prevent Ike from being pressed about specific plans, so he permitted correspondents to ask no questions. Ike thought it would be difficult to end the fighting with a "positive and definite victory without possibly running the grave risk of enlarging the war"; nonetheless, America would "see it through." But the visit did force him to the conclusion (as he wrote in his memoirs) that "we could not stand forever on a static front and continue to accept casualties without any visible results. Small attacks on small hills would not end wars." Eisenhower clearly now shared John Foster Dulles's view that a gesture of considerable magnitude was needed to persuade the Communists to accept peace. But Ike was looking beyond conventional infantry actions. Prior to Eisenhower's arrival, General Clark's staff had worked up new contingency plans for prosecuting the war, including increasing the size of the ROK Army from sixteen divisions to twenty (640,000 men); again considering the use of Chinese Nationalist troops; and "serious consideration" of the use of atomic weapons.³ But Clark was given no opportunity to discuss these contingencies—OPLAN 8-52—with Eisenhower. To Clark, this was "the most significant thing about the visit of the President-elect. . . .⁴ The question of how much it would take to win the war was never raised. It soon became apparent, in our many conversations, that he would seek an honorable truce."

From Seoul, Eisenhower flew to Wake Island, where he boarded the cruiser USS *Helena* for a relaxing three-day cruise to Hawaii. Most of the future Cabinet was aboard—including John Foster Dulles, who had stayed in New York as part of the deception operation—and the impression given the press was of lofty strategy sessions, with Korea paramount among the issues. Emmet John Hughes, who sat in on some of the conferences, found a "somewhat dismaying contrast between their actual substance and their public appearance."⁵ Dulles was the dominant figure, and he could speak for hours on foreign policy or any other subject. "Dulles apparently made one consistent impact upon Eisenhower," Hughes concluded. "He bored him."

As Eisenhower headed back to the mainland, he received advice from an expected source: General Douglas MacArthur, who told a convention of the National Association of Manufacturers he had a plan to end the war and that, if asked, would outline it to Eisenhower. Ike immediately cabled his acceptance of MacArthur's idea for an "informal meeting in which my associates and I may obtain the full benefits of your thinking and experience." On December 17 (at a meeting in Dulles's home, a convenient neutral site) MacArthur gave Eisenhower a memorandum of several thousand words' length. The key point was a "two-party conference" between Eisenhower and Soviet Premier Stalin. The United States would demand unity for both Germany and Korea and a two-power guarantee of their neutrality, as well as that of Austria and Japan. Unless the Soviets accepted:

> It would be our intention to clear North Korea of enemy forces. This could be accomplished through the atomic bombing of enemy military concentrations and installations in North Korea and the sowing of fields of suitable radio-active materials, the by-product of atomic manufacture, to close major lines of enemy supply and communications leading south from the Yalu, with simultaneous amphibious landings on both coasts of Korea.

China's military and industrial facilities would also be bombed.

Eisenhower listened noncommittally, obviously wary of saying anything either to encourage or to reject MacArthur. He finally said:

> General, this is something of a new thing. I'll have to look at the understanding between ourselves and our allies, on the prosecution of this war

because if we're going to bomb bases on the other side of the Yalu, if we're going to extend the war we have to make sure we're not offending the whole . . . free world or breaking faith.[6]

One person who emphatically did not like news of MacArthur's "secret plan" was Truman. At a press conference Truman challenged MacArthur or anyone else having a "reasonable plan" to submit it to him "at once." General Omar Bradley, the JCS chairman, sent MacArthur a crisply polite note inviting him to send his views to superiors. (Although Bradley did not point up the fact, as a general officer MacArthur remained subject to military discipline; a general, even when he leaves active duty, continues as an officer.) MacArthur declined on the somewhat flimsy ground that the Truman administration did not have sufficient time to make any worthwhile use of his plan. Truman had his own views: He thought both Eisenhower's Korean trip and the meeting with MacArthur "a piece of demagoguery."*

But as 1953 dawned, Eisenhower faced the same problem as had the outgoing administration: how to devise a peace formula that would adhere to the principles which brought America and the UN into the war and at the same time be palatable to a recalcitrant enemy.

"Asians Against Asians"

The change of administrations gave the Joint Chiefs the opportunity for a broad restudy of war policies, and the generals and Pentagon staff officers quickly realized the new President's immediate intentions: that he would "Koreanize" the war as swiftly as possible as an alternative to the dominant American role. As Ike had said in one of his campaign speeches:

> There is no sense in the UN, with America bearing the brunt of the thing, being constantly compelled to man those front lines. That is a job for the Koreans. We do not want Asia to feel that the white man of the West

*Relations between Truman and Eisenhower had been deteriorating since mid-campaign, when the general peremptorily rejected the President's traditional offer of periodic foreign policy briefings. By inauguration day, January 20, 1953, they were barely on speaking terms. Eisenhower refused Truman the courtesy of entering the White House before their drive together to the inaugural stand and then had the further ill grace to say, "I wonder who is responsible for my son John [an army major] being ordered to Washington from Korea? I wonder who is trying to embarrass me?" "The President of the United States ordered your son to attend your inauguration," Truman replied. "If you think somebody was trying to embarrass you by this order, then the President assumes full responsibility."

is his enemy. If there must be a war there, let it be Asians against Asians, with our support on the side of freedom.

The consensus at the Defense Department, after considerable tinkering with staff studies and position papers, was that the administration should increase the ROK military to about 655,000 men, including twenty army and one marine divisions.[7] (The ROK Army had fourteen active divisions at the start of the year.) It was hoped these infusions of troops would enable the United States to begin withdrawing some of its own men, although their equipment would be left in Japan for possible emergency use. Supporting such an enlarged ROK defense establishment would cost an estimated $1 billion a year, a sum that gave Eisenhower's budget planners pause. But by March 1953 plans were well along to increase vastly the strength of the ROKs.

Then there occurred on March 5 potentially the most significant event of Eisenhower's first year in office, in terms of his dealing with the Communist world. Premier Joseph Stalin, the unchallenged strong man of the Soviet Union for almost three decades, died suddenly of a cerebral hemorrhage. Eisenhower immediately saw the death as providing an opening toward peace. He wrote in his memoirs: "The new leadership in Russia, no matter how strong its links with the Stalin era, was not completely bound to blind obedience to the ways of a dead man."

But weeks of careful and frustrating diplomatic, political, and military maneuvering would precede peace in Korea. Unbeknownst to the enemy, however, the United States now had a significant new nuclear weapon in its arsenal. In mid-January scientists at the New Mexico nuclear testing grounds excitedly reported the first successful detonation of an atomic warhead of a size suitable for use in battlefield artillery —meaning that nuclear weapons could be used for tactical as well as strategic purposes. The news caused a swift rethinking of nuclear policy by the JCS, who had frequently considered the nuclear option the past two years, only to reject the use of atomic bombs as impractical. Although the Joint Chiefs were not ready to make a formal recommendation on use of the new tactical weapons, carefully worded paragraphs in a March 27 study showed a distinct shift in their thinking:

> The efficacy of atomic weapons in achieving greater results at less cost of effort in furtherance of U.S. objectives in connection with Korea points to the desirability of re-evaluating the policy which now restricts the use of atomic weapons in the Far East.
>
> In view of the extensive implications of developing an effective conventional capability in the Far East, the timely use of atomic weapons should be considered against military targets affecting operations in Korea, and operationally planned as an adjunct to any possible military course of action involving direct action against Communist China and Manchuria.[8]

Another concurrent staff study suggested the efficacy of convincing the Chinese and the North Koreans that the UN Command intended to launch a major offensive should armistice talks not be resumed and completed.[9] The JCS on May 19 recommended air and naval operations "directly against China and Manchuria," including use of nuclear weapons.[10] Timing was of the utmost importance, the Joint Chiefs felt. All the necessary operations, including "extensive strategical and tactical use of atomic bombs," should be undertaken so as to "obtain maximum surprise and maximum impact." A gradual escalation, starting with a naval blockade and working up to a ground offensive, would minimize chances of success. The National Security Council approved these recommendations the next day, on May 20.

By coincidence, the NSC action came as Secretary Dulles was on a trip to the Middle East and Asia. He chose India as the forum at which to warn of the use of atomic weapons. In a conversation with Prime Minister Nehru, Dulles suggested that Chinese Premier Chou En-lai be warned that failing an early settlement, the United States would bomb Manchurian sanctuaries north of the Yalu. Dulles also mentioned America's successful testing of nuclear artillery shells, in a fashion that implied strongly it would not hesitate to use these weapons in North Korea.

In yet another move against China—this one done in the full glare of publicity—Eisenhower announced that the Seventh Fleet would no longer stand between Formosa and the mainland. "This order implies no aggressive intent on our part," Eisenhower said. "But we certainly have no obligation to protect a nation fighting us in Korea." The Central Intelligence Agency was authorized to increase raids against the mainland by Nationalist guerrillas who were armed, trained, and transported by the Americans. Soon the official New China News Agency complained loudly about "adventurous American imperialists supporting the running dogs of the tyrant Chiang." By the Chinese's own count, more than 200 such raids were launched against the mainland the first five months of 1953.

The new administration clearly had given the enemy an incentive to look for a way out of the war. And a signal was not long in coming.

Operation Little Switch[11]

In December 1952 the League of Red Cross Societies, meeting in Geneva, had urged both the UN and the Communists, as a "good will gesture" toward peace, to consider exchanging sick and wounded prisoners. Both the Soviets and the Chinese voted against the resolution, which attracted little public attention. But in Tokyo General Mark Clark saw possible propaganda advantage in pressing the idea. This was done, by Clark, on February 22.

In following weeks, hard on the heels of Stalin's death, the new Soviet premier, Georgi M. Malenkov, showed signs that his government might be more flexible toward the West. The evidence was through a series of faint signals discernible only to the most skilled of Kremlinologists. For instance, the Soviet radio publicly acknowledged for the first time since 1945 that the United States and Great Britain had played a major role in the Second World War. The Soviets agreed to help the British secure the release of diplomats and missionaries confined in North Korea. Then came two extraordinary developments.

On March 28 Premier Kim Il Sung of North Korea and General Peng Teh-huai, head of the Chinese Communist "volunteers," surprised Clark by accepting his offer to exchange the sick and wounded POWs. But they went a step further: This exchange should lead to settlement of the entire POW issue and an armistice "for which people throughout the world are longing." The Joint Chiefs authorized Clark to pursue the offer, but cautiously.

On March 30 the Communists supplied an even greater surprise. Premier Chou En-lai, in a broadcast over Peking Radio, said this initial exchange could be extended to settlement of the entire war. Chou repeated the Communist objection to any Chinese or North Korean POWs being retained by the UN. He would not concede that any Communist prisoners had refused repatriation. Then, in the next breath, he said that any who did so should be handed over to a "neutral state" for further screening. And two days later, on April 1, Soviet Foreign Minister V. M. Molotov praised the "entire fairness" of the Chou proposal and offered to cooperate in carrying it out.

The Chinese move was fraught with ambiguity.[12] Which was the "neutral nation" Chou had in mind? Did he intend that the POWs be interned in South Korea or in a neutral zone or be taken elsewhere? How would the "just solution" be reached in the cases of the soldiers refusing repatriation? Nonetheless, the JCS directed Clark to explore the lead and "take at face value every offer that it made to us." Clark was dubious, saying that "it would be completely naive on our part not to anticipate any and every form of chicanery" once the enemy got down to specific bargaining.

But liaison officers, meeting at Panmunjom, swiftly reached an agreement on what the UN called Operation Little Switch. On April 11 they agreed the UN would return 700 Chinese and 5,100 Korean prisoners, while the enemy would return 450 Korean and 150 non-Korean soldiers. The prisoners were brought to Panmunjom beginning on April 20, and by May 3 Little Switch was effectively completed.

Many of the American and ROK prisoners came out in pitiable condition—emaciated veritably to skeleton size, their wounds untreated for months, even years, some demented by the strain of captivity and their mistreatment. The Communist invalids, to the contrary, sought to embarrass the UN to the very last. Many refused a new issue of clothing because the letter *P*—for "prisoner"—had not been stenciled on the shirts. Nor would they subject themselves to a final dusting with DDT powder by UN personnel. As they rode away from Panmunjom, they threw away their UN-issued rations of tooth powder, soap, and cigarettes. And some tore and cut their clothing to give the impression they had been mistreated by the UN.

But the important point was that the negotiations had enjoyed their first major thaw. Peculiarly, having given the Chinese the prod that alarmed them into serious talks, Dulles seemed to have second thoughts. In a conversation with Emmet John Hughes, Dulles did not think that American interests would be served by a truce in Korea. "We'd be sorry," he said. "I don't think we can get much out of a Korean settlement until we have shown—before all Asia—our clear superiority by giving the Chinese one hell of a licking." Hughes, finding this comment incredible, mentioned it to Eisenhower, who exclaimed, "If Mr. Dulles and his sophisticated advisers really mean that they cannot talk peace seriously, then I am in the wrong pew." He felt that Dulles "is just too worried about being accused of sounding like Truman and Acheson."

Now the prisoner negotiations took on a momentum of their own, with the Communists and the UN sparring over the composition of the "neutral" commission or nation which would receive the POWs, and the procedures to be followed. The UN wanted a traditional neutral such as Switzerland, with POWs refusing repatriation to be held no longer than sixty days. Clark was instructed to stress two points: that the United States would not compromise on forced repatriation and that it would not "countenance prolonged and inconclusive negotiations."

The full delegations faced each other at Panmunjom on April 26, their first direct meeting in six months. But the talks quickly bogged down again on three points. The Chinese would not accept Switzerland; they wanted the POWs to be removed from Korea during the screening process; and they wanted six months to persuade their prisoners to return. Pressed to name their choice of a neutral nation, the Chinese finally suggested India, Burma, Indonesia, or Pakistan, the latter of which the United States accepted. Next the Chinese abandoned their demand that the POWs be taken out of Korea and cut the screening period from six to four months. And just as suddenly they abandoned the idea of a single-nation neutral and asked for a Neutral Nations Repatriation Commission (NNRC), composed of Poland, Czechoslovakia, Switzerland, Sweden, and India.[13]

Clark felt this concession to be important, even though parts of it remained fuzzy.[14] He saw it as a sign the Communists truly wanted an armistice. The main hanging point, to Clark, was the long time limit for screening. He worried the Chinese would try to move the POW repatriation issue into a postarmistice conference. He also saw no chance that the South Korean government would permit armed personnel from Communist satellites to work in its country.

Although Clark sensed his negotiators were on the brink of success, he asked Washington's permission to lay down a final proposal—a single neutral nation to screen the POWs, in Korea, and with a ninety-day limit. Otherwise, his command would unilaterally release North Korean POWs—the ones not wishing repatriation—within thirty days and would begin "increased military pressures" on the enemy.

What Clark proposed was sensitive. Already Far East Air Force planes had bombed dams in North Korea to free floodwaters which destroyed highways and railroads. For instance, on May 13 planes hit a dam north of Pyongyang, and the resulting floodwaters destroyed or damaged more than six miles of rail lines, five railway bridges, and two miles of a major highway. Some five square miles of rice fields also were destroyed. Now Clark wished to go a step further: to bomb dams with the express purpose of destroying croplands through flooding, thereby cutting food supplies for both the Communist military and civilian population. The JCS did not object. Clark now had a new card to play against the enemy.

As the Communists mulled Clark's last offer, the UN Command was suddenly confronted with a new crisis that threatened to scuttle the entire truce talks: a flat rebellion by President Syngman Rhee.

Rhee's Last Stand

Rhee was hurt, confused, heartsick the spring months of 1953. For almost three years he had been a puppet president in his own land— a man the Americans would cajole from time to time but ignore when convenient for them. Ambassador John J. Muccio, the American he perhaps trusted the most, had been gone since November 1952, replaced by Ellis Briggs, a skilled diplomat but a stranger. Rhee knew exactly what the new President, Eisenhower, intended to do: to make a peace and leave Korea divided. So Rhee, to the utter frustration of the American community, set out to sabotage the peace talks.

In person and through spokesmen, Rhee stated his position forcefully and repeatedly.[15] He would "never" agree to an armistice that did not require withdrawal of all Communist Chinese forces from Korea; require the disarming of North Korean forces; stipulate clearly that no "third power" could assist the North Koreans in any international conference dealing with Korea; and fully recognize and protect the sovereignty and territorial integrity of South Korea. The Communists, of course, would accept no such conditions, especially unilateral disarming of North Korea while Rhee still had more than a dozen well-armed divisions. In the agonized words of a JCS historical study, "No amount of logic, persuasion, or protest by the U.S. or the UN was able to move the obdurate President Rhee from his single-minded and potentially suicidal course."[16]

The closer the talks seemed to fruition, the more vociferous were Rhee's complaints. Anti-American rallies became frequent and large, with Rhee calling for unilateral action by the Korean people. At one rally, in early April, he declared that "regardless of what happens at Panmunjom, our objective remains the same—our permanent objective is to unify Korea from the south to the Yalu River. . . . [Y]ou must continue to fight until you reach the Yalu."

To General Clark, the most immediate danger was that Rhee would withdraw his delegates from the UN negotiating team, an act which almost certainly would cause the Communists to abandon the talks. Clark also feared a withdrawal of ROK forces from UN control, which would endanger the military situation. He did concede that Rhee's fears had some legitimacy. For instance, given the reality of Russo-Sino power, would the United States return to South Korea's aid if war erupted again? But Clark had no doubts Rhee would use his army independently if he thought he had a chance of achieving his objectives. "He [is] dangerous because of his general unpredictability and his tendency to act on occasion without adequate prior consideration of the consequences," Clark cabled the JCS on April 16.[17] As a means of mollifying Rhee, Clark suggested an immediate offer of postwar economic and military aid and a promise to continue to seek Korean unification by political, peaceful means.

In contrast with his shaky domestic situation during past confrontations with the United States, this time Rhee appeared to have the solid, if not unanimous, support of other Korean politicians. On April 21 the National Assembly supported Rhee's objective of unifying Korea by invading the North. Bolstered by this mandate, three days later Rhee informed President Eisenhower that if the UN permitted the Chinese to remain south of the Yalu, he would withdraw his forces from the UN Command and fight on alone.[18]

Clark, after several meetings with Rhee, concluded that Rhee was bluffing, although apparently to an unintended extreme.[19] In discussions with the president, Clark emphasized that he was supporting a twenty-division army for South Korea and that Rhee's demand for a formal security pact with the United States could be discussed after the armistice. Clark apparently convinced Rhee at a meeting on May 13 that the United States was bent upon signing an armistice, regardless of whether the ROKs agreed. "He is bargaining now to get a security pact, to obtain more economic aid, and to make his people feel he is having a voice in the armistice negotiations," Clark cabled the JCS.

The Prisoner Logjam Broken

With Operation Little Switch completed, on April 26 the Communists pushed the talks a bit farther along—deciding "to strike while the iron was hot," in General Clark's words—with a sweeping new proposal. The Communists assembled their largest delegation of the war, including, for the first time, a *Pravda* correspondent. General Nam Il proposed that three months after signing of an armistice, prisoners refusing repatriation and demanding political asylum would be moved to a neutral state. Over the next six months agents of their government could try to persuade them to return home. Any refusing would continue to be held while a "political conference" tried to settle their fate.

Clark thought this proposal absurd.[20] "Boiled down to its essentials," he said, "this meant that to win political asylum a prisoner would have to submit to a minimum of nine months' imprisonment after the armistice and then have to sit indefinitely in a prison camp while UN and Communist politicians . . . tried to agree on what to do with him." The prisoners had no assurance any such conference would ever be held, and Clark was doubtful that one ever would. In the end the POWs would accept repatriation just to get out of the prison camp.

Nam Il's proposal killed optimism inspired by Little Switch, and Clark complained that the Communists had sought a "sneak diplomatic victory." Furthermore, POWs freed during Little Switch reported some 400 sick or wounded American and ROK prisoners had not been returned, a breach of faith that angered UN negotiators.

Realizing he had gone down a blind path, Nam Il revised his proposal on May 7. The POWs would be left in Korea during the screening, but they would still be subjected to persuasion by agents of their government, under Indian supervision. Clark countered that the Chinese would be turned over to the neutrals, but Korean nonrepatriates would be released the day of the signing of the armistice. Nam called this proposal a "step backwards," and his negotiators railed at the UN team for a full four days until a recess was called.

Then came a decision from Washington that stunned Clark and convinced him that the Eisenhower administration had decided to make concessions previously unacceptable:

I was instructed to agree to turn over to the neutral repatriation commission all Korean as well as Chinese non-repatriates—a point that made many in the ROK government feel that we had betrayed them. In addition, I was instructed to agree to the Communist demand that all disputes within the Repatriation Commission be decided by a majority vote rather than by unanimous vote. This gave the Communists an edge since India, although avowedly neutral, recognized and was sympathetic to Red China.[21]

But Clark was still to insist on the principle of no forcible repatriation and ensure that no intimidation could be used against the prisoners. Further, the only armed neutral troops permitted in Korea would come from India. If the UN proposal were not accepted by the Communists, the talks would be terminated.

To Clark and Ambassador Briggs fell the unpleasant chore of informing President Rhee of the change of American bargaining policy. Predictably he reacted with rage. "I am deeply disappointed," he told the Americans. He would never allow Indian troops, or those of any other "neutral" nations, in ROK rear areas. He concluded:

You can withdraw all UN forces, all economic aid. We will decide our own fate. We do not ask anyone to fight for us. We made our mistake perhaps in the beginning in relying upon diplomacy to assist us.

Sorry, but I cannot assure President Eisenhower of my cooperation under the present circumstances.[22]

As Briggs stated later, "the venerable Korean statesman had us over an A-frame, and he knew it."[23] Clark agreed. "Behind all of Rhee's spoken and unspoken threats was the psychological whammy he had on us. He knew that no matter what happened we could not, after three years of war, after all the blood and treasure we had lost, let Korea go to the Reds by default because of a quarrel 'in the family.'" But with the ROKs manning two-thirds of the front, a sudden decision by Rhee to withdraw them from UN control would throw the military situation into chaos.

Thus concurrent with the armistice negotiations the American command commenced planning a two-track strategy—a carrot and a stick —in how to deal with Rhee. Clark and other officers realized (but did not philosophically accept) the clear directive being given them by Washington. Eisenhower had won by a popular mandate that demanded he end an unpopular war, and he was moving to do so on terms that would have been politically impossible for the weaker Truman administration.

One track of the strategy, the "stick," was devised in the Far East.[24] At Clark's direction, General Maxwell D. Taylor (a veteran airborne officer who had replaced Van Fleet as Eighth Army commander in

February) began planning for what the military considered the "worst possible contingency"—that Rhee might withdraw the ROKs from UN control. Plan Everready, written in EUSAK headquarters, approved by Clark, and forwarded to Washington, was an even tougher version of the Rhee-removal scheme first studied in 1952, when the Truman administration considered removing the South Korean president by force. Everready envisioned three contingency situations: (I), in which ROK forces were not responsive to UN directives; (II), in which ROK forces took independent action; and (III), the most extreme, in which ROK forces and the civilian population became "openly hostile" to UN forces.

Under Condition I, U.S. and UN forces would move to protect vital areas around major cities; naval and air forces would go on alert; and intelligence coverage of the ROK Army and government would be increased. Under II, some "protective" withdrawals would be made to secure bases; ROK security units would be disarmed and replaced by trusty UN troops; and civilian movements would be controlled.

Condition III called for the most extreme measures. Clark outlined this phase of Everready in a May 27 cable to the Joint Chiefs:

> President Rhee would be invited to visit Seoul or elsewhere—anywhere to get him out of Pusan [the temporary ROK capital]. At an appropriate time, the UN commander would move into the Pusan area and seize between five and ten key ROK officials who have been leaders in Rhee's dictatorial actions . . . and take over control of martial law through the Chief of Staff, ROK army, until it is lifted.

If Rhee did not agree to accept the UN armistice terms, "he would be held in protective custody, incommunicado. . . ." The UN Command would move to establish a government under the prime minister, Chang Taek Sang; if he refused, a military government would be set up, under either the ROK Army or the UN directly.

Everready was received favorably by the Joint Chiefs and State Department officials and then presented to Secretaries Dulles and Charles E. Wilson for review on May 29. Their decision reflected a good deal of protective caution. They declined to authorize *directly* the portion of the plan calling for Rhee's detention. But Dulles and Wilson did direct the JCS to inform Clark that in the event of a "grave emergency," he was authorized to *"act as necessary* [emphasis added] to insure the integrity of your forces."[25] Given the tenor of Clark's recommended actions, these words constituted *de facto* authorization to put Rhee out of the way in an emergency and were so interpreted by Clark.

At the same meeting Dulles, Wilson, and the generals discussed another track—the "carrot"—that might entice Rhee to change his mind and in a manner that would not cause him loss of face. One fear haunting Rhee, a legitimate one, was South Korea's ability to protect itself once the fighting ended, and the United States began cutting its military forces. Rhee clearly felt the United States and the UN had betrayed him by not pressing the war to military victory that would reunite Korea. So Dulles and Wilson asked Clark, through the JCS, whether Rhee would support the armistice in return for a long-term security pact under which America would insure the defense of the ROK in the event of further Communist attacks. Clark agreed this might make Rhee "fall into line."[26] He also now felt that Rhee would not take "serious unilateral actions" without advance warning to the UN.

President Eisenhower decided the next day—May 30—to make the offer of a security pact formal, contingent upon Rhee's acceptance of the armistice terms. But he did not wish the proposal publicized lest it become embroiled in the peace talks.

At Panmunjom, meanwhile, negotiations proceeded apace, and on June 5 the Communists indicated general agreement with the UN proposals of May 25. Clearly only the clearing of a few trivial details awaited a formal signing. General Clark hastened off to inform Rhee what was about to happen, to soften what he knew would be a harsh psychological blow to the old president.

Clark realized right away the session would be a rough one: When Rhee was in a conciliatory mood, his Austrian-born wife, Francesca, would join their conversations, clad in a flowing Korean dress. This day Mrs. Rhee was not in sight; only the president and a small dog were there. ("Only the pup seemed glad to see me, perhaps as a fellow-tenant of his dog house," Clark recollected.[27])

As Clark cabled the Joint Chiefs later that day, he made "absolutely no progress" in persuading Rhee to accept the armistice terms.[28] "I have never seen him more distracted, wrought up, and emotional. He told me he was not feeling well, was tired and that he had not slept all night."

Clark tried, unsuccessfully, to reassure Rhee, but he emphasized "that my government is determined to go ahead and conclude an armistice on our May 25 terms, that agreement on the POW question is imminent, and that there are only a few remaining questions to be settled." Ambassador Briggs would bring in a personal letter from Eisenhower later in the day to outline steps the United States would take to support South Korea, "short of continuing the fighting to secure the unification of Korea."

Rhee heatedly replied the "U.S. is making a great mistake in adopting these tactics of appeasement." The ROK government would never accept the armistice terms; it would "fight on, even if it meant suicide, and he would lead them." He now felt "free to take such steps as he deems appropriate."

Clark pressed for elaboration on the latter point, but Rhee "was too emotional to do so." He was evasive when asked specifically whether he would leave the ROK Army under the UN. Clark told him "how futile it would be for him to attack alone, for he . . . does not have the necessary logistical support, that it would result in destruction of himself and his country." Rhee retorted that his country "would become another China [meaning a Communist state]; it is inevitable and he and his people may as well die now as later."

Reporting on the conversation to Washington, Clark emphasized that although he was uncertain whether Rhee had decided to wreck the peace, "he has the capability of violating the armistice terms to the great embarrassment of the UN." The ROK president was "utterly unreasonable and gave no ground whatsoever. He himself is the only one who knows how far he will go but undoubtedly he will bluff right up to the last.

"I see no solution at this time, other than to await developments." And such "developments" were to come swiftly.

Rhee "Solves" the POW Problem

On June 8 the UN and the Communists finally struck a deal on repatriation. Any prisoner who wished to return home could do so in sixty days, with no force or threats either to effect or to prevent repatriation. Those not choosing repatriation within sixty days would be turned over to the neutral commission for ninety days, during which they would be subject to "explanations" from their governments about repatriation in the presence of a neutral representative. After this ninety-day period the nonrepatriates would be held for yet another thirty days while the political conference (provided one ever assembled) discussed their fate. And after this period those still unrepatriated would be declared to have civilian status, and the neutral commission would help them relocate.

The debate over voluntary repatriation had delayed peace for more than a year, during which time more than 100,000 UN troops, plus uncountable thousands of Chinese and North Koreans, were killed or wounded. The resultant formula, complex though it was, did provide the safeguards the United States had sought at the outset (although Clark was dubious about the ability of the Chinese nonrepatriates to withstand blandishments from the Communist interviewers who would screen them). Some mechanics remained—chiefly the creation of the neutral screening commission. Then, with one audacious stroke, President Rhee rendered much of the detailed negotiations moot.

For weeks General Clark had feared—and so warned Washington—

that Rhee might order a mass release of North Korean prisoners who did not wish to return to their homeland. He was powerless to prevent any such action: The prisoner compounds were guarded by ROK troops, with only a handful of Americans working in the camps' administrative headquarters. Clark did not have the manpower to replace the ROKs with more reliable guards. Besides, he felt strongly that firearms should "not be used against professed anti-Communists who were basically on our side. I was not going to be a party to the mass slaughter with machine guns of these people."[29]

Just after midnight on June 18, Sergeant Tim Maddox, on duty at the vast Pusan POW compound, decided to walk a few hundred yards to his quarters for a paperback book to while away the predawn hours.[30] He heard the shuffle of hundreds of feet and the murmur of low-pitched but excited voices. Maddox hurried to the side of the main compound enclosure. "The gate was wide open," he said, "and the North Korean prisoners were running through on the double, carrying their ditty bags. I ran over to one of the ROK noncoms—they were just standing, watching—and asked what the hell was happening. He just shrugged and smiled."

Maddox aroused the handful of other Americans at the compound, but nothing could be done. Within a few hours it was empty, as were three other camps elsewhere in South Korea. A total of 25,000 North Koreans nonrepatriates vanished into the night.

No one in Korea—from Rhee on down—even pretended that the breakouts were not sanctioned. ROK soldiers and police met the escapees outside the gates, gave them civilian clothes and food, and directed them to hiding places in private homes. Government radio instructed citizens to shelter them and to warn them against the approach of U.S. soldiers who set out in search of the former POWs. Somewhat less than 1,000 of the escapees were caught. During the next hours U.S. troops assumed guard duty, with instructions to use nontoxic irritants to prevent further escapes. But the breakouts continued; after four days, the POW population had dropped from 35,400 North Koreans to fewer than 9,000.*

Rhee's audacious action dumbfounded both Eisenhower and Dulles, who immediately feared the Communists would use the escapes as an excuse to shatter an armistice that only hours before had seemed safely in hand. In a public statement Dulles decried Rhee's action as a "violation of the authority" of the UN Command. He veritably pleaded that the Communists not fault the United States for Rhee's handiwork: "We have conducted our negotiations for an armistice in good faith and we have acted and are acting in good faith." In a private cable Ike spoke

---

*Despite the UN Command's abhorrence of the use of force, 61 POWs died and another 116 were injured in the mass escapes.

sternly to Rhee, saying his "violation . . . creates an impossible situation for the UN command. If continued, such a course of action can only result in the needless sacrifice of all that has been won for Korea by the blood and bravery of its magnificent fighting forces."[31] Eisenhower warned that the UN was ready to "effect another arrangement" to end the war—i.e., that any further such behavior could leave the ROKs standing alone in the postarmistice period, with no U.S. assistance.

The major unknown, of course, was the Communist reaction, and analysts anxiously monitored broadcasts over the next several days. On June 28 the New China News Agency said that the "Syngman Rhee 'tail' has been wagging furiously, and has pushed the armistice to the edge of the precipice. Whether it is the 'head' that commands the 'tail,' or vice versa, is up to Washington to *decide and answer* [emphasis added]." Analysts interpreted this statement as an indication that the Communists would gladly listen to an explanation at Panmunjom, which was quickly offered and accepted. Another NCNA broadcast, on July 8, said the United States was obliged to insure "that no such incidents occur *again*"—that is, China was willing to let the episode pass.

But could Rhee be persuaded not to create other incidents? Eisenhower had urged him to visit Washington for personal talks, but Rhee declined because of the press of the war. So on June 25 Eisenhower had dispatched to South Korea a special emissary, Walter Robertson, a courtly gray-haired Virginian who carried the title of assistant secretary of state and the reputation of being a man of infinite tact and patience. Robertson's mission was one of the most delicate in American diplomatic history, for his persuasive powers the next days could determine whether the Korean War continued—or ended.

What Walter Robertson took to South Korea was a tough message indeed: that if Rhee were to remain intransigent on abiding with the truce, the UN would get out of Korea. The UN was in complete readiness to make an agreement with the Communists independently of the Republic of Korea, to withdraw all UN troops, and to go ahead with the POW exchange. The reasoning was that if Rhee could be convinced, once and for all, that the United States meant business on withdrawing, he might change his attitude.

But conveying this threat involved ticklish political maneuvering. Under no circumstances was the enemy to learn that the UN was ready to leave Rhee standing alone if necessary to secure an armistice. A key part of the UN postarmistice strategy, it shall be recalled, was the so-called greater sanctions statement warning against the consequences of a Communist renewal of the war. The Joint Chiefs warned Clark that if the ROKs did not assure compliance with the armistice before its signing, other nations fighting in the war would not agree to the statement.

Now the burden of persuading Rhee to go along with the UN lay with

Robertson. For hours, days, Robertson sat and listened to the elderly president pour out his seemingly uncountable grievances with the United States. The first days the American did not even try to answer; he told another diplomat later, "I simply stuck my shoulder out there and let Rhee cry on it."

Robertson's Friendly Persuasion

Even as Robertson flew across the Pacific, the Communists launched an offensive that underlined the Republic of Korea's inability to continue the war on its own, without American support. The drive was the largest since the spring of 1951, and it was aimed directly at ROK troops in the center of the Eighth Army lines—three Chinese armies totaling almost 100,000 men versus five Korean divisions of half that number. To EUSAK intelligence, the purpose seemed to be to level out a bulge in the front line that would give the Communists stronger positions after the armistice. General Mark Clark saw another reason entirely: "There is no doubt in my mind that one of the principal reasons—if not the one reason—for the Communist offensive was to give the ROKs a 'bloody nose,' to show them and the world that *puk chin*—go north—was easier said than done."[32]

The offensive succeeded in pushing back the targeted ROK troops several thousand yards; there it stalled under the shattering impact of UN artillery, which hit the Chinese with more than 2.7 million rounds in June, highest monthly total of the war by a million rounds. But the intense fighting was to continue through the first days of July, and the Chinese willingness to accept heavy casualties unquestionably shook Rhee's resolve to continue the war alone. And Robertson sought to pick out, from the cascade of Rhee's complaints, points on which the United States could yield ground and make acceptance of the truce more palatable.[33]

One handicap was that Rhee seemed incapable of making up his mind on exactly what he wanted. The first day they talked, on June 27, Rhee laid down four stipulations: that the remaining anti-Communist Korean prisoners be moved to the demilitarized zone and turned over to the neutral commission; that a time limit of ninety days be put on the political conference; that the United States give economic aid to the Republic of Korea and help it build its army to twenty divisions; and that the United States "guarantee" a mutual defense pact.

None of these points posed any major problems to the Americans. In a personal message to Rhee on June 27, President Eisenhower promised the Korean nonrepatriates would be moved to the DMZ "if logistically feasible." The United States could not unilaterally impose a time limit on the political conference, but it would "consider" withdrawing if nothing had happened in ninety days. It would give the requested military and economic aid. Finally, it would be willing to negotiate a mutual defense treaty but could not "guarantee" one because of the necessary consent of the U.S. Senate.

Rhee's response to the Eisenhower message was cordial. "Well"—he smiled at Robertson—"the President has met all my views."[34] Robertson and Clark reduced Eisenhower's letter to a formal *aide-mémoire* which they sent to Rhee after the meeting.

That evening Robertson and Clark returned to Rhee's residence for a dinner and a presumed *pro forma* ratification of the agreement Rhee seemingly had accepted only hours earlier. To their consternation, Rhee met them with a list of difficult new demands. Twenty divisions for the ROK Army would not be enough; he wished a force equal to those of "an immediate neighbor in view" (he apparently meant North Korea but did not say so). If the political conference did not succeed in uniting Korea within ninety days, the United States should join South Korea in resuming military operations. The South Koreans would remain under UN control only so long as the goal was that of "settling the war with victory."

In a disheartened cable to Washington after the dinner meeting (one for which the Americans understandably had little appetite) Clark and Robertson reported that Rhee was obviously trying to prolong the negotiations. The Communists and the UN had been in agreement on the armistice for twenty days. During that time the UN had suffered some 17,000 battle casualties, 3,333 of them killed—all because of Rhee's intransigence. Now they wished to resume negotiations with the Communists on the few remaining details, regardless of what Rhee felt. Washington officials agreed.

Robertson, meanwhile, resumed his hand-holding sessions with Rhee, and the more he heard, the more alarmed he became. Unlike Clark, Robertson did not think Rhee was bluffing. "I consider it inadvisable to make a threat of withdrawal unless we are willing to carry it out," he cabled on July 2. "Rhee is a zealous, irrational and illogical fanatic and might well call our bluff."[35] Neither Clark nor Robertson felt that any prominent ROK generals would be willing to "risk their necks" by moving against Rhee unless they were given stronger assurances of U.S. support than could then be provided.

Rhee now began tugging at details. He flatly denied ever entertaining intentions to leave the UN Command (an outright misstatement); all he declared was the *right* of the Republic of Korea, as a sovereign nation, to protect its interests. He insisted that Chinese as well as Korean nonrepatriates be moved to the DMZ, this to avoid "having Indian troops set foot on Korean soil." He was now vague on just what he

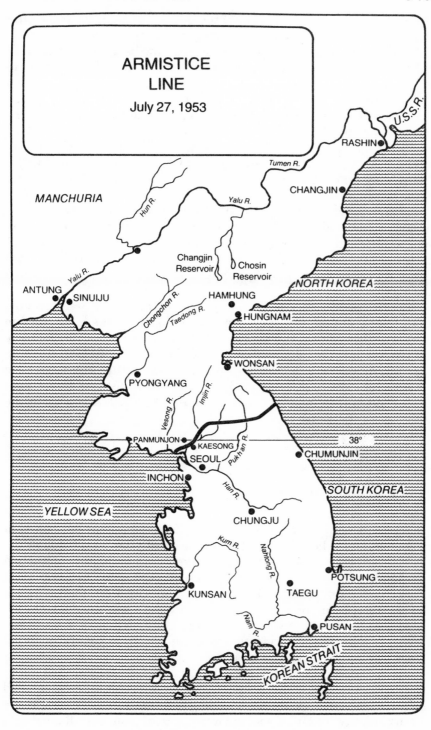

ARMISTICE
LINE
July 27, 1953

U.S.S.R.

RASHIN

Tumen R.

MANCHURIA

Yalu R.

CHANGJIN

Hun R.

Changjin
Reservoir

Chosin
Reservoir

NORTH KOREA

ANTUNG

Yalu R.

SINUIJU

Chongchon R.

HAMHUNG

Taedong R.

HUNGNAM

WONSAN

PYONGYANG

Vesong R.

Imjin R.

PANMUNJON

KAESONG

Puk'han R.

38°

CHUMUNJIN

SEOUL

INCHON

SOUTH KOREA

Han R.

YELLOW SEA

CHUNGJU

Kum R.

Nahtong R.

POTSUNG

KUNSAN

TAEGU

Nam R.

PUSAN

KOREAN STRAIT

expected the United States to do if the political conference failed after ninety days, but he no long demanded a resumption of the war.

Robertson prodded and poked, and each time he got the ROK president to agree with a specific point, he immediately reduced it to writing. The dozens of cables between Washington and its emissaries during the first days of July showed an almost urgent desire to get Rhee's commitment to accept the armistice and leave ROK troops under the UN without specifying a time limit. With such a document in hand, an armistice could be concluded, and then the postwar problems addressed. And once the fighting stopped, Clark felt Rhee would find it "extremely difficult to make up his mind" to resume the war on his own.[36]

Finally, on July 9, Rhee yielded. He told Robertson, in writing, that although he could not sign the armistice, "we shall not obstruct it, so long as no measures or actions taken under the armistice are detrimental to our national survival." He would "endeavor to cooperate fully and earnestly in the political and peaceful achievement of reunification of our nation. . . ."

Robertson had succeeded. On July 12, 1953, the United States and the ROK jointly announced they had reached agreements for a truce in Korea, for handling of the nonrepatriates, and for future collaboration.

Privately the UN Command informed the Communists—in response to a question—that it "will not give support during any aggressive action of units of ROK army in violation of the armistice." Robertson's persuasion and iron-eared patience had persevered. Once again the war was on the brink of settlement.

Finale at Panmunjom

Heavy rains fell before dawn on July 27 at Panmunjom but halted at daybreak, and a hesitant sun could occasionally be seen through the heavy cloud cover. Carpenters had worked until midnight completing the building constructed for the armistice ceremony. General Mark Clark insisted on two final details: removal of two Communist "peace doves" (then being used as propaganda symbols worldwide) from the gables of the pagoda-style building and construction of a south entrance, so that the UN delegation would not have to pass through the enemy section to enter the building.

Shortly before ten o'clock a UN honor guard, smartly turned out in white gloves, scarves, and helmets, men from each nation which had fought in the war, lined the walk leading to the entrance. There was one glaring absence: No ROK soldiers were present. Syngman Rhee would honor the armistice, but he would not sign it. At the opposite end of the building were clustered relatively dull-looking Communist soldiers clad in olive-drab fatigue uniforms and canvas shoes.

Precisely at the hour the parties entered the building from the opposite sides. Keyes Beech felt that "a casting director couldn't have selected two more striking opposites" than the principals. The chief UN delegate, Lieutenant General William K. Harrison, "might have been a Baptist preacher in Tennessee." Nam Il, tall and thin, was "resplendent in dress blues, his high-necked tunic buttoned to the top, his chest glittering with medals." The UN party walked in casually, as if on a stroll, and lolled into their seats, whereas the Communists and North Koreans "sat straight and rigid like students at a graduation ceremony."

On one of the tables at the head of the room was a small UN flag and nine blue-bound copies of the agreement. Here Harrison took his seat. Nam Il sat at a parallel table, this one with a North Korean flag and nine copies. They exchanged neither a word nor a nod. They picked up pens and began signing. Not too far in the distance could be heard the boom-boom-boom of UN artillery.

At 10:12 A.M. the task was completed, and Harrison glanced at the press table and permitted himself a small smile of satisfaction. He and Nam rose to leave at the same time, and their eyes briefly met and locked. But neither man spoke.

The Korean War was to last a few minutes less than twelve hours longer, until ten o'clock that evening, local time.

Anthony Ebron, a corporal in the 5th Regiment of the 1st Marine Division, had heard scuttlebutt about peace for so many weeks he did not pay much attention to reports that an armistice was imminent.[37] "For two or three days we had been out on assault missions, trying to get the most favorable positions. Those last few days were pretty bloody. Each time we thought the war was over we'd go out and fight again.

"The day it ended? We shot off so much artillery that day the ground shook. One of my best buddies was killed that day by a Commie artillery round. Then, that night, the noise just stopped. We knew it was over."

Forty minutes before the cease-fire another batch of marines near Panmunjom saw Chinese digging trenches less than 100 yards in front of their lines.[38] They were ordered not to shoot. "Don't start anything you can't stop," directed Lieutenant Colonel Joseph Hill, the battalion commander. The marines did not shoot—but they spent the last minutes of the war amusing themselves by throwing rocks at the Chinese.

At ten o'clock the sky was suddenly lit by dozens of multicolored flares: white star clusters, red flares, yellow flares, the pyrotechnics signifying the end of a thirty-seven-month conflict.[39] The moon was full that night, and marine Martin Russ thought it "hung low in the sky like a Chinese lantern." He crawled out of his foxhole to enjoy his first moments of peace in Korea.

Marines shed their helmets and flak jackets. Shrill voices drifted up the hillside. "The Chinese were singing," Russ realized. "A hundred yards or so down the trench, someone began shouting the Marine Corps hymn at the top of his voice. Others joined in, bellowing the words." It was noisy and off-key fun.

Later some Chinese wandered over to the marines' position and offered candy and handkerchiefs as gifts. The marines stared back. They said nothing. They offered no gifts. Peace was enough.

The Korean War had cost the United States 142,091 casualties—33,629 dead; 103,284 wounded; and 5,178 captured or missing.

Peace: An Afterword

For the first time the United States had concluded a war in which it could not claim success. There were no celebrations. News of the armistice signing flickered across the news lights in Times Square; people stopped to read the announcement, shrugged, and walked on; unlike V-E and V-J days, no cheering throngs assembled. Public statements from the White House were muted for fear of offending Rhee's pride. General Mark Clark told newsmen, "I cannot find it in me to exult in this hour." Eisenhower clearly had carried out his campaign promise to end the war, but the settlement did nothing to bolster the American national spirit.

Criticisms came swiftly, even from the President's own party. Senator William Jenner of Indiana called the armistice "the last tribute to appeasement," while Representative Joe Martin of Massachusetts, the House speaker, remarked, "You cannot go into a military campaign with any hope of success without victory as its objective." Senator William Knowland of California disputed Eisenhower's claim that the war was a victory for "collective security," noting that the United States and South Korea supplied 95 percent of the manpower for the war.

Perhaps the unhappiest American was Harry S. Truman, who cloaked his immediate rage in politic and uncharacteristic silence.[40] He knew the nation was so grateful for peace that any criticisms would be dismissed as ill-tempered. But to friends in later years he decried the "Republican glamour boy" and said that if he had agreed to an armistice on terms accepted by Ike, "They [the Republicans] would have tried to draw and quarter me." Truman did not quibble with the armistice terms, which were essentially what he had sought when the talks began in 1951. But he felt he had been pilloried from office because of Republican charges of a "no-win" war policy. Now Eisenhower had unblinkingly accepted a "no-win" conclusion. Other Democrats spoke out publicly. A young Texas senator, Lyndon B. Johnson, asserted that an armistice that "merely releases aggressive armies to attack elsewhere . . . [is] a fraud." But liberals who had supported Truman and Acheson in going to the defense of South Korea saw that very act as a Democratic strongpoint. Richard H. Rovere summed up the convictions of liberals faithful to the Roosevelt-Truman concept of peace through collective action:

> In Korea, the United States proved that its word was as good as its bond —and even better, since no bond had been given. History will cite Korea as the proving ground of collective security, up to this time no more than a plausible theory. It will cite it as the turning point of the world struggle against Communism.

In his last sentence Rovere overspoke, and considerably, but Korea did provide the Western world a brief respite from armed conflict with Communist expansion. One factor was a stern warning the United States issued through the UN on August 7, 1953, on any Communist attempt to revive the Korean War: "The consequences of such a breach of the armistice would be so grave that, in all probability, it would not be possible to confine hostilities within the frontiers of Korea."

Only one portion of the armistice agreement was fulfilled, that of disposition of POWs. Operation Big Switch began at Panmunjom on August 5, and a month later the UN had returned 75,823 prisoners (70,183 North Koreans, 5,640 Chinese). The enemy in turn surrendered 12,773 men, 3,597 of them Americans, 7,862 South Koreans, and the remainder from other nations.

The prisoners refusing repatriation consumed far more time and energy. On September 23 the UN turned over 22,604 POWs (14,704 Chinese, the others North Koreans) to the Neutral Nations Repatriation Commission in the DMZ; the Communists delivered 359 nonrepatriates, mostly South Koreans. As the UN expected, the Chinese representatives had scant success in "explaining" to their former troops why they should return home. Only 137 opted for repatriation. When the Communists showed signs of dragging out these talks in hope of winning back more troops, the UN simply released the prisoners. Most of the Chinese promptly went to Formosa, where many joined the Nationalist Army; the Koreans went to South Korea.

Of the 359 UN nonrepatriates, only 10 chose to return home—2 Americans, 8 Koreans. The remainder, 325 Koreans, 21 Americans, and 1 Briton, remained with the Communists.*

*The Americans promptly were dubbed turncoats and subjected to vilification and from-afar analysis by the press. Over the next two decades at least a dozen of them chose to return to the United States, where after brief publicity they slipped into anonymity.

On another issue, that of arms stabilization, the Communists simply refused to permit observers to visit the ten designated ports of entry in North Korea. Meanwhile, Polish and Czech members of the neutral commission sought strict application of the inspection agreement in South Korea. This one-sided situation continued for several years, until the United States announced in 1957 it intended to proceed with modernization of the ROK Army.

Under the armistice the political conference on the future of Korea should have convened on October 27, 1953. Such was not the case (to no one's surprise). The Communist bloc in the UN pressed for a large round-table conference, including the Soviet Union, that would discuss a broad range of Asian problems. The United States, noting that the armistice specifically referred to a conference of "both sides" to the Korean War, asked the USSR if it agreed to be so identified. The Soviets declined. Eventually Korea was discussed, to no avail, at a multinational conference that opened in Geneva in April 1954. By now Korea had receded in public importance, for the conference devoted most of its time to the partition of Vietnam, an action that was supposed to end what was then called the war in Indochina.

Syngman Rhee was to cling to the South Korean presidency until 1960, in a regime that became increasingly oppressive. He continually blustered about resuming the war (no one took him seriously), and as the decade ended, even admirers thought him senile. Protests and student riots finally drove him into exile in Hawaii in 1960; he died there in 1965.

The Republic of Korea, by most objective accounts, remains politically a rather abject country, where succeeding presidents have gained office either through military coups or one-candidate elections. Freedom of press, speech, and political action is veritably unknown, and agents of the Korean Central Intelligence Agency (KCIA) routinely track down and kill dissidents, even those living abroad. On the positive side, Korea is known as an "economic garden spot" of Asia, one which does some $10 billion in trade with the United States annually. But considerable serpents reside in the garden. South Korea continues to enjoy wide political support among American conservatives, as former President Jimmy Carter found when he was unable to carry through a campaign pledge to withdraw the 40,000-odd American troops still garrisoned there as a trip-wire force.

In North Korea, Kim Il Sung continues as an unchallenged, if severely aged, strong man. He alternately blusters about "uniting Korea in my lifetime"—under his rule, of course—and tries to coax the unconvinced South Koreans to the conference table. North Korea is one of the few remaining Stalinist states, and it is capable of creating chilling international incidents (as it did in 1968, when it seized the intelligence ship USS *Pueblo,* killing a crewman in the process and then holding the eighty-two officers and men in brutal captivity for ten months). Troops from both Koreas still skirmish across the demilitarized zone, where UN and Communist delegates meet sporadically in meaningless "peace" talks. "Two scorpions separated by some trenches and strands of barbed wire," a State Department official describes the two nations.

A Personal Observation

The nondecisive climax of the Korean War understandably left many Koreans—especially the country's national leaders—emphatically unhappy that the United States did not achieve its once-declared goal of uniting the country. To have done so, as noted earlier, bore political and military costs two administrations were unwilling to pay. Nonetheless, Korean discontent was acute in the years immediately after the war. Syngman Rhee, for one, liked to repeat the old Korean proverb about the fate of a shrimp caught in the battle of the whales.

But South Korea is a nation doggedly faithful to the United States (even though its leaders apparently find little virtue in such features of the American governmental system as free elections and political action). ROK troops fought alongside Americans in Vietnam with a ferocity that impressed anyone who wandered into their sector. South Korea remains a bone in China's throat—a reminder that the United States responded militarily once to aggression in that particular part of the world and could do so again should the target be an even more important nation, Japan. Korea, nonetheless, remains an unknown to most Americans, and much of what they think or hear of it is unfavorable— the homeland of the weird sect of "Moonies" who harass people on the street and in airports; the wellspring of the money that financed the miniscandal known as Koreagate, in which the Korean government bought the favors of innumerable congressmen; a regime that is on Amnesty International's annual black-hat list.

In August 1979 I saw another side of the South Korean psyche. A friend arranged for me to tag along with a group of retired ROK generals who were in New York on what was formally entitled "Consolatory Mission to Korean Veterans in Hospital/Korean-American Goodwill Visiting Mission." A Korean public relations woman explained that the purpose was "simply to say thanks to American soldiers who fought in Korea who are now in veterans' hospitals." (The Koreans were sorely in need of goodwill: Koreagate was in the headlines, and President Carter still talked of pulling U.S. troops out of the country.)

In any event the Koreans assembled an entourage of elderly generals, parchment-skinned octogenarians clad in mufti, Korean business and professional people from the New York area, and several publicists and set out for the Veterans Administration hospital on New York's East Side, where several war veterans were said to be patients.

No one thought to tell the veterans what was planned in their honor. Time and again the group, perhaps a dozen people, would sweep into a ward or room where resided one of the veterans. The lead general, a former chief of staff of the ROK Army, would step forward, bow politely, and proceed to read a long proclamation in fluent (and incomprehensible to the veteran) Korean. Some of the men, obviously alcoholics brought in for detoxification, recoiled as if they had suddenly been thrust into an Asian version of a Fellini nightmare, or as if the Korean cops had arrived to call them to account for some long-forgotten crime in Seoul and they were hearing a version of a *Miranda* rights warning. None actually rose from their beds and ran, although many looked outright nervous. After the proclamation the general would pin a medal on the patient's pajamas, and an interpreter only then would mercifully tell the veteran what the happening was all about.

After watching several of these presentations, I lagged behind the party to talk with one of the veterans, in hope of getting an anecdote I could use in this book. "Korean War," one of them said. "Jesus, you know, I was there for eight months, almost nine, and I have to think awhile to even let you know what outfit I was with." He paused. "These Koreans, though, they sure haven't forgotten, have they?" No, they have not.

The first draft of this book exceeded 2,000 manuscript pages; even cut to somewhat half that length, it remains a formidably sized volume. Rather than further increase the girth, I have attempted to hold notes to a minimum. If a source is obvious in the text or derived from contemporary press accounts of more or less public happenings, I do not repeat it in the notes. This includes public statements of Presidents Truman and Eisenhower, which are to be found in the *Public Papers* series issued by the Government Printing Office, and floor comments in Congress, which are in the *Congressional Record*.

Archival collections which proved valuable were the Harry S. Truman Library, Independence, Missouri (HSTL); the Dwight D. Eisenhower Library, Abilene, Kansas (DDEL); the Army War College, Carlisle, Pennsylvania (AWC); the Nimitz Library at the U.S. Naval Academy, Annapolis, Maryland (NL); the History and Museums Division, Headquarters U.S. Marine Corps, Washington Navy Yard, Washington, D.C. (USMCHC); and the Modern Military Records Branch of the National Archives and Records Service, Washington, D.C. The bulk of the cables quoted in this book—many declassified the past several years through the use of the Freedom of Information Act by myself and other researchers—are to be found in the National Archives.

The military services' official histories were of immense and continuing value, for in many instances they draw upon internal documents and notes unlikely to be discovered by the most diligent of civilian researchers. The U.S. Army volumes published as of mid-1981 are *South to the Naktong, North to the Yalu*, by Roy E. Appleman; *Policy and Direction: The First Year*, by James F. Schnabel; *Truce Tent and Fighting Front*, by Walter G. Hermes; and *Military Advisors in Korea*, by Robert K. Sawyer. The U.S. Marine Corps series is comprised of five volumes, individual titles of which are cited in the notes, by Lynn Montross, Nicholas A. Canonza, Pat Meid, James M. Yingling, Hubard D. Kuokka, and Norman W. Hicks. The naval and air force histories, of which I made less use, are cited in the notes.

Military and diplomatic declassification procedures, unfortunately, contain the pitfalls endemic to any bureaucratic actions, especially in the national security field. For instance, an FOIA request produces a cable or memorandum of conversation which in turn refers to other documents. Or, even more galling, one discovers that a document still considered classified at one repository is in open files at another. Fortunately a backstop exists for the Korean War. The Historical Division of the Joint Chiefs of Staff is in the process of compiling a long history of the influence the JCS have had on national policy. Volume III, by James F. Schnabel and Robert J. Watson, *The Korean War*, dated April 12, 1978, was declassified in 1979. The document is more than 1,200 pages of single-spaced typescript and is a veritable shopping list for documents to ferret out and read. Both authors are skilled military historians, and their narrative adds much to the understanding of the raw documentation. Further, the authors had access to diplomatic cables the State Department is in the process of declassifying for its long-overdue volume *Foreign Relations of the United States, Korea 1951*. The 1950 volume was issued in 1976; the 1951 volume was scheduled for 1979, and as of mid-1981 no one in the State Department seems to know when it will appear. Hence the Schnabel-Watson paper is valuable because it permits a reading of portions of documents still considered secret or top secret by a sister agency of government. Citations *SW* hereafter, with a Roman numeral indicating the chapter (i.e., *SW-I*, for Chapter One). Other volumes in the *Foreign Relations of the United States* series, chiefly those dealing with U.S.-Korea relations in the postwar period, are *FRUS*.

For purposes of intelligibility, I have translated military cables into straightforward English by adding articles and punctuation in the conventional form and by spelling out words abbreviated in the original text. The American commander in the Far East (first MacArthur, then Ridgway and Clark) wore two major hats: commander in chief, Far East Command, CINCFE; and commander in chief, United Nations Command, or CINCUNC. All used these titles more or less interchangeably in cables to the Joint Chiefs of Staff, or JCS. Two other frequently used abbreviations in the notes are *OH*, for oral history; and *DIS*, FEC, for *Daily Intelligence Summary*, Far East Command. "Princeton Seminar" refers to a series of conversations Dean Acheson had with former colleagues when writing his memoirs; transcripts of these talks are at HSTL. "Postpresidential interviews" are transcripts of conversations President Truman had with David M. Noyes and William Hillman, who wrote his two-volume memoirs. The one referred to most frequently here is Volume II, *Years of Trial and Hope* (Garden City: Doubleday, 1956), *HST-II* hereafter. Many of the persons who helped me with this book, either with interviews or in obtaining research material, are cited in the chapter notes. I would like to give especial thanks to Lynn Eden, of the University of Michigan; Elizabeth Sporkin; Tom Kelley; Dr. Ray S. Cline; Brigadier General Eugene M. "Mike" Lynch; Brigadier General Francis Farrell; General Oliver P. Smith (who, although too ill for an interview, permitted me to copy his 800-plus page war diary and other documents); Lieutenant General Alpha Bowser; Hans Tofte; Robert Edson; Irene King; Christine Herdell; Lucille Cohen; Thomas Mechling; Chayon Kim; Harold and Doris Swenson; Colonel George H. Chase; Elizabeth Safly; Dennis Bilger; Erwin Mueller; Pauline Testerman and Dr. Benedict K. Zobrist, the Harry S. Truman Library; John E. Wickman, the Dwight D. Eisenhower Library; Alice S. Creighton, the Nimitz Library, the United States Naval Academy; Brigadier General Edwin H. Simmons, Sergeant William Judge, and Ben Frank, the History and Museums Division, Headquarters United States Marine Corps; Dr. Richard J. Sommers, Colonel Donald P. Shaw, and Phyllis S. Cassler, United States Army Military History Institute, Carlisle Barracks; Paul H. Nitze, Charles Burton Marshall, Dianna Goldstein, the Westover branch, Arlington County Library; Paul Dickson, William D. Hickman, Robert D. Heinl, Jr., and Edward J. Reese, Modern Military Branch, Military Archives Division, National Archives and Records Service; Carl Marcy; Pat Holt; Francis O. Wilcox; N. B. Schnapper; Tom Hyman; Edward T. Chase, Jean Pohoryles, Pam Lyons, Hugh Howard, and Pearl Hanig of The New York Times Book Company; Carl D. Brandt; and to Dr. Robert F. Ryan of Arlington, Virginia, for sound medical guidance, literary and otherwise.

Chapter One

1. Robert T. Oliver, *Syngman Rhee* (New York: Dodd, Mead, 1955), p. 9; Oliver, *Rhee* hereafter. Relied upon Oliver, Rhee's friend and confidant, for much of the early biographical material on the Korean president. Historical background on Korea from Oliver and from George M. McCune with Arthur L. Grey, Jr., *Korea Today*, (Cambridge, Mass.: Harvard University, 1950).

2. Ross Y. Koen, *The China Lobby* (New York: Harper & Row, 1974), p. 7.

3. Theodore Roosevelt, *Autobiography* (New York: Putnam, 1917), p. 318.

4. Koon Woo Nam, *The North Korean Communist Leadership* (Montgomery, Ala.: University of Alabama Press, 1974); discussion of the early years of the Communists in Korea is drawn from Nam.

5. Baik Bong, *Kim Il Sung: A Political Biography* (New York: Guardian, 1970), three volumes. This official state biography is the source for the heroic claims about Kim's career.

6. Nam, *NK Leadership*, p. 111.

7. Acheson, Princeton Seminar, HSTL.

8. Oliver, *Rhee*, p. 163.

9. *Ibid.*, p. 164.

10. Quotations from Cairo and Teheran conference communiqués are in *FRUS: Conferences at Cairo and Teheran, 1943*.

11. Cordell Hull, *Memoirs* (New York: Macmillan, 1948), Vol. II, p. 1596.

12. State Department memorandum, "Korea: Occupation and Military Government; Composition of Forces," March 29, 1944, *FRUS, 1944,* Vol. 5, pp. 1224–28.

13. "Briefing Book Paper," *Conferences at Yalta and Malta, FRUS, 1945,* pp. 358–59.

14. Winston Churchill, *Triumph and Tragedy* (Boston: Houghton Mifflin, 1953), p. 344.

15. Charles Bohlen, *Witness to History* (New York: Norton, 1976), p. 196.

16. Rusk, Memorandum for State Department Division of Historical Policy Research, July 12, 1950, *FRUS-KOREA 1950,* p. 1039.

17. State Department *(SD)* cable, Langdon, Seoul, to Secretary Byrne, November 26, 1945. Background on the occupation is derived from *FRUS 1945-49*; A. Wigfall Green, *The Epic of Korea* (Washington, D.C.: Public Affairs Press, 1950) (Green was a political officer of the occupation and criticized its policies sharply); and Frank Baldwin, ed., *Without Parallel* (New York: Pantheon Books, 1973).

18. *FRUS 1945,* Vol. VI, pp. 1129–33.

19. Mark Gayn, *Japan Diary* (New York: William Sloane Associates, 1948), p. 341.

20. Memo, JCS to secretary of defense, "Military Importance of Korea," September 23, 1947.

21. "Review of the World Situation As It Relates to the Security of the United States," Central Intelligence Agency, February 12, 1948, p. 9.

22. Muccio *OH,* HSTL; Muccio's impressions of Rhee are from the same source.

23. The Defense-State battle over troop levels in Korea is in numerous cables, *FRUS* 1947, 1948, and 1949 volumes.

24. Muccio *OH.*

25. Matthew Ridgway, *The Korean War* (Garden City, N.Y.: Doubleday, 1967), pp. 10–12. Ridgway, *Korean War* hereafter.

26. Douglas A. MacArthur, *Reminiscences* (New York: McGraw-Hill, 1964), p. 322. MacArthur, *Reminiscences* hereafter.

27. London *Daily Mail* (March 1, 1949).

28. Dean Acheson, *Present at the Creation* (New York: Norton, 1969), p. 377. Acheson, *Present* hereafter.

29. *Ibid.,* p. 753.

30. *Ibid.,* p. 374.

31. Background on the U.S. military advisers is from Major Robert K. Sawyer, *Military Advisors in Korea: KMAG in Peace and War* (Washington, D.C.: Office of the Chief of Military History, 1962). Hereafter Sawyer, *Military Advisors.*

32. Muccio *OH.*

33. Guerrilla activity in South Korea, and countermeasures by the ROK Army, are detailed in *DIS,* FEC, 1948–50, various dates.

34. The curious Fatherland Front affair is described in Harold J. Noble, *Embassy at War* (Seattle: University of Washington Press, 1964), Noble, *Embassy at War* hereafter; and Noble's "The Reds Made Suckers of Us All," *Saturday Evening Post* (August 9, 1952).

35. Muccio to State, June 10, 1950, *FRUS-KOREA 1950,* pp. 101–02.

36. UN Commission on Korea to UN secretary-general, June 25, 1950, *United States Policy in the Korean Crisis* (Washington, D.C.: Department of State, 1950).

37. Interview, Dr. Ray S. Cline-JCG, February 12, 1980; also, Ray S. Cline, *Secrets, Spies and Scholars* (Washington, D.C.: Acropolis Books, 1976). CIA prewar evaluations of events in Korea are in the monthly series "Review of the World Situation As It Relates to the Security of the United States," various dates 1948–50; these are summary papers prepared chiefly for the President of the United States.

38. FEC G-2 reports are from *DIS,* FEC.

39. Frank Kluckhorn, "Heidelberg to Madrid—the Story of General Willoughby," *The Reporter* (August 19, 1952).

* * *

Chapter Two

1. Roy E. Appleman, *South to the Naktong, North to the Yalu* (Washington, D.C.: Office of the Chief of Military History Department of the Army, 1961), pp. 7–18. Appleman, *South* hereafter.

2. Interview, Jin Hak Kim—JCG, August 19, 1979.

3. Sawyer, *Military Advisors,* p. 115.

4. Oliver, *Rhee,* pp. 300–01.

5. Jack James, "The Korean Invasion," *Editor & Publisher* (July 22, 1950).

6. Margaret Truman, *Harry S. Truman* (New York: William Morrow, 1973), pp. 453–54. *Margaret* hereafter.

7. Truman to Woodward, June 24, 1950, HSTL.

8. Ayers diary, HSTL.

9. Beverly Smith, "Why We Went to War in Korea," *Saturday Evening Post* (November 10, 1951). Smith's article about the first critical ten days of the war benefited from White House cooperation, and I relied heavily upon it in bringing together documents and recollections from other sources. Equally valuable for a first-days account is Glenn D. Paige, *The Korean Decision* (New York: The Free Press, 1968), a classic study of crisis decision making.

10. Joseph and Stewart Alsop, *The Reporter's Trade* (New York: Reynal, 1958), p. 147.

11. Hickerson *OH,* HSTL.

12. Memorandum for record, "Statement About Korea," by Lieutenant Colonel Chester V. Clifton, June 26, 1950, *SW-II,* p. 64.

13. Hearings, *Military Situation in the Far East,* Senate Armed Services and Foreign Relations Committee, 82nd Congress, First Session (Washington, D.C.: Government Printing Office: 1951), Vol. IV, p. 2572. "The MacArthur hearings," popularly. *Military Situation* hereafter, with Roman numerals for volume numbers.

14. Acheson *Present; HST-II; Margaret;* and Ayers diary, HSTL.

15. Hickerson *OH,* HSTL.

16. Memorandum of conversation with Dean Rusk, by John W. Hizenga of State Department Division of Historical Policy Research, August 7, 1950, *FRUS-Korea 1950,* p. 128.

17. *FRUS-Korea 1950,* p. 128 fn.; p. 131.

18. The initial North Korean advance is described in Appleman, *South,* pp. 19–35.

19. Smith, quoted in *Time* (July 17, 1950).

20. Allison, Dulles papers, Princeton University Library; John Allison, *Ambassador from the Prairie* (Boston: Houghton Mifflin, 1973), pp. 129–30; Allison, *Ambassador* hereafter.

21. Noble, *Embassy at War,* p. 19.

22. Muccio *OH,* HSTL.

23. J. Lawton Collins, *War in Peacetime* (Boston: Houghton Mifflin, 1969), p. 11, Collins, *War in Peacetime* hereafter; *Record of JCS Actions,* JCS, April 1951 (a summary of substantive contacts between the JCS and MacArthur from the war's start to his firing in April 1951, submitted to the committee for hearings, *Military Situation).*

24. TT-3417, transcript of JCS telecon with CINCFE, June 25, 1950.

25. Bradley memorandum to other members JCS, June 25, 1950, quoted in *SW-II,* p. 71.

26. Ayers diary, HSTL.

27. Postpresidential interviews, HSTL. The account of Truman's flight back to Washington also draws upon *HST-II;* Snyder's comments are in Francis H. Heller, ed., *The Korean War: A 25-Year Perspective* (Lawrence, Ks.: Regents Press of Kansas, pp. 17–21. Heller, ed., *Korean War* hereafter.

28. Kennan, Princeton Seminar, HSTL.

29. Memorandum, "Estimate of the Military Situation in Light of Events in Korea," Joint Strategic Plans Committee, July 14, 1950, summarizes intelligence available on June 25.

30. *Khrushchev Remembers,* Strobe Talbott, trans. & ed. (Boston: Little, Brown, 1970), pp. 367–70.

31. Acheson, *Present,* p. 406.

32. Memorandum, untitled, from Estimates Group of Office of Intelligence Research, Department of State, June 25, 1950; *FRUS-KOREA 1950,* p. 148.

33. State to U.S. Embassy, 618 NIACT, Moscow, June 25, 1950, *FRUS-KOREA 1950*, p. 148.

34. Acheson to Muccio, 619 NIACT, June 25, 1950, *FRUS-KOREA 1950*, pp. 156–57.

35. Various cables between State and U.S. Delegation to the UN, June 25, 1950, *FRUS-Korea 1950;* allied doubts are expressed in Memorandum of Conversations by Charles P. Noyes, adviser on Security Council affairs to the delegation, pp. 144–47.

36. Trygve Lie, *In the Cause of Peace* (New York: Macmillan, 1954), pp. 327–32. Lie, *Cause of Peace* hereafter.

37. George F. Kennan, *Memoirs 1925–50* (Boston: Atlantic Monthly Press, 1967), p. 513.

38. DA TT 3416, transcript of telecon with CINCFE, June 25, 1950.

39. *Soldier: Memoirs of Matthew B. Ridgway* (New York: Harper & Bros., 1956), p. 192. Ridgway, *Soldier* hereafter.

40. Hickerson *OH,* HSTL.

41. Muccio *OH,* HSTL; Sawyer, *Military Advisors,* pp. 118–25; Appleman, *South,* pp. 38–40; and Noble, *Embassy at War.*

42. Allison *OH,* Princeton; Allison, *Ambassador,* pp. 128–31.

43. Noble, *Embassy at War;* Muccio *OH,* HSTL.

44. "Memorandum of Conversation at the White House, June 26, 1950," Acheson papers, HSTL.

45. Richard L. Strout, *TRB: Views and Perspectives on the Presidency* (New York: Macmillan, 1979), pp. 87–88.

46. "Memoranda of Conversations, Acheson with Senators Tom Connally and Alexander Wiley and Representative John Kee," June 26, 1950, Acheson papers, HSTL.

47. Five cables, Muccio to State, June 26, 1950: Embtel 953; unnumbered; 957 NIACT: 966 NIACT; and 967 NIACT; *FRUS-KOREA 1950*, pp. 168, 170, 173, and 176.

48. The fullest account of the June 26 Blair Meeting meeting is "Memorandum for the Record," by Jessup, in *FRUS-KOREA 1950*, pp. 178–83; also, Truman and Acheson memoirs and *Military Situation.*

49. Allison *OH,* Princeton; Allison, *Ambassador,* pp. 136–39.

50. Ayers diary, "Memoranofm of Conversation with President Truman, aboard *Williamsburg,* July 1, 1950," HSTL.

51. Diary of Major General Earle E. Partridge, June 25, 1950, quoted in Robert F. Futrell, *The United States Air Force in Korea 1950–53* (New York: Duell, Sloan and Pearce, 1961), p. 24. Futrell, *Air War* hereafter. (This is the "official" air force history, although historian Futrell notes it was approved "without a suggestion for changing so much as a single word.") Much of the air war material in this and succeeding chapters is derived from Futrell.

52. Muccio *OH,* HSTL, for his evacuation of embassy; cables State–Seoul and Seoul–State *FRUS-KOREA 1950,* June 26 and 27, 1950.

53. The evacuation of Seoul is described in Keyes Beech, *Tokyo and Points East* (New York: Doubleday, 1954), pp. 103–22; Marguerite Higgins, *War in Korea* (New York: Doubleday, 1951), pp. 17–22; *The New York Times* (June 29, 1950), Crane's account; *Time* (July 3, 1950), Gibney's account; Appleman, *South,* pp. 30–34; and Sawyer, *Military Advisors,* pp. 125–126.

Chapter Three

1. Kennan, Princeton Seminar, HSTL.

2. "Notes of Meeting with Congressional Leaders," White House, June 27, 1950, HSTL; also Acheson, Princeton Seminar, HSTL.

3. Lie, *Cause of Peace,* pp. 332–33.

4. Muccio *OH,* HSTL; Noble, *Embassy at War,* p. 171.

5. Sawyer, *Military Advisors,* p. 127; arrival of the Church party, same source.

6. MacArthur, *Reminiscences,* pp. 331–34; Major General Courtney Whitney, *MacArthur: His Rendezvous with History* (New York: Knopf, 1956), pp. 325–33, Whitney, *Ren-*

dezvous hereafter; Major General Charles A. Willoughby and John Chamberlain, *MacArthur, 1941–1951* (New York: McGraw-Hill, 1954), pp. 356–61, offer what could be called the "official" account of MacArthur's visit to the front. Appleman, *South,* pp. 44–46, is more restrained and also less complete.

7. David Douglas Duncan, *This Is War* (New York: Harper & Row, 1951), p. 191.

8. Roy MacCartney of Australian Associated Press, quoted in Collins, *War in Peacetime,* p. 18.

9. Appleman, *South,* p. 44.

10. *SW-II,* pp. 109–10.

11. "Memorandum of Conversation, NSC Meeting, June 28, 1959," by Jessup, Acheson papers, HSTL.

12. Noble, *Embassy at War,* p. 187.

13. Collins, *War in Peacetime,* p. 19.

14. Ridgway, *Korean War,* pp. 21–22.

15. Higgins, *War in Korea,* pp. 33–34.

16. An analysis of MacArthur's delay in reporting to Washington, and requesting troops, is in *SW-II,* Appendix, "General MacArthur's Message of 30 June 1950."

17. Memorandum, Admiral Davis to JSSC, June 28, 1950.

18. Memorandum, Hillenkoetter, director of central intelligence, to White House, untitled, June 27, 1950.

19. Memorandum for the secretary of the army, "Situation in the Far East," from Major General Charles L. Bolte, assistant chief of staff, G-3, June 28, 1950. The Bolte memorandum outlines Plan Offtackle as well.

20. JCS position paper 1776/6, June 29, 1950.

21. Minutes of this meeting remained classified as of July 1981, but the account given in Beverly Smith, "Why We Went to War in Korea," is cited as authoritative by *SW-II,* authors of which read but could not quote directly the classified material. Hence the source for this section is Smith, endorsed by *SW-II,* p. 106.

22. *HST-II,* p. 341.

23. U.S. Embassy, Moscow, to Acheson, 1767 NIACT, June 29, 1950, *FRUS-KOREA 1950,* pp. 229–30.

24. CINCFE C 56942 to DA for JCS, June 30, 1950.

25. Collins, *War in Peacetime,* pp. 20–21.

26. DA TT 3444, with CINCFE, June 30, 1950.

27. Collins, *War in Peacetime,* p. 22.

28. Pace *OH,* HSTL.

29. *Military Situation,* Part II, Sherman testimony.

30. Memorandum, "President's Call to Pace, and Call from Louis Johnson," June 30, 1950, Elsey papers, HSTL.

31. *HST-II,* p. 343.

32. Memorandum, "Meeting in Cabinet Room with Representatives of State, Defense and Number of Congressmen," June 30, 1950, Elsey papers, HSTL.

33. Heller, ed. *Korean War,* Harriman quoted, pp. 104–06; Battle, pp. 106–07.

34. Memorandum, "Congressional Resolution," July 16, 1951, Elsey papers, HSTL.

35. Acheson, Princeton Seminar, HSTL.

36. *SW-II,* pp. 122–25.

37. *Military Situation,* Part IV, Johnson testimony.

Chapter Four

1. Appleman, *South,* pp. 60–76; also, Smith file, Office Chief of Military History, Washington, which includes transcripts of interviews with Smith and other men of his task force, as well as after-action reports and correspondence.

2. MacArthur, *Reminiscences,* p. 336.

3. Interview, Brigadier General Eugene M. "Mike" Lynch-JCG, May 14, 1980. Lynch

served as aide and personal pilot for Generals Walker and Ridgway; his insights added much to my understanding of both men, especially Walker.

4. Appleman, *South,* p. 417.

5. Noble, *Embassy at War,* p. 311.

6. Major General William F. Dean as told to William L. Worden, *General Dean's Story* (New York: Viking, 1954). *Dean's Story* hereafter.

7. *Time* (July 17, 1950). Marguerite Higgins of the New York *Herald Tribune,* who was at the scene, gave Shadrick temporary fame as the war's "first casualty."

8. *Dean's Story,* pp. 23–25.

9. Appleman, *South,* p. 84.

10. CINCFE C 57061 to DA for JCS, July 2, 1950.

11. JCS 84876 to CINCFE, July 3, 1950.

12. CINCFE C 57218 to DA for JCS, July 5, 1950.

13. JCS 85058 to CINCFE, July 6, 1950.

14. Appleman, *South,* pp. 101–08.

15. John G. Westover, ed., *Combat Support in Korea* (Washington, D.C.: Combat Forces Press, 1955).

16. *Ibid.*

17. Because of stay-behind agents and line crossers, the CIA managed to obtain markedly detailed accounts of life in the ROK capital after the North Korean occupation. This section is based upon the CIA's "Daily Intelligence Reports" of July 4, 5, 6, 9, 12, 14, 19, and 28, and August 9, 15, and 30.

Chapter Five

1. Intelligence Memorandum, "Effects of a Voluntary Withdrawal or Elimination of U.S. Forces from Korea," Central Intelligence Agency, July 10, 1950.

2. Interview, Cline—JCG.

3. Memorandum, "Some Recent Developments with Regard to Soviet Personnel Abroad," Hillenkoetter, director of central intelligence, to Truman, July 8, 1950.

4. CINCFE CX 57481 to JCS, July 9, 1950.

5. Position paper JCS 1776/27, July 10, 1950.

6. This section on the draft and mobilization draws from an essay, John Edward Wiltz, "The Korean War and American Society," in Heller, ed., *Korean War,* pp. 112–17; Eric Goldman, *The Crucial Decade* (New York: Vintage, 1960); and my own preliminary research for a social history of the 1950's that evolved, for reasons stated in "A Word About Origins," into the book at hand.

7. *Time* (July 24, 1950).

8. "Memorandum for General Bolte: Report of Trip to the Far East Command," July 19, 1950, written by Lieutenant Colonel D. D. Dickson, who accompanied Generals Collins and Vandenberg.

9. Appleman, *South,* pp. 214–18.

10. O. H. P. King, *Tail of the Tiger* (Caldwell, Id: Caxton Printers, 1961).

11. Relman Morin, Associated Press, San Francisco *Chronicle* (July 21, 1950).

12. *Eighth Army War Diary,* July–August 1950, HSTL.

13. Noble, *Embassy at War,* pp. 000-000; also Muccio *OH,* HSTL.

14. Account of Dean's capture is from *Dean's Story,* pp. 59–82.

15. Quoted *Time* (October 15, 1951).

16. Letter to Representative Joseph Martin, October 18, 1949, *Congressional Record,* October 25, 1949.

17. Foster Rhea Dulles, *American Policy Towards Communist China 1949–1959* (New York: Crowell, 1972).

18. K. M. Pannikar, *In Two Chinas: Memoirs of a Diplomat* (London: George Allen and Unwin, Ltd., 1955).

19. Whitney, *Rendezvous,* p. 369.

20. William Sebald, *With MacArthur in Tokyo* (New York: W. W. Norton, 1965), pp. 122–24. Sebald, *With MacArthur* hereafter.

21. *HST-II*, p. 354.

22. *U.S. News & World Report* (August 1, 1950).

23. Sebald, *With MacArthur*, pp. 124–25.

24. *Time* (August 14, 1950).

25. MacArthur, *Reminiscences*, pp. 340–41.

26. SecDef WAR 88014 to CINCFE, August 4, 1950.

27. Whitney, *Rendezvous*, p. 376.

28. Harriman, Princeton Seminar, HSTL.

29. Harriman memo to Truman on Far East trip, undated, but late August 1950 from context, HSTL.

30. Lowe's observation of MacArthur, "Memorandum for Record," Ridgway, March 9, 1951, Ridgway papers, AWC.

31. *HST-II*, p. 354.

32. *SW-X*, p. 506.

33. Baldwin *OH*, NL.

34. Truman diary, September 12, 1950, HSTL.

35. Ayers diary, July 1, 1950, HSTL.

36. *Ibid.*, July 3, 1950, HSTL.

37. Acheson, Princeton Seminar, HSTL.

38. Acheson, *Present*, pp. 423–24.

39. "Memorandum for Record of Events of August 26, 1950," Acheson papers, HSTL. The remainder of the happenings that day is from the memo and Acheson's Princeton Seminar comments.

40. Charles Ross (White House press secretary), memorandum dictated to George Elsey, September 12, 1950, Elsey papers, HSTL.

41. Interview, Cline—JCG.

Chapter Six

1. Strategy of the Pusan Perimeter defense from Appleman, *South*, and Collins, *War in Peacetime*.

2. Interview, Lynch—JCG.

3. *DIS*, FEC, August 3, 4, and 6, 1950.

4. The account of the 25th Infantry Division, and its ill-fated 24th Regiment, Appleman, *South*, and Collins, *War in Peacetime*.

5. *The New York Times* (November 28, 1950).

6. *DIS*, FEC, August 11, 1950.

7. *Ibid.*, August 10, 1950.

8. *Time* (August 20, 1950).

9. *DIS*, FEC, August 13, 1950.

10. Appleman, *South*, p. 206.

11. *Ibid.*, pp. 207–08.

12. Hanson Baldwin, in *The New York Times* (August 2, 1950).

13. Willoughby, *MacArthur*, pp. 361–64.

14. "North Korean 6th Infantry Division," InterRept 33-6, Allied Translator and Interpreter Service (ATIS), Far East Command.

15. Fight for Hill 342 in Lynn Montross and Nicholas A. Canzona, *U.S. Marine Operations in Korea 1950–53*, Vol. I, *The Pusan Perimeter* (Washington, D.C.: Historical Branch, Headquarters U.S. Marine Corps, 1954), pp. 103–17. *USMC-I* hereafter.

16. James Bell, in *Time* (August 28, 1950).

17. *USMC-I*, p. 183.

18. Manring's account, *The New York Times* (August 18, 1950); *Life* (September 4, 1950); *Time* (August 28, 1950).

19. Charles and Eugene Jones, *The Face of War* (New York: Prentice-Hall, 1951), pp. 45–49.

20. "Advanced General Headquarters, NKPA," ATIS report, Issue 4, translating documents captured by 8th Cavalry Regiment, September 6, 1950.

21. John Osborne, in *Time* (August 21, 1950).

22. Beech, *Tokyo and Points East*, pp. 139–40.

23. "Analysis, Kim Il Sung Speech," Foreign Broadcast Information Service, Central Intelligence Agency, August 15, 1950.

Chapter Seven

1. MacArthur, *Reminiscences*, p. 334.

2. Montross and Canzona, *U.S. Marine Operations in Korea 1950–1953*, Vol. II, *The Inchon-Seoul Operation*, p. 6, *USMC-II* hereafter. Montross-Canzona details marine planning for Inchon.

3. CINCFE C 58473 to DA for JCS, July 23, 1950.

4. Shepherd *OH*, USMCHC.

5. Admiral Radford's account, quoted in Robert Debs Heinl, Jr., *Victory at High Tide* (Philadelphia: Lippincott, 1968), p. 20. *Victory at High Tide* is the definitive account of the Inchon operation, lacking only material that was later declassified.

6. Collins via CINCFE C 57814 to DA for JCS, July 14, 1950.

7. Hearings, "The National Defense Program: Unification and Strategy," House Armed Services Committee, October 1949.

8. *The New York Times* (October 20, 1949).

9. CINCFE CX 58327 to JCS, July 21, 1950.

10. Davis *OH*, USMCHC.

11. Bowser *OH*, USMCHC.

12. Smith *OH*, USMCHC.

13. Andrew Geer, *The New Breed* (New York: Harper & Row, 1952), p. 104.

14. Bowser *OH*, USMCHC.

15. DA WAR 88594 to CINCFE, August 12, 1950.

16. CINCFE CX 58327 to JCS, July 21, 1950.

17. DA TT 3573, transcript of telecon with CINCFE, July 23, 1950.

18. *Military Situation*, Part IV, Sherman testimony.

19. Memorandum, "Interim Guidance for Support of Far East Command Campaign in Korea," August 7, 1950, G-3, Department of the Army.

20. MacArthur, *Reminiscences*, p. 347.

21. Numerous accounts exist of the August 23, 1950, meeting, and they agree in substance, if not in detail. This account draws heavily from Heinl, *Victory at High Tide*, who interviewed several of the surviving participants; MacArthur, *Reminiscences*; Collins, *Peace in Wartime*; General Oliver Smith's war diary; and Malcolm W. Cagle and Frank A. Manson, *The Sea War in Korea* (Annapolis, Md.: United States Naval Institute, 1957). Both authors were naval commanders at the writing; their book is the "official" navy history of the war. MacArthur's summation remarks, which were not transcribed, are an amalgamation from his *Reminiscences* and the other cited sources.

22. Smith *OH*, USMCHC.

23. Harriman memo to Truman on Far East trip, August 1950, HSTL.

24. Harriman, Princeton Seminar, HSTL.

25. JCS 89960 to CINCFE, August 28, 1950.

26. Harriman, Princeton Seminar, HSTL.

27. JCS 90639 to CINCFE, September 5, 1950.

28. CINCFE C 62213 to DA for JCS, September 6, 1950.

29. JCS 90908 to CINCFE, September 7, 1950.

30. MacArthur, *Reminiscences*, p. 351.

31. CINCFE C 62423 to DA for JCS, September 8, 1950.

32. JCS 90958 to CINCFE, September 8, 1950.

33. Brigadier General Lynn D. Smith, "A Nickel After a Dollar," *Army* (September 1970); same source for subsequent references to Smith's journey.

34. Shepherd *OH,* USMCHC.

35. Appleman, *South,* p. 490.

36. Shepherd *OH,* USMCHC.

37. Smith *OH,* USMCHC.

38. Bowser *OH,* USMCHC.

39. Appleman, *South,* p. 509.

40. Summary Report, "Operation Trudy Jackson, September 1950," Far East Division, Central Intelligence Agency, Tokyo, September 23, 1950; also Heinl, *Victory at High Tide,* pp. 67–69.

41. Cagle-Manson, *Sea War in Korea,* pp. 91–94; also, James A. Field, Jr., *United States Naval Operations, Korea* (Washington, D.C.: Department of the Navy, 1962), pp. 191–95.

42. *Time* (September 25, 1950) had its traditional eye for colorful detail in describing MacArthur's demeanor during the invasion. The *Time-Life* correspondent on MacArthur's flagship was Carl Mydans, skilled observer as well as photographer. Correspondent Frank Gibney went ashore in the marine assault wave and did some of the most vivid coverage of the war.

43. Howard Handleman of International News Service, quoted in Heinl, *Victory at High Tide,* p. 76.

44. Pilot quotes are from Press Releases 443 and 446, Far East Command, September 15 and 16, 1950, respectively. Despite the presence of scores of correspondents, FEC press officers did not want a single detail to escape mention.

45. *USMC-II,* pp. 87–92.

46. Bowser *OH,* USMCHC.

47. Technical Sergeant Allen G. Mainard, "Sea Wall," *Leatherneck* magazine (September 1957).

48. Marguerite Higgins, in New York *Herald Tribune* (September 16, 1950).

49. James Bell, with the second marine assault wave, in *Time* (September 25, 1950).

50. Bruce Jacobs, *Korea's Heroes: The Medal of Honor Story* (New York: Berkley Medallion, 1961, rev. ed.), pp. 28–29; also, *USMC-II,* p. 106.

51. Memorandum, Simmons, March 28, 1955, USMC Historical Branch.

52. Shepherd *OH,* USMCHC.

53. Staff Sergeant Robert W. Tallent, "Inchon to Seoul," *Leatherneck* magazine (January 1951).

54. *USMC-II,* pp. 147–51; Staff Sergeant Robert W. Tallent, "Gunsmoke Reveille," *Leatherneck* magazine (January 1951).

55. Burke Davis, *Marine!: The Life of Lieutenant General Lewis B. (Chesty) Puller* (Boston: Little, Brown, 1962), pp. 261–64, Davis, *Marine!* hereafter; Bowser *OH,* Smith *OH,* Shepherd *OH,* USMCHC; Percy Wood, in Chicago *Tribune* (September 18, 1950); and Heinl, *Victory at High Tide,* tell of MacArthur's shore visit.

56. Shepherd *OH,* USMCHC.

57. Appleman, *South,* pp. 542–63.

58. Telecon, Walker with Hickey, September 21, 1950, quoted in Schnabel, *Policy and Direction: The First Year* (Washington, D.C.: Office of the Chief of Military History, Department of the Army, 1963), pp. 175–76. *Schnabel, Policy and Direction* hereafter.

59. *Time* (October 9, 1950).

60. Interview, Robert Edson—JCG, December 8, 1979.

61. Smith *OH,* USMCHC.

62. Bowser *OH,* USMCHC; *OH* source for other Bowser comments on Seoul recapture.

63. Davis, *Marine!,* p. 275.

64. Smith *OH,* USMCHC.

65. Noble, *Embassy at War,* p. 311.

66. Smith *OH,* USMCHC.

67. Ridgway, *Korean War,* pp. 42–44.

* * *

Chapter Eight

1. Acheson, *Present,* p. 445.
2. *HST-II,* p. 341.
3. Draft memorandum, "U.S. Courses of Action in Korea," Joint Strategic Planning Committee, JCS, July 31, 1950.
4. Draft memorandum, untitled, Policy Planning Committee, Department of State, July 25, 1950.
5. "Memorandum for General Bolte, Report of Trip to Far East Command," Lieutenant Colonel D. D. Dickson, July 19, 1950.
6. JCS misgivings about NSC 81 are discussed in *SW-V,* p. 227.
7. "Memorandum of Meeting with Ambassador Chang," Dean Rusk, September 8, 1950, Acheson papers, HSTL.
8. Rhee quoted in Collins, *War in Peacetime,* p. 163.
9. *Department of State Bulletin,* July 10, 1950.
10. CINCFE C 64159 to JCS, September 23, 1950.
11. JCS 92801 to CINCFE, September 27, 1950.
12. *The New York Times* (September 30, 1950).
13. JCS 92985 to CINCFE, September 29, 1950. Marshall wrote the message in longhand and marked it "EYES ONLY FOR CINCFE."
14. CINCFE C 65118 to DA for JCS, October 1, 1950.
15. Acheson, *Present,* pp. 453–54.
16. JCS 93079 to CINCFE, October 1, 1950.
17. Collins, *War in Peacetime,* p. 155. MacArthur's strategic planning for his advance is in Collins and Appleman, *South.*
18. Appleman, *South,* p. 611.
19. Lieutenant Colonel Melvin B. Voorhees, *Korean Tales* (New York: Simon & Schuster, 1952), p. 212–13.
20. Interview, Lynch—JCG.
21. Smith *OH,* USMCHC.
22. Walter Karig, Malcolm Cagel, and Frank A. Manson, *Battle Report: Volume VI, The War in Korea* (New York: Rinehart & Company, 1952), pp. 348–49. Karig, *Battle Report* hereafter.
23. "Memorandum of Conversations," Rusk with Sir Oliver Banks, British ambassador, and Lord Arthur W. Tedder, British Embassy, October 4, 1950, subject, "Korean Operations," Acheson papers, HSTL.
24. Memorandum, Tedder to Bradley, October 5, 1950.
25. Bradley, handwritten notation on memo cited line above.
26. Acheson, *Present,* p. 450.
27. *Military Situation,* Part III, Acheson testimony.
28. Acheson, *Present,* p. 454.
29. Collins, *War in Peacetime,* p. 149.
30. Of the many books on the Philby-Burgess-Maclean spy ring, the most comprehensive is Andrew Boyle, *The Fourth Man* (New York: Dial, 1980).
31. Interview report, Washington field office, Federal Bureau of Investigation, July 13, 1951, Burgess-Maclean file, case summary.

Chapter Nine

1. Appleman, *South,* and Collins, *War in Peacetime.*
2. Appleman, *South,* p. 645.
3. *Time* (October 30, 1950).
4. *DIS,* FEC, October 20, 1950.
5. Lynn Montross and Nicholas A. Canzona, *United States Marine Operations in*

Korea, 1950–1953, Vol. III, *The Chosin Reservoir Campaign* (Washington, D.C.: Historical Branch, Headquarters Marine Corps, 1957), p. 30. *USMC-III* hereafter. *USMC-III* source also for marine withdrawal from South Korea and voyage to eastern coast.

6. Collins, *War in Peacetime,* p. 169. Of the dozens of professional military critiques I read of the marine deployment during research of this book, I found not a single one defending MacArthur's decision. The marines were apoplectic. Smith and Bowser *OH*s, USMCHC.

7. Collins, *War in Peacetime,* p. 177.

8. CINCFE 66839 to EUSAK, October 19, 1950.

9. Freeman *OH,* AWC.

10. Don Whitehead, Associated Press story, various American newspapers (October 23 and 24, 1950).

11. CINCUNC CX 67291 to all commanders, October 24, 1950.

12. JCS 94933 to CINCFE, October 24, 1950.

13. CINCFE C 67397 to JCS, October 25, 1950.

14. *Military Situation,* Part II, Collins testimony.

15. State to U.S. Embassy, Seoul, October 21, 1950, quoted in *FRUS-KOREA 1950,* p. 987.

16. JCS 94799 to CINCFE, October 21, 1950.

17. CINCFE C67154 to JCS, October 22, 1950.

Chapter Ten

1. Muccio *OH,* HSTL.

2. *HST-II,* pp. 362–63.

3. Murphy *OH,* HSTL.

4. Pace *OH,* HSTL.

5. Whitney, *Rendezvous,* pp. 384–86.

6. MacArthur, *Reminiscences,* p. 361.

7. "Memorandum of Conversation with the President," October 19, 1950, Acheson papers, HSTL.

8. Acheson, Princeton Seminar, HSTL.

9. Pace *OH,* HSTL.

10. *Time* (October 23, 1950).

11. Whitney, *Rendezvous,* p. 386.

12. MacArthur, *Reminiscences,* p. 361.

13. Muccio *OH,* HSTL.

14. "Wake Island," Truman memorandum, April 4, 1951, Elsey papers, HSTL.

15. Whitney, *Rendezvous,* p. 387.

16. "Wake Island," Truman memorandum cited in note 14.

17. Baltimore *Sun* (October 22, 1950).

18. *Time* (May 14, 1951).

19. Murphy *OH,* HSTL.

20. Whitney, *Rendezvous,* p. 391.

21. Muccio *OH,* HSTL.

22. "Substance of Statements Made at Wake Island Conference on October 15, 1950," compiled by General Omar Bradley, chairman, JCS, for use of Senate Armed Services Committee and Foreign Relations Committee, printed May 2, 1951, as committee document.

23. Whitney, *Rendezvous,* pp. 388–89.

24. Joseph E. Johnson of State Department, Princeton Seminar, HSTL.

25. MacArthur, *Reminiscences,* p. 363.

26. Muccio *OH,* HSTL.

27. Murphy *OH,* HSTL.

28. Ayers diary, October 19, 1950, Ayers papers, HSTL.

29. Pace *OH,* HSTL.

Chapter Eleven

1. "The USSR and the Korean Invasion," CIA Intelligence Memorandum (IM) 300, June 28, 1950.

2. "Soviet Capabilities with Respect to Japan in the Light of U.S. Commitment in Korea," CIA IM 314, July 7, 1950.

3. "Consequences of the Korean Incident," CIA IM 320, July 8, 1950.

4. "Review of the World Situation," CIA, July 19, 1950.

5. Memorandum, untitled, Hillenkoetter, director of central intelligence, to Truman, August 1, 1950.

6. "Soviet Preparations for Major Hostilities in 1950," CIA IM 323-SRC, August 25, 1950. This paper was prepared by a highly sensitive CIA branch, the Special Research Center, which apparently relied upon agents operating within the Soviet Union.

7. DIS for White House, CIA, September 1, 1950.

8. Situation Summary, CIA, September 22 and September 29, 1950.

9. Ibid., September 29, 1950.

10. Memorandum, untitled, Smith, director of central intelligence, to Truman, October 12, 1950.

11. Situation Summary, CIA, October 27, 1950.

12. Harry Rositzke, The CIA's Secret Operations (New York: Reader's Digest Press, 1977), p. 53.

13. "U.S.-UK Chiefs of Staff Meeting," October 23, 1950, minutes.

14. Stratemeyer to Chief of Staff, USAF, October 20, 1950; this message describes the reconnaissance missions of both October 18 and October 19.

15. Quotations in following section are from DIS, FEC, September and October 1950.

16. Pannikar, In Two Chinas, p. 108.

17. Memorandum, "Conversations between Indian Representatives in Peking and Chinese Communist Officials," Merchant, September 27, 1950, Acheson papers, HSTL.

18. Pannikar, In Two Chinas, p. 110.

19. Memorandum, "Threat of Chinese Intervention in Korean Conflict," Johnson to Rusk, October 3, 1950, Acheson papers, HSTL.

20. Cable, Kirk to State, 492, October 3, 1950, Acheson papers, HSTL.

21. Cable, Wilkinson to State, 708, October 2, 1950, Acheson papers, HSTL.

22. Chapin to State, 490 NIACT, October 3, 1950, Acheson papers, HSTL.

23. Memorandum of Conversation, "Chinese Participation in Korean Debate," John Allison of U.S. Delegation to UN, October 4, 1950, Acheson papers, HSTL.

24. JCS 93709 to CINCFE, October 9, 1950.

25. "The Position and Actions of the United States with Respect to Possible Further Soviet Moves in the Light of the Korean Situation," report by Joint Strategic Study Committee, August 9, 1950; adopted by NSC under same title, August 25, 1950.

26. "Threat of Full Chicom Intervention in Korea," CIA briefing paper for Wake Island Conference, October 12, 1950.

27. Burke OH, NL.

28. Talbott, Khrushchev Remembers, pp. 371–72.

Chapter Twelve

1. DIS, FEC, November 9, 1950.

2. Ibid., October 28 and 29, 1950.

3. Nitze, Princeton Seminar, HSTL.

4. Appleman, South, p. 677.

5. DIS, FEC, November 3, 1950.

6. Johnson OH, AWC.

7. Freeman OH, AWC.

8. *Ibid.*

9. New York *Herald Tribune* (November 3, 1950).

10. Milburn *OH,* AWC.

11. Appleman, *South,* pp. 699–704, tells of the battalion's plight; also, correspondent Homer Bigart, who was at Unsan, in New York *Herald Tribune* (November 3, 1950).

12. Jacobs, *Korea's Heroes,* pp. 101–02.

13. "Enemy Documents Captured by ROK 1st Division November 26, 1950," ATIS analysis 11, undated.

14. CINCFE C 68285 to DA for JCS, November 4, 1950.

15. *Air War,* Futrell, pp. 209–10.

16. "Memorandum of Conversation between Mr. Acheson and Mr. Lovett, November 6, 1950, 10:20 A.M.," Lovett, Acheson papers, HSTL.

17. CINCFE C 68396 to DA for JCS, November 6, 1950.

18. *HST-II,* pp. 375–76.

19. JCS 95949 to CINCFE, November 6, 1950.

20. CINCFE C 68465 to DA for JCS, November 7, 1950.

21. Marshall to CINCFE, DEF 95961, November 7, 1950.

22. CINCFE C 68506 to DA for SecDef, November 8, 1950.

23. Roy K. Flint, "The Tragic Flaw: MacArthur, the Joint Chiefs, and the Korean War," Ph.D. dissertation, Duke University, 1976, University Microfilms, Ann Arbor.

24. Smith *OH,* USMCHC.

25. Description of the terrain leading to the reservoir, and background on the marine tactical planning, Smith *OH* and Smith, *Aide-Mémoire, Korea* (Smith *A-M* hereafter), JCG files; a slightly truncated version of the *A-M* is at USMCHC.

26. Bowser *OH,* USMCHC.

27. The marines' first encounter with the Chinese is in *USMC-III,* pp. 99–117, and Geer, *New Breed,* pp. 270–93.

Chapter Thirteen

1. "On the Protracted War," *Selected Works of Mao Tse-tung* (New York: International Publishers, 1954), Vol. II, p. 183.

2. Gene Hanrahan and Edward L. Katzenbach, Jr., "The Revolutionary Strategy of Mao Tse-tung," *Political Science Quarterly* (September 1955), reprinted in Franklin Mark Osanka, ed., *Modern Guerrilla Warfare* (New York: Free Press of Glencoe, 1969), pp. 177–84.

3. Robert Leckie, *Conflict* (New York: Avon, 1963), p. 161.

4. Acheson, *Present,* p. 466.

5. Bradley, Princeton Seminar, HSTL.

6. JCS 96060 to CINCFE, November 8, 1950.

7. CINCFE C 68465 to DA for JCS, November 7, 1950.

8. CINCFE 68572 to DA for JCS, November 9, 1950.

9. Memorandum, "Chinese Communist Intervention in Korea," JCS to secretary of defense, November 9, 1950.

10. Memorandum for the President, November 10, 1950, meeting of NSC, HSTL.

11. Richard E. Neustadt, *Presidential Power* (New York: John Wiley & Sons, 1960), pp. 127–28.

12. Memorandum of conversation, "General MacArthur's Concept of the Korean War," by Sebald, November 14, 1950, Acheson papers, HSTL.

13. Memorandum of conversation, "Korean Military Action," by Muccio, November 17, 1950, Acheson papers, HSTL.

14. Memorandum, "Resolutions in the United Nations to Provide Certain Assurances to the Chinese Communists," JCS to secretary of defense, November 8, 1950.

15. *SW-VI,* pp. 309–11.

16. Schnabel, *Policy and Direction,* p. 266; *SW-VI,* p. 312.

17. Memorandum, "State-Defense High-level Briefing on Korea," Bolte for General Collins, November 20, 1950.

18. Memorandum, "U.S. Courses of Action with Respect to Korea," G-3, Department of Army, to Collins, November 28, 1950.

19. Memorandum, untitled, Rusk to Acheson, undated, but internal wording suggests November 24, 1950, Acheson papers, HSTL.

Chapter Fourteen

1. Smith *A-M.*

2. Leckie, *Conflict,* p. 171.

3. Smith *A-M.*

4. *Time* (December 4, 1950).

5. Whitney, *Rendezvous,* p. 416.

6. MacArthur, *Reminiscences,* p. 372.

7. Higgins, *War in Korea,* p. 176.

8. Colonel Sid Huff with Joe Alex Morris, *Fifteen Years with MacArthur* (New York: Paperback Library, 1964), p. 133; Whitney, *Rendezvous,* pp. 416–17.

9. Interview, Lynch—JCG.

10. *Ibid.*

11. *DIS,* FEC, November 10, 1950.

12. *Ibid.,* November 12, 1950.

13. *Ibid.,* November 15, 1950.

14. *Ibid.,* November 7, 1950.

15. Intelligence Digest 16:31, FEC, January 1952, quoted in Appleman, *South,* p. 770.

16. Ridgway, *Korean War,* pp. 60–65.

17. Smith *OH,* USMCHC.

18. Geer, *New Breed,* p. 247.

19. Davis *OH,* USMCHC.

20. Bowser *OH,* USMCHC.

21. Litzenberg *OH,* USMCHC.

22. Smith *OH,* USMCHC.

23. *USMC-III,* pp. 131–35.

24. Smith *OH,* USMCHC.

25. *Ibid.*

26. Smith, letter to General Cates, November 15, 1950, contained in Smith *A-M.*

27. Smith *A-M.*

28. *Ibid.*

29. Davis, *Marine!,* pp. 297–98.

30. Michener, in his Introduction to Beech, *Tokyo and Points East,* p. 12; letter, Herman to JCG, June 18, 1980.

31. Leckie, *Conflict,* p. 172.

32. S. L. A. Marshall, *The River and the Gauntlet* (New York: Time Reading Program ed., 1962), pp. 31–38. Marshall did some of the most vivid battle writing of the war. He was in Korea as a consultant to the Operations Research Office of Johns Hopkins University, as an infantry operations analyst working from EUSAK G-3 (Operations). Marshall, *River and Gauntlet* hereafter.

33. T. R. Fehrenbach, *This Kind of War* (New York: Macmillan, 1963), pp. 304–14. Fehrenbach, an infantry commander during the war, did extensive interviews for this book, told from the vantage point of the foot soldier and his officers. I am indebted to his work for his insight into the thinking of infantrymen, plus specifics of the episodes cited in the notes.

34. Marshall, *River and Gauntlet,* p. 163.

35. Leckie, *Conflict,* p. 175.

Chapter Fifteen

1. *USMC-II,* pp. 151–71, and Smith *A-M* detail the marine advance and planning.
2. *DIS,* FEC, February 4, 1951.
3. Beech, *Tokyo and Points East,* pp. 191–92.
4. Geer, *New Breed,* p. 270.
5. Interview, Charles G. Higgins—JCG, May 17, 1978.
6. Interview, Brenton Case—JCG, May 17, 1978.
7. Geer, *New Breed,* pp. 275–76.
8. Fehrenbach, *This Kind of War,* p. 363.
9. Smith *A-M.*
10. Geer, *New Breed,* p. 309.
11. Smith *OH,* USMCHC.
12. Bowser *OH,* USMC.
13. Smith *A-M.*
14. *USMC-II,* pp. 177–85.
15. Philip N. Pierce, "The Hill," *Leatherneck* magazine (April 1962).
16. Jacobs, *Korea's Heroes,* pp. 55–57.
17. Pierce, "The Hill."
18. *USMC-III,* p. 194.
19. Davis *OH,* USMCHC; Medal of Honor citation files, Davis and Barber, USMCHC.
20. Smith *OH,* USMCHC.
21. Bowser *OH,* USMCHC.
22. Beech, *Tokyo and Points East,* pp. 196–97.
23. *Ibid.,* p. 188.
24. Smith *OH,* USMCHC.
25. Interview, Franklin Moore—JCG, May 19, 1978.
26. Geer, *New Breed,* p. 337.
27. Interview, Barry Lester—JCG, July 17, 1977.
28. Beech, *Tokyo and Points East,* p. 198.
29. *USMC-III,* p. 271.
30. Bowser *OH,* USMCHC.
31. Beech, *Tokyo and Points East,* p. 200.
32. Smith *A-M.*
33. Smith *OH,* USMCHC.
34. Smith *A-M.*
35. Smith *OH,* USMCHC.
36. Higgins, *War in Korea,* pp. 182–83.
37. Geer, *New Breed,* p. 351.
38. *USMC-III,* p. 291.
39. G. L. Coon, "Versatility," *Leatherneck* magazine (March 1951).
40. Interview, Leland Gordon—JCG, July 17, 1977.
41. Smith *A-M;* Smith *OH,* USMCHC. Memorandum, "Air Drop and Construction of Treadway Bridge at the Penstocks South of Funchilin Pass," Smith papers, USMCHC.
42. *USMC-III,* p. 319.
43. *Ibid.,* p. 321.
44. Fehrenbach, *This Kind of War,* p. 372.
45. *Time* (December 25, 1950).
46. Westover, *Combat Support in Korea,* p. 171.
47. "Compilation of Battle Experiences Reported by Various Armies in their Operation Against U.S. Forces in Korea," Document 204141, Headquarters 500th Military Intelligence Group, FEC, March 1951.

Chapter Sixteen

1. CINCFE 69953 to JCS, November 28, 1950.

2. *HST-II*, p. 385.

3. Goldman, *Crucial Decade*, p. 178.

4. "Memorandum of Conversation, NSC Meeting, November 28, 1950," by Jessup, Acheson papers, HSTL.

5. JCS 97592 to CINCFE, November 29, 1950.

6. JCS 97594 to CINCFE, November 29, 1950.

7. Collins, *War in Peacetime*, p. 22.

8. Schnabel, *Policy and Direction*, pp. 278–79.

9. CINCUNC C 50095 to DA for JCS, November 30, 1950.

10. Bradley handwritten comments on message cited above.

11. CINCUNC C 50107 to JCS, November 30, 1950.

12. JCS 97772 to CINCFE, November 30, 1950.

13. *Military Situation*, Part III, Bradley testimony.

14. Collins, *War in Peacetime*, p. 211.

15. John Stebbins, ed., for the Council on Foreign Relations, *The United States in World Affairs, 1950* (New York: Harper's, 1951), pp. 411–13.

16. William S. White, *The Taft Story* (New York: Harper's, 1954), pp. 173–74.

17. John W. Spanier, *The Truman-MacArthur Controversy* (New York: Norton, 1965), p. 154.

18. Untitled memorandum, December 14, 1950, Elsey papers, HSTL; Acheson, *Present*, p. 485, has a slightly different version.

19. Lester Thurow, "How to Wreck the Economy," *New York Review of Books* (May 14, 1981).

20. "Memorandum of Conversation, Acheson and Lovett, December 2, 1950," Acheson papers, HSTL.

21. Memorandum, Collins to JCS, November 20, 1950.

22. Memorandum, Lalor to Joint Strategic Survey Committee, November 28, 1950.

23. "Memorandum of Conversation with Baron Silvercruys, November 30, 1950," Rusk to Acheson, Acheson papers, HSTL.

24. *HST-II*, p. 396.

25. 3194 NIACT, U.S. Embassy London to Acheson, November 30, 1950, Acheson papers, HSTL.

26. Austin to State, 902, November 29, 1950, Acheson papers, HSTL.

27. Austin to State, 916, November 30, 1950, Acheson papers, HSTL.

28. "Notes on Meeting in JCS Conference Room, Pentagon, 8:30 A.M., December 1, 1950," by Jessup, Acheson papers, HSTL.

29. "Meeting of the President and Members of Congress, 11 A.M., Friday, December 1, 1950," Elsey papers, HSTL.

30. "Soviet Intentions in the Current Situation," *National Intelligence Estimate 11*, CIA, December 2, 1950.

31. "Memorandum of Conversation of White House Meeting, December 2, 1950," by Jessup and Battle, Acheson papers, HSTL.

32. "Acheson to Certain Diplomatic and Consular Offices," December 2, 1950, *FRUS-KOREA 1950*, p. 1298.

33. Austin to Acheson, cable 930, December 1, 1950, Acheson papers, HSTL.

34. "Highlights of the Korean Situation, December 2, 1950," JCS.

35. CINCUNC C 50332 to JCS, December 3, 1950.

36. "Memorandum of Conversation, Meeting at Pentagon, 9:30 A.M., December 3, 1950," by Jessup, Acheson papers, HSTL.

37. Acheson, *Present*, p. 475.

38. Ridgway, *Korean War*, pp. 61–62.

39. Acheson, *Present*, p. 474; also, Memorandum of conversation, "Report of the Secretary's Meeting at the White House," executive secretariat, Department of State, December 3, 1950, Acheson papers, HSTL.

40. JCS 97917 to CINCFE December 3, 1950.

41. JCS 98172 to CINCEUR *et al.*, December 6, 1950.

42. Acheson, *Present,* p. 478.

43. "U.S. Delegation Minutes of the First Meeting of President Truman and Prime Minister Attlee, December 4, 1950," Acheson papers, HSTL.

44. Memorandum, "Truman-Attlee Talks," by Jessup, on conversations evening of December 4, 1950, between Attlee, Acheson, and aides, Acheson papers, HSTL.

45. Memorandum of conversation, "Meeting in the Secretary's Office, December 5, 1950, 10 A.M.," by McWilliams, December 5, 1950, Acheson papers, HSTL.

46. Memorandum, "Truman-Attlee Talks," December 5, 1950, Acheson papers, HSTL.

47. "U.S. Delegation Minutes of Fifth Meeting of President Truman and Prime Minister Attlee, December 7, 1950," Acheson papers, HSTL.

48. Memorandum for record, untitled, by Jessup, December 7, 1950, records exchange between Truman and Attlee, with notation "This information not incorporated in official account of meeting. This is single copy to be retained by Mr. Battle in the Secretary's office," Acheson papers, HSTL.

49. Memorandum, untitled, Bradley to Collins, December 1, 1950.

50. JCS WAR 97929, personal for Collins via CINCFE, December 3, 1950.

51. Memorandum, Hickey to Collins, summarizing MacArthur-Collins conversation of December 4, 1950.

52. Collins C 50371 to JCS, December 4, 1950.

53. Memorandum, "Report on Visit to FEC and Korea, December 4–7, 1950," Collins to JCS, December 8, 1950.

54. Collins, *War in Peacetime,* pp. 230–32.

55. *Ibid.,* p. 233.

56. Stebbins, *United States in World Affairs, 1950,* p. 415.

57. "Memorandum for the President on NSC Meeting of December 11, 1950," President's Secretary's File, HSTL.

58. CINCFE 51052 to DA for JCS, December 12, 1950.

59. Memorandum, "United States Position Regarding the Terms of Any United Nations General Assembly Cease-Fire Resolution for the Korean War," JCS to Marshall, December 12, 1950.

60. *SW-VIII,* pp. 383–84.

61. Interview, General Francis W. Farrell—JCG, June 2, 1980.

Chapter Seventeen

1. Ridgway, *Korean War,* pp. 79–81.

2. Ridgway *OH,* AWC.

3. "Memorandum of Meeting with MacArthur in Tokyo, December 26, 1950," Ridgway papers, AWC.

4. *HST-II,* p. 371.

5. Memorandum of conversation, by Battle, December 27, 1950, summarized Acheson's account of White House meeting of previous day and discussions with State subordinates (especially Rusk) on options to be pursued.

6. Memorandum, JCS to Marshall, December 27, 1950; also discussed in *SW-VIII,* p. 396.

7. JCS 99935 to CINCFE, December 29, 1950.

8. Whitney, *Rendezvous,* p. 432.

9. MacArthur, *Reminiscences,* p. 378.

10. "Consequences of the Early Employment of Chinese National Forces in Korea," *National Intelligence Estimate NIE-12,* CIA, December 27, 1950.

11. Whitney, *Rendezvous,* p. 432.

12. CINCFE C 52391 to JCS, December 30, 1950.

13. CINCFE C 52715 to DA personal for Collins, January 4, 1951.

14. Ridgway's thoughts on turning around the UN Command are in his *Korean War,* pp. 85–94, and *OH,* AWC.

15. Letter, Ridgway to Collins, January 5, 1951, Ridgway papers, AWC.

16. Ridgway *OH,* AWC.

17. Letter, Ridgway to Collins, January 8, 1951, Ridgway papers, AWC.

18. Letter, Ridgway to Gilmer, March 12, 1951, Ridgway papers, AWC.

19. Ridgway *OH,* AWC.

20. Freeman *OH,* AWC.

21. "Memorandum on Inspection Trips to 2nd Division, 9 and 13 January, 1951," Almond to Ridgway, January 14, 1951, Ridgway papers, AWC.

22. "Memorandum on Conferences of Senior Aides, January 8, 1951," Ridgway papers, AWC.

23. Letter, MacArthur to Ridgway, January 16, 1951, forwarding Haislip's directive, Ridgway papers, AWC.

24. *Time* (March 5, 1951).

25. Minutes, conference at EUSAK headquarters, January 8, 1951, Ridgway papers, AWC.

26. Letter, Ridgway to MacArthur, January 6, 1951; refused, MacArthur to Ridgway, January 7, 1951; Ridgway papers, AWC.

27. Ridgway, *Korean War,* p. 100.

28. Interview, Lynch—JCG.

29. Letter, Ridgway to Hickey, January 8, 1951, Ridgway papers, AWC.

30. Letter, Johnson to Ridgway, February 16, 1951, Ridgway papers, AWC.

31. Letter, Ridgway to Johnson, February 23, 1951, Ridgway papers, AWC.

32. Notes on briefing of 1st Marine Division officers, January 9, 1951, Ridgway papers, AWC.

33. JCS 80680 to CINCFE, January 9, 1951.

34. Whitney, *Rendezvous,* p. 435.

35. CINCUNC C 53167 to DA, January 10, 1951.

36. *HST-II,* p. 434.

37. Acheson, *Present,* p. 515. *Military Situation,* Part II, Sherman testimony; Marshall testimony on succeeding sentence.

38. *Military Situation,* Part II, Sherman testimony, Marshall testimony.

39. Collins, *War in Peacetime,* p. 248.

40. Memorandum, "Preparations of Instructions to FEC," January 10, 1951, Acheson papers, HSTL; JCS version discussed *SW-VIII,* p. 413.

41. *HST-II,* pp. 434–36.

42. Whitney, *Rendezvous,* pp. 437–39.

43. *Military Situation,* Part I, Marshall testimony.

44. Ridgway, *Korean War,* pp. 105–08.

45. CINCFE 54197 to EUSAK, February 4, 1951.

46. *Time* (February 12, 1951).

47. Freeman *OH,* AWC; background on French Foreign Legion from *Soldier of Fortune* magazine (February 1979); Fehrenbach, *This Kind of War,* 390–96.

48. Letter, Ridgway to MacArthur, February 3, 1951, Ridgway papers, AWC.

49. Memorandum for the record, February 24, 1951, Ridgway, Ridgway papers, AWC.

50. Voorhees, *Korean Tales,* p. 36.

51. *Ibid.,* p. 59.

52. Letter, Adam A. Komosa to JCG, July 25, 1980.

53. MacArthur statement text, undated and untitled, March 1951 by context, Ridgway papers, AWC.

54. Feis and Acheson, Princeton Seminar, HSTL.

55. *SW-IX,* pp. 447–79.

56. CINCFE 55315 to DA for JCS, February 11, 1951.

57. MacArthur, *Reminiscences,* p. 384.

58. CINCFE CX 55610 to DA for JCS, February 15, 1951.

59. JCS 84026 to CINCFE, February 21, 1951; also, memorandum, "Draft Dispatch to CINCFE," Lalor, February 21, 1951.

60. CINCFE 56453 to JCS, February 26, 1951.

61. JCS 84577 to CINCFE, March 1, 1951.

62. Schnabel, *Policy and Direction,* p. 340.

63. CINCFE 56709 to JCS, March 1, 1951.

64. Acheson, *Present,* pp. 512–14.
65. Stebbins, *United States in World Affairs 1950,* p. 85–86.
66. *Department of State Bulletin,* January 29, 1951.
67. Acheson, *Present,* p. 517.
68. *Ibid.,* p. 517.
69. *SW-IX,* pp. 459–62, summarizes the interdepartmental debate.
70. CINCUNC 57090 to JCS for UN, March 2, 1951.
71. Memorandum, "United States National Objectives and Policy in Asia," NSC to NSC senior staff, March 15, 1951.
72. Interviews, Hans Tofte—JCG, various dates February–November 1980; memorandum, "CIA Covert Action Build-up in Japan and Korea, 1950–1951," by Hans Tofte, 1964; memorandum, "Evasion and Escape Organization and Guerrilla Operations in Korea 1950–1951," by Tofte, February 23, 1980; letters, Tofte—JCG, February 4 and 23, 1980. Tofte also supplied JCG with numerous photographs of guerrilla training camps (see photographic section).
73. *Final Report of the Selection Committee to Study Governmental Operations with Respect to Intelligence Activities,* United States Senate, 94th Congress, 2d Session, Part IV, pp. 6–9 (the so-called Church Committee).

Chapter Eighteen

1. Whitney, *Rendezvous,* p. 419.
2. Interview, Charles Burton Marshall—JCG, April 22, 1980.
3. Whitney, *Rendezvous,* p. 462.
4. Acheson, Princeton Seminar, HSTL.
5. *HST-II,* p. 438.
6. Letter, Lovett to Acheson, March 31, 1951; the State-Defense discussions also discussed *SW-IX,* pp. 469–71.
7. JCS 86276 to CINCFE, March 20, 1951.
8. CINCUNC C 58203 to DA for JCS, March 21, 1951.
9. *Record of JCS Actions Relative to Korea,* p. 101.
10. *HST-II,* p. 440.
11. Press statement, FEC, March 25, 1951, reprinted in *Military Situation,* Part V.
12. *The New York Times* (October 18, 1951).
13. Whitney, *Rendezvous,* p. 467.
14. Willoughby, *MacArthur,* p. 422.
15. *Military Situation,* Part I, Marshall testimony.
16. *HST-II,* p. 442.
17. Acheson, Princeton Seminar, HSTL.
18. *Ibid.,* quoting Truman.
19. JCS 87636 to CINCFE personal for MacArthur, March 21, 1951.
20. *HST-II,* p. 443.
21. *Ibid.,* p. 446.
22. Acheson, Princeton Seminar, HSTL. The account of the discussions leading to MacArthur's firing is from Acheson, *Present;* Acheson's Princeton Seminar, HSTL, comments; *HST-II;* Truman diary entries; and *Military Situation.*
23. Planning paper, JCS 1776/202, March 30, 1951; memorandum, "Military Action in Korea," Sherman to Bradley, April 4, 1951; and memorandum, JCS to Secretary Marshall, same title, April 5, 1951.
24. Memorandum, untitled, Bradley for JCS files, April 23, 1951.
25. Cabell Phillips, *The Truman Presidency* (New York: Macmillan, 1956), pp. 346–47.
26. Walter Trohan, *Political Animals* (Garden City, N.Y.: Doubleday, 1975), pp. 252–53.
27. Elsey *OH,* HSTL.
28. Pace *OH,* HSTL.
29. Sebald, *With MacArthur,* p. 226.

30. Huff, *Fifteen Years with MacArthur,* pp. 5–7.

31. "Memorandum for Diary," April 12, 1951, Ridgway papers, AWC.

Chapter Nineteen

1. Trohan, *Political Animals,* p. 255.

2. Interview, Pat Holt—JCG, June 17, 1980.

3. Memorandum, untitled, Marshall to Nitze, April 11, 1951.

4. Memorandum, April 11, 1951, "MacArthur Chronological File," Ayers papers, HSTL.

5. Merle Miller, *Plain Speaking* (New York: Berkley-Putnam, 1974), p. 313.

6. Acheson, *Present,* p. 524.

7. Memorandum for President, William J. Hopkins, May 8, 1951, analyzing White House mail, PSF, HSTL.

8. Michener, in introduction to Beech, *Tokyo and Points East,* p. 9.

9. Elsey *OH,* HSTL.

10. Memorandum, Hechler to Carroll, April 17, 1951, Elsey papers, HSTL.

11. Memorandum, "Records of the MacArthur Hearing," Elsey to Truman, July 5, 1951, Elsey papers, HSTL; letter, Elsey to Schlesinger, July 20, 1951.

12. Memorandum, "Preparations for Forthcoming Congressional Hearings," April 26, 1951, Colonel E. F. Cress, secretary, Joint Strategic Survey Committee, to JCS.

Chapter Twenty

1. Direct quotations from the hearing are from two sources: the record as printed by the two Senate committees immediately following the hearings as *Military Situation in the Far East,* 3,691 pages in six volumes; and the official stenographic transcript in the National Archives, declassified by the two Senate committees in the mid-1970's. Very little testimony was censored from the printed record—1.4 percent of that of MacArthur, and 4 percent of Marshall, according to a computation by the JCS. For reasons of economy and space, specific page references are not cited.

2. Rovere-Schlesinger, The *MacArthur Controversy,* p. 180.

3. Interview, Francis O. Wilcox—JCG, October 12, 1979.

4. *Daily Report,* Foreign Broadcast Information Service, CIA, March 23, 1951.

5. Letters, Maverick to Truman, June 15, 1951, and Seay to Truman, undated, but June 1951 from context, HSTL.

Chapter Twenty-one

1. Interview, Charles Burton Marshall—JCG.

2. Rusk, Washington *Post* (May 22, 1951).

3. Theodore White, *In Search of History* (New York: Harper & Row, 1978), p. 395.

4. Acheson, *Present,* p. 532.

5. Interview, Marshall—JCG.

6. Acheson, *Present,* pp. 532–33.

7. Memoranda of conversations, "Briefing of Ambassadors," State Department, June 5

and June 8, 1951, HSTL. Memoranda of these periodic briefings for nations with troops serving in the UN Command are unsigned but apparently were written by John Hickerson of the State Department's Bureau of United Nations Affairs. *Briefing of Ambassadors* hereafter.

8. *Briefing of Ambassadors,* June 27, 1951.

9. NIACT 3784, Kirk to Rusk, June 27, 1951, Acheson papers, HSTL.

10. *Briefing of Ambassadors,* June 29, 1951.

11. Memorandum of conversation, State-Defense representatives meeting of June 29, 1951, by U. Alexis Johnson, State Department, quoted *SW-XI,* p. 568.

12. *Briefing of Ambassadors,* June 29, 1951.

13. *Ibid.,* July 3, 1951.

14. Joint Intelligence Committee memorandum 581/1, untitled, July 2, 1951.

15. CS 66188 to DA for JCS, July 2, 1951.

16. *SW-XI,* pp. 577–79.

17. CINCFE C 65800 to JCS, June 26, 1951.

18. Collins, *War in Peacetime,* pp. 306–07.

19. Matthew Ridgway, "My Battles in Peace and War," *Saturday Evening Post* (February 25, 1956).

20. JCS 95353 to CINCUNC, personal for Ridgway, June 30, 1951.

21. Memorandum, Ridgway to General and Flag Officer Members of UN Delegation, July 6, 1951, Ridgway papers, AWC.

22. Hermes, *Truce Tent,* p. 21.

23. Admiral C. Turner Joy, *How Communists Negotiate* (New York: Macmillan, 1955), pp. 4–5.

24. Pawel Monat, *"Russians in Korea: The Hidden Bosses,"* *Life* magazine (June 27, 1960).

25. Joy, *How Communists Negotiate,* p. 14.

26. *Transcript of Proceedings,* "Armistice Proposal in Korea," July 10, 1951. The army's transcript of the peace negotiations covers more than 15,000 typewritten pages. Direct quotations from the negotiations are either from these typescripts or from the summaries of each session prepared by Joy for transmittal by Ridgway to the JCS.

27. Hermes, *Truce Tent,* p. 26.

28. Memorandum for diary, July 11, 1951, Ridgway papers, AWC.

29. Hermes, *Truce Tent,* pp. 27–28.

30. Joy, *How Communists Negotiate,* p. 18.

31. CINCFE C 66323 to JCS, July 4, 1951.

32. *Briefing of Ambassadors,* July 20, 1951.

33. *Ibid.,* July 18 and 20, 1951.

34. CINCFE C 68428 to JCS, August 6, 1951.

35. Memorandum on conversations between Truman, Bradley, and Lovett, by Colonel Edwin H. J. Carns, deputy secretary to JCS, July 21, 1951.

36. CINCFE CX 67390 to JCS, July 20, 1951.

37. *SW-XI,* pp. 585–86.

38. JCS 96930 to CINCFE, July 21, 1951.

39. CINCFE 68672 to JCS, August 10, 1951.

40. JCS 98713 to CINCFE, August 11, 1951.

41. CINCFE C 68437 to JCS, August 6, 1951.

42. Memorandum, "Meeting of President Truman with Congressional Leadership," June 11, 1951, Elsey papers, HSTL.

43. DA TT 5018, transcript of telecon with CINCFE, August 4, 1951.

44. CINCFE C 68437 to DA for JCS, August 6, 1951.

45. JCS 98216 to CINCFE, August 6, 1951.

46. Kinney report to Ridgway and Joy, quoted in CINCFE C 69575 to JCS, August 25, 1951.

47. Ridgway, *Korean War,* pp. 192–94; *SW-IX,* pp. 193–96.

48. *Briefing of Ambassadors,* September 18, 1951.

49. JCS 81246 to CINCFE, September 12, 1951.

50. CINCUNC 51575 to JCS, September 25, 1951; DA TT 5193, transcript of telecon with CINCFE, September 26, 1951.

51. Memorandum, "Report on Trip to Japan and Korea with General Bradley," Bohlen to Acheson, October 4, 1951; memorandum, "Trip of General Bradley to Japan and Korea," Bradley to JCS, October 9, 1951.

52. CINCFE C 55841 and C 55852 to JCS, both October 25, 1951, and CINCUNC C 55922 to JCS, October 26, 1951.

53. CINCUNC 420 to JCS, November 4, 1951 (from advanced headquarters, UNC).

54. CINCUNC 430 to JCS, November 8, 1951 (from advanced headquarters, UNC).

55. JCS 85537 to CINCFE, October 30, 1951.

56. *SW-XII*, pp. 640–42.

57. JCS 86291 to CINCFE, November 6, 1951.

58. CINCFE CX 56810 to JCS, November 7, 1951; CINCFE 430 to JCS, November 8, 1951 (from advanced headquarters, UNC).

59. *Briefing of Ambassadors*, October 26, 1951.

60. *Ibid.*, November 6 and 9, 1951.

61. JCS 86654 to CINCFE, November 9, 1951.

62. Hermes, *Truce Tent*, p. 118.

63. JCS 86797 to CINCFE, November 13, 1951.

64. CINCFE 57216 to JCS, November 13, 1951.

65. JCS 86804 to CINCFE, November 14, 1951.

66. Joy, *How Communists Negotiate*, pp. 173–74.

67. Collins, *War in Peacetime*, p. 331.

68. Hermes, *Truce Tent*, p. 119.

69. Collins DA 88293 to Truman, Key West, November 29, 1951.

Chapter Twenty-two

1. Hermes, *Truce Tent*, pp. 123–28.

2. Joy, *How Communists Negotiate*, p. 66.

3. Truman (through Naval Aide *Williamsburg*) to JCS, December 8, 1951.

4. JCS 89118 to Naval Aide *Williamsburg* for Truman, December 8, 1951.

5. JCS 89173 to CINCFE, December 10, 1951.

6. CINCUNC 588 to DA for JCS, December 18, 1951 (from advanced headquarters UNC).

7. JCS 90083 to CINCFE, December 19, 1951.

8. CINCFE C 60584 to DA for JCS, January 1, 1952.

9. Memorandums of conversations, Rome, November 28 and 29, 1951, Nash to Bradley, December 19, 1951.

10. JCS 90083 to CINCFE, December 19, 1951.

11. CINCUNC C 60961 to DA, January 7, 1952.

12. JCS 91600 and 91602 to CINCFE, both January 19, 1952.

13. Hermes, *Truce Tent*, pp. 136–37.

14. CINCFE C 6603 to JCS, July 8, 1951.

15. *SW-XII*, pp. 680–82.

16. Memorandum, meeting with the President, October 29, 1951, Acting Secretary of State James E. Webb.

17. CINCFE C 58702 to DA, December 5, 1951.

18. CINCFE CX 59188 to DA for JCS, December 12, 1951.

19. CINCUNC C 59943 to DA for JCS, December 22, 1951.

20. JCS 90157 to CINCFE, December 20, 1951.

21. CINCFE C 60059 to JCS, December 24, and C 60193, December 26, 1951.

22. JCS 92059 to CINCFE, January 15, 1952.

23. Joy, *How Communists Negotiate*, pp. 91–93.

24. JCS 90216 to CINCFE, February 27, 1951.

25. CINCFE C 52613 to DA for JCS, January 3, 1951.

26. General Mark W. Clark, *From the Danube to the Yalu* (New York: Harper &

Brothers, 1954), Clark, *From Danube* hereafter, and Ridgway, *Korean War;* both contain detailed sections on the organization and troubles of the Koje-do POW camp.

27. CINCUNC C 66832 and C 66838 to DA, both April 12, and CINCUNC C 66864 to DA, April 13, 1952.

28. Hermes, *Truce Tent,* p. 174.

29. Clark, *From Danube,* pp. 33–45, details the misfortune of Dodd.

30. Memorandum, "Comments on *Truce Tent and Fighting Front,"* Boatner to adjutant general, Department of the Army, January 1967, Haydon Boatner papers, AWC.

31. "Communist Bacteriological Warfare Propaganda," Special Paper 4, Office of Intelligence Research, State Department, June 16, 1952.

32. James Angus MacDonald, "The Problems of United States Marine Corps Prisoners of War in Korea," Master of Arts thesis, University of Maryland, College Park, Md., 1961, Nimitz Library, United States Naval Academy, Annapolis. MacDonald, "Problems of USMC POWs" hereafter.

33. Dean, *Dean's Story,* p. 276.

34. MacDonald, "Problems of USMC POWs."

Chapter Twenty-three

1. *HST-II,* pp. 488–91.

2. Eisenhower to Hazlett, June 21, 1951, DDEL.

3. Whitney, *Rendezvous,* p. 399.

4. C. L. Sulzberger, *A Long Row of Candles* (New York: Macmillan, 1969), p. 769.

5. Townsend Hoopes, *The Devil and John Foster Dulles* (Boston: Atlantic Monthly Press, 1973), p. 124. The Dulles papers now in the public domain are thin, especially for his years as secretary of state. *The Devil* is a shrewd analysis of his pre-1953 years, written by a man who worked on defense and foreign policy matters for the Truman, Eisenhower, and Johnson administrations. I relied heavily on Hoopes in trying to understand a most mystical figure in American diplomacy.

6. *HST-II,* p. 498.

7. Untitled memorandum, October 1952, Elsey papers, HSTL, details Eisenhower's public record on Korea and his misrepresentations in campaign speeches. Oddly, this abundant rebuttal material was never put to effective use.

8. Brownell *OH,* DDEL.

9. Emmet John Hughes, *The Ordeal of Power* (New York: Atheneum, 1963), p. 33.

10. *HST-II,* p. 501.

11. Muccio *OH,* HSTL.

12. Muccio to State, (Pusan 817) February 19, 1952.

13. CINCUNC CX 64241 to DA for JCS, February 25, 1952.

14. JCS 90215 to CINCFE, February 27, 1952.

15. DA 902912 to CINCFE, March 6, 1952.

16. Pusan 893 to State, March 14, 1952; Pusan 939 to State, March 28, 1952. (U.S. Embassy cables came from wherever Rhee happened to be conducting his government.)

17. *SW-XIV,* pp. 785–87.

18. CINCUNC GX 6204 TAC KCG to CSUSA, June 2, 1952. The generals used this high-security cable channel because of the discussion of "military action" against Rhee and his government.

19. CINCUNC CX 50748 to CG EUSAK, 24 June; CINCUNC CS 50901 to DA for JCS, June 27, 1952; CINCUNC CS 51399 to DA for JCS, July 5, 1952.

20. *SW-XIV,* pp. 796–97.

21. CINCFE C 60326 to DA for JCS, December 28, 1951.

22. CINCFE 302 to JCS, March 1, 1952, special channel message.

23. Memorandum, "Communist Short Term Intentions in Korea," SE-25, assistant chief of staff, G-2, to assistant chief of staff, G-3, Department of the Army, April 25, 1952.

24. Clark, *From the Danube,* pp. 98–99.

25. CINCFE C 69181 to JCS, May 27, 1952.

26. Memorandum, "Employment of Chinese Nationalist Forces in Korea and Supply Priorities in Connection Therewith," Lovett to JCS; JCS, August 25, 1952.

27. Memorandum for record, "Meeting with the President on Korean Situation," Lovett, September 15, 1952.

28. Memorandum, "State-Defense Conference on Korean Armistice Negotiation, September 17, 1952," by Admiral Fechteler, same date.

29. Memorandum, "White House Meeting on Status of Korean Truce Negotiations," no signature or date, but context shows September 24, 1952.

30. JCS 919368 to CINCFE, September 25, 1952.

Chapter Twenty-four

1. Merriman Smith, *Meet Mr. Eisenhower* (New York: Harper & Bros., 1954), pp. 51–58.

2. Clark, *From the Danube*, p. 230.

3. CINCUNC OPLAN 8-52, October 15, 1952; letter, Clark to Collins, October 9, 1952; OPLAN 8-52 had its genesis in a Joint Strategic Planning Committee study, JCS 1776/310 August 29, 1952, that stated in the event of a heightened UN offensive, "it would be necessary to authorize the use of atomic weapons against military targets in the Far East."

4. Clark, *From the Danube*, p. 233.

5. Hughes, *Ordeal*, p. 51.

6. Eisenhower *OH*, Dulles papers, Princeton.

7. Memorandum, "Briefing for the Secretary of Defense Designate by the Chief of Staff," December 17, 1952, *SW-XVI*, pp. 941–42.

8. Memorandum, "Future Courses of Action in Connection with the Situation in Korea," JCS to Wilson, March 27, 1953.

9. Memorandum, "Possible Actions to Impress Communists in Korea of UN Offensive Intentions in Event Armistice Negotiations Break Down," JCS to Wilson, May 4, 1953.

10. Memorandum, "Courses of Action in Connection with the Situation in Korea (Analysis)," JCS to Wilson, May 19, 1953.

11. *SW-XVI*, pp. 962–63.

12. JCS 93534 to CINCUNC, April 1, 1953.

13. CINCUNC ZX 36484 to DA for JCS, May 7, 1953.

14. CINCUNC CX 62301 to DA for JCS, May 8, 1953.

15. CINCFE C 61736 to DA for JCS, April 4, 1953.

16. *SW-XVI*, p. 984.

17. CINCFE C 61976 to DA for JCS, April 16, 1953.

18. Clark, *From the Danube*, p. 261; Hermes, *Truce Tent*, pp. 442–43.

19. CINCFE CX 62406 to DA for JCS, May 13, 1953.

20. Clark, *From the Danube*, p. 260.

21. *Ibid.*, p. 267.

22. CINCUNC to DA for JCS, May 26, 1953.

23. Ellis Briggs, *Farewell to Foggy Bottom* (New York: David McKay, 1964), p. 231.

24. JCS planning paper, JCS 1776/373, June 5, 1953; memorandum for the record, "Conference on the Current Difficulties with the ROK Government Due to Their Dissatisfaction with Armistice Terms," by Major General C. D. Eddleman, army G-3.

25. DA 940238 to CINCFE (Collins exclusive for Clark), May 30, 1953.

26. CINCFE CX 62747 to DA for JCS, May 30, 1953.

27. Clark, *From the Danube*, p. 275.

28. CINCFE CX 62890 to JCS, June 12, 1953.

29. Clark, *From the Danube*, p. 274.

30. Interview, Timothy J. Maddox—JCG, October 18, 1979.

31. Eisenhower to Rhee, June 18, 1953, draft for State Department, DDEL.

32. Hermes, *Truce Tent*, p. 477.

33. State Department records of the Robertson mission remain classified; this account

is constructed from CINCFE cables reporting on his meetings with Rhee, summarized in *SW-XVII,* pp. 1017–22.

34. CINCUNC to DA for JCS, June 28, 1953.
35. CINCUNC CX 63449 to DA for JCS, July 2, 1953.
36. *SW-XVII,* p. 1027.
37. Interview, Anthony Ebron—JCG, August 17, 1979.
38. Beech, *Tokyo and Points East,* pp. 226–27.
39. Martin Russ, *The Last Parallel* (New York: Rinehart & Company, 1957), p. 320.
40. Postpresidential interviews transcript, HSTL.

INDEX